GENERAL MANAGEMENT

Processes and Action
Text and Cases

David A. Garvin
Harvard Business School

Mc
Graw
Hill

Boston   Burr Ridge, IL   Dubuque, IA   Madison, WI   New York   San Francisco   St. Louis
Bangkok   Bogotá   Caracas   Kuala Lumpur   Lisbon   London   Madrid   Mexico City
Milan   Montreal   New Delhi   Santiago   Seoul   Singapore   Sydney   Taipei   Toronto

McGraw-Hill Higher Education

A Division of The **McGraw-Hill** Companies

GENERAL MANAGEMENT: PROCESSES AND ACTION

Published by McGraw-Hill, an imprint of The McGraw-Hill Companies, Inc. 1221 Avenue of the Americas, New York, NY, 10020. Copyright © 2002 by David A. Garvin. All rights reserved. No part of this publication may be reproduced or distributed in any form or by any means, or stored in a data base or retrieval system, without the prior written consent of The McGraw-Hill Companies, Inc., including, but not limited to, in any network or other electronic storage or transmission, or broadcast for distance learning.

Some ancillaries, including electronic and print components, may not be available to customers outside the United States.

This book is printed on acid-free paper.

2 3 4 5 6 7 8 9 0 DOC/DOC 0 9 8 7 6 5 4 3 2 1

ISBN 0-07-243241-1

Publisher: *John Biernat*
Sponsoring Editor: *Marianne Rutter*
Editorial Assistant: *Tammy Higham*
Marketing manager: *Lisa Nicks*
Project manager: *Jean R. Starr*
Production supervisor: *Carol A. Bielski*
Coordinator of freelance design: *Mary Kazak*
Cover design: *Kiera Cunningham*
Associate supplement producer: *Vicki Laird*
Producer, Media technology: *Melissa Kansa*
Printer: *R. R. Donnelley & Sons Company*
Typeface: *10/12 Times Roman*
Compositor: *TechBooks*

Library of Congress Cataloging-in-Publication Data

Garvin, David A.
    General management: processes and action/David A. Garvin.
        p. cm.
    Includes index.
    ISBN 0-07-243241-1 (alk. paper)
    1. Industrial management. 2. Industrial management—Case studies. I. Title.
HD31. G344 2002
658–dc21

                                                                          2001030301

To Lynn

Preface

General Management: Processes and Action (GMPA) focuses on implementation and the way that general managers get things done. Typically, they work through processes—sequences of tasks and activities that unfold over time, like strategic planning, business development, and budgeting—to move their organizations forward and achieve results. Skill at influencing the design, direction, and functioning of processes is therefore essential to effective general management, and the aim of GMPA is to develop in students a deeper understanding of these activities and their links to performance. It does so by describing a number of critical organizational and managerial processes, outlining their basic elements and operating characteristics and exploring how they are best influenced and led. Throughout, the focus is on high-level processes that are of interest to general managers; for this reason, virtually all case protagonists are division presidents or higher.

The course is divided into six parts, following the categories and frameworks described in the Introduction. Each corresponds to an essential task of general management and the associated processes for carrying it out. The first two sections deal with administrative processes—those recurrent tasks, activities, and systems that general managers use to set broad direction and goals. Module I focuses on strategic processes, while Module II examines resource allocation processes. They are closely related. Strategic processes help managers establish organizational purpose, ensure alignment across levels and functions, and provide ways for capabilities and competitive positioning to evolve over time. Cases in this section explore a range of issues, including new business creation, strategic planning, forecasting, and acquisition screening and integration. Resource allocation processes are discussed next because of their role in supporting strategy. For strategy to be effective, personnel and funds must be allocated to the appropriate businesses, products, and markets. Here, most cases focus on the development and execution of budgets—how managers set priorities, rank projects, and manage the associated interpersonal conflicts and organizational politics.

The next two modules focus on behavioral processes. Typically, these patterns of behavior become programmed into the organizational fabric; over time, they become accepted as "the way we do things around here." Modules III and IV focus on two representative examples of these types of processes: decision making and organizational learning. Decision-making processes determine how individuals and organizations overcome conflicts, choose among alternatives, and reach agreement. A variety of approaches are possible, and the cases in this section compare the strengths and weaknesses of different modes of decision making, as well as the general manager's role in guiding them. Learning processes determine how individuals and organizations create, acquire, interpret, transfer, and retain knowledge; they also may take a variety of forms. The approaches examined in this module include experimentation, benchmarking, and learning from past successes and failures.

The final two sections of the course shift attention from the organization to individuals. Module V focuses on managerial processes—the patterns of behavior, influence, and action that general managers use to oversee the work of subordinates and ensure that goals are achieved. Here, a critical contrast is between formal and informal approaches, and between processes for managing hierarchical and lateral relations. Some managers use tightly specified control systems to monitor and direct employees; others rely on qualitative information and personal contacts. The strengths and weaknesses of these approaches are explored, as are the associated management styles. Equally significant differences exist between the challenges of managing hierarchically—down to subordinates and up to bosses—and managing laterally to peers, who are either fellow division managers or functional heads. The cases and readings in this section compare the associated management processes and required skills. Among the most critical are negotiating and selling, coaching and development, and setting agendas and direction.

Finally, the last module of the course focuses on change processes. The challenges of initiating and leading change are described in a number of settings, including rapid growth, maturity, and decline. All require new behaviors and ways of working, and all place extraordinary demands on general managers. Cases in this section describe successful managers mobilizing their organizations, unfreezing past practices, developing commitment, integrating isolated fiefdoms, and crafting new strategies. A concluding class then assesses the implications of adopting a process perspective for the role and performance of general managers.

Acknowledgments

A casebook is a complex project with many contributors. I would like to thank the many people who helped bring this particular project to completion.

Several of my colleagues assisted by writing cases, articles, and technical notes and then providing permission to include them here. I would like to thank Sumantra Ghoshal and Philippe Haspeslagh for "Note on the Major Appliance Industry in 1988" and "Electrolux: The Acquisition of Zanussi," Richard Vancil for the cases on which Ellis International and Peterson Industries are based, Francis Aguilar for the case on which Americhem is based, Lynda Applegate and Julie Hertenstein for "Westinghouse Electric Corporation: Automating the Capital Budgeting Process," Jay Lorsch for "British Steel," Jack Gabarro and Anne Harlan for "Note on Process Observation," L.J. Bourgeois III and Kathleen Eisenhardt for the articles on decision making in high-velocity environments, and Paul Lawrence for "Millipore Corporation (A)." I would also like to thank the *Harvard Business Review* and *Sloan Management Review* for permission to reprint articles of mine, as well as those written by others. All of us owe a special debt to the many managers who participated in interviews, provided data, and agreed to let their stories be told. Without them, this casebook would not exist.

I would like to offer special thanks to my research associates, Jeffery Berger, Artemis March, Michael Roberto, Donald Sull, and Jonathan West, who were with me on the front lines developing new material. They contributed in countless ways, helping me frame the issues, develop the stories, interview the protagonists, and write up the findings. The cases in this book are a testimony to their insights and skills.

The entire project took nearly six years. During that period, the directors of Harvard Business School's Division of Research provided continued funding, encouragement, and support. My colleagues in the general management area read several cases and articles in draft form and suggested improvements and revisions. My secretary, Andrea Truax, typed each and every case—many, many times—with a remarkable combination of accuracy, speed, and good cheer. My MBA and executive students identified the strengths and weaknesses of each of the cases and the best ways to teach them, while uncovering many of the most important lessons. And, as always, my wife and daughters provided a stimulating, loving setting in which to get the work done. I am grateful to all of these people for helping to bring this book to life.

About the Author

David A. Garvin is the Robert and Jane Cizik Professor of Business Administration at the Harvard Business School, where he teaches general management in the MBA and Advanced Management programs. He has also taught in many corporate executive programs and consulted with companies around the world on organizational learning, leadership, and strategic change. He is the author or coauthor of nine books, including *Learning in Action, Education for Judgment,* and *Managing Quality;* 25 articles, including "The Processes of Organization and Management," "Building a Learning Organization," and "Quality on the Line"; and four videotape series, including *Working Smarter* and *Putting the Learning Organization to Work.*

Garvin is a three-time winner of the McKinsey Award, given annually for the best article in the *Harvard Business Review,* and a winner of the Beckhard Prize, given annually for the best article on planned change and organizational development in the *Sloan Management Review.* From 1988–1990 he served as a member of the Board of Overseers of the Malcolm Baldrige National Quality Award, and from 1991–1992 he served on the Manufacturing Studies Board of the National Research Council.

Contents

MODULE 6
Change Processes   **520**

Cases

Index   **623**

Introduction:

The Processes of Organization and Management

Managers today are enamored of processes. It's easy to see why. Many modern organizations are functional and hierarchical; they suffer from isolated departments, poor coordination, and limited lateral communication. All too often, work is fragmented and compartmentalized, and managers find it difficult to get things done. Scholars have faced similar problems in their research, struggling to describe organizational functioning in other than static, highly aggregated terms. For real progress to be made, the "proverbial 'black box,' the firm, has to be opened and studied from within."[1]

Processes provide a likely solution. In the broadest sense, they can be defined as collections of tasks and activities that together—and only together—transform inputs into outputs. Within organizations, these inputs and outputs can be as varied as materials, information, and people. Common examples of processes include new-product development, order fulfillment, and customer service; less obvious but equally legitimate candidates are resource allocation and decision making.

Over the years, there have been a number of process theories in the academic literature, but seldom has anyone reviewed them systematically or in an integrated way. Process theories have appeared in organization theory, strategic management, operations management, group dynamics, and studies of managerial behavior. The few scholarly efforts to tackle processes as a collective phenomenon either have been tightly focused theoretical or methodological statements or have focused primarily on a single type of process theory.[2]

[1]B.S. Chakravarthy and Y. Doz, "Strategy Process Research: Focusing on Corporate Self-Renewal," *Strategic Management Journal* 13 (special issue, Summer 1992), pp. 5–14, quote from p. 6.

[2]L.B. Mohr, *Explaining Organizational Behavior* (San Francisco: Jossey-Bass, 1982); P.R. Monge, "Theoretical and Analytical Issues in Studying Organizational Processes," *Organization Science* 1, no. 4 (1990), pp. 406–430; A.H. Van de Ven, "Suggestions for Studying Strategy Process: A Research Note," *Strategic Management Journal* 13 (special issue, Summer 1992), pp. 169–188; and A.H. Van de Ven and G. Huber, "Longitudinal Field Research Methods for Studying Processes of Organizational Change," *Organization Science* 1, no. 3 (1990), pp. 213–219.

Yet when the theories are taken together, they provide a powerful lens for understanding organizations and management:

First, processes provide a convenient, intermediate level of analysis. Because they consist of diverse, interlinked tasks, they open up the black box of the firm without exposing analysts to the "part–whole" problems that have plagued earlier research.[3] Past studies have tended to focus on either the trees (individual tasks or activities) or the forest (the organization as a whole); they have not combined the two. A process perspective gives the needed integration, ensuring that the realities of work practice are linked explicitly to the firm's overall functioning.[4]

Second, a process lens provides new insights into managerial behavior. Most studies have been straightforward descriptions of time allocation, roles, and activity streams, with few attempts to integrate activities into a coherent whole.[5] In fact, most past research has highlighted the fragmented quality of managers' jobs rather than their coherence. A process approach, by contrast, emphasizes the links among activities, showing that seemingly unrelated tasks—a telephone call, a brief hallway conversation, or an unscheduled meeting—are often part of a single, unfolding sequence. From this vantage point, managerial work becomes far more rational and orderly.

My aim here is to give a framework for thinking about processes, their impacts, and the implications for managers. I begin at the organizational level, reviewing a wide range of process theories and grouping them into categories. The discussion leads naturally to a typology of processes and a simple model of organizations as interconnected sets of processes. In the next section, I examine managerial processes; I consider them separately because they focus on individual managers and their relationships, rather than on organizations. I examine several types of managerial processes and contrast them with, and link them to, organizational processes, and identify their common elements. I conclude with a unifying framework that ties together the diverse processes and consider the implications for managers.

ORGANIZATIONAL PROCESSES

Scholars have developed three major approaches to organizational processes. They are best considered separate but related schools of thought because each focuses on a particular process and explores its distinctive characteristics and challenges. The three categories are (1) work processes, (2) behavioral processes, and (3) change processes (see the sidebar on organizational processes).

---

[3]A. H. Van de Ven, "Central Problems in the Management of Innovation," *Management Science* 32, no. 5 (1986), pp. 590–606.

[4]L. R. Sayles, *Leadership: Managing in Real Organizations,* 2nd ed. (New York: McGraw-Hill, 1989).

[5]C. P. Hales, "What Do Managers Do?," *Journal of Management Studies* 23, no. 1 (1986), pp. 88–115; and H. Mintzberg, *The Nature of Managerial Work* (New York: Harper & Row, 1973).

Three Approaches to Organizational Processes

Work Processes
- "A process is thus a specific ordering of work activities across time and place, with a beginning, an end, and clearly defined inputs and outputs: a structure for action."
T.H. Davenport, *Process Innovation* (Boston: Harvard Business School Press, 1993), p. 5.
- "Process. Any activity or group of activities that takes an input, adds value to it, and provides an output to an internal or external customer."
H.J. Harrington, *Business Process Improvement* (New York: McGraw-Hill, 1991), p. 9.

- "We view processes as the direction and frequency of work and information flows linking the differentiated roles within and between departments of complex organization."
J.R. Galbraith and R.K. Kazanjian, *Strategy Implementation: Structure, Systems, and Process* (St. Paul, MN: West, 1986), p. 6.

Behavioral Processes
- "The key to understanding what makes an organization more or less effective is how it does things . . . One must understand various processes—how goals are set, how the means to be used are determined, the forms of communication used among members, their processes of problem solving and decision making, how they run meetings and groups, how superiors and subordinates relate to each other, and ultimately how leaders lead."
E.H. Schein, *Process Consultation: Its Role in Organization Development,* 2nd ed. (Reading, MA: Addison-Wesley, 1988), p. 15.

- "Decision making is an organizational process. It is shaped as much by the pattern of interaction of managers as it is by the contemplation and cognitive processes of the individual."
L.R. Sayles, *Managerial Behavior* (New York: McGraw-Hill. 1964), p. 207.

Change Processes
- "Process is a way of giving life to data by taking snapshots of action/interaction and linking them to form a sequence or series . . . Process is the analyst's way of accounting for or explaining change."
A. Strauss and J. Corbin, *Basics of Qualitative Research* (Newbury Park, CA: Sage, 1990), pp. 144, 148.

- "A good process theory describes, at least in broad outline, plausible time parameters associated with change within and between the phenomena of interest . . . At the center of all dynamic analysis is the assessment of change over time."
P.R. Monge, "Theoretical and Analytical Issues in Studying Organizational Processes," *Organization Science,* vol. 1, no. 4, 1990, pp. 408, 426.

- "Study of organizational change tends to focus on two kinds of questions. (1) What are the antecedents or consequences of change in organizational forms or administrative practices? (2) How does an organizational change emerge, develop,

> grow, or terminate over time? . . . The second question requires a 'process theory' explanation of the temporal order and sequence in which a discrete set of events occurred based on a story or historical narrative."
>
> A.H. Van de Ven and G.P. Huber, "Longitudinal Field Research Methods for Studying Processes of Organizational Change," *Organization Science,* vol. 1, no. 3, 1990, p. 213.

Work Processes

The work process approach, which has roots in industrial engineering and work measurement, focuses on accomplishing tasks. It starts with a simple but powerful idea: Organizations accomplish their work through linked chains of activities cutting across departments and functional groups. These chains are called processes and can be conveniently grouped into two categories: (1) processes that create, produce, and deliver products and services that customers want, and (2) processes that do not produce outputs that customers want, but that are still necessary for running the business. I call the first group "operational processes" and the second group "administrative processes." New-product development, manufacturing, and logistics and distribution are examples of operational processes, while strategic planning, budgeting, and performance measurement are examples of administrative processes.

Operational and administrative processes share several characteristics. Both involve sequences of linked, interdependent activities that together transform inputs into outputs. Both have beginnings and ends, with boundaries that can be defined with reasonable precision and minimal overlap. And both have customers, who may be internal or external to the organization. The primary differences between the two lie in the nature of their outputs. Typically, operational processes produce goods and services that external customers consume, while administrative processes generate information and plans that internal groups use. For this reason, the two are frequently considered independent, unrelated activities, even though they must usually be aligned and mutually supportive if the organization is to function effectively. Skilled supply chain management, for example, demands a seamless link between a company's forecasting and logistics processes, just as successful new-product development rests on well-designed strategy formation and planning processes.

The work processes approach is probably most familiar to managers. It draws heavily on the principles of the quality movement and reengineering,[6] both of

---

[6]For discussions of processes in the quality literature, see H.J. Harrington, *Business Process Improvement* (New York: McGraw-Hill, 1991); E.J. Kane, "IBM's Quality Focus on the Business Process," *Quality Progress* 19 (April 1986), pp. 24–33; E.H. Melan, "Process Management: A Unifying Framework," *National Productivity Review* 8, no. 4 (1989), pp. 395–406; R.D. Moen and T.W. Nolan, "Process Improvement," *Quality Progress* 20 (September 1987), pp. 62–68; and G.D. Robson, *Continuous Process Improvement* (New York: Free Press, 1991). For discussions of processes in the reengineering literature, see T.H. Davenport, *Process Innovation* (Boston: Harvard Business School Press, 1993); M. Hammer and J. Champy, *Reengineering the Corporation* (New York: Harper Business, 1993); and T.A. Stewart, "Reengineering: The Hot New Managing Tool," *Fortune* 23 (August 1993), pp. 40–48.

which focus on the need to redesign processes to improve quality, cut costs, reduce cycle times, or otherwise enhance operating performance. Despite these shared goals, the two movements are strikingly similar on some points, but diverge on others.

The similarities begin with the belief that most existing work processes have grown unchecked, with little rationale or planning, and are therefore terribly inefficient. Hammer, for example, has observed: "Why did we design inefficient processes? In a way, we didn't. Many of our procedures were not designed at all; they just happened . . . The hodgepodge of special cases and quick fixes was passed from one generation of workers to the next."[7] The result, according to one empirical study of white-collar processes, is that value-added time (the time in which a product or service has value added to it, as opposed to waiting in a queue or being reworked to fix problems caused earlier) is typically less than 5 percent of total processing time.[8]

To eliminate inefficiencies, both movements suggest that work processes be redesigned. In fact, both implicitly equate process improvement with process management. They also suggest the use of similar tools, such as process mapping and data modeling, as well as common rules of thumb for identifying improvement opportunities.[9] First, flow charts are developed to show all the steps in a process; the process is then made more efficient by eliminating multiple approvals and checkpoints, finding opportunities to reduce waiting time, smoothing the handoffs between departments, and grouping related tasks and responsibilities.[10] At some point, "process owners" with primary responsibility for leading the improvement effort are also deemed necessary. Their role is to ensure integration and overcome traditional functional loyalties; for this reason, relatively senior managers are usually assigned the task.[11]

The differences between the two movements lie in their views about the underlying nature and sources of process change. The quality movement, for the most part, argues for incremental improvement.[12] Existing work processes are assumed to have many desirable properties; the goal is to eliminate unnecessary steps and errors while preserving the basic structure of the process. Improvements are continuous and relatively small scale. Reengineering, by contrast, calls for radical change.[13] Existing work processes are regarded as hopelessly outdated; they rely on work practices and a division of labor that take no account of modern information technology.

---

[7]M. Hammer, "Reengineering Work: Don't Automate, Obliterate," *Harvard Business Review* 68 (July–August 1990), pp. 104–112.

[8]J.D. Blackburn, "Time-Based Competition: White-Collar Activities," *Business Horizons* 35 (July–August 1992), pp. 96–101.

[9]E.H. Melan, "Process Management in Service and Administrative Operations," *Quality Progress* 18 (June 1985), pp. 52–59.

[10]Davenport (1993), chap. 7; Hammer and Champy (1993), chap. 3; Harrington (1991), chap. 6; and Kane (1986).

[11]Hammer and Champy (1993), pp. 108–109; Kane (1986); and Melan (1989), p. 398.

[12]Moen and Nolan (1987); and Robson (1991).

[13]Davenport (1993), pp. 10–15; and Hammer and Champy (1993), pp. 32–34.

For example, the case management approach, in which "individuals or small teams . . . perform a series of tasks, such as the fulfillment of a customer order from beginning to end, often with the help of information systems that reach throughout the organization," was not economically viable until the arrival of powerful, inexpensive computers and innovative software.[14] For this reason, reengineering focuses less on understanding the details of current work processes and more on "inventing a future" based on fundamentally new processes.[15]

Perhaps the most dramatic difference between the two approaches lies in the importance they attach to control and measurement. Quality experts, drawing on their experience with statistical process control in manufacturing, argue that well-managed work processes must be fully documented, with clearly defined control points.[16] Managers can improve a process, they believe, only if they first measure it with accuracy and assure its stability.[17] After improvement, continuous monitoring is required to maintain the gains and ensure that the process performs as planned. Reengineering experts, on the other hand, are virtually silent about measurement and control. They draw on a different tradition, information technology, that emphasizes redesign rather than control.

Insights for Managers.   The work processes perspective has led to a number of important insights for managers. It provides an especially useful framework for addressing a common organizational problem: fragmentation, or the lack of cross-functional integration. Many aspects of modern organizations make integration difficult, including complexity, highly differentiated subunits and roles, poor informal relationships, size, and physical distance.[18] Integration is often improved by the mere acknowledgment of work processes as viable units of analysis and targets of managerial action.[19] Charting horizontal work flows, for example, or following an order through the fulfillment system are convenient ways to remind employees that the activities of disparate departments and geographical units are interdependent, even if organization charts, with their vertical lines of authority, suggest otherwise.

In addition, the work processes perspective provides new targets for improvement. Rather than focusing on structures and roles, managers address the underlying

---

[14]T. H. Davenport and N. Nohria, "Case Management and the Integration of Labor," *Sloan Management Review* 35 (Winter 1994), pp. 11–23, quote from p. 11.

[15]I. Price, "Aligning People and Processes during Business-Focused Change in BP Exploration," *Prism* (fourth quarter, 1993), pp. 19–31.

[16]Kane (1986); and Melan (1985) and (1989).

[17]H. Gitlow, S. Gitlow, A. Oppenheim, and R. Oppenheim, *Tools and Methods for the Improvement of Quality* (Homewood, IL: Irwin, 1989), chap. 8.

[18]P.F. Schlesinger, V. Sathe, L.A. Schlesinger, and J.P. Kotter, *Organization: Text, Cases, and Readings on the Management of Organization Design and Change* (Homewood, IL: Irwin, 1992), pp. 106–110.

[19]J. Browning, "The Power of Process Redesign," *McKinsey Quarterly* 1, no. 1 (1993), pp. 47–58; J.R. Galbraith, *Organization Design* (Reading, MA: Addison-Wesley, 1977), pp. 118–119; and B.P. Shapiro, K. Rangan, and J.J. Sviokla, "Staple Yourself to an Order," *Harvard Business Review* 70, July–August 1992, pp. 113–122.

processes. An obvious advantage is that they closely examine the real work of the organization. The results, however, have been mixed, and experts estimate that a high proportion of these programs have failed to deliver the expected gains.

My analysis suggests several reasons for failure. Most improvement programs have focused exclusively on process redesign; the ongoing operation and management of the reconfigured processes have usually been neglected. Yet even the best processes will not perform effectively without suitable oversight, coordination, and control, as well as occasional intervention. In addition, operational processes have usually been targeted for improvement, while their supporting administrative processes have been overlooked. Incompatibilities and inconsistencies have arisen when the information and plans needed for effective operation were not forthcoming. A few companies have used the work processes approach to redefine their strategy and organization. The most progressive have blended a horizontal process orientation with conventional vertical structures.[20]

Behavioral Processes

The behavioral process approach, which has roots in organization theory and group dynamics, focuses on ingrained behavior patterns. These patterns reflect an organization's characteristic ways of acting and interacting; decision-making and communication processes are examples. The underlying behavior patterns are normally so deeply embedded and recurrent that they are displayed by most organizational members. They also have enormous staying power. As Weick observed, behavioral processes are able to "withstand the turnover of personnel as well as some variation in the actual behaviors people contribute."[21]

All behavioral processes share several characteristics. They are generalizations, distilled from observations of everyday work, and have no independent existence apart from the work processes in which they appear. This makes them difficult to identify but explains their importance. Behavioral processes profoundly affect the form, substance, and character of work processes by shaping how they are carried out. They are different, however, from organizational culture because they reflect more than values and beliefs. Behavioral processes are the sequences of steps used for accomplishing the cognitive and interpersonal aspects of work. New-product development processes, for example, may have roughly similar work flows yet still involve radically different patterns of decision making and communication. Often, it is these underlying patterns that determine the operational process's ultimate success or failure.[22]

---

[20]For example, see A. March and D.A. Garvin, "Arthur D. Little, Inc." (Boston: Harvard Business School, case no. 9-396-060, 1995).

[21]K.E. Weick, *The Social Psychology of Organizing,* 2nd ed. (Reading, MA: Addison-Wesley, 1979), p. 34.

[22]S.C. Wheelwright and K.B. Clark, *Revolutionizing Product Development* (New York: Free Press, 1992).

Next I discuss three categories of behavioral processes, selected for their representativeness and rich supporting literature: decision-making, communication, and organizational learning processes. All involve the collection, movement, and interpretation of information, as well as forms of interpersonal interaction. In most cases, the associated behaviors are learned informally, through socialization and on-the-job experience, rather than through formal education and training programs.

Decision-Making Processes.   Of all behavioral processes, decision making has been the most carefully studied. The roots go back to the research and writings of Chester Barnard and Herbert Simon, who argued that organizational decision making was a distributed activity, extending over time, involving a number of people.[23] Because it was a process rather than a discrete event, a critical management task was shaping the environment of decision making to produce desired ends. This, in itself, is still a surprising insight for many managers. All too often, they see decision making as their personal responsibility, rather than as a shared, dispersed activity that they must orchestrate and lead.[24]

These early writings spawned a vast outpouring of research on decision making; eventually they coalesced into the field of strategic process research.[25] One group focused on the structure of decision-making processes: their primary stages, and whether stages followed one another logically and in sequence or varied over time with the type of decision.[26] The goal was a model of the decision process, replete with flow charts and time lines, that mapped the sequence of steps in decision making and identified ideal types. For the most part, the results of these studies have been equivocal. Efforts to produce a simple linear flow model of decision making—in the same way that work processes can be diagrammed using process flow charts—have had limited success. Witte, for example, studied the purchase process for new computers and found that very few decisions—4 of 233—corresponded to a standard, five-phase, sequential process. He concluded that simultaneous rather than sequenced processes were the norm: "We believe that human beings cannot gather information without in some way developing alternatives. They cannot avoid evaluating these alternatives immediately, and in doing this, they are forced to a decision. This is a package of operations."[27]

---

[23]C. I. Barnard, *The Functions of the Executive* (Cambridge: Harvard University Press, 1938), pp. 185–189, 205–206; and H. A. Simon, *Administrative Behavior,* 3rd ed. (New York: Free Press, 1976), pp. 96–109, 220–228.

[24]L. A. Hill, *Becoming a Manager* (Boston: Harvard Business School Press, 1992), pp. 20–21.

[25]For reviews, see J. L. Bower and Y. Doz, "Strategy Formulation: A Social and Political Process," in D. H. Schendel and C. H. Hofer, eds., *Strategic Management* (Boston: Little, Brown, 1979), pp. 152–166; and A. S. Huff and R. K. Reger, "A Review of Strategic Process Research," *Journal of Management* 13, no. 2 (1987), pp. 211–236.

[26]H. Mintzberg, D. Raisinghani, and A. Théorêt, "The Structure of Unstructured Decision Processes," *Administrative Science Quarterly* 21 (June 1976), pp. 246–275; P. C. Nutt, "Types of Organizational Decision Processes," *Administrative Science Quarterly* 29 (September 1984), pp. 414–450; and E. Witte, "Field Research on Complex Decision-Making Processes—The Phase Theorem," *International Studies of Management and Organization* 2 (Summer 1972), pp. 156–182.

[27]Witte (1972), p. 179.

Mintzberg et al. and Nutt, in their studies of strategic decision making, found it equally difficult to specify a simple sequence of steps.[28] After developing general models of the process, they identified a number of distinct paths through them, each representing a different type or style of decision making.

A second group of scholars adopted a more focused approach. Each studied a particular kind of decision, usually involving large dollar investments, to identify the constituent activities, subprocesses, and associated management roles and responsibilities, as well as the contextual factors shaping the process. Much of this research has examined the resource allocation process, with studies of capital budgeting, foreign investments, strategic planning, internal corporate venturing, and business exit.[29] This research has led to two important insights:

First, it has forced scholars to acknowledge the simultaneous, multilevel quality of decision processes. While sequential stages can be specified, they are incomplete as process theories and must be supplemented by detailed descriptions of the interaction of activities, via subprocesses, across organizational levels and through time. Bower, for example, identified three major components of the resource allocation process—definition (the development of financial goals, strategies, and product–market plans), impetus (the crafting, selling, and choice of projects), and determination of context (the creation of structures, systems, and incentives guiding the process)—and then went on to describe the linkage among these activities and the interdependent roles of corporate, divisional, and middle managers.[30] A simple stages model was unable to capture the richness of the process: the range of interlinked activities, with reciprocal impacts, that were unfolding at multiple organizational levels. This finding has obvious implications for managers because it suggests that effective resource allocation—as well as most other types of decision making—requires attention to the perspectives and actions that are unfolding simultaneously above and below one's level in the organization.

Second, this body of research focused attention on the way that managers shape and influence decision processes. By describing the structural and strategic

[28]Mintzberg et al. (1976); and Nutt (1984).

[29]For studies on capital budgeting, see R. W. Ackerman, "Influence of Integration and Diversity on the Investment Process," *Administrative Science Quarterly* 15 (September 1970), pp. 341–351; and J.L. Bower, *Managing the Resource Allocation Process* (Boston: Harvard Business School, Division of Research, 1970). For studies on foreign investment, see Y. Aharoni, *The Foreign Investment Decision Process* (Boston: Harvard Business School, Division of Research, 1966). For studies on strategic planning, see P. Haspeslagh, "Portfolio Planning: Uses and Limits," *Harvard Business Review* 60 (January–February 1982), pp. 58–74; and R. Simons, "Planning, Control, and Uncertainty: A Process View," in W.J. Bruns, Jr., and R.S. Kaplan, eds., *Accounting and Management: Field Study Perspectives* (Boston: Harvard Business School Press, 1987), pp. 339–367. For studies on internal corporate venturing, see R.A. Burgelman, "A Process Model of Internal Corporate Venturing in the Diversified Major Firm," *Administrative Science Quarterly* 28 (June 1983), pp. 223–244; and R.A. Burgelman, "Strategy Making as a Social Learning Process: The Case of Internal Corporate Venturing," *Interfaces* 18, no. 3 (1988), pp. 74–85. For studies on business exit, see R.A. Burgelman, "Fading Memories: A Process Theory of Strategic Business Exit in Dynamic Environments," *Administrative Science Quarterly* 39 (March 1994), pp. 24–56.

[30]Bower (1970).

context—the rules by which the game is played, including the organization's goals, values, and reward systems—and showing how it is formed through actions and policies, scholars have demonstrated how senior managers are able to have a pronounced impact on decisions made elsewhere in the organization. While behavioral processes like decision making have great autonomy and persistence, they can, according to this line of research, be shaped and directed by managerial action.

Another stream of research has explored the quality of decision making. Scholars have studied flawed decisions to better understand their causes, examined the factors supporting speedy decision making, and contrasted the effectiveness of comprehensive and narrow decision processes.[31] These studies have noted certain distinctive problems that arise because organizational decision making is a collective effort. Janis, for example, citing foreign policy debacles such as the Bay of Pigs, noted that when members of a decision-making group want to preserve social cohesion and strive for unanimity, they may engage in self-censorship, overoptimism, and stereotyped views of the enemy, causing them to override more realistic assessments of alternatives.[32] However, certain techniques that introduce conflict and dissent, such as devil's advocacy and dialectical inquiry, have been found to overcome these problems in both controlled experiments and real-world situations.[33]

After the Bay of Pigs fiasco, President Kennedy explicitly reformed the national security decision-making process to include devil's advocacy and dialectical inquiry, and used both techniques to great effect during the Cuban Missile Crisis.[34] Similarly, Bourgeois and Eisenhardt found that successful, speedy decision making relied on rational approaches, the development of simultaneous multiple alternatives, and the use of up-to-date operating information to form judgments.[35] For managers, the implications of this line of research should be

----

[31]G. T. Allison, *Essence of Decision* (Boston: Little, Brown, 1971); I.L. Janis, *Victims of Groupthink* (Boston: Houghton Mifflin, 1972); L.J. Bourgeois, III, and K.M. Eisenhardt, "Strategic Decision Processes in High-Velocity Environments: Four Cases in the Microcomputer Industry," *Management Science* 34, no. 7 (1988), pp. 816–835; K.M. Eisenhardt, "Speed and Strategic Choice: How Managers Accelerate Decision Making," *California Management Review* 32 (Spring 1990), pp. 39–54; J.W. Fredrickson and T.R. Mitchell, "Strategic Decision Processes: Comprehensiveness and Performance in an Industry with an Unstable Environment," *Academy of Management Journal* 27, no. 2 (1984), pp. 399–423; J.W. Fredrickson, "The Comprehensiveness of Strategic Decision Processes: Extension, Observations, Future Directions," *Academy of Management Journal* 27, no. 4 (1984), pp. 445–466; and I. Nonaka and J.K. Johansson, "Organizational Learning in Japanese Companies," in R. Lamb and P. Shrivastava, eds., *Advances in Strategic Management*, vol. 3 (Greenwich, CT: JAI Press, 1985), pp. 277–296.

[32]Janis (1972).

[33]A.C. Amason, "Distinguishing the Effects of Functional and Dysfunctional Conflict on Strategic Decision Making: Resolving a Paradox for Top Management Teams," *Academy of Management Journal* 39, no. 1 (1996), pp. 123–148; D.M. Schweiger, W.R. Sandberg, and J.W. Ragan, "Group Approaches for Improving Strategic Decision Making," *Academy of Management Journal* 29, no. 1 (1986), pp. 51–71; and D.M. Schweiger, W.R. Sandberg, and P.L. Rechner, "Experimental Effects of Dialectical Inquiry, Devil's Advocacy, and Consensus Approaches to Strategic Decision Making," *Academy of Management Journal* 32, no. 4 (1989), pp. 745–772.

[34]Janis (1972), pp. 146–149.

[35]Bourgeois and Eisenhardt (1988).

obvious: the need to introduce healthy conflict and competing perspectives to ensure more effective, timely decision making.

Together, these studies have shown that decision-making processes are lengthy, complex, and slow to change. They involve multiple, often overlapping stages, engage large numbers of people at diverse levels, suffer from predictable biases and perceptual filters, and are shaped by the administrative, structural, and strategic context. Their effectiveness can be judged, using criteria such as speed, flexibility, range of alternatives considered, logical consistency, and results, and they are subject to managerial influence and control. Perhaps most important, these studies have shown that decision making, like other behavioral processes, can be characterized along a few simple dimensions that managers can review and alter if needed. A company's decision-making processes may be slow or fast, generate few or many alternatives, rely primarily on operating or financial data, engage few or many organizational levels, involve consensual or hierarchical resolution of conflicts, and be tolerant of or closed to divergent opinions.

Communication Processes.   Social psychologists and sociologists have long studied communication processes, dating back to the original human relations experiments at the Hawthorne Works of Western Electric, the pioneering studies of Kurt Lewin, and the efforts of the National Training Laboratories to establish the field of organizational development.[36] The field currently covers a broad array of processes and interactions, including face-to-face, within-group, and intergroup relationships.

The efficacy of these relationships invariably rests on the quality and richness of interpersonal communication and information-processing activities: how individuals and groups share data, agree on agendas and goals, and iron out conflicts as they go about their work.[37] These processes frequently become patterned and predictable. But because they are embedded in everyday work flows, they are not always immediately apparent. Like decision-making processes, they reflect unconscious assumptions and routines and can often be identified only after repeated observations of individuals and groups. Moreover, the underlying processes are quite subtle, as Schein has observed:

> Many formulations of communication depict it as a simple problem of transfer of information from one person to another. But . . . the process is anything but simple, and the information transferred is often highly variable and complex. We communicate facts, feelings, perceptions, innuendoes, and various other things all in the same "simple" message. We communicate not only through the spoken and written word but through

---

[36]E.H. Schein, *Process Consultation: Its Role in Organization Development,* 2nd ed. (Reading, MA: Addison-Wesley, 1988), pp. 17–19.

[37]D.G. Ancona and D.A. Nadler, "Top Hats and Executive Tales: Designing the Senior Team," *Sloan Management Review* 31 (Fall 1989), pp. 19–28; and D.C. Hambrick, "Top Management Groups: A Conceptual Integration and Reconsideration of the 'Team' Label," in B.M. Staw and L.L. Cummings, eds., *Research in Organizational Behavior,* vol. 16 (Greenwich, CT: JAI Press, 1994), pp. 171–214.

facial expressions, gestures, physical posture, tone of voice, timing of when we speak, what we do not say, and so on.[38]

Because of these complexities, communication processes are best characterized along multiple dimensions. Schein has provided a relatively complete set of categories, including frequency and duration, direction, triggers and flow, style, and level and depth.[39] Some patterns can be captured through the tools of communication engineering, which model communication networks and present a picture of a group's information linkages and flows in the same way that work processes are often mapped.[40]

A few studies have pursued an intermediate level of analysis, combining activities into subprocesses. These subprocesses fall into two distinct categories: those needed for task management and work accomplishment and those for building the group and maintaining its relationships.[41] Examples of the first include information giving and seeking and opinion giving and seeking, and examples of the second include harmonizing and compromising. Several scholars have used these categories to develop simple self-assessment forms for evaluating group processes and have then linked the results to group effectiveness.[42]

Together, these studies provide a relatively complete set of categories for diagnosing and evaluating communication processes. Like decision-making processes, they can be characterized along a few simple dimensions. Here, too, managers can use the dimensions to profile their organizations and identify areas needing improvement. The nature, direction, and quality of discussion flows are important, as are the interrelationships among group members, their stances toward one another, and the tenor and tone of group work.

Organizational Learning Processes.   A wide range of scholars, including organizational theorists, social psychologists, manufacturing experts, and systems thinkers have studied organizational learning processes.[43] There is broad agreement that organizational learning is essential to organizational health and survival,

---

[38]Schein (1988), p. 21.

[39]Ibid., pp. 22–39.

[40]O. Hauptman, "Making Communication Work," *Prism* (second quarter, 1992), pp. 71–81; and D. Krackhardt and J.R. Hanson, "Informal Networks: The Company behind the Chart," *Harvard Business Review* 71 (July–August 1993), pp. 104–111.

[41]Ancona and Nadler (1989), p. 24; Schein (1988), p. 50.

[42]D. McGregor, *The Professional Manager* (New York: McGraw-Hill, 1967), pp. 173–174; and Schein (1988), pp. 57–58, 81–82.

[43]R.L. Daft and G.P. Huber, "How Organizations Learn: A Communication Framework," in S.B. Bacharach and N. DiTomaso, eds., *Research in the Sociology of Organizations,* vol. 5 (Greenwich, CT: JAI Press, 1987), pp. 1–36; C.M. Fiol and M.A. Lyles, "Organizational Learning," *Academy of Management Review* 10, no. 4 (1985), pp. 803–813; G.P. Huber, "Organizational Learning: The Contributing Processes and the Literatures," *Organization Science* 2, no. 1 (1991), pp. 88–115; B. Levitt and J.G. March, "Organizational Learning," *Annual Review of Sociology* 14 (1988), pp. 319–340; and P. Shrivastava, "A Typology of Organizational Learning Systems," *Journal of Management Studies* 20, no. 1 (1983), pp. 7–28.

involves the creation and acquisition of new knowledge, and rests ultimately on the development of shared perspectives (often called "mental models"). Most scholars have described these activities abstractly, without trying to group or categorize them. But there are persistent underlying patterns. The way an organization approaches learning is as deeply embedded as its approaches to decision making and communication.[44]

Four broad processes are involved: knowledge acquisition, interpretation, dissemination, and retention. In each area, companies appear to rely on relatively few approaches that fit their cultures and have been adapted to their needs. Over time, these approaches become institutionalized as the organization's dominant mode or style of learning. According to Nevis et al.: "Basic assumptions about the culture lead to learning values and investments that produce a different learning style from a culture with a different pattern of values and investments."[45]

Knowledge, for example, may be acquired in many ways. Each approach involves distinctive tools, systems, and behaviors and is associated with a particular learning style. The underlying processes differ accordingly. Companies like DuPont have focused their efforts on brainstorming and creativity techniques; others, like Boeing and Microsoft, have become adept at learning from their own internal manufacturing and development experiences. AT&T and Xerox have gained considerable skill at benchmarking competitors and world leaders; others, like Royal Dutch/Shell, have used hypothetical planning exercises to stimulate learning. Similar distinctions exist for the processes of knowledge interpretation, dissemination, and retention. Retention, for example, may be through written records or tacitly understood routines, and the organization's memory may be accessed by a range of indexing and retrieval processes.[46]

Organizational learning processes thus share many of the same characteristics as decision-making and communication processes. Activity is distributed throughout the organization, unfolds over time, involves people in diverse departments and positions, and rests on a few critical subprocesses or routines. It too is "an organizational process rather than an individual process" and can be classified

---

[44]P.M. Brenner, "Assessing the Learning Capabilities of an Organization" (Cambridge, MA: MIT Sloan School of Management, unpublished master's thesis, 1994); Daft and Huber (1987), pp. 24–28; D.A. Garvin, "Building a Learning Organization," *Harvard Business Review* 71 (July–August 1993), pp. 78–91; Levitt and March (1988), pp. 320; and E.C. Nevis, A.J. DiBella, and J.M. Gould, "Understanding Organizations as Learning Systems," *Sloan Management Review* 37 (Winter 1995), pp. 73–85.

[45]Nevis et al. (1995), p. 76.

[46]T. Kiely, "The Idea Makers," *Technology Review* 96 (January 1993), pp. 32–40; M.A. Cusumano and R.W. Selby, *Microsoft Secrets* (New York: Free Press, 1995); Garvin (1993); J. Simpson, L. Field, and D.A. Garvin, "The Boeing 767: From Concept to Production (A)" (Boston: Harvard Business School, case 9-688-040, 1988); R.C. Camp, *Benchmarking* (Milwaukee, WI: ASOC Quality Press, 1989); R.E. Mittelstaedt, Jr., "Benchmarking: How to Learn from Best-in-Class Practices," *National Productivity Review* 11 (Summer 1992), pp. 301–315; A. De Geus, "Planning as Learning," *Harvard Business Review* 66 (March–April 1988), pp. 70–74; Huber (1991), pp. 105–107; Levitt and March (1988), pp. 326–329; and J.P. Walsh and G.R. Ungson, "Organizational Memory," *Academy of Management Review* 16, no. 1 (1991), pp. 57–91.

into distinctive modes or styles.[47] In fact, when combined together, the three behavioral processes are often complementary and synergistic. They interact in predictable ways, producing clusters of characteristics that are mutually reinforcing.

In the microcomputer industry, for example, the most effective firms were able to make quick decisions.[48] Their ability to do so rested on several mutually reinforcing activities. Decision making was rational and analytical, based on multiple alternatives and real-time operating information. Communication was open and wide ranging, with discussions that relied on shared ideas, pooled information, and the judgment of a few trusted counselors, but vested final authority with the chief executive officer (CEO). Organizational learning was guided primarily by external scanning and search. There is an important message here for managers. Just as administrative and operational processes must be complementary and supportive, so too must behavioral processes.

Unfortunately, managers frequently assume that restructuring or reengineering work processes will be accompanied by simultaneous, virtually automatic changes in behavior. Such changes are usually considered essential for successful transformations.[49] But because they reflect deeper forces, these behaviors normally remain in place unless the underlying processes are tackled explicitly. Managers must recognize that successful improvement programs require explicit attention to the organization's characteristic patterns of decision making, communication, and learning. Tools for stimulating change include simulations, exercises, observations, and coaching; each may be applied at the individual and organizational levels.

Change Processes

The change process approach, which has roots in strategic management, organization theory, social psychology, and business history, focuses on sequences of events over time. These sequences, called processes, describe how individuals, groups, and organizations adapt, develop, and grow. Change processes are explicitly dynamic and intertemporal. Unlike the relatively static portraits of work and behavioral processes, they attempt "to catch reality in flight."[50] Examples of change processes include the organizational life cycle and Darwinian evolution.

All change processes share several characteristics. They are longitudinal and dynamic, designed to capture action as it unfolds, with three components always present: "a set of starting conditions, a functional end-point, and an emergent process of change."[51] Change processes therefore answer the question, "How did

---

[47]Shrivastava (1983), p. 16.

[48]Bourgeois and Eisenhardt (1988); and Eisenhardt (1990).

[49]B. Blumenthal and P. Haspeslagh, "Toward a Definition of Corporate Transformation," *Sloan Management Review* 35 (Spring 1994), pp. 101–106.

[50]A.M. Pettigrew, "Longitudinal Field Research: Theory and Practice," *Organization Science* 1, no. 3 (1990), pp. 267–292, quote from p. 270.

[51]Van de Ven (1992), p. 80.

x get from here to there?" Often, a story or narrative is required to provide coherence and explain the underlying logic of the process.[52] Most descriptions of change also divide time into broad stages or phases. Each stage consists of groups of activities aimed at roughly similar goals, and the transition between stages may be smooth or turbulent.[53]

Studies of change have focused on four broad areas: creation, growth, transformation, and decline.[54] Each period represents a critical stage in the individual or organizational life cycle, and, over time, the life cycle has become the organizing framework for the field. Scholars remain divided, however, about the pattern and flow of events over time. The primary question is whether change processes proceed through incremental steps—what Gersick has called "a slow stream of small mutations"—or through alternating periods of stability and revolutionary change.[55] Ultimately, the choice is between traditional Darwinian theories and those based on a newer, punctuated equilibrium framework. While the subject is still under debate, evidence supporting the latter view is accumulating rapidly.[56]

Whatever their focus, change processes fall into two broad categories: autonomous and induced. Autonomous processes have a life of their own; they proceed because of an internal dynamic. The entity or organism evolves naturally and of its own course. In some cases, the direction of change is preordained and inevitable. In others, transitional periods create flux, and the entity may evolve in multiple, unexpected ways. Processes in the former category include an organization's evolution from informal, entrepreneurial start-up to a more structured, professionally managed firm. Processes in the second category include organizational and industry shifts that result from revolutionary changes

---

[52]Van de Ven and Huber (1990).

[53]C.J.G. Gersick, "Revolutionary Change Theories: A Multilevel Exploration of the Punctuated Equilibrium Paradigm," *Academy of Management Review* 16, no. 1 (1991), pp. 10–36.

[54]For studies on creation, see D.N.T. Perkins, V.F. Nieva, and E.E. Lawler, III, *Managing Creation: The Challenge of Building a New Organization* (New York: Wiley, 1983); S.B. Sarason, *The Creation of Settings and the Future Societies* (San Francisco: Jossey-Bass, 1972); and A.H. Van de Ven, "Early Planning, Implementation, and Performance of New Organizations," in J.R. Kimberly, R.H. Miles, and associates, *The Organizational Life Cycle* (San Francisco: Jossey-Bass, 1980), pp. 83–134. For studies on growth, see W.H. Starbuck, ed., *Organizational Growth and Development: Selected Readings* (Middlesex, England: Penguin, 1971). For studies on transformation, see J.R. Kimberly and R.E. Quinn, eds., *New Futures: The Challenge of Managing Corporate Transitions* (Homewood, IL: Dow Jones-Irwin, 1984); A.M. Mohrman, Jr., S.A. Mohrman, G.E. Ledford, Jr., T.G. Cummings, E.E. Lawler, III, and associates, *Large-Scale Organizational Change* (San Francisco: Jossey-Bass, 1989). For studies on decline, see D.C. Hambrick and R.A. D'Aveni, "Large Corporate Failures as Downward Spirals," *Administrative Science Quarterly* 33 (March 1988), pp. 1–23; R.I. Sutton, "Organizational Decline Processes: A Social Psychological Perspective," in B.M. Staw and L.L. Cummings, eds., *Research in Organizational Behavior,* vol. 12 (Greenwich, CT: JAI Press, 1990), pp. 205–253; and S. Venkataraman, A.H. Van de Ven, J. Buckeye, and R. Hudson, "Starting Up in a Turbulent Environment," *Journal of Business Venturing* 5, no. 5 (1990), pp. 277–295.

[55]Gersick (1991), p. 10.

[56]M. Crozier, *The Bureaucratic Phenomenon* (Chicago: University of Chicago Press, 1964), p. 196; Gersick (1991); H. Mintzberg, "Patterns in Strategy Formation," *Management Science* 24, no. 9 (1978), pp. 934–948; Starbuck (1971), p. 68; and Van de Ven (1992).

in technology.[57] In both cases, Selznick has observed, managers must be attentive to the path and timing of development: "Certain types of problems seem to characterize phases of an organization's life-history. As these problems emerge, the organization is confronted with critical policy decisions."[58] Appropriate action depends, in large part, on fitting behavior to the conditions and requirements of the current stage.[59] An obvious example is knowing when to introduce policies, procedures, and systems into a loosely knit, entrepreneurial firm. Too early, and growth may be stifled; too late, and the organization may already have spun out of control.

Unlike autonomous processes, induced processes do not occur naturally but must be created. All planned change efforts therefore fall into this category. While they are triggered in different ways, such efforts, once underway, unfold in a predictable sequence. Each step is accompanied by distinctive challenges and tasks, with striking parallels in different theorists' descriptions. Induced change processes are commonly divided into three basic stages.[60] The first is a period of questioning, when the current state is assessed and energy applied to dislodge accepted patterns. The second stage is one of flux, when old ways are partially suspended and new approaches are tested and developed. The third is a period of consolidation, when new attitudes and behaviors become institutionalized and widely adopted. Again, it is critical that managers develop actions appropriate to the current stage and know when it is time to shift to a new stage. Examples of three-part theories include Beckhard and Harris's present state, transition state, and future state; Lewin's and Schein's unfreezing, changing, and refreezing; and Tichy and Devanna's awakening, mobilizing, and reinforcing.[61]

We can thus classify change processes on a few simple dimensions: They may be autonomous or induced, and involve slow incremental evolution or alternating periods of stability and revolutionary change. Complete process descriptions

---

[57]L.E. Greiner, "Evolution and Revolution as Organizations Grow," *Harvard Business Review* 50 (July–August 1972), pp. 37–46; and M.L. Tushman and P. Anderson, "Technological Discontinuities and Organizational Environments," *Administrative Science Quarterly* 31 (September 1986), pp. 439–465.

[58]P. Selznick, *Leadership in Administration* (Berkeley: University of California Press, 1957), pp. 103–104.

[59]M.L. Tushman, W.H. Newman, and E. Romanelli, "Convergence and Upheaval: Managing the Unsteady Pace of Organizational Evolution," *California Management Review* 29 (Fall 1986), pp. 29–44.

[60]R.M. Kanter, B.A. Stein, and T.D. Jick, *The Challenge of Organizational Change* (New York: Free Press, 1992), pp. 375–377.

[61]R. Beckhard and R.T. Harris, *Organizational Transitions,* 2nd ed. (Reading, MA: Addison-Wesley, 1987); K. Lewin, *Field Theory in Social Science* (New York: Harper, 1951); E.H. Schein, *Professional Education* (New York: McGraw-Hill, 1972), pp. 76–84; and N. Tichy and M. Devanna, *The Transformational Leader* (New York: Wiley, 1986).

EXHIBIT 1   An Organizational Processes Framework

	Work Processes	*Behavioral Processes*	*Change Processes*
Definition	• Sequences of activities that transform inputs into outputs	• Widely shared patterns of behavior and ways of acting/interacting	• Sequences of events over time
Role	• Accomplish the work of the organization	• Infuse and shape the way work is conducted by influencing how individuals and groups behave	• Alter the scale, character, and identity of the organization
Major categories	• Operational and administrative	• Individual and interpersonal	• Autonomous and induced, incremental and revolutionary
Examples	• New-product development, order fulfillment, strategic planning	• Decision making, communication, organizational learning	• Creation, growth, transformation, decline

---

also include the precise sequence, duration, and timing of stages, as well as the nature and number of activities and participants at each stage.[62]

A Recap of Organizational Processes

The three major approaches to organizational processes have much in common (see Exhibit 1). Each views processes as collections of activities, involving many people, that unfold over time. Each involves repeated, predictable sequences or patterns. And each takes a holistic approach, grouping individual activities and decisions in coherent, logical ways. The latter quality is especially important because it suggests that processes provide managers with a powerful integrating device, a way of meshing specialized, segmented tasks with larger organizational needs.

Despite these similarities, the three types of processes capture different organizational phenomena and are best viewed as complementary pieces of a larger puzzle. They can, in fact, be combined into a single framework that includes both cross-sectional and dynamic elements. (For a unified portrait of organizations as collections and reflections of processes, see Exhibit 2.)

A process view of organizations offers several advantages. First, it provides a disaggregated model of the firm, but does so in ways that make the analysis of

---

[62]A. Abbott, "A Primer on Sequence Methods," *Organization Science* 1, no. 4 (1990), pp. 375–392; Monge (1990); A. Strauss and J. Corbin, *Basics of Qualitative Research* (Newbury Park, CA: Sage, 1990), chap. 9; and Witte (1972).

EXHIBIT 2   A Diagram of Organizational Processes

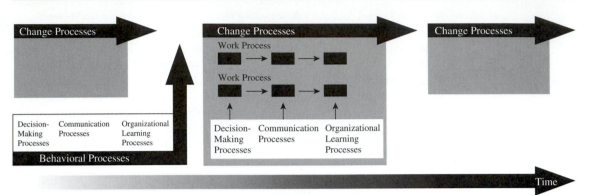

implementation more tractable and explicit. Put another way, if organizations are "systems for getting work done,"[63] processes provide a fine-grained description of the means. Second, the diagram suggests the intimate connections among different types of processes and the futility of analyzing them in isolation. It is extraordinarily difficult—and, at times, impossible—to understand or alter a single process without first taking account of others on which it depends.[64]

Perhaps most important for managers, a process view of organizations changes the focus of both analysis and action. All too often, managers' first response to problems is to pin responsibility on an individual or department. Yet because processes shape the vast majority of organizational activities, they are frequently the true sources of difficulty. Accountability must therefore shift to a higher level: to those with wide enough spans of control to oversee entire processes. This principle has long been a staple of the quality movement, where it has been applied to operational processes. The preceding arguments suggest that managers need to be equally attentive to administrative, behavioral, and change processes. As a general rule, responsibility for these processes must shift to senior members of the firm.

Approaches to organization design must change as well. Most texts on the subject focus on tasks and structures, with detailed discussions of roles, positions, levels, and reporting relationships.[65] They say relatively little about processes or about how the work actually gets done. The implicit argument seems to be that organization design is largely a matter of architecture: drawing the right boxes and connecting them appropriately. A process perspective suggests that far more

[63]C. Perrow, "A Framework for the Comparative Analysis of Organizations," *American Sociological Review* 32, no. 2 (1967), pp. 194–208, quote from p. 195.

[64]D. A. Garvin, "Leveraging Processes for Strategic Advantage," *Harvard Business Review* 73 (September–October 1995), pp. 76–90.

[65]See, for example, Galbraith (1977); and Schlesinger, Sathe, Schlesinger, and Kotter (1992).

attention should be paid to organizational functioning, and that design efforts should begin by attending to processes and only later should shift to the structures needed to accommodate them.

Finally, this approach suggests that managers are continually enmeshed in organizational processes. The result is a delicate balancing act. On the one hand, managers are constrained by the processes they face, forced to work within their boundaries and preestablished steps to get things done. On the other hand, they try to influence and alter these processes to gain advantage. This continual shifting from "statesman" to "gamesman" is what makes management such a challenging task.[66] It also suggests another, quite different use of the world *processes*.

MANAGERIAL PROCESSES

Management is often described as the art of getting things done. But because organizations are complex social institutions with widely distributed responsibility and resources, unilateral action is seldom sufficient.[67] Managers therefore spend the bulk of their time working with, and through, other people.[68] They face a range of challenges: how to get the organization moving in the desired direction, how to gain the allegiance and support of critical individuals, and how to harmonize diverse group interests and goals. In the broadest sense, these are questions of process: They involve how things are done, rather than the content or substance of ideas or policies.

The mechanics of implementation thus lie at the heart of this definition of processes. The focus is on the way that managers orchestrate activities and events and engage others in tasks so that desired ends are realized (see the sidebar on managerial processes, p. 20). Action is the key, and process is implicitly equated with skilled professional practice. Not surprisingly, this use of the term *process* appears in a wide range of professions where there is need for artistry, subjectivity, and careful discriminations. Architects, for example, engage in the design process; scientists employ the scientific process; and psychologists engage in the counseling process. Like management, each activity involves complex, contingent choices about how best to transform intentions into results.

Managerial processes, however, involve additional complications. Many scholars agree that "organizations . . . are fundamentally political entities,"[69] composed of diverse groups with their own interests that come into conflict over agendas

---

[66]W. G. Astley and A. H. Van de Ven, "Central Perspectives and Debates in Organization Theory," *Administrative Science Quarterly* 28 (June 1983), pp. 245–273, quote from p. 263.

[67]C. A. Bartlett and S. Ghoshal, "Beyond the M-Form: Toward a Managerial Theory of the Firm," *Strategic Management Journal* 14 (special issue, Winter 1993), pp. 23–46.

[68]Hales (1986); Mintzberg (1973); Sayles (1989); and L. R. Sayles, *Managerial Behavior* (New York: McGraw-Hill, 1964).

[69]J. Pfeffer, "Understanding Power in Organizations," *California Management Review* 34 (Winter 1992), pp. 29–50, quote from p. 29.

Descriptions of Managerial Processes

• "Managing is a social process. It is a process because it comprises a series of actions that lead to the accomplishment of objectives. It is a social process because these actions are principally concerned with relations between people."
W.H. Newman, C.E. Summer, and E.K. Warren, *The Process of Management* (Englewood Cliffs, NJ: Prentice-Hall, 1972), p. 12.

• "Whether proposing a change in the executive compensation structure, establishing priorities for a diverse group of business units, consolidating redundant operations, or preparing for plant closings, a senior executive's conscious thoughts are foremost among the processes for accomplishing a change or implementing a decision: 'Who are the key players here, and how can I get their support? Whom should I talk to first? Should I start by getting the production group's input? What kind of signal will that send to the marketing people? I can't afford to lose their commitment in the upcoming discussions on our market strategy.'"
D.J. Isenberg, "How Senior Managers Think," *Harvard Business Review* 62 (November–December 1984), pp. 82–83.

• "Most of the literature of general management has separated the positional aspects [of the chief executive officer's function] from the managerial ones. In positional frameworks, the problem of managing is described in terms of getting the firm from one position to another. . . . In the managerial framework, attention is focused on how goals are developed, on how resources are allocated, and on how the efforts of individuals are coordinated to achieve particular goals and patterns of allocation. Managerial frameworks focus on the process of management more than on the overall direction followed by the company."
J.L. Bower and Y. Doz, "Strategy Formulation: A Social and Political Process," in D.H. Schendel and C.H. Hofer, eds., *Strategic Management* (Boston: Little, Brown, 1979), p. 153.

---

and resources.[70] In such settings, successful managers must align and harmonize competing interests, while cultivating commitment and motivation. Skillful managers therefore spend relatively little time issuing ultimatums or making big decisions. Rather, they engage in an extraordinary number of fragmented activities, tackling pressing issues or small pieces of larger problems.[71] Often, the

---

[70]Crozier (1964); J.G. March, "The Business Firm as a Political Coalition," *Journal of Politics* 24, no. 4 (1962), pp. 662–678; Sayles (1989); and M.L. Tushman, "A Political Approach to Organizations: A Review and Rationale," *Academy of Management Review* 2 (April 1977), pp. 206–216.
[71]Hales (1986); J.P. Kotter, *The General Managers* (New York: Free Press, 1982); Mintzberg (1973); and H.E. Wrapp, "Good Managers Don't Make Policy Decisions," *Harvard Business Review* 45 (September–October 1967), pp. 91–99.

process requires building and using interpersonal networks, as well as "skillful maneuvering" to overcome political obstacles.[72]

The challenge for managers, then, is to shape, prod, and direct their organizations, through words and deeds, so that larger goals are realized. The approaches they use—which were once the subject of courses on administrative practice— are managerial processes. They have an underlying logic that is easily missed when scholars focus on taxonomies of discrete tasks and activities, rather than unifying threads.[73] Moreover, because these processes require flexibility and a sensitivity to context, they seldom unfold in the same set sequence or maintain the same character on every occasion.[74]

Empirical studies of managerial processes fall into two broad categories. One group has taken an anthropological approach focusing on a single manager in action, with vivid descriptions of his or her behavior. Case studies in business policy fall into this category, as do studies by insiders or journalists who have gained unusual access to a company.[75] The associated processes have usually been idiosyncratic and highly individualistic, reflecting the distinctive character of the managers studied. Such nuanced, textured descriptions provide invaluable insight into the processes of management but permit few generalizations.

A second group of empirical studies, usually by scholars, has sought broader conclusions. Typically, they have reviewed the time commitments and activities of a few managers, grouped them into categories according to purposes and goals, and then applied a process perspective. Three broad processes have dominated this literature: direction setting, negotiating and selling, and monitoring and control.

Direction-Setting Processes

Direction setting, the most widely recognized managerial activity, has appeared, in some form, in most empirical studies of managerial work.[76] It involves charting an organization's course and then mobilizing support and ensuring alignment

---

[72]E.M. Leifer and H.C. White, "Wheeling and Annealing: Federal and Multidivisional Control," in J.F. Short, Jr., ed., *The Social Fabric* (Beverly Hills, CA: Sage, 1986), pp. 223–242.

[73]Hill (1992); and Kotter (1982).

[74]W. Skinner and W.E. Sasser, "Managers with Impact: Versatile and Inconsistent," *Harvard Business Review* 55 (November–December 1977), pp. 140–148.

[75]Examples include *The Soul of a New Machine,* featuring Tom West, the leader of a project to build a new minicomputer at Data General Corporation, and *My Years with General Motors,* written by Alfred Sloan, who resurrected General Motors in the more than 20 years that he served as the company's chief executive and chairman. See J.T. Kidder, *The Soul of a New Machine* (Boston: Little, Brown, 1981); and A.P. Sloan, Jr., *My Years with General Motors* (New York: Doubleday, 1963).

[76]Mintzberg (1973), p. 92; Sayles (1964), chap. 9; and Hales (1986).

with stated goals. Kotter's description of how general managers met this challenge is representative.[77] All the managers he studied began by developing an agenda, collecting information from a wide range of sources, and then assimilating it and forming a few broad thrusts or general goals. They then worked hard to frame messages, using diverse communication media and opportunities, to ensure that members of the organization developed a shared understanding of the new objectives. Often, these activities occurred within the broad parameters of the organization's planning or goal-setting process, although much work was informal and unstructured, tailored to the unique skill of the manager and the distinctive demands of the situation. Gabarro and Simons reached similar conclusions in their studies of the "taking charge" process of new executives, where individualized managerial action was coupled with established organizational processes.[78]

Together, these empirical studies have shown that direction-setting processes have several components: learning about the organization and its problems through a broad range of interactions, assessments, and continued probing; framing an agenda to be pursued during the manager's tenure through conscious reflection and intuitive experience; and aligning individuals through communication, motivation, rewards, and punishments, often using new or established organizational processes. Critical process choices that the manager makes include which information sources to tap, which communication media and supporting systems to emphasize, and which approaches to use in framing, testing, and revising initiatives.

Negotiating and Selling Processes

Once the manager sets a direction, negotiating and selling processes are necessary for getting the job done. They work in two directions, horizontally and vertically. Because horizontal flows link the activities of most departments, employees frequently rely on individuals outside their work groups for essential services and information.[79] Formal authority is normally lacking in these relationships, and managers must use other means to gain cooperation. This usually requires building a network of contacts and then working with the appropriate individuals to negotiate the "terms of trade" for current and future interactions.[80] Various approaches are used to gain support, including currying favor, creating dependence, providing quid pro quos, and appealing to compelling organizational needs.

---

[77]Kotter (1982).

[78]J.J. Gabarro, *The Dynamics of Taking Charge* (Boston: Harvard Business School Press, 1987); and R. Simons, "How New Top Managers Use Control Systems as Levers of Strategic Renewal," *Strategic Management Journal* 15, no. 3 (1994), pp. 169–189.

[79]Sayles (1964).

[80]Hill (1992); Kotter (1982); F. Luthans, R.M. Hodgetts, and S.A. Rosenkrantz, *Real Managers* (Cambridge, MA: Ballinger, 1988); and Mintzberg (1973).

Successful negotiating requires an understanding of "the strengths and weaknesses of others, the relationships that are important to them, what their agendas and priorities are."[81] Issues must be shaped and presented in ways that are palatable to individuals and groups with differing interests and needs. Sayles, who has conducted the most extensive research on these processes, noted that they usually began with "missionary work," in which potential buyers and sellers were identified for possible future use.[82] A surprising range of contacts was necessary because horizontal relationships fell into so many different categories. All, however, required skilled salesmanship: the ability to interest outsiders in a project, gain exceptions from staff groups, and convince support specialists to invest time and resources. For this reason, the most critical process choices involved framing and presentation: deciding how to solicit help and present proposals in ways that appealed to others yet met one's basic objectives.

Selling is also required in a vertical direction. Middle managers must normally convince their superiors of the value of their proposals if they hope to see them enacted; to do so, they frame projects to highlight urgency and need, bundle them in ways that increase the likelihood of acceptance, and assemble coalitions to provide credibility and support.[83] This activity is not confined to middle managers. Chief executives engage extensively in selling, for it is often the only way they can gain acceptance of their strategies and plans.[84]

Monitoring and Control Processes

Once operations are underway, managers engage in a third set of processes, designed to ensure that their organizations are performing as planned. Such oversight activities are necessary because business environments are inherently unstable; they generate any number of unexpected shocks and disturbances. Monitoring and control processes detect perturbations, initiate corrective action, and restore the organization to its previous equilibrium.[85] Typically, managers begin with efforts to sense problems and formulate them clearly, followed by probes to clarify the problems' precise nature and underlying causes.[86] They collect information through their own contacts, others' contacts, observation, and re-

---

[81]D.J. Isenberg, "How Senior Managers Think," *Harvard Business Review* 62 (November–December 1984), pp. 80–90, quote from p. 84.

[82]Sayles (1964).

[83]J.E. Dutton and S.J. Ashford, "Selling Issues to Top Management," *Academy of Management Review* 18, no. 3 (1993), pp. 397–428; and I.C. MacMillan and W.D. Guth, "Strategy Implementation and Middle Management Coalitions," in R. Lamb and P. Shrivastava, eds., *Advances in Strategic Management,* vol. 3 (Greenwich, CT: JAI Press, 1985), pp. 233–254.

[84]D.C. Hambrick and A.A. Cannella, "Strategy Implementation as Substance and Selling," *Academy of Management Executive* 3, no. 4 (1989), pp. 278–285.

[85]Mintzberg (1973), pp. 67–71; and Sayles (1964).

[86]Isenberg (1984); and M.A. Lyles and T.I. Mitroff, "Organizational Problem Formulation: An Empirical Study," *Administrative Science Quarterly* 25 (March 1980), pp. 102–119.

views of records.[87] At times, they use formal organizational processes, like variance reporting; more often, effective monitoring is nonroutine and conducted as part of other, ongoing interactions.[88] Here, critical process choices include the information sources to tap, the data to request, the questions to pose, and the amount of time to allow before drawing conclusions and initiating corrective action.

Recapping Managerial Skills

These three processes have different purposes, tasks, and critical skills (see Exhibit 3). Although most managers treat them as distinct challenges, at a deeper level, they have much in common. All depend on rich communication, pattern recognition, a sensitivity to relationships, and an understanding of the organization's power structure. Perhaps most important, all managerial processes involve common choices about how to involve others and relate to them as the organization moves forward. They are the essence of the manager's craft and can be applied equally effectively to direction setting, negotiating and selling, and monitoring and control.

The variables are few, but the combinations are virtually limitless. Whatever the issue, all managerial processes involve six major choices that a manager must make:

1. **Participants.** (Whose opinions should I seek? Whom should I invite to meetings? Who should participate in task forces? Which groups should be represented?)
2. **Timing and sequencing.** (Whom should I approach first? Whom should I invite next? Which agreements should I solicit before others? How should I phase events over time?)
3. **Duration.** (How much time should I devote to information collection? How much time should I give to individuals and groups for their assignments? How should I pace events to build momentum?)
4. **Framing and presentation.** (How should I describe and interpret events? How should I heat up issues or cool them down? How should I frame proposals for superiors, subordinates, and peers? What questions should I ask to gain information?)
5. **Formats.** (Should I make requests in person or over the phone? Should I communicate information through speeches, group meetings, or face-to-face encounters?)
6. **Style.** (How should I induce others to cooperate? How should I utilize and distribute rewards and punishments? What tone should I take when dealing with superiors, subordinates, and peers?)

---

[87]Sayles (1964), p. 170.
[88]Mintzberg (1973), pp. 67–71.

EXHIBIT 3   A Managerial Processes Framework

	Direction-Setting Processes	*Negotiation and Selling Processes*	*Monitoring and Control Processes*
Purpose	• Establish organizational direction and goals	• Obtain needed support and resources	• Track ongoing activities and performance
Primary task	• Developing an agenda	• Building a network	• Collecting information
Critical skills	• Synthesis, priority setting, communication	• Timing and sequencing, framing and presentation	• Questioning and listening, interpreting data

There are many possible answers. This variety helps explain why management, like many other professions, continues to be more an art than a science.[89] In the face of massive uncertainty, managers must make complex choices with few precedents or guidelines; the resulting processes seldom repeat themselves exactly. Moreover, seemingly minor variations in processes can have major impacts. Changes in sequencing, with one critical individual or department contacted before another, or shifts in format, with written memoranda replacing face-to-face meetings, often produce dramatically different coalitions and results.[90] The subtlety of these distinctions, plus the enormous range of possibilities, is what makes managerial processes so difficult to master. But, by thinking in process terms, managers are much more likely to link together their activities to produce the desired ends.

IMPLICATIONS FOR ACTION

The process perspective fills an important gap. Most research on organizations either employs highly aggregated concepts like strategy or focuses on low-level tactics and tasks. Researchers often ignore the middle ground. Processes, by contrast, are intermediate-level concepts that combine activities into cohesive wholes, yet offer a fine-grained, differentiated perspective. They are also inherently dynamic. Because processes unfold over time, they capture linkages among activities that are often lost in static models and cross-sectional analyses. A process approach encourages thinking in story lines rather than events; the appropriate metaphor is a movie rather than a snapshot.[91]

For this reason, the approach is unusually helpful in addressing implementation problems. Managers can articulate the required steps in a process, as well as improvements. By contrast, traditional lists of roles and responsibilities leave the associated activities unspecified or undefined. Job descriptions framed in process terms should therefore make it easier for untrained individuals to step

[89]D. A. Schön, *The Reflective Practitioner* (New York: Basic Books, 1983), chaps. 1, 2, and 8.
[90]MacMillan and Guth (1985); and Bower and Doz (1979), pp. 152–153.
[91]Mohr (1982), p. 43.

EXHIBIT 4   A Framework for Action

		Organizational Processes	
	Work Processes	*Behavioral Processes*	*Change Processes*
Direction-Setting Processes	• Are there clear goals for operational and strategic performance?	• Are there well-specified approaches to communication, decision making, and learning?	• Is there a clear rationale, direction, and path of change?
Negotiation and Selling Processes	• Have we obtained the necessary agreements and resources from upstream and downstream departments?	• Is there widespread acceptance of the desired approaches to communication, decision making, and learning?	• Are others in the organization convinced that change is needed and that the proposed changes are the right ones?
Monitoring and Control Processes	• Do we know how well our performance matches plans?	• Do we know how well our current behaviors match the desired approaches to communication, decision making, and learning?	• Do we know whether critical milestones have been reached and planned changes have been implemented?

Managerial Processes (left vertical label)

into new jobs and acquire necessary skills.[92] Managers should be able to focus their questioning of peers and subordinates on issues more directly related to the organization's operation.[93] And a sensitivity to processes should give managers clearer guidelines about how and when to intervene effectively in others' work.[94]

We can combine the major organizational and managerial processes into a simple, integrating framework (see Exhibit 4). The framework consists of diagnostic questions that allow managers to assess the effectiveness of their, and their organization's, approaches to action. For example, the question "Is there a clear rationale, direction, and path of change?" asks managers to determine whether direction has been set effectively for a particular change process. Similarly, the question "Have we obtained the necessary agreements and resources from upstream and downstream departments?" assesses whether negotiation and selling have been conducted effectively for a given work process. Together, the questions provide a reasonably complete framework for evaluation.

---

[92]E. D. Chapple and L. R. Sayles, *The Measure of Management* (New York: Macmillan, 1961), pp. 49–50.

[93]Garvin (1995).

[94]E. H. Schein, *Process Consultation: Lessons for Managers and Consultants* (Reading, MA: Addison-Wesley, 1987); and Schein (1988).

The framework has two primary uses:

First, it can help managers decide where, when, and how to intervene in their organization's activities. To do so, they should work down the columns of the matrix, asking each question in turn to isolate the likely source of difficulties and identify appropriate remedial actions. Consider, for example, a company experiencing customer service problems. Because customer service is an operational (work) process, the questions in the first column provide guidance. If the answers suggest that problems can be traced to unclear goals, managers need to invest time in setting and clarifying objectives. If the problems reflect a lack of support from upstream designers and manufacturing personnel, managers need to devote time to cross-departmental negotiations and salesmanship. If the problems signify slow, limited customer feedback, managers need to upgrade the processes for monitoring and collecting information.

Managers can use the same approach for less tangible processes like decision making. Suppose that decision making is currently parochial and unimaginative, and managers have decided to improve the process by encouraging dissent and constructive conflict. Progress, however, has been slow. Because decision making is a behavioral process, managers should use the questions in the second column to diagnose the problem. If the answers suggest that difficulties can be traced to unclear concepts (e.g., "We don't know how to distinguish constructive from unproductive conflict"), managers should focus on improved direction setting. If the difficulties reflect underlying disagreements about the appropriateness of the desired behaviors (e.g., "We are a polite company and see no reason to argue with one another"), managers should focus on selling the new approaches. If the difficulties are caused by poor awareness of current practices (e.g., "We don't need to do anything differently because we already entertain diverse viewpoints and debate issues in depth"), managers need sharper real-time feedback and monitoring. Here, too, the matrix provides managers with a powerful lens for identifying the underlying sources of problems and for framing responses in process terms.

Second, the matrix helps managers identify their personal strengths and weaknesses. Because direction setting, negotiation and selling, and monitoring and control are very different processes, few managers are equally adept at all three. One way to identify areas needing work is for managers to proceed across the rows of the matrix, asking the relevant diagnostic questions about diverse organizational activities.

For example, to assess direction-setting skills, a manager might look at a number of operational processes under his or her control to see if clear goals have been established, might review a variety of decision-making and communication processes to see if preferred approaches were clearly described and understood, and might assess several current change initiatives to see if the rationale, direction, and paths of change were clear. A series of "no's" in a row means that the manager needs to improve direction setting. As with the previous assessments of organizational processes, managers can conduct these evaluations working alone in their offices, teams of executives responsible for related projects or programs can work in groups, or entire departments or units can work collectively. In general, the size of the evaluating group should correspond to the scope of the process under review, and the larger the group, the more likely that formal approaches to data collection such as surveys, questionnaires, and diagnostic scales will be needed.

Clearly, a process perspective has much to offer. It sheds light on many pressing questions of organization and management while providing a number of practical guidelines. Here I present a starting point, a taxonomy and frameworks for defining, distinguishing, and classifying the major types of processes. Used wisely, they will improve managers' ability to get things done.

ACKNOWLEDGMENTS

I would like to thank Christopher Bartlett, Joseph Bower, Robert Burgelman, Roland Christensen, Michael Cusumano, Alison Davis-Blake, Lynn Garvin, Donald Hambrick, Carl Kaysen, Ashish Nanda, Philip Rosenzweig, Malcolm Salter, Leonard Sayles, Leonard Schlesinger, David Upton, Richard Walton, Gerry Zaltman, and two anonymous referees for helpful comments on earlier drafts of this article, and the Division of Research, Harvard Business School, for financial support.

Module 1

Strategic Processes

OVERVIEW

Strategic decisions are big decisions; they are "concerned with the long-term health of the enterprise."[1] Typically, they focus on which businesses and markets to enter, which products and services to offer, and which capabilities and competencies to pursue. Entire courses in business policy and competitive analysis are devoted to identifying and applying the proper frameworks and tools for making these choices correctly. Much less attention, however, is usually paid to the underlying processes of strategy formulation, programming, and deployment.

Strategy formulation is the task of crafting strategy. The process is both analytical and intuitive, a combining of facts, feelings, and data in ways that lead to unexpected insights and approaches. At heart, it remains a rather mysterious, creative act that is difficult to describe or direct.[2]

Strategic programming is far more concrete; it is the process organizations follow when they "engage in formal planning, not to create strategies but to program the strategies they already have, that is, to elaborate and operationalize their consequences."[3] Programming involves the specification of policies and plans, as well as the associated task of setting goals and objectives. Put another way, if formulation is about "deciding where you want your business to go," programming is "figuring out how to get there."[4]

Strategy deployment, by contrast, is concerned with implementation: the actions managers must take in order to translate plans into reality. At times, the

---

[1]Alfred D. Chandler, Jr., *Strategy and Structure* (Cambridge, MA: MIT Press, 1962), p. 11.

[2]Henry Mintzberg, *The Rise and Fall of Strategic Planning* (New York: Free Press, 1994), especially chap. 6.

[3]Ibid., p. 333.

[4]Shona L. Brown and Kathleen M. Eisenhardt, *Competing on the Edge* (Boston: Harvard Business School Press, 1998), p. 3.

task is simple, such as communicating a new vision or appropriating required funds. At other times, the task is dauntingly complex, such as establishing a new division or integrating an acquisition into an established organization. But in either case, the work of strategy has not been completed until these actions have been taken.

To a large extent, strategic success depends on having all three processes in place and working smoothly. Activities must unfold in a sequence that generates the required analyses, decisions, and actions. The proper choices are unlikely to materialize on their own. Even when the choices are obvious—a desirable capital investment, perhaps, or a promising untapped market—there are invariably questions of how to ensure that execution is targeted and trouble free. In fact, success normally requires a seamless link between upstream and downstream activities. The best strategic processes are highly interdependent; they recognize that ideas are only of value if they can be put into practice. According to scholars,

> a well-conceived strategy is one that is *implementable.* For that reason, implementation must be considered *during* the formulation process, not later, when it may be too late. A tendency to treat formulation and implementation as two separate phases is the root of many failed strategies.[5]

OUTLINE

"Arthur D. Little, Inc." (ADL), the first case in this module, introduces the concept of processes and considers the links to strategy. The case features the very first consulting company in the United States, which maintained its number-one ranking in the industry for nearly a century. Despite its great success, ADL operated for many years with few formal processes. The organization was atomized and fragmented; consultants were treated as free agents; policies were virtually nonexistent; and required practices were few. Then, in the 1980s, the industry changed in fundamental ways, and ADL was left behind. The case describes the reorientation initiated by a new CEO and his introduction of formal business processes. ADL's performance soon improved dramatically. But at the time of the case questions remained about whether these processes constituted a full-fledged strategy, or whether additional steps were needed.

The next two cases, "R.R. Donnelley: The Digital Division" and "Allstate Chemical Company: The Commercialization of Dynarim," describe a common but difficult strategic challenge facing mature companies: how to create new businesses, especially when they require fundamentally different capabilities and skills. At Donnelley, the company was trying to shift from expensive offset and

---

[5]Donald C. Hambrick and Albert A. Cannella, "Strategy Implementation as Substance and Selling," *Academy of Management Executive*, vol. 3 (1989), p. 278. Italic in original.

gravure presses, geared to long, unchanging production runs, to digital presses with their smaller, customized orders. At Allstate, the company was moving from commodity chemicals, which required massive capital investments and efficient production, to specialty chemicals, which were applications-oriented and were sold primarily on the basis of product performance. Both cases explore the associated new business development processes—from concept through production—using a single, detailed example. Both therefore cover the entire sweep of strategy formulation, programming, and deployment. Both also describe the roles played by various levels of management as these processes unfold over time. The primary contrast between the two cases is that at Donnelley the digital business was created independently, with little organizational support and no obvious home, while at Allstate a new entity, the Commercial Development group, was established to serve as the hothouse and breeding ground for new chemical businesses.

The fourth case in the module, "Time Life Inc.," focuses on a different strategic challenge. Time Life is a diversified media company with interests in books, music, video, and television. For many years, it was run as "a loosely confederated conglomerate," with few linkages among the divisions. At the time of the case, however, multimedia products were emerging that required far more interdivisional cooperation. Managers at Time Life also had to learn to make better use of their common corporate assets, such as the customer file and the brand, that all divisions drew upon. To that end, the CEO gathered his direct reports and asked them to craft and deploy a corporate strategy, which had never before existed. The group made considerable progress, but conflicts remained. These issues came to a head with a potential multimedia product, True Crime, which, because of its sensitive and possibly sensationalist subject matter, pitted the staff of the book division against members of the video and television division.

The next two cases, "Watermill Ventures" and "Electrolux: The Acquisition and Integration of Zanussi," shift attention to external sources of growth. Rather than developing new businesses on their own, companies today frequently seek out mergers and acquisitions. Surprisingly, most of these efforts are unsuccessful and fail to produce the anticipated gains.[6] In part, the problem is one of process: managers who do not follow the necessary steps when screening, selecting, and integrating acquisitions.[7] Watermill Ventures and Electrolux are notable exceptions; both have long records of successful acquisitions, as well as carefully tuned acquisition screening, selection, and integration processes. Both cases describe these processes in detail, but in

---

[6]F. M. Scherer and David Ross, *Industrial Market Structure and Economic Performance*, 3rd ed. (Boston: Houghton Mifflin, 1990), chap. 5.

[7]Philippe C. Haspeslagh and David B. Jemison, *Managing Acquisitions* (New York: Free Press, 1991); David B. Jemison and Sim B. Sitkin, "Acquisitions: The Process Can Be a Problem," *Harvard Business Review* 64, March–April 1986, pp. 107–116; and David B. Jemison and Sim B. Sitkin, "Corporate Acquisitions: A Process Perspective," *Academy of Management Review* 11 (1986), pp. 145–163.

different settings. Watermill Ventures is a small turnaround firm, with only six employees, that buys troubled companies in diverse industries, retains their management teams, imposes new planning and control systems, and then orchestrates an intensive strategy development process. Electrolux, by contrast, is a multinational appliance maker that expands by acquiring companies in its core business, installing top managers of its own choosing, and then rationalizing and revitalizing the newly acquired operations by imposing an already developed strategy. Yet the two companies are remarkably similar in the acquisition processes they follow and their attempts to link strategy formulation and implementation.

The last class in the module combines two readings, "Emerson Electric: Consistent Profits, Consistently" and "Xerox Charts a New Strategic Direction," that describe strategic planning processes in fine-grained detail. Despite a superficial similarity, the processes have very different objectives. At Emerson Electric the task is strategic programming, while at Xerox the task is strategy formulation. The two companies also face very different competitive environments and are led by CEOs with contrasting styles. These factors play a further role in shaping the direction and character of the two planning processes, as well as the required skills of participants. They also highlight an important lesson of the module: No one type of process is appropriate for all needs. There is seldom a single, best solution. Instead, processes, like organizations, are far more likely to succeed if they have been designed to fit the circumstances.

THEMES

Modes of Strategy Making

Just as strategies can be classified as being of different types, so too can strategic processes. They take three main forms: entrepreneurial, adaptive, and planning.[8] In the entrepreneurial mode, the strategic process is characterized by bold leaps forward. The primary goal is growth, and there is an active search for new opportunities, often long before problems are apparent. Power is centralized in the hands of a senior executive, who develops an integrated, unifying vision. R. R. Donnelley provides a vivid example. Rory Cowan, the number-two person at the company, single-handedly developed a vision of the digital business, well before his colleagues recognized the opportunity; he then sold it aggressively throughout the organization. Cowan also orchestrated the strategy deployment process, first by ensuring that resources and people were committed to the cause and then by overseeing the final business design.

---

[8]Henry Mintzberg, "Strategy-Making in Three Modes," *California Management Review* 16 (1973), pp. 44–53, and Henry Mintzberg and James A. Waters, "Of Strategies, Deliberate and Emergent," *Strategic Management Journal* 6 (1985), pp. 257–272.

In the adaptive mode, clear goals do not exist, and a single bold vision is lacking. For this reason, the strategic process consists of incremental decisions and small steps. They reflect the division of power among members of a complex coalition—typically, the members of the senior management team—and the limited authority of the CEO or division general manager to proceed unilaterally. Progress comes from reactive solutions to problems, rather than foresight and the anticipation of emerging opportunities. Time Life presents a vivid example, as does Arthur D. Little. At Time Life, John Fahey, the CEO, moved slowly and tentatively to develop a corporate strategy. He had little choice, since he was constrained by the autonomy and authority of his division managers, who had considerable power but competing perspectives, as well as the lack of a clear vision of the multimedia future. True Crime presented him and his team with a problem that highlighted these difficulties while serving as a catalyst for action. Charlie LaMantia, the CEO of Arthur D. Little, faced a similar situation and proceeded in similar ways. Because power at ADL was largely in the hands of section and unit managers, LaMantia too had to work adaptively and incrementally, tackling opportunities as they arose. Rather than developing and pursuing a grand vision, he simply "fixe[d] the next thing that [was] most wrong."

In the planning mode, the strategic process is characterized by systematic analysis, often provided by financial experts or strategic planners. Rational approaches dominate, and the costs and benefits of competing proposals are carefully compared. Leaders strive to articulate their goals as clearly as possible and then plan execution in fine detail. Emerson Electric provides the best example in the module, although there are elements of this approach in Electrolux's planning for the acquisition of Zanussi. At Emerson, division managers were required to formulate detailed sales and investment plans, using a series of preestablished charts and templates; they then had to defend their proposals in the face of hostile questioning by the CEO. The proposals that stood up best were those backed by systematic analysis and a deep understanding of the numbers.

The existence of these three modes of strategy making has important implications for managers. To begin, many executives need to broaden their perspectives, mastering a wider range of approaches to strategic problems. At too many companies today, strategic planning and strategy making are thought to be identical. Yet formal planning is not always the best way to produce a successful strategy. As the Donnelley and Time Life cases make clear, other methods, under the right circumstances, can be equally effective.

Managers must also recognize that these three approaches demand different talents, skills, and personal profiles. Enterpreneurial strategy making requires vision—the ability to see the big picture, play with concepts and ideas, and motivate others through passion and personal commitment. Adaptive strategy making requires political acumen—the ability to understand divergent perspectives, form enduring coalitions, and employ power when necessary. Planned strategy making requires discipline—the ability to think rationally and systematically, break complex problems into smaller pieces, and administer an orderly, programmed process. To succeed at multiple modes, managers therefore need a broad array of skills, as well as knowledge about when each approach is best applied. They must also learn to employ the skills in combination. This is particularly true of adaptive and planned approaches, which require a careful balancing of flexibility and discipline. Managing, after all, "requires a light deft touch—to direct in order to realize intentions while at the same time responding to an unfolding pattern of action. The relative emphasis may shift from time to time but not the requirement to attend to both sides of the phenomenon."[9]

A Contingency Approach

Contingency theory has a long and venerable history in the social sciences.[10] Briefly stated, it argues that different environments impose different demands on organizations; as a result, no single organizational design is uniformly superior. Some environments, for example, are unchanging and mature; they require designs that support stable, efficient operations and steady, incremental improvement. Other environments are fluid and rapidly changing; they require designs that accommodate flexible, responsive operations and large, innovative changes. The critical concept is "fit"—the degree to which the organization's design matches the needs of the environment. The importance of fit for superior performance is now widely accepted. Most studies, however, have focused on the structural features of organizations, such as the number of administrative levels and functional versus divisional forms. Surprisingly little has been said about processes.

One exception is the work of Burns and Stalker.[11] They describe two systems of management, organic and mechanistic, which are easily applied to processes. Organic systems (processes) involve large, holistic tasks, loosely defined responsibilities, network structures of authority, control, and communication, and mobilization through employee commitment and enthusiasm. Mechanistic systems (processes) involve specialized, highly differentiated tasks, well-defined responsibilities, hierarchical structures of authority, control, and communication, and mobilization through employee loyalty and the acceptance of oversight, direction, and rules. Together, these two types stake out opposite ends of a spectrum; they are best thought of as differences of degree rather than discrete, clearly separable categories.

---

[9]Mintzberg and Waters, "Of Strategies, Deliberate and Emergent," p. 271.

[10]For reviews, see Jay R. Galbraith, *Organization Design* (Reading, MA: Addison-Wesley, 1977), pp. 28–32, and W. Richard Scott, *Organizations: Rational, Natural, and Open Systems*, 3rd ed. (Englewood Cliffs, NJ: Prentice-Hall, 1992), pp. 88–90.

[11]Tom Burns and G. M. Stalker, *The Management of Innovation* (Oxford: Oxford University Press, 1961).

What does this have to do with management? Burns and Stalker argue that organic systems are best suited to uncertain, unpredictable environments, especially those where judgment is necessary and adaptability and flexibility are essential. Mechanistic systems, by contrast, are best suited to stable, predictable environments where efficiency and reliability are the goals and each project or assignment is very much like the one that preceded it. In other words, Burns and Stalker argue for a fit between process characteristics and the demands of the environment.

Examples of this fit—as well as illustrations of the two ideal types—are present throughout the module. Allstate Chemical used a highly organic process to research, develop, and market specialty chemicals, a business in which it was completely lacking in experience and precedents. Xerox did the same to ensure open-minded creativity in the formulation of a new strategy for document processing. Emerson Electric, on the other hand, used a far more mechanistic process for strategic planning, one that was well suited to the company's predictable, mature businesses. Electrolux used an equally mechanistic process for screening and integrating acquisitions in the appliance industry.

Companies are not required to stick with these approaches indefinitely. As the environment changes, so too should the choice of process. Several cases in the module show companies shifting from organic to mechanistic processes in the interests of greater efficiency. Arthur D. Little, for example, moved from a collection of unarticulated, loosely organized processes to a clearly defined business process matrix with standardized activities and assigned process owners. R.R. Donnelley similarly shifted from a loose, ad hoc approach to technology development to a disciplined process with clearly articulated milestones, gates, and deliverables.

These cases convey three important lessons. First, as has already been mentioned, there is no single best approach to process design. This is as true of strategic processes as it is of any other type of processes. Sometimes, they are best kept organic and loosely structured; at other times, they work best when they are tightly scripted and precisely defined. The proper approach depends on the circumstances.

Second, the three modes of strategy making can be linked to this contingency framework. In most cases, entrepreneurial approaches to strategy making are organic, planning approaches are mechanistic, and adaptive approaches fall somewhere in the middle of the spectrum. Each is therefore best used in certain environments.

Third, managers should recognize that they are not bound forever to an organic or mechanistic approach. They can alter their approaches over time, as the Arthur D. Little and R.R. Donnelley cases suggest. Such changes are frequently essential as organizations adapt to rapidly changing environments. But they should be approached with care. These changes are normally difficult and demanding, requiring new competencies and skills as well as fundamentally different ways of thinking and working. Often, they require new people as well.

The Theory of the Business

Given the preceding discussion, it should come as no surprise that general managers today must be able to quickly size up the environments facing their organizations. This is particularly important during times of transition, when new needs are just emerging. Then, the future is only apparent in the broadest of outlines, and considerable judgment is required. As Harvard's Dean Stanley Teele often observed, in such settings "management is the art of making meaningful generalizations out of inadequate facts."

The cases in this module show executives sizing up and then responding to a wide range of environmental shifts. In most cases, the shifts have been so substantial that the underlying rules of the game—what Peter Drucker calls the "theory of the business—have been called into question. A theory of the business is no more than an implicit set of assumptions about markets, customers, competitors, technology, and the organization's mission and competencies, shared by a company's managers, that provides a frame for interpreting events and making decisions.[12] These assumptions are powerful, conservative forces. Typically, they have been in place for years. According to Drucker,

> Every organization, whether a business or not, has a theory of the business. Indeed, a valid theory that is clear, consistent, and focused is extraordinarily powerful . . . The theory of the business explains both the success of companies like General Motors and IBM . . . and the challenges they have faced. In fact, what underlies the current malaise of so many large and successful organizations worldwide is that their theory of the business no longer works . . . Put another way, reality has changed, but the theory of the business has not changed with it.[13]

At ADL, for example, the company's long-held theory of the business was developed during its fledgling years, when the company took root and prospered. At its core was a collection of independent, autonomous consultants, facing an environment of limited competition and excess demand. Consultants could therefore pick and choose assignments. Usually, they selected the most challenging, unfamiliar problems, and then used their intelligence and generic problem-solving skills to develop solutions. There was little need for integration or corporate support, little concern for specialized knowledge, little focus on long-term client relationships, and little attention to implementation. This model served the company well until the 1970s, when there were significant shifts in the industry and the environment. Competitors began to bundle products and services. Their consultants began to specialize in a small number of techniques, topics, or industries. Large, multinational customers began to demand consistency across geographical regions as well as increased attention

---

[12]Peter F. Drucker, "The Theory of the Business," *Harvard Business Review* 72 (September–October 1994), pp. 95–104.
[13]Ibid., pp. 96, 98.

to implementation. Faced with these challenges, ADL had to modify its prevailing theory of the business, as well as the associated strategy, structure, and organizational processes.

Other cases in the module describe equally dramatic changes. Each required managers to reassess their longstanding theories of the business because they suddenly found themselves playing a different game. At Allstate, the game changed from commodity chemicals to specialty chemicals. At Time Life, the game changed from stand-alone book, music, video, and television products to multimedia bundles and integrated Internet offerings. And at Electrolux, the game changed from isolated national markets to global and pan-European competition.

The ability to identify and capitalize on such changes is vital to strategic success. In fact, skill at identifying the prevailing theory of the business and evaluating its fit with market and organizational realities is one of the hallmarks of effective general managers. The associated analytical tools taught in most first-year strategy courses are not reviewed here.[14] But the task is also interpretative and creative; it involves synthesis as well as analysis. Managers must be able to "wade into the swarm of events that constitute and surround the organization and actively impose some order . . . developing models for understanding . . . , bringing out meaning, and . . . assembling conceptual schemes."[15] The critical talent—what some scholars have termed "strategic recognition"—is as much art as science.[16] Inferences, for example, are often based on limited, fragmentary evidence. Large conceptual leaps are frequently required. Intuition and holistic thinking are as important as running the numbers. For these reasons, virtually every case in this module provides practice in strategic recognition. The problem must first be diagnosed; then, implications must be drawn for action. Among the critical questions: Is our current theory of the business still valid? Does it mesh with market realities? What aspects of the environment are changing, and how (if at all) must we modify traditional approaches? How can we begin the process of moving from the old theory to the new?

The last question is often the most difficult. Managers must learn to think about the transition in concrete terms, identifying ways of introducing new approaches while displacing old ones. They must create forums for fostering new ways of thinking, provide settings that are hospitable to new ways of working, and craft business and management processes that are responsive to new

---

[14]Among the most important techniques are situation audits; environmental assessments; and strengths, weaknesses, opportunities, and threats (SWOT) analysis. For representative discussions, see Kenneth R. Andrews, *The Concept of Corporate Strategy*, rev. ed. (Richard D. Irwin, 1980), chap. 3, and George A. Steiner, *Strategic Planning* (New York: Free Press, 1979), chap. 8.

[15]Karl E. Weick and Richard L. Daft, "The Effectiveness of Interpretation Systems," in K. S. Cameron and D. A. Whetten, eds., *Organizational Effectiveness* (New York: Academic Press, 1983), p. 74.

[16]Robert A. Burgelman and Andrew S. Grove, "Strategic Dissonance," *California Management Review* 39 (1996), pp. 8–28.

demands. At R. R. Donnelley, Rory Cowan and his team addressed each of these needs as they tried to move the organization toward digital printing. They created a venture capital fund that placed senior Donnelley executives on the boards of key companies to cultivate a more entrepreneurial perspective. They formed a new, freestanding division to ensure that the digital business developed its own distinctive ways of working. They retooled the technology development process to add discipline to business planning. And they crafted innovative compensation schemes to convince established divisions to draw on the services of the new division.

Strategic Challenges

While strategic challenges come in many guises, two appear prominently in this module: growth and integration. They are singled out because of their special relevance to general managers. Department heads typically see only part of the puzzle and cannot be held accountable for these broader, organizationwide goals. Only general managers, responsible for the overall health of the business or enterprise, are charged with putting all the pieces together.

Growth.   Growth, for example, invariably requires coordinated action from many functions and departments. R&D must develop new technologies, marketing must target new customers, operations must devise new equipment, and finance must find new sources of capital or cash. Putting these pieces together is surprisingly difficult, especially for large companies that have reengineered or downsized their way to success. The required mind-set is completely different, as are the required skills. They are forward looking and constructive rather than reactive and responsive.[17]

How, then, should managers pursue growth? To begin, they must recognize that there are multiple paths, with three main options: expanding current businesses, creating new businesses, and acquiring established businesses. Arthur D. Little, Time Life, Emerson Electric, and Xerox provide examples of the first approach; R.R. Donnelley and Allstate Chemical provide examples of the second approach; and Watermill Ventures and Electrolux provide examples of the third approach. No one approach is superior, since each has predictable strengths and weaknesses. In any given situation, they can be compared using the tools of competitive analysis.[18] What is seldom recognized, however, is that the three approaches also demand very different strategic processes.

---

[17]Gary Hamel and C. K. Prahalad, *Competing for the Future* (Boston: Harvard Business School Press, 1994), chap. 1.

[18]Michael Porter, *Competitive Strategy* (New York: Free Press, 1980), esp. chap. 16, and Michael Porter, *Competitive Advantage* (New York: Free Press, 1985), esp. chap. 4.

When a company chooses to grow by expanding its current businesses, the strategy is usually well established. Growth comes from product-line extensions, new service offerings, increased capacity, and better marketing, not from radical changes in direction or design. The critical tasks are positioning, planning, and resource allocation—delivering on a known strategy, not finding new ways of competing. At Time Life, for example, *True Crime,* the proposed book and television series, presented managers with difficult choices of brand positioning. At Emerson Electric, a key responsibility of division managers was to define, develop, and defend new capital investment proposals that met demanding financial targets. In both cases, creative approaches to strategy formulation were of far less importance than disciplined strategic programming and strategy deployment.

Companies that choose to grow by creating new businesses face quite different challenges. Innovative ways of thinking and working are required, and continuing with current practice is normally unhelpful and misleading.[19] The essential skill is the ability to think "outside of the box" and generate previously unexplored options. The process must also be flexible and allow for continual revision, since few companies "get it right the first time" when they tackle major innovations. Time must therefore be available for learning, and the strategy formulation process must be allowed to proceed through multiple iterations.[20] Both R.R. Donnelly and Allstate Chemical show such processes in action. In each case, new strategies went through long periods of incubation and development, and new products and services were repeatedly prototyped, tested, evaluated, and refined.

When companies choose to grow through acquisitions, all three strategic processes are critical. In the formulation stage, criteria must be developed that allow for the careful screening of potential acquisition candidates since managers have a common tendency to rationalize the relevance and fit of companies that come to their attention. In the programming stage, plans must be suitably detailed since managers frequently fail to pin down the precise sources of synergies, cost savings, and other anticipated benefits. In the implementation stage, disciplined execution must be combined with real-time readjustments since managers invariably discover unexpected—and usually unpleasant—surprises. Especially when failing companies are to be turned around or acquired sites are to be integrated with established operations, the hard work of mergers often begins *after* the deal is done.[21] Both Watermill Ventures and Electrolux

---

[19]This is particularly true when radical, disruptive technologies are involved. See Clayton M. Christensen, *The Innovator's Dilemma* (Boston: Harvard Business School Press, 1997), for further discussion.

[20]For a discussion of the importance of iterations in both strategy and product development, see David A. Garvin, *Learning in Action* (Boston: Harvard Business School Press, 2000), esp. chaps. 3 and 5.

[21]Claudia H. Deutsch, "The Deal Is Done. The Work Begins." *New York Times,* April 11, 1999, sec. 3, pp. 1, 6.

show these processes in action, as well as the critical links between the upstream tasks of screening and selection and the downstream tasks of implementation and alignment.

Integration.   Integration—"the achievement of unity of effort among the major functional specialists in a business"—is a related challenge.[22] Here, too, general managers are often the only ones in the organization with the needed holistic perspective. Others are frequently more interested in narrower goals and objectives. The problem is hardly confined to functional managers. In large, multidivisional corporations, even division presidents frequently pursue their own local interests while slighting larger corporate concerns.

All too often, the result is limited cooperation and a lack of alignment. CEOs frequently cite fragmentation as a major problem in their senior management teams.[23] This generates inefficiency and confusion in several guises: divergent product, market, and regional policies, even though divisions have common customers; inefficient, duplicative use of resources; excessive, unmanaged demands for common corporate assets such as the brand; inability to leverage local learning and experience; and limited success in developing integrated products and services. The ADL and Time Life cases provide vivid examples of these problems.

General managers thus face a difficult dilemma: how to balance local needs, which point toward specialization and autonomy, with organizational needs, which demand collaboration, coordination, and give and take. Often, the challenge is to create "one company" out of assorted fiefdoms and independent units. Successful general managers use a variety of techniques to improve integration. Among the approaches discussed in this module are the introduction of common strategic and operational processes (as at ADL and Emerson Electric); the involvement of senior managers in cooperative, unifying activities like strategy formulation (as at Time Life, Xerox, and Watermill Ventures); the development of integrated, multibusiness products (as at Time Life and Electrolux); and the redrawing of organization charts to ensure collaborative roles and joint work (as at Allstate and Time Life). All of these approaches, it should be emphasized, are designed to improve organizational alignment through the development of common interests, activities, and agendas.[24]

---

[22]Paul R. Lawrence and Jay W. Lorsch, "New Management Job: The Integrator," *Harvard Business Review* 45 (November–December 1967), p. 142. For a more comprehensive discussion, see Paul R. Lawrence and Jay W. Lorsch, *Organization and Environment* (Boston: Harvard Business School Press, 1967).

[23]Donald C. Hambrick, "Fragmentation and the Other Problems CEOs Have with Their Top Management Teams," *California Management Review* 37 (Spring 1995), pp. 110–127.

[24]John P. Kotter, *A Force for Change* (New York: Free Press, 1990), chap. 2.

Case 1-1

ARTHUR D. LITTLE, INC.

On the afternoon of September 6, 1995, Charlie LaMantia, president and CEO of Arthur D. Little, Inc. (ADL), an international management consulting, product development, and environmental, health, and safety consulting firm, was pondering the agenda for the upcoming bimonthly meeting of his senior leadership and management (SLAM) team, which had been chartered to set ADL's strategy, policy, and procedures. In the several years ADL had begun to focus its three lines of business around seven "core processes," and had enjoyed considerable financial success (see Exhibit 1). But SLAM team members were still debating whether a complete corporate strategy was in place. Since LaMantia hoped that the issue would be squarely faced in the team's next session, he began jotting down what he believed were the elements of ADL's strategy:

- Three businesses, organized into seven directorates.
- Each business grown as a stand-alone winner.

- Developing a clear identity in the marketplace for each business and for the firm as a whole.
- Developing cross-business synergy/products/practices.
- Integrating management consulting directorates worldwide around "one strategy."
- Developing world-class functional capabilities (marketing, HR, etc.) at the corporate level and deploying them to operations.
- Learning and applying best practices for the seven core processes across the firm.

LaMantia found himself humming as he wrote, and recognized the tune as Peggy Lee's "Is That All There Is?" Smiling wryly, he wondered, Should there be more?

This case was prepared by Artemis March under the direction of David A. Garvin.

EXHIBIT 1   Revenue and Income Growth (000s)

Revenues by Line of Business	1995 Est.	1994	1993	1992
Management Consulting	$340,261	$271,627	$228,759	$206,587
Environmental, Health, and Safety Consulting	60,260	58,521	52,736	56,159
Technology and Product Development/ Cambridge Consultants Limited	73,141	69,881	64,746	61,217
Other	31,485	32,480	39,092	42,968
Total	505,147	432,509	385,333	366,931

From 1990 to 1994, net income grew at a compound rate of 28 percent per year, and the share value increased at an 18 percent annual compound growth rate.

Source: ADL

Company and Industry Background[1]

History

In 1886, chemists Arthur Dehon Little and Roger Griffin set up a chemical laboratory in Boston, Massachusetts, to conduct "investigations for the improvement of processes and the perfection of products." MIT-trained Little envisioned their contribution to "industrial progress" as marrying scientific and academic research findings to the veritable explosion of untested and poorly understood ingredients and products being developed for the marketplace—thereby bridging the gap between theory and practice. In so doing, Little and Griffin pioneered two broader concepts: selling knowledge as a service, and performing research on contract. Early examples were the invention of nonflammable motion picture film, whose rights were sold to Eastman Kodak, and helping General Motors organize its first central engineering laboratory.

In 1909, the firm was incorporated as Arthur D. Little (Roger Griffin died in 1893). Seven years later, having sold new stock, it was able to build new laboratory facilities and office space in Cambridge, adjacent to MIT. That year the firm also adopted the winged acorn as its symbol, trading on the aphorism "giant oaks from little acorns grow." When 40 years later the company moved to the outskirts of Cambridge, it named its complex Acorn Park. The buildings there were brick-over-cinder block, resembling, according to one account, "the science wing of a poorly endowed university." Another observer noted: "ADL is Cambridge, not a downtown, corporate style. It is a culture that hates glitz. Things are ostentatiously understated."

During its first century, ADL's business consisted primarily of analytical testing and creative problem-solving work on technical problems, and technology and new product development, espe-

cially in pharmaceuticals, energy/petrochemicals, and pulp and paper. In the 1920s, ADL pioneered an odor classification system and a "flavor profile" that turned taste and odor analysis into a transferable skill taught to hundreds of companies, launching a stream of assignments that produced a wide range of new food products and flavors. At one point the firm even manufactured and sold precision laboratory equipment.

During World War II, ADL took on more than 100 assignments for the government, including the development of a process for converting salt water into fresh water. It also developed a probabilities-based method of searching for enemy submarines, an early example of operations research, which became increasingly important to the company postwar. ADL was one of the first to apply these methods to management issues such as logistics and supply chain management. To help perform this work, the organization supplemented its scientists and technicians by hiring people whose backgrounds were in economics, organization, and planning. By the end of the 1950s, they were part of a growing management consulting practice. In the following decade, ADL established a petroleum economics practice, pioneering in pollution control and environmental protection, the safe disposal of hazardous wastes, and analysis of the social and economic effects of environmental regulation. With the energy crisis of the 1970s, this practice took off.

By 1995, the company had 2,700 professional employees on four continents, 51 offices, and over $500 million in revenues. Acorn Park housed more than 150 laboratories, and nearly 3,000 patents had been received by employees, including several for such well-known processes as manufacturing blown glass fibers, the foundation of Fiberglas™. The tenth largest consultancy in Europe, where it grossed $120 million, ADL ranked among the top 20 consulting firms worldwide.

Organization and Management

The zest for tackling "impossible" problems plus the commitment to hands-on problem solving

---

[1]*Some material in this section is drawn from E. J. Kahn, Jr., The Problem Solvers: A History of Arthur D. Little, Inc. (Boston: Little, Brown and Company, 1986).*

forged a company in which, some said, "Everyone consulted, and the managers managed when their consulting didn't get in the way."

Organization Structure. From its earliest days, sole practitioners at ADL actively responded to opportunities in their areas of expertise and interest. Eventually, the more entrepreneurial and successful built little businesses, called units, of 5–15 people. If it became large enough (e.g., with $3 million in revenues), a unit usually became a section, headed by a section manager; sections typically contained between two and four units. By the 1980s, there were about 40 sections, each a $5–$10 million business.

Unit managers primarily attended to their consulting teams' billability. But they drew their real power from selling work and serving as consulting project leaders. Section managers were considerably more powerful; they essentially ran their own small businesses, although a section's P&L did not include overhead or working capital costs. They could hire and fire employees and determine which clients, projects, and capital-equipment they wanted. Section managers often became vice presidents, although that title did not hold great weight, since titles meant little at ADL during this period.

Early in the 1950s, ADL attempted a divisional organization, aggregating sections into six or seven divisions. According to John Magee, who became CEO in 1974, that structure was abandoned in 1973 because the divisions "had become very competitive, fighting over leads and capital resources, and actively disliked one another." Magee wanted to build a leadership group more aligned with the company than with the units. Accordingly, he formed a corporate staff group of senior vice presidents, most of whom had been division heads. One of the latter was Charlie Kensler, who was appointed the first chief professional officer (a COO-type role established to guide ADL's professional activities). Section managers, who nominally reported to Magee, in fact reported to Kensler, making him, in effect, ADL's chief operating officer.

Cases. The work at ADL revolved around projects (called cases). Harland Riker, who had built ADL's European business and in 1995 was chairman of ADL International, summarized the period through the mid-1980s:

> We had a profound preoccupation with the case, and we took great pride in the freshness of our approach to each case. We were the arithmetic sum of the cases. We had no sense of the client other than as the details of the case.

Jeff Traenkle, a senior vice president and since 1992 chief financial officer, added: "The case leader was always king. The president couldn't tell him how to run a case or whom to use." Because ADL had no central staffing process, professionals had to get themselves invited onto case teams, which consisted of diverse experts assembled for a particular task. And because case leaders could pick anyone for their teams, including the chairman of the board, senior people might well find themselves, on a particular case, reporting to someone junior. Those asked could decline, but few did. Most projects involved a few people for two or three months, and much of the work was performed at Acorn Park. Even when ADL handled larger projects, involving 50 or more people, the work remained problem oriented, technically based, and highly customized.

Managing Leads. Demand for ADL services remained high well into the 1970s, with business often arriving unsolicited. A telephone line connected directly to the contracting office rang often, as companies called to see if ADL could solve tough problems. At the same time, there was a growing "pickiness" in choosing assignments and intense, often bitter, competition over leads. Leads arrived by two routes: a client contacted an ADL staff member directly; or the lead came into the company through the contracting office phone. The latter were labeled "over the transom" and were a prime source of contentiousness, according to both Traenkle and Al Wechsler, senior vice president and, since 1981, chief professional officer. Those contacted directly by clients typically treated the lead as their own; the first time the company might learn of it was when the contracting office reviewed the proposal. Not surprisingly, lead finders often suggested themselves or close colleagues as case leaders. In the 1970s, to bring order to this process and sort out how case leaders were selected, Magee established the Lead Management Group (LMG).

The LMG comprised several permanent and several rotating members and was run by the chief professional officer, assisted by the chief contracting officer. It established the principle that leads belonged to the company, not to individuals: Anyone getting a lead was to immediately report it. Three nights a week, LMG members reviewed the leads, meeting the following morning to discuss them. Lead finders still proposed a case leader (often themselves) and key staff, but the LMG had veto power over the case leader, which it exercised about 10 percent of the time. The LMG's impact, however, was far broader. It reduced the hoarding of leads, staked the company's claim to lead ownership, brought the lead selection process into view, looked disapprovingly at the "buddy system" of case assignments, and significantly influenced case team staffing. As such, although it intervened infrequently, it had much perceived power. Tammy Erickson, a senior vice president, recalled: "The most powerful, visible, prestigious process in the company was the LMG. The highest honor you could get, the most sought-after position, was to be one of its rotating members."

Culture and Incentives. Because ADL deeply prized the challenge of solving knotty problems in widely disparate fields, the ability to do so was a particular source of pride for employees. For decades, ADLers who exercised that ability found a deeply valued camaraderie, both inside and outside the office—even as they fought fiercely over leads. The twin freedoms of being able to pursue their own interests and be their own boss were, for many, the primary rewards for establishing a niche

at ADL. And because they were drawn to unique, cutting-edge problems—in the 1970s, the company's motto was "There is hardly anything that is not our business"—they rarely leveraged their problem-solving methods. Ladd Greeno, another senior vice president, recalled:

> Clients were asking us to solve problems. "Gee, nobody has ever done this," they would say. "Can you?" If another client asked us, a second time, to solve a similar problem, we might do it. By the third time, we weren't interested.

Riker added:

> We placed a premium on the Eureka! solution rather than on any systematic learning from what went on before. There were no limits on the brief, and no necessity to relate one case to another.

Since everyone, from the chairman on down, was expected to consult, the operative rule was, "Sell a little [business], do a little [consulting work]." There were few constraints. One long-term consultant summed up the times with a twofold rule: "One, you never wanted to see your manager—since you only saw him if you were in trouble. Two, you kept your numbers decent—sell $300,000 a year, stay 70 percent billable."

ADL had two primary financial targets at this point: billability levels and profit margins. Not only was inadequate billability grounds for dismissal, but unit members' billability levels largely determined unit managers' modest bonuses (all bonuses were set by the chief professional officer and CEO). Section managers, who could receive sizable bonuses, were accountable for their sections' financial performance, which Kensler monitored closely. The primary factor was meeting percent profit margin targets; growth was distinctly secondary in the bonus equation.

If a section manager or case leader drew upon people from other sections for a case, the revenue for their full billing rate multiplied by their billable hours accrued to the other section(s); if case leaders went to an outside contractor, the revenue still accrued to their own section. Section managers worked around this formula by hiring either specialized resources, such as their own environmental, health, and safety experts, or general resources, such as MBAs, to conduct work formerly filled by specialists in finance, strategy, or marketing. Also, because revenue followed the individual, the building of branch offices (which were profit centers) was constrained. Branch managers had two options as a result: hiring the best people from ADL, thus gaining little revenue from the assignment, or increasing revenues by hiring locally, thus risking inadequate performance.

Competition

Since ADL was the first consulting firm in the United States and remained, until 1979, number one, for many years its only competition came from such early players as Booz Allen and Hamilton (founded in 1914), A. T. Kearney (1926), and McKinsey & Company (1930). During the 1980s, however, hundreds of new firms sprung up, and the industry rocketed from $2 billion in annual revenues to an estimated $14.5 billion. Firms like McKinsey became a powerful global presence, presenting a single face to clients everywhere, while accounting firms such as Arthur Andersen formed dedicated management consulting arms. Strategy boutiques like the Boston Consulting Group capitalized on trendy solutions such as the experience curve, then time-based management, and, more recently, reengineering. These companies recruited on campuses, trained professionals in standardized programs, developed products and methodologies that could be reused for new clients and projects, and adopted sophisticated marketing strategies supported by publications, articles, and books that promised answers to whatever dilemmas plagued corporations— particularly in the arena of "change." Oral presentations supplanted written reports, client teams worked more on-site, and facilitation and intervention skills were increasingly used. Faced with these forces, ADL's overall position slowly deteriorated (see Exhibit 2).

In fact, a volatile pattern of earnings had always characterized management consulting. This was particularly true of ADL because of its focus on short, discrete projects. The company rarely had a backlog of more than a couple of months' work. Even in 1995 LaMantia would observe:

> It is a very fragile, very volatile business. For 109 years, we have been about to go out of business within three months. If you lose sight of the short term for even a month, you are in serious trouble.

By the early 1980s, continuing pressure for billability and margins only intensified internal competition for the most interesting leads. Morale steadily sank, and many people left. ADL's ancillary businesses, such as Decision Resources (which provided research materials in technical areas) and Pilgrim Health Associates (a health care administrator) were targeted for growth, rather than the core business. The business press ran several critical articles, and the ADL board became restive for change. Magee recalled, "We overdid the profit emphasis and underrecognized the need to invest and grow. Our management consulting activities got flabby; we were harvesting the past."

The Transition Years

LaMantia Returns

In September 1986, Charlie LaMantia returned to ADL as president. (About a year later, the company fended off a takeover bid and went private; in July 1988, LaMantia added the title of CEO while Magee remained chairman.) LaMantia had built a large, profitable section focused on energy, environmental, and chemical process technology during his 14 years at ADL, before leaving in 1981 to run Koch Process Systems. Trained as a chemical engineer, he noted that process thinking had been a constant throughout his work:

> If you'd asked me what I was 20 years ago, I would have said I was a process engineer; from an engineering point of view, the stuff flows through pipes, not people, but the concepts are similar.

EXHIBIT 2 Rankings of Consulting Firms, 1978–1993, by Worldwide Revenues ($ in millions)*

1978		1982		1987		1993	
Firm	Revenues	Firm	Revenues	Firm	Revenues	Firm	Revenues
Arthur D. Little	$121	Arthur Andersen	$218	Arthur Andersen	$838	McKinsey	$1,274
Booz Allen	115	Booz Allen	210	Marsh & McLennan	530	Coopers & Lybrand	1,002
Arthur Andersen	114	McKinsey	145	McKinsey	510	Ernst & Young	922
McKinsey	100	Arthur D. Little	141	Towers Perrin	465	Price Waterhouse	876
Coopers & Lybrand	83	Towers Perrin	120	Peat Marwick	438	Andersen Consulting	858
Touche Ross	72	Mercer Cos.	120	Booz Allen	412	Deloitte & Touche	792
Peat Marwick	70	Peat Marwick	112	Coopers & Lybrand	381	KPMG Peat Marwick	769
Towers Perrin	60	Ernst & Whinney	85	Ernst & Whinney	374	Mercer Cos.	600
Arthur Young	53	Coopers & Lybrand	79	Price Waterhouse	345	Gemini	516
Ernst & Ernst	51	American Management Systems	65	Saatchi & Saatchi	267	Towers Perrin	450
Hay	42	Hay	60	Touche Ross	248	Booz Allen	400
Reliance	42	Reliance	59	Wyatt	237	Arthur Andersen	395
Price Waterhouse	33	Price Waterhouse	57	Arthur D. Little	218	Wyatt	349
A.T. Kearney	30	Hewitt	54	Deloitte Haskins	209	BOG	340
BOG	27	BOG	50	Arthur Young	204	CSC Consulting	312
		SRI	50	Bain	200	Arthur D. Little	301

*1978 and 1982 figures include all consulting revenues; 1987 and 1993 figures are management consulting revenues only. Note also that the revenue figures attributed to ADL management consulting in 1993 do not match those of Exhibit 1 because different classification schemes are used.

Source: Consultants News

A colleague added:

> Charlie [is] at heart a process thinker who unconsciously thinks of organizational processes as hydraulics. He has a strong will, pays attention to operations, and uses numbers to sniff out problems—he is a ground-level operator who works off the tangible. Most of all, he is a shrewd businessman who thinks he is running a business, not a religion.

Traenkle concurred, with a chuckle: "Charlie is his own CFO. He really appreciates the economics of the firm."

Erickson cited another important aspect of LaMantia's initial approach: "He brought a spirit of inquiry. Charlie was willing to question why we did things the way we always had." Another manager observed, "He fixes the next thing that is most wrong." And "most wrong" for LaMantia, upon his return, was ADL's approach to financial planning and reporting. ADL had no overall operating statement showing revenues, costs, and profits; reports showed variance to plan, but not the plan itself. "You couldn't tell if they were making money, or how much," recalled LaMantia. "All anyone knew was their own plan, not the other guy's." Further, the performance of Acorn Park's sections could not be compared to European offices' since the latter carried full overhead costs, including facilities, while these costs appeared only at the corporate level in Acorn Park. LaMantia wanted a companywide method of allocating costs. He was also angered by managers blaming an antiquated accounting system for what he suspected were substantive issues in performance.

LaMantia's first initiative in the financial area was overhauling and tightening the planning and budgeting system, as well as the accounting system, coupled with quick cost cutting. For example, he began charging managers 15 percent for working capital use. Jack Burns, ADL's controller, explained: "When Charlie came, there were no penalties for not collecting your accounts receivable. When he charged 15 percent it soon brought our working capital down 4 percent which amounted to a $12 million improvement in cash flow at that time." LaMantia also jettisoned a tracking process

that cost $250,000 to operate yet recovered only about 40 percent of costs for such items as postage, telephone, and shipping that were to be charged back to clients. Instead, he imposed a surcharge on clients' bills, thereby recovering about 90 percent of the costs. In addition, he began pruning ADL's ancillary businesses.

Over the next few years, LaMantia began articulating a broader agenda for change, concentrating on six broad themes: staff development, quality, overhead, compensation, marketing, and P&L leadership. In June 1988 he took his senior managers off-site to begin exploring these concerns. Task forces were formed for each topic, headed by a senior vice president (who collectively were known as the Corporate Management Group, or CMG). Many task force members were section managers, and some, like Greeno and Erickson, participated in two or three groups. LaMantia personally stayed "very involved [in the task forces' work] and they knew it. I was trying to drive the process, but didn't know all the answers." One of the most important groups was the staff development task force headed by Harland Riker because of its impact on ADL's subsequent organization and management.

Staff Development Task Force

Historically, human resources (HR) and human resource development had been loosely managed at ADL. Over the course of a year, Riker's task force studied a range of HR issues, including senior leadership, professional career structure, role expectations and performance standards, professional training, and recruitment, selection, and hiring. Special attention was devoted to overcoming resistance, especially among technologists, to the idea of career "stages," for they threatened a deep-seated egalitarianism at ADL. But these stages were necessary for business and competitive reasons, as Riker explained:

> If you leave the clients to a case leader, the latter will do a discrete piece of work. But it is the client relationship, not the case, that is our asset. We needed someone to manage the client, and someone else to handle the assignment.

The group's central recommendation was that ADL adopt a professional career structure that would be common worldwide, yet flexible enough for different practices. The task force proposed three firmwide stages—consultant, senior consultant, and director. Specific functions, responsibilities, and performance expectations were broadly defined for each stage. Directors, for example, were expected to attract a certain amount of new business, demonstrate continued excellence in client work and practice development, and contribute significantly to staff development as well as to corporate and business leadership. The task force emphasized that these stages should not be confused with temporary titles such as practice leader, which reflected one's role on a particular client assignment.

The task force also recommended establishing seven directorates (described below), whose primary responsibility would be designing and managing the staff development programs, including worldwide professional training, for their respective practices and offices. Because this recommendation dovetailed neatly with ongoing CMG discussions about the need for a compensation plan tied to an organizational entity smaller than the company, the directorates were approved and in palce by spring 1989.

To assign roles within the new organizational structure, the CMG first reviewed the current section leaders and appointed most of them directors, dividing them among the seven directorates; out of this group, the CMG named one director "chair" for each directorate. The chair and his or her newly designated directors then assigned the position of director, senior consultant, or consultant to each member of their directorate. Riker recalled the pain involved in this selection process:

> No one wants to sit down and slot people into categories. Some people left because they felt humiliated in not having been made a director. Yet when those tough choices were not made at the beginning, the pruning came later.

A New Organization Structure

The directorates were composed from practices with common functional expertise or geography; they, in turn, were grouped into three businesses.

Directorates.   Five of the seven directorates were in management consulting; four of these were regionally based, while the fifth, Energy, was a global practice focused on the oil and gas industries. These five directorates provided consulting services in strategy, customer service, supply chain management, information technology, manufacturing, finance, organization, and technology and innovation to clients in the chemicals, pharmaceuticals/health care, automotive, telecommunications, and other industries. The North American Management Consulting (NAMC) and European Management Consulting (EMC) practices were in mature consulting markets, while Latin America and Asia/Pacific were embryonic businesses in emerging markets. All, however, covered a wide sweep. NAMC, for example, was formed from 10 sections ("practices") that concentrated on strategy and operations and had a long history of vigorous internal competition.

The Environment Health and Safety (EHS) Directorate consisted of five sections that had begun collaborating even before they were formally grouped together. EHS section managers had set up a practice leaders council in 1988; it became the core of the new EHS Directorate formed the following year. The new directorate was headed by Ladd Greeno, one of the five section managers. EHS work was scientifically based, often drawing upon its own laboratory efforts and field studies. For example, EHS scientists had developed a method of a chemical fingerprinting that was used to trace the contamination from the massive Exxon Valdez oil spill and distinguish it from preexisting environmental degradation.

Finally, ADL's oldest laboratory-based businesses became the core of the Technology and Product Development (TPD) Directorate. These businesses had long operated research and development laboratories that developed new technologies and products on contract, and solved complex technical problems. Their hands-on involvement with clients had grown much more collaborative as technologies and products had become more sophisticated. Some clients were small firms with limited R&D capabilities, while others were larger organizations seeking the multidisciplinary expertise that TPD could provide.

Although the original charter of the directorates was limited to staffing and human resources, their role expanded rapidly. "The minute the directors started to meet," Erickson recalled, "they started talking about other problems they were facing, and grabbed the ball." Over the next two or three years, the directorates migrated to full line authority and P&L status. The chairs of the directorates also developed roles with more formal authority and were assigned new titles, becoming Directorate Managing Directors (DMDs). Erickson's progression was typical. A section manager and vice president, she became both a director and the chair of the NAMC Directorate in 1989, reporting, along with 10 other section managers, to a CMG member. In 1992, she was named DMD of NAMC, and her section and its 10 managing directors reported to her. A year later, she gave up her section responsibilities to focus on the DMD role.

Lines of Business.   Although ADL described itself as a multidimensional consulting organization with a wide range of expertise and a worldwide network of resources, market research showed that its identity was fragmented and confused. In a memo to staff in early 1988, LaMantia emphasized the need to think more rigorously about the balance among functional skills, geography, and industry—that is, what, where, and for whom services were offered. By 1990, convinced that ADL had to abandon the idea that it was one, large undifferentiated business, he asked Ranganath Nayak, a senior vice president who then headed ADL's operations work, to lead a CMG discussion about what made a business a business. The group developed a number of criteria, including types of clients and engagements, how services were sold, the kinds of people hired and the training required, competitors, and pay scales. "We put these criteria up on the board," LaMantia recalled, "and any way you measured it, we seemed to be in three distinct lines of business: EHS, TPD, and management consulting." There was some debate over whether consulting should be two businesses, separated into strategy and operations, but Nayak argued strongly that because "our advice to clients is to integrate strategy and operations, we need to integrate them as well."

The emergent view was that the main job of each business was to be a "winner in its own right." Each should be able to go head-to-head with the best competitors in its area and be among the tops in the field. Each should also look for synergies with the other businesses.

The Seven Core Processes

The DMDs soon realized they lacked critical information needed to manage the directorates effectively. Operational information was hard to access and unintegrated, control and monitoring information was incomplete, and strategic and planning information was scarce. Thus, in 1991, Erickson, Greeno, David Lee, the head of TPD, and Tom Sommerlatte, the head of European Management Consulting, invited Larry Chait, an ADL expert in information systems, to work with them as an internal consultant, using a method called strategic information value analysis (SIVA) to identify their information gaps and develop projects for filling them. This effort built on an earlier presentation by LaMantia in which he had identified seven priorities for the company: "focus our strategies, establish a product development process, strengthen our marketing, improve our key account management, improve our human resource processes, use our resources effectively, and have fun." The seven core processes that emerged from the SIVA project were closely aligned with LaMantia's list.

The SIVA Project.   SIVA helped companies understand their information needs by focusing on the work itself, independent of organization structure or assigned responsibilities. A process of identifying, categorizing, and prioritizing the work and the information needed to conduct it led eventually to the creation of an "information supply matrix." Its four rows pertained to the type of information needs (strategic, analytical, controlling, and operational), and were standard for any SIVA matrix. The columns were the major "functions" of work activity the client identified, such as "manufacturing components" or "distributing finished products." To develop the ADL matrix, Chait worked intensively with the DMDs for three months; to collect additional data, he and his associates also interviewed 34 senior ADL employees in a wide range of positions.

Ultimately, this analysis produced seven categories or "functions" that virtually exhausted the work of the directorates: (1) marketing services (later called "generating awareness and leads"); (2) managing client relationships; (3) developing services; (4) delivering services; (5) acquiring, developing, and managing staff resources; (6) managing finances; and (7) managing strategy and organization. Each category was further subdivided into narrower activities by the four types of information needs. (Exhibit 3, pp. 52–53, shows a recent version of the matrix.) To identify information project priorities, Erickson, Greeno, and Lee used a color coding system to indicate the columns and cells needing the most support in the matrix, based on the quality of information currently available. The key cells were "managing strategy and organization," especially at the controlling and operational levels; "acquiring, developing, and managing staff," especially at the analysis and operational levels; and, in general, "managing client relationships."

A crucial terminological shift occurred early in these discussions. In place of the word *function,* the DMDs began using the term *business processes,* and began referring to the matrix as a "business process matrix." The concept of processes had already surfaced at ADL several months earlier when Nayak led a group that developed a model of the "high performance business"; LaMantia then used the model to set priorities for the firm. The core premises of the model were that both stakeholder satisfaction (including that of shareholders, customers, and employees) and superior performance were achieved through excellence in work processes—chains of value-adding activities that cut across the entire organization. As Nayak noted, "Achieving value for stakeholders without trading off one against the other is something you do by process improvement."

Following their work with Chait, the DMDs began to apply and leverage the process matrix. Erickson began by using process profiles for strategic positioning of NAMC, while Greeno used processes primarily as a way to better organize and manage EHS.

Processes at NAMC.   The value of process thinking quickly became evident during the summer of 1992, when NAMC's leaders decided to analyze competitors using the matrix. To determine their own strategic positioning, they first assessed competitor firms by their strengths and weakness in the seven core processes. After several iterations, two distinct patterns of process excellence emerged: product/awareness, and client/staff. Firms in the former category, like Index and Monitor, were distinguished by their superiority in the processes "developing services" and "generating awareness and leads." Typically, these firms employed a service delivery process based on standardized methodologies and placed limited emphasis on long-term management of client relations. By contrast, firms using the second (client/staff) model, such as McKinsey and Bain, built their practice by managing long-term client relationships, while also investing heavily in the acquisition and development of staff resources. At these firms standard tools and products were presented as interesting insights or used as excuses to see clients, rather than serving as the focus of the engagement.

NAMC then began to apply the business process matrix to its own activities and discovered that it did not show outstanding strength in either the product/awareness or client/staff model. The group decided that a choice was necessary, and focused initially on the client/staff model. Implementation was slow, however, because the group found it difficult to translate the positioning strategy into concrete products, investments, and actions.

Processes at EHS.   Greeno too used process profiles to examine the competition and EHS's own strengths and weakness, but moved quickly to matters of organization and management. Drawing upon NAMC's models, he first determined that EHS fit the product/awareness profile, even though it was a small player in a fragmented market. Because of weakness in the "awareness" part of the profile, "generating awareness and leads" was identified as a process priority. One result was the decision to host a two-day training course on "environmental audits" (an area for which EHS was renowned) for 1,000 people annually from client organizations.

Next, Greeno began evaluating internal integration and management using the seven processes. He quickly discovered that EHS's vertical organizational structure was leading to fragmentation and redundancy, and that he and his section managers had the same job. Not only were section managers working with their individual unit managers separately on their entire range of business issues, Greeno himself was working with the section managers on the same set of issues. He recalled:

> We were treating ourselves as a collection of $3 million businesses, but we were really a $40 million business. Looking forward, I wanted to build the structure and infrastructure, the processes and systems, for a $100 million business.

To achieve these objectives, Greeno phased out the EHS sections and recombined the pieces of the business. He then formed a directorate management group (DMG) consisting of himself and three other directors, all former section heads. The four directors became responsible for one or two

processes apiece, and the DMG evaluated the progress of the business as a whole, as well as assessing process strengths and weaknesses. Greeno noted: "We could not manage processes seriously at a small scale because it would give us nothing more than incremental improvement. Managing processes effectively requires having the scale for specialization." The primary role of the DMG thus became process management. Members were formally assigned "process ownership," and their performance evaluation was heavily weighted in this area.

Corporate Management

Since LaMantia's return in 1986, the senior vice presidents who had originally constituted the CMG had retired one by one, to be replaced by the DMDs. The cumulative impact was substantial, as LaMantia recalled: "The senior management of the company and the senior management of operations were becoming one, as opposed to the operating managers being managed by the senior management." In response, LaMantia began reshaping ADL's corporate management structure, strategy, and philosophy.

SLAM Team

In January 1994, LaMantia renamed the CMG the Senior Leadership and Management (SLAM) team and assigned it the role of setting strategy, policy, and procedures for the entire company. He also created an Office of the President to oversee the businesses and directorates, reduce his span of control, and assist in such delicate matters as deciding compensation for DMDs (see Exhibit 4 for an organization chart and a listing of SLAM team and Office of the President members). SLAM was to explore and decide such questions as how ADL should invest its capital, including commitments to marketing and product development, and whether, when, and where to open new offices. The group also devised a new variable compensation plan to help attract and retain staff and created a new ownership structure that would bring

EXHIBIT 3   Business Process Matrix

	Manage the Strategy and Organization	Generate Awareness and Leads	Manage Client Relationships
Strategic	Develop business/directorate strategy Design the organization Establish staff strategy Develop pricing strategy Develop organizational communication strategy Develop regional office strategy Develop measurement/control strategy	Understand market needs Identify target market segments Determine positioning Develop brand identity Define marketing mode mix Develop linkages among businesses	Identify target industry sectors Identify key and target accounts Develop "client lifecycle" strategy Develop account portfolio
Planning and Analysis	Establish goals and measures Establish staff strategy Create responsibilities for implementing strategy Develop quality standards Define information systems needs Develop internal operational procedures Analyze competitors	Make service/market investment decisions Identify emerging issues/key unmet needs Develop practice marketing plans Develop service marketing plans Develop geographic market marketing plans Develop business/directorate marketing plans Establish marketing policies and methods Analyze ADL image Manage marketing database	Understand client needs and environment Develop proposal strategy Develop account plans Design communication plans Analyze client portfolios
Measuring and Controlling	Monitor achievement of operating strategy Monitor alignment of staff with strategy Assess/control quality Measure quality Assess I/T effectiveness Monitor compliance with policy/procedures	Measure marketing effectiveness Track execution of marketing plans Monitor competition Monitor service relevance Control expenditures versus budget Monitor conversion rates	Monitor account performance Monitor conversion rates Monitor client feedback Assess client communications Approve proposals Control investment versus budget
Operational	Build partnership within organization Build teams Continually improve internal processes Share knowledge/experience Align staff with strategy Tailor strategy to short-term business conditions Develop information systems Manage infrastructure Coordinate/communicate horizontally Communicate downward Communicate upward	Publish articles Manage mailing list Give seminars Maintain trade/industry association relationships Manage media relationships Generate market awareness Conduct promotional campaigns Conduct sales calls Generate leads Perform lead triage Sell to new prospects Write proposals Price proposals Do direct mailing Do telemarketing Conduct marketing events Develop credentials materials	Foster client relationships Leverage client relationships Identify new business opportunities Write proposals Price proposals Sell business (convert proposals) Get client feedback Follow up on client feedback Send bills Collect bills Provide billing backup Resolve account conflicts

Develop Services	Deliver Services	Manage Staff Resources	Manage Finances
Develop service strategy Identify new service offerings Identify themes Withdraw from nonstrategic services	Develop service delivery/value model Establish professional standards	Set human resource philosophy Establish staff development strategy Establish long-term staff profile Establish staff acquisition strategy Develop total remuneration strategy	Develop long-term financial goals Develop long-term ownership goals Develop dividend policy
Plan specific new services Compare competitive services	Develop case plans Customize service for client Analyze service delivery Analyze client feedback	Develop recruiting program Set staffing policies Forecast staffing needs Establish compensation policies Develop career plan/path program Develop individual career paths Design training Establish welfare/pension policies	Develop operating budgets Develop capital budgets Reforecast operations
Assess services acceptance Control investments versus budget	Control cases versus case plans Review client deliverables Collect service feedback	Measure staff performance Measure staff satisfaction Assess training effectiveness Approve hiring plans Monitor individual career paths Fulfill government requirements Assess recruiting effectiveness Assess staff productivity	Measure operating results Control working capital Control capital budget Control operating costs Track capital assets
Develop and codify methodologies Develop tools Enhance services Develop service training materials Disseminate information about services internally	Manage cases Form case teams Demonstrate value added Perform case work Conduct case reviews Provide feedback Produce and deliver case results Maintain archival files Maintain product experience (e.g., quals) Report regularly to client Maintain intellectual assets Manage case-related risks and liabilities	Recruit staff Enhance staff satisfaction Hire staff Assimilate staff Set staff goals Review staff Counsel and mentor staff Promote/reward staff Provide nonmonetary rewards and recognition Develop training materials Conduct training programs Execute compensation plan Communicate with staff Maintain relationships with university placement offices Address underperforming staff Adjust staffing to business conditions	Manage working capital Manage expenses Acquire assets Allocate costs Manage overruns, write-offs, and discounts Manage professional service income Manage payroll Manage cash and investments

EXHIBIT 4 Organization Chart

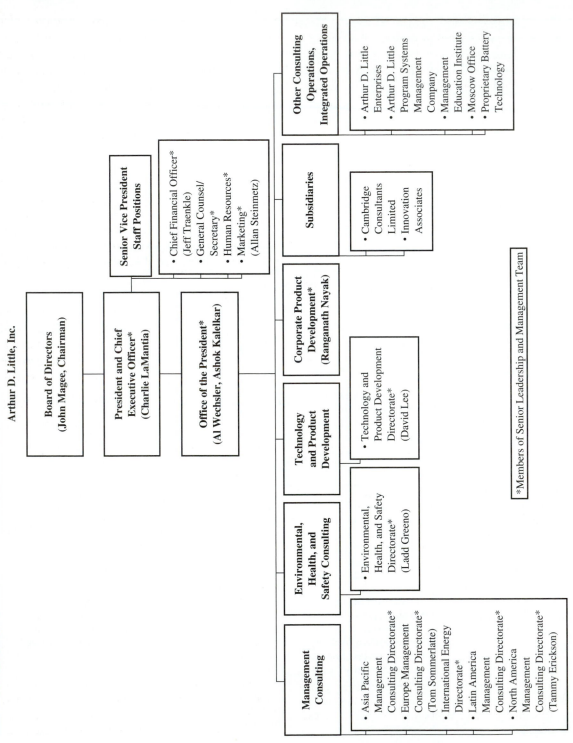

Arthur D. Little, Inc.

Board of Directors
(John Magee, Chairman)

President and Chief Executive Officer*
(Charlie LaMantia)

Office of the President*
(Al Wechsler, Ashok Kalelkar)

Senior Vice President Staff Positions
- Chief Financial Officer* (Jeff Traenkle)
- General Counsel/ Secretary*
- Human Resources*
- Marketing* (Allan Steinmetz)

Management Consulting
- Asia Pacific Management Consulting Directorate*
- Europe Management Consulting Directorate* (Tom Sommerlatte)
- International Energy Directorate*
- Latin America Management Consulting Directorate*
- North America Management Consulting Directorate* (Tammy Erickson)

Environmental, Health, and Safety Consulting
- Environmental, Health, and Safety Directorate* (Ladd Greeno)

Technology and Product Development
- Technology and Product Development Directorate* (David Lee)

Corporate Product Development*
(Ranganath Nayak)

Subsidiaries
- Cambridge Consultants Limited
- Innovation Associates

Other Consulting Operations, Integrated Operations
- Arthur D. Little Enterprises
- Arthur D. Little Program Systems Management Company
- Management Education Institute
- Moscow Office
- Proprietary Battery Technology

*Members of Senior Leadership and Management Team

Source: ADL

54

non-U.S.–based senior staff to parity with American-based staff. Ashok Kalelkar, a member of the Office of the President and a SLAM team member, observed: "This was a big change. In the past, everything was done locally, and our offices behaved almost as if they were franchisees." Another team member noted:

> In the old structure, we couldn't engage with these issues. The top had the power, but lacked consensus and was too removed from daily operations to use it. The units had the ability to see the issues and to act, but not the scale to take advantage of it.

As for his own role, LaMantia observed:

> Around here, almost everything requires participation and consensus to make it happen. So I spend a lot of time traveling around the world, talking and listening to staff. That, coupled with an extensive staff feedback process, helps us decide what we ought to be working on. Then I formally set the agenda. I also must decide who sits at the table, how they are performing, who stays on the team. We don't vote on that.

Managing through Processes

Process thinking had steadily gained ground at the corporate level. LaMantia had immediately embraced the seven processes emerging from the high performance business model and the SIVA project, but others at the corporate level were initially resistant. Kalelkar recalled: "It was a tough sell. The group felt that there wasn't a simple formula for running a complex business like ours." LaMantia, however, persisted, and in 1991 began to organize ADL annual reports around "our seven critical processes." He also used them to shape the agenda of SLAM team meetings. LaMantia believed that, over time, processes had become a "way of thinking" at ADL. He observed:

> We can talk across the organization because even though the businesses differ, they each have the same processes. We have a common language and approach for discussing issues and understanding how different aspects of what we do relate to each other.

One test of a process, he suggested, was whether the same process could be used in all three businesses. Moreover, since ADL sold process-focused services, LaMantia believed that it was important to tell clients, "We practice what we preach."

LaMantia had also found processes to be a way to "keep going deeper." His early initiatives, for example, had kept overhead flat by focusing on cost control and eliminating unnecessary or redundant expenditures. But as LaMantia pointed out, "They did not examine overhead itself from a process point of view." A new initiative, Operation Second Wind, was being considered for that purpose. Through it, the overhead a process generated would be considered an investment to be selectively managed to produce faster growth, not simply a cost to be reduced. Similarly, LaMantia sought improvements in the process "acquiring, developing, and managing staff resources." Having the right people in the right place at the right time was a topic he frequently raised with the SLAM team. In response, the group had developed a set of leading indicators that would provide staffing guidance for DMDs. LaMantia commented:

> Next I wanted them to define how they will apply these leading indicators. Which ones will they use, and how will they manage the process? My approach is not to insist on uniformity across directorates but to define a minimum process that they can elaborate, using their initiative and judgment. Ultimately, hiring is a judgment call.

Riker, who had headed the original staff development task force, saw it as consistent with his group's recommendations:

> The process perspective leads you to different questions and activities than a functional one. You think about selection, hiring, training, and career stages, not personnel actions. Activities like staff development get taken seriously, and we see what it takes to do it . . . Those activities were not taken seriously before.

At the same time, there were debates and discussions within SLAM about process definition, process ownership, and process measurement. Some team members believed that progress in these areas was slower than needed, and that "process think-ing" needed to be moved forward more aggressively.

Process Definition. Recalling the processes' origins in the SIVA project, one SLAM team member noted, "Our seven 'processes' are not really processes, but buckets of like activities . . . they do not reflect sophisticated thinking about how processes work. You could not reengineer them." (See Exhibit 5 for a list of characteristics describ-ing a well-connected process used by some ADL consultants.) Chait agreed, in part: "Remember, what we have is an information-needs matrix that was relabeled a business process matrix. Our goal was to help the organization be comfortable with it, take ownership of it, and act through it; if they do that, it has served its purpose."

According to Nayak, now senior vice president in charge of product development, well-defined processes required an output of value to stake-holders, and the activities creating the output had to be linked. This meant defining the output and how to measure it, and then working backward to create value chains of activities. He elaborated:

You have to develop a broad understanding among process owners because each person's work will affect the others' since their processes are interlinked. Some reengineering firms will tell you that a collection of processes is like a layer cake; you can take one layer at a time and fix it. In truth, it's more like a marble cake, with a swirled pattern. You therefore need an educational process so process owners understand what all the processes are, how they link up, the outputs they want to create, and where they are right now in terms of quality or quantity of output. Then you need joint agreement among them on what concrete performance improvement is sought within, say, 18–24 months—so you have something concrete you are going to achieve, rather than just saying you are simply going to improve the process. Agreeing on the output also means agreeing on the resources required to execute it. Without that agreement, people will back off as soon as you try to get process improvement underway.

EXHIBIT 5   Characteristics of a Well-Connected Process

1. The overall process is well understood, appropriately documented, and routinely executed with minimal variability.

2. Technology is aggressively employed to maximum advantage.

3. Hand-offs are minimized; tasks are combined and responsibility for large portions/all of the process is vested in single individuals/groups, without regard to traditional organizational boundaries.

4. Tasks within the process are performed on a continuous, rather than a batch, basis.

5. The "capacity" of participants within the process is carefully balanced to avoid bottlenecks and delays.

6. Tasks are performed simultaneously, in parallel, rather than in sequence whenever possible.

7. Decisions necessary within the context of the process are vested in the individuals who actually perform each task, eliminating all rubber-stamp approvals.

8. The process includes robust channels of lateral communication designed to mitigate typical interfunctional barriers and eliminate lengthy, chain-of-command hierarchical communications.

9. Control mechanisms are concentrated in the early parts of the process and focus on prevention rather than rework.

10. Measures of process effectiveness occur throughout the process and are communicated to all process participants, encouraging continuous improvement of the process.

Source: ADL

Nayak believed that at ADL "developing services" and "delivering services" came closest to meeting these criteria and being true processes. In "developing services," for example, one output was product-specific training programs designed so that someone who had been through the training would know how to deliver the service to a client. A second output was the documentation of products and services in sufficient detail so that a staff member could use the documentation to write a proposal or guide a client engagement. A set of these detailed road maps had been developed over the past two years by the management consulting directorates, and took the form of eight compact books. The enormity of the task lay in converging and consolidating the 200 services that 1,000 management consultants offered into a reasonable number of articulated, standardized products.

Process Ownership. By 1994, process management and ownership were being pursued with varying degrees of effort by each of the directorates. To formalize the approach at the corporate level, LaMantia appointed several SLAM team members process owners. For example, Nayak was assigned "developing services," Traenkle was assigned "managing finances," Wechsler was assigned "delivering services," and LaMantia himself assumed ownership of "managing strategy and organization." Each individual was to be the catalyst, driver, integrator, and overseer of their process throughout all the directorates, and was charged with ensuring that best practices were identified and adopted across the company. Wechsler commented on the distinction between corporate and directorate-level responsibilities:

> The directorate staff will take responsibility for managing and improving the processes within their directorate. We at SLAM will look more broadly at the company's processes and subprocesses, identify where they are weak, what is missing, where they can be improved, and will find the best practices and put them in place.

During subsequent SLAM meeting discussions, best practices in areas such as training, performance assessment, or product development were unearthed from individual directorates, and their elements were analyzed and discussed. The result was a template, extracted from the particulars of practice, that became the minimum standard against which all other directorates were challenged to improve their processes. Thus, a case management training program developed by EHS became the best practice standard companywide for training case leaders, as did EHS's staff review process. SLAM team process owners were expected to guide the transfer, although the process was still in its infancy.

Process Costing. In 1995, at LaMantia's suggestion, Erickson, Traenkle, and Burns were assigned responsibility for a SLAM project to determine whether earlier exploratory work on process costing was applicable to all of ADL. The basic thrust of this approach (which, in theory, resembled activity-based costing) was to allocate overhead expenses to the appropriate activities performed in each of the seven processes. Without this allocation, it was difficult to determine how much was being spent on each process. LaMantia was a strong supporter of the concept, and viewed process costing as a tool for "managing investment rather than controlling costs." As such, it fit nicely with Operation Second Wind. It was anticipated that by 1996 all operating statements could be examined from a process standpoint, since the necessary accounting frameworks were already under development (see Exhibits 6a and 6b).

Planning Processes

Because ADL was privately held, its stock value had to be set by an outside valuation service. As a result, LaMantia observed, "twice a year we get a report card on how we've done." The value of the firm was based on expectations for future growth in earnings and cash flow, which, in turn, were based on the company's recent financial performance, its track record against long-term plan, and strategies in place for the future. To ensure that ADL performed well, LaMantia had developed a 10-year valuation model, with long-term targets of 15 percent annual growth in earnings and stock

---

EXHIBIT 6a Templates for Process Costing

Consulting Activities
Summary of Labor Distributed
June, 1995

Directorate: DXXX XXXXXXXXXXXXX

	Month to Date			Year to Date		
	Actual	**Prior Year**	**Actual Index**	**Actual**	**Prior Year**	**Actual Index**
Direct Labor						
Service Delivery						
Service Development						
Manage Client Relationships						
prospects						
projects						
Generate Awareness						
Acquire, Develop Staff						
Manage Strategy and Org.						
Vacation, Illness, etc.						
Other Administrative Activities	_____	_____	_____	_____	_____	_____
			100%			100%
Indirect Labor						
Service Delivery						
Service Development						
Manage Client Relationships						
prospects						
projects						
Generate Awareness						
Acquire, Develop Staff						
Manage Finances						
Manage Strategy and Org.						
Vacation, Illness, etc.						
Other Administrative Activities	_____	_____	_____	_____	_____	_____
			100%			100%
Total Labor Distributed						

Source: ADL

value, that he used to monitor the business and provide input for corporate investment decisions.

In addition, each business and business segment was required to develop a five-year strategy that was renewed annually. Each also engaged in a detailed financial planning process that projected revenues, staffing, expenses by process, and income from operations; set growth goals; and requested investment dollars. These plans then rolled up to the corporate level, where investment requests were screened and balanced against the funds available, based on the 10-year valuation model. At this time, trade-off decisions were made. Some initiatives were favored over others, and funds might be shifted across businesses or segments. Reforecasts were required every quarter to track changing business conditions and ensure that adjustments in investment levels were made in real time.

EXHIBIT 6b   Templates for Process Costing

**Consulting Activities
Overhead Expense Summary
June, 1995**

Directorate: DXXX XXXXXXXXXXXXXX

Business Process	Expense Category	Month to Date		Year to Date	
		Actual	Prior Year	Actual	Prior Year
Generate Awareness	Material Reproduction				
	Travel				
	PR Advertising	____	____	____	____
Manage Client Relationships	Travel				
	Meals & Entertainment				
	Seminars, Conferences	____	____	____	____
Acquire, Develop Staff	Training				
	Travel				
	Employee Welfare				
	Hiring Bonus				
	Relocation				
	Recruiting	____	____	____	____
⋮	⋮				
Total					

Source: ADL

Brand Positioning

In LaMantia's view, the three lines of business needed to be linked by more than processes and planning alone. A unifying brand identity was also required. He observed: "Our blessing and curse is that we are broader than any of our competitors. For that reason, it is more difficult for the marketplace to have a clear image of what ADL can do." To address the problem, LaMantia looked outside the firm and hired Jeff Dunn, an experienced marketer who had worked previously at Bank of Boston and Time, Inc. Dunn quickly began surveying customers to find the attributes they desired in consultants. His goal was to develop a clearer picture of ADL's distinctive value added, and to begin crafting a brand identity. In 1993 Dunn left for a position elsewhere, and Allan Steinmetz, an expert in brand positioning from Andersen Consulting, was hired in his place. With the help of the SLAM team, Steinmetz completed the brand identity work and developed an integrated communications strategy.

ADL's brand identity was forged from its long tradition of learning and creating new solutions; its target audience was "discoverers" who wished to reinvent their organizations. It also built on NAMC's analysis of the migration of value in the marketplace—from providing information to facilitating change—and recognized that ADL could "jump over" the current focus on change and plant itself squarely in the future by emphasizing learning. The new positioning statement read, in part:

> For clients who are interested in reinventing their companies, enhancing the learning potential of their people, and creating long-lasting leadership, Arthur D. Little provides experienced and knowledgeable people who are pathfinders, working with clients side by side to achieve lasting results.

EXHIBIT 7   Business Positioning Statements

Management Consulting	Environmental, Health, and Safety Consulting	Technology and Product Development
Arthur D. Little's global Management Consulting Group works side by side with leading organizations to help them accelerate their learning, create positive change, and achieve lasting results.	Arthur D. Little helps its clients meet their environmental, health, and safety challenges by integrating our technological expertise with management vision. We work side by side with our clients, enhancing their organizations' strengths with our experience and knowledge.	Arthur D. Little's Technology and Product Development Directorate can help you leverage technology to gain competitive advantage. We work with our clients side by side to ensure knowledge transfer, and then we help them use their technological lead for strategic benefit.
• We strive for client satisfaction and value by providing objective, creative solutions in a spirit of partnership that enhances learning and knowledge transfer. • More than 75 percent of the Fortune 100 companies (or their global equivalents) have trusted Arthur D. Little's proven expertise. • By applying out global knowledge of best practices, we help our clients achieve sustained competitive advantage. • Working with you, our world-class management consultants put our industry-focused knowledge of strategy, process design, and resource and organizational alignment to work to enhance your vision and turn it into reality.	• Our team approach draws on our world-class consultants across functional, geographic, and industry lines to put the right skills and experience to work on each assignment. • Our long-standing client relationships demonstrate our success in fulfilling our commitment to meeting clients' needs. • Through knowledge transfer and training, we help out clients learn and improve their EHS skills and capabilities. • Our clients consider us their consultants of choice because we help them develop practical solutions, improve EHS performance, and achieve sustained business advantage.	• Since 1886, our world-class technologists have worked with clients in a wide range of engineering, manufacturing, and laboratory environments. We offer industry knowledge, hands-on expertise, and a track record of successful innovation. • We provide fast access to a vast knowledge base and can help you apply both emerging and existing technologies to create innovative products and technological solutions. • Because we understand both your business and the requirements of your customers, we can help you make the right strategic decisions about acquiring, developing, and using technology to improve your bottom line.

Source: ADL

This identity was then carried into all marketing, advertising, publications, and corporate literature (see Exhibit 7). For the first time ever, ADL launched a major advertising campaign. And in August 1995, it acquired Innovation Associates, a leading consulting firm in the area of organizational learning.

"One Strategy" for Management Consulting. Prior to 1993, ADL's management consulting businesses were largely autonomous. But in December 1993, at the instigation of Riker and LaMantia, a meeting was held at Pennyhill, U.K., aimed at bringing together the North American and European consulting directorates. After the meeting LaMantia observed: "It was incredible! It couldn't have happened three years ago. They were ready to 'link arms.'" Sommerlatte concurred: "In the past, Europe was part of the company but did not feel ownership. Now we are represented on the SLAM team, and our leaders own ADL shares. That makes for real integration in both operations and spirit."

The Pennyhill meeting was the first step in developing a single approach to management consulting, called "One Strategy," in which ADL consultants would provide most of their value in change and learning. Differentiation would be based on the firm's traditional strengths in service delivery and staff quality, supported by extensive work standardizing and documenting ADL products and services. ADL's high percentage of experienced senior staff on each team assignment and intensive investments in continued training would also be highlighted, since most competitors saturated their assignments with junior-level consultants.

"Is That All There Is? Should There Be More?"
Despite these steps forward, several SLAM team members remained concerned about ADL's corporate strategy. They raised questions in three areas: the strategy's concreteness, growth and resource allocation, and cross-business integration.

Concreteness.   In their client work, ADL consultants defined a strategy as a path for getting from "here" to a future vision, together with a year-by-year timetable against which progress could be assessed. The issue for some was whether there was any way of telling whether there had been progress in implementing ADL's strategy. While there were clear financial milestones, one SLAM member observed: "The strategy has no other measurable things connected to it."

Growth/Resource Allocation.   Historically, each of the directorates had been largely self-funding. But the Latin American Management Consulting DMD had recently proposed that SLAM take resources from less rapidly growing regions, such as North America, and apply them to Latin America, which was growing far more rapidly and was constrained by the number of available staff. "We have not done a lot of formal cross-allocation," noted LaMantia. "Most of the necessary trade-offs get made during the financial planning process."

Integration.   The issue of cross-business opportunities (called cross-selling) was also under debate. Some believed that the tradition of independent businesses made sense:

> We are three businesses, not three product lines. Cross-selling just doesn't seem to work. The shared relationship among us is at the value level: commitments to customers, to quality, to customer satisfaction, and to ethics.

Others, however, claimed that ADL was significantly underrealizing its cross-business possibilities and favored the development of integrated services. In fact, SLAM had recently decided to appoint corporate marketing managers, whose job would be to develop business in selected fields for every area of the company. For his part, LaMantia spoke increasingly about relating the businesses in a deeper way by working through two processes, "generating awareness and leads" and "developing services":

> We need to come up with approaches and products that involve more than one of our businesses; right now, we have only one multibusiness product, minimalist manufacturing, and one cross-business practice, utilities. We need to be able to represent the full capabilities of the firm to the client.

There were strong pressures from the marketplace encouraging this shift, as a SLAM team member observed: "Our clients don't care if we are in three businesses, or where we are based; they are operating global companies and want help where they want it when they want it." For this reason, a number of ADL consultants wanted the organization's axis to revolve around global industry practices, with each practice including people from all three businesses.

The sunset blazed over Acorn Park as Charlie LaMantia packed up his notes for the forthcoming SLAM team meeting. He was immersed in thought. Did ADL now have a complete corporate strategy? Were the seven processes really the glue holding the three businesses together? How *did* processes and strategy fit together?

Case 1–2

R. R. DONNELLEY & SONS:
THE DIGITAL DIVISION

"My biggest worry," said Barbara (Barb) Schetter, vice president and general manager of R.R. Donnelley's Digital Division, "is that we don't become an orphan. We could build up the division and even meet our revenue numbers, yet still not be embraced by the rest of the organization." Indeed, by early June 1995, many group and division managers at the $4.9 billion printing giant had yet to sign on to the strategic potential of digital technology or accept the Digital Division as the most appropriate locale for the business. Some still saw digital printing as a technology in search of a market. Others had indicated that if they did decide to embrace digital printing, they might do so on their own.

These concerns were very much on the minds of Schetter and Mary Lee Schneider, the division's director of marketing, as they sat down for a meeting on June 7, 1995. In two weeks Schneider was scheduled to make a presentation to one of Donnelley's business groups, Book Publishing Services, which was deciding whether to move into digital technology on its own or to bring its digital work to the division. Schetter and Schneider were hoping to craft a plan that would convince the Books Group to come to them. But they were still struggling to find convincing arguments and the right set of incentives.

Company and Industry Background

R.R. Donnelley & Sons was founded in 1864. By 1995, it had become the world's largest commercial printer, with 41,000 employees in 22 countries. A privately held, family-run, Chicago-based company for almost a century, Donnelley went public in 1956; the first outsider was named chairman 20 years later. Donnelley had begun printing telephone directories and the Montgomery Ward catalog in the late 1800s and still generated 60 percent of its revenues from directories, catalogs, and magazines (see Exhibits 1 and 2). Its major customers were telephone operating companies, retail and direct-mail merchandisers, and publishers of books, magazines, and software. In 1995, the company was organized into 38 divisions; the divisions, in turn, were collected into eight business groups, which were part of three sectors.

Organization and Incentives

At Donnelley, manufacturing and sales were the core functions. Schneider observed:

> In this company, you either make it or you sell it. Our divisions are therefore organized around manufacturing assets [i.e., plants].[1] The trim size of the magazine, the binding requirements of the book— that's how we look at structure.

Highly autonomous, division managers were vice presidents who could choose the printing jobs they wanted to run and the equipment they wanted to buy. They sought the most profitable jobs because they were held accountable for operating profit, based on targets set during the budgeting

---

This case was prepared by Artemis March under the direction of David A. Garvin.

Copyright © 1996 by the President and Fellows of Harvard College. Harvard Business School case 396-154.

[1]*Although the fit was not perfect, Donnelley employees used the terms division, plant, and assets interchangeably.*

EXHIBIT 1   Financial Highlights ($ in thousands, except per share data)

	Year Ending December 31	
	1994	*1993*
Operating Performance		
Net sales	$4,888,786	$4,387,761
Earnings from operations	459,431	415,607[a]
Net income	268,603	245,920[a]
Operating cash flow[b]	582,066	520,724[a]
Per Common Share		
Net income	$ 1.75	$ 1.59[a]
Dividends	0.60	0.5
Other Selected Financial Data		
Capital investments	$ 545,651	$ 484,25
Working capital	551,480	424,47
Total assets	4,452,143	3,654,02
Total debt to total capitalization ratio	38.6%	27.8
Return on average equity	14.1%	13.3%[a]

[a]Excluding the effects of one-time items in 1993 for a restructuring charge, required accounting changes for postretirement benefits and income taxes, and the deferred income tax charge related to the increase in the federal statutory income tax rate.

[b]Operating cash flow represents net income from operations, excluding one-time items, plus depreciation and amortization.

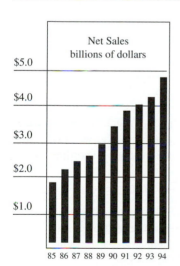

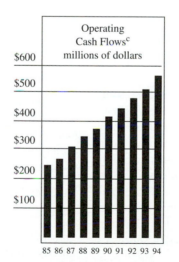

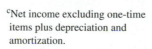

[c]Net income excluding one-time items plus depreciation and amortization.

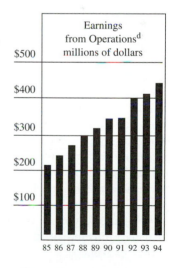

[d]Excluding one-time items.

Source: Annual Report

EXHIBIT 2   Sales and Customers by Business Category (% of consolidated sales)

Catalogs	*Magazines—18%*	*Books—13%*	*Metromail—5%*
Lands' End	*TV Guide*	Random House	Procter & Gamble
L.L. Bean	*Family Circle*	Simon & Schuster	FirstCard
Eddie Bauer	*Time*	Harcourt Brace	Mutual of Omaha
J. Crew	*Glamour*	Harper Collins	Whirlpool
	People	Bantam Doubleday	
31%	*Reader's Digest*		
Retailers	*Telephone Directories—12%*	*Financial—5%*	*Software/Hardware—16%*
Wal-Mart	Sprint	Merrill Lynch	Microsoft
JC Penney	Ameritech	Smith Barney	IBM
Kmart	Nynex	Paine Webber	WordPerfect
Service Merchandise	Bell Atlantic	Goldman Sachs	Quicken
Toys 'R Us	Southwestern Bell	Schwab & Co	
	US West		

Source: R.R. Donnelley

---

process. Division P&Ls reflected plant revenues and costs, as well as allocations of corporate and selling expenses. Because most salesforces were aligned with business groups rather than divisions, each had a sales expense ratio that was applied to the work it sold into any plant.

Until 1991, division managers' incentive compensation was tied to their particular division's profit performance. This formula was subsequently changed in the oldest parts of the company, such as commercial printing, where the assets of individual divisions were similar and could be used for the same type of work. In these parts of the company, division-level incentives became groupwide in 1991, and sectorwide in 1993. As Jeff Majestic, financial director of the Information Services Group, explained:

> We couldn't move work around when each division wanted to maximize its own profitability. Now the division directors ask, "What is the most profitable way to run this job for Donnelley?" because they

can make the best decision for the company without its affecting their incentive pay.

With few exceptions, division managers reported to business group presidents. Each business group contained several plants (divisions), as well as its own salesforce and such staff functions as marketing and finance. Group P&Ls were therefore the aggregate of their plants' P&Ls, and business presidents' incentive compensation was tied to the profits and losses of those plants. According to one senior manager:

> This incentive system creates a tremendous bias for the business group presidents to deploy their sales forces to fill their assets. The salesforce is an expense to its home group; you only benefit from it if they sell against your assets.

Salespeople worked solely on commission and were paid no matter what they sold or to whose assets the work was assigned. Technically, salespeople were free to sell work that was printed at any plant in the Donnelley system. But because sales managers' incentives, like those of business group presidents, were tied to the profitability of their particular group, there was considerable pressure to fill the home group's plants with profitable jobs. In a typical group, the salesforce sold 80 percent to 95 percent of its volume to its own plants.

In total, Donnelley's salesforce numbered nearly 500 people. They were often described as the company's greatest strength; they sold primarily to print buyers, whose first consideration tended to be cost per page. Salespeople developed considerable knowledge about their customers, particularly on the operational side; they might become quite involved, for example, in helping a catalog customer reduce inventory and shorten cycle times. Most of Donnelley's upper management had come from Sales, and many sales representatives did extremely well financially. CEO John Walter reportedly said that after being a sales representative, it took him six jobs to make equivalent money. Marketing, a recent innovation at Donnelley, for the most part supported the salesforces and focused on current customer needs, rather than creating long-term strategies.

Sectors were also a relatively recent addition to the organization. They were formed in 1993, when the president of Donnelley resigned. Instead of naming a successor, Walter clustered the business groups into three sectors: Commercial Print, Networked Services, and Information Resources. Each business group president reported to one of the three sector presidents, who were also executive vice presidents of the corporation. Together, Walter, the sector presidents, and key corporate staff formed Donnelley's Management Committee.

The Traditional Print Business

Donnelley's traditional businesses were geared to long printing runs on gravure and offset/web presses. These enormous machines, dubbed "heavy iron," required large capital investments. A typical offset press cost $12 million, and a gravure press

cost considerably more. Offset presses used film and plates and were cost-effective for runs of 25,000 to 500,000, while gravure presses used etched copper cylinders and were employed for run lengths of 500,000 or more.

The company considered long-term relationships with customers to be the key to its commercial printing business. About 70 percent of this business was based on contracts of 3 to 10 years. Donnelley's strategy was to secure multiyear "enabling contracts," worth tens of millions of dollars, from select customers and to then build a plant specifically for each one, with equipment dedicated to its needs. Resource allocation likewise followed this opportunistic approach. While most people at the company viewed enabling contracts as the secret of the firm's success, others raised concerns. Allen Cubell, director of strategic planning for the Commercial Print Sector, noted: "You get an emergent strategy based on opportunities, as opposed to selecting the right opportunity based on a strategic assessment of alternatives."

The traditional print business was one of high fixed and low variable costs: The longer the run length on heavy iron, the lower the cost per page. Technology projects initiated by the corporate Technology Center and the divisions kept Donnelley's $3.7 billion asset base at the forefront of these traditional, electromechanical print technologies, while allowing some tailoring and customization. Majestic explained what customized binding equipment could do, using a Donnelley customer, the *Farm Journal*, as an example:

Subscribers to this magazine include farmers of all kinds, and our customer wants to target the variable portions of the magazine to each of their interests. At the same time, we want to save the customer money. We do that by mailing according to zip code—in fact, by carrier route. Our binding lines allow us to assemble different versions of the magazine according to subscribers' interests, and then have them come off the equipment in zip code sequence, all correctly addressed. In total, we do 66,000 versions of the *Farm Journal!*

Industry Shifts and New Technologies

Industry trends were moving increasingly toward such local, targeted communications, often called "mass customization." Long-time customers such as *TV Guide* wanted shorter runs, more versions, tailored inserts, and greater use of color. Newer customers like Microsoft put a premium on speed, simultaneous global distribution, and the ability to revise materials quickly. All customers faced sharply rising postal rates and paper prices, which, along with increased inventory, warehousing, and shipping costs, were creating incentives to develop alternative, electronic media and new channels of distribution.

Imaging technologies had been fairly stable since the development of offset/web printing in the 1960s, but major changes were underway, largely because of the rapid spread of office computing. Schetter noted: "Last year, for the first time more paper was produced on desktops than on web presses." Desktop publishing, which emerged on a large scale in the late 1980s, integrated many craft-based, front-end, editorial and prepress operations, and triggered their migration away from traditional production sites in the publishing and printing industries. The economic impact was significant, as Schneider observed: "The craft side of the business that we made big money on—stripping, color correction, etching—has migrated to the hands of the document creator."

Filmless printing technologies, such as digital four-color and computer-to-plate, were expected to have an even more profound impact. By eliminating the demanding intermediate steps of converting to film, these technologies would significantly reduce cycle times and chemical pollution. Digital four-color printing went the furthest, eliminating plates altogether and printing directly from computer files. It allowed short run, four-color printing in which the image was infinitely customizable, and could be delivered in variable quantities as often as desired. This capability, together with the low cost (approximately $200,000 in 1995) and small size of digital presses meant that they did not need to operate in a manufacturing environment but could be sited at distribution points anywhere in the world, even on customers' own premises. Rory Cowan, president of the Information Resources Sector and a staunch advocate of digital technology, summarized the likely impact: "Digital technology will atomize the printing industry the way the microprocessor did the computer industry." In 1995, digital growth was forecast at around 16 percent annually, while traditional printing was expected to grow by 3 percent.

Emerging Competition

In 1995, at least 55,000 printing companies operated worldwide. Most had fewer than 25 employees. Donnelley, with 6 percent of the $80 billion print market, was larger than its next nine rivals combined. Threats, however, were emerging from several directions, largely because of new technologies and new entrants to the business.

Online service providers and software packagers were making four-color images available electronically, at the same time that color printers were improving rapidly in quality and migrating to homes and small businesses. Smaller printing companies were building alliances, among themselves and with firms that had high-capacity networks for transmitting files. For example, AT&T had recently forged a multiparty agreement in which Adobe Systems and Quark provided the software to compose documents directly on computers; Xerox provided the software to compress and decompress document files before and after transmission; and digital print manufacturers provided the hardware. Moore Graphics and EDS had announced similar plans. Pulled together, these offerings provided the infrastructure to support networks of local printing companies and link them with retail chains such as Sir Speedy. Schetter explained the implications: "Digital print is rapidly migrating to retail. With these alliances, a small printer can now look like a very large printer."

The Digital Vision

One Donnelley executive alert to these changes was Rory Cowan, who over the years had championed a series of efforts, including the formation of the Digital Division, to focus the company's attention on the opportunities of digital technology. Cowan joined Donnelley in 1986, when the company he then owned, CSA Press, was acquired by the printing giant. Ten years earlier, while still in business school, he had bought CSA from his father and grown it into a $20 million printer of documentation books and bundles for the software industry. In 1987, Cowan was named senior vice president of sales for Documentation Services (soon renamed Global Software), Donnelley's first major nontraditional business group. Global Software served companies such as Microsoft, Apple, and IBM that needed to reproduce and distribute technical documentation in a variety of formats worldwide. By 1990, the business had quintupled in sales to several hundred million dollars, and Cowan was promoted to group vice president.

Throughout this period, Cowan attempted to build his new business in parallel with the old. Rather than directly challenging the traditional organization and values, he preferred, in his words, "to create a new business and have it drip on the culture." He viewed Donnelley as being "like IBM in 1983—PCs are coming in, but management has grown up in a mainframe world." Global Software therefore sought and developed a younger breed of managers, more of them women and all of them comfortable with computers. Epitomizing the breed was Janet Clarke, manager of the group's hardware salesforce, who in 1985 had sought out IBM's PC division and made a crucial $50 million sale.

In 1991, Cowan was promoted again and became Donnelley's sole executive vice president. He was effectively the number two person in the company, with responsibility for Global Software, Books, Financial, Information Services, and Metromail, as well as the corporate Technology Center. Meanwhile, he was becoming convinced that "value was leaving the book" and began exploring how Donnelley's traditional scale advantages could be preserved in a digital future.

A New Business Model

As Cowan saw it, digital presses were an essential enabling technology, but were unlikely, by themselves, to provide Donnelley with enduring competitive advantage. Instead, he believed that economies of scale would come from an information architecture that linked Donnelley with upstream "content owners" and downstream customers. Donnelley would become an electronic warehouse and distributor, with the critical ability to print on demand. In the early 1990s, Cowan began developing the broad outlines of a new business model based on these concepts, with distributed digital printing at its core.

In the new world, publishers would send data files of their manuscripts to Donnelley, where they would be retained in a database. When a bookstore needed copies of a particular book, it would contact Donnelley, and the files would be printed in the appropriate numbers, bound, and shipped; Donnelley would simultaneously send a check to the publisher for the necessary royalties. This process eliminated a range of costly steps, including warehousing and inventory, that represented roughly 60 percent of book publishers' costs. The approach also avoided the usual mismatching of demand and inventory. Because data files could be printed anywhere in the world—preferably in a print-on-demand (POD) site that Donnelley located near the final point of sale—end-user stock could be replenished within 24 hours. To make the model work, Donnelley would need to develop and control four database systems: a transaction management system for triggering and managing the purchasing process; a system for royalty accounting and payment; an object-oriented database for managing the intellectual property; and a manufacturing database for directing the digital printing presses.

The underlying economics and selling process would be fundamentally different from traditional printing. Once the digitalized document was in the database, virtually no time or setup costs would be required to convert it to a final product in nearly any quantity. Cost per copy would thus be independent of run length, constant rather than declining. Costs would be higher than offset/web or gravure for long runs, but lower for short runs. Moreover, on-demand printing would have an enormous effect on customers' total system costs when warehousing, transportation, obsolescence, and throwaways were factored in. Total cycle time would be reduced by an order of magnitude—from 20 days to 2 or 3, and, if necessary, to a single day. Customization also offered the opportunity for more tailored marketing and better sales, so new selling approaches were likely to be needed.

For these reasons, Cowan suspected that a new division, dedicated to this approach, would be required, rather than simply spreading digital technology throughout the company. He recalled:

> I did not want to put two digital presses in every plant. They wouldn't see the light of day. They would be wonderful toys, but would be swallowed up if they were scattered.

Economic and Technical Validation

Between 1991 and 1993, Cowan began selling his vision within the firm, particularly to senior management. He established a venture capital fund to invest in new print-related technologies and put a Donnelley executive on the board of each venture. He asked the corporate Technology Center to research the capabilities and costs of new imaging technologies, to determine Donnelley's potential competitive advantage in a "digital future." A small group of technologists were assigned the task. They soon dubbed themselves the Field of Dreams Team, after the movie that spawned the phrase "build it, and they will come."

The team began by establishing close contact with technology suppliers such as Xeikon, a Belgian manufacturer of digital presses that was partially funded by Cowan's venture capital fund.

Team members provided direction for Xeikon's development work, as well as oversight and monitoring. When prototypes became available, they conducted over 200 beta tests, using data files solicited from Donnelley customers. These tests produced estimates of throughputs, machine stability, and the readiness of the technology for full-scale manufacturing. Costs were higher than expected: The presses were expensive, required skilled and dedicated operators, and used more toner than anticipated. Nonetheless, for run lengths of 2,000 or less, digital's per-unit costs were lower than the costs of offset printing.

Traditionally, Donnelley's competitive advantage had come from the scale economies associated with heavy iron. Cowan asked the team to determine whether scale advantages existed in digital technology, based on investments in information architecture and databases rather than the manufacturing process itself. Surprisingly, team members found that, in addition to these economies, Donnelley's ability to negotiate volume discounts and its efficiencies in using sophisticated production control systems and multiple presses provided advantages even in manufacturing. As team member Grant Miller noted, "We found that scale is good, and that we could make money at digital printing."

As part of their ongoing work, the team made numerous presentations about the technology to Donnelley marketing staff and customers. Miller alone made presentations to more than 60 major customers. He recalled:

> Internally, people thought digital was a good idea, but no one wanted it because it was outside their core business. They all had some potential digital work, but didn't know enough about the markets and were scared of an unproven technology. Customers, on the other hand, almost jumped up and down, even though they too didn't know what to do with the new technology, or were themselves just starting to convert to digital format.

To improve the odds of successful adoption, Cowan sought to link the Technology Center's work more closely with Donnelley's businesses. In 1993, he asked Schetter, who was then running a Financial Services printing facility, to join the Tech Center and informally manage the emerging digital effort. The goal, Cowan indicated, was to find a home for digital within Donnelley, or at least to spark a major digital program. One early candidate for this role, the Magazines Group, shelved its digital initiative just prior to launch because the new sector president wanted the group to focus on long-run, high-volume markets instead. Shortly thereafter, Donnelley launched an ambitious reengineering effort, with important consequences for digital's development.

Reengineering the Technology Development Process

Between January and April 1994, seven teams worked to reengineer the processes of the corporate center. One, headed by James (Jim) Turner, who had come to Donnelley from IBM and was senior vice president for technology and head of the Technology Center, was assigned the task of improving the technology development process. Schneider, who had been actively involved in the Magazine Group's canceled digital program, was also a member of the team.

The Existing Process
The group quickly discovered, Turner recalled, "that all the technology development processes were ad hoc." Projects were not chosen on the basis of customer needs, nor were their economics carefully screened. Instead, senior managers with clout got their projects funded, particularly when they were identified and championed early in the budgeting cycle. One result was that resource decisions were often governed by a "first pig to the trough" mentality. Bootleg projects gained momentum once they secured highly placed sponsors; at that point they were rarely canceled. Technology projects seldom had financial gatekeepers, and there were no formal reviews of how development money was being spent. Division and marketing managers played a minor role in guiding technology development. Turner summarized the traditional approach:

> There were no limits on spending, no deliverables, and you could spend as much as a million dollars investigating a technology. No one was looking. There were no gates at the beginning. No one was saying "go/no go."

After analyzing 10 years of projects, the team also discovered that Donnelley, while often first with new technologies, rarely realized their full market potential. Miller explained:

> We at the Tech Center would roll the technology out to one plant; they would try it, we would refine it, and then we'd take it to the next plant. With 38 plants, that takes a long time. They also wind up with different versions, and we had to support them all.

Manufacturing managers could, and often did, say: "We'll take it later after you've gotten the bugs out," or, "We'll do our own version on our own equipment." The reengineering team discovered that divisions were spending, on their own, an amount equal to the Technology Center's budget, primarily on information systems technology and incremental technology improvements that were not transferred or transferable to other divisions. As a result, no one technology or information system worked across the company or across groups in a sector; some did not even work across closely related divisions.

The Redesigned Process
To overcome these problems, Turner's team devised a new process, guided by the objectives of greater speed, improved financial data and checkpoints, and better connections with the divisions. The underlying philosophy, Turner noted, was that "discipline does not have to mean bureaucracy."

The new process consisted of four structured phases. Each phase concluded with a formal review that specified deliverables to be met before the next phase could begin (see Exhibits 3 and 4). The divisions were offered incentives to take a broader, shared approach: corporate would pay half the bill if projects were at least sectorwide, and all projects were assigned to cross-functional teams, with representatives from marketing, manufacturing, and

EXHIBIT 3 Technology Development Process

New Process Overview

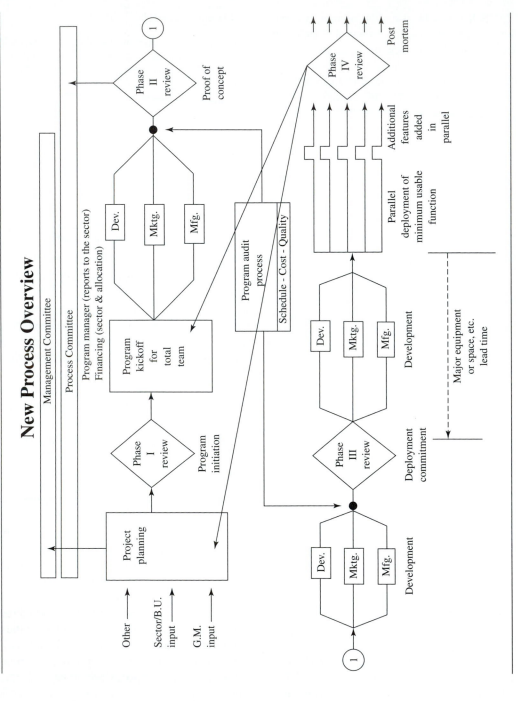

Source: R.R. Donnelley

EXHIBIT 4 Deliverables for Phase Reviews

Phase I (Program Initiation)[a]	Phase II (Proof of Concept)	Phase III (Deployment Commitment)	Phase IV (Post Mortem)

• SWAG[b] analysis
  • Financial benefits
  • Cost of development/deployment
  • Capital requirements
  • Revenue stream
  • Cost savings
• Schedule of development/deployment
• Make vs. buy
• Skilled set of people
• Initial market assessment
• Set maximum $ that can be spent prior to next justification
• Approval by Sector President/Sr. V.P. Technology
	• Rigorous financial review
	• Detailed
	  • Development schedule
	  • Deployment schedule
	  • Cost of development/deployment
	  • Capital requirements
	  • Cost savings
	  • Ongoing cost estimates
	  • Revenue stream
	  • Marketing plan
	  • Implementation plan
	• Completed program audit
	• Determine capital commitment, lead time to meet deployment schedule.
	• Set maximum $ that can be spent prior to next justification
	• Approval by Sector President/Sr. V.P. Technology
		• Final financial
		  • Financial justification
		  • Deployment schedule
		  • Capital requirements
		  • Market assessment
		• Completed second program audit
		• Approval by Sector President/Sr. V.P. Technology
		• OK to deploy
			• Metrics
			• Actual vs. planned of
			  • Costs
			  • Schedules
			  • Function vs. release
			  • Field performances
			  • Incident reports
			  • Installation problems
			• Lessons learned
			• Roles and responsibility problems
			• Process problems

[a]Up to $100,000 can be spent without completing Phase 1 requirements
[b]SWAG = "scientific wild-assed guess"

Source: R. R. Donnelley

71

development. Teams operated through a matrix. Developers continued to report to the Technology Center, while marketing and manufacturing representatives continued to report to their business groups. But they all also reported to a program manager, who was appointed by the appropriate sector or group president. Together, the program managers met monthly to decide on future projects, with Turner acting as their self-described coach and mentor. He observed:

> The program managers run this process; they are the ones empowered to make decisions. If there are complaints from the business presidents, I say to them, "The program managers report to you. You go after them if you're not getting value."

The process was triggered when a new technology or concept was deemed worthy of investigation. An ad hoc Technology Center team was formed and could spend up to $100,000 of strategic development funds to investigate the idea. Preliminary project and financial planning had to be completed within two months; the idea was not to be studied to death. At the end of two months, the project faced a Phase I review in which Turner, the relevant business groups, vendors, and other key players decided whether a formal program should be initiated. If the decision was "yes," a program manager and cross-functional team were assigned. There were no limits on how much money this team could request to prove the concept in the next phase; the point was to move as quickly as necessary. Phase II and III reviews were rigorous financial checkpoints, and no project could receive major funding without first completing a successful Phase III review. Once a project passed a review, it had a green light until the next one; the only person empowered to stop a project between reviews was the program manager. Turner observed:

> With this system we are inviting senior management to stop meddling in technology programs. In the past, that was understandable, given our poor financial discipline. But not with the new process.

Turner believed strongly in the broad applicability of these techniques; he was convinced that the redesigned process could even be extended to new business creation:

> I see project management as being identical with process management, whatever the process. It's the Deming cycle: plan—do—check—get feedback. That's process management in a nutshell, and it's also what good project management is all about. You could even run a new business through this process; you'd just present business plans at phase reviews instead of simple IRRs.

From Vision to Reality

The digital project was the first to tie into the newly revised technology development process. In April 1994, Barb Schetter was named program manager, with the objective of creating a new digital color printing business. She continued to report informally to Cowan. Because the project was already underway, it was grandfathered in at Phase III of the development process, and its Phase III review was scheduled for June. Schetter observed:

> Until we developed this new approach to technology development, digital was wandering. Then all of a sudden, we were catapulted into a process that gave us structure, hurdles, and credibility, allowing us to set dates, have meetings with general management, and get through the CFO's office.

The project's cross-functional team included Schneider for marketing, Lew Waltman for manufacturing, and Miller for development. They quickly dubbed themselves the Trapeze Team because they felt that they were "working without a net." The scheduling of the Phase III review meant that the team had to establish the existence of a market, identify possible applications, construct a deployment schedule and funding plan, and define the scope of the business in only two months. Every week, the team held day-long meetings, assembling cost estimates, integrating plans, crafting a preliminary design, rolling up projected costs and revenues, and generating an IRR that, in Schetter's words, "showed ourselves and others that we could roll out a division that could make money." During this period the team also began securing several digital presses, determining where the facility would be located, defining the database and transaction systems, obtaining the necessary capital appropriations, and creating a marketing plan.

Meanwhile, Schetter was making the case for a dedicated digital division to Cowan and other members of senior management. She recalled her reasoning—and the reaction to it:

> We had to get moved out of the Tech Center and into a P&L area where we would also get HR and financial resources. I thought digital should be its own stand-alone business unit, with its own complete P&L, because our finances and marketing would be so dramatically different and because, with growth, we would become huge. They said absolutely not; they saw digital only as a [manufacturing] division.

Following the Phase III review, Schetter redoubled her efforts. This time, in addition to Cowan, she targeted Bart Faber, president of the Information Services Group (ISG), and asked to be moved there. On July 1, 1994, she was successful: Schetter was named vice president and general manager of the Digital Division, reporting directly to Faber. The division would have its own P&L, with marketing and a freestanding salesforce reporting to Schetter.

The Information Services Group

ISG, digital's new home, was characterized by Faber as a

> greenhouse group that incubates small, internally generated divisions and manages a portfolio of venture capital investments. Those investments are our over-the-horizon radar to look at new technologies that may impact our core businesses and new ways that our customers will distribute information.

The businesses were unified, in part, by the goal of creating a "scaleable digital architecture," in which a single database drove outputs to diverse media. Faber observed: "Selling information in only one medium doesn't give you enough revenue to build a robust business model; you have to reslice it and remarket it." Daniel Hamburger, ISG's vice president for marketing and business development, added:

> We are laying a digital architecture for the company. Eventually, even commercial printing will be done by this new technology. From the same image database, we will be able to print at any scale, using any print technology, or deliver the image in any other form the customer wants—CD-ROM, fax, or online. The entire process, including the formatting for a particular medium, will be automated.

Faber had established several additional criteria for these new businesses: They should have the potential to grow twice as fast as the corporation, reach at least $100 million in sales, and achieve an above-average ROA. Because each ISG division was unique and their plants did not produce interchangeable work, division managers' incentives focused on divisional, rather than group, performance.

ISG's 60-member salesforce, which sold about 85 percent of its $280 million volume outside the group's divisions, was often challenged to get their work into non-ISG plants. Faber observed:

> We are not tied to heavy iron, and other group's plants often throw my reps' stuff out. To succeed, they have to offer better priced, more profitable work. So my reps tend to be tougher, to leap on new businesses that are struggling for work, and still answer the phone when they call.

The ISG salesforce targeted industries such as financial services, pharmaceuticals, and health care, where the primary focus was not publishing; salespeople worked not only with purchasing agents but with marketing and senior managers, trying to meet their business and print requirements. As such, they tended to bundle together Donnelley products and to include database services in the package.

In addition to the group salesforce, each of ISG's divisions had its own small, dedicated salesforce. Faber noted:

> I have found that if a new business doesn't have control over its sales destiny, it has little chance of succeeding. It will wind up a second- or third-tier priority in most of Donnelley's other sales organizations. We have learned to build a dedicated salesforce for all our new businesses.

Building the Division

On becoming vice president and division general manager, Schetter's first decision was to "pick a date and drive to it." She chose November 11, 1994, noting that "with even a few digital presses we could be up and running; not perfect or full scale, but by then we could be a real business." Funding was delayed by several months, however, as the $40 million budget was finalized, and the start date for the new operation was moved to January 1995.

Operations and Technology

Memphis, Tennessee, was chosen as the site of the first digital facility, primarily because it was the central processing and distribution point of Federal Express. By locating close to the FedEx runway, the division gained several hours of work time each day and could offer rapid, reliable delivery even without dispersed print-on-demand (POD) facilities or a complete database management system. In essence, Memphis offered "virtually distributed manufacturing" from a single location.

Manufacturing director Lew Waltman's immediate task was to test and operationalize the digital technology. Eleven digital presses were selected from three vendors. Each had strengths for different kinds of jobs, and the aim was to integrate the presses into an operation that would be the industry's low-cost digital producer. As Waltman noted, the challenge was enormous:

> There are very few pieces of this model anchored in any way. You cannot go somewhere else, observe for

a day, and say, "Yes, we're running it properly." The equipment is new, and most of it is unproven.

Working with a third-party vendor, Waltman and his team also began building the transaction system and database to hold customers' content. A customer's order would trigger the transaction system, which would then access the right content, send it to the appropriate digital press, and pull together the printed pieces for the customer. New functional capabilities were added rapidly. By mid-1995, the system could accommodate Macintoshes as well as the original PC-based machines, and would soon be reconfigured so customers could do their own invoicing. In addition, the division developed three software tools that allowed customers to manipulate and vary the content in Memphis's database without ever leaving their offices. Target-IT allowed customers to pick, pull, and compose their own pages, depending on what they wanted to promote in a particular week. Send-IT allowed customers to sent orders by dragging and dropping an icon on their desktop computers, while Order-IT allowed them to assemble the order itself.

These developments aligned closely with Faber's view of the division's purpose:

> The Digital Division is an attempt to take three distinct value creation devices—a content management system, a transactions management system, and digital imaging technology—and combine them to create a new product. They have a very different value that way, and allow us to get significantly higher margins. If we simply put Xeikon presses in each of our existing divisions, we would end up selling short-run printing jobs the same way that we sell longer runs—as images on pieces of paper. With the atomization of the printing industry, that wouldn't be very profitable.

Organization, Reporting Relationships, and Roles

In August 1994, Walter and Cowan asked Janet Clarke, now a Donnelley senior vice president, to head the Digital Division and become Schetter's boss (see Exhibit 5 for a partial organization chart).

EXHIBIT 5 Partial Organization Chart, 1995

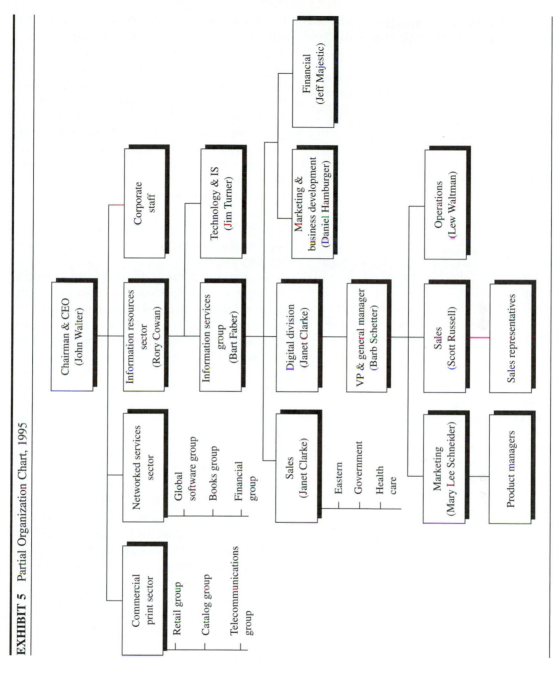

Source: R.R. Donnelley

Clarke would report directly to Faber and would also manage half of the ISG salesforce. Faber explained.

> By adding a sales animal like Janet to the mix, we covered the major weakness of a strong and seasoned team, added some capabilities we didn't have, and ensured our getting better sales performance. We could hold Janet responsible for some value.

Clarke added: "This was a people decision, not a strategy or structure decision." Schetter agreed, noting:

> Janet provides the balance. She is building the business from a customer base. She doesn't say to me, "I need a transaction system at less than $X per order." That's what Bart does. Rather, Janet asks, "Are we ready to sell?" Right now the issue is revenues, but once we get them, it will be our ability to deliver. The delivery of the Digital Division—that's my responsibility and not anyone else's.

Clarke, who was based in New York, described her role:

> I spend my time as little as possible on whether capital appropriations will be approved, or whether the plug will be pulled on the equipment or the project management of the administrative system. I have a weekly conference call with Barb and her direct reports, and I go to Chicago fairly often. But my focus is on external sales, on things outside our radar scope, and for that, the best place is New York.
>
> My job is to create robust revenue streams that use the advantages of the division and make it grow the way Global Software did in the 1980s. My job is to leverage digital for the whole company. I see the division as an incubator, from which I can figure out the opportunities for proliferating the technology and can then integrate them into the business.

Clarke felt accountable for meeting revenue and marketing plan objectives, for monitoring technical and financial performance against the division plan, for aligning the division strategy with company objectives, and for keeping the division's efforts broad enough to be transformational. She had chosen not to focus on internal lobbying at the sector or executive level and had asked Faber to manage these relationships. She would, however, meet with senior-level customers to influence their thinking—what she called an "education and demand-creation function." She would also meet with customer influencers (such as consultants and advertising agency presidents) as a route to "backing into" their customers. Like Cowan and Faber, she would monitor technology developments, verifying her perceptions with investment bankers and analysts. Her role in dealing with "stray cats at a high level," as she called them, was "catalytic . . . keeping Rory's vision . . . and being an ambassador for the company."

To supplement these efforts, Clarke organized her portion of the ISG salesforce into three vertical teams: health care, federal government, and the eastern U.S. region, with the latter encompassing retail banking, credit cards, and high-end consumer marketing. She not only spent time with her sales managers and representatives but also made sales calls, especially when a potential new customer or new area was involved.

In addition to Clarke's ISG salesforce, the Digital Division was seeking revenue through Donnelley's other salesforces, for which Schneider, now the division's director of marketing, and her product managers provided technical and product support. The Digital Division was also building its own small salesforce under Scott Russell, who had been at Xerox for 11 years and was hired by Schetter as sales manager in April 1995. By June, he was actively searching for six sales reps who, in his words, were both "hunters and farmers—people who can aggressively go after business, who have the confidence and know-how to close hard and professionally, and can farm and build relationships."

Marketing and Sales Strategy

Target Markets. To identify target markets, Schetter and Schneider developed a matrix from interviews with customers and Donnelley's marketing directors. Potential applications for short-run digital printing were first characterized by operating characteristics (e.g., turnaround time, paper requirements, repetitive database needs). The technology's capabilities were then mapped against these cells, and targets were established; they were continually updated based on experience in the marketplace. The primary near-term candidates were customers already using a digital format such as desktop publishing but who were encountering problems such as high physical distribution costs or high information obsolescence. Other potential candidates were those with unmet printing needs such as a desire for overnight delivery to multiple sites, increased customization of print materials, or growing need for color. Based on this analysis, magazine reprints, corporate literature, marketing and product literature for pharmaceuticals and health care, and advance, liquidation, and prospecting catalogs were identified as target markets for 1995.

Positioning.   Because the Digital Division would offer services that were quite different from Donnelley's traditional businesses, new marketing strategies were required. The division was not selling specific printing jobs in well-defined markets; instead, it offered a business capability that allowed customers to carry out printing in new ways, resulting in cost reductions and revenue enhancement. As Schneider put it: "We sometimes say we're not selling printing anymore; we're selling a marketing tool. We are teaching people to do things differently."

In most companies, the process of disseminating corporate literature and documents, whether for direct selling purposes or general information, was undermanaged, if managed at all. Typically, people scattered throughout the organization made piecemeal decisions about the production and distribution of reports, pamphlets, advertising, and other printed material. The result was literature that was costly to produce, expensive to inventory, and frequently out of date. Digital printing offered a much more effective approach, one that was likely to reduce the total costs associated with documents and printing. Moreover, by introducing new capabilities—the creation of short-run, on-demand, customized materials—digital printing could also increase customers' revenues by allowing greater market segmentation and more focused selling. To profit from these opportunities, however, most customers had to rethink the way that they conceived, produced, stored, and distributed their print materials.

To illustrate, Schneider cited a telephone operating company that produced generic corporate publications and marketing materials. These documents had never been customized and quickly became outdated. There were lengthy time gaps between updates, and salespeople had to root among "dead documents," stashed in dozens of cubby-holes, before sales calls. The digital alternative, Schneider noted, was an infinitely customizable "living document database"; electronic inventory would replace physical inventory, and each sales office would have a terminal with a "window into the materials of theirs that we have in Memphis." She elaborated:

> We're teaching them to think of their information as something that is alive and needs to be updated. There are two pieces—the content and the customers—and they need to be well matched. We're telling them to reengineer the way they gather and produce their information, publish it, and store it, so that the content is current and targeted to individual customers.

Unfortunately, the activities that Schneider hoped to reengineer—which she termed the "literature management process"—had not yet been identified as a process by most customers. Thus, a major aspect of selling the division's services was helping customers recognize that they already had an implicit process for creating, managing, storing, and distributing literature, and that with digital technology the process could be reengineered to reduce total costs and enhance revenues. This required sophisticated positioning, as

Clarke explained:

> We are selling to customers who sell to customers, rather than to people whose business is publishing. In essence, we are providing tools for marketing. So instead of calling on customers in the print procurement area, who only want to know the price per page, we are talking to senior people about their systems costs and total competitive advantage.

Consultative Selling. The multiple selling challenges, in turn, affected the sales approach. According to Russell:

> I don't want print reps on my salesforce; it's not about printing. I want people who can find the right members of the organization, articulate digital's advantages, make them aware of their need for services, and help them see things in a new way. Our job is to lead customers, not be led by them. We don't want to meet current customer requirements, but to ferret out deeper, unmet needs and then satisfy them.

In fact, Schneider had discovered that if she or her product managers could provide proof of revenue enhancement, companies became more open to re-thinking their literature management process. She observed:

> Our goal with a customer is to get to a prototype job and compare the response it generates with their usual response rate. In every case so far, we have gotten a significantly higher rate—maybe two or three times what the customer was getting before. With that evidence, inertia is overcome, and it's like a runaway train. We suddenly have a champion within the organization.

To develop additional sales opportunities and better cross-industry data, the division was funding research with five partner–customers to measure the response rates of generic versus customized marketing messages.

Like Clarke, Schneider and Russell also viewed client influencers, such as consulting firms and advertising agencies, as an important leverage point and planned to focus sales attention there. Russell noted:

> These channels magnify and expand our reach. We are in start-up mode, so people are at a premium, and we need to engage outsiders to spread our message. I also discovered very quickly that focusing on channels was a way to avoid conflict with the traditional Donnelley salesforce. With corporate clients, I was running into, "That's our account," or, "We have a big deal pending there and we don't want anything else going on there right now" all the time.

Mobilizing Sales. In fact, the Digital Division had to motivate three overlapping and potentially conflicting salesforces: the division's own sales reps, the ISG salesforce, and the salesforces of other business groups. One problem was that if Russell or Clarke wanted an existing account reassigned to someone in their own group—who would then get credit for the sale—they first had to petition an account adjudication board. Schneider noted, "If you go through too many of those, you get a bad reputation as a group." Faber, however, was comfortable with the situation and saw the need for diverse salesforces. He observed:

> In my view, it's better to have sales conflict and overcoverage than to be missing sales. The tension keeps everybody on their toes. It can be a little messy, but creation usually is.

One fallout of Donnelley's complex incentive structure was that business group leaders, sales managers, and sales representatives did not always see eye to eye. Clarke explained:

> Getting the middle of the organization to buy in is tough. Business group presidents and sales managers will not encourage their people to spend time selling the services of the Digital Division because the profits will accrue to another group. We therefore focused our incentives at the rep level because we needed the support of the complete Donnelley salesforce.

To that end, Clarke had proposed an aggressive commission plan to motivate other groups' reps to sell work into Memphis. It included a "kicker," to be paid by the Digital Division, based on the page price of the work sold relative to a preestablished page price. Although more aggressive than most plans, such incentives were not uncommon, as Faber explained:

> When you are trying to get new businesses going, you really have to provide sales reps with special incentives. You are offering products and services that they don't know anything about. So you have to spend money to make it lucrative for them to learn about your business and become interested in it.

Challenges of Internal Acceptance

By June 1995, the Memphis facility was up and running. But expected sales had not yet materialized, and the Digital Division was under intense financial pressure. Faber wanted to see profits by the fourth quarter and a breakeven year in 1996. He noted:

> We at Donnelley demand early profits from our new businesses. It's hard to be unprofitable around here for even a few years, unless you are making clear progress and it's part of long-term plan. I have to run digital as a strong stand-alone business because a marginal or unsuccessful organization won't convert anybody. The best way to convince people at Donnelley is to be successful.

As a result, Faber was not in favor of expanding the division or building other print-on-demand (POD) sites until Memphis was working well.

Schetter, by contrast, believed that the Digital Division represented an entirely new model, where the traditional incremental approach to investment was unlikely to succeed. She observed:

> You have to have large databases that integrate the software of multiple operating systems at multiple geographic locations. Our success depends on developing these new skill sets, which are hard to find. We need an organized approach to expansion beginning right now.

Schetter's biggest concern, however, was being embraced by the business groups. She explained:

> We have not, as a company, stood up and said, "Short-run, on-demand, color printing and the associated delivery systems are a strategic initiative." There is no companywide roll-out plan. We had envisioned a real pull for this capability, throughout Donnelley and from multiple customers. Instead, it has been more "wait and see" from the Management Committee. They say, "Let's see" if the business model proves out. "Let's see" if the transactions processing system pans out. Instead of taking a companywide position that digital is a strategic necessity, they're waiting for enablers who will pay the bill, and have said to the business group presidents, "You can use the Digital Division if you want, or you can do it on your own."

An immediate issue had arisen with the Books Group, which had a single digital press that had received few resources. Within 60 days, the group would decide whether it would invest in digital printing on a larger scale or move its growing digital business to the Digital Division. Schetter and Schneider were trying to develop a presentation that would convince Books managers that the Digital Division offered the better opportunity. The question was, what arguments and incentives would be most effective?

Case 1–3

ALLSTATE CHEMICAL COMPANY: THE COMMERCIALIZATION OF DYNARIM

In February 1986, Pete Kennedy, director of the Dynarim project, and his boss, Eric Reinhalter, sat down with Jack Cousins, president of Allstate Chemical Company, to discuss the future of the new Dynarim product. Dynarim, a liquid resin fabricated into structural parts by a new molding technology, now had repeat orders approaching $1 million. The project had been housed in an incubator group called Commercial Development for the past two years, but it could not remain there indefinitely. Cousins therefore wanted to review its status and future location, even though a move was not yet imminent.

Company Background

Allstate Chemical in the 1970s

Allstate Chemical Company (ACC) produced commodity and specialty chemicals, and distributed commodity chemicals for virtually every major chemical producer in the United States. Its distribution philosophy, supported by the largest distribution network in the country, was "Tell us what you want, and we will get it to you." ACC itself supplied about 15 percent to 20 percent of the product sold through its network. Distribution accounted for about half of total revenues. Another 15 percent of sales came from the production of diverse specialty chemicals such as adhesives, foundry products, and electronics chemicals, most of which ACC had acquired during the last decade. Like Allstate's existing divisions, these additions operated with considerable autonomy and possessed the full range of functions needed for P&L accountability. (See Exhibit 1.)

This case was prepared by David A. Gravin.

EXHIBIT 1   Selected Financial Data (numbers are in millions of dollars)

	1985	*1984*	*1983*	*1982*	*1981*
Sales and Operating Revenues	$1,500	$1,500	$1,200	$1,200	$1,300
Operating Income	70	55	0	30	40
Identifiable Assets	500	500	420	400	460
Funds Provided from Operations	60	50	20	45	50
Additions to Plant, Property and Equipment	40	20	20	30	35
Depreciation, Depletion and Amortization	25	25	20	20	15
All figures have been rounded.					

Source: 1985 Annual Report

Relationship with the Corporation

Allstate Chemical was a wholly owned subsidiary of the $8 billion Allstate Oil Corp. (AOC). During most of the 1970s, according to Jack Cousins, who became president of ACC in mid-1983,

> Chemicals were not perceived as a significant growth or investment area. It was tacitly understood that our mission was to provide a positive cash flow to the corporation for use in other areas.

Refinery closings and divestment of some oil-producing properties in the late 1970s reduced the pressure on ACC to be a cash provider and generated funds for reinvestment in businesses other than oil. For the first time, chemical distribution and specialty chemicals were targeted for reinvestment and growth. Corporate expected a high return from the chemical business—12 percent to 13 percent ROI—as well as long-term growth. This sometimes produced conflicts: $4 million per year for a development project, for example, translated into 1/2 percent less ROI.

Strategic Shift toward Specialty Chemicals in the 1980s

Such pressures from AOC were one of several factors leading ACC management to decide that its future lay in specialty chemicals (coupled with a continued focus on distribution) rather than commodities. Because of differences between the two types of chemicals, major organizational and policy changes were required to support the shift.

Customers bought commodity chemicals to meet a specification and because the price was right. Products were generic, and the market determined their price. Purchasing departments made the buying decisions, largely on the basis of price, quality, and delivery. Commodities were sold to end users and fabricators. Because the cost of the chemical was a key part of these customers' costs, a supplier that was 1–2 cents high usually lost the business. This emphasis on cost led to in-house manufacturing, in which, one manager noted, "Life revolves around the plant because

low cost wins the game." Although high volume had brought ACC healthy profits, margins were less than for specialties, where performance set the price.

In specialties, the approach was usually to start from the customer's use and work backward. Applications were critical. Specialty chemicals were usually a small part of the price of the customer's product; as long as products performed as needed, business was not lost over pennies. Purchasing played a largely administrative role because decisions to buy or specify critical ingredients were made by design engineers and plant people. These demands increased the need for marketing and technical staff. Because specialties were sold in the tens of millions of pounds per year rather than in billions, they were more likely to be made in batches than by continuous processes. This enormously reduced the scope and cost of capital investment—from hundreds of millions of dollars to tens of millions. But commodity plants could not be converted to specialty production. Specialties, however, allowed a company to forego in-house manufacturing, particularly in the early, risky stages of a product's life. Cousins explained:

> With an uncertain new product, why own a plant when you can rent a reactor? You would only want to bring manufacturing in-house if you had a well-established, high-volume product, or if you couldn't protect the technology, or if the manufacturing sequence was very complex and an outside company couldn't do it right or very consistently.

In specialties, ACC management felt it was important to be a leader rather than a follower. An early entrant could not only gain market share, set the price and ground rules, and gain lead time; it could also dictate the performance parameters a competitor would need to exceed to displace it. Later entrants had to provide significantly better performance because their products were seldom "drop-ins" for the customer's equipment and process. Switching costs might include new molds, or repiping, and, most significantly, requalification testing, which could take years and cost millions of dollars. Second entrants also had to overcome reluctance to change from the known to the unknown.

Between 1980 and 1985, Allstate closed and sold several commodity businesses, including plants, and added specialties by acquiring and building facilities and using outside processors. Specialties doubled from 15 percent of Allstate's business to 30 percent, while distribution of commodities continued to account for about half of the company's sales. George Prince, general manager of the Polyesters Division, which now derived most of its profits from specialties, commented on what the changes had meant for his division:

> You have much more exposure in the corporation when you're identified as a division that needs to be grown. We have made timely acquisitions that fit our technological and customer base, and we intend to make more since the corporation is now willing to fund them. Our staff has increased dramatically. Two years ago, we did no market development. But now, for example, we are trying to get engineers to design in our resins for the Pontiac Firebird, and that requires marketing.
>
> Specialties are also more quality oriented, and there's been more emphasis on how we control processes and how we report data to customers. For that reason, we do all of our own specialty manufacturing and are investing in things like computer control of reactors. Our productivity has gone up because we're not making off-spec product.

Research, 1977–1986

Formation of Venture Research

Until 1977, Allstate Chemical had no significant central research organization. Small research groups in each division focused on short-term technical service to customers. Under the impetus of Cousins, who was then administrative vice president for research, engineering, and finance, 25 percent of the company's research budget and people were pulled from the divisions to form Venture Research (VR).

VR's charter was to develop projects that would lead to major new businesses, with "major" defined as at least several hundred million dollars in annual sales. The group was to look for home runs outside existing division interests. Initially, Cousins and other senior managers wanted VR to focus on breakthrough process changes for producing high-volume, commodity chemicals. To head VR, Allstate recruited Dick Winthrop, whose process work at a competitor had won several industry awards.

Research Strategy: From Process/Commodity Focus to Product/Specialty

Process research required a broad range of chemical and engineering skills, a large commitment of people for long periods, and heavy investments in capital equipment. During the research stage, for example, this might mean building a series of reactors of increasing size, each of which could study a larger number of process variables. If the researchers succeeded in creating a commercially viable reaction, engineers would then have to create the equipment to make it. Process research typically started with petrochemicals that could be refined from crude oil (such as benzene) and sought cheaper ways to produce derivative monomers (such as styrene) or polymers (such as polystyrene) by significantly reducing the costs of raw materials, of capital, or both.[1]

VR's initial strategy aimed to replicate what Winthrop had accomplished at Sohio. Process changes had so dramatically lowered Sohio's price for a high-volume monomer that they had "knocked the bottom out of the market," as one manager put it. Although Allstate did develop two new

---

[1]*Monomers are small molecules (i.e., molecules having low molecular weight), usually in liquid form. Also called resins or prepolymers, they are an intermediate product that needs further processing (polymerization plus molding into a part) to make a final product. Monomers are the bricks and mortar for constructing the polymer "house." Polymers are large molecules that have been put together to create a solid material that, when molded, has desired properties such as stiffness or strength.*

processes, neither achieved commercial success. In one case, the cost advantage was not large enough; in the other, ACC had to compete with potential customers' captive monomer production. The 1981–1983 industry recession and the domestic industry's shift to offshore production dealt the final blows to ACC's process/commodity research strategy. Cousins ruefully acknowledged: "It took us five years and $50 million to see that this was the wrong way to go."

As process research was cut back, VR slowly gravitated toward product/specialty research. By 1984, its charter had shifted to supporting and strengthening the divisions. Prince described Polyesters' changing relationship to VR:

> We used to do almost no new-product development; what we did was handholding, fire-fighting, and low-level product improvement to satisfy specific customer needs. Now we are identifying market opportunities and developing new chemistries for which we want VR's expertise. We want them to do original chemistry, to invent new polymers that we develop for the market. Therefore, we need close contact to see that they are on track—we don't want them doing any blue-sky stuff. So when we see an opportunity for expanding our product line, I lobby Jack and the others, and they go to Dr. Winthrop and tell him to work on it.

Less capital intensive than process research, polymer research normally involved working with a certain type of chemistry (such as esters, urethanes, or alcohols) to produce either an entirely new molecule or improvements in the performance of existing molecules. Results were typically the product of years of studying such basic phenomena as what made adhesives work. According to Cousins, the shift in research strategy was brought about by a combination of "SEP oversight, reviews of projects, yelling, and handholding."

Strategic Expansion Project (SEP) Board

Shortly after becoming president, Cousins established the Strategic Expansion Project Board to oversee research. Its members were Cousins and five group vice presidents, and its charter was to identify and fund those research projects that had significant strategic and commercial potential. The board looked for projects that fit Allstate's strength in technology or markets, and could open up new businesses. Such projects had to be more than mere line extensions, which remained the responsibility of divisions. VR could still fund projects at a relatively low level from its own budget, but continued funding or significant expansions of the work required board approval. SEP-approved projects were funded from "Jack's budget" until they broke even.

With this mechanism, the company's chief operating officers supported the start-up costs of new businesses from company rather than division profits, and exercised control over funding. If necessary, the board could kill a project that was not showing significant progress or whose commercial potential had waned. Cousins was satisfied that commercial considerations now guided Allstate's research in new areas. He noted, however, that "Dick Winthrop doesn't totally approve of this approach. There are areas he would like to expand that don't have a chance of succeeding commercially. But he knows that I will not approve a test-tube project." Winthrop conceded that "they have shelved a few projects I would like to have continued," but pointed out the board's usefulness in giving VR direction:

> They advise us of areas to keep away from, and give me guidance on time frames and capital expenditures so that I, in turn, can provide better guidance to the projects. The cross-play between divisions is valuable, and they may see areas we don't know about. But I would like them to do more in the way of suggesting areas of R&D that would be good for Venture Research.

One of VR's earliest polymer projects—and one that did gain SEP approval—was eventually commercialized as Dynarim. In the beginning, however, Dynarim was a molecule without a purpose or a home.

The RIM Polymer Project

V110: A Neat Molecule with No Use, 1976–1980

Originally, the project had sought to plug a hole in the high end of Allstate's ester product line. In 1976, Hank Benoit and Joe Finnigan, both research chemists, were asked to create a molecule that would outperform competitors' vinyl esters. Benoit and Finnigan invented a family of low molecular weight, liquid resins. During the next few years, they explored innumerable variations in the family's chemistry and spatial configuration; eventually, they narrowed the field to four molecules. By 1980, Winthrop had selected one of the four, V110, as clearly superior. Yet despite agreement among the co-inventors, their section head, Ron Church, and Winthrop that they had a "neat molecule," and despite efforts to involve the divisions, no one was interested in or could find applications for V110.

The polymer had excellent properties when molded: strength, stiffness, and resistance to high temperatures. But it was too brittle for commercial use without the addition of other materials. Fiberglass reinforcement eliminated the brittleness, but processing difficulties with the fiberglass resin sometimes created consistency problems with the product. These problems disappeared if a new molding technique, reaction injection molding (RIM), was used instead of conventional compression molding. But fabricators were resistant to the different type of fiberglass handling required to make large RIM parts.

Adding RIM Technology

RIM technology and equipment were first developed in Europe. By 1980, approximately 500 machines had been installed in the United States, with ownership distributed about equally between multiple independent molders and a few captive producers, mostly in the auto industry. By contrast, compression (or press) molding equipment was owned primarily by 20 major end users, six of whom dominated the business. The differences in equipment distribution reflected the technologies' cost differences. Press molding required enormous heat and pressure, and thus enormous equipment and energy, to make parts. RIM, on the other hand, could fabricate large parts using smaller, cheaper equipment. For a part 8 inches by 5 feet (such as an automobile bumper), the contrast was between a 750-ton, $400,000 machine and a 25-ton, $200,000 machine. RIM's energy costs, molding costs, and tooling costs were much lower as well.[2] The major reason for these differences was that RIM polymerized the liquid monomers (the reaction), and formed them into a solid part (injection molding) in one step, rather than the two required by compression molding.

Not all monomers, however, were suitable for use in this process. Because the reaction occurred very quickly, RIM required liquid materials, such as urethane, that flowed easily at room temperature and reacted quickly with an isocyanate. The Allstate V110 team realized that its molecules so reacted, and thus made the link to RIM. Moreover, the result was a rigid product that could be used for structural parts, unlike the usually floppy, urethane-based products. Winthrop commented:

> Once we recognized the technological opportunity, it took six months to get the project redirected and the chemists working on tailoring a molecule for RIM use. We also needed someone who knew plastics markets to head the commercial development of the RIM project [the new name of the V110 project].

Market and Applications Development, 1980–1983

Pete Kennedy was recruited from Du Pont in August 1980 to identify market opportunities for V110, to reorient Allstate's chemists to those

---

[2]*RIM had even greater cost advantages over injection molding, the third major molding technique. Huge clamping forces were required for injection molding, making it inappropriate for large parts. For most purposes, the primary comparison was therefore between RIM and compression molding.*

markets, and to develop a business strategy. Cousins commented:

> We knew we had a neat molecule in one of our VR projects, but we didn't know how to talk to the market. We had always made interesting molecules and then tried to figure out how to use them. Now, instead of working in a vacuum, we needed to bring information from the market into the lab. But we weren't set up to do that. So we hired Pete Kennedy, a hybrid, a Ph.D. chemist with street experience, who understood pricing and marketing, and who knew the auto market.

Initially, there was some uncertainty about whom Kennedy should work for. As a first step, Cousins decided to place him within the VR organization, reporting to Winthrop.

Kennedy began visiting design engineers and materials people in the automotive and aerospace industries to identify their needs for V110-based materials, to generate and validate industry interest, and to develop market pull. He encouraged customers to test Allstate's materials and worked with molders to make prototypes. He also began to create an applications laboratory, noting that it "is one of the first things you add when you want to commercialize a product." Such a laboratory duplicated customers' facilities, running parts on the same kinds of equipment and then testing them. For this reason, within a few months of his arrival Kennedy got approval to buy a RIM machine for $80,000. A VR project manager pointed out the importance of an applications laboratory, which was a new concept for Allstate:

> You need both a pilot plant and an applications laboratory for product development. The applications or field support staff provide know-how to the customer and to the molder. They show him how to make the part, and demonstrate that it won't tear up his equipment. They give customers the comfort of knowing their parts can in fact be made.

Kennedy identified a wide range of materials that could be of use to customers. The project broadened from V110 to a larger category of potential products: high-performance engineering materials that could be RIMed.[3] A few of these would displace existing urethane and thermoplastic materials, but most would try to displace metal. Kennedy commented:

> I am not committed to V110, but to a market with opportunities for new chemistries. I have an open strategy on materials. I want to create engineering-type RIM polymers that customers want. If my product becomes obsolete, I want to be the one to obsolete it.

Despite his charter to tailor V110 to the market, Kennedy initially lacked both staff and authority. The four research chemists still reported to Ron Church. Friction between the two slowed the project. Benoit recalled:

> When Kennedy joined us, there was a period of severe adjustment. I resisted him for six months before I saw the light. Then I began to see that we needed to work toward performance requirements to commercialize a product. Before, we had just varied things willy-nilly: "Gee, what happens if we do this?" But when Kennedy talked to customers, they would say, "We need *X*, can you formulate it to do that?" Of course, they don't give you clear specifications. They are more likely to say, "If I can bang it against the side of my desk and it doesn't crack, it's good," rather than tell you what tensile strength they want. So you need to translate such comments into something concrete. Pete Kennedy can do that.

By stimulating market interest, Kennedy built internal credibility for the project. And by building

---

[3]*Polymers could be divided into three groups on the basis of broad performance capabilities. At the low end were plastics used in applications such as packaging, toys, and housewares. Engineering materials were higher-performance polymers that stood up to certain temperatures, were chemically resistant, and had desirable characteristics for particular work applications. Structural polymers were a subset of engineering materials. Usually reinforced, they could substitute for metal and be designed into structures where they performed load-bearing functions. V110 was a structural engineering polymer.*

relationships with individual chemists and helping them solve technical problems, he began reorienting RIM research toward market needs.

Product and Process Development, 1980–1983
Because molders resisted using fiberglass reinforcement, Kennedy wanted to begin work on a new resin that did not require it. Top management soon wanted the RIM team to cut back pilot runs for V110 process specification so it could devote most of its energy to creating such a molecule. But, because Kennedy also felt Allstate had "to have a product we could make and a way we could make it," he thought it was just as imperative to do extensive applications development on V110 materials and define a manufacturing process for that molecule as it was to start work on a new molecule. He therefore went down two tracks: initiating work on a molecule that did not require fiberglass reinforcement while doing as much applications work and as many pilot runs as he could get through. He summarized his approach: "No one said 'no,' and I didn't ask." In the words of his eventual boss, Eric Reinhalter, Kennedy

> went from using "springs and mirrors" to "officially condoned bootlegging." He began operating, perhaps subconsciously, as the general manager of a business that did not yet exist, talking to customers, making prototypes, and looking into manufacturing possibilities.

Process development entailed two major tasks: specifying the process variables, and getting a manufacturing organization in place. Allstate's pilot plant, which was run by VR, could make virtually any chemical Allstate made or was likely to. Batches of V110 made in the pilot plant were studied to identify key variables and their interactions, or used for prototypes and customer evaluations. By the end of 1983, Kennedy felt that Allstate still needed to understand much more about these interactions to define "the window within which we could safely operate" the V110 process, which included a very flammable reactant.

Eventually, commercial-scale manufacturing of V110 would be necessary. Since Allstate had no reactor available with the right capabilities, Kennedy opted for toll processing—manufacture of the chemical by an outside processor under contract. Allstate management often used toll processors, and Kennedy found it appropriate at this stage of V110 development: "Before we make any dedicated capital investment that could become obsolete, I want to be sure that the product has a stable position and its chemistry is the final one."

A Market-Driven Technology Strategy
Guiding product development toward market-based performance targets was a new approach to research at Allstate. Through presentations and one-to-one meetings with chemists, Kennedy advocated this approach in the 1980–1983 period. He recalled:

> I was saying, "Make me a molecule that does these things." This was scary to chemists because they didn't have a basic molecule to work from. Instead, they had all of nature to deal with, so they didn't even know where to begin. Most were impressed with the elegance of the analysis, but found it hard to use. Even today, it hasn't become part of our working environment; when Venture Research designs a new molecule, it still does it the old way.

The method articulated by Kennedy provided a starting point for structuring the approach to polymer design. It established product performance targets and then identified process parameters that immediately eliminated much chemistry from consideration. The researchers then concentrated their search within those classes of polymers whose spatial relationships made them likely to meet the desired performance and process parameters. (See Exhibit 2.)

One of Kennedy's tools for communicating this approach was a positioning chart for RIM resins. (See Exhibit 3.) For each of seven key attributes, such as stiffness, he compared the performance

---

EXHIBIT 2   Key Steps in Market-Driven Technology Strategy for Engineering RIM Resins

---

1. PRODUCT PERFORMANCE TARGETS:

Establish performance characteristics the product must meet.

For Engineering RIM polymers, seven such characteristics and their ranges were established, including:

flexural modulus (stiffness)   250,000 – 500,000 psi
tensile strength   8,000 psi (minimum)
etc.

A resin had to meet all seven characteristics within the target range, giving considerable latitude for trade-offs, experimentation, and judgment, resulting in multiple resins with a different balance of properties.

2. PROCESS PARAMETERS:

Establish boundaries within which the resins must fall in order to be processed on equipment chosen.
RIM processing equipment required:

a. Materials must be liquid (low viscosity) at operating temperatures in order to flow properly.
b. Individual components must be transportable as liquids at temperatures less than 300°F.
c. There must be no by-products because all reactions will take place very quickly in the mold.

This eliminated many materials from consideration.

3. POLYMER ARCHITECTURE:

Because broad classes of spatial relationships are associated with certain performance features, it is possible to eliminate whole classes of polymers from consideration and concentrate on those most likely to meet targets.

With regard to RIM materials:

a. Linear polymers tended to be stiff, have high viscosity, and high melting points, features that made them prime candidates for RIM resins. Branched linear polymers, being less stiff, lower in viscosity, and having lower melting points than unbranched, were easily eliminated from consideration, whatever their chemistry.
b. Higher molecular weight polymers were always tougher, and longer molecules had higher molecular weight. However, getting the molecular weight up required more cycle time, thereby increasing manufacturing costs. Was it possible to design a molecule that acted like longer/higher weight molecules but in fact required less molecular weight? Yes, if one constructed it to take advantage of certain kinds of bonding between molecules whose effect took the place of single, large molecules.

CONCLUSION:

It is possible and efficient to design polymers to fit market-determined performance features and hardware requirements by concentrating one's research in areas most likely to pay off according to a structural analysis linking polymer morphology with performance tendencies.

---

ranges covered by existing thermoplastics and RIM materials with those that were currently unserved. For example, thermoplastics covered almost the entire range of stiffness, but existing RIM materials showed major gaps in this area. Such gaps, which could be met by engineering-type RIM resins, would become the focus of Allstate's research and the basis for refining and varying the V110 family of molecules.

The Formation of Commercial Development

After setting up the SEP Board and clarifying Venture Research's role, Cousins considered other ways to link research more closely with marketing. One was to push the specialty divisions to become more market-sensitive. A second was to let Venture

EXHIBIT 3   RIM Resin Positioning

A shows that IM materials cover the whole performance spectrum for this feature.
B shows major holes in the performance spectrum being met by existing RIM materials, c. 1980–1981.
C shows how Allstate proposes to fill those gaps in areas most important to market (300–1,500 range).

PERFORMANCE TARGETED FOR ALLSTATE REACTIVE RESINS

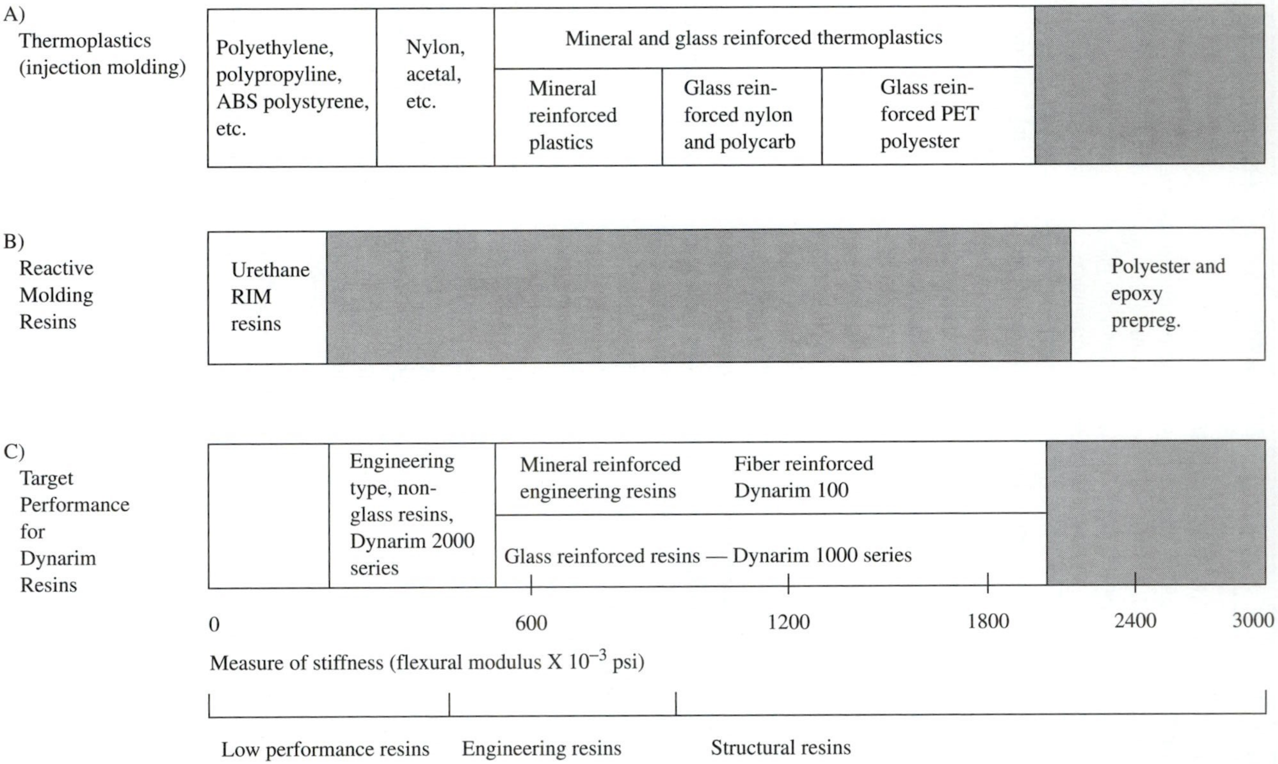

A)
Thermoplastics (injection molding)

Mineral and glass reinforced thermoplastics

| Polyethylene, polypropyline, ABS polystyrene, etc. | Nylon, acetal, etc. | Mineral reinforced plastics | Glass reinforced nylon and polycarb | Glass reinforced PET polyester |

B)
Reactive Molding Resins

Urethane RIM resins

C)
Target Performance for Dynarim Resins

| Engineering type, non-glass resins, Dynarim 2000 series | Mineral reinforced engineering resins | Fiber reinforced Dynarim 100 |
Glass reinforced resins — Dynarim 1000 series
Polyester and epoxy prepreg.

Measure of stiffness (flexural modulus X 10^{-3} psi)

0   600   1200   1800   2400   3000

Low performance resins   Engineering resins   Structural resins

Research develop its own marketing efforts, an option he rejected because "they tend to be naive about marketing, and research management might not listen." The third option, which was eventually adopted, was to create a high-level group with the commercialization of new businesses as its main charter, and the spread of marketing as a secondary goal.

CD Leadership and Organization

To head this new group, called Commercial Development (CD), Cousins wanted

> a marketing animal with on-the-ground success in markets and technologies similar to ours. He had to know enough technology to talk with Research. His personal makeup had to be consistent with our culture—laid back and informal.

In Eric Reinhalter, he found someone who had developed, marketed, and sold applications for polymer materials to large end users for over 20 years. Originally he was slated to report to the SEP Board; but after insisting that he have one formal boss, Reinhalter was assigned to report directly to Cousins, and joined the company in January 1984. He commented:

> I felt that a clear reporting relationship to one senior manager was essential. Jack's choice that it be him sent a signal that CD would be an important new effort, and it has worked well for both of us. I keep Jack informed, but he manages me by exception rather than on a day-to-day basis. I also defer to the SEP Board—of which I am a member—and it treats me as an unequal equal.

Transfer of RIM to CD

Reinhalter was offered three projects; he accepted them all. Of these, RIM was the most mature and the only one with a product. The CD group began quite small; it consisted of the technical people Reinhalter inherited from the three projects, plus three business analysts. Kennedy was immediately appointed sole project manager for RIM. He observed:

> I now had a boss who understood business and marketing. Eric validated my feelings about what I

had been doing—that markets were key. The project now had a place in the organization and it fit the new strategic direction.

One of Reinhalter's early initiatives was a contest to name V110 to give it a new, commercial identity and team mentality. The winner was "Dynarim." Dynarim referred to the entire family of RIM resins, and Dynarim 1100 referred to V110 specifically.

If RIM had not been housed within Commercial Development, it would have been sent to a division. That option, however, had little support. There was no obvious fit with any existing division; and RIM would have had to compete with more established profitable products for funds and attention.

The Role of CD

Cousins had given CD a deliberately broad charter. He wanted it to manage two or three projects at a time ($2–$4 million per year per project meant more were too expensive), to guide research, and to bring more of a marketing perspective to the company. But he had only rough guidelines for deciding when projects should be transferred into and out of CD. He did not want to saddle a division with foreign technologies, products, or markets. He was also inclined to put a project in CD if a division lacked critical skills to make the project successful; he commented, "With RIM, for example, we put it in CD because we didn't have market development skills in the divisions." Once projects were assigned to CD, Cousins wanted it to be a portfolio manager, providing research and marketing direction, functioning as an intermediary between VR and the divisions. Most of all, Cousins wanted to avoid redundancy:

> If a division already has a certain capability, we shouldn't set up anything in CD that duplicates it. I don't want CD to worry about process development or manufacturing—that's a distraction. I don't want a self-contained business unit; I want them to develop a product that can be handed off to a division. For example, why should we recreate a custom manufacturing facility for Dynarim when we already have six or eight divisions set up to manufacture?

George Prince summarized his view of CD's role:

> CD should work with chemistries we in the divisions don't practice but which are akin to our markets. Process development should take place before a project goes too far: Is there a known process? Do we have the equipment? The expertise? This should be coordinated—the marketing by CD, the chemistry by VR, and the engineering and manufacturing by a division. CD should do very little manufacturing, but they need to be able to scope out what's required.

Before a product was handed off to a division, Prince thought that its commercial feasibility needed to have been demonstrated:

> First you need a commercial process, and the demonstration that it is economically feasible. Then a division can take it and commercialize it. But if it's still hard to meet specifications consistently on scaled-up production, then we shouldn't take it.

While he thought it was possible in some cases for a product to be handed off directly from Venture Research to a division, Prince felt that CD, with greater resources for product and market development, could generally take a project earlier than a division. He commented: "If Venture Research can take a product from A to H, then CD might need to get it to L or M before a division takes it."

According to CD's own mission statement, its goal was to identify, develop, and commercialize profitable new business opportunities. In Reinhalter's view, this meant CD had to be active in four areas:

> We have to develop the product, get it made, develop the market, and have applications people who go to the customer. Applications development is the norm in specialties; you have to work with the customer to make the part. Marketing includes everything needed to sell the product: creating demand from the end user, calling on molders who fabricate it—whatever it takes. We must also demonstrate the ability to sell the product and to make it. But it can actually be made anywhere; we just need someone on the team who is responsible for getting it made right and who can deal with any problems.

The growth in staff for the RIM project reflected these priorities. Between 1984 and 1986, applica-

tions development expanded to nine people, research (renamed product development) to eight, and marketing to five. The marketing and sales people both developed markets and handled accounts. One manufacturing engineer served as liaison with the toll processor.

Reinhalter distinguished between three key manufacturing activities: demonstrating manufacturability, process development, and production responsibility. Demonstrating the manufacturability of a new product was, in his view, the responsibility of the seller. Thus, Winthrop had to convince Reinhalter a product could be made, and he in turn had to convince the SEP Board and Cousins. Both paper exercises and physical demonstrations were usually required. Process development then followed. Reinhalter believed it should be done by whomever had the most expertise, but in practice, it usually fell to the group with the greatest interest. Reinhalter commented:

> CD should not be manufacturing intensive; it needs only enough process development expertise to get a particular job done. With Dynarim, I would have been happy to have an existing division handle it, but none stepped forward—they all had jobs already. So we developed the process and transferred it to production.

Kennedy supported this approach, with qualifications. He too wanted to minimize CD's work-in-process development, but at the same time wanted to be certain the product fit tight parameters. He commented:

> I have no product until I can make it. You must tie down the interface between manufacturing and product performance, so you can't turn it over to someone who doesn't know that a 700 viscosity gives you a different product from 600. But I will do the minimum necessary to assure myself that I have the product I want. If I can get this from a division, fine; if I have to go outside, I will; and if I have to do it myself, I will.

Finally, once it became clear that a potential new business had emerged, full-scale manufacturing was necessary. Reinhalter wanted clear responsibility for manufacturing lodged somewhere in the company. But he cared less about where it was lodged than that there was someone who could be held accountable.

Although Reinhalter agreed with CD's original charter, he felt the mission had become less clear over time. "We have to decide if the plate is full enough already. Should we keep adding more? Do we really want to move things in and out?" He also pointed to a possible conflict between CD's original charter and the recruitment and motivation of staff. Reinhalter argued that operating people who had a personal stake (which he called "psychological ownership") in a program would do a better job than "pass-through people," but recognized they would probably have trouble letting go of projects.

The Dynarim Project, 1984–1986

Kennedy developed a strategic plan in 1984 with the goal of becoming the worldwide leader in engineering-type RIM materials. He argued that RIM hardware had opened up new opportunities for high-performance materials, that a large, unserved market for such materials already existed, and that Allstate was far ahead in grasping this opportunity and developing the required products. Accordingly, applications development on the Dynarim 1100 series expanded; by 1985, heavy product development was under way on the Dynarim 2000 series as well. Molecules in the 1100 series were iterations based on the original V110 chemistry and were targeted for large, structural, nonappearance parts used in transportation equipment. Dynarim 2000 was based on a new chemistry that could be used with or without reinforcement; it would eventually take RIM resins into such markets as cabinetry for business and medical equipment.

During 1984–1985, interest in Dynarim picked up at General Motors for use as tire covers (the platform covering the well in which spare tires were placed, which became the floor of the trunk). Covers for several models were tested, and the first order, for use in selected Cadillacs, Oldsmobiles, and Buicks, came in April 1985. A year later repeat orders had generated $1.4 million in sales. Kennedy was confident that business would soon expand, both to other auto models, and to additional parts. In both areas, testing and evaluation were well under way.

Toll processing continued to be the manufacturing method of choice, despite the cost premium of 10 cents per pound and the need to share proprietary information. Patents on Dynarim reduced anxiety about sharing such information. Toll processing was also consistent with Cousins' desire to reduce capital intensity, and his view that manufacturing was not a competitive key, at least at that time.

Managing a toll processor required skills similar to those needed to manage an in-house manufacturing operation; these included getting raw materials to the processor, paying bills, and handling off-spec production. It also required the ability to identify appropriate processors in the first place, and then to negotiate and administer contracts. Because the manufacturing engineer assigned to the RIM project was only 24 years old and had little experience in these areas, an engineer from Polyesters acted as a consultant.

Allstate managers thought they might want to bring Dynarim manufacturing in-house within three to five years. Some of the factors that would shape the decision would be the size of the required investment (about $2.5 million to convert an existing plant, $5 million to build a new one), the company's willingness and ability to make the investment, whether Allstate had a plant with the right equipment that was underused at the time, EPA regulations, and projected volume.

Future Dynarim Decisions

Eventually, decisions would have to be made about moving Dynarim out of Commercial Development. Issues involved timing, location, and the size of the group to be moved. But no one felt decisions were needed soon. Reinhalter, for example, observed:

It's not important to me to define the future if the trend is right. I am not preoccupied with whether or not Dynarim goes to a division, although I would prefer to leave it where it is until it's obvious that it's time to change. When there's a compelling reason to move, it should be obvious—for example, if we need a sales force. But if you change, don't screw up what made it work before.

Cousins also felt no urgent need to move Dynarim to a division. But he cautioned:

Leaving it forever in CD is not an option, although I'm perfectly comfortable with it in CD this year and next. Polyesters probably wouldn't even want it right now because they are profit oriented and Dynarim is still losing money. But I don't want CD to spend all its time on RIM, either.

Reinhalter's primary concern was keeping the project team intact, or at least allowing whoever wanted to move with the product to be able to do so. Reinhalter explained:

I don't want to lose the momentum that's been built by having critical mass. I worry about culture change. Pete Kennedy built an environment here—I just added to it—where we do more than we think we can. The "can do" attitude has generated extremely rapid progress, and that could get lost if the team were broken up.

Although Polyesters remained the division most likely to receive Dynarim, an alternative was for it to go to a new division. The choice was complicated because Dynarim had already spun off a new product, Dynatech, that was being developed in Polyesters. In the long run, there were three possibilities: Dynarim could join its sister product in the Polyesters division; the two products could form the basis of a new division; or Dynatech could remain in Polyesters while Dynarim became the core of a new business unit.

Dynatech's chemistry was identical to Dynarim 1100's for the V110 molecule was the foundation of both products. Dynarim, however, was then RIMed, forming a polymer and a part in a single operation, while Dynatech was to be used in compression molding. Once the Dynatech project had a marketable product, press-molding fabricators would buy V110 resin, combine it with a fiberglass resin to form a sheet-molding compound (SMC), and then mold a part. The resulting parts would be

similar in performance to Dynarim,[4] and thus superior to vinyl ester's performance. Compared with other SMCs, Dynatech's fumes would be much less noxious, an advantage in dealing with environmental regulations. Finnigan thought the use of compression molding gave Dynatech a financial advantage as well:

If a fabricator were starting from scratch, it would make sense to buy RIM equipment for large parts. But few of them have RIM equipment yet, while lots of them have heavily depreciated press-molding equipment. With both products, we can cover all the bases.

Dynatech had emerged from an SEP-funded project in 1984 that focused on polyester fabrication processes. The project had been instigated by Finnigan, who saw an opportunity for Polyesters to do something with the V110 chemistry. The year's work convinced Prince that Dynatech was a commercially feasible product, and Polyesters then picked up its funding. Prince described the difference between his division's acceptance of Dynatech in 1985 and its resistance to Dynarim in 1984:

Both Dynatech and Dynarim will concentrate on the transportation industry, with automotive being our initial target. We already market our specialty polyesters to domestic auto producers and work with the press molders that fabricate auto parts. While we have lots of expertise in compression molding, we know little about RIM and have no relationships with RIM molders. So Dynatech fit our customers' business and equipment without our having to fiddle, while Dynarim would have required our hiring several people we couldn't afford.

———————

[4]*Kennedy disputed this in part, pointing out that the vertical walls of large press-molded parts were weaker than the walls of similar parts that had been RIMed. These differences resulted from the rates at which resins flowed in the two processes. In Kennedy's view, the consequence was that Dynarim could cross over more easily into Dynatech markets than the reverse. Prince disagreed; he believed that RIM products were restricted to non-appearance applications, while Dynatech could be used in appearance applications such as car fenders.*

Markets for Dynatech and Dynarim 1100 overlapped—although just how, and to what extent, was still unclear. Currently, both products were expected to replace metal in nonappearance structural applications in transportation and other equipment. Estimates of potential crossover in each direction varied. Most Allstate managers viewed the overlap as broadening Allstate's market coverage, rather than as a source of competitive problems. In fact, both Dynatech and Dynarim had based applications engineers in the same Detroit office. These people talked to one another constantly, exchanged leads, and, according to Reinhalter, seldom fought over applications. In most cases, the line dividing the two products was obvious: the size, shape, and volume of a part usually dictated whether RIM or compression molding should be used. If product choice was not resolved at this level, customers were likely to make the decision. Reinhalter pointed out, "Our customers are very sophisticated, so they know which method is better for their application. They also have preferred molders or fabricators that they want to use."

While end-user applications were similar for the two products, there were subtle, but in Kennedy's view, critical, distinctions between the required marketing processes. RIM was strongly end-user driven, while Polyesters' SMCs were more processor driven. Kennedy observed:

> The SMC community is relatively small and composed of big, influential processors who create a credible supply for, say, a General Motors. GM determines only the performance specs, and leaves it to the processor to choose particular materials from particular vendors. Quality is controlled by the processors' skill. We, on the other hand, want the end user to specify a particular material; the specifications are for a particular formulation, not just for performance. Quality would then be controlled by the materials.

While Prince acknowledged that, in the past, Polyesters had tried to sell against performance specifications, Allstate's new emphasis on specialties was affecting the division's marketing approach:

> We now spend time with end users, talking with their engineers to try and get our resins designed into products. We want them to tell fabricators to make the parts from our resins; then we work with molders to make it easy for them to do so.

These considerations affected the eventual location of the two new products. Cousins, for example, thought the organizational separation of the two was "fine for now"; but he noted that eventually they were "likely to become the same business." Because of the similarity of product and end-user markets, Cousins indicated he "would have no hesitation putting the two products together."

Prince, on the other hand, believed that the size of the eventual Dynarim market was a key consideration in deciding where it should go. If it appeared that that market would be $50–$100 million, then Dynarim had grounds for becoming a new division. But if it looked more like a market of $5–$15 million, Prince believed it made more sense to "graft Dynarim onto an existing division," most likely Polyesters because "our ultimate customers are similar."

Reinhalter and Kennedy both favored continued separation of the two products. Surface similarities, they argued, were less important than differences in how the two were marketed, sold, distributed and used. Therefore, Dynatech was best handled by Polyesters, while Dynarim would be better off as the core of a new division. RIM technology, they added, did not fit within the existing corporate structure, and was properly the basis of a new business unit. If a division like Polyesters were to absorb Dynarim, it would then have to add a significant number of RIM specialists—possibly by absorbing most of Kennedy's group in the process.

Although Kennedy and Reinhalter felt the immediate issue was achieving commercial success with Dynarim, they knew such success would reopen the location issue. To create a new division, they would have to develop strong arguments favoring the separation of the two products.

Case 1–4

TIME LIFE INC. (A)

As the video screen faded to black, all eyes turned to John Fahey, Time Life's president and chief executive officer. The group in Fahey's office included most of the firm's top management. They had gathered on January 22, 1993, to view a selection of revised TV advertisements for the *True Crime* book series and decide whether they should be used. Time Life sold series of books, videotapes, records, and compact disks by mail, and *True Crime* was its first attempt to tap the public desire for graphic accounts of famous crimes and criminals. Market tests suggested that the series would be a solid success and perhaps a major hit, the first in nearly six years.

Yet Fahey and others in the room were troubled. Did the ads (or for that matter *True Crime* itself) fit Time Life's strategy? Would the series undermine the company's image as a provider of quality family material? Fahey had already temporarily halted shipment of the book series and suspended TV advertising, following hostile mail from viewers who had seen early versions of the advertisements and felt that they glorified violence. Now he needed to decide whether to proceed with the new version of the ads—and even whether to proceed with *True Crime* itself.

Background

Time Life Books was founded in 1961 as an offshoot of *Time* and *Life* magazines. Both were prominent national publications in post–World War II America. Their publishers believed that books on similar subjects to those covered by the magazines, using similar material, could be sold readily to their more than eight million subscribers. The books would combine the reporting and editorial standards of *Time* with the photojournalism for which *Life* was renowned.

From the beginning, Time Life offered subscribers series of books on subjects of educational, historical, and topical interest. Series explored broad themes and built into a substantial library, usually 20 volumes on a single topic. Early successes included *The Time Life Nature Library, The Second World War,* and *Great Ages of Man.* These series, together with the associated marketing approach, became known as the continuity concept. After purchasing the first book in a series, subscribers received mailings of subsequent books, on the same broad subject, every other month. These could be accepted, in which case the subscriber was billed, or returned without charge. Over time these efforts produced a large mailing list—in 1993, the list contained four million names—as well as specialized computer systems and distribution facilities for serving the needs of a business based on repeated mailings to the same customers.

Time Life cultivated a reputation for authenticity, reliability, and clarity. A 1991 Image Study concluded: "The underpinnings of Time Life Books' image is the notion that the products are worthwhile and useful . . . 'educational,' though not necessarily in a scholarly or academic sense." Fahey put it more succinctly: "We're known for taking a large body of knowledge, including complicated concepts, and making it accessible." Facts were checked carefully and exhaustively. Expert consultants, often leading academics, researchers, and freelance writers, were engaged to ensure that text and graphics were

---

This case was prepared by Jonathan West under the direction of David A. Garvin.

accurate and understandable. Photographers were dispatched to remote sites to capture exactly the right shot. Specialists were engaged to produce intricate illustrations, sometimes costing thousands of dollars per page. According to a new-product development manager:

> The core of our business is research. We go the extra nine yards and track down every possible source. For instance, I did some picture research for a book on Labrador and called around to find anybody who'd ever been there with a camera—missionaries, bush pilots, tourists, a few professional photographers. Being where the action is is the essence of our culture.

From the start in 1961, consumers liked the product. The appeal proved to be international as well. Before long, the company had distribution networks in Europe, Australia, Asia, and South America and published in 30 languages. However, in the late 1960s growth began to slow. Many series petered out after the first few volumes, contributing little or no profit, and there were fewer big hits. A breakthrough came in 1972, when Time Life introduced *Foods of the World,* the first series to depart from traditional themes. It was followed a few years later by *Home Repair,* a huge hit, and several similar series. But trouble returned in the late 1970s and continued—with some ups and downs—into the 1980s. Profits turned to losses. In part, the problem was poor controls over international operations, but there was also a drought of successful new book series. Time Life's management was divided about the underlying cause. Some felt that the compnay simply needed fresh ideas. Others worried that the very concept of continuity books had been exhausted, rendered obsolete by the proliferation of information and new entertainment sources available to consumers. As the managing editor put it at the time: "All the good series have been done."

In 1982 Time Life's parent, Time, Inc., toyed with the idea of closing it entirely, and Time dispatched Reginald Brack from corporate headquarters with a simple mandate: "Fix it or sell it."

Brack decided that the business could be salvaged by reducing costs, particularly by cutting overhead through outsourcing many aspects of the production process. Most of the existing top management was replaced, and the editorial staff was trimmed by over 100 people. Brack also drove down production costs through measures such as bulk paper buying and less expensive binding. By the mid-1980s, the company had stemmed its losses and returned to profitability with the hit series *Mysteries of the Unknown,* which featured parapsychology, the occult, and other unexplained phenomena.

In 1982, shortly after Brack's arrival, music was added to the product line in an attempt to leverage the company's strengths in direct response marketing and continuity publishing. Like books, the music division developed and then offered customers series of tapes, records, and later compact disks organized around a central theme. Early successes included series on the music of the 1950s, 1960s, and 1970s. Each was a steady seller, with 40 to 50 separate volumes. In 1989, following the success of music, a video division was added to the company. It too was conceived as a way of pushing additional products through the direct mail channel established by books. Initially, all videotapes were sourced from outside the firm, and, because the division had to pay relatively little to license existing material, it generated immediate profits. Fahey observed: "At that time, we were the only game in town." In recognition of these new media, Time Life Books changed its name to Time Life, Inc., in 1990.

Meanwhile, in 1989 the parent company merged with Warner Brothers to create Time Warner, a media and entertainment giant with interests in books, music, television, movies, and theme parks. The merger raised the possibility that Time Life might undertake multimedia projects. As a first step, in 1992, it moved to produce its own video and television series. Thirty million dollars were allocated to the division for creating new documentaries, and Time Life hired its own experienced television producer.

Fahey had occupied the top slot at Time Life since January 1989. He had joined Time Inc.'s controller's department in 1976. After stints in *Time* magazine's circulation department, various financial positions for Home Box Office, Time's pay-TV subsidiary, and Time Inc., he had moved, in 1984, to Time Life Books as vice president and chief financial officer.

The View from Corporate

Challenges

By 1992 it was clear to Fahey that Time Life was "a wholly different animal" than it had been five years earlier. It was no longer focused on a single product line or unified by a common culture, but had mushroomed into a collection of largely independent businesses—in Fahey's words, "a loosely confederated conglomerate." Each division had its own market, strategy, and positioning, and each was becoming more of a "hit-driven business," with a small number of offerings providing the bulk of profits. Yet at the same time, the total number of products had more than tripled. Because they drew on common corporate resources, divisional conflicts were beginning to surface. Fahey felt that the underlying issues—how best to use the Time Life brand, which division would get the first shot at good ideas, who would get to mail to selected names on the house file, and how often— would only worsen with time. Systems issues were a special stumbling block. They were closely linked to the organization's critical processes of finding, selling, and servicing customers and were utilized by all divisions. But many systems were dated, having been created to serve the needs of continuity book publishing. To date, there had been limited progress on common systems, and little attempt by the divisions to follow through on systems strategy once it was developed. Moreover, investment dollars were limited, and Time Life could afford to upgrade its systems only at a slow, incremental rate.

Nor were customers completely satisfied. According to market research, Time Life products were well regarded, but the continuity system was not. It offered insufficient choice to subscribers, made returns difficult, provided only adequate customer service, and did not reward superior customers. Younger customers were especially dissatisfied. Fahey was convinced that, despite a wealth of statistical studies, "we still don't feel the customer in our guts." He had initiated a quality process in 1991 to address these needs, but progress was slow. Perhaps most important, the organization was not yet taking full advantage of its assets. In Fahey's view, the future belonged to multimedia, and Time Life had a distinct edge:

> We are good at finding out what people are interested in, doing all the research, bringing the information together, and then repackaging it in any form that customers wish to receive it . . . We have a basic process that is going to be extremely valuable in the world of multimedia . . . and there's a tremendous opportunity if we define ourselves correctly and get everyone to buy in.

To address these concerns, Fahey invited seven of his top officers to form a Corporate Strategy Committee in March 1992. In a letter to the new group's members, which included the three division heads, three corporate vice presidents (marketing services, human resources, and finance), and the Time Warner Libraries publisher, he outlined his thinking:

> To date we have managed the company in a decentralized fashion from both strategic and operating perspectives. I'm not suggesting that Time Life will henceforth be managed centrally—it would not be right or effective—but the time is here for more focused strategic development and implementation.
> I perceive a huge and exciting opportunity for the company and quite frankly for each of us. The issues we will need to tackle include clarifying our vision and goals, developing an integrated and focused blueprint for achieving our goals, agreeing on a systems strategy and coming up with a prescription for managing Time Life's relationship with its customers—making *customer first* a reality.

On May 7, 1992, after several preliminary meetings had identified the need for better cooperation and integration, Fahey gathered the Corporate Strategy Committee for an afternoon at a local hotel to begin the process of formulating and implementing a companywide strategy. The group met for six hours, with a follow-up meeting the next week guided by a consultant. At both meetings, participants expressed general support for the concept of integration. Most members agreed that Time Life's businesses shared at least some features: a common customer base, reliance on intellectual property, a need for effective customer service systems, and the Time Life brand. This meant that any form of integration would probably include a common "attitude," organizational structures to leverage shared resources, a united voice to customers, and agreements on brand positioning. The latter issue was especially vexing and prompted considerable debate. For some time, management had worried that the brand was being "stretched." In music, for example, the Time Life brand had first been attached to classical music and then to rock 'n roll; now rap music was under discussion. Where, if at all, should the brand's boundaries be drawn? The last successful book series, *Mysteries of the Unknown,* had raised similar concerns. Many in the editorial department had been uneasy about attaching the Time Life name to psychic phenomena, arguing that a second brand might perhaps be needed to handle such products.

Considerable time was also spent discussing the issue of "strategic integration." Participants were divided on what the term meant and whether integration should involve ideas, processes, or organizational structure. A number of joint projects had, in fact, already taken place, but they had occurred largely by chance. Time Life managers rarely sat down to share ideas outside their divisions, and Fahey had personally provided much of the necessary coordination. Yet despite their recognition of the need for improved integration, several committee members voiced concerns. Would new-product development, which was currently conducted independently by each business, be integrated? And, if so, would the process become bureaucratic and uncreative? Candice Carpenter, president of the video and television division, was especially uneasy, fearing that an integrated product development process could become a bureaucratic obstacle stifling creativity. She believed that video and television could "leverage" the editorial department's resources to store, retrieve, and use data and ideas, but doubted whether a joint product development structure could speedily identify the biggest potential hits in her media. Because the time frames and requirements were quite different for television and books, Carpenter worried that joining the two would be problematic, and that the slower, more deliberate, book development process would dominate. John Hall, then head of the music division, expressed similar concerns. He could see little or no benefit to his business from joint product development work. The meetings concluded without determining the precise degree or kind of integration needed, but with general acceptance of the goal.

In the following weeks discussion continued, largely in an exploratory mode. Each member of the Corporate Strategy Committee prepared two brief documents—a vision of Time Life in the year 2002, and a description of what the corporate strategy statement should and should not be— for discussion at the next group meeting. There was broad agreement that the future of Time Life required a full range of media and technologies, continued skill at direct marketing, a beefed-up editorial and research capability, and more flexible and diverse offerings to customers. The extent of the corporate strategy, however, provoked considerable debate. It was defined variously as "a map to get us to our destination," "a message to the staff clarifying our agenda," "a very broad statement that thematically brings us together," and "a planned approach to create competitive advantage for the company." There was considerable confusion about the operational requirements of such a strategy, and how much autonomy each division would have to forgo.

Strategic and Organizational Changes

In August 1992, after continuing discussions but few substantive changes, Fahey decided to push forward on two fronts. First, he asked the Corporate Strategy Committee to jointly develop a series of "strategic imperatives." These imperatives were aimed at the future; they were efforts that Time Life must pursue to be successful long term. In total, the group crafted eight imperatives: (1) continue to develop a diversified portfolio of book, music, television, video, and eventually new media options; (2) make customer service a competitive advantage again; (3) refine and improve new-product development processes; (4) build winning business formulas beyond 20-volume continuity series; (5) build the customer file; (6) bring a more integrated, sophisticated approach to promotions of the customer file; (7) invest in new business systems; and (8) continue global expansion. These imperatives were expected to guide the divisions as they conducted their own planning and budgeting processes for the year.

Fahey also asked the Corporate Strategy Committee to consider a reorganization plan. He developed the first version himself; it was subsequently modified and fine-tuned by the group as a whole. The reorganization and associated staffing changes were announced to the organization in October 1992 (see Exhibit 1). There were three major shifts, as well as a number of reinforcing moves at middle management levels. First, all support services were pulled together into one group, to be headed by Mary Davis, who was named executive vice president and chief operating officer. Davis had been president of the books division for the past year, having come from Time, Inc., where she had been general manager of *Life* magazine, vice president of manufacturing, and most recently in a special corporate quality assignment. She would now be responsible for customer service, fulfillment, marketing support, warehousing and distribution, finance, and human resources. In a letter to the staff, Fahey explained the rationale for the move:

> Mary's primary responsibility will be to further our quality objectives by improving customer service (both external and internal customers) and to bring a strategic focus to operating issues that are cross-divisional in their scope. Examples of the latter would be the management of our customer file, systems development efforts, and inbound and outbound telemarketing strategy and technology.

Second, the editorial department was separated organizationally from books. The new editorial department would continue to be responsible for the entire range of activities necessary to produce the text and graphics for Time Life's books, which currently took about 95 percent of its time, but would also provide research support to other divisions. Tom Flaherty, the managing editor of books, would become editor-in-chief, reporting directly to Fahey. In his letter to the staff, Fahey observed:

> This change in reporting recognizes that our editorial resources will increasingly provide support across divisional bounds, including books, video, and TV. Of course, when an edit team or individual is assigned to a project, those staffers will be accountable to the division that assigns the project (i.e., Domestic Books for a book series).

Finally, to replace Mary Davis at books, John Hall moved from the music division, where he had been president, and a new hire took his place. Fahey explained: "John's marketing skills and product development expertise will significantly aid the resurgence of our book business."

Over the next few months the Corporate Strategy Committee continued to meet. It was renamed the Policy Committee and, with the addition of Flaherty, gathered every two weeks to discuss issues of corporate strategy, use of the Time Life brand, and new products. Davis simultaneously established an Operations Group; it met weekly and quickly identified a number of high priority projects, including improving customer service and responsiveness on the company's "800" telephone number; setting aggressive new targets for delivery

EXHIBIT 1 Organization Charts

Before 1992 reorganization

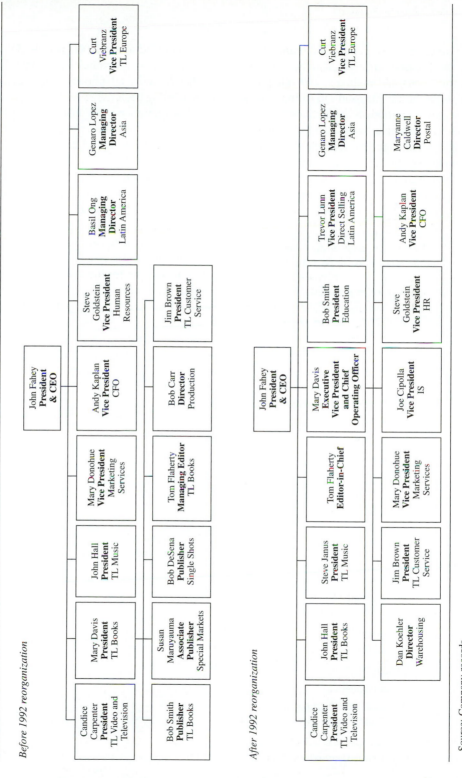

After 1992 reorganization

Source: Company records

times and order processing; commissioning studies to assess the lifetime value of customers, the impact of promotions and mailings, and other ways to optimize the house file; and launching a series of human resource initiatives that involved training, compensation, organization and staffing changes, and the quality management process. Meanwhile, division managers began to address the strategic needs of their businesses, while working together on a small number of joint projects. Hall summarized the status of the organization in early 1993:

> If you think of a spectrum with individual fiefdoms at one end and total integration at the other, we're somewhere in the middle. We're peacefully coexisting, and the competition between the divisions is gone. But we're not totally developed . . . More than any other place I've been, this organization thrives on successes. We're very goal oriented, and until we have a multimedia success total acceptance won't come.

Divisional Views

In 1993 Time Life consisted of three major divisions—books, music, and video/TV—along with an editorial group and operations staff. In total,

they employed about 2,000 people. Of these, 550 were based in the Alexandria, Virginia, head office; another 700 were telephone salespeople at a nearby telemarketing center; 325 were located at the Richmond, Virginia, and Indianapolis distribution centers; and the remainder were overseas, spread among Europe, Asia, and Australia.

Time Life Music

The music division had experienced steady growth since its start in 1982, and seemed well on its way to meeting its goal of becoming "the largest nonclub direct marketer of music." In 1992 it had revenues of $86 million and accounted for over a third of Time Life's net income for the year (see Exhibit 2). Profit margins were above 12 percent. The division had launched successful continuity series covering a broad range of composers and styles, including classical, rock and roll, rhythm and blues, jazz, and country. Moreover, unlike the book division, which had remained wedded to continuity series, music had broadened its offerings to include sets and single shots. Sets consisted of three to nine records or compact disks, drawn from a preexisting continuity series, that were packaged, advertised, and sold as a

---

EXHIBIT 2   Financial Summary: Revenue by Line of Business

	Net Revenue ($ millions)		
	1990	*1991*	*1992*
Books	$167.3	$163.2	$124.1
Music	58.2	82.6	86.4
Video and TV	36.3	55.1	88.9
Total Domestic	$261.8	$300.9	$299.4
Europe	134.1	150.7	168.6
South Pacific	21.8	25.0	25.4
Asia	8.9	11.2	16.2
Latin America	—	—	—
Total International	$164.8	$186.9	$210.2
Total Worldwide	$426.6	$487.8	$509.6

Source: Company records

single bundle. Single shots were single volumes advertised and sold on their own. Although each had been started only two years earlier, sets now contributed 20 percent of the music division's profits, while single shots contributed 5 percent.

With the reorganization, Steven Janas succeeded Hall as president of the music division. Janas held both undergraduate and graduate degrees in music and had come to Time Life from Home Box Office, where he had spent a decade building its direct marketing capability. After several months learning the business, he summarized his early impressions:

> I'm overwhelmed by the sophistication of the business. There's expertise in systems, warehousing and distribution, marketing services, and media and creative. The editors and consultants here are some of the most knowledgeable people about music I've ever seen. And we have strong relationships with all of the major labels and sources of product. Now I understand why a number of people, including record companies, have tried to set up continuity programs and failed. I don't think anyone besides Time Life could do this successfully. In fact, I don't really see competition for us in the continuity business.
>
> At the same time, I'm underwhelmed by the diversity of products we market. We're just not as attuned to popular culture as we should be. The three rock and roll series carried us for a long time, but they will only take us so far. We need to think more creatively about new products.

The music division employed the same creative and development process used by the book division, and Janas had no immediate plans to alter it. But he did plan a change in reporting relationships. Previously, new-product development and marketing had been separate functions in music, with each reporting directly to the president. Janas planned to eliminate new-product development as a separate department and to give each of the division's two marketing vice presidents their own product development person. In addition, he wanted to establish a new position for business development. The person hired into that position would have a bold mandate: to expand into new markets including retail products, other types of music merchandise such as rock and roll clothing and collectibles, and new types of continuity products such as music games.

Time Life Video and Television

Like the music division, the video and television division was thriving. In 1992, its fourth year of operation, it had revenues of $89 million. Profit margins continued to rise and were above 15 percent. Originally, the division had been created to push product through the existing fulfillment system, while leveraging Time Life's direct marketing skills. The earliest products were therefore off-the-shelf videotapes, produced by others, that the division licensed, marketed, and sold. Offerings were quite diverse, including documentaries in military history as well as James Bond movies. Yet the business was profitable from the start, largely because it was able to draw on the company's extensive customer file, experience in direct mail and broadcast advertising, and hard-to-duplicate fulfillment system. The economics were also unusually favorable. With an average up-front investment of $100,000 for an entire multivolume series and a selling price of $20 per tape, breakeven volumes were in the thousands. Cash flow was healthy and positive from the beginning because of the high proportion of credit card purchases (55 percent versus 5 percent for books) and low inventory requirements (turns of 12.1 per year versus 1.2 for books).

Over time, the division focused increasingly on documentaries. Major successes included several series from PBS, such as "The Civil War", and "Trials of Life," a huge hit about violence in nature. At the same time, the division moved to broaden its activities. Off-the-shelf products were supplemented by "versioned" products, in which existing shows were edited or revised for video release. Next came several experiments with coproduction, in which Time Life made larger investments up front—$2.5 million or more—in return for a significant editorial voice. Breakeven volumes rose substantially, but so did potential returns because the company now received a percentage of all future sales. In each of these areas, the division capitalized on the traditional Time Life strengths of marketing and distribution. But it also added skills in sourcing and product selection, and the ability to draw on relationships in the television and film industry.

Finally, in 1992 division managers asked Time Warner for permission to produce their own television shows. In their request for funds, they made three broad arguments: (1) margins were higher for in-house production than for off-the-shelf, versioned, or coproduced product because the returns did not have to be shared with the owner of the property, (2) in-house production provided a defense against competition from interactive television, which might ultimately allow viewers to call up movies or other shows on demand, bypassing the direct response channel completely, and (3) in-house production allowed the bundling of products from multiple media, with Time Life able to offer packages of television documentaries, books, compact disks, and videotapes that could be sold as a unit. The latter argument was regarded as especially important. Bundling was the first step toward offering true multimedia products; it also provided access to a vast market. "The Civil War," for example, had appeared as a television documentary, book, and videotape series. The package had generated $30 million in sales, and Ken Burns, the producer, had indicated that in the future he would be looking for companies that offered him access to multiple media through "one-stop shopping." Time Warner responded to these arguments by allocating $30 million to the division for original television productions. Carpenter then hired Joel Westbrook, an experienced television producer, to spearhead the effort, and set a goal of generating 30 percent of divisional revenues from this source by 1995. High profits were expected as well. The first three productions, for example, at a cost of $16 million, were projected to yield a net income of $11 million.

Creative and Production Processes.   While television, videotape, and book production followed many similar steps, there were important differences, especially in the economics of the businesses and sources of value added (see Exhibit 3). A single hour of documentary television was a massive undertaking, involving 100 to 200 people and costing $400,000 to $800,000. It began with an idea, called the "high concept," that explained in one or two sentences how the subject would be treated. Research was then undertaken to develop and expand the concept; often, outside experts were used. Eventually, a "treatment" was developed. It explained, in anywhere from one to hundreds of pages, what the show was about and became the basis for a pitch to broadcasters and potential program sponsors. Because of the large up-front costs, producers tried to cover as much of the investment as they could by preselling to both domestic and foreign broadcasters. Ideally, at least 50 percent of the cost would be covered. That way, risk was reduced, and significant earnings from the "back end," such as retail or direct response videotapes that were sold after the show was aired, would ensure a profit. The selling process was time consuming, averaging six months, and involved extensive meetings. Westbrook explained: "Television is a relationship business. Everything is a personal sale to the gatekeepers and decision makers who control the flow of product."

Once the sale was made, preproduction began. Because each show was a business unto itself, careful planning and project management were required. Locations were scouted, a production crew was hired, the necessary equipment was secured, and a schedule was developed. Meanwhile, the script was under development, usually by a collection of independent writers and expert consultants. Once the script was completed, production began and continued for several weeks, and often months. After completing production and final editing, the show was delivered to broadcasters and aired. In total, the entire development process usually took at least two years, and considerably more if a large amount of time was devoted to research.

EXHIBIT 3 Comparative Product Value-added Chains

Business activity	Time Life Books		Video Distribution		Television	
	Success factors	Value-added	Sucess factors	Value-added	Success factors	Value-added
Concept organization	• Understand customers and information needs	▨▨		☐		☐
Creation	• Match needs and editorial content • High quality, fact based • Collectible • Test marketing	☐	• Relationships • Timeliness/ Aggressiveness • Scale • Deal negotiating • Recognize entertainment value	▨▨▨	• Relationships • Timeliness/ Aggressiveness • Scale • Deal negotiating • Recognize entertainment value	▨▨
Sourcing		☐	• Pre-sold equity • Audience targeting	☐	• Pre-sold equity	☐
Marketing	• Brand name • List quality • Attractive promotions and packaging	☐		☐		☐
Distribution	• Direct marketing continuity system • Low cost per order	☐	• Flexible multiproduct distribution system • Low cost per order		• Low cost per order	
Fulfillment	• Continuity product fulfillment system	▨	• Flexible fulfillment system • Customer service	☐	• Continuity fulfillment	☐
Backend marketing		☐	• Premarketing and backend management	☐		☐

▨ = Critical value-added activity

Source: Marakon Associates

Opportunities and Problems.   Carpenter and her management team faced two primary tasks: ensuring a continual flow of new products, and establishing the television business as a viable competitor. Video products had far shorter life cycles than books. Three seasons was about the most that could be expected from even a strong success, including both original production and mail order sales. Moreover, because of the smaller size of the market, it took a larger number of video products to generate a given level of revenues than was true of music or books. For this reason, new products generally accounted for more than 50 percent of divisional profits each year, and the division's strategic plan concluded:

> Video is forced by its financial dynamics to be extremely outward in its focus. Whether sourcing off-the-shelf, or coproducing, we are dependent upon alliances with producers, distributors, and television networks. This . . . keeps us in the market, and constantly infused with fresh ideas . . . [we] require a very effective, very pumped-up product development capability which can develop a new portfolio of successful products every year.

A key issue for management was attracting and retaining the highly dynamic and creative people who could continue to turn out new products. According to Carpenter, video and television was a "star" business, dependent on a small number of critical people, where "managing really matters. Creative people need lots of care, feeding, and recognition, and usually they don't get it. But when they do, they blossom." The culture was freewheeling and open, decision making was rapid, and most employees were relatively young. Yet they commanded high salaries. This was even more true of television production, where the industry's most successful producers could earn more than $300,000, plus substantial bonuses for hit shows. The differences between the salaries of television employees and the staff in book publishing concerned both Fahey and Carpenter, who felt that they could emerge as issues as the company moved increasingly to multimedia projects.

Several of the new television documentaries were, in fact, joint products involving editorial and video staff. All were tied to book series. Among the projects under development were shows on *Native Americans, Lost Civilizations,* and *True Crime*. In each case, Carpenter had established an editorial board, consisting of three to four members of the editorial staff, two television experts, and two video marketing experts, to formally bring the editorial group into the process of shaping program content. Because the division preferred to bring editors into the process after the related book series were already well along, extensive research was already complete. This provided a number of competitive advantages, as Carpenter explained:

> When we pitch an idea to a potential investor, we might already have two years of research under our belt. That's not true for our competitors, so we can offer shorter time-to-market. Our editors also have fantastic contacts. For instance, for *True Crime,* they already had access to [notorious serial killer] Ted Bundy's mother. And because they've already done the research, they know which stories will work and which are dead ends. They've already located the best archives and the best consultants. As an entry strategy, these assets are invaluable.

Westbrook agreed, noting the special advantages in the selling stage:

> Our link with Time Life books gives the buyer a comfort level. Whenever you're selling to someone, it's a leap of faith. What we're able to say is, "It's not going to be awful because we have the knowledge." Traditional networks can't do that. They don't have a lot of editors because, with their diverse set of productions, it doesn't make sense to maintain a standing army of researchers.

The relationship was still in its formative stages, however. Most editors had a relatively low regard for the amount of research conducted for television—as one put it, "Their idea of research is two graduate students and a library card"—and the editorial boards had been in existence for only nine months. At least one previous joint project had foundered because editors considered it to be too superficial, while division members regarded it as staid and heavy. Yet according to Carpenter, there had already been significant progress: "There were all these people in editorial who thought we were Martians. They found that we were intelligent, which they didn't know, and that we had some aesthetic sense." But because the video and television division did not pay for the use of materials of research generated by the books division, there was still grumbling. Carpenter had attempted to build fees for intellectual property developed by editors into contracts, but they had been rejected by buyers.

Time Life Books

Books remained central to Time Life and continued to be the largest sources of revenues, although profits had fallen sharply in recent years. Profit margins had dropped to less than half their level three years earlier and were now below 10 percent. The division remained, for the most part, a direct-response continuity publisher.

Continuity Publishing. Continuity publishing had three major components. First, the company maintained a significant editorial staff to develop ideas, conduct research, and package material as multi-volume series. The editorial group contained 130 people, and nearly 95 percent of their time was devoted to books. Unlike traditional publishing, where single authors and single volumes were the norm, continuity publishing involved multiple volumes on related topics, developed by teams of editors and writers using the same broad research base. The challenge was to parcel out the ideas so that they supported strong individual books as well as a compelling series—as one manager put it, "to slice the bologna as thin and as unobjectionably as possible." Most research was completed before the first volume was published, and the usual series required an up-front investment of $4 million. The development of a full, 20-volume series could cost more than $6 million. To break even, a series usually had to sell at least several hundred thousand copies, which meant that most customers were buying at least four or five volumes in the series; by comparison, trade books normally broke even at around 10,000 copies.

The second element of Time Life's continuity system was its direct response marketing capability. A consolidated marketing services group had been created in 1989, right after Fahey became CEO; it numbered 110 people and functioned, in Janas's words, "as a full-service, in-house advertising agency." The group conducted marketing research, created and sent direct mail brochures, carried out telemarketing, bought broadcast time (since many products were advertised on television), and managed and mined the data files, which listed all customers who had ever bought from Time Life. List management was a specialized, sophisticated activity, and over the years marketing services had developed a number of formulas for predicting the success of series from early market tests, as well as various ways to segment the list to ensure high response rates for different kinds of products. For example, formulas had been developed for predicting "average take" (the number of volumes, on average, that customers would buy in a series, and therefore a key to profitability), the proportion of customers who would "pay and stay," return rates for unbought volumes, and expected nonpayment rates (abbreviated "ku," for "killed us"). Occasionally, outside lists were purchased and their names were added to the master file. According to Mary Donohue, vice president of marketing services, this was necessary to avoid "overpromoting the file," with too many mailings to the same set of customers.

The third element of continuity publishing required a distinctive fulfillment system. Because volumes were sold as part of a series, the warehousing and distribution system had to be able to trigger shipments of the next book in the series to individual customers every six weeks. It also had to be able to track and log in returned, unpurchased volumes. This was an exceedingly complex task, requiring expensive, customized hardware and software, and had historically been one of the primary barriers to entry.

Creative and Production Processes. Producing a continuity book series required teams of 15 to 20 editors, writers, and researchers working together for several years. Editors usually drew up a list of at least 20 volumes for every proposed new series. Most series required six new volumes per year, or one every other month. If the series succeeded, it could be in active production for 3 or more years, and might continue to be printed and marketed for as long as 20 years. As many as five series were typically in production at any one time.

Creating products that could sustain such interest on the part of buyers called for substantial investments of time, effort, and money. Hall observed: "It's tough to come up with 20-volume ideas." Great care had to be taken to ensure that the product met the expectations of its readers, and that it could stand the test of time. Production of a new book series thus involved many sequential steps. (See Exhibit 4 for a flow chart of the editorial and production process.) The very first stage was the generation of series concepts. According to Tom Flaherty, managing editor:

> Concepts usually emerge through the efforts of a champion within editorial. Initially, it's a labor of love. We've tried everything to help the process—brainstorming, memos, meetings to get ideas—but most concepts still come from the same small group of people.

Next, every idea was subject to detailed scrutiny and market testing. Only a handful of proposed concepts survived all hurdles. Four main types of tests were conducted, each at a different stage of development: concept tests, title preference tests, dry tests, and wet tests. In concept tests, the basic idea for a series was first fleshed out in a few paragraphs by editorial staff and the book division's new-product development experts; several series concepts were then presented to customers in mail and telephone surveys for their reactions. These tests generated consumer rankings of the proposed series and a willingness to continue developing those with favorable results. Next came title preference tests, in which

more complete descriptions of each book, including titles, outlines, and extensive descriptions of the proposed content, were shown to selected samples from the firm's mailing list to determine their preferences. Here, an important goal was to identify the most desired books in the series, so that the sequence of volumes would stimulate continued, multivolume purchases and high average take. Then, in dry tests, mock-ups of possible advertising for the most promising concepts were mailed to potential customers and actual orders sought (but not delivered). The launch decision ("go" or "no go") was based on the results of dry tests. Finally, in wet tests, which were not always used, the first four volumes of a series were produced and delivered in order to understand repeat purchase patterns and further clarify average take. Overall, the entire testing process took between one and one-half and two years.

Once ideas were given the go-ahead, research and book preparation could begin. Most actual manuscripts were prepared by freelancers. However, Time Life staff generated detailed chapter outlines, potential graphics placements, and information packets for writers. After the series editor accepted a manuscript, an assistant editor checked it and obtained consultants' input to verify accuracy and comprehensiveness. Consultants were usually experts in the particular subject matter of the series—academics and other scholars, or prominent practitioners. Various editors then substantively edited the text, double-checked the content, and worked to incorporate research changes and consultant suggestions. After it was approved, the manuscript went through layout, typesetting, and proofreading.

While manuscript preparation was under way, a picture team worked to create accompanying graphics. At all stages of the work, Time Life editors sought to use original material. Working from the book outline, a picture editor and associate, along with assistant editors for research, put together a plan for illustrating the book. Once the plan—the picture outline—was approved, the art director started work on layouts, which were approved by the series editor. The research editor and the picture editor worked

EXHIBIT 4   Steps in Producing a Time Life Book

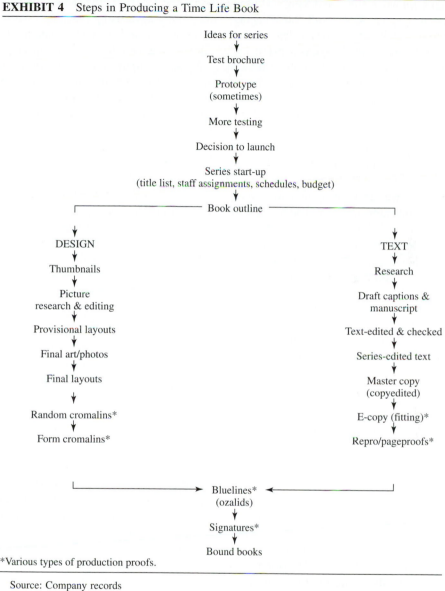

Ideas for series
↓
Test brochure
↓
Prototype
(sometimes)
↓
More testing
↓
Decision to launch
↓
Series start-up
(title list, staff assignments, schedules, budget)
↓
Book outline

DESIGN
↓
Thumbnails
↓
Picture
research & editing
↓
Provisional layouts
↓
Final art/photos
↓
Final layouts
↓
Random cromalins*
↓
Form cromalins*

TEXT
↓
Research
↓
Draft captions &
manuscript
↓
Text-edited & checked
↓
Series-edited text
↓
Master copy
(copyedited)
↓
E-copy (fitting)*
↓
Repro/pageproofs*

Bluelines*
(ozalids)
↓
Signatures*
↓
Bound books

*Various types of production proofs.

Source: Company records

to find images and set up photography shoots; the art director assigned freelance artists when necessary. These were then combined with the manuscript in final production. In total, the entire process, including manuscript and graphics preparation, usually took eight to nine months for each book.

Problems and Opportunities.   The book division was facing serious financial problems. Revenues had declined 35 percent since 1990, and profits had fallen 65 percent. In 1993 the division seemed unlikely to break even. The most obvious problem was a lack of successful new products. The division had not had a major hit since 1987, and there had been relatively few new series. One result was an aging product portfolio, the oldest the division had offered customers in a decade. Direct response advertising was also generating weaker sales. Customers drawn from the house list, for example, were buying fewer books in a series, causing a drop in the average take of nearly 20 percent since 1991. Television advertising, despite substantial outlays, was also significantly less effective, and rented lists were bringing in only half the orders they had in 1987.

Morale was low, especially among editors. Many felt that their status was declining (a little more than a decade earlier, the editorial group had had a separate reporting line, bypassing the president of Time Life and going directly to Time Inc.'s managing editor in New York) and there was a perceived loss of respect for editorial values. Editors were concerned about a shift away from the firm's founding philosophy, toward pop culture and greater marketing control. The problem was exacerbated by the cultural gap between the video and books divisions and the great success that the former enjoyed. Flaherty commented:

> They were the new kids on the block, the glamour group, and we saw that they were making a lot of money and having a good time doing it. Meanwhile, there was a heavy level of paranoia about the demise of books.

Opinions were divided about the cause of the problem. Some felt that the issue was fundamental, reflecting market changes and a decline in the appeal of continuity publishing. According to this argument, consumers wanted flexibility and choice, rather than predictable mailings of a 20-volume series. Unfortunately, that approach brought economic problems. When consumers were given the freedom to choose books in a series rather than forced to make a yes or no choice on a particular volume, the response rate fell 30 percent to 40 percent. The division also faced increased competition for consumers' leisure time and spending, not only from other publishers but also from diverse media and entertainment options that had appeared in the

1970s and 1980s. At the same time, the volume of direct mail advertising reaching consumers' mailboxes had expanded sharply, making it more difficult for Time Life to have an impact.

A second group saw the situation more favorably. In their view, the early 1990s were a replay of events two decades earlier. In each case, the demise of books was widely anticipated (as one manager put it, "this was considered a dead business in 1972, 1982, and 1992") and each time a hit series had emerged to revitalize the division. According to this argument, books had simply had a streak of bad luck; with time, another hit series would come along and profits would return. In fact 1989 had been a record year for the division, and profits had declined only since then.

Hall did not accept either of these arguments. In his view, the problem was one of attitude and approach. He commented:

> When John Fahey asked me to take this role, it was his assessment that the business needed a marketing and new product injection. And he was certainly right . . . The books division has lost creativity. It has become machine-like, not as the result of a single event or change, but gradually, over time. Things were just added to the system, which slowed it down . . . The energy level and aggressiveness that I saw in music just aren't here.

Action Plan. Hall was considering an ambitious, four-pronged program to revitalize the division. As a first step, he wanted to change the way that new concepts were generated. Historically, this stage of development had relied heavily on a small set of people who had a reputation for generating good ideas. In Hall's view, the approach was unanchored and relied too heavily on inspiration. He wanted marketing and competitive information to figure more prominently in the early analysis, with assessments of market trends and Time Life's representation in critical market segments suggesting possible new products. His goal was "to guide the process, without destroying the serendipity," while also making concept development more of a collective responsibility, involving groups outside of editorial.

Second, Hall planned to reduce reliance on the current market research process, which he regarded as slow and cumbersome and a primary reason why so few new products had been produced in recent years. Rather than relying on elaborate and repeated tests, managers in the future needed to be closer to the market and willing to make rapid, independent decisions based on less-comprehensive information. The entire development process was also being examined. A fast-track process had been used to produce several volumes that were needed to meet the scheduled airings of public television series; it was being studied for possible lessons. The process relied on a dedicated team, considerable simultaneous development, the use of photographs rather than commissioned art, a larger writing staff, a preestablished story line drawn from the television series, and an increased budget. Information technology experts were also being consulted, although Hall had doubts about their ability to reengineer the process successfully.

Third, Hall planned to broaden the division's product offerings using the same approach he had used at music, introducing sets and single shots and lessening the reliance on continuity series. Sets and single shots barely existed in books; custom publishing, however, aimed at special projects, such as *Mrs. Fields' Cookie Book,* that took existing materials and repackaged them as new products, already contributed one-fifth of revenues and one-half of profits. Hall planned to expand these activities by encouraging a more entrepreneurial, flexible approach, even if it meant selling through bookstores rather than via direct mail. He explained:

> In the past, we called ourselves a continuity publisher. But we're both a publisher and a direct marketer. That means we should be able to take others' books through our direct marketing channel, and also to publish books of our own that we can sell through different channels. We need to protect ourselves in the slim years when, God forbid, we don't have a hit continuity series.

Finally, Hall felt it was necessary to bring new thinking, and perhaps new people, into books

marketing, product development, and editorial. Several moves had already been made in the marketing area, and a search was under way to fill a critical new-product development position. Editorial, however, remained a concern. Hall observed:

> Editorial leadership here has been very status-quo oriented. We have a lot of people who have risen to the top and are very comfortable sitting there. We are going to turn up the heat on those people and make them feel that they are personally responsible for selling books for the company . . . My instinct now is to make the changes happen fast.

True Crime

The *True Crime* project began in the book division. Market research suggested a healthy public appetite for books on crime and criminals, and the goal was to combine Time Life's traditional standards of accuracy and careful investigative reporting with graphic details and vivid images (see Exhibit 5). Each volume in the series was designed to investigate a particular type of crime, including serial killers, mass murderers, cultists, the Mafia, and crimes of passion. By January 1993 six volumes had been researched, developed, and test-marketed, and were ready for shipment. Meanwhile, the video and television division had pitched the idea of a television series on the same subject to broadcasters and received an encouraging response. Development had started on the television series in May 1992, and three treatments were now in hand. Videotape sales were anticipated at a later date.

Early tests suggested that the book series would be a major hit. In fact, in the week after the first television advertisements hit the air, Time Life received more orders than it had for any other series in the company's history. But at the same time, Fahey began to receive concerned letters from viewers, who felt that Time Life was glorifying law breaking and promoting violence by giving excessive attention to mass murders and other criminals. While the number of letters was relatively small, they came at a bad time: Time

---

EXHIBIT 5   *True Crime* Marketing Report (Excerpts)

Overview

True Crime was developed as a mass market product targeted to the huge audience of people who read *True Crime* paperbacks, watch the many "Tabloid" television shows and are fascinated by the shocking murders and crimes that dominate our news headlines. It is a series that has refused to die despite many setbacks and one that has undergone numerous revisions from its conception in 1983 until its successful test today. Perhaps the market has finally caught up with the series.

The series is designed to be an exciting but responsible investigation of modern crime, particularly those crimes involving passion and murder. It seeks to answer the question, "What is it that turns seemingly normal men and women to destructive anti-social behavior and crime?" This is a subject that fascinates the American public. *True Crime* paperbacks flood the bookstores every month, occasionally hit the hardcover bestseller list and dominate both network and syndicated television. It is a lucrative subject for movies (witness *The Silence of the Lambs* and the spate of gangster movies in the early 1990s). Grisly murders obligingly keep the subject current in the news.

Although there are no specific mail order products to track (*Reader's Digest* does not publish in the category and Book of the Month Club rarely offers *True Crime* books), the Literary Guild frequently offers *True Crime* in its promotions. TLB Europe has expressed enthusiasm (300,000 starts) for this series, but it has not yet been tested there.

Competition

There is no direct competition in direct response. There is, however, enormous paperback competition. Television also offers plenty of weekly crimes to satisfy the *True Crime* fan. Hardcover sales are moderate. To date, this is a paperback and television market.

Concept Development

Concept Development focus groups were held in early 1989 to probe the strengths and weaknesses of three different approaches to crime . . . Consumers wanted "thrilling blockbuster style balanced by Time-Life's authority and dignity." They were most interested in violent crimes involving individual victims, and they wanted to be able "to walk around the crime and understand it from all perspectives."

Warner, the parent company, had recently been in the public eye because of inflammatory lyrics in a recording by the rap singer Ice-T and a racy new book of photographs of Madonna. In fact, concerns about the series had earlier risen internally. During the development of *True Crime,* members of the editorial group had expressed misgivings about the topic and proposed treatment. But the strong market tests had prevailed, leaving Fahey with the current predicament. He observed:

> This problem came about because of market research–based publishing. People told us that they wanted blood, guts, and gore. We needed a hit to revitalize the business, and all our research pointed to this topic.

To buy time, Fahey asked the book division to temporarily halt release of the series. He also requested revised television advertisements, and it was this version that the group had just screened in Fahey's office. They were less graphic than previous versions, but still dramatic. Now, Fahey had to weigh several arguments. On the one hand, there were the potential profits and boost to morale that the books division would gain from a hit (see Exhibit 6). Estimated profits ranged from $8 million to $17 million, with the videotape and television series expected to contribute an additional $7 million. This alone might mean that the company should take the risk and proceed. Fahey was also loathe to do anything that would discourage the efforts of the video and television division to continue to build in-house

EXHIBIT 6 *True Crime* Book Series Financial Summary

Five-Year Sales Plan

Assumptions used in this forecast are:

1. Launch price $12.99. Increased to $14.99 in year three, assuming that price testing supports this change.
2. 1H93 mini-launch.
3. Rollout in Mass Media delayed until 2H93 when the backend is established.
4. 20-volume series length.
5. Average takes are based on analysis of *Mysteries of the Unknown* performance at launch and current economic environment. Fatigued each year as price increases.
6. 3% increase in selling cost in mail and 2.5% in cost of goods.

Executive Summary

($ millions)	Base Case	Aggressive Case
Net revenues	$38.2	$68.2
Trading income	$31.3	$57.0
Promotion spending	($20.8)	($37.4)
Contribution to overhead	$10.5	$19.6
Edit	($ 5.2)	($ 5.2)
Domestic profits	$ 5.3	$14.4
International profits	$ 3.0	$ 3.0
Total profits	$ 8.3	$17.4
Orders (000s)	765	1,457
Average take	4.37	4.15
Shipments (000s)	3,344	6,044

capabilities and collaborate with editorial and books personnel. The division had identified *True Crime* as an important vehicle for establishing its credibility, and its managers were much less worried about the topic and proposed advertising than their counterparts in books. Fahey did not want to reinforce the impression that Time Life was too stodgy to succeed in television. Moreover, he knew that success with the book, television, and videotape series would provide further momentum for multimedia projects and cooperation across divisions.

Still, there were concerns about the brand. Fahey knew that this series, and television in general, required more provocative advertising than the books

division had historically used. But he was worried that an adverse image might be created for the whole company by the proposed advertisements, and, indeed, by the series itself. He commented:

We know what the public wants and we can give it to them. We accept that we're becoming more controversial; with the videotape "Trials of Life," for instance, our television ads showed vivid scenes of violence in nature and produced a runaway hit. I don't want to serve as the guardian of the brand or to stop *True Crime* because of tradition. We need to move forward. But we also have to protect our image. My role is difficult; the word "guardian," after all, has both positive and negative connotations.

Case 1–5

WATERMILL VENTURES

Watermill Ventures (WMV) was a partnership formed in 1993 to acquire and then turn around underperforming businesses. Three years later, Steven (Steve) Karol, Watermill's founder, was growing increasingly concerned about the small number of completed acquisitions—only Crossville Rubber Products in 1994, and Gulf States Steel in 1995. Karol was evaluating two alternatives for stimulating the deal flow: rethinking, and perhaps loosening, the company's selection criteria, and keeping the criteria intact but casting a wider net so that more acquisition candidates were reviewed. Among other actions, he had established a website (**http://www.watermill.com**) to broaden Watermill's base of contacts. But he was considering what other steps were needed as well.

Company Background

Watermill Ventures was one of a number of businesses known informally as the Karol companies. The first, HMK, was launched by Steve's father in 1977. Using family money as equity capital, it acquired companies needing help, improved their operations, and then continued to operate them at a profit. Most were small manufacturers in mature industries, such as Sheffield Steel, Suburban Manufacturing, and Business Interiors. Steve Karol became president and CEO of HMK in 1983, after his father's death. He later sold several of its businesses to his younger brother, William (Bill) Karol, who then became president and CEO of his own KODA group. Over time, the Karol companies acquired more than 30 businesses, building a strong track record with lenders by consistently improving performance and meeting all fiduciary responsibilities.

After considerable reflection in the early 1990s, Steve Karol decided to split off HMK's main acquisition arm into Watermill Ventures, forming a group of limited liability companies. Whereas HMK's approach was to buy, fix, grow, and hold companies, WMV would buy, fix, grow, and then, within four to seven years, take public or sell the companies it had acquired. It would include equity capital from high net worth investors, as well as relying on family money. Karol's plan was to acquire an average of two companies per year, grow to a revolving portfolio of about eight companies, and then harvest an average of two of the most successful turnarounds annually.

By early 1996, WMV had eight professional staff members. Three were managing directors: Steve Karol, Bill Karol, and Dale Okonow, an attorney and MBA with a background in mergers and acquisitions. Bill Karol took primary responsibility for the front end of the deal flow—sourcing acquisitions, structuring deals, and making sellers and lenders comfortable. Okonow took over once a letter of intent was signed, playing the lead role on negotiations, contracts, and due diligence. Steve Karol had primary responsibility for strategy development, both during the selection process and after a company was acquired.

The Watermill Approach

Watermill Ventures sought companies with distinctive profiles, and turned them around using techniques that the Karols had refined through years of experience. Acquisition candidates were

This case was prepared by Artemis March under the direction of David A. Garvin.

all in relatively mature industries, positioned at critical transition points in their evolution, and underperforming relative to their potential and to competitors. Typically, they faced difficult situations that ensured a low purchase price. To improve their operating performance, WMV introduced strategic thinking and a new system of management, called "professional entrepreneurship." Steve Karol summarized the approach:

> Fifty percent of the value you obtain in an acquisition is in the way you buy it. If you buy well, the odds are there won't be much competition, and you won't have to negotiate. The other 50 percent of value comes from doing something with companies once you get them. We've developed a strategic process that helps lost companies find their way.

WMV therefore looked for troubled manufacturers and value-added distributors in industries such as textiles, rubber, steel, chemicals, pulp and paper, paints and coatings, and office furniture. It had ruled out high technology because of the large R&D investments required. Nor was it interested in companies in industries with very short life cycles, fashion businesses, or real estate. Initially, WMV had imposed size limits of $20 to $200 million in sales, but in 1996 these were broadened to $30–$500 million. Steve Karol commented on the shift: "It's easier to turn around a company having more substance. Besides, there is so much money out there chasing deals in the upper size ranges that there's space for us to move up a little."

Market Life Cycle: The S-Curve

WMV's primary stethoscope for identifying companies of interest was the S-curve or industry life cycle. The S-curve graphically depicted the evolution of an industry or market, beginning with a period of slow growth, followed by steady acceleration. Eventually, growth peaked, and the industry began to decline. Another competing S-curve was always starting somewhere during the current life cycle; often, it rendered existing products and processes obsolete. Five-inch disk drives, for example, eventually supplanted eight-inch drives, just as minimills soon pulled demand away from integrated steel bar producers.

At WMV the S-curve was divided into four quadrants, which the company referred to as Q1, Q2, Q3, and Q4. Each mapped out an important stage of the life cycle. Q1 represented the incubation period, when the industry was first becoming established; Q2 represented adolescence, when growth was rapid; Q3 represented maturity, when competition often shifted to cost; and Q4 represented old age and decline, when consolidation typically occurred. At the beginning of the century, a complete Q1-to-Q4 cycle might take 50 years; by the mid-1990s the period could be as short as six months.

In searching for acquisitions, WMV was particularly interested in identifying companies in Q3 and Q4 that had failed to negotiate certain critical industry transitions. These transitions were usually marked by periods of what Karol called "dynamic change," or shifts in the relative growth rates of industry supply and demand. Karol believed that these periods were important because they signaled the need to run a business differently and led to predictable problems at established companies. Two types of problems were of special interest because they represented desirable turnaround opportunities: "founder's trap" and "midlife crisis." (See Exhibit 1.)

Founder's trap was partly a state of mind in which the founder of a business, having enjoyed great success in the early stages of the life cycle, was unable to listen, change, or adjust to the new requirements of maturity. Often, the critical problem was the company's inability to make the transition from entrepreneurship to professional management. Managers might, for example, have become skilled at adding new capacity, but as the market shifted into later stages of the life cycle, growth in demand slowed, and new skills would be necessary, including tighter discipline, improved market segmentation, and better systems for strategic planning, budgeting, and cost control. Many founders were unable to recognize these needs and make the necessary adjustments.

EXHIBIT 1   S-Curves and the Industry Life Cycle

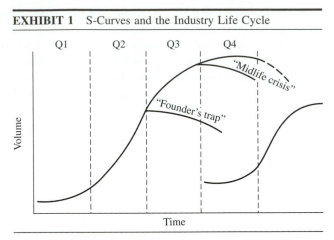

Source: Watermill Ventures

Midlife crises, by contrast, occurred in the fourth stage of the life cycle, when demand growth was low or negative and supply had stabilized. Often, systems and strategies appropriate to Q3 had by this time become fixed and unyielding, just when the company needed to reinvigorate itself with a more entrepreneurial spirit. Flexibility was essential, for previously unidentified niches had to be found and exploited, or else the company had to take the lead in consolidating the industry. Karol described the psychological dilemma: "You recognize you are mortal, but you refuse to acknowledge it. You accelerate your demise by refusing to adapt and act appropriately."

Use of the S-Curve.   According to Karol, WMV's leverage from the S-curve came from the fact that the company believed in it, gave considerable thought to its implications, and acted on the ideas. Watermill actively sought founder's trap and midlife crisis acquisitions, and used the S-curve to help identify them. Karol explained: "The S-curve helps to predict industry dynamics and tells us the company behaviors required for success." He elaborated:

> The strategy we need to put in place at an acquisition will depend, first of all, on where the company is on the S-curve. For example, if they're in Q4 and there are some niches available, then

segmentation and repositioning are part of the answer. If there aren't any niches, then they must become a consolidator and the low-cost producer. In either case, they need to reinvent themselves.

Watermill had tried to use these techniques prospectively, analyzing industry S-curves in advance and then targeting acquisition candidates, but lacked the staff to do so on an ongoing basis. Most front-end screening was conducted by a single individual, Ben Proctor, the company's director of acquisitions, with Bill Karol's assistance. Steve Karol described their approach:

> We go fishing; Ben and Bill are out casting on a daily basis. If we get a nibble, then we do analysis and decide whether we want to throw the fish back. Even if we could do it prospectively, it would violate the other half of our equation, which is to buy it right. If you are the initiator of a transaction, you will probably pay more than if it comes to you.

Proctor concurred:

> This is by nature an opportunistic business. When you have a good gut feel about a company, then you go back and do the work on the industry, its life cycle, and performance characteristics, and you analyze the company in that framework.

Underperformance

WMV was especially interested in companies that were underperforming compared with others in their industry. It used two tools to make the determination. The first, called the "underperforming scale," was a rough intuitive estimate of whether the company was in the right performance zone. Later, when profitability and market share data had been collected, Watermill developed a more refined measure, the "normative band of performance," that compared the company's results to industry norms. Proctor contrasted the two approaches: "The underperforming scale is broader and shallower than the band. It takes account of future strategic positioning, the balance sheet, and other factors. The band, by contrast, is strictly a P&L analysis."

Underperforming Scale.   Ratings were done on a simple 0-to-10 scale, with 0 indicating severe problems ("can't survive") and 10 indicating outstanding performance ("can't be challenged"). Typically, WMV looked for companies that fell into the 2–6 (or yellow) range. Karol explained: "We don't play in the red zone (0–1) because it's too risky, and there's too much money chasing companies in the green zone (7–10)." WMV's goal was to find companies that could be purchased at an acceptable price because they were experiencing problems, yet still had turnaround potential. Proctor elaborated on the factors he weighed when rating a company:

> The most important is current operating profit performance as a percentage of sales. But I also try to get a feel for their strategic positioning, as well as their basic financials. Do they differentiate their product? Are they losing market share? What is their cost position? Do they have balance sheet issues, such as contingent liabilities? Are they having cash problems?

Normative Band of Performance.   The normative band of performance was invoked later in the assessment process, when WMV wanted to determine the upside potential of an acquisition. The technique had originally been developed by Bain and Com-

pany to assess potential profitability, and represented a refinement of the growth-share matrix pioneered by The Boston Consulting Group. At WMV, it played a wider role; as Proctor explained: "The normative band has become the framework and language we use to discuss an acquisition's possibilities."

The task began by defining an industry segment and then plotting the performance of participants on two dimensions, profitability and relative market share. Once outliers were eliminated, the result was a broad band of expected (or typical) performance for companies in that market segment (see Exhibit 2). Bain was able to draw on considerable industry data to generate these bands; Watermill, by comparison, could often produce only a few data points, such as the most and least profitable companies in the industry. Relative market share was particularly difficult to come by. It was defined as the ratio of a company's market share to the share of the industry leader (or, in the case of the leader, the ratio of its share to that of the next largest competitor). For example, in a billion dollar industry, where the leader's sales were $250 million and the next largest competitor's sales were $200 million, the leader's relative market share would be 1.25 (.25/.20) and the next largest competitor's would be .8 (.20/.25).

Once the band was plotted, Watermill used it to qualify potential acquisition candidates. Karol explained:

> If a company is above the band, we are not interested because there is nowhere to go but down. We don't buy companies at the top of their game, or pay high multiples for past performance. If they are in the band, we might go forward, depending on how much we think we can do with the company. But what we are really looking for is companies that are below the band.

Buying It Right

Buying it right meant avoiding auctions and bidding contests, which WMV was usually able to do because there were few competitors for the

---

EXHIBIT 2   Normative Band of Performance

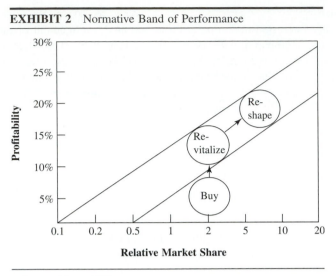

Source: Watermill Ventures

---

companies it sought. The reasons often had to do with what Karol called "hair on the deal"—a range of messy problems that dissuaded most other investors. Bill Leaver, a vice president who worked with Okonow on financial structures, contracts, and labor negotiations, elaborated:

> Our value added is in the deal structure, and looking at companies that other buyers don't want. Hairy deals are hard to do. We have one now, for example, that is an ESOP, has gone through Chapter 11, is union owned, has three sets of unsecured creditors, and involves a state agency.

Watermill was not put off by such companies, providing its strategic assessment suggested that it could do something about the problems and significantly increase the company's performance. Watermill was willing to look at these situations—or, more precisely, look *through* them—to determine whether strategic repositioning and a different approach to management might make a difference.

If so, time was usually required for a turnaround, suggesting a second element of buying it right: knowing how to structure deals so that the interests of both investors and banks were covered in a downturn. Okonow explained:

We look at what a company will return in a down cycle, and that tells us what we'll pay. Then, we try to build in enough cushion, enough liquidity, to see us through these periods. Liquidity is the key for us. What I lose sleep over is if all of our businesses would go down at the same time, and what I focus on is not getting crunched in a downturn. We try to get friendly lenders who understand this going into the deal, and don't switch lenders for a few basis points. In fact, we've been working with the same lenders for a decade.

Strategic Thinking

Strategic analysis began as soon as a company became a target for serious consideration. The focus was on crafting a compelling, integrated story, as Proctor explained:

> From the moment we begin discussing a company in the acquisition committee, Steve will start talking about what "the story" is—for example, what's causing the problems, what are the possibilities for repositioning, does the company have the capacity to implement the new strategy? The story will begin to take shape in people's minds before we have much documentation. In fact, we tend to get to the letter-of-intent stage without it being fully crystallized. We have a sense that there's a story

there, and a pretty good idea of the outline, but it won't be until we are in due diligence that it gets filled in and fully checked out. Developing the story to our satisfaction takes longer and is more difficult than doing financial analysis or models.

Steve Karol took the lead in crafting the story and framing strategic questions. His major themes were S-curve positioning, relative market share, and opportunities for increased segmentation, and he paid special attention to assessing the markets currently served, growth segments, market positioning, and the general nature of the fit between the company, its customers, and competitors. All questions had the same end: understanding the kind of operating and revenue improvements that might be gained from strategic repositioning. This dialogue continued throughout the screening and acquisition process. For example, when Watermill first began considering a potential acquisition in the custom rubber mixing business, there was broad discussion of how it might fit with Crossville Rubber. Following a site visit, the acquisition committee probed deeper, asking, "How do they *really* fit with Crossville?" George O'Conor, Watermill's chief technology officer, observed: "Unlike many investors and fund managers, we develop a company's new business strategy before we acquire it. So we do a lot more thinking and spend a lot more time up front."

Professional Entrepreneurship

Professional entrepreneurship was a management system originally developed at HMK. It sought to balance autonomy and innovation with discipline and control by coupling the skills of professional management with an entrepreneurial mind-set. It had three elements: a distinctive approach to planning, incentives that were keyed to meeting plan, and a system for tracking and monitoring performance.

The approach had emerged from Steve Karol's thinking about entrepreneurship as a system or culture in which people managed opportunities rather than assets and were skilled at handling the associated risks. At WMV, he observed, the critical

risks involved the operating plan: "We buy high-risk companies that are highly leveraged financially, and cannot afford a downside surprise. Our managers must hit their plan. I want them to be willing to bet their house on it."

All plans had to generate sufficient cash to meet strategic goals, yet not violate any covenants that were imposed by financial institutions. Karol imposed two other requirements as well. Every annual plan had to be derived from a company's strategic plan, with operating goals that were based on the strategy. Plans also had to be bottom up. Sales, for example, established sales and marketing targets, manufacturing established productivity and yield targets, and these and other numbers bubbled up to the company's executive committee, where overall goals were established.

To further control risk, Karol wanted his managers to "sandbag" him—that is, to build small buffers or contingencies into their plans. These buffers introduced a certain looseness into the numbers, but gave managers greater assurance that their goals would be met. Unlike conventional sandbagging, however, which was undercover and illicit, these sandbags were openly placed and agreed to. Everyone knew where they were and how much cushion was involved. Okonow described the process:

> We are very explicit about where the cushions go. They're not on controllable items, like production efficiency; there we want to be very accurate and push performance to the edge. Instead, we allow little cushions on things that are noncontrollable or less controllable at the operating level. Take scrap, which our steel mills buy at market price. If we think it's going to cost $127 per ton, we'll allow them to build in a small sandbag by projecting the purchase price at $130 per ton.

To reinforce this philosophy, the incentive system was keyed to meeting plan. Senior managers at acquired companies who hit their targets received an additional 25 percent of their salary in cash. If they exceeded their targets, they received incremental increases in their bonuses up to a cap, usually 50 percent of their salaries. Karol considered these bonuses a small price to pay, and had found them to be an effective way of focusing the executive team on performance rather than politics. He observed:

> Most people are capable of taking some risk if they know the risk is being managed. You lose those who are cautious when they think there's no net under them. You lose the risk takers when they think there is too much control. What we've tried to do is construct a balance between the net and the controls so that a normal person can operate effectively.

To monitor performance against plan, WMV requested daily and monthly reports from its companies. Daily reports covered sales, margins, bookings, and critical balance sheet information. Monthly reports contained both quantitative and narrative material. The quantitative sections compared results to plan for every item on which managers had specific targets, while the narrative portions focused on issues that the company was facing, threats and opportunities that it had identified, and current initiatives. These reports were expected to be shared with all employees, and cascade throughout the organization.

Deal Flow, Screening, and Acquisition Processes

Watermill had to continually seek out sources and develop potential leads. Proctor, with Bill Karol's oversight, was taking on more and more of the front-end responsibility for deal flow and screening. Bill Karol compared their roles: "Ben prequalifies the substance of the deal—the S-curve, pros and cons, the numbers—and I prequalify the process: Can we buy it right? Only then do we take it to the acquisition committee for consideration."

Stimulating the Deal Flow
The primary source of leads were intermediaries. They ranged from small business brokers who made cold calls pitching $10 million deals to companies like Goldman Sachs that had professional mergers-and-acquisitions departments and large numbers of brokers. To receive notifications of new

deals, a buyer first had to become known to these intermediaries and gain credibility with them. Proctor observed: "It's a numbers game; the more contacts you have, the better off you will be in terms of deal flow." Over the past two years, he had built Watermill's database of qualified intermediaries from 100 to 400 names.

The database was just a starting point, however. Proctor explained: "It's an 80/20 rule, if not 90/10. If you have 400 names in the database, there are probably 40 you are really dealing with." The key to better deal flow, he believed, was for Watermill to define itself more clearly in the marketplace and become better known to a group of higher quality intermediaries. He observed: "We have to make sure we are listed correctly—as buyers of mature, turnaround opportunities in a broad range of manufacturing industries." Proctor had found face-to-face contact to be the single biggest factor in getting an intermediary to think of Watermill when it was sending out deal announcements.

The Screening and Acquisition Process
The process of screening and analyzing deals involved six, largely sequential activities: lead development, target formation, financial modeling, site visit(s), letter of intent, and due diligence. (See Exhibit 3.) In addition, once a company became an active lead, it cycled through the acquisition committee every week until it was dropped. The process worked like a funnel, as companies were progressively winnowed out. In a typical year, 300–500 potential deals might be considered, and 80–100 might pass the first screen. Of these, 40–50 companies might become targets, with half of them receiving at least one site visit. Offers might then be made to 10–15 companies, with the expectation that fewer than half would be signed.

Lead Development.   To begin, Proctor tried to identify companies that fell within Watermill's size and industry parameters, yet were not so healthy as to be "too good for us." The first information about a deal was often little more than a few sentences

EXHIBIT 3   Screening and Acquisition Process

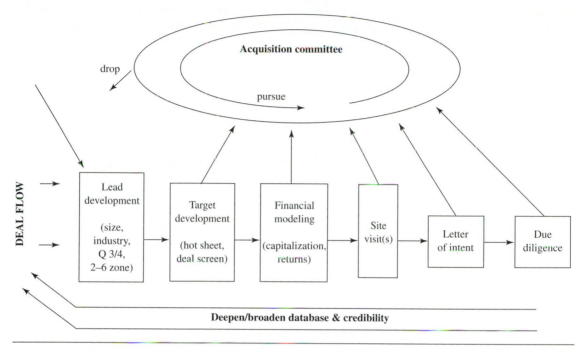

Source: Casewriter

or a paragraph that came in by fax. If, based on this information, the industry appeared to be in Q3 or Q4, Proctor called the broker to get additional data, and initiated direct contact with the seller as soon as possible. He looked for balance sheet information to gauge whether the asset base would permit financing the acquisition, and market share and P&L data to assess overall performance. Irregular or cyclical earnings were preferred, and companies were screened out if they ranked higher than 6 on the underperforming scale. Proctor then developed a lead sheet on any companies that looked promising. He observed: "If something might remotely fit our criteria, I post the lead to Lotus Notes and introduce it at the next acquisition committee meeting, without any consideration of the technical aspects of the strategy or the normative band of performance." He estimated that he spent about a half-hour on this first-cut screening.

Target Formation and Development.   If the initial screening suggested that the company could be financed and was between 2 and 6 on the underperforming scale, Proctor then investigated it in more detail. At this point, the lead became a target. Proctor normally signed a confidentiality agreement with the intermediary or seller to gain access to additional information and received a book on the company, further materials from the seller, or made a site visit to collect needed data. To structure his assessments, he spent about an hour generating "hot sheets" and "deal screens."

A hot sheet was a company's financial history for the past three or four years, taken, if possible, to the level of cash flow. It also included next year's financial plan. Because it was based on more complete information than the initial screening, it permitted more reliable estimates of performance, price, and financing needs. A deal screen, by contrast, was a way of structuring the nonfinancial analysis. It included about a dozen key questions, many of them related to the S-curve. The potential for market growth was addressed, and niches or pockets of opportunity were identified for possible repositioning. Other questions probed the degree of market fragmentation or industry consolidation, and asked for estimates of the company's relative market share. The seller's motivation was also assessed; it might be related to founder's trap or a midlife crisis. There were also questions comparing the seller's price expectations with Watermill's assessment of its asset base and financeability, as well as evaluations of management tenure and the currency of technology.

Acquisition Committee.   The acquisition committee was WMV's primary decision-making body. In it, members explored the strategic and financial possibilities of a deal, developed the strategic story and proposed repositioning, and made decisions about whether to pursue, table, or drop an acquisition candidate. The committee met weekly for several hours and was composed of the eight Watermill principals: the two Karols, Okonow, Leaver, Proctor, O'Conor, Jeff Stein, a director who focused on finance and operations, and Bill Fitzgerald, a vice president who handled tax matters. Proctor developed the agenda and ran the sessions as structured brainstorming sessions.

In most cases, there was broad agreement about whether or not to pursue a deal, usually because the data and supporting analysis were convincing. For example, the group was uniformly positive about the acquisition of a printing company until serious problems about its asset quality surfaced during due diligence; then, all members changed their views. Decision making was not, however, by consensus because that approach had not worked well at HMK. As Steve Karol put it: "The sticking point is that the one who says no ends up with a veto." WMV therefore took a different tack when someone in a minority position felt strongly. Karol explained:

If someone thinks we've found a great deal but others are not convinced, the person who says they really like the company becomes its champion. They carry the process forward: "I'm going to prove to you that this is a good deal." If, on the other hand, almost everyone wants to pursue a deal but one person is adamantly opposed, then the burden is on that person to continue to show us the errors of our ways. We encourage both types of dissenting behavior all the way through our decision-making process. Why? Because you never know—the dissenter may be right.

When a target was first brought to the acquisition committee, the goal was to flesh out a rough outline of the turnaround story. Proctor presented candidates and fielded questions; Steve Karol probed on market and S-curve issues; and the accountants asked primarily financial questions. The focus was on the S-curve, the company's positioning in the industry, and its performance relative to the normative band. If the committee thought there might be a fit with WMV, they usually suggested a ballpark price. Proctor then called the intermediary or seller, and was often asked to send a letter of interest or come down for a look. Visits were sometimes made for the purpose of gathering material to develop the story; they were likely when there was no book on the company, information was hard to come by, or the story was a complicated one. If this new information generated further excitement within the committee, Proctor began to develop a financial model of the company.

Financial Model.   A financial model ran 8–10 pages, and combined marketing and financial analysis. Most deal groups did not develop a full financial model until after they signed a letter of intent; WMV, by contrast, never got to the letter-of-intent stage until it had a model in hand. Two of the key elements in the WMV model were the capitalization page and the returns page.

The capitalization page was a tool for estimating what WMV should pay for the company, what it could borrow to finance it, and the interest charges and other financial responsibilities the company could safely handle. Proctor calculated the borrowing base, capitalization requirements, and projected liquidity for the first two years, which gave Bill Karol the foundation for thinking about the financial structure of the deal. The returns page showed expected returns during the ownership period. Using generic assumptions—for example, a six-year exit, selling at a multiple of five to seven, and the like—it also showed the price WMV could expect when it sold the company.

Site Visit(s). Before a letter of intent was signed, there was always one, and sometimes two, site visits. Proctor almost always went on these trips, as did Bill Karol if he were available; if he was not, Steve Karol or Okonow accompanied Proctor. Bill Karol described the form of a typical, day-long meeting:

> I talk to the CEO, who usually has the CFO with him. Other managers come and join them, and we always make sure to include sales and marketing. I prefer to meet with people one-to-one, and then meet with them again in a group to see how their answers change.

A critical goal of this visit was to determine whether the company's problems were fixable. Proctor explained:

> We want to make sure that they're not heading into the red zone and we can't get that sense without talking to management directly. We need to know *why* they are below the band—or, in point of fact, if they really are below it. The band may turn out to be in a different position than we thought it was. Perhaps no one in the industry is making any money.

The other objective of the first site visit was to establish whether it was even possible to do the kind of repositioning and market segmentation needed to improve the company's operating performance. Did the strategic scenarios that Watermill was considering have any basis in reality? Was there a base of skills on which WMV could build? Bill Karol noted that he often surprised

companies on these visits by asking so many questions about marketing and operations. Most other buyers focused almost exclusively on the numbers.

The second site visit went into even more depth on market segmentation and competitive positioning. Questions were more fine-grained and focused. WMV wanted to gain confidence in its financial model—for example, had it made the right assumptions about the value of inventory and receivables? While it did not share its emerging thinking about strategy, it tried to check whether the seller was comfortable with the assumptions and projections it was making. For example, was 10 percent annual growth for the next three years a reasonable expectation? In addition, Watermill conducted a more comprehensive examination of the company's facilities, identifying bottlenecks and constraints and gauging capital requirements so that it could estimate cash flow more accurately during the turnaround period.

Letter of Intent. If the site visit(s) went well and the acquisition committee felt comfortable with the strategic and financial story that had emerged, one of the principals talked with the intermediary or seller about issuing a letter of intent. For WMV, this meant a commitment to conclude the deal unless due diligence brought new, conflicting data to light. WMV sought a letter of intent that would give it an exclusive for 60, 90, or 120 days to do the additional research that would be used to confirm the information provided by the seller and would make or break the deal.

Due Diligence. The goals of due diligence were to collect in-depth information that allowed Watermill to further assess the risks of the acquisition, confirming or disconfirming all critical aspects of the deal. At this time, Bill Karol began working with banks to put the financial structure together; coupled with the earlier strategy work, these materials became the package presented to potential investors. If the deal closed, Watermill then went to its investor base and raised the necessary equity capital.

The Process in Action: The Acquisition of Gulf States Steel

Gulf States Steel, Inc. (GSS), was founded in 1904 in Gadsden, Alabama, as a fully integrated producer of wire products. Over the next 80 years, it had a series of owners and a long history of undercapitalization, leading to several bankruptcies. It also evolved into a producer of both plates (for heavy capital equipment) and sheets (hot-rolled, cold-rolled, and galvanized for a wide range of customers). A new owner resurrected the company between 1986 and 1994 by renegotiating union and supplier contracts and investing $200 million in capital improvements, including a continuous caster. During this period, John Lefler was recruited from U.S. Steel to oversee the manufacturing operation and facility upgrade. He observed:

> If this had been U.S. Steel, it would have cost $400 million to do the same work. The difference is that at Gulf States we buy used equipment, upgrade it with the original manufacturer, and install it ourselves. Our people have very good skills.

In 1992 Lefler instigated an extensive reengineering process that made Gulf States the lowest cost sheet producer in the United States, and one of the low-cost producers of plate. A year later he became president. However, for unrelated reasons the owners' partnership unraveled in 1994, and GSS was put up for sale.

Evaluating the Acquisition.   Gulf States presented Watermill with a difficult dilemma. It did not perfectly match the company's selection criteria, yet still seemed to be a desirable candidate. At the time, Watermill's upper limit for acquisitions was $200 million in revenues; Gulf States' revenues were $480 million. Could Watermill's infrastructure handle such a large company? Would it unbalance the investment portfolio? Nor was Gulf States a classic underperformer. It enjoyed a low-cost position, and even with 1.3 million tons of capacity had averaged 96 percent utilization for the past five years, compared with 85 percent for the industry. Proctor recalled: "Gulf States was making $75 million before interest and taxes, already had good management, and had just taken $28 a ton out through cost reengineering. We knew we could not expect a great leap in band performance."

On the other hand, there were elements of the deal that did fit the WMV profile. Gulf States was an inwardly focused, production-oriented company positioned in Q4; there were a number of unexploited marketing opportunities. Despite a highly diversified customer base and a strong position in the Southeast, where there were very few competitors, Gulf States had pursued only limited segmentation. About two-thirds of its tonnage went to sheet, which was a highly competitive, lower-margin product. In plate, it suffered cost penalties because 40 percent of its products came from ingots rather than continuous casting. Moreover, most competitors were switching to a new technology that threatened to make Gulf States obsolete. Leaver summarized the arguments:

> Gulf States was outside our band, but because of our underlying strengths in other areas, we said, "Let's go for it." We understood steel because HMK has long owned a steel company. Cyclicality scares the hell out of most people, but it doesn't scare us; you can manage your way through a cycle if you have a financial structure that works. Besides, Gulf States had taken out an enormous amount of costs during the past four years, but had received no valuation for it. The owners looked at it as a steel mill, and didn't know how to position it strategically. When Ben looked at what the company would have earned in earlier years if the cost restructuring had already been in place, we saw the multiple going through the roof.

Steve Karol had championed the project from the beginning. He recalled:

> Gulf States fit our criteria in many respects, so it was not really out of bounds. True, it was much larger than our parameters and was doing well, but some of the performance at the time was buoyed by the market. More fundamentally, it had a strategic dilemma. Gulf States was an integrated mill well into Q4, yet many believed that in the new world of

minimills, the old integrated model wouldn't work anymore. So we bought a company that no one else wanted, and were able to get it at an extremely low price. We then immediately embarked on a strategic planning process to reposition the company and take advantage of its Q4 strengths.

Strategy Development

Karol described strategy as "the science of positioning your company so it is successful," and the process he led at acquired companies relied on a host of well-known strategic concepts and tools. Karol had pulled these ideas together into a chart that served as a rough, linear map of what was in practice an iterative process (see Exhibit 4). The most recent version of the chart highlighted two important aspects of his approach: its foundation in research and its organization as a funnel. Karol believed that structured research about a company's strengths and weaknesses, markets, competitors, and technology must inform every aspect of strategy development and must become ingrained in managers. He also believed that action plans should be the outcome of a process that funneled or narrowed over time, moving from broad concepts like purpose and vision to targeted questions of competitive positioning and culminating eventually in highly specific action plans.

EXHIBIT 4   Strategic Framework

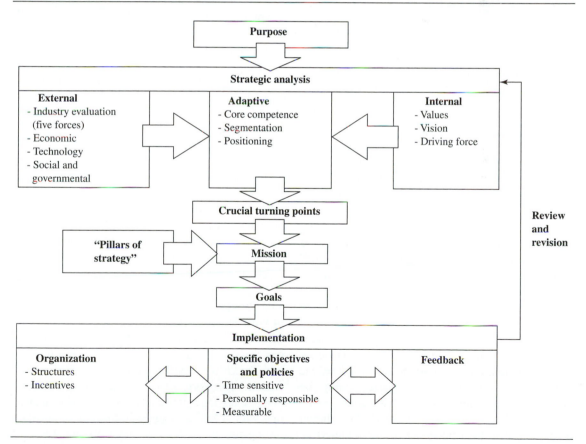

Source: Watermill Ventures

One of the first themes that Karol asked managers to explore was their underlying sense of the company's direction. His goal was to bring focus and coherence to their efforts because he had found, when working with "strategically challenged" companies, that factions of people were invariably moving in conflicting directions on issues such as pricing, distribution, plant configuration, customer relations, and product development. For this reason, Karol viewed the strategic process as essential for building a senior team that owned the strategy and worked together to implement it. He had strong views on the subject: "If I had to choose, I would prefer a bad strategy implemented effectively by a great group of people over a great strategy and lousy implementation." Karol was sensitive to his own role in leading the process:

> When you own the pen, what gets written tends to be in your handwriting. I've learned the hard way that in those situations, I can't err by being too neutral, but I can be too opinionated. After all, the walls of the room will be covered with charts that I've written, so I'm going to be represented in any event. If, in addition, I try to put myself on the walls, it's going to be *my* strategy, not theirs.

Six concepts provided the foundation for WMV's approach to strategy development: purpose, vision, values, driving force, core competencies, and goals. Purpose was why a company existed—its value to society, as contrasted with its value to shareholders. Karol explained: "Purpose answers the 'why' question. Why do you exist? Why does the world need specialty steel? What value do you add to society? What does society do with your product or service?" Vision referred to where the company could be in the future, which was often quite different from its current positioning and performance. Values provided guidance for action. When discussing them, Karol contrasted the product recalls of Tylenol and Perrier, noting the difference that Johnson & Johnson's credo made. He did not dictate what a company's values should be, but insisted that managers agree on a shared set of principles. Driving force was an idea adopted from the writer and consultant Michel Robert. Robert argued that one and only one motive or engine could drive a company, and that a choice had to be made among 10 possible approaches or driving forces. For example, a company could be product/service concept driven, building its business around a single product or service; user/customer class driven, focusing its business on a specific category of end users or customers; production capacity/capability driven, investing heavily in plant and facilities and then maintaining high levels of capacity utilization; or sales/marketing-method driven, basing its business on a unique selling or marketing approach. Each of these driving forces gave a company momentum in a particular direction and allowed it to draw critical lines between the products, markets, and users it would pursue and those it would not. Karol observed: "If strategy is positioning your company so that it can be successful, choosing a driving force is the way you focus the company on that position." Finally, core competencies were the skills and abilities a company needed to perform well to achieve its purpose.

These abstract ideas were translated into action using three additional concepts: turning points, mission, and goals. Turning points were the key opportunities, threats, and challenges that a company had to navigate successfully to move from vision to reality. Once they were identified and ranked, a mission could be derived, giving the company a clear direction and a definable list of goals to be accomplished. These, in turn, were further refined and then assigned to individuals with due dates, milestones, and specific targets.

The Process in Action: Strategy Development at Gulf States Steel

Immediately after acquiring Gulf States, Karol began the strategic process. He scheduled a meeting with the GSS executive team in June, and even assigned homework. Over the next seven months, Gulf States vice presidents and general managers met with WMV executives in three sessions, each lasting two days. All were held off-site. Between meetings, managers conducted extensive research and analysis, and they met weekly over lunch to review their progress.

First Meeting: June 3–4, 1995. Prior to the meeting, participants were asked to read excerpts from several books on strategy, including Robert's work on driving force. They were also asked to interview customers, suppliers, and employees about Gulf States' strengths and weaknesses. To ensure objectivity' managers hired a market research firm to conduct the customer interviews. The results showed that employees had a sharply different profile of the company's strengths and weaknesses than did customers.

Early in the session, Karol outlined the basics of the strategy development process and introduced a number of concepts. One Gulf States manager recalled:

> We felt lost in all that purpose and vision stuff, and had a tough time figuring out where he was going. Finally, Steve changed the order that he usually followed, and went directly to driving force. We then spent a lot of time talking about who we are, who we're not, what we should do, and what we shouldn't do.

The group continued the discussion over dinner and the following morning. As they dug into Robert's work, many felt that for the first time, they could see themselves reflected in the abstract literature. The team concluded that Gulf States was a production capacity/capability–driven company that had to optimize its heavy investment in facilities by running at or near capacity. At the same time, managers recognized that they had to become more market driven, and perhaps think differently about the segments they served.

Once the driving force was clarified, managers defined their purpose, and then the required core competencies. They developed two: being the low-cost producer, and vertical marketing, which meant identifying, selecting, and serving desirable market segments and customers. The group then decided to commission a major marketing survey to find out how their customers saw them. Managers listed 15 attributes for each product, and asked to be rated

against the best competitor on each one; they also requested rankings of the importance of each attribute to customers. Finally, the group developed 18 homework assignments for themselves; they were to be completed before the next meeting or combined with the market survey (see Exhibit 5). The meeting concluded with the drafting of a vision statement, based on the kind of company that managers saw Gulf States becoming.

Second Meeting: November 14–15, 1995. During the morning of the first day, the group revisited and slightly revised their vision statement; they then drafted a set of company values. After an interim report from the marketing consultants, Karol introduced Michael Porter's five forces model, and the GSS team spent considerable time applying it to each of their major products and markets.

In the afternoon, the group went outside and participated in a "paint ball" exercise that Karol had arranged. Dressed in old clothes and safety equipment, participants were divided into two groups and equipped with harmless paint guns; the objective was to score points by shooting (i.e., splattering with paint) members of the opposing team. Neither group could cross the line into the other's territory; halfway through the exercise, the teams changed sides and played again. Karol's team was the clear winner. Later, the group discussed the results. John Russ, vice president and general manager for sheet products, recalled: "We learned that if you have a strategy and work as a team, you'll win the game." Lefler elaborated:

> Steve's team took better advantage of the landscape and topography, as opposed to just firing bullets. They made a strategic decision about how to use the field to their advantage and were better able to look at the situation, develop a strategy, and move quickly.

Gulf States managers began referring to this approach as OODA—observe, orient, decide, and act—and added it to their list of desired core competencies.

In the middle of the second day, the group began developing a basic strategy, the Gorilla and

EXHIBIT 5   Homework Assignments between Strategy Meetings

Item	Description	Responsibility	Date
1.	List market segments that GSS could dominate.	ALL	8/24
2.	Develop subsidiary missions.	ALL	10/18#
3.	List advantages of minimill over integrated.	ALL	8/17
4.	List advantages of integrated over minimill.	ALL	8/17
5.	Needs versus capabilities—technicolor chart.	ALL	10/18#
6.	Study capital costs of strategy change to product differentiation—Is there a market to support it?	JFM/JWD/JOR/PPP	10/18#
7.	Develop competitive landscape for each market segment.	MARKET STUDY	10/4#
8.	Research technology opportunities, e.g., strip casting.	JPM/JWD/JOR/PPP	9/14
9.	Draft vision/purpose statement.	JDL	8/24
10.	Benchmarking—best in class by process.	JPM/JWD/JOR/PPP	9/14
11.	Implementation plan.	ALL	10/18
12.	Finalize vision statement.	ALL	8/24
13.	Develop action plans to increase competitive advantage.	ALL	#
14.	Develop action plans to deal with weaknesses.	ALL	#
15.	Ways to maximize opportunities.	ALL	#
16.	Action plan to deal with threats/problems.	ALL	#
17.	Segment customers by appropriate categories.	BUSINESS UNIT	10/4#
18.	Other customers/other competitors in segments.	BUSINESS UNIT	10/4#

= awaits market study

Source: Gulf States Steel

the Chihuahua, that they named after a slightly off-color story told by Bill Leaver the previous evening. The Gorilla was the steel mill, which had to be fed constantly to maintain efficiency. But throughput and high yields would not be enough to ensure Gulf States success against minimills or larger steel producers. The Chihuahua, small, gutsy, scrappy, and responsive, represented the other half of the equation—the marketplace and the voice of the customer: the small lots, odd shapes, narrow and light gauges, difficult chemistry, and superior customer service that, if done well, would make Gulf States the supplier of choice. (See Exhibit 6.) Karol reflected on the decision:

The Gorilla and the Chihuahua didn't come out of nowhere. It was the result of our detailed and concrete discussions of the external environment. That's why we contrasted ourselves with minimills, identifying what we could do better and where we were vulnerable. We also listened to what our customers were telling us and asked, what are the things they don't get from anybody else that they really want? Ultimately, strategy grows out of these details.

With the "pillars of strategy" defined, attention shifted to turning points, and the group developed a dozen priorities, including assorted upgrades to facilities and installing world-class information technology to run the business from order entry to payment. They then drafted a mission statement,

---

EXHIBIT 6 The Gorilla and the Chihuahua

GULF STATES STEEL

Pillars of strategy

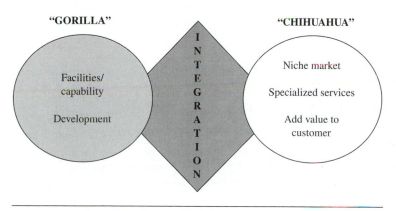

Source: Gulf States Steel

---

which was a broad set of directive and implementable goals, took a rough cut at specific goals, and developed homework assignments to be completed before the third meeting. Assignments included further analyzing customers and products and reviewing the agreed upon turning points, mission, and goals. A consultant attending the meeting suggested an additional task: developing matrices to assess the profitability of products by volume, customer size, order size, product size, and markets served.

Third Meeting: January 29–30, 1996. After minor revisions to the strategy, goals, vision, and mission statements, the greater part of the third meeting was spent analyzing the matrices that had been developed to assess product profitability. Few patterns were visible for sheet products because pricing concessions were often required to secure orders. In plate, on the hand, particular segments and sizes were clearly more profitable than others. These matrices became the basis for deciding which market segments Gulf States would

pursue and which it would pull back from; they also led to further revisions of the mission statement and goals. John Duncan, vice president and general manager of plate, recalled: "When we put together the matrices, they dispelled a lot of old notions, and we began rethinking our product priorities. For example, we thought our sheet segments were more profitable than they actually were." Collins added: "We concluded that we had to do more in plate, where our strengths and the opportunities are, as well as in the more value-added areas of sheet." Joe Magee, vice president and general manager of steel making, summarized the discussion: "The big thing here was the market analysis. No one had ever put one-tenth the effort that Watermill did into thinking through where we wanted to go and how we should be positioned."

The matrices also played a major role in shifting investment priorities. In the past, Gulf States had usually split capital between products. In fact, Lefler observed, "We often put sheet ahead because that's where the most trouble was." As a result of the strategic process, the approach to investment changed dramatically. Lefler recalled:

> When we sat down as a group, it was clear that the best decision economically was to move other investments earlier, in front of several sheet projects. The need to change our priorities was made easier by having everyone working together, conducting analysis that showed the differences in margins and the possibility of improving them even further through segmentation and new technology.

Duncan was extremely gratified by the vote, noting the difference in receptivity that the new owners and strategic process had made:

> Awhile ago I put together a long-range plan to invest in new technology, but the former owners weren't interested. Yet without this technology, we would be obsolete in three or four years. With Watermill I was allowed to present my proposal at the strategic planning meetings, and management bought in. We would never have gotten to this point without the strategic process. It got everyone looking at the plant as a whole.

Lefler agreed, citing the impact on managers' attitudes and perspectives. In the past, he observed, Gulf States had been told what to do by its owners, but now, for the first time, the senior team had come to their own view of "who we are. As we gathered and analyzed information, we began to shift from thinking reactively to proactively." Russ elaborated on the same point: "Before, we had just gone with the market. But after we spent time discussing what we could do well, what we wanted to do well, and what we needed to do to succeed, we began to see that we could dictate our own destiny."

Stimulating the Deal Flow

In March 1996, despite their satisfaction with the progress at Gulf States, Watermill's principals were becoming uneasy. They had not closed a deal in nearly a year, and many felt that the company's credibility was at stake. But what exactly was the problem? Was it that Watermill did not see enough deals, that it was not seeing the right deals, or that it was not seeing them soon enough? Or were Watermill's selection criteria simply too restrictive?

Part of the answer, Proctor believed, lay in "better refining and focusing our marketing efforts while broadening our base of contacts." He had already increased the intermediary database to 400 names, and planned to add another 100 every year. He had also been educating intermediaries about the kinds of deals that Watermill was looking for, and even helped them prescreen deals in their offices using the underperforming scale. Proctor had been speaking frequently at trade meetings and conferences, was refocusing the company's marketing materials, and was gaining confidence that "our name recognition is improving. People are getting to know that we are one of the few groups whose processes and financing are exclusively set up for underperforming companies."

To support these efforts, Watermill had decided to establish its own website. As of May 1, 1996, anyone with access to the Internet could be introduced to WMV's principals, acquisition criteria, and underperforming scale, as well as gaining background information on the operating companies of HMK, KODA, and WMV. Several of these companies had their own Web pages, which could be accessed directly from WMV's. In its first week, over 1,000 people visited the site. Most were intermediaries and brokers, while a few were sellers. O'Conor noted: "Ben is steering people to the website, and they are educating themselves about us."

But even with improved marketing and better access to intermediaries, increasing the deal flow posed a challenge. At WMV, all employees wore several hats. Karol observed:

> In most large buyout groups, everyone goes after their own deals and competes for funding in the acquisition committee. But at Watermill we have one focal point, Ben and Bill, who find all of our deals. That means we tend to have less flow than companies with more pipes. Besides, when Ben brings in a deal, he also works on the team that finances it. Who's getting the next deal while he's out financing the one we've got?

There was the further issue of Watermill's selection criteria, and whether they should be loosened or relaxed. Proctor asked: "Should we broaden our criteria to look at other troubled industries—high-tech, retailing, fashion—things that haven't historically been our strong suit?" A few months earlier he had been leaning in that direction; now, however, he was less inclined to alter the criteria. He argued: "The deal-doing business is a Q3 business with tremendous competition. We have to define our niche and stick to our guns."

Steve Karol was also considering whether Watermill should loosen its financing criteria. He observed: "It's not the deal flow that worries me; it's winning the bids. Because there is so much money chasing deals, it's driving up the price, and we are losing out." In 1995, Watermill had issued six letters of intent; none were signed because the deals went to others who made higher bids. Karol described the dilemma: "To make a return, we have to stick to what we do best. Yet the market is telling us that if we want to buy anything, what we think we do best may have to change."

Case 1–6

NOTE ON THE MAJOR APPLIANCE INDUSTRY IN 1988

The major appliance industry consisted of a fairly large number of products, including kitchen appliances such as cooking-ranges (both gas and electric), refrigerators, freezers, microwave ovens and dishwashers; and laundry products such as washing machines and dryers. The basic technologies and designs for most of these products, except for the microwave oven, were developed before the Second World War. Over the last four decades, technological advances in this business had primarily focused on the development of new features, improving energy efficiency, product standardization, and the exploitation of new materials. Given the consistently low or even zero rate of growth in the overall industry in recent years, competition had been particularly fierce and average profitability had been poor. Producers who were unable to achieve competitive cost positions or speciality niches had found it difficult to survive. An additional feature of the industry had been the increasing importance of distribution in the total cost structure, resulting from increasing concentration in distribution channels and a general shift of bargaining power from the manufacturers to the distributors and retailers.

Initially characterized by a high level of fragmentation, the industry was evolving toward increasing concentration, with seven companies accounting for over 50 percent of the global market (see Exhibit 1). Over 70 percent of the worldwide demand for household appliances was concentrated in three markets: the United States, Europe, and Japan. Each of these markets had developed along

This case was prepared by Sumantra Ghoshal and Philippe Haspeslagh, Associate Professors at INSEAD and Dag Anderson, Nicola de Sanctis, Beniamino Finzi, and Jacopo Franzan. It is intended to be used as a basis for class discussion rather than to illustrate either effective or ineffective handling of an administrative situation. The cooperation of the Electrolux company and its executives is gratefully acknowledged.

Copyright © 1989 INSEAD-CEDEP, Fontainebleau, France. Revised 1990.
Financial support from the INSEAD Alumni Fund European Case Programme is gratefully acknowledged.

EXHIBIT 1   The Seven Global Appliance Producers and Their Sales in 1987

Company	Sales in 1987 US $ billion
Electrolux/Zanussi/White	5.10
General Electric	4.35
Matsushita	4.18
Whirlpool	3.95
Bosch-Siemens	2.20
Philips	2.00
Maytag-Hoover	1.58

similar lines but had remained relatively isolated from the others due to differences in customer tastes and preferences, divergent technical standards, and the relatively high cost of transportation for most products of the industry except for a few items such as room air conditioners and microwave ovens.

The North American Market

In 1988, the North American market for household appliances was valued at approximately $12 billion. Whereas strong consumer spending and favorable pricing had allowed for a unit growth of about 3 percent during the 1986–1988 time period, industry observers were expecting a decline in total industry shipments over the next two to three years. Indeed replacement demand (accounting for over 75 percent of industry shipments) had been above normal levels, implying some borrowing of future business.

Overcapacity in the U.S. market had already resulted in a wave of mergers and acquisitions in the 1980s. Of some 230 mostly single product line manufacturers operating in the late 1940s, less than 10 remained, and of these 4—GE, Whirlpool, Maytag, and White, a subsidiary of Electrolux—accounted for 90 percent of the business. In 1986, Whirlpool completed its purchase of KitchenAid, White Consolidated was acquired by Electrolux, and Maytag merged with Magic Chef—all within six months. By now most of the survivors produced and sold all the major appliances.

Only one of the U.S. producers—Whirlpool—had started to position itself as a global appliance manufacturer. In contrast to companies like GE and Maytag, which had limited their operations to the United States and its adjacent markets such as Mexico and Canada, Whirlpool believed that significant presence in all the key regional markets was essential for its long-term survival in this business. As a result, it had pursued an aggressive strategy of geographic expansion. In 1985, it took a majority interest in Inglis, Canada's second-largest appliance company. In 1986, it acquired a 65 percent interest in Aspera, an Italian compressor manufacturer, and raised its equity interests in three Brazilian companies. Finally, in 1988, it bought into a strong presence in Europe by acquiring a 53 percent stake in Philips' major appliance business, with an option to buy out the remainder.

Besides increasing concentration, two other trends characterized the present situation in the U.S. household appliance market: a push toward full-line marketing leading to growing interfirm sourcing, and increasing competition in the high-price segments.

Strategic components such as compressors had a significant weight in the cost structure of domestic appliances. Their production is a scale intensive activity: For example, doubling compressor production can reduce unit costs by about 15 percent. Strength in component production, therefore, was a vital source of competitive advantage in this business. The resulting search for volume in component production had led to a widespread practice of private-labeling and cross-sourcing among the U.S. manufacturers.

Simultaneous to their search for cost reduction, companies attempted to improve profitability by focusing on the relatively stable and profitable high-end segment of the market. GE's Monogram line and White's Euroflair lines—both introduced in 1988—were developed specifically for this segment. Maytag traditionally served this niche and recently announced its commitment to further upgrade its product lines to strengthen the company's image among the more sophisticated and less price-sensitive buyers. Whirlpool—historically strong in the midprice segment but weak at the high end—had also made a determined effort to overcome this weakness through its acquisition of KitchenAid and its more expensive product lines.

One special case in the industry was Sears, which held a dominant position in the distribution end of the household appliances business in the United States, controlling some 25 percent of the retail trade. In order to preserve its bargaining power, the company actively influenced the structure of the supplier industry. The formation of Whirlpool, for example, was the result of a Sears initiative to merge two existing companies so as to create a single viable rival to GE. During the last three years, Whirlpool distributed more than 50 percent of its U.S. sales through Sears. Montgomery Ward, another large department store chain, had similar ties with manufacturers who supplied it with private label products.

Recently, specialized appliance and/or consumer electronics chains had made inroads against both the department stores and independant dealers on the basis of aggressive pricing. Industry observers regarded this development as leading not only to increased price pressure on the manufacturers, but also to facilitating eventual entry by foreign manufacturers.

The Japanese Market

With a population of 122 million people, Japan was second only to the United States as a single national market for household appliances. Matsushita was the market leader in nearly all product categories.

Hitachi and Toshiba were fighting for second position while Sharp, Mitsubishi, and Sanyo competed in the third tier. Exhibit 2 shows the market shares of the leading Japanese manufacturers for the main product categories.

Distribution of household appliances in Japan continued to be a very complex and fragmented system involving a host of small and large actors such as trading companies, producer-owned sales companies, several layers of wholesalers, and different types of retailers. Most wholesalers carried the brands of a single manufacturer. The leading appliance producers had tightly controlled distribution networks with their own sales companies and a large number of company-owned outlets that sold a diverse range of consumer products produced by the company including household appliances. Exhibit 3 shows the number of sales companies and retailers that were owned or controlled by the five leading Japanese competitors. This distribution system was, however, slowly changing, with the emerging independent supermarkets, speciality stores, and discount chains gradually increasing their share of the retailing market at the cost of the company-owned retail outlets.

In contrast to their own actions in other businesses such as consumer electronics, Japanese producers had been relatively slow in internationalizing their domestic appliance business. So far their international activities had been limited to the neighboring Asian and Pacific markets and, except for microwave ovens and air conditioners, they had

---

EXHIBIT 2   Market Shares (%) of Leading Japanese Manufacturers in 1984

	Refrigerators	*Microwaves ovens*	*Laundry machines*	*Electric ranges*
Matsushita	27.0	28.5	25.1	27.6
Toshiba	18.1	10.9	15.7	18.1
Hitachi	14.7	13.2	17.5	15.3
Sharp	13.0	31.9	9.0	8.3
Mitsubishi Electric	10.0	4.4	9.6	14.8
Sanyo Electric	9.2	2.9	13.0	10.2
Others	7.9	8.2	10.0	5.7

EXHIBIT 3   Distribution Networks of Leading Japanese Appliance
Manufacturers in 1984

Company	Number of sales companies in Japan	Number of company-owned retail shops in Japan
Matsushita	101	27,000
Toshiba	22	12,000
Mitsubishi Electric	14	5,500
Sanyo Electric	11	4,500
Sharp	1	3,800

---

made little effort to develop market shares in Europe or the United States. However, this was expected to change soon since many of the largest companies had now given explicit warning of their intentions to build up a strong global presence. The following statement by the general manager of Matsushita's corporate overseas office reflected this commitment: "Foreign makers are right to expect that Matsushita and other Japanese companies will enter the United States and European markets soon enough. The traditional makers won't be number 1 and number 2 forever." Even more direct evidence of the emerging Japanese vivacity was manifest in the words of John Bennigsen, director of marketing and sales of Toshiba consumer products in the

United Kingdom: "Every time I go to Japan, I lick my lips over the prospect of bringing some of our products to Europe. I think it is fair to say that we are seriously considering the European market."

The European Market

The overall market for household appliances in Europe was characterized by very low or, in some instances, even negative growth. As shown in Exhibit 4, the penetration levels for most products were extremely high in most key markets. There were significant differences among the various products, however, and while annual demand growth for washing machines was .4 percent between 1978 and

---

EXHIBIT 4   Penetration Levels in Selected European Countries, in 1981 (*) and 1985 (% of Households)

Country	Washing machines		Dishwashers		Refrigerators		Freezers		Microwave ovens
	1981	1985	1981	1985	1981	1985	1981	1985	1985
D	90	95	25	33	95	98	52	61	4
F	81	84	19	28	96	97	30	39	2
B	80	83	16	19	93	95	45	51	2
NL	87	91	11	13	98	98	44	52	na
I	88	95	16	18	89	95	28	35	na
UK	80	87	3	8	94	98	31	43	15
S	65	72	21	25	94	98	66	76	na

*1978 figures for The Netherlands, Italy, and United Kingdom
1979 figures for Sweden

1983, that for microwave ovens was as high as 40 percent during the same period. Similarly, while demand in countries like the United Kingdom and Holland has been stagnant, other countries such as Spain have registered significant growth.

In 1970, there were 695 producers of household appliances in Europe. By 1988, while some 300–350 fringe producers continued to survive, six companies—Electrolux Zanussi (25 percent), Philips Bauknecht (13 percent), Bosch-Siemens (12 percent), Merloni-Indesit (10 percent), Thomson (6 percent), and AEG (4 percent)—controlled 70 percent of the market. Currently, there was a manufacturing overcapacity of between 20 and 40 percent in Europe for the different product categories, and most companies had to struggle with low or even negative profitability in this business. AEG, Thompson, and some of the Italian manufacturers had survived only because of direct and indirect government subsidies. Lately, East European producers had vigorously attacked the low-price segments for products like refrigerators and cooking-ranges. Except in the microwave oven market, Japanese imports had not yet made any major inroads. As a production platform, Italy held the number one position with 39 percent of total European production, West Germany was second with 22 percent, France third with 11 percent, followed by the United Kingdom with 10 percent.

Major European competitors in the household appliances business could be categorized into three broad groups:

1. Companies that produced and sold in single national markets (national players).
2. Companies that produced primarily in a single country, but marketed in many countries through exports (exporters).
3. Companies that produced and marketed in several countries within Europe and outside (global or regional players).

GEC's Hotpoint division was a typical example of a national player. It was the leader in the washing-machine and dishwasher markets in the United Kingdom and probably one of the most profitable appliance producers in Europe with an operating margin of over 12 percent. Hotpoint only competed in the U.K. market, where it had a niche as a low-cost producer with a strong marketing organization. Managers of Hotpoint supported the company's nationally focused approach by pointing out the very limited penetration of international brands in the different European countries. Although these brands were often available in all major national markets, they typically commanded very small market shares in comparison to the brands of the local producers. To some extent, this was due to differences in customer tastes and national technical standards, which had made product standardization difficult. In the case of washing machines, for example, spin-speed and method of loading were two features for which different national customers had traditionally expressed very different preferences. High transport costs of the bulky finished products, high and fixed costs of advertising required to develop and support pan-European brands, the difficulty of obtaining shelf space in the retailers' showrooms, and the need for a fairly extensive after-sales service network were among the others factors that had so far helped the national players at the cost of the exporters and the global players.

A clear example of the exporter strategy was provided by Merloni, a manufacturer based in central Italy. Between 1984 and 1986, Merloni doubled its production and reached an output level of 1.6 million units, achieving the highest level of worker productivity in Europe (741 units per worker/year). Merloni believed that in the long run, its formula of centralized high-scale production in low-cost Italy with decentralized and differentiated marketing efforts in the different national markets would prove superior to both the national player and the integrated global producer–marketer strategy. To support this strategy, in 1987 Merloni acquired Indesit, a large but financially strapped Italian producer, which had strong marketing presence in a number of neighboring countries.

Electrolux provided a good illustration of the global players' strategy. The company believed that global-scale volume was absolutely vital for long-term survival in this business, and that local or regional production was necessary to build and maintain adequate market shares in all the major markets. While acknowledging the need to respond to the differences in tastes and preferences of national customers, they believed that those differences were narrowing and that market characteristics would converge. They also believed that by developing the ability to transfer and leverage product concepts, components, and manufacturing techniques from one market to another, they could develop insurmountable advantages over others with more new product launches and shorter development cycles. In the words of Mr. Anders Scharp, Electrolux's CEO, "Even if national differences persist for some years to come, there are many other ways of benefiting from economies of scale. For example, coordination of component production, such as compressors, motors, and pumps can quickly produce cost benefits . . . Besides, even at the finished product level, the trend is quite clear: new products are more international."

Case 1–7

ELECTROLUX: THE ACQUISITION
AND INTEGRATION
OF ZANUSSI

In recounting the story of Electrolux's acquisition of Zanussi, Leif Johansson, head of Electrolux's major appliance division, had reasons to feel pleased. Through financial restructuring and operating improvements Zanussi had, in only three years since the acquisition, gone from a massive loss of Lit. 120 billion in 1983 to a tidy profit of Lit. 60 billion in 1987[1]—a turnaround that astounded outside analysts and was perhaps more impressive than the expectations of even the optimists within Electrolux. More important was the progress made in integrating Zanussi strategically, operationally, and organizationally within the Electrolux group, while protecting its distinct identity and reviving the fighting spirit that had been the hallmark of the proud Italian company. Having been the first to suggest to President Anders Scharp that Electrolux should buy financially troubled Zanussi, Johansson had a major personal stake in the operation's continued success.

By early 1988, however, the task was far from complete. Not everything was going well at Zanussi: The company had recently lost some market share within Italy to Merloni, its archrival, which had taken over domestic market leadership following its acquisition of Indesit, another large Italian producer of household appliances. There had been some delays in Zanussi's ambitious program for plant automation. Moreover, a recent attitude survey had shown that, while the top 60 managers of Zanussi fully supported the actions taken since the acquisition, the next rung of 150 managers felt less motivated and less secure. It was not clear whether these problems were short term in nature and would soon be resolved, or whether they were the warning signals for more basic and fundamental maladies.

Though Leif Johansson felt it useful to review the integration process, his concerns focused on the next stage of the battle for global leadership. The industry was changing rapidly with competitors like Whirlpool and Matsushita moving outside their home regions (see accompanying "Note on the Major Appliance Industry in 1988"). At the same time some local European competitors like GEC-Hotpoint in the United Kingdom or Merloni (Ariston) in Italy were making aggressive moves to expand their shares in a relatively low-growth market. The Zanussi takeover and the subsequent acquisition of White Consolidated in the United States catapulted Electrolux to the top of the list of the world's largest producers of household appliances.

The challenge for Johansson now was to mold all the acquired entities into an integrated strategy and organization that would protect this leadership role and leverage it into a profitable worldwide operation.

---

[1] $1 = Lit. 1170 = SEK 5.85 (*International Financial Statistics, December 1987*).

Electrolux

In 1962, Electrolux was on a downward curve. Profits were falling and the company had not developed any significant in-house research and development capability. Compared with other appliance manufacturers such as Philips, Siemens, GEC, and Matsushita, it had a limited range of products: The core business was made up of vacuum cleaners and absorption-type refrigerators. These refrigerators were increasingly unable to compete with the new compressor-type refrigerators developed by the competitors, and sales of the once highly successful lines of vacuum cleaners were rapidly declining.

That same year ASEA, a company in the Wallenberg network (an informal grouping of major Swedish companies in which the Wallenbergs—the most influential business family in Sweden—had some equity shares) sold Electro-Helios to Electrolux for shares and thereby became a major shareholder. Electro-Helios was a technological leader in compressor-type refrigerators and a significant producer of freezers and cooking-ranges. This led to a major expansion of Electrolux's role in the Swedish household appliance market, but the company found itself in financial difficulty again due to rapid expansion of production capacity during a period of severe economic downturn.

In 1967 Hans Werthén was appointed CEO of Electrolux. In the next two decades he and the other two members of what was known as the "Electrolux Troika," Anders Scharp and Gösta Bystedt, would manage to develop the company from a relatively small and marginal player in the business into the world's largest manufacturer of household appliances.

Growth through Acquisitions

At the core of the dramatic transformation of Electrolux was an aggressive strategy of expansion through acquisition. At the beginning, Electrolux concentrated on acquiring firms in the Nordic countries, its traditional market, where the company already had a dominant market share. Subsequent acquisitions served not only to strengthen the company's position in its household appliance activities, but also to broaden its European presence and open the way to entirely new product areas. Exhibit 1 illustrates Electrolux's major acquisitions between 1964 and 1988.

With more than 200 acquisitions in 40 countries, and 280 manufacturing facilities in 25 countries, the Electrolux Group had few equals in managing the acquisition and integration processes. The company generally bought competitors in its core businesses, disposing of operations which either failed to show long-term profit potential or appeared to have a better chance of prospering under the management of another company. In addition, Electrolux always tried to ensure that there were sufficient realizable assets available to help finance the necessary restructuring of the acquired company. Thus, from the beginning of the 1970s up to 1988, the group made capital gains from selling off idle assets of more than SEK 2.5 billion.

At the same time, Electrolux had maintained flexibility in order to pick up new product areas for further development. A typical example of this was the chain-saw product line that came with the acquisition of the Swedish appliance manufacturer Husqvarna in 1978. By developing this product line through acquisitions and in-house development, Electrolux emerged as one of the world's leading chain-saw manufacturers with about 30 percent of the global market. Another example was provided by the new business area of outdoor products (consisting mainly of forestry and garden products), which had been grown from the small base of the Flygmo lawnmower business through the acquisition of firms like Poulan/Weed Eater in the United States and Staub/Bernard Moteur in France.

The two most notable departures from the strategy of buying familiar businesses had been the 1973 acquisition of Facit, a Swedish office equipment and electronics maker, and the 1980 purchase of Gränges, a metal and mining company. Both companies were in financial trouble. Electrolux had difficulty in fully mastering Facit. After having brought the profit up to a reasonable level, it was sold off to Ericsson in 1983. The borrowing

EXHIBIT 1 1987 Turnover by Product Line

Million Swedish kroner

White goods 28,476

Aluminum products 5,853

Vacuum cleaners 5,571

Forestry products 2,394

Food-service equipment and vending machines 2,356

Building materials services products 1,810

Garden products 1,761

Cleaning equipment 1,756

Air conditioners 1,793

Components 1,717

Car safety products – White 1,711

Leisure bathroom equipment 1,286

Kitchen appliances 1,691

Laundry services and equipment 1,132

Industrial laundry products 1,128

Materials handling equipment 1,140

Commercial laundry equipment 1,068

Commercial refrigeration equipment 790

Sewing machines 633

Sterilization and disinfection equipment 462

International Mining (360)

Agricultural implements (360)

Home electronics 236

(of which vending machines 211)

Sales billion Swedish kronor

Major company acquisitions and divestments since 1962

Companies shown beneath the drops have been sold

Year

1962 63 64 65 66 67 68 69 70 71 72 73 74 75 76 77 78 79 80 81 82 83 84 85 86 87 88

Electrolux Corp. vacuum cleaners

ElektroHelios white goods

Getinge sterilization equipment

Atlas white goods Elektra ranges

Flymo garden products ASAB, cleaning services

Euroclean, commercial cleaning equipment

Kent commercial cleaning equipment Quatfass, food-service equipment

Kreft/Seigas, absorption refrigerators

Ballingslov, kitchen & bathroom cabinets Vaxjo Rostfritt, disinfection equipment

Facit, office machines Wascator, industrial laundry equipment

Eureka, vacuum cleaners Emerson Quiet Kool, air-conditioners

Martin, kitchen ranges Tornado, vacuum cleaners

Husqvana, sewing machines, white goods Partner, chainsaws

Tvattman, laundry services

Therma, white goods, commercial appliances

Jonsered/Pioneer, chainsaws Tappan, household appliances

Columbus Dixon, commercial cleaning equipment Granges, metals

Oceanic, radio/TV Voss, kitchen ranges

Parts-Phone, vacuum cleaners Lequeux, sterilization products

Hugin, cash registers Norlett, garden products Progress, vacuum cleaners

Camping Freeze, caravan refrigerators ZK Hospital, disinfection equipment

Volund, industrial laundry equipment

Zanussi, household & commercial appliances, industrial products

Klippan, safety belts Sumak, commercial refrigeration equipment

Duo-Therm, air-conditioners Staub/Bernard Moteur, garden products

Zanker, washing machines Beijer Bygg, building materials

Poulan/Weed Eater, forestry & garden products

White, household appliances, industrial products Gotthard, scrap recycling

Tricity/Stott Benham, white goods, food-service equipment

Design & Manufacturing, dishwashers

Bruynzeel, materials handling equipment Unidad Hermetica, compressors

Corbero/Domar, white goods Alpeninox, food-service equipment

Britax/Kolb/Cooldrive, safety belts Alfatec, vacuum cleaners A & E Systems, caravan enhancements

Granges Kraft, hydro electric power

Facit, office machines Hugin, cash registers

Platzer (Granges division), contractors

Emerson Quiet Kool, air conditioners

Metallverken/Wirsbo (formerly Granges divisions) metals tubes

Oceanic radio/TV

necessary to buy Gränges, combined with the worldwide economic downturn and rising interest rates, pushed Electrolux into a sobering two-year decline (1981–1983) of its profit margin. However, through the Gränges takeover Electrolux also acquired new businesses for future growth. An example was the manufacturing of seat belts, now concentrated in the subsidiary Electrolux Autoliv. Nevertheless, the acquisition of Gränges would be the last diversifying acquisition.

Even though Electrolux had dealt with a large number of acquisitions, specific companies were seldom targeted. In the words of Anders Scharp, "You never choose an acquisition, opportunities just come." The company made it a practice to simulate what the merger combination with other companies would result in should they come up for sale. The financial aspects of an acquisition were considered to be very important. The company usually ensured that it paid less for a company than the total asset value of the company, and not for what Electrolux would bring to the party.

Based on their experience, managers at Electrolux believed that there was no standard method for treating acquisitions: Each case was unique and had to be dealt with differently. Typically, however, Electrolux moved quickly at the beginning of the integration process. It identified the key action areas and created task forces consisting of managers from both Electrolux and the acquired company in order to address each of the issues on a time-bound basis. Such joint task forces were believed to help foster management confidence and commitment and create avenues for reciprocal information flows. Objectives were clearly specified, milestones were identified, and the first phase of integration was generally completed within three to six months so as to create and maintain momentum. The top management of an acquired company was often replaced, but the middle management was kept intact. As Anders Scharp explained, "The risk of losing general management competence is small when it is a poorly performing company. Electrolux is prepared to take this risk. It is, however, important that we do not change the marketing and sales staff."

Electrolux Prior to the Acquisition of Zanussi

The activities of the Electrolux group in 1984, prior to the acquisition of Zanussi, covered 26 product lines within five business areas, namely household appliances, forestry and garden products, industrial products, commercial services, and metal and mining (Gränges). Total sales revenue had increased from SEK 1.1 billion in 1967 to SEK 34.5 billion in 1984. The household appliance area (including white goods, special refrigerators, floor-care products, and sewing machines) accounted for approximately 52 percent of total Group Sales in 1984. Gränges was the second largest area with nearly 21.5 percent of total sales. The third area, industrial products, provided heavy equipment for food services, semi-industrial laundries, and commercial cleaning.

By the 1980s Electrolux had become one of the world's largest manufacturers of white goods with production facilities in Europe and North America and a small presence in Latin America and the Far East. The Group's reliance upon the Scandinavian markets was still considerable. (See Exhibit 2.) More than 30 percent of sales came from Sweden, Norway, and Denmark. European sales, focusing mainly on Scandinavia and Western Europe, constituted 65 percent of total Group sales. The United States had emerged as the single most important market with 28.9 percent (1987) of total sales.

Electrolux's household appliances were manufactured in plants with specialized assembly lines. Regional manufacturing operations were focused on local brands and designs and established distribution networks. Sales forces for the various brands had been kept separate, though support functions such as physical distribution, stocking, order taking, and invoicing might be integrated. With increasing plant automation and product differentiation, the number of models and the volume produced in any given plant had risen sharply. As described by Anders Scharp, "We recognized that expansion means higher volumes, which create scope for rationalization. Rationalization means better margins, which are essential to boost our competitive strength."

One important characteristic of Electrolux was the astonishingly small corporate headquarters at

EXHIBIT 2   Electrolux Group Key Data

1. Group Sales and Employees Worldwide

Nordic Countries

	Sales SEKm	No. of Employees
Sweden	11,128	29,456
Denmark	1,735	3,078
Norway	1,505	1,299
Finland	1,445	1,563
	15,813	35,396

Rest of Europe

	Sales SEKm	No. of Employees
Great Britain	6,377	10,589
France	5,098	8,753
West Germany	4,045	3,317
Italy	3,684	15,282
Switzerland	1,818	1,814
Spain	1,445	2,851
Netherlands	1,238	1,016
Belgium and Luxembourg	913	1,040
Austria	392	958
Portugal	96	193
Others	604	41
	25,710	45,854

Asia

	Sales SEKm	No. of Employees
Japan	707	1,175
Saudi Arabia	215	738
Hong Kong	152	1,340
Philippines	150	525
Kuwait	147	2,220
Taiwan	119	2,178
Malaysia	72	1,833
Thailand	56	15
Singapore	50	556
Jordan	28	137
Lebanon	22	35
Others	720	1,729
	2,438	12,481

North America

	Sales SEKm	No. of Employees
USA	19,488	29,750
Canada	1,580	2,150
	21,068	31,900

Latin America

	Sales SEKm	No. of Employees
Brazil	302	6,215
Venezuela	208	1,032
Peru	181	750
Colombia	104	1,865
Mexico	66	1,735
Ecuador	34	232
Guatemala	24	31
Others	443	198
	1,362	12,058

Africa

	Sales SEKm	No. of Employees
	414	

Oceania

	Sales SEKm	No. of Employees
Australia	497	2,216
New Zealand	114	557
Others	14	—
	625	2,773
TOTAL	67,016	140,462

(*continued*)

EXHIBIT 2   *(concluded)*

2. Sales by Business Area

	1987 SEKm	*1986 SEKm*	*1985 SEKm*	*% OF TOTAL sales of 87*
Household appliances	39,487	31,378	19,200	58.6
Commercial appliances	5,619	4,250	3,348	8.3
Commercial services	2,893	2,504	2,266	4.3
Outdoor products	4,475	2,909	2,990	6.6
Industrial products	11,784	9,087	9,232	17.5
Building components	3,172	2,962	2,652	4.7
Total	67,430	53,090	39,688	100.0

3. Operating Income after Depreciation by Business Area

	1987 SEKm	*1986 SEKm*	*1985 SEKm*	*% OF TOTAL sales of 87*
Household appliances	2,077	1,947	1,589	49.2
Commercial appliances	484	349	260	11.4
Commercial services	169	172	132	4.0
Outdoor products	421	241	373	10.0
Industrial products	910	474	657	21.5
Building components	164	138	126	3.9
Total	4,225	3,321	3,137	100.0

Lilla Essingen, six kilometers outside the center of Stockholm, and the relatively few people who worked in central staff departments. The size of headquarters was a direct outcome of the company's commitment to decentralization. "I believe that we have at least two hierarchical levels fewer than other companies of the same size," said Scharp, "and all operational matters are decentralized to the subsidiaries." However, most strategic issues, such as investment programs, and product range decisions were dealt with at headquarters. The subsidiaries were considered to be profit centers and were evaluated primarily on their returns on net assets as compared with the targets set by the corporate office. Presidents of the diversified subsidiaries reported directly to Scharp, while others reported to the heads of the different product lines.

The Acquisition of Zanussi

In June 1983, Leif Johansson, the 32-year-old head of Electrolux's major appliance division,

received a proposal from Mr. Candotti, head of Zanussi's major appliance division in France, from whom he had been "sourcing" refrigerators for the French market. The proposal called for the investment of a small amount of money in Zanussi so as to secure future supplies from the financially troubled Italian producer. The next day Johansson called Anders Scharp to ask "Why don't we buy all of it?," thereby triggering a process that led to the largest acquisition in the history of the household appliance industry and in the Swedish business world.

Zanussi

Having begun in 1916 as a small workshop in Pordenone, a little town in northeast Italy, where Antonio Zanussi produced a few wood-burning cookers, Zanussi had grown by the early 1980s to be the second-largest privately owned company in Italy with more than 30,000 employees, 50 factories, and 13 foreign sales companies. Most of the growth came in the 1950s and 1960s under the leadership of Lino Zanussi, who understood the necessity of having not only a complete range of products but also a well-functioning distribution and sales network. Lino Zanussi established several new factories within Italy and added cookers, refrigerators, and washing machines to the product range. In 1958 he launched a major drive to improve exports out of Italy and established the first foreign branch office in Paris in 1962. Similar branches were soon opened in other European countries and the first foreign manufacturing subsidiary, IBELSA, was set up in Madrid in 1965. Through a series of acquisitions of Italian producers of appliances and components, Zanussi became one of the most vertically integrated manufacturers in Europe, achieving full control over all activities ranging from component manufacturing to final sales and service. It is rumored that, during this period of heady success, Zanussi had very seriously considered launching a takeover bid for Electrolux, then a struggling Swedish company less than half Zanussi's size.

The company's misfortunes started in 1968 when Lino Zanussi and several other company executives died in an air crash. Over the next 15 years the new management carved out a costly program of unrelated diversification into fields such as color televisions, prefabricated housing, real estate, and community centers. The core business of domestic appliances languished for want of capital, while the new businesses incurred heavy losses. By 1982, the company had amassed debts of over Lit. 1300 billion and was losing over Lit. 100 billion a year on operations (see Exhibit 3 for the consolidated financial statements during this period).

Between 1982 and 1984, Zanussi tried to rectify the situation by selling off many of the loss-making subsidiaries, reducing the rest of the workforce by over 4,400 people, and focusing on its core activities. However, given the large debt burden and the need for heavy investment in order to rebuild the domestic appliance business, a fresh injection of capital was essential and the company began its search for a partner.

The Acquisition Process

The process of Electrolux's acquisition of Zanussi formally commenced when Enrico Cuccia, the informal head of Mediobanca and the most powerful financier in Italy, approached Hans Werthén on November 30, 1983, about the possibility of Electrolux rescuing Zanussi from impending financial collapse. It was not by chance that the grand old man of Mediobanca arrived in Sweden. Mr. Cuccia had close links to the Agnelli family—the owners of Fiat, the largest industrial group in Italy—and the proposal to approach Electrolux came from Mr. Agnelli, who wanted to save the second largest private manufacturing company in his country. As a board member of SKF, the Swedish bearing manufacturer, Agnelli had developed a healthy respect for Swedish management and believed that Electrolux alone had the resources and management skills necessary to turn Zanussi around.

In the meanwhile, Electrolux had been looking around for a good acquisition to expand its appliance business. Its efforts to take over AEG's appliance business in Germany had failed because the conditions stipulated for the takeover were found to be too tough. Later, Electrolux had to back away from acquiring the TI group in the United Kingdom because the price tag was too high. Zanussi now represented the best chance for significant expansion in Europe. "It was a very good fit," recalled Anders Scharp. "There were not many overlaps: we were strong where Zanussi was weak, and vice-versa." There were significant complementarities in products, markets, and opportunities for vertical integration. For example, while Electrolux was well established in microwave ovens, cookers and refrigerator-freezers, Zanussi was Europe's largest producer of "wet products" such as washing machines, traditionally a weak area for Electrolux. Similarly, while Electrolux had large market shares in Scandinavia and Switzerland where Zanussi was almost completely absent, Zanussi was the market leader in Italy and Spain, two markets that Electrolux had failed to crack. Zanussi was also strong in France, the only market where Electrolux was

EXHIBIT 3   Consolidated Financial Statements for Zanussi Group

Consolidated Income Statement for Zanussi Group (in million SEK)

	1980	1981	1982	1983
Sales	3826	4327	4415	5240
Operating cost	−3301	−3775	−3957	−4654
Operating income before depreciation	525	552	458	586
Depreciation	−161	−98	−104	−130
Operating income after depreciation	364	454	354	456
Financial income	192	330	284	279
Financial expenses	−407	−489	−647	−627
Income after financial items	149	295	−9	108
Extraordinary items	−53	−228	−223	81
Income before appropriations	96	67	−232	189
Appropriations	−53	−42	−409	−382
Income before taxes	43	25	−641	−193
Taxes	−7	−7	−10	−10
Net income	36	18	−651	−203

Consolidated Balance Sheet for Zanussi Group (in million SEK)

	1980	1981	1982	1983
Current assets excl. inventory	1559	1987	1811	2108
Inventory	965	1054	999	956
Fixed assets	1622	1539	2366	2902
Total assets	4146	4580	5176	5966
Current liabilities	1590	1832	1875	2072
Long-term liabilities	1273	1441	1864	2349
Reserves	259	301	472	627
Shareholders' equity	1024	1006	965	918
Total liabilities and shareholders' equity	4146	4580	5176	5966

losing money, and had a significant presence in Germany where Electrolux had limited strength except in vacuum cleaners. Finally, while Electrolux had historically avoided vertical integration and sourced most of its components externally, Zanussi was a vertically integrated company with substantial spare capacity for component production that Electrolux could profitably use.

From November 30, 1983, until December 14, 1984, the date when the formal deal was finally signed, there ensued a 12-month period of intense negotiation in which, alongside the top management of the two companies, Gianmario Rossignolo, the chairman of SKF's Italian subsidiary, took an increasingly active role. The most difficult parts of the negotiations focused on the following three issues.

Union and Work Force Reduction.   At the outset, the powerful unions at Zanussi were against selling the company to the "Vikings from the North." They would have preferred to keep Zanussi independent, with a government subsidy, or to merge with Thomson from France. They also believed that under Electrolux management all important functions would be transferred to Sweden, thereby denuding the skills of the Italian company and also reducing local employment opportunities.

In response to these concerns, Electrolux guaranteed that all Zanussi's important functions would be retained within Italy. Twenty union leaders were sent from Sweden to Italy to reassure the Italians. The same number of Italian union leaders were invited to Sweden to observe Electrolux's production system and labor relations. Initially, Mr. Rossignolo signed a letter of assurance to the unions on behalf of Electrolux confirming that the level of employment prevailing at that time would be maintained. Soon thereafter, however, it became obvious that Zanussi could not be made profitable without work-force reductions. This resulted in difficult renegotiations. It was finally agreed that within three months of the acquisition Electrolux would present the unions a three-year plan for investments and reduction in personnel. Actual retrenchments would have to follow the plan, subject to its approval by the unions.

Prior Commitments of Zanussi.   A number of problems were posed by certain commitments on the part of Zanussi. One major issue was SELECO, an Italian producer of television sets. A majority of shares in SELECO were held by REL, a government holding company, and the rest were owned by Zanussi and Indesit. Zanussi had made a commitment to buy REL's majority holdings of SELECO within a period of five years ending in 1989. Electrolux had no interest in entering the television business but finally accepted this commitment despite considerable apprehension.

Another major concern was the unprofitable Spanish appliance company IBELSA owned by Zanussi. Zanussi had received large subsidies from the Spanish government against a commitment to help restructure the industry in Spain, and heavy fines would have to be paid if the company decided to pull out. Once again, Electrolux had to accept these terms despite concern about IBELSA's long-term competitiveness.

Nevertheless, there was one potential liability that Electrolux refused to accept. In the later stages of the negotiations, an audit team from Electrolux discovered that a previous managing director of Zanussi had sold a large amount of equipment and machinery to a German company and had then leased them back. This could potentially lead to severe penalties and large fines, as the actions violated Italian foreign exchange and tax laws. Electrolux refused to proceed with the negotiations until the Italian government had promised not to take any punitive actions in this case.

Financial Structure and Ownership.   Electrolux was not willing to take over majority ownership of Zanussi immediately since it would then be required to consolidate Zanussi into group accounts and the large debts would have major adverse effects on the Electrolux balance sheet and share prices. Electrolux wanted to take minority holdings without relinquishing its claim to majority holdings in the future. To resolve this issue, a consortium was organized that included prominent Italian financial institutions and industrial companies such as Mediobanca, IMI, Crediop, and a subsidiary of Fiat. The consortium took on a large part of the shares (40.6 percent), and the Friuli region bought another 10.4 percent. This allowed Electrolux to remain at 49 percent. While the exact financial transactions were kept confidential since some of the parties opposed any payment to the Zanussi family, it is believed that Electrolux injected slightly under $100 million into Zanussi. One-third of that investment secured the 49 percent shareholding, and the remainder went toward debentures that could be converted into shares at any time to give Electrolux a comfortable 75 percent ownership. An agreement with over 100 banks that had some form of exposure to Zanussi assured a respite from creditors, freezing payments on the Italian debt until January 1987. At the same time the creditors made considerable concessions on interest payments.

One of the most important meetings in the long negotiation process took place in Rome on November 15, 1984, when, after stormy discussions between the top management of Electrolux and the leaders of the Zanussi union, a document confirming Electrolux's intention to acquire Zanussi was jointly signed by both parties. During the most crucial hour of the meeting, Hans Werthén stood up in front of the 50 union leaders and declared: "We are not buying companies in order to close them down, but to turn them into profitable ventures . . . and, we are not the Vikings, who were Norwegians, anyway."

The Turnaround of Zanussi
It was standard Electrolux practice to have a broad but clear plan for immediate postacquisition action well before the negotiation process for an acquisition was complete. Thus, by August 1984, well before the deal was signed in December, a specific plan for the turnaround and the eventual integration of Zanussi was drawn up in Stockholm. As stated by Leif Johansson, "When we make an acquisition, we adopt a centralized approach from the outset. We have a definite plan worked out when we go in and there is virtually no need for extended discussions." In the Zanussi case, the general approach had to be amended slightly since a feasible reduction in the employment levels was not automatic. However, clear decisions were taken to move the loss-making production of front-loaded washing machines from France to Zanussi's factory in Pordenone. On the other hand, the production of all top-loading washing machines was to be moved from Italy to France. In total, the internal plan anticipated shifting production of between 600,000 and 800,000 product units from Electrolux and subcontractors' plants to Zanussi, thereby increasing Zanussi's capacity utilization. Detailed financial calculations led to an expected cost savings of SEK 400–500 millions through rationalization. Specific plans were also drawn up to achieve a 2–3 percent

reduction in Zanussi's marketing and administrative costs by integrating the organization of the two companies in different countries.

Immediate Postacquisition Actions
On December 14, a matter of hours after the signing of the final agreement, Electrolux announced a complete change in the top management of Zanussi. The old board, packed with nominees of the Zanussi family, was swept clean and Mr. Gianmario Rossignolo was appointed as chairman of the company. An Italian, long experienced in working with Swedish colleagues because of his position as Chairman of SKF's Italian subsidiary, Rossignolo was seen as an ideal bridge between the two companies with their vastly different cultures and management styles. Carlo Verri, who was Managing Director of SKF's Italian subsidiary, was brought in as the new Managing Director of Zanussi. Rossignolo and Verri had turned around SKF's Italian operations and had a long history of working together as a team. Similarly, Hans Werthén, Anders Scharp, Gösta Bystedt and Lennart Ribohn joined the reconstituted Zanussi board. The industrial relations manager of Zanussi was the only senior manager below the board level to be replaced. The purpose was to give a clear signal to the entire organization of the need to change work practices.

Consistent with the Electrolux style, a number of task forces were formed immediately to address the scope of integration and rationalization of activities in different functional areas. Each team was given a specific time period to come up with recommendations. Similarly, immediate actions were initiated in order to introduce Electrolux's financial reporting system within Zanussi, the clear target being to have the system fully in place and operative within six months from the date of the acquisition.

Direct steps were taken at the business level to enhance capacity utilization, reduce costs of raw materials and components purchased, and revitalize local sales.

Capacity utilization: It was promised that Electrolux would source 500,000 units from Zanussi including 280,000 units of household appliances, 200,000 units of components, and 7,500 units of commercial appliances. This sourcing decision was given wide publicity both inside and outside the company, and a drive was launched to achieve the chosen levels as soon as possible. By 1985, 70 percent of the target had been reached.

Cost cutting in purchases: Given that 70 percent of production costs were represented by raw materials and purchased components, an immediate program was launched to reduce vendor prices. The assumption was that vendors had adjusted their prices to compensate for the high risk of supplying to financially distressed Zanussi and should lower their prices now that that risk was eliminated. A net saving of 2 percent on purchases was achieved immediately. Over time about 17 percent gains in real terms would be achieved, not only for Zanussi, but also for Electrolux.

Revitalizing sales: Local competitors in Italy reacted vigorously to the announcement of Electrolux's acquisition of Zanussi. Anticipating a period of inaction while the new management took charge, they launched an aggressive marketing program and Zanussi's sales slumped almost immediately. After consulting with Electrolux, the new management of Zanussi responded with a dramatic move of initially extending trade credit from 60 to 360 days under specified conditions. Sales surged immediately and the market was assured once and for all that "Zanussi was back."

Agreement with the Unions

In the next phase, starting from February 1985, the new management turned its attention to medium and long-term needs. The most pressing of these was to fulfill a promise made to the unions before the acquisition: the presentation of a complete restructuring program. This program was finalized and discussed with the union leaders on March 28, 1985, at the Ministry of Industry in Rome. It consisted of a broad analysis of the industry and

market trends, evaluation of Zanussi's competitive position and future prospects, and a detailed plan for investments and workforce reduction. The meeting was characterized by a high level of openness on the part of management. Such openness, unusual in Italian industrial relations, took the unions by surprise. In the end, after difficult negotiations, the plan was signed by all the parties on May 25.

The final plan provided for a total reduction of the workforce by 4,800 employees (the emergency phone number in Italy!) to be implemented over a three-year period (2,850 in 1985, 850 in 1986, and 1,100 in 1987) through early retirement and other incentives for voluntary exit. In 1985, as planned, the workforce was reduced by 2,850.

Paradoxically, from the beginning of 1986 a new problem arose. With business doing well and export demands for some of the products strong, a number of factories had to resort to overtime work and even hired new skilled workers, while at the same time the original reduction plans continued to be implemented. Management claimed that there was no inconsistency in these actions since the people being laid off lacked the skills that would be needed in the future. With the prospect of factory automation clearly on the horizon, a more educated and skilled workforce was necessary and the new hires conformed to these future needs. Some of the workers resisted, and a series of strikes followed at the Porcia plant.

Management decided to force the issue and brought out advertisements in the local press to highlight the situation publicly. In the new industrial climate in Italy, the strategy proved effective and the strikes ended. In 1987, the company made further progress in its relationship with the unions. In a new agreement, wage increases were linked to productivity and no limits were placed on workforce reductions. Further, it was agreed that the company could hire almost 1,000 workers on a temporary basis, so as to take advantage of the subsidy provided by the government to stimulate worker training through temporary employment. It was clear that Zanussi management benefited significantly from the loss of union power that was a prominent feature of the recently changed industrial scene in Italy. However, its open and transparent approach also contributed to the success by gaining the respect of trade union leaders, at both the company and national levels.

Strategic Transformation: Building Competitiveness

The new management recognized that, in order to build durable competitive advantage, more basic changes were necessary. The poor financial performance of the company before the acquisition was only partly due to low productivity, and sustainable profits could not be assured through workforce reduction alone. After careful analysis, three areas were chosen as the focal points for a strategic transformation of Zanussi: improving production technology, spurring innovations and new product development, and enhancing product quality.

Improving Production Technology. Recalling his first visit to Zanussi, Halvar Johansson, then head of Electrolux's technical R&D, commented: "What we found on entering Zanussi's factories was, in many respects, 1960s technology! The level of automation was far too low, especially in assembly operation. We did not find a single industrial robot or even a computer either in the product development unit or in the plant. However, we also discovered that Zanussi's engineers and production personnel were of notably high standards." As part of a broad program to improve production technology, Electrolux initiated an investment program of Lit. 340 billion to restructure Zanussi's two major plants at Susegana and Porcia.

The Susegana restructuring proposal foresaw an investment of Lit. 100 billion to build up the facility into a highly automated, high-capacity unit able to produce 1.2 million refrigerators and freezers a year. The project was expected to come onstream by the end of 1988. The Porcia project anticipated a total investment of about Lit. 200 billion to build a highly automated, yet flexible plant capable of producing 1.5 million washing machines per year.

This project, scheduled for completion in 1990, was the largest individual investment project in the history of the Electrolux group. When onstream it would be the largest washing machine factory in the world. Both projects involved large investments to build flexibility through the use of CAD-CAM systems and just-in-time production methodology. As explained by Carlo Verri, "The automation was primarily to achieve flexibility and to improve quality, and not to save on labor costs."

Implementation of both the projects was somewhat delayed. While the initial schedules may have been overoptimistic, some of the delays were caused by friction among Zanussi and Electrolux engineers. The Electrolux approach of building joint teams for implementation of projects was seen by some Zanussi managers as excessive involvement of the acquiring company in tasks for which the acquired company had ample and perhaps superior capabilities. Consequently, information flows were often blocked, resulting in, for example, a more than one-year delay in deciding the final layout of the Susegana factory. The delays were a matter of considerable concern to the top management of Electrolux. On the one hand, they felt extensive involvement of Electrolux's internal consultants to be necessary for effective implementation of the projects, since Zanussi lacked the requisite expertise. On the other hand, they acknowledged Zanussi's well-established engineering skills and the need to provide the local engineers with the opportunity to learn and to prove themselves. They also worried about whether the skill levels of the local workforce could be upgraded in time for operating the new units and looked for ways to expedite the training process.

Innovation and New-Product Development. Zanussi had built its strong market presence on the reputation of being an innovator. This ability had, unfortunately, languished during the lean period. Both Rossignolo and Verri placed the greatest emphasis on reviving the innovative spirit of the company, and projects that had idled for years due to lack of funds were revitalized and assigned high priority.

The results were quite dramatic and a virtual torrent of new product ideas emerged very quickly. The most striking example was a new washing machine design—the "Jet System"—that cut detergent and water consumption by a third. The product was developed within only nine months and the new machine was presented at the Cologne fair in February 1986. Through a direct television link with Cologne, Carlo Verri himself presented the assembly line at Pordenone where the Jet System was to be mass produced. By July 1986, demand for the new machine had reached the level of 250,000 per year and the company was facing delivery problems.

While the Jet System was the most visible outcome of the new emphasis on innovation, other equally important developments were in the pipeline. For example, the company developed a new rotary compressor to replace the reciprocating compressors that were being used in refrigerators. A major drive was also underway to improve product design and features through the introduction of IC chips. Interestingly, most of these proposals came not from the sophisticated and independent research center of the company, but from development groups located within the line organizations that produced the products. How to maintain the momentum of innovation was a major concern for Verri, particularly as the company moved into the larger and more complex projects necessary for significant technological breakthroughs.

Enhancing Product Quality.   Quality enhancement was viewed as the third leg of the strategy for long-term revitalization of Zanussi. At Electrolux, high quality was viewed as an essential means of achieving the primary objectives of the company: satisfied customers, committed employees, and sound profitability. Zanussi had a good reputation for quality, but the standards had slackened during the turmoil faced by the company for almost a decade prior to the acquisition. Committed to the policy that quality levels must be the same within the group no matter where a product was produced, Electrolux initiated a major drive to enhance product quality at Zanussi and set extremely ambitious

targets to reduce failure rates and postsales service requirements. The targets were such that incremental improvements did not suffice for their attainment and a new approach towards quality was necessary. The technical staff of Electrolux provided requisite guidance and assistance and helped set up the parameters for a series of quality improvement programs launched by Zanussi.

Carlo Verri was involved in these programs on an almost day-to-day basis. First, he headed the working group that set up the basic policy on quality for the entire Zanussi organization. In accordance with this policy, a Total Quality (TQ) project was started in May 1986 and a series of education and training programs was introduced in order to diffuse the new philosophy and policy to all company employees. Supplier involvement was an integral part of the TQ project. As described by Verri, "Supplier involvement was crucial. Zanussi's suppliers had to demonstrate their commitment to effective quality control. This meant that all the procedures for quality assurance, for tracking down failures etc., had to be approved by us. In other words, suppliers had to have the capability to provide self-certification for the quality of their products. They had to provide service within days rather than weeks, given that our plants were becoming automated. Our gains in flexibility and quality through new production techniques could be lost if the suppliers did not become equally efficient."

Organizational Revitalization; Changing Attitudes

One of the biggest challenges faced in the turnaround process lay in the area of revitalizing the Zanussi organization. During the troubled years the management process at Zanussi had suffered from many aberrations. Conflicts had become a way of life, and information flow within the organization had become severely constrained. Most issues were escalated to the top for arbitration, and the middle management had practically no role in decision making. Front-line managers had become alienated because of direct dealings between the workers and senior managers via the union leaders. Overall, people had lost faith in the integrity of the system, in which seniority and loyalty to individuals were seen as more important than competence or commitment to the company.

In addition, the acquisition had also created a strong barrier of defensiveness within the Zanussi organization. In its own acquisitions Zanussi typically eliminated most of the middle management in the acquired companies. As the acquired company it expected similar actions from Electrolux. Moreover, some Zanussi managers were not convinced of any need for change. They believed that Zanussi's financial problems were caused not by any strategic, operational or organizational shortcomings, but by the practices of the previous owners, including diversion of overseas profits through a foreign holding company in Luxembourg.

Finally, most of the managers were also concerned that both Rossignolo and Verri, with their backgrounds in the Italian subsidiary of a Swedish company, "were closer to Stockholm than to Pordenone."

In an attempt to overcome these barriers, Verri and the entire executive management group at Zanussi participated in a number of team-building sessions that were facilitated by an external consultant. These meetings gave rise to a number of developments that constituted the core of the organizational revitalization of Zanussi.

Statement of Mission, Values, and Guiding Principles.
One of the direct outcomes of the team-building meetings was a statement of Mission, Values, and Guiding Principles developed to serve as the charter for change (see Exhibit 4). The statement identified the four main values of the company: to be close to the clients and satisfy them through innovation and service; to accept challenges and develop a leader mentality; to pursue total quality not only in production but in all areas of activity; and to become a global competitor by developing an international outlook. Apart from these specific points, the statement also confirmed the new management's commitment to creating a context that would foster transparent and coherent behavior at both the individual and company levels under all circumstances. As described by Rossig-

nolo, "We adopted the Swedish work ethic—everybody keeps his word and all information is correct. We committed ourselves to being honest with the local authorities, the trade unions and our customers. It took some time for the message to get across, but I think everybody has got it now."

Management Development Workshops.
In order to improve the flow of information among senior managers and to co-opt them into the new management approach, a set of management development workshops was organized. The 60 most senior managers of Zanussi, including Verri, participated in each of three two-day workshops that were held between November 1985 and July 1986. The next tier of 150 middle managers of the company were subsequently exposed to the same program.

Middle Management Problems.
An organizational climate survey in 1987 revealed an interesting problem. The top 60 managers of the company confirmed strong support for the mission statement and the new management style. Conversely, the 150 middle managers, who seemed to feel threatened by the changes, appeared considerably less enthused. Their subordinates—about a thousand front-line managers and professional employees—like the top management, fully approved the change and demanded greater involvement. In response to this problem, it was decided that the 60 top managers should establish direct communication with the 1,000 front-line managers, bypassing the middle management when necessary. The decision was made known within the organization and a clear signal was sent to the middle managers that they should get on board or else they would risk missing the boat. At the same time, a special training program was launched for the front-line managers and professional employees in order to broaden their management skills and outlook.

Structural Reorganization.
Before the acquisition, Zanussi was organized in five "sectors," with the heads of each sector reporting to the managing director. The sectors, in turn, controlled the

---

EXHIBIT 4 Mission, Values, and Guiding Principles of Zanussi

Mission

To become the market leader in Europe, with a significant position in other world areas, in supplying homes, institutions, and industry with systems, appliances, components, and after-sales services.

To be successful in this mission, the company and management legitimization must be based on the capability to be near the customer and satisfy his needs; to demonstrate strength, entrepreneurship, and creativity in accepting and winning external challenges; to offer total quality on all dimensions, more than the competition; and to be oriented to an internal vision and engagement.

Values

Our basic values, ranked, are:

1. To be near the customer; 2. To accept challenges;
3. To deliver total quality; 4. With an international perspective.

Our central value, underlying all of the above, is transparence, which means that Zanussi will reward behavior which is based on constantly transparent information and attitudes, safeguarding the interests of the company.

Guiding Principles

1. A management group is legitimized by knowing what we want, pursuing it coherently, and communicating our intent in order to be believable.
2. Shared communication means shared responsibility, not power and status index.
3. The manager's task is managing through information and motivation, not by building "power islands."
4. Time is short: the world will not wait for our "perfect solutions."
5. Strategic management implies:

   - Professional skills.
   - Risk-taking attitudes and the skill to spot opportunity.
   - Integration with the environment and the organization, flexibility, and attention to change.
   - Identification with the mission of the firm, and helping in the evolution of a culture that supports it.
   - Teamwork ability.
   - Skill in identifying strengths and weaknesses.

Policies to Be Developed

Specific policies were being developed in the following areas to support the implementation of the above mission, values, and guiding principles: personnel, image and public relations, administration, purchasing, asset control, legal representation, R&D and innovation, and information systems. Members of senior management were assigned responsibility for developing policies in each of these areas, with completion expected by the end of 1986.

---

operating companies in their business areas. In practice, the sector managers were closely involved with the day-to-day operations of the companies under their charge. Both the managing director at the corporate level and the different sector managers had strong staff organizations to support their activities.

Verri abandoned the sector concept, even though the operating companies continued to report to the former sector managers who were now called managing directors. However, staff at the sector level were virtually eliminated and the operating companies were given full responsibility and authority for taking all operating-level decisions. Similarly, staff at the corporate level were also reduced very substantially, and the heads of planning, finance and control, organization and human resources, general administration, and legal and public affairs all reported directly to Verri. The four managing directors, the five heads of major corporate staff departments, and Verri constituted the executive management group of Zanussi. As chairman, Rossignolo concentrated primarily on external relations.

Integration of the Two Companies

As described by Leif Johansson, "With the acquisition of Zanussi, the Electrolux group entered a new era. In several respects we were able to adopt a completely new way of thinking." Much of the new thinking emerged from the discussions and recommendations of the task forces that had been appointed, involving managers from both companies, to look at specific opportunities for integrating the activities of the two organizations. In total, eight such task forces were formed: two each for components, product development, and commercial appliances, and one each for the marketing function and management development. Each of these task forces had met three to four times, typically for half a day each time. Their recommendations formed the basis for the actions that were taken to integrate the production and sales operations of the two companies, rationalize component production, and develop specialization in product and brand development within the entire Electrolux group. At the level of individuals, a bridge had been built between the top management of Electrolux and the senior management team of Zanussi, and further actions were underway for creating similar understanding and mutual respect among managers lower down in the two organizations.

Electrolux Components Group (ECG)

Following Electrolux's acquisition of White Consolidated in the United States in March 1986, an international task force consisting of managers from Electrolux, White, and Zanussi was created to explore the overall synergies that could be exploited within the activities of the three companies. The task

force concluded that integration opportunities were relatively limited at the level of finished products because of factors such as differences in customer preferences and technical standards and the high transportation costs. However, at the component level there were many similarities in the needs of the three companies, implying greater scope for standardization and production rationalization. As a result of this analysis, the Electrolux Component Group was formed at the beginning of 1987 as part of the newly created industrial products division at Electrolux. The group was made responsible for the coordination and development of all strategic components used by Electrolux worldwide. Since over 50 percent of the group's component production came from Zanussi, Verri was appointed head of this group in addition to his responsibilities as managing director of Zanussi, and the group headquarters were located in Turin, Italy. In order to preserve and enhance the competitiveness of the component sector, it was decided that 50 percent of the component group's sales must be made to outside parties and at least 20 percent of the internal requirement for components must be sourced from outside the newly formed group.

Integration of Production

At Electrolux, production, sales, and marketing had traditionally been integrated market by market. After the acquisition of Zanussi, all these activities will be reorganized into international product divisions and national marketing/sales companies.

The larger volumes from the combined operations made it feasible to switch to a system in which large-scale specialized plants, equipped with flexible manufacturing technology, would each produce a single product for the entire European market. This new "one product–one factory" strategy was exemplified by the new plants in Susegana and Porcia. Each of the product divisions carried full responsibility not only for manufacturing, but also for development and internal marketing of their products. In order to coordinate long-term development among these 43 divisions, three coordinators were appointed for "wet," "hot," and "cold" products respectively. Based in Stockholm without staff, each of these coordinators would be on the road most of the time.

Integration of Sales/Marketing

Similarly, it was decided to create single umbrella companies over the separate sales/marketing organizations in all countries. Given the long-standing history of competition between the Electrolux and Zanussi organizations, this would turn out to be a difficult and complex process. It was planned that in each country the stronger organization would absorb the weaker one. This did not mean, however, that the head of the larger organization in each country would automatically receive the top slot in the combined organization. A number of complaints arose on both sides over this issue, which became a source of much irritation. For example, it was because of this that Candotti, who had been the first to approach Electrolux for investment in Zanussi, resigned. In what remained a source of considerable frustration, Zanussi continued to operate through directly controlled sales companies in Germany, France, Denmark, and Norway.

Coordination among the marketing companies was achieved through an equally lean coordinating structure reporting to Leif Johansson, with an Italian manager coordinating all European countries and a Swedish manager looking after the rest of the world.

To facilitate operational coordination between sales and production, a number of new systems were developed. One, the Electrolux Forecasting and Supply System (EFS), involved the automatic coordination of sales forecasts and delivery orders. By 1988 computer links with EFS would be established in all European Sales subsidiaries and factories. The Zanussi evaluation system was changed to that of Electrolux, in which both sales and factories were assessed on the basis of return on net assets (RONA) rather than on a profit and cost basis. An overall RONA target of 20 percent was set for the Group as a whole.

Brand Positioning and Product Development

One of the consequences of Electrolux's history of international expansion through acquisitions was a proliferation of brands, not only in Europe but also in the United States, where the acquisition of White had brought a number of brands. The task of coor-

dinating these brands, some of which were local, others regional, and a few international, would fall to the two marketing coordinators, working closely with Leif Johansson and a task force involving product styling and marketing managers. The challenge was complicated by the fact that even the international brands did not always have the same position from market to market. Zanussi, for example, was not a brand name in Italy itself, where its products sold as "Rex." And its image in Sweden was not nearly as upscale and innovative as in other countries like the United Kingdom.

The approach chosen in Europe was to group the brands in four brand-name families, each targeted at a particular customer profile and destined to become a separate design family (see Exhibit 5). Two of these families would be international brands, based respectively on Electrolux and Zanussi, and the other two would regroup a number of local brands (see Exhibit 6). The goal was to develop an integrated pan-European strategy for each brand-name family. For the international brands, the strategy would involve high-scale production of standardized products in focused factories and coordinated positioning and marketing across different countries. For the families representing a collection of national brands, the products would again be standardized as far as possible so as to allow manufacturing on a regional scale; but each brand would be "localized" in its country through positioning, distribution, promotion, and service.

Mutual Respect and Understanding among People

Since the acquisition Anders Scharp, Lennart Ribohn, and Leif Johansson had ensured that they jointly visited Pordenone at least once every two months for a two-day review of Zanussi's activities and progress. Hans Werthén and Gösta Bystedt also visited Zanussi, though much less frequently. The visitors would typically spend some time touring one or another of Zanussi's facilities and then move on to preplanned meetings with Zanussi's top management. Over time these meetings had built a strong bridge of mutual respect between the two groups and helped diffuse some of

EXHIBIT 5   Customer Profiles

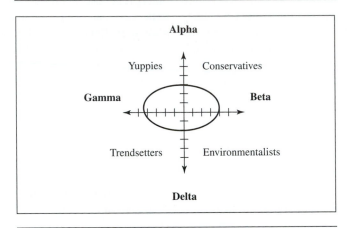

the early apprehensions. As described by a senior manager of Zanussi, "The top management of Electrolux really understands numbers. They look at a few key numbers and immediately grasp the essentials. That was very good training for us— we had the habit of analyzing and analyzing, without coming to any conclusions . . . Besides, the top two or three people in Electrolux have the ability of immersing themselves in a particular problem and coming up with a solution and an implementation plan. They are also so obviously excited by what they do, their enthusiasm is very contagious." For most senior managers at Zanussi these meetings provided stronger evidence than could any words that the top management of Electrolux did not consider the acquisition as a conquest but rather as a partnership. "We have had a lot of exchanges, and have learnt a lot from them, but we have not had a single Swedish manager imposed on top of us here."

At the next level of management the joint task forces had helped build some relationships among individuals, but the links were still weak and apprehensions remained. "We don't know them, but our concern is that the next level of Electrolux managers may be more bureaucratic and less open. To them we might be a conquest," said a senior manager of Zanussi. "In the next phase of inte-

gration, we must develop bridges at the middle and I frankly do not know how easy or difficult that might be."

Future Requirements.   Whereas the acquisition of Zanussi and White Consolidated had catapulted Electrolux into a clear lead in the industry, the race was far from over. After initially failing to reach agreement with Philips in 1987, Whirlpool had come back in early 1988 agreeing to buy out 53 percent of Philips' appliance operations as a first step to taking full control. Upon full completion Whirlpool would have paid or assumed debt totaling $1.2 billion for activities that in 1987 were generating $70 million pretax preinterest income on sales of $2 billion. The Japanese had started moving outside Southeast Asia. In the meantime, local European competitors such as GEC and Merloni were ensuring good returns and, more importantly, were gaining back market share.

All of this was taking place in a mature industry highly dependent on replacement demand. Industry analysts expected that, even in a moderately growing economy, appliance shipments would be on a downward trend for the next couple of years. Given the concentration of buyers and the shift toward specialized retailers, raw materials price increases were more and more difficult to pass on.

EXHIBIT 6   The Brand-Name Families

α
Alpha

Electrolux

β
Beta

Husqvarna   ZANKER

therma   ARTHUR MARTIN

Zoppas (Belgium, Italy)

γ
Gamma

Elektro Helios   ATLAS

Elektra   FAURE (Quelle)

CASTOR   privileg

VOSS   Zoppas (Norway, France)

STRÖMBERG   MARYNEN

δ
Delta

ZANUSSI
REX

Case 1–8

EMERSON ELECTRIC: CONSISTENT PROFITS, CONSISTENTLY

Charles F. Knight

When I meet with people outside Emerson, I'm often asked: What makes Emerson tick? That question typically reflects an interest in the company's consistent financial performance over the past three-and-a-half decades—but my answer deals with issues that go far beyond financial statements.

Simply put, what makes us "tick" at Emerson is an effective management process. We believe we can shape our future through careful planning and strong follow-up. Our managers plan for improved results and execute to get them. Driving this process is a set of shared values, including involvement, intensity, discipline, and persistence. We adhere to few policies or techniques that could be called unique or even unusual. But we do act on our policies, and that may indeed make us unusual.

Several assumptions underlie our management process. We believe, for example, that profitability is a state of mind. Experience tells us that if management concentrates on the fundamentals and constantly follows up, there is no reason why we can't achieve profits year after year—even in manufacturing businesses that many observers consider mature and unglamorous. We also believe that companies fail primarily for nonanalytical reasons: Management knows what to do but, for some reason, doesn't do it. That is why Emerson has a strong action orientation; we see to it that our strategies get implemented properly.

A third belief is that the "long term" consists of a sequence of "short terms." Poor performance in the short term makes it more difficult to achieve strong performance in the long term. The basis of management is management from minute to minute, day to day, week to week. Finally, it is crucial to "keep it simple." While effective management is simple in theory, it's difficult in practice. As Peter Drucker has noted, managers seem naturally inclined to get caught up in complicated ideas and concepts—ideas that look great on paper but just don't work. A corporation has to work hard to have a simple plan, simple communications, simple programs, and simple organizations. It takes real discipline to keep things simple.

My answer, therefore, to those who ask what makes us tick is far-reaching in its implications but uncomplicated in its substance: what we do at Emerson to achieve consistent performance at high levels is just solid management, rigorously executed. Interestingly enough, given our consistent performance, the dynamic impact of Emerson's approach to management is sometimes overlooked. Wall Street analysts, for example, tend to portray our stock as a good investment, but they also consider us a conservative and unchanging company. Yet a close look at what Emerson has accomplished in recent years reveals that we have changed a great deal.

For example, through our Best Cost Producer Strategy, we have spent more than a quarter of a billion dollars on restructuring and now have best cost positions in all of our major product lines.

We've moved from an export-led to an investment-led international strategy, resulting in a rise of international sales from about 20 percent to about 40 percent in the past five years. As a result of a $1.6 billion investment in technology during the 1980s, new products—those introduced in the past five years—as a percent of sales have increased from 9 percent to 20 percent. All the while, we've adhered to the discipline of constantly increasing earnings, earnings per share, and dividends per share.

The driving force behind all that change is a simple management process that emphasizes setting targets, planning carefully, and following up closely. The process is supported by a long-standing history of continuous cost reduction and open communication and is fueled by annual dynamic planning and control cycles. Finally, it is nourished by strongly reinforced cultural values and an approach to organizational planning that is as rigorous as our approach to business planning. It is an environment in which people at all levels can and do make a difference.

The Basics of Our Approach

In my view, the job of management is *to identify and successfully implement business investment opportunities that permit us to achieve the financial targets we set*. That definition is carefully phrased, and it constitutes the foundation of our approach to management.

The first step is to "set financial targets," since almost everything we do is geared toward reaching our financial objectives. When I came to Emerson in 1973, the company was already a strong performer whose stock traded at a premium relative to other industrial companies. We wanted to maintain this performance. We analyzed Emerson's historical record and the records of a set of "peer companies" that the stock market valued highly over the long term for growth and consistency. We concluded that, to maintain a premium stock price over

---

Emerson's Record

During the past several decades, St. Louis, Missouri–based Emerson Electric Co. has posted an enviable record for a U.S. manufacturing company. In 1991, Emerson marked its 34th consecutive year of improved earnings and earnings per share and its 35th consecutive year of increased dividends per share—a performance matched by only a handful of manufacturing companies in the world and unmatched by any U.S. company that makes comparable products or serves similar markets.

Since 1956, Emerson's persistence has rewarded investors, yielding an annual total return that has averaged 19.1 percent. According to a recent study by A.T. Kearney, Emerson is one of only 11 U.S. corporations that outearned its cost of capital during each of the past 20 years and one of only 22 industrial companies whose ratio of market price to book value ranked in the top 20 percent of U.S. corporations during each of the past 10 years.

Although it is one of America's leading manufacturing corporations, Emerson is hardly a household name. Many products bearing its brand names are better known commercially than Emerson itself. Among them are Skil, Dremel, and Craftsman power tools, Ridgid professional plumbers' tools, In-Sink-Erator waste disposals, Copeland compressors, Rosemount instruments, and Browning, Morse, Sealmaster and U.S. Electric Motors in the power transmission market.

Emerson's 40 divisions make a wide range of electric, electromechanical, and electronic products for industry and consumers. The divisions are collected into eight businesses: fractional horsepower electric motors; industrial motors and drives; tools; industrial machinery and components; controls and components for heating, ventilating and air conditioning equipment markets; process control equipment and systems; appliance components; and electronics and computer support products and systems.

long periods of time, we needed to achieve growth and strong financial results on a consistent basis—no swings of the pendulum, just constant improvement starting from a high level.

Consistent high performance requires ambitious and dynamic targets. Every year we reexamine our growth targets to see whether they remain valid, and we have recalibrated our growth objectives several times because the business environment has changed, or Emerson has changed, or we've learned something that causes us to see the world a little differently. In the early 1970s, for example, the general level of economic activity, plus the energy shocks and their inflationary aftermath, forced us to rethink our nominal and real growth rates. In recent years, we've targeted growth rates relative to economic growth as a whole, based on revenue targets above and beyond economy-driven expectations.

We have not modified our other financial goals, despite pressure to do so. During the 1980s, for example, we were criticized because we refused to increase our debt position. Given the then-prevailing attitudes toward leverage, our financial position appeared unduly conservative. But we regard our finances strategically: Maintaining a conservative balance sheet is a powerful competitive weapon. When we see an opportunity that we can finance only by borrowing, we have the capacity. By the same token, we're not encumbered by interest payments, which are especially burdensome during economic downturns—as the experience of the 1990s bears out so far.

Once we fix our goals, we do not consider it acceptable to miss them. These targets drive our strategy and determine what we have to do: the kinds of businesses we're in, how we organize and manage them, and how we pay management. At Emerson, this means planning. In the process of planning, we focus on specific opportunities that will meet our criteria for growth and returns and create value for our stockholders. In other words, we "identify business investment opportunities."

From a management standpoint, the most important decision a company makes is the level at which it plans and controls profits. For a corporation of our size, approaching $8 billion in sales, we are relatively decentralized. Our division presidents are responsible for identifying business investment opportunities and planning and controlling profits by product line. We do not have groups or sectors or other combinations commonly found in large, diversified companies. Although we recently adopted a new structure that gathers similar divisions into businesses to exploit common distribution channels, organizational capabilities, and technologies, we never aggregate financial reports for purposes of planning or controlling profits at levels between the division and the corporation as a whole.

Once we identify business investment opportunities, the next step is to "successfully implement" them. This is where many companies fail. Often implementation goes astray because the people who plan are separated from the people who have the

---

Emerson's Best Cost Producer Strategy

In recent years, the Best Cost Producer Strategy has been fundamental to Emerson's profitability and its success in global markets. Developed in the early 1980s, the strategy consists of six elements:

☐ Commitment to total quality and customer satisfaction.

☐ Knowledge of the competition and the basis on which they compete.

☐ Focused manufacturing strategy, competing on process as well as product design.

☐ Effective employee communications and involvement.

☐ Formalized cost-reduction programs, in good times and bad.

☐ Commitment to support the strategy through capital expenditures.

responsibility to make the plans work. The plans go to the bottom of an operations manager's drawer, and that's the end of them. At Emerson, the people who plan are the people who execute. They have ownership and involvement; it's their plan, not a corporate plan. That ownership makes all the difference.

Sometimes companies fail to execute because people are not permitted to complete the implementation. Systems in other companies may require putting good people on a fast track, giving them more responsibility, and promoting them. As a result, people are not permitted to stay involved long enough to complete what they start. In contrast, we try to focus on jobs and projects rather than status; we compensate people based on the importance of their jobs, not on the number of people reporting to them or the arbitrary need for a promotion.

The structure and everyday operation of Emerson embodies this basic approach: Set tough targets, plan rigorously to meet them, and follow through on the plans.

Two Underlying Principles

The first pieces of our management process were put in place during the 1950s, when my predecessor, W.R. "Buck" Persons, established two fundamental principles—continuous cost reduction and open communication—as central to everyday management.

The first of the two has correctly been described as a "religion" and "a way of life" at Emerson. Every year for the past three-and-a-half decades (in good times and bad), the company has set cost-reduction goals at every level and required plant personnel to

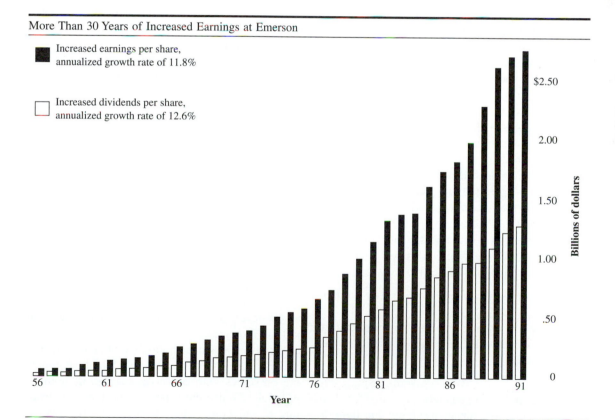

More Than 30 Years of Increased Earnings at Emerson

■ Increased earnings per share, annualized growth rate of 11.8%

□ Increased dividends per share, annualized growth rate of 12.6%

identify the specific measures necessary to achieve those objectives. Over that period, Emerson's cost-reduction programs have targeted improvements of 6 percent to 7 percent a year, in terms of cost of sales. During the 1980s, when fierce global competition challenged many of our businesses, we redoubled our efforts, aiming for still higher levels of annual improvement. Our present cost-reduction goals, developed by each division, average about 7 percent of the cost of goods sold.

We identify the programs that will give us 70 percent to 80 percent of our cost-reduction targets before the year starts. We know exactly what we're going to do: We'll install this machine tool to streamline that process, saving two-and-a-half man-years; we'll change this design on that part, saving five ounces of aluminum per unit at 75 cents a pound; and so on. Division and plant management report every quarter on progress against these detailed targets. Although this entire saving does not reach the bottom line, without this program combined with price changes, we would not be able to stay ahead of the inflation that affects our costs, and our margins would drop.

The second principle—open communication—is also fundamental to the management process. For decades, Emerson division presidents and plant managers have met regularly with all employees to discuss the specifics of our business and our competition. We continue this practice today because we believe people are more likely to be receptive to change if they know why, when, and how it's coming; they need to be involved in the process.

As a measure of communication at Emerson, we claim that every employee can answer four essential questions about his or her job:

1. What cost reduction are you currently working on?
2. Who is the "enemy" (who is the competition)?
3. Have you met with your management in the past six months?
4. Do you understand the economics of your job?

When I repeated to a business journalist the claim that every employee can answer these questions, he put it to the test by randomly asking those questions of different employees at one of our plants. Each employee provided clear and direct answers, passing both the journalist's test and ours.

Communication is a two-way street. We listen to employees and make changes when we hear a better idea. We also conduct, and spend a lot of time analyzing, opinion surveys of every employee. At many plants, survey information reaches back for decades and is a valuable resource that enables us to track trends. I personally review a summary of every opinion survey from every plant. When I spot a downward trend, I immediately ask the managers in charge for an explanation. It has to be a good one.

Best Cost Producer

Continuous cost reduction and effective communication became two central elements of Emerson's Best Cost Producer Strategy, which we developed during the early 1980s to meet global competition. The four other elements of this strategy are an emphasis on total quality, a thorough knowledge of the competition, a focused manufacturing strategy, and a commitment to capital expenditures.

The Best Cost Producer Strategy begins with a recognition that our customers' expectations for quality, broadly defined, are getting higher every day. To remain competitive, we have to meet or exceed the highest standards in the world for product performance, on-time delivery, and service after the sale. In this context, for example, the ideal of "zero defects" is not some high-tech dream: We've gotten to the point where defects are counted in parts per million—and I'm not just referring to electronic products. For example, on one of our electric motor lines, we have consistently reached fewer than 100 rejects per one million motors.

We also stress the importance of analyzing and understanding the competition. Simply comparing ourselves with ourselves teaches us nothing of value. We use the products and the cost structure of our competitors as the measures against

Return on Equity: Emerson vs. Standard & Poor's 500

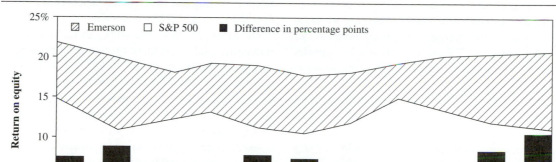

which we assess our performance. We do this in detail, legally and ethically, by taking apart competitors' products, analyzing the cost of components, knowing regional labor rates and freight costs, and more. If we want to make intelligent decisions about investing millions of dollars in a new plant to make circular saws, we must assemble as clear a picture as possible of the cost structures and overall plans of both our domestic and global competitors.

Once we understand the needs of our customers and the plans of our competitors, we develop a focused manufacturing strategy to produce more competitively and to provide better service. Among other things, this strategy means staying close to customers and vendors, helping them achieve their goals as well as our own. It also means that we compete on process, not just product design; that we focus strictly on manufacturing and aren't afraid to say so; that we address the issue of our installed manufacturing base and are willing to relocate plants, invest in technology, and make other tough decisions when necessary.

Finally, we support the elements of our Best Cost Producer Strategy through an ongoing program of capital investments. This commitment to capital ex-

penditures is crucial: It's the only way to improve process technology, increase productivity, gain product leadership, and achieve critical mass regularly. This investment program is made possible by our strong cash flow and balance sheet, which we view as a major competitive asset; effective asset management plays a major role in freeing up the needed cash.

These elements of strategy are not especially new or original. We think the key to success is closely tracking performance along these dimensions and attacking deviations immediately. Ten years ago, Emerson was not globally competitive in all its major product lines. Today we are, thanks to the intensity of our manufacturing approach and to the management process through which we make it work.

Making the Future Happen—Planning and Control

At Emerson, rigorous planning has been essential to the company's success since the 1950s; it's no coincidence that our long record of improved annual earnings dates from the same period. As CEO, more than half of my time each year is blocked out strictly for planning. Emerson President and Chief Operating Officer Al Suter and other senior managers spend even more time in planning sessions. We devote so much time to planning because that is when we identify business investment opportunities in detail—and because good planning takes time.

Each fiscal year, from November through June, selected corporate officers, Al Suter, and I meet with the management of every division for a one- or two-day planning conference, usually held off-site. These division conferences are the culmination of our planning cycle. The mood is confrontational— by design. Though we're not trying to put anyone on the spot, we do want to challenge assumptions and conventional thinking and give ample time to every significant issue. We want proof that a division is stretching to reach its goals, and we want to see the details of the actions division management believes will yield improved results. Our expectations are high, and the discussions are intense. A division president who comes to a planning conference poorly prepared has made a serious mistake.

Corporate management sets the stage. We require only a few standard exhibits, including a "value measurement chart," a "sales gap chart," and a "5-back-by-5-forward" P&L statement. (See Exhibits 1 through 4, which are reproductions of actual Emerson charts). While the list is short, it takes substantial planning and backup data to develop these exhibits. To prepare properly requires that division presidents really understand their business. Every piece of data we ask for is something division management needs to know itself.

The value measurement chart captures on a single page such vital data as long-term sales and profit growth, capital investment, and expected return. The chart displays the amount and type of investment and return on capital over the preceding five years, allowing us to see quickly the return on incremental capital. Add to this a forecast of capital investment and returns over the next five years, and we can see whether the division is earning, or expects to earn, a return on total

capital greater than our cost of capital. In other words, we can tell in a glance whether the division is creating stockholder value.

The sales gap chart and sales gap line chart display current sales and make projections for the next five years based on an analysis of the sources of growth: the market's natural growth rate, the division's change in market penetration, price changes, new products, product line extensions, and international growth. Should the projected growth not meet or exceed our target, the division faces a gap. Then it is management's job to tell us the specific steps it will take to close the gap.

The 5-back-by-5-forward P&L chart arrays current-year results in the context of five years of historical information and five years of projections. This exhibit shows not only sales growth but also gross profit margin, SG&A expense, operating profit margin, capital turnover, and returns on sales and capital. We look at 11 years' worth of data to spot trends. If they're down, then we want to see why we can't make the margins we used to make and what actions will bring them back. If they're up, we ask, "How much further can we drive them?"

Together, those charts tell us basic information about the business, alert us to any problems, and provide clues to the steps divisions must take to outperform the competition and produce results for stockholders. Beyond the required exhibits, the planning conference belongs to the division presidents. We're there to help them improve their plans and their results. We want to hear division management's views of customers and markets; its plans for new products; its analysis of the competition; and the status of such manufacturing issues as quality, capacity, productivity, inventory levels, and compensation.

We also believe in the logic of illogic. Often, a manager will give a logical presentation on why we should approve a plan. We may challenge that logic by questioning underlying assumptions illogically. The people who know their strategies in detail are the ones who, after going through that, are able to stand up for the merits of their proposal. In the end, the test of a good planning conference is whether

EXHIBIT 1 The Value Measurement Chart Assesses Value Creation at a Glance*

	Line No.	5th Prior Year Actual FY 1986		Current Year Expected FY 1991		5th Year Forecast FY 1996		5 Year Increment Historical CY vs. 5th PY		5 Year Increment Forecast 5th Yr vs. CY		10 Year Increment 5th Yr vs 5th PY	
		Amt.	% Sales	Amt.	% Sales	Amt.	% Sales	Amt.	% Sales	Amt.	% Sales	Amt.	% Sales
		A	B	C	D	E	F	G	H	I	J	K	L
Growth Rate and Capital Requirements													
Working capital operating—Y/E	1127	117.1	29.8%	120.2	21.8%	153.3	18.5%	3.1	1.9%	33.1	12.0%	36.2	8.3%
Net noncurrent assets—Y/E	1128	92.9	23.6%	150.0	27.2%	221.6	26.8%	57.1	35.9%	71.6	26.0%	128.7	29.6%
Total operating capital—Y/E	1129	210.0	53.4%	270.2	48.9%	374.9	45.3%	60.2	37.9%	104.7	38.0%	164.9	37.9%
Average operating capital	1130	201.1	51.1%	267.1	48.4%	370.4	44.7%						
Incremental investment	1584							66.0		103.3		169.3	
Net oper. prof. aft. tax (NOPAT)	1119	33.4		49.5		79.0		16.1		29.5		45.6	
Return on incremental investment								24.4%		28.6%		26.9%	
NOPAT growth rate								8.2%		9.8%		9.0%	
Capital growth rate								5.8%		6.8%		6.3%	
Rate of Return													
Return on Total Capital = $\dfrac{\text{NOPAT}}{\text{Avg. Oper. Cap.}}$		16.6%		18.5%		21.3%							
Net sales	0001	393.2		552.2		827.9		159.0		275.7		434.7	
Sales growth rate								7.0%		8.4%		7.7%	
NOPAT margin		8.5%		9.0%		9.5%		10.1%		10.7%		10.5%	
Operating capital turnover [T/O]		1.96		2.07		2.24		2.41		2.67		2.57	
Cost of capital	3000	12.0%		12.0%		12.0%							
Capital charge (L1130 × L3000)	3001	24.1		32.1		44.4		8.0		12.3		20.3	
Economic profit (L1119 − L3001)		9.3		17.4		34.6		8.1		17.2		25.3	

*In millions of dollars

EXHIBIT 2 The Sales Gap Chart Forecasts Five-Year Plans* . . .

	Line No.	Prior Year Actual FY 90 (A)	Current Year Expected FY 91 (B)	Forecast FY 92 (C)	FY 93 (D)	FY 94 (E)	FY 95 (F)	FY 96 (G)	5 Year Source of Growth % (H)	5 Year Company Annual Growth % (I)
Current year domestic sales base @ 10/1 prices	1		305.7	305.7	305.7	305.7	305.7	305.7		
Served industry—growth/(decline)	2			3.0	24.6	39.0	49.6	58.3	21.1%	3.6%
Penetration—increase/(decrease) (including—new line extensions/buyouts)	3			6.3	14.1	21.0	29.8	37.6	13.6	2.0
Price increases—current year through 5th year	4		3.3	7.6	14.7	21.6	29.5	38.0	12.6	1.7
Incremental new products — Prior 5 year introduction	5		16.1	16.4	17.7	17.4	17.5	19.0	1.1	
Incremental new products — Current year through 5th year	6		1.4	5.6	11.6	18.5	25.9	34.2	11.9	
Other	7		3.1	1.4	1.6	2.3	2.5	2.8	-0.1	
Total Domestic	8	363.7	329.6	346.0	390.0	425.5	460.5	495.6		8.5
Current year international sales base @ 10/1 prices	9		202.9	202.9	202.9	202.9	202.9	202.9		
Served industry—growth/(decline)	10			(0.1)	8.8	17.0	24.8	35.4	12.9	3.3
Penetration—increase/(decrease) (including—new line extensions/buyouts)	11			(0.5)	18.8	27.2	36.2	45.1	16.4	3.6
Price increases—current year through 5th year	12		2.0	4.9	8.5	12.5	16.9	21.7	7.1	1.4
Incremental new products — Prior 5 year introduction	13		6.9	7.1	6.7	7.1	8.0	9.2	0.8	
Incremental new products — Current year through 5th year	14		1.1	4.5	6.3	10.1	14.3	16.9	5.7	
Currency	15		9.3						-3.4	
Other	16		0.4	0.8	0.7	0.9	1.0	1.1	0.3	
Total International	17	204.3	222.6	219.6	252.7	277.7	304.1	332.3	100.0	8.3
Total Consolidated	18	568.0	552.2	565.6	642.7	703.2	764.6	827.9		8.4
Annual Growth %—nominal			-2.8%	2.4%	13.6%	9.4%	8.7%	8.3%		
15% Target—nominal	19			635.0	730.2	839.8	965.7	1,110.6		15.0
Sales gap—over/(under)	20			(69.4)	(87.5)	(136.6)	(201.1)	(282.7)		
U.S. Exports (excluding to foreign subsidiaries)	21	35.3	31.3	33.7	35.9	39.9	43.9	47.6		8.7
Foreign subsidiaries (excluding sales to U.S.)	22	169.1	191.4	185.8	216.8	237.8	260.3	284.7		8.3

Domestic Excluding Exports (rows 1–8)

International Excluding Sales to U.S. (rows 9–17)

Gap (rows 19–20)

*In millions of dollars

162

EXHIBIT 3   While the Sales Gap Line Chart Projects Sales Growth Against Other Targets

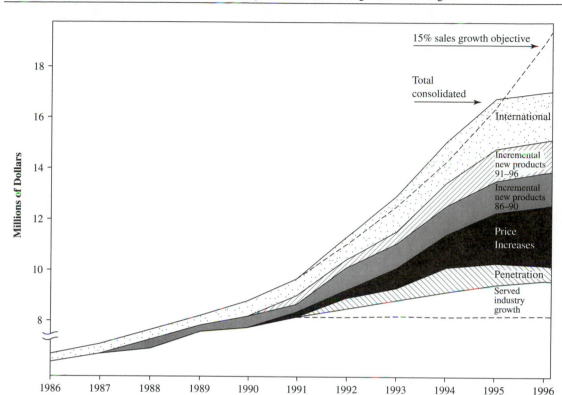

it results in managers taking actions that will have a significant impact on the business.

Since operating managers carry out the planning, we effectively establish ownership and eliminate the artificial distinction between strategic and operating decisions. Managers on the line do not—and must never—delegate the understanding of the business. To develop a plan, operating managers work together for months. They often tell me that the greatest value of the planning cycle lies in the teamwork and discipline that the preparation phase requires.

The Measure of Managers

The measure of Emerson managers is whether they achieve what they say they will in a planning conference. We track the implementation of our plans through a tight control system. That system starts at the top, with a corporate board of directors that meets regularly and plays an active role in overseeing our business. Management of the company is directed by the office of the chief executive (OCE), which presently consists of me, Al Suter, Vice Chairman Bob Staley, Vice Chairman Jan Ver Hagen, the seven other business leaders, and three additional corporate officers. The OCE meets from 10 to 12 times each year to review and discuss issues facing the divisions individually as well as the corporation as a whole.

Input from the divisions arrives in the form of their president's operating reports (PORs), monthly submissions that summarize the divisions' results

EXHIBIT 4 The 5-Back-By-5-Forward Chart Provides 11 Years of P&L Measures*

	Line No.	Actual/Restated					Current Year Expected FY 91	Forecast				
		5th PY FY 86	4th PY FY 87	3rd PY FY 88	2nd PY FY 89	Prior Year FY 90		Next Yr FY 92	2nd Yr FY 93	3rd Yr FY 94	4th Yr FY 95	5th Yr FY 96
		A	B	C	D	E	F	G	H	I	J	K
Order entries	1143	71,363	77,057	92,716	100,164	126,591	128,247	142,612	157,972	173,743	189,856	207,133
Sales backlog (year end)	1144	13,310	14,051	17,098	16,534	29,334	29,842	31,509	33,082	34,805	36,591	38,363
Net sales	0001	71,163	76,316	89,669	100,728	113,791	127,739	140,945	156,399	172,020	188,070	205,361
Annual growth %—nominal			7.2%	17.5%	12.3%	13.0%	12.3%	10.3%	11.0%	10.0%	9.3%	9.2%
—real							11.3%	7.8%	8.4%	6.7%	6.8%	6.1%
Cost of sales	0009	36,802	39,382	46,487	51,593	60,003	67,651	74,432	82,109	89,966	98,173	106,997
% to sales		51.7%	51.6%	51.8%	51.2%	52.7%	53.0%	52.8%	52.5%	52.3%	52.2%	52.1%
Gross profit	0010	34,361	36,934	43,182	49,135	53,788	60,088	66,513	74,290	82,054	89,897	98,364
% to sales		48.3%	48.4%	48.2%	48.8%	47.3%	47.0%	47.2%	47.5%	47.7%	47.8%	47.9%
SG&A expenses	0011	21,773	22,558	26,246	29,941	32,163	36,150	40,169	44,887	49,714	54,366	59,555
% to sales		30.6%	29.6%	29.3%	29.7%	28.3%	28.3%	28.5%	28.7%	28.9%	28.9%	29.0%
Operating profit	0012	12,588	14,376	16,936	19,194	21,625	23,938	26,344	29,403	32,340	35,531	38,809
% to sales		17.7%	18.8%	18.9%	19.1%	19.0%	18.7%	18.7%	18.8%	18.8%	18.9%	18.9%
Other [inc.]/ded. [excl.int.]	0235	423	1,090	1,395	1,232	1,488	1,764	1,766	1,794	1,530	1,438	1,423
Earnings before interest & taxes	0240	12,165	13,286	15,541	17,962	20,137	22,174	24,578	27,609	30,810	34,093	37,386
% to sales		17.1%	17.4%	17.3%	17.8%	17.7%	17.4%	17.4%	17.7%	17.9%	18.1%	18.2%
Interest (income)/expense, net	0230	(771)	(1,041)	(1,127)	(1,326)	(1,781)	(2,224)	(2,330)	(2,576)	(2,734)	(2,903)	(3,070)
Pretax earnings	0015	12,936	14,327	16,668	19,288	21,918	24,398	26,908	30,185	33,544	36,996	40,456
% to sales		18.2%	18.8%	18.6%	19.1%	19.3%	19.1%	19.1%	19.3%	19.5%	19.7%	19.7%
Income taxes	0016	5,445	6,785	7,788	8,447	9,668	10,551	11,753	13,101	14,497	15,948	17,387
Effective tax rate		42.1%	47.4%	46.7%	43.8%	44.1%	43.2%	43.7%	43.4%	43.2%	43.1%	43.0%
Net earnings	0017	7,491	7,542	8,880	10,841	12,250	13,847	15,155	17,084	19,047	21,048	23,069
% to sales		10.5%	9.9%	9.9%	10.8%	10.8%	10.8%	10.8%	10.9%	11.1%	11.2%	11.2%
Return on total capital	1324	20.4%	19.7%	20.3%	23.6%	23.8%	25.1%	26.1%	28.0%	30.1%	32.0%	33.9%
ROTC excluding goodwill	1323	27.3%	28.0%	27.2%	30.6%	31.5%	32.5%	32.9%	34.7%	36.6%	38.3%	40.2%

*In thousands of dollars

and immediate prospects (see Exhibit 5). We view the budget process used by many companies as static. In contrast, the POR is a dynamic tool: We update expected annual results each month and make rolling comparisons against historical and projected performance.

The divisions themselves are governed by their own boards of directors, with a member of the OCE serving as chairman. Other members of the board include the division president and the president's direct reports. The division boards are partly a legacy of Emerson's growth through acquisition, but more important, they are a reflection of the level at which we plan and control profits. The boards meet monthly to review and monitor performance. In addition, the president and chief financial officer of each division meet quarterly with corporate operating and financial management to discuss short-term operating results and lock in on the current quarter; we call these sessions "president's councils."

Each division president, along with appropriate staff, meets once a year with senior corporate officers for separate financial reviews. These reviews occur late in the fiscal year and are a review of performance against financial plan, with a detailed financial plan of the coming year.

At the financial review, we push the divisions to think through different scenarios and to plan and advance actions that different contingencies will require. We use a technique called ABC budgeting: An A budget applies to the most likely scenario, a B budget to a possible lower level of activity, and so on. As a result, our managers know well ahead that, if their business environment changes, they have a well-thought-through set of actions they can take to protect profitability. This contingency planning is particularly helpful in an economic downturn; we are not paralyzed by bad news because we've already planned for it.

Information generated for and during the division planning conferences and financial reviews becomes raw material for the corporate planning conference. We consolidate the data and take a fresh look at the aggregate at our corporate "preplanning

conference" about a month before the corporate planning conference, which is held in late September near the start of each fiscal year.

For the preplanning conference, we combine input from the divisions with an analysis of the macroeconomic environment. The annual planning conference itself, which includes corporate management and the top officers of each division, serves primarily as a vehicle for communication. Corporate officers share overall results and communicate the financial plan for the coming year as well as the strategic plan for the next five years. It is an ideal setting for sharing success stories and for challenging conventional wisdom.

So the wheel turns full circle, and we do it all over again. This may sound repetitive and boring. But paying attention to detail makes Emerson successful.

Management Development

We manage organizational needs with the same intensity as we manage our businesses. Emerson's approach to the development of people is founded on two principles: First, the corporation has the obligation to create opportunities for talented individuals; and second, these individuals have the obligation to create their own careers. We provide the opportunities; it's up to our people to take advantage of them.

Our organization planning reflects the critical importance we attribute to human resource issues and our dissatisfaction with standard, off-the-shelf appraisal and compensation packages. We rely primarily on two techniques.

The first is the organization review, which is part of the annual planning and control cycle for each division. This review is an annual half-day meeting centering on basic human resource issues in a division. In preparation, a division will evaluate all managers who are department heads or higher, assessing them according to specific performance criteria. At the meeting, we talk about key managers' length of service in a particular assignment, their potential to move to a more difficult job, and specific responsibilities they might assume.

EXHIBIT 5 The President's Operating Report Updates Expected Annual Results*

Line No.		Current Year						Prior Year		Act % Exp Over/(Under) Prior Year
		Actual or Expected	% Sales	Prior Expected	% Sales	Forecast	% Sales	Actual	% Sales	
		1st Quarter Ending December 31								
1	Intercompany sales	36		36		34		37		−2.7%
2	Net sales	29,613		29,613		29,463		25,932		14.2
3	Gross profit	14,065	47.5%	14,065	47.5%	3,790	46.8%	12,384	47.8%	13.6
4	SG&A expenses	8,312	28.1	8,312	28.1	8,281	28.1	7,650	29.5	8.7
5	Operating profit	5,753	19.4	5,753	19.4	5,509	18.7	4,734	18.3	21.5
6	Earnings before interest & tax	5,280	17.8	5,280	17.8	5,048	17.1	4,343	16.7	21.6
		2nd Quarter Ending March 31								
7	Intercompany sales	5		5		9		56		−91.1%
8	Net sales	33,324		33,324		31,765		26,661		25.0
9	Gross profit	15,283	45.9%	15,283	25.9%	14,812	46.6%	12,518	47.0%	22.1
10	SG&A expenses	9,301	27.9	9,301	27.9	8,937	28.1	7,395	27.8	25.8
11	Operating profit	5,982	18.0	5,982	18.0	5,875	18.5	5,123	19.2	16.8
12	Earnings before interest & tax	5,785	17.4	5,785	17.4	5,612	17.7	5,918	18.4	17.6
		3rd Quarter Ending June 30								
13	Intercompany sales	25		25		39		146		−82.9%
14	Net sales	32,845		32,845		33,424		30,678		7.1
15	Gross profit	15,353	46.7%	15,353	46.7%	15,664	46.9%	14,310	46.6%	7.3
16	SG&A expenses	8,916	27.1	8,916	27.1	9,399	28.2	8,424	27.4	5.8
17	Operating profit	6,437	19.6	6,437	19.6	6,265	18.7	5,886	19.2	9.4
18	Earnings before interest & tax	6,126	18.7	6,126	18.7	5,645	16.9	5,378	17.5	13.9

EXHIBIT 5 *(concluded)*

Line No.		Current Year						Prior Year		Act % Exp Over/(Under) Prior Year
		Actual or Expected	% Sales	Prior Expected	% Sales	Forecast	% Sales	Actual	% Sales	
		4th Quarter Ending September 30								
19	Intercompany sales	94		94		94		25		276.0%
20	Net sales	36,611		36,611		35,722		30,521		20.0
21	Gross profit	17,109	46.7%	17,109	46.7%	16,832	47.1%	14,576	47.8%	17.4
22	SG&A expenses	10,537	28.7	10,537	28.7	10,029	28.1	8,695	28.5	21.2
23	Operating profit	6,572	18.0	6,572	18.0	6,803	19.0	5,881	19.3	11.7
24	Earnings before interest & tax	6,122	16.7	6,122	16.7	8,146	22.8	5,498	18.0	11.3
		Fiscal Year Ending September 30								
25	Intercompany sales	160		160		176		264		−39.4%
26	Net sales	132,393		132,393		130,374		113,792		16.3
27	Gross profit	61,810	46.7%	61,810	46.7%	61,098	46.9%	53,788	47.3%	14.9
28	SG&A expenses	37,066	28.0	37,066	28.0	36,646	28.1	32,164	28.3	15.2
29	Operating profit	24,744	18.7	24,744	18.7	24,452	18.8	21,624	19.0	14.4
30	Earnings before interest & tax	23,313	17.6	23,313	17.6	24,451	18.8	20,137	17.7	15.8
31	Pretax earnings	25,154	19.0	25,154	19.0	24,771	19.0	21,918	19.3	14.8
32	Net Earnings	14,361	10.8	14,361	10.8	14,024	10.8	12,250	10.8	17.2
		Expected 1st Quarter Next Fiscal Year								
33	Intercompany sales	67		65				36		86.1%
34	Net sales	32,830		32,311				29,613		10.9
35	Gross profit	15,142	46.1%	15,143	46.9%			14,065	47.5%	7.7
36	SG&A expenses	9,179	27.9	9,217	28.6			8,312	28.1	10.4
37	Operating profit	5,963	18.2	5,925	18.3			5,753	19.4	3.7
38	Earnings before interest & tax	5,628	17.1	5,619	17.4			5,280	17.8	6.6

*In thousands of dollars

167

We try to identify young people who look like "high potentials" and develop plans to offer them a series of assignments that will enhance and augment their skills. Finally, we try to ensure that the division has—or knows how to get—the specific human resource skills it will need to implement its strategy. If a business plans to open an operation in Eastern Europe, for example, we want a demonstration that it has the organization and personnel capacity to succeed there.

The second technique is one we adapted from a major engineering construction firm. We maintain an organization room at headquarters, where we keep personnel charts on every management team in the entire company, corporate and division (see Exhibit 6). Every year we update this information, which covers more than a thousand people, on the basis of organization reviews. The charts include each manager's picture and are color coded for areas such as function, experience, and career path. They provide a powerful visual aid to human resource planning. When a position opens, we know quickly which candidates are most qualified and which people might succeed the candidates we move up.

Both of these organization planning techniques support our focus on follow-through and implementation by letting us know when people should not be moved. For the benefit of implementation, we avoid moving people who are in the middle of important assignments.

Emerson's management personnel come from four sources. The first—and by far the largest group—consists of long-term employees. We believe that operating the company successfully requires management continuity. The typical Emerson division or corporate officer is in his or her late 40s and has about 15 years of service. About 85 percent of promotions come from within Emerson; we believe that this approach to management development contributes to good morale and helps our culture remain cohesive. A second major source of personnel is acquisitions. Many of our division presidents and business leaders joined the company this way; if they stick around—and, in most cases, they do—they tend to thrive in the Emerson system.

Third, every year we recruit 10 to 20 high-potential young people and put them in jobs for which they are not yet qualified. The best make it; the others don't. It's that simple. We carefully track othese people, and we retain a majority of them; some have become division presidents and corporate officers. Finally, we hire experienced people for certain jobs because we believe that occasionally bringing in new thinking is very important. We also hire from the outside when we need specialized experience that we do not have internally.

To keep people motivated and involved, we've tried to avoid problems that can paralyze corporations—things like organization charts and large headquarters staffs. We don't have a published corporate organization chart at Emerson. No such piece of paper exists because we want people communicating around plans, projects, and problems, not along organization lines.

I am a believer in small, talented, functionally oriented corporate staffs. But we work hard at not loading up on staff because a large staff creates work. For every person we hire at corporate, we have to hire others in the divisions. A number of years ago, one of the best staff people I've ever known came to me with a list of programs Emerson's operating management wanted to implement and the seven people he would need to hire to help carry out these initiatives. I sat down with him and said, "Let's cut the number of programs in half. How many people do we need to hire now?" He said, "Three." Then I said, "Let's cut the number of programs in half again. Now how many people do we need to hire?" He said, "None." As it turned out, we were able to complete all the programs the businesses wanted with no additions to corporate staff.

There are two lessons to be learned from this story. The first is, don't underestimate the capacity of well-managed organizations to get important things done—less important things probably will not get done, but important things will. And the second is, don't burden very talented staff people with a lot of administrative responsibility; the loss of their productivity is rarely worth the extra capacity the additional people provide.

EXHIBIT 6   Emerson's Personnel Profile

Legend

1	Department Head				
2	Jane H. Doe				
3	10			4	75
5		6	2		7

8	7	9	John T. Smith	10	②	11	50
8		9		10	◯	11	
8		9		10	◯	11	

(1) Position Title
(2) Incumbent Manager
(3) Incumbent's Years of Service
(4) Incumbent's Base Salary (in $M)
(5) Incumbent's Performance (see Coding)
(6) Incumbent's Readiness for Promotion
(7) Incumbent's Potential (see Coding)
(8) Replacement's Years of Service
(9) Replacement's Name
(10) Replacement's Degree of Readiness
      for Promotion
(11) Replacement's Base Salary (in $M)

Performance Coding (Number 5)

(Orange/Gold) (1) Outstanding:
Awarded only to those managers who have made significant, easily recognizable contributions; performance so clearly outstanding as to be obvious to all. Results obtained far in excess of the requirements and indicate early promotion potential. Rating must be supported with specifics.
Note: A "good" manager may have an outstanding year and be rated "outstanding." However, the manager whose performance exceeds requirements but does not make a "significant" contribution should be rated "commendable."

(Green)   (2) Commendable:
Performance exceeds expectations. Employee's day-to-day performance "excellent," but no special contribution can be cited.

(Blue)   (3) Competent:
Performance completely satisfactory and sufficient in every respect. Meets all end results expected of a seasoned and well-qualified employee.

(Yellow)   (4) Adequate:
Results not yet completely meeting requirements of all objectives. Results fall somewhat below expected levels of accomplishment. Need for further development recognizable, but progress clearly evident.

(Red)   (5) Needs Improvement:
Unacceptable performance. Results noticeably below the expected level; may have to be replaced if no major improvement.

(White)   (6) New in Position:
No evaluation.

Potential Appraisal (Number 7)

(Orange/Gold) (1) Outstanding:
Qualifications for advancing to high-level (executive) position—"high performance."

(Green)   (2) Exceeds Expectations:
Clear potential for advancing to high-level position or for substantially increased responsibilities at present level.

(Blue)   (3) Some Potential:
Potential to handle expanded responsibilities at present level and perhaps one level higher.

(Yellow)   (4) Limited Potential:
At or near capacity in present position or limited due to personal factors.

(Red)   (5) Not Promotable:
Below average potential.

(White)   (6) New in Position:
Not evaluated.

Degree of Readiness Coding (Number 10)

(1) Ready Replacement
    Within 30 days (nominal orientation)
(2) Pending Replacement
    Within 1 year (after specific experience in select areas)
(3) Future Replacement
    Within 3 years (after specific experience or development)
(4) No movement
    No upward movement or increased responsibilities foreseen

So, whenever someone considers hiring additional personnel, the presumption is that the answer will be no. In 1991, Emerson has about the same number of people at headquarters—approximately 300—as it did in 1980, when the company was one-fifth its current size.

Emerson's compensation policies help involve and motivate our people. Simply, we pay for results. Each executive in a division earns a base salary and is eligible for a year-end "extra salary," which is based on the performance of the division according to measurable objectives. This extra compensation is calculated as a multiple of an extra salary "centerpoint," which we establish as part of the total compensation target at the beginning of each year. Depending on how well the division performs, the multiplier applied to the centerpoint ranges from 0.35 to 2.0. If the division hits its forecasted target for performance—numbers based on commitments that were mutually agreed on during the annual financial review—the multiplier is 1, and members of the management team will receive their centerpoint extra salary. Doing better increases the multiplier, and doing worse lowers it.

The formula for computing compensation targets changes over time, depending on the needs of the business. At present, sales and margin have a 50 percent weighting, with inventory turnover, international sales, new product introductions, DSOs (a measure of accounts receivable), and individual management objectives accounting for most of the rest. Other factors that may be included in the formula are geared to the economics of a particular division. In addition, stock options and a five-year performance share plan make up an important part of the total compensation package.

Systematic Process—and Benefits

Emerson's annual planning and control cycles provide important advantages in addition to good plans and tight controls: The process fosters teamwork, communication, understanding of the business and the marketplace, improved management skills, and focus on the fundamentals; it serves as an ongoing mechanism to identify and assess management talent; and it helps assimilate new acquisitions into the company.

The most important benefit, of course, is the bottom line. The proof lies in constantly improving results and long-term, high levels of total return to stockholders. We are opportunists, constantly on the lookout for new management techniques. When a new idea surfaces—such as a method of measuring value creation or focusing factories or a statistical process control technique—we take a hard look. If we think the idea has merit, we'll adapt it into our management process and operations.

Occasionally, I'm asked whether the Emerson management process is exportable to other companies. The quick answer is yes—it happens every time we make an acquisition—but it is never easy. As has happened here, building a smooth-running operation will entail years of effort and piece-by-piece construction.

The process cannot be installed all at once, nor is it necessarily appropriate for all other companies. But nothing we do has a geographic or national basis; the sources of competitive success are the same in Japan, Germany, the United States, or any other strong manufacturing economy. A company that puts the pieces in place will see progress and results. We believe that planning will pay off if management implements it aggressively, that the results of the process will reward the intensity of the effort, and that people will respect and respond to tough challenges.

One final, basic point: Never underestimate the cumulative impact of incremental change and the gathering forces of momentum. When you grind it out a yard at a time, you are in fact moving ahead. I can't say it will work for everybody, but at Emerson we view it as the only way to manage.

Case 1–9

XEROX CHARTS A NEW STRATEGIC DIRECTION—EXCERPTS

Carol Kennedy

The Myth of the Paperless Office

The paperless office, that technological mirage that beguiled us in the 1970s, is not going to happen. Xerox Corporation, a company built on the single most profitable invention in U.S. history—the photocopier—has designed its strategy for the 1990s around the firm assumption that the paper document will continue to be "the primary tool of the office" and its principal measure of work output.

After a period of restructuring and corporate soul-searching in the early 1980s that succeeded in reversing a serious Japanese threat to its survival in the mass copier market, Xerox adopted intensive new planning techniques to identify its strengths for the future in office products and systems. Out of these has come a new strategic direction for the company, based on a family of technologies covered by the term *document processing*.

Xerox has concluded that, for most businesses, enormous investments in information systems have not paid off in increased productivity because office technology, in most cases, reaches only a small portion of a company's information base—up to 80 percent of which is carried on paper. Former Xerox president Paul A. Strassmann, an internationally recognized guru on information technology, has pointed out that paper usage in U.S. offices has been growing steadily since 1946 at three times the rate of the country's GNP, and shows no sign of slowing down. Instead of replacing paper, electronic workstations have actually generated more of it.

Documents, in the words of Roger E. Levien, Xerox vice president responsible for corporate strategy, are "the lifeblood of the office, its raw material and its final product." Document processing, as the new strategy defines it, is broadly the technique of building bridges for documents to pass easily between the two worlds of paper and electronics, to enable a company to make the best use of its entire information base. Although electronic printers enable computer-held data to be transmitted to paper, going in the reverse direction is less easy. Huge amounts of data are therefore being held on paper, electronically inaccessible to many parts of a company.

Technology, says Levien, is just beginning to close this loop. The next big step will be for paper documents to be converted to electronic documents—not simply as images but with words, graphs, charts, and pictures, scanned into digital storage systems to be called up as required and reformatted, edited, or put together in a brand-new document. Xerox has the technology, and its strategy for the remainder of the century will be to deliver products and systems to the market that bridge the present chasms between paper and electronic filing and retrieval.

It is potentially an enormous market. Including electronic printing, Xerox president Paul Allaire estimates it at around $80 billion by 1995—10 times its present size. Allaire believes that small companies, even doctors' and lawyers' offices, could be part of it within 10 years.

Linking Electronic and Paper Documents

In the larger business context, Allaire states:

> Connecting the company's document base to its electronic environment is a key to realizing the full

Reprinted from Long Range Planning, *Vol. 1, C. Kennedy, "Xerox Charts a New Strategic Direction," pp. 395–398, copyright 1997, with permission from El Sevier.*

potential of its investments in information systems. We believe that a company's ability to gain a competitive edge in the future will depend on its ability to effectively utilise its entire information base. Our strategy is designed to enable our customers to do that—by providing products and software that will enhance the case with which people can create, reproduce, distribute and file documents, and by enabling users to move seamlessly back and forth between electronic and paper documents.

In Allaire's view,

> the biggest requirement in industry today is to improve office productivity. It has not kept up with productivity improvements on the manufacturing side. To compete in the nineties, a company has to be cost-effective in all areas: for most businesses, most of the jobs are in the white-collar area.

David T. Kearns, chairman and chief executive officer of Xerox since 1982, enlarged on this theme when he explained some of the basic findings that emerged from the first major strategy review, "Xerox '95."

> It will become increasingly imperative for American businesses to improve office productivity. Office expenditures now account for about 75 percent of the national wage. They are the largest expense item in business today, and they are increasing.
>
> While data processing and communications have automated many office functions very well, this is not true in the document area. With office workers spending 30 to 70 percent of their time interacting with documents, this area accounts for a large percentage of office costs.
>
> Paper will continue to be the primary medium for documents well into the future.
>
> We can expect electronics costs to continue to fall and capability to continue to rise at incredible rates over the next 5 to 15 years. This will make new document processing applications affordable for most businesses.

Kearns, a man with a crusading belief in quality that extends to dinner-table arguments with his wife over whether 100 percent fault-free quality is consistently attainable (he thinks it is; she doubts it), has achieved something remarkable, if not unique, in U.S. industry. By his quality cultural revolution in the company, coupled with fierce cost cutting and decentralizing the businesses, he has made Xerox the only U.S. corporation to regain market share lost to Japanese competitors. (In 1986, a hard year for the office equipment industry, Xerox increased overall market share in copiers.) That battle, although won, instilled awareness of the need for longer and deeper planning horizons. Kearns explains how the strategy emerged:

Narrowing the Focus

> We took a long, hard look at our weaknesses. We saw that we were not going to succeed selling office information systems that were computing or communications oriented. We also recognized that we could not sell "generic" systems. Nobody buys a generic anything—they buy something to help them meet a specific need. We saw that our initial strategy—offering operating systems that were developed uniquely for our equipment—was the wrong way to go.
>
> We considered our strengths, too. This company began in the document image processing business, and that has always been our greatest strength. We also have tremendous knowledge and experience in the information systems business, having pioneered many of the important advances in the application of information processing to the office. We believe our expertise in the office, and particularly in the document area, gives us an important edge over companies that will attempt to compete in this market from a data processing or telecommunications point of view.

Several alternative strategies were considered, as Roger Levien explains in detail later. There were some vigorous differences of opinion over how broad or narrow the company's focus should be, and over how quickly Xerox customers would take to the new concept of document processing. "I can't say we all agreed on all the points we debated, but we did get a pretty good consensus," says Kearns. "We ended up by narrowing the focus of the company considerably. We reorganized to reflect our new emphasis on document processing, cutting back on a number of programs and bolstering or consolidating others."

The Strategic Reconnaissance

The idea of "Xerox '95" was to establish a 10-year corporate strategy, based on the company's best assessments of where office technology and global markets were heading.

. . .

Xerox '95 got under way in August 1985 with a series of meetings between unit and corporate management, conducted off-site from the Stamford headquarters. Before the first of them, David Bliss of the corporate strategy office asked each of 15 senior corporate managers a basic question: "How did they see a successful Xerox 10 years ahead? What would be the critical external and internal forces affecting that view, and what were Xerox's current strengths and weaknesses?"

"We took everyone's answers and put them on the same page," said Levien. "Then we stripped away the names of the respondents, so that you could see the range of the answers given, and we gave them back to each participant before the meeting." Kearns chaired the round-table gathering, which opened with a video of Joe Wilson, the company's founder, giving his personal vision of the future.

"We used that one-day meeting to discuss key issues like the nature of success, critical success factors, and what businesses we should be in," said Levien. "It became clear there was a wide range of views, even among those 15 people, about what a success Xerox would be, 10 years on."

Between the first meeting in August and the second in November, more questionnaires were constructed in the corporate strategy office. They posed such questions as "What kinds of products do you think we should sell? In what geographic regions? What are the critical success factors?"

The "High Concepts"

"In analysing those questionnaires, we thought we had found a number of underlying world views on implicit strategies for the company," Levien recalled. From those,

> We isolated four strategic themes that we thought a group among the respondents were implicitly pursuing. For each of these we gave a brief

description, using the Hollywood notion of a "high concept."

(A high concept is a one-sentence encapsulation of a movie theme such as "great white shark terrorizes beach community" for *Jaws*.)

> One of these strategies, for example, was for Xerox to be a complete financial animal, to look at each business purely on its short-term returns and to get out of any business which couldn't promise a profit fairly quickly. In other words, to manage a portfolio as a conglomerate would, strictly according to the profitability of each element, without any synergy.
>
> Another was to put together a complex set of businesses which could compete across the board with an IBM. Another was to "mind our knitting"; to be a first-class copier and printer business and forget about anything else. The fourth was to emphasize our distribution channels and build on that.
>
> We then took 16 people and divided them into groups of four and asked each group to take one of those four strategies and spend the first part of the afternoon elaborating it in some detail. Each group contained one person who was a strong supporter of that strategy and one who was not too enthusiastic about it. When they came back and made their presentation, using flip charts and spelling out the strategy in further detail, it became apparent that support for this or that strategy depended largely on that person's view of the world.
>
> One key issue that emerged was the future of paper: Was paper going to play an important role in the office in the future?

In between this second one-day meeting and the third in the series, which covered a three-day weekend, more work was done at corporate level on external economic and political research. The assignment was to spell out in more detail the four strategic alternatives . . .

The Consensor

At the weekend meeting, groups of four were asked to decide what they felt were the most important external and environmental influences likely to affect the company's future strategy. These were then "polled" anonymously by a device called a consensor, a small box with two dials numbered 0 to 7 on which individuals registered the issues in terms of numerical rating. A central console read the settings, consolidated them and displayed the result as a bar chart on a screen.

> We used the consensor to narrow the group of 20–25 assumptions about the world down to a handful, perhaps a dozen, which people agreed were the key assumptions about the external environment. That became what we call our "view of the world." There are now 24 assumptions of that kind which we keep evergreen; these are our beliefs about the external environment which we see as strategically critical and which we continue to monitor in the corporate strategy office.

Those 24 assumptions—about the future of paper, the way competition is seen as likely to evolve, the way marketing channels may develop and other key factors—became a small printed booklet within Xerox, highly classified to outsiders. It was the blueprint upon which Xerox would build its strategy for the 1990s.

The last stage of that weekend meeting began with members of the corporate strategy office sitting with each of four small groups discussing in detail the four "high concept" strategies and analyzing them through to financial and market projections. On the Saturday evening, each person was given an hour to collect his thoughts and then the group gathered round a large table. Kearns asked each in turn to spend five minutes describing which strategy, or combination of strategies, he favored and why. The result was 15 different options. After dinner, a small group gathered with Kearns to discuss them before retiring to bed. On the Sunday morning Kearns gave his verdict on which strategic direction the company should follow.

The whole exercise was typical of Kearns's methods, said Levien: "He likes to build teams, he likes to listen, but he's willing to make the tough decisions himself."

Out of this came the strategy built around document processing, although Kearns did not use those words when making his choice. The corporate strategy office took the direction he had outlined and formulated a one-page "statement of strategic intent." That was followed, in 1986, by an exercise called "strategy validation," in which the ideas in that statement of intent were rigorously tested, with external consultants as well as internally. A thick and detailed document resulted, and further refinements were made as the 1986 planning process unfolded.

In January 1987, coinciding with another corporate restructuring, principally in the marketing area, a second Xerox '95 meeting was held that produced a very precise statement of missions and boundaries for each of the business units as well as for overall strategic direction . . .

"We are continuing these Xerox '95 meetings twice a year to bring senior management together, and in 1989 we will probably start working on a Xerox 2000," said Levien.

References

Gary Jacobson and John Hillkirk, *Xerox: The American Samurai* (New York: Macmillan, 1986).

Benchmark, Xerox quarterly publication (Spring 1988).

Meeting of the Research Board, San Francisco, March 4, 1987.

Remarks by Paul A. Allaire, *Business Week* 22 (June 1987).

Roger E. Levien, *Making Strategic Concepts Work*, Xerox Corporation.

Resource Allocation Processes

OVERVIEW

Without resources, strategies exist in name only. As a leading scholar has observed:

> Finally, daily, somebody must decide to take action that will consume corporate resources . . . Plans are nice, but nothing really happens—physically—until the resources are expended.[1]

Only after research programs are funded, capital is allocated, and marketing and advertising dollars are committed do strategies have any chance of becoming a reality. Until then, they are little more than empty promises.

The associated processes usually involve some form of budgeting. At times, these activities are difficult to separate from strategic programming, and the terms are occasionally used interchangeably. But budgeting normally comes later in the planning cycle and involves many more organizational levels. It picks up where programming ends, providing the resources that bring goals to life. For most managers, the line between the two is reasonably clear because of differences in specificity and ownership. Unlike forecasts and plans, budgets are stated in dollar terms, cover well-defined (and usually short) periods, are reviewed and approved by upper management, can only be changed under specified conditions, and involve commitments that serve as the basis for individual, unit, and departmental performance evaluations.[2]

Equally important, budgeting involves explicit rankings and comparisons. The process is one of "internal selection."[3] Programs and projects are compared; some

---

[1]Richard F. Vancil, *Implementing Strategy: The Role of Top Management: Teacher's Manual* (Boston: Division of Research, Harvard Business School, 1982), p. 112.

[2]Robert N. Anthony and John Dearden, *Management Control Systems,* 4th ed. (Homewood, IL: Richard D. Irwin, 1980), pp. 368–369.

[3]Robert A. Burgelman, "Fading Memories: A Process Theory of Strategic Business Exit in Dynamic Environments," *Administrative Science Quarterly* 39 (1994), pp. 24–56, and Robert A. Burgelman, "A Process Model of Strategic Business Exit: Implications for an Evolutionary Perspective on Strategy," Strategic *Management Journal* 17 (1996), pp. 193–214.

are deemed more important than others and are awarded a larger share of available funds. Not every proposal is funded, and few managers receive all of the dollars they request. This winnowing process is crucial to understanding the distinctive challenges of resource allocation. Because selection is involved, there are certain to be winners and losers, and unit and department heads will go to great lengths to secure funding. Politics, posturing, and gamesmanship are virtually inevitable, and strategic goals can be easily subverted. To combat these problems, resource allocation processes are normally designed with two ends in mind. They are vehicles for management control—"assuring that the organization carries out its strategies efficiently and effectively"—as well as for direction setting and planning.[4] As we shall see later, these goals occasionally conflict, resulting in predictable difficulties and challenges.

OUTLINE

"Ellis International Division: Patrick O'Brian," the first case in the module, introduces resource allocation processes and considers their impact on organizational performance. Patrick O'Brian, the recently appointed president of a large, multinational consumer goods company's Latin America and Far East Division, has installed a new resource allocation process, called Continuous Planning and Review (CP-R), to improve the division's market planning and control. Extensive documentation and data collection are now required for all new products, including detailed product profiles, market assessments, and advertising plans and budgets. Individual roles and responsibilities have also been clearly defined, so that headquarters and field personnel, as well as managers at different organizational levels, know when approvals and consultation are necessary.

This system has succeeded in resurrecting the division, which was struggling for years because of a lack of discipline. The prevailing sales culture, with its emphasis on meeting short-term budgets no matter what the cost, has been replaced by systematic forward planning. Efficiency has become the goal, and O'Brian has decreed that there will be no more "one-market products or one-product markets." The resource allocation process has played a critical role in this transition, helping managers develop new skills while limiting the excesses of the past.

But there are concerns. Some believe that the new resource allocation process is burdensome and bureaucratic. An entrepreneurial manager in Mexico has just developed a new nutritional product with great potential; in his zeal to get the project launched, he has not completed all of the steps in the CP-R process. In response, O'Brian has delayed the product launch and reprimanded the manager in question, insisting that all steps in the process be followed. Has he overreacted? The source of the problem is still unclear. Was it the initiator of the project, who failed to follow required procedures? The Mexican country manager, who failed to communicate divisional requirements down to field personnel and the project's special needs

---

[4]Anthony and Dearden, *Management Control Systems,* pp. 6–7.

up to headquarters staff? Or was it O'Brian himself, who insisted on a rigid acceptance of procedures and tolerated no exceptions? These questions lie at the heart of the case, for they illustrate the diverse roles played by managers at different levels in the organization as resource allocation processes unfold over time.

The next case in the module, "Americhem: The Gaylord Division (A)," takes this theme a step further. It explores the challenges of leading the resource allocation process when diverse, conflicting interests must be resolved. Americhem, a large chemical company, has just installed a zero-base budgeting system, in which annual budgets are computed from scratch each year rather than based on small changes from prior years' funding.[5] Discussions at the Gaylord Division, composed of three businesses with vastly different profitabilities, growth rates, and funding requirements, have been tense and competitive, as business leaders have argued selfishly for increases in their share of the pie. Staff groups have been equally uncooperative. They too have found it difficult to accurately compare the costs and benefits of adding or subtracting people from different areas. In no case has a common, agreed-upon standard emerged for resolving arguments and making choices.

Here too, the underlying causes of the problem remain unclear. Was it the lack of a clear strategy and unambiguous priorities? Was it managers' unfamiliarity with the new budgeting process? Or was it poor leadership by the division president, who failed to clarify his agenda, communicate his goals, and orchestrate the (admittedly difficult) interpersonal dynamics? There are a number of action questions as well. Now that the process has stalled, how should the division president get discussions back on track? How should he overcome the resistance of line and staff managers? Where should he compromise, and where should he stand firm? And what should he do next time to ensure that the process goes more smoothly?

"Westinghouse Electric Corporation: Automating the Capital Budgeting Process (A)" provides partial answers to these questions. It describes a complex, multilevel budgeting process with several innovative features. Two are especially distinctive: the company's use of a Capital Review Committee (CRC) to react to proposals roughly midway through proceedings, and the committee's use of a novel voting technology that allows members to evaluate a large number of projects in a short period of time. The CRC is an advisory group, composed of a dozen middle managers from diverse functions and departments, that reviews written proposals, listens to presentations, and provides feedback to senior managers about both individual projects and aggregate budgets. Some of their recommendations are binding; others are merely advisory. In combination, they offer a wealth of objective, independent information—a form of checks and balances—that serves as a counterweight to the gamesmanship and self-serving behavior that so often arise during budgeting discussions.

The voting system assists in this process. By combining a simple, standardized scoring sheet with bar-code technology providing easy and immediate input, the voting system enables CRC members to rate every project quickly and anonymously. Their scores are then compiled—after all presentations are finished,

---

[5]Ibid., pp. 382–384.

individual ratings are printed out, together with summary and comparative statistics, and are discussed by the group as a whole. In this way, over 200 proposals can be evaluated during a single, two-day CRC meeting.

The final case in the module, "Peterson Industries: Louis Friedman," describes a resource allocation process that deploys engineering personnel rather than capital. Peterson is a leading producer of products made from specialty plastics. Innovation and product development have long been keys to the company's success. In recent years, engineering talent has become the limiting resource, and Louis Friedman, the president, has come to play a central role in evaluating projects and allocating engineers from a central pool. The case describes several of his recent decisions, as well as a number of proposed reforms. One of the central problems has been the perceived looseness of the process: the difficulty of making crisp resource allocation decisions, especially at the top of the organization, where there has been limited detailed information about the merits of competing proposals. Subjectivity and managerial reputation have determined many of the choices. In addition, there have been questions about the proper role of division general managers in shaping and championing projects and the best way to structure the compensation system so that it produces superior resource allocation decisions.

THEMES

A Multilevel, Multifunctional Process

Perhaps *the* distinguishing feature of resource allocation is that it is a distributed activity. Many people are involved, and many choices must be made throughout the organization. Both line and staff managers play pivotal roles. In fact, in most companies it is almost impossible to find a single person or a central authority responsible for resource allocation.[6] According to a classic study:

> [It] is a very long social process, not solely an intellectual exercise . . . composed of many small acts, carried out by different people at divergent points of time . . . The problem is not defined in any unique way. In fact, every participant may see the problem differently, according to his interests and values. The decision process may be defined as a bargaining process among the various participants.[7]

Bargaining proceeds through two critical stages: definition and impetus.[8] During the definition stage, projects are formulated and defined. During the impetus

---

[6]Walter Kuemmerle, *Home Base and Foreign Direct Investment in Research and Development*, unpublished doctoral dissertation, Graduate School of Business Administration, Harvard University, 1996, chap. 4.

[7]Yair Aharoni, *The Foreign Investment Decision Process* (Boston: Division of Research, Graduate School of Business Administration, Harvard University, 1966), pp. 219–220.

[8]The descriptions of these stages, as well as the descriptions of the roles played by participants, are drawn from Joseph L. Bower, *Managing the Resource Allocation Process* (Boston: Harvard Business School Press, 1986).

stage, they are presented and sold. The process concludes when choices are made by upper management.

As the process unfolds, participants are drawn from different organizational levels, and they play very different roles. Three are critical. At the corporate level, managers are responsible for setting broad strategic direction, establishing and communicating financial goals, and designing and shaping the context in which resource allocation decisions are made. They create the settings, targets, and incentives that govern the process. Examples in this module include O'Brian of Ellis International and Friedman of Peterson Industries. At the divisional level, managers are responsible for integration. They play a Janus-like role,[9] communicating corporate needs downward and product/market and business needs upward. Examples include Barnes, the Mexican country manager at Ellis, and Kells, the vice president and general manager of Peterson's peripherals business. At the operating level, managers are responsible for initiating ideas, developing proposals, and selling projects to their superiors, who are generally division general managers. Examples include Rao, the creator of Ellis's new nutritional product, and LeGoff, one of the product managers in Peterson's peripherals business.

This distribution of activity has several important implications. First, it suggests that resource allocation processes can seldom be controlled through conventional, hierarchical means. Orders and directives are of little use because authority is so diffused. Instead, the most effective approach is to change the context in which resource allocation takes place, altering the goals, incentives, and assessment criteria that managers use when making decisions. The Peterson case shows how altered financial incentives shape the allocation process, while Westinghouse shows the impact of changed assessment criteria.

Second, this description of the resource allocation process highlights the critical role of division general managers. Their position in the middle of the organization provides a powerful vantage point: They are highly enough placed to understand what corporate managers need and will accept, but close enough to the grass roots to remain in touch with marketplace realities. At times, in fact, they are well ahead of the rest of the organization; occasionally, they actively precipitate a change in corporate priorities by shifting around resources. Intel's move from a memory company to a microprocessor company was led by its division managers, who shifted resources and manufacturing capacity to the latter, more highly valued activity even as top managers continued to believe that memory chips were their salvation.[10] Making these choices properly—achieving the right balance "between creative innovation and predictable goal achievement"[11]—is one of the central challenges of resource allocation. As the Americhem case suggests, these choices are often squarely in the hands of

---

[9]Janus was an ancient Roman deity, thought to preside over beginnings and endings, who was commonly represented with two faces pointing in opposite directions.

[10]Burgelman, "Fading Memories," pp. 43–49.

[11]Robert Simons, *Levers of Control* (Boston: Harvard Business School Press, 1995), p. 29.

division general managers. At the Gaylord Division, the general manager has to decide whether his limited resources are best spent sustaining a mature, highly profitable business or growing two young businesses that will require heavy advertising and R&D spending while providing few short-term profits.

Competing Goals

Nor are these the only tensions that arise during budgeting discussions. Often, there are fierce debates about whether targets have been set too high or too low. These debates are more than simple differences of opinion; they also reflect the fact that budgets play multiple roles. Budgets can be used for planning, motivation, evaluation, coordination, and education.[12] Not surprisingly, these roles—particularly the first three—are frequently in conflict.

When budgets are used for planning, the primary goal is accuracy. Managers will state plans with precision and will propose targets that are realistic and achievable. When budgets are used for motivation, the primary goal is stretch. Managers will try to push beyond easy, visible goals and will seek out targets that are difficult but potentially attainable. When budgets are used for evaluation, the primary goal is assured performance. Managers will tend to understate what they think is achievable and will propose targets that are relatively easy to meet.

Clearly, a single budgeting system will have trouble meeting all three goals simultaneously. Planning and motivation are in conflict, as are motivation and evaluation. A process designed for planning requires realism and predictability; a process designed to motivate managers requires optimism and hope. When motivation is the goal, all targets should be just beyond reach; when evaluation is the goal, few managers will suggest targets that are not already within grasp. Ellis, Americhem, and Peterson provide examples of these conflicts. In each case, managers can be seen arguing for more generous allocations even as their superiors are demanding greater accuracy or stretch.

There are other trade-offs as well. Managers frequently make short-term operating decisions that undermine long-term goals. Invariably, resources are at stake. According to a study of several major corporations:

> The conflict is basic. The attainment of long-range goals often involves resource commitments that that may adversely affect profits in the current period, even though these investments may provide significant returns in later years. Additionally, achievement of long-range goals may require adherence to a specific strategy—such as a market, product, or labor relations strategy—that in certain economically difficult years might cause higher-than-normal expenses. In the short run, these expenses reduce profits; but, in the long run, they are "investments" designed to pay off.[13]

[12]M. Edgar Barrett and LeRoy B. Fraser, III, "Conflicting Roles in Budgeting in Operations," *Harvard Business Review* 55 (July–August 1977), pp. 137–146.

[13]Robert L. Banks and Steven C. Wheelwright, "Operations vs. Strategy: Trading Tomorrow for Today," *Harvard Business Review* 57 (May–June 1979), p. 113.

All too often, the short term wins. Managers postpone capital outlays and defer or reduce necessary operating expenses. But such behavior is not inevitable, as the Westinghouse and Peterson cases suggest. Problems can be minimized by tightly linking strategy development and resource allocation processes, fostering a deep understanding of strategic objectives in lower- and mid-level managers, holding explicit discussions of short- and long-term trade-offs, and incorporating both short- and long-term goals in performance evaluation and compensation systems.

Politics and Gamesmanship

Politics are a fact of organizational life. Individuals and departments have differing interests and goals; they will invariably frame issues, argue positions, and lobby and align with other groups to increase the odds that their needs will be met. Why? Because they are competing for resources and believe that they are engaged in a zero-sum game. "As long as organizations continue as resource-sharing systems where there is an inevitable scarcity of those resources, political behavior will occur."[14] In most cases, such behavior is viewed negatively, for it suggests self-serving, manipulative actions that come at the expense of others. But this need not be the case. Politics has positive—or at least neutral—overtones as well.[15] Decisions that are made politically may be said to involve compromise, accommodation, and bargaining rather than rational analysis.[16] These forces need not be dysfunctional and may even result in a larger common good.

Both forms of politics can be seen in the cases of this module. Westinghouse, for example, has established its multifunctional Capital Review Committee to inject balanced and diverse views into discussions of investment proposals. Because the committee's recommendations are advisory, and because presenters are given ample opportunity to revise their proposals after presenting to the committee, politics—in the sense of a healthy "give and take" among diverse, conflicting opinions—has played a benign and largely supportive role.

Similarly, politics can shape the resource allocation decisions of senior managers in positive, useful ways. In the absence of hard data, senior managers must often base their budgeting decisions on the commitment and support of presenters. Initially, they must rely on "gut feel" and guesswork. But because the process is repeated at regular intervals, they can seldom be fooled for long. Most soon develop a reasonably clear picture of their subordinates' predilections and

---

[14]Andrew M. Pettigrew, *The Politics of Organizational Decision-Making* (London: Tavistock, 1973), p. 20.

[15]For comparisons of the neutral and negative definitions of politics, see Jeffrey Gandz and Victor V. Murray, "The Experience of Workplace Politics," *Academy of Management Journal* 23 (1980), pp. 237–251.

[16]Michael L. Tushman, "A Political Approach to Organizations," *Academy of Management Review* 2 (1977), p. 207.

profiles. They learn who makes extravagant, unsupported promises and who consistently delivers.[17] In such settings, basing resource commitments on credibility and track record is both necessary and appropriate. The willingness of respected division leaders to go to bat for certain projects—what scholars have called "organizational championing"—thus becomes a key guide to their likely effectiveness, especially when technologies are new, innovative, and only dimly understood at the top.[18] This form of politics can be seen clearly in the Peterson case, where Friedman, the president, has based several budgeting decisions, especially those involving the peripherals division, on the commitment and performance of the division managers supporting the project.

Of course, such behavior can be taken to extremes. When resource choices are made primarily on the basis of "show and tell"—fancy presentations rather than solid analysis—little good is likely to result. Politics then takes on a decidedly unhealthy air. The integrity of the process is quickly undermined, and managers soon come to accept "the cynical view that your project is as good as the performance you can put on at funding time."[19] Various forms of gaming—"engaging in behaviors to influence the measure that do not further organizational goals"— may also arise. Among the most popular are building in slack in anticipation of cutbacks, tying your fate to more popular departments or divisions, and shifting funds between categories to reduce the amount requested for any single project.[20] Some of these behaviors can be seen at Americhem, as both line and staff managers put the most favorable spin on their requested allocations.

There are a number of remedies for these problems. All involve tinkering with the resource allocation process in ways that encourage more careful, thoughtful submissions. New steps can be added to the process, with all budget requests accompanied by a sensitivity analysis showing the expected impact on performance of slightly larger and slightly smaller allocations. Choices among projects would then have a rational basis, eliminating unproductive politics and arm-twisting.[21] A zero-base system, in which budgets are built from the ground up rather than allocated from current positions or levels, serves a similar purpose, leveling the playing field and forcing every department to justify its expenditures beyond a certain baseline level.[22] Analytical tools—decision grids, scoring

---

[17]In fact, a careful scholarly study of the resource allocation process reached the following conclusion: "The ability to judge other managers and the quality of their work emerges . . . as one of the key attributes of a manager." See Bower, *Managing the Resource Allocation Process*, pp. 301–302.

[18]Robert A. Burgelman, "A Process Model of Internal Corporate Venturing in the Diversified Major Firm," *Administrative Science Quarterly* 28 (1983), pp. 238–239.

[19]Paul Sharpe and Tom Keelin, "How SmithKline Beecham Makes Better Resource Allocation Decisions," *Harvard Business Review* 76 (March–April 1998), p. 45.

[20]Simons, *Levers of Control,* pp. 82–84.

[21]Sharpe and Keelin, "How SmithKline Beecham Makes Better Resource Allocation Decisions," pp. 45–57.

[22]Zero-base budgeting systems have a mixed record in practice, largely because they demand so much management time. See Simons, *Levers of Control,* p. 171.

templates, and standardized submission forms—are also useful for imposing order, structuring what would otherwise be a loose, undisciplined set of activities. The process can be designed to include a heavy interactive component, ensuring that proposals—and performance—are discussed regularly and routinely, when changes can still be made easily, rather than at widely spaced intervals, when irreversible commitments have already been made. All of these approaches are on display in the cases of this module, showing that the political impacts of resource allocation depend, to a large extent, on how the process has been designed and managed.

Case 2–1

ELLIS INTERNATIONAL DIVISION: PATRICK O'BRIAN

Sitting at breakfast, Patrick O'Brian was going over in his mind the key issues that were likely to come up during the day. The sun was just beginning to peek through the branches of the fir trees beyond the parking lot of the Middletown Sheraton. Across the top of the menu propped in the holder at the next table was the date: Thursday, August 10, 1993.

Throughout the week, management personnel from headquarters and field offices of Ellis International, Latin America/Far East Division (LA/FE), had been attending the mid-August quarterly review meeting. As division president, O'Brian had scheduled for that day individual agreement sessions with six of his overseas directors. There would be much ground to cover. It was essential that the important questions not be lost in a myriad of details. O'Brian also wanted to be sure that he assumed the appropriate role with regard to each critical issue, and that he was clear in his mind on the roles of others.

Of particular concern was a program in Mexico to develop and launch Alpha, a new nutritional product. Several other policy questions of greater

moment would be dealt with in the next 18 hours. Among them were the approach to be taken on a partial divestment of equity in Indonesia, the approval of capital financing for two product introductions in Australia, and a move to broaden the division's product line in a dynamic Japanese market. But the Alpha situation required special attention because it touched upon the way in which the division's formal management system was working.

"It's ironic," O'Brian mused. "Our management system calls for the explicit assignment of work roles to the various managers within the division who must contribute to the attainment of a certain objective. Yet, with regard to Alpha, there seems to be some misunderstanding about who is responsible for each role, and what that means in terms of managing the project."

This case was prepared by David A. Garvin.

Background

O'Brian had been president of Ellis International, Latin America/Far East, since 1984. A native of New York, he had studied chemistry at Notre Dame before working for Union Carbide. In 1971, at 29, he joined Wellsprings Inc., a diversified company engaged in the development, manufacturing, and marketing of proprietary medicines and toiletries, ethical pharmaceuticals, veterinary products, laboratory and diagnostic chemicals and equipment, and plastic packaging. (See Exhibit 1 for WI's organization chart.)

O'Brian: "As one of WI's nine operating divisions, we are given considerable independence in running our business, so long as we contribute to the company's goals of stable growth, improving profitability, and product excellence. Wellsprings' original business, starting in 1920, was built around Ellis ColdRelieve and subsequently other proprietary drugs in the cold remedy area. But in order to achieve more stability and growth the company began to diversify in the 1950s. As a result, a number of other products have been added to WI's lines, but the Ellis divisions, which handle proprietary health and personal care products, continued to be the mainstay of the business (see Exhibit 2).

"When I became division general manager in 1984, Ellis International, LA/FE was having difficulty sustaining adequate growth and profitability. During the previous two years we had missed our budgets by wide margins. My initial analysis of the situation was that the division had an inadequate budget system, ineffective tracking and control mechanisms, and a lack of action-oriented reporting. So we instituted a budget manual, undertook improvements in the database for planning, initiated a program to improve communications, and overhauled our reporting system. As a result, it was extremely frustrating when we didn't make our budgets the next two years either.

"I had not experienced this type of failure before, and it led me to a far-ranging examination of what the division's business was and how we went about

accomplishing it. Joan Lake, my executive vice president, had expressed her concern. I told her I would like to initiate some fundamental changes. She promised her support and wished me success. The pressure to deliver was now really on my back.

"Our business strategy was based on running with products already developed by other divisions within the company. In essence, it was an extension of our highly successful export business of the mid-to-late 60s, but it no longer fit the requirements of our expanding and changing markets. During the early 80s we had set up manufacturing and distribution operations in a large number of countries, and as a result the management emphasis had been on sales generation to cover the rather substantial overhead.

"My challenge was to refocus the division's resources and energies into more productive and successful patterns. I became convinced that we should stop running and pushing products in favor of returning to a more comprehensive marketing stance. We had to put major emphasis on analyzing consumer needs, to identify or develop products to satisfy those needs. We had to improve communications to the consumer that the product was available and superior in meeting his needs. Measurement of our success would then shift from sales volume shipped to distributors and focus on consumer awareness and retail take-off.

"I also decided the division should concentrate on fewer products with higher profitability potential and higher volume potential across the countries. This meant encouraging our overseas operating units to reduce the number of low-volume and low-margin items in their product line, to shift away from price-controlled categories, and to consider introducing products that were highly successful in other markets. It has become something of a slogan that 'we can't afford one-market products or one-product markets.' This required that we become proficient in the transfer of strategy and expertise among the markets.

"To bring about these changes, we had to introduce significant improvements in our organization and management practices. This message emerged clearly from a division management conference which I convened in November of 1986 to look at

EXHIBIT 1 Wellsprings, Inc., Organization Chart

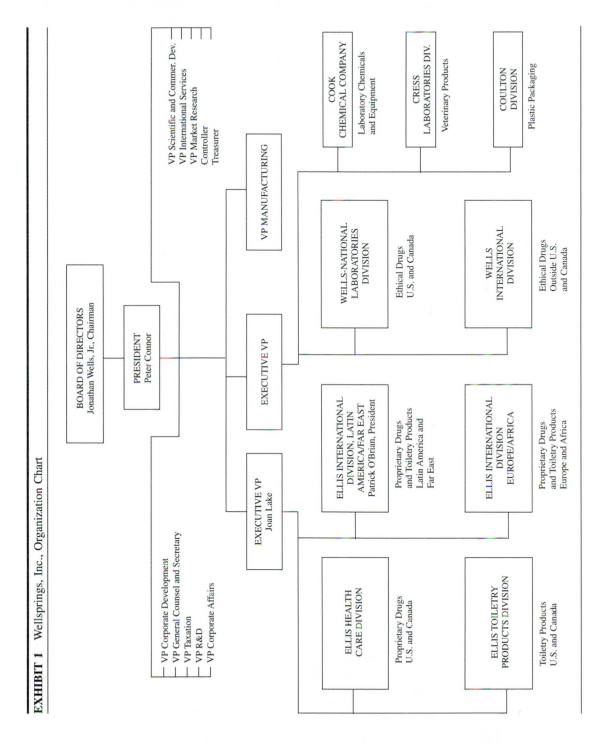

BOARD OF DIRECTORS
Jonathan Wells, Jr., Chairman

PRESIDENT
Peter Connor

VP Corporate Development
VP General Counsel and Secretary
VP Taxation
VP R&D
VP Corporate Affairs

VP Scientific and Commer. Dev.
VP International Services
VP Market Research
Controller
Treasurer

VP MANUFACTURING

EXECUTIVE VP

EXECUTIVE VP
Joan Lake

WELLS-NATIONAL
LABORATORIES
DIVISION

Ethical Drugs
U.S. and Canada

WELLS
INTERNATIONAL
DIVISION

Ethical Drugs
Outside U.S.
and Canada

ELLIS INTERNATIONAL
DIVISION, LATIN
AMERICA/FAR EAST
Patrick O'Brian, President

Proprietary Drugs
and Toiletry Products
Latin America and
Far East

ELLIS INTERNATIONAL
DIVISION
EUROPE/AFRICA

Proprietary Drugs
and Toiletry Products
Europe and Africa

ELLIS HEALTH
CARE DIVISION

Proprietary Drugs
U.S. and Canada

ELLIS TOILETRY
PRODUCTS DIVISION

Toiletry Products
U.S. and Canada

COOK
CHEMICAL COMPANY

Laboratory Chemicals
and Equipment

CRESS
LABORATORIES DIV.

Veterinary Products

COULTON
DIVISION

Plastic Packaging

EXHIBIT 2 Selected Financial Data

WELLSPRINGS

				Year Ending June 30		
Category	*1988*	*1989*	*1990*	*1991*	*1992*	*1993*
Net sales ($ thousands):						
Total	1,110,768	1,152,882	1,317,382	1,491,754	1,672,008	1,989,922
Consumer products only	548,906	627,208	729,944	878,608	1,015,934	1,211,884
Consumer products sold abroad only	264,726	233,710	414,454	482,684	542,688	N/A
Percent of contribution to income[a]						
Consumer products	57.5	55.9	58.4	70.1	71.5	79.9
Ethical products	35.7	35.5	33.2	25.3	26.0	18.7
Other products	6.8	8.6	8.4	4.6	2.5	1.4

ELLIS INTERNATIONAL, LA/FE

							Year Ending June 30					
Category	*1982*	*1983*	*1984*	*1985*	*1986*	*1987*	*1988*	*1989*	*1990*	*1991*	*1992*	*1993*
Net sales ($ millions)	64	76	70	82	90	100	114	126	172	212	224	272
Controllable marketing expense as percent of sales	13.6	12.7	14.2	14.2	14.9	15.4	15.7	16.1	13.1	14.9	15.5	17.6
Operating profit as percent of sales	13.6	9.0	9.6	12.6	7.3	9.1	9.4	10.5	12.1	14.6	16.7	15.1
ROAE	N/A	N/A	N/A	N/A	N/A	N/A	13.5	15.4	18.5	24.2	28.5	27.3

[a]Income before taxes and allocation of central administrative expense.

our organizational problems. The following summary of that session was presented some time back at a meeting in which we shared some of our experiences with a sister division.

The 1986–1987 Situation as Defined by Managers

"Managers were by no means unanimous in their views, but some of the feelings that were most often put forward can be summarized as follows:

1. Managers were influenced too much by immediate circumstances or events. Managing consisted of disposing of one crisis quickly enough to be ready for the next.
2. Almost without exception managers brought out one topic that they felt was of prime importance to them: 'Making this year's budget.'

   Managers expected their budgets to be revised in detail arbitrarily at headquarters. Managers felt they were judged only on whether or not the current year's budget was achieved in their markets.
3. Corporate and division objectives were known to have been slated for sales and profit growth. However, this was not the starting point for planning or budgeting within the markets.
4. They overall feeling about 'knowing where they were going' was that immediate problems did not allow time to worry to any great extent about the *long-term* future.
5. They believed that as long as everyone carried on as they had been doing, there was no reason for any serious doubts about the *short-term* future.
6. Headquarters staff (division and corporate) was essentially 'reaching over the shoulder' of both line management and functional counterparts in markets—emphasis was on audit ('police') and problem-solving ('intervention') activities, self-generated, or on behalf of corporate or division management.

"Clearly, we needed to delegate more responsibility for key managerial decisions, especially in marketing, to our operating units, but we lacked the focus, discipline, and procedural mechanisms to assure that such delegation would produce positive results.

"George Scott joined the division as finance director shortly thereafter and went to work on improving and systematizing our financial reporting and planning practices. Even before that, I had started working on ways to bring more rigor and discipline to our marketing activities in line with the new view of our business strategy. I set up the headquarters marketing departments to help me manage this new approach. The essence of the approach is reflected in a memo I issued in 1991 that formalized a classification of our products into three categories, each of which we had found to require different management approaches. The first, which we call development products, are those that are not currently being sold in commercial volume in any of our markets but promise to be winners. The main job of the HQ marketing directors is to assure that enough of these products are successfully introduced and spread throughout the division to provide us growth in future years. In the jargon of our management system, the development product program is 'prime moved' by our HQ marketing directors.

"Commercial products are those currently marketed successfully in several regions. They provide the bulk of our current business, but we have to watch their product life cycle and be especially wary of declining profitability in price-controlled markets under the pressure of cost inflation. Our HQ staff plays only a supporting role in the management of these products, with the Prime Movers being in the overseas operating units.

"Nondivisional products are those associated with only one market, with unknown or no potential for expansion to others (our insecticide line in Australia is a good example). We want our people overseas who handle these products to make them fully self-supportive while meeting our policies and standards. If they can't, we must divest the products. Generally they cannot rely on division resources, and support for these products that they themselves provide must not divert their own resources or attention from the expansion of profitable commercial products and the introduction of promising development products.

"Given the diversity of our markets and of the local personnel working in each of them (see Exhibit 3 for LA/FE organization chart), as well as the inherent difficulties in obtaining timely information flows that would allow markets to learn from each other and HQ staff to provide adequate support, we have developed a set of elaborate, formalized, and rather standardized management procedures. Through them we have been trying to professionalize our management and clarify the relationship between the various country operations and the headquarters' departments."

Ellis International, LA/FE's CP-R Management System

Ellis International, LA/FE employed an extensive formalized system of planning and control to direct and coordinate its widely scattered operating units. The system, known affectionately as CP-R (continuous planning and review), was not put in place all at once. O'Brian built up the division's management capacity piece by piece over a period of several years. He moved management personnel around to make better use of talent. He brought in additional help, especially in the marketing management area. He worked closely with his headquarters staff to develop an all-encompassing marketing methodology which could be applied consistently throughout the division and serve as a link for coordination with other functions. He worked individually with each manager reporting directly to him to develop a mutual understanding about the nature of managers' responsibilities. He knew that as the division grew, effective delegation of decision making to the appropriate levels would be indispensable. To assist in making this possible and to improve coordination, he established a work role assignment process. And to energize the division, he instituted a series of periodic management meetings tied to a detailed planning and review system that looked backward 12 months and forward three years, with a complete update every quarter.

Over the years, the division gained substantial experience with the various components of this process. Eventually, much of it became formalized in a series of manuals: the Product Marketing Guides, the Manager's Guides, and the Planning and Review Guide.

O'Brian: "The key to our management process is its thoroughness, combined with its flexibility. Take the Marketing Guides, for example. For each of our major products we develop a guide that includes eight separate documents. The first two, the Product Profile Statement (PMG-1) and the Product Marketing Policy (PMG-2), are developed by one of the marketing directors and his staff at division headquarters as a standardized blueprint for the product across the division. They serve as a basis for planning the expansion or introduction of the product in a market.

"The Product Data Book (PMG-3) and Product Marketing Assessment Statement (PMG-4) are developed by each regional or country unit handling or interested in introducing the product, to assess its appropriateness and potential in the local market. The regional market managing director is assigned the Approver role for the PMG-3, but because of its strategic importance, the PMG-4 is approved by the division president. The assessment in these two documents includes the discussion of reasons for deviations from the policies or standards set for the products in PMGs 1 and 2, if any are deemed necessary.

"The remaining PMG documents, covering specific aspects of marketing, advertising, promotion, and sales and distribution strategy in a given market, are put together to refine the assessment of the feasibility of the product in that market, and then to serve as the basis for the management of the product once it is introduced.

"The elaboration of each PMG document must be preceded by extensive research work. This might involve analysis of market conditions, product development, consumer attitude surveys, packaging design and testing, and so forth. Once the PMG package has been completed for a given product in a given market, however, all the pertinent results of this work are brought together in one place and are

EXHIBIT 3 Division Organization Structure

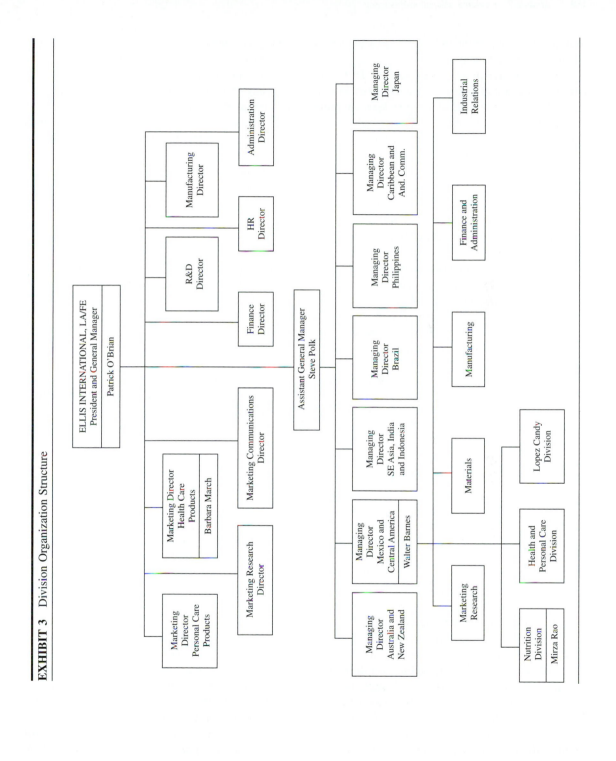

available for assessment and reference by managers throughout the division.

"As one of our product managers at HQ, who has had substantial field experience, likes to say, 'The PMG system doesn't let you take anything for granted. We are forced to go through all the steps and as a result we don't make those mistakes that used to slip by when we tried to finesse a difficult part of the marketing planning process.' But at the same time, each overseas operating unit is free to adapt the product policy to its own circumstances, giving us substantial built-in flexibility. And each exception to standard practice is thus made explicit.

"The marketing management process is embedded within a wider planning and review process, through which we obtain agreement on business financial objectives and functional operational objectives for each regional or country market, and between those markets and the division headquarters. These objectives in turn are tied to explicitly formulated strategic objectives for each unit and the division as a whole.

"The process also provides procedures for the continuing review, analysis, testing, and reporting of performance and progress toward achieving division and market objectives and standards. We have found it necessary to break with WI's traditional annual planning and budgeting cycle. It isn't dynamic enough for our markets, nor does it take a systematic enough look at the prospects for three, four, and five years out. So we have opted for our own system, which calls for quarterly updates and includes the prior year, the current year, and the next three years. (See Exhibit 4 for graphic representation of the CP-R planning cycle.)

"Once operational objectives are set, we use succinct but explicit Work Programs following a standard format. These serve to draw together from all involved parts of the organization the information required so that we can view each program as a whole. This lets us test and evaluate the risk/cost/benefit relationship of the operational objective and the Work Program for its achievement. We can also assure efficient use and timing of resources, and

identify conflicts between the demands of various Work Programs for limited resources.

"The Work Programs, of course, quickly multiply. They can cover objectives related to development products and commercial products within various markets. They can touch on issues of personnel development, improving inventory management, building new facilities, managing an acquisition or divestment, and so on and so forth. The roles our managers are called upon to play will vary from one Work Program to another. As a result, we have found it indispensable to devise a mechanism for keeping our wires untangled. We assign all concerned parties a specific role in each Work Program, Action Plan, or other formal CP-R scheduling document. The four roles are: Approver, Prime Mover, Concurrer, and Contributor. The terms are all positive by design. We want to get things done, not get them hung up.

"The Prime Mover, as the name implies, is the manager with the action. Quite frequently he or she will be at a third or fourth level in our hierarchy. This allows us to get around the rigidity of a chain of command and recognize the important and indispensable contribution to be made by those who actually push the work to its completion.

"The Approver is a higher-level manager than the Prime Mover—frequently, but not always his or her immediate superior. The Approver's job is to assure that the measures taken by the Prime Mover are in line with division policies and overall objectives. And especially in the case of relatively inexperienced Prime Movers, the Approver will take care to see that serious mistakes that might damage the division or the subordinate's career are avoided.

"Concurrers, of which there can be more than one on any given job, supply technical or specialized judgment to the Prime Mover. Their agreement is necessary prior to the implementation of any decision involving their area of expertise, although unresolvable disagreements can be referred to higher management. This perhaps is the one area where we still have to learn to do the job better. There is at times a tendency for Concurrers to behave as vetoers rather than positive collaborators.

EXHIBIT 4   CP-R Planning Cycle

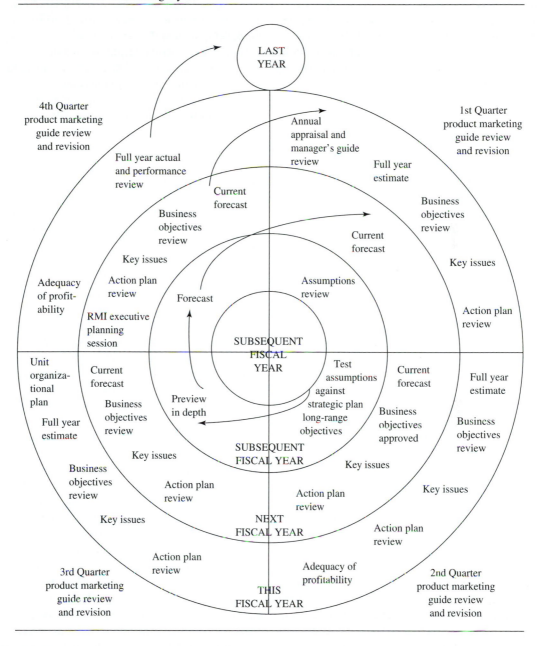

But by making the roles explicit, we find that such behavior becomes visible and can be dealt with. (Exhibit 5 presents the definitions of the work roles as they are set forth in the CP-R Manual.)

"I personally find the work role assignment process very valuable. By nature I am inclined to get involved in the details of every task. But now that the roles are formally specified, it has become commonplace for some of my directors to remind me to stay off their turf when I start getting too involved. There are days when I will be with one of them in two successive meetings in which our formally assigned roles change. It really helps us change gears."

Barbara March also found the CP-R management system of much help. As marketing director for Health Care Products, she had several hats to wear and many markets to work with. March had been with WI for 15 years since receiving her MBA from Cornell. Most of her career so far had been within the marketing function with the Ellis domestic Health Care Division. She had been in her present job for the last three years.

March: "I have enjoyed this job very much. While some people might find it difficult to move from the less formally structured management process in a domestic division to LA/FE with its CP-R system, I have found it invigorating. Patrick is a great guy to work for. He is bright, competent, and has a very professional approach to management. He has involved me deeply in the development and refinement of the division's marketing management approach and the techniques and procedures needed to carry it out. These are brought together in the PMG process.

"Working with Patrick on the elaboration of my Manager's Guide has made it possible to see where I can concentrate my efforts most productively for the division. It also has helped me see where my actions and those of my department affect the outcomes of other units and in what ways we are dependent on them. (Exhibit 6 shows one page from March's Manager's Guide.)

"As I see it, I have three main responsibilities. First, as part of Patrick's management team, I help him as he feels the need on a broad set of general issues along with the other division headquarters directors. Then, more specifically, I assist him in the development of the marketing function throughout the division in the Health Care area.

"Second, I am responsible for the adequate functioning of the division's activities aimed at business development in the health care field, including, more recently, nutritional products. My staff and I look for new ideas or products both from our people abroad and from outside the division or even outside the company. We undertake projects on our own to translate some of these ideas into physical products backed by a marketing strategy and marketing materials that can be tested in a trial market. Then we get the cooperation of one of our overseas units to test and launch it.

"For example, just over a year ago the Australian Board of Health relaxed limitations on the advertisement of liquid cold remedies. Australia saw this as an opportunity for itself, and we saw it as a good opportunity for the division, especially as we had indications that similar policy changes were in the making in some other countries in our half of the world. At division headquarters we pooled information worldwide on WI's capabilities in this area. Working with our Australian marketing staff, we did some consumer survey work. Out of this we concluded that SleepWell, which was being sold successfully in the United States and Europe, had promising potential. We then drew up a plan that would allow us to launch the product successfully in Australia within nine months. Members of my department and I, as well as other HQ staff members, traveled to Sydney several times during the subsequent months working very closely with, and providing assistance to, our local people out there. It required a concentrated joint effort, but we were successful in launching the product, which we call EasyRest in that market, within the time period specified. We beat the competition into the market by several weeks. We used the PMG process very successfully as an aid in getting all the pieces together, and the CP-R process helped get all the actors collaborating in a timely fashion. Manufacturing and

EXHIBIT 5   Work Role Definitions

Approver:	*Prime Mover:*	*Concurrer:*	*Contributor:*
The individual delegated the authority and responsibility by a higher management level to make the management decision to undertake, regulate, or terminate an activity at any phase and to accept or reject recommendation for further action.	The individual responsible to the Approver and delegated authority by the Approver for the management coordination and follow-through of all phases of the activity, from planning through implementation to evaluation of results. The Prime Mover makes recommendations for further action to the Approver and recommends Concurrers and selects Contributors.	Responsible to the Approver for providing to the Prime Mover judgment on the validity of those aspects of the activity within the scope of his or her expertise, and for contributing to the timely completion and quality of the activity. There can be more than one Concurrer.	Responsible to the Prime Mover for providing resources on aspects of the activity required or requested by the Prime Mover. There normally will be more than one Contributor. Contributors do not take part in the decision process.
The Approver assures adherence to policies and procedures. He or she approves or rejects requests for exceptions to policy, or endorses them for referral to higher authority if the exception is beyond his/her approval scope.	The Prime Mover is responsible to the Approver for adherence to policies and procedures and for prompt identification and justification of exceptions to policy.	Discusses with the Prime Mover areas of disagreement to reach a mutually acceptable agreement. If agreement cannot be reached between the Prime Mover and Concurrer, they jointly discuss with the Approver, who makes the decision or establishes the basis for resolution. If disagreement continues between the Concurrer and the Approver (and Prime Mover) on matters of technical expertise or exceptions to policy within the scope of the Concurrer's expertise, either the Approver or the Concurrer may refer the matter to higher management authority.	Each manager and supervisor who, because of his/her expertise or resources, recognizes themself as a Contributor to a particular work activity must also exercise initiative in assuming this work role. If not designated he or she should approach the Prime Mover and secure the Prime Mover's agreement to his or her involvement as Contributor.
Consistent with Delegation of Authority, the Approver retains responsibility for performance and designates Concurrers.		It is the responsibility of each manager and supervisor to exercise individual initiative in assuming the role of Concurrer for a particular work activity that involves his/her expertise. If not nominated, he or she should approach the Prime Mover and secure both the Approver's and Prime Mover's agreement to his/her involvement as Concurrer.	

EXHIBIT 6   Excerpt from March's *Manager's Guide*

Key Result Area: **KEY TASK #1**   Position: Div. Marketing Dir.
Tomorrow's Products   Page
                                                                       Date:
                                                                       Revised: December 6, 1991

KEY TASK #1

As Prime Mover to ensure that sufficient viable ideas for
Development Products are being identified and acted
upon at least to meet future Division growth needs.

STANDARDS OF PERFORMANCE	EVIDENCE OF ACHIEVEMENT
a. When there is an approved plan, consistent with division objectives and strategy, for long-term business development of the field of activity, including product development, acquisition, and licensing.	a. GM approval of HQ Marketing Preview in Depth (PID) for the category.
b. When there is an ongoing program to track and screen, against division criteria and objectives for the category, new product activity within the Ellis divisions.	b. Individual performance reviews against action plans. Minutes of meetings within the program.
c. When there is an ongoing program to test objectives and screening criteria and to identify or generate ideas for prospective development products.	c. Individual performance reviews against action plans. Minutes of meeting within the program.
d. When all ideas that pass the screening against divisional criteria are promptly referred to R&D for exploratory feasibility.	d. R&D approved projects.
e. When 80% of the recommendations of the Active Development State are approved and allocated the necessary resources on the basis of reasonable or supportable quantified statements of cost and potential benefits/risks.	e. GM approvals of not less than 80% of submitted project guides.
f. When the marketing checkpoints included in assigned Active Development Projects are adequate to validate continuance, to select an alternative course or to terminate, and when appropriate action is taken when each checkpoint is reached.	f. GM approval of action plan. Indvidual performance reviews against action plans.
g. When no assigned Active Development Project is significantly delayed, has its cost increased, or fails because of inadequate or delayed marketing information or because of failure to provide, promptly, requested and agreed-upon HQ market support or resources.	g. Individual performance reviews against action plans.
h. When, at all times, there is at least one development product of the assigned category on the Active Development State (or under negotiation for license/acquisition **and** at least one other undergoing testing (including test marketing) each with a first sustaining year national contribution **total** for **major** markets in excess of $1 million, at a contribution ratio, growth rate, investment level, and ROAE equal to or better than criteria for the category and whose resource requirements are within the capabilities of the division and the major markets.	h. Project guides and action plans.

marketing EasyRest in Australia is now primarily the responsibility of our people out there, although in our third role as a resource department on marketing we will continue to be available to assist our people in Australia if and when they need it.

"Back to the issue of business development: when our overseas units have a substantial nondivision business segment that warrants product development as part of its long-term strategy, we allow them to develop such products within our policies, procedures, and standards, and try to support them in every way we can. The PMG system provides us with regular feedback reports, and through it we are assured that a thorough review is made of all aspects of the product that could make it successful or cause it to flounder. Several of our units, especially Australia, Mexico, and India, are strong in new product development, but they still each have some shortcomings. We try to capitalize on their strengths by letting them take a lot of initiative and operate quite independently, while we remain available to help whenever it's needed.

"This job allows me to act both as a marketing staff director and as an operating director for the new product development program. This is challenging and personally satisfying. I know that my counterpart for Personal Care Products feels the same way. It is what attracted him to come to WI. It would be nearly impossible to carry out this dual role without the work role assignment approach of the CP-R system. Since it started being used regularly in the division, the amount of wasted time and effort has dropped considerably. Delays in communication between the field and headquarters have also been reduced substantially."

Walter Barnes, managing director in Mexico since 1989, while committed to the CP-R system, was less enthusiastic about it. Of his 20 years with WI, he had spent about half in manufacturing and marketing management, first with WI domestic and then with international. For the last 10 years, he had held various field management positions in Latin America.

Barnes: "CP-R certainly has a lot going for it, but it does cause us some problems. The quarterly management review meetings are tremendously helpful. We get a lot of problems resolved, and are able to adjust our objectives often enough to keep an even keel in a very volatile political and economic environment. But there is an overload of paperwork. My financial director has to keep records for me under the CP-R system, but since we also service the Mexican office of Wells International, he has to follow a different setup for them.

"And then there is the language barrier. Most of our Mexican management people have a working knowledge of English, but we conduct our business in Spanish and as a result they find it hard to tune in to the CP-R system, which is all in English. Some of the terminology can't even be translated. Then, of course, there is a cultural barrier in almost all LA/FE overseas locations. Some are not comfortable with such explicitly assigned responsibilities, with everyone's performance open to the general view, especially if they are accustomed to use a more personalized form of supervision.

"We are trying to apply the CP-R system to our operations, but so far it has been more difficult than we anticipated. However, I feel it will be worth all the effort.

"Some of our managers feel CP-R is really an extension of Patrick O'Brian, that he makes it work by pure willpower, and they're sure we are all the better for it. The division's performance certainly has improved. In part it's a big advantage, but in part it may be a drawback that Patrick knows so much about our market and our operations. He has a tendency to get too involved from time to time in the details of running our business. Maybe Mexico is a special case. He spent 18 months here in 1979 to 1980 as director."

Corporate/Division Relations

Although WI went public in 1946, the Wells family maintained a strong ownership position and an active role in the company's corporate management. Jonathan Wells, Jr., chairman of the board since 1976, had previously been a vice president, administrative vice president, and president (1967–1976). The company had a long tradition of hiring top-of-the-class graduates from leading colleges and moving them through a management career ladder, starting in field sales, thus "developing our own managers." Vice Chairman James Weingarten, who was president from 1979 to 1980, and Peter Connor, president since 1975, both had followed this path.

Top management, therefore, had a strategy of monitoring the growth and development of its young managers carefully, placing them in key positions as they showed an ability to handle the challenges at that level, giving them basic guidance as to overall corporate objectives, and allowing them substantial freedom to manage their own shops. As Joan Lake, executive vice president for the Ellis divisions, put it: "The most important part of my job is on the people side. The better the people, the less I have to be involved in day-to-day operations."

Corporate officers had an open-door policy toward key operating managers and expected them to bring up any problems or opportunities that required attention at any time. They also traveled and visited field operations from time to time, with particular interest in staying in touch with management personnel at various levels. Peter Connor made it a habit to have lunch once or twice a month with junior managers from various divisions at the Ellis headquarters.

Formal reviews of divisional plans and performance were limited to the following three areas:

1. Previews-in-Depth (PIDS) of a particular business or market, initiated by the Operating Committee (president, executive vice presidents, vice president for manufacturing services, and controller). Such a planning exercise would look at all facets of that part of the business going out three to five years into the future.
2. The Step Planning Process, designed to spread planning and budgeting activities out over the year. For Step 1, in late January, the divisions would highlight for top management the key problems and opportunities for the coming fiscal year. Step 2, around March, involved the presentation of recommended plans of action in light of the discussions during Step 1. In

May, Step 3 was undertaken, involving the presentation, analysis, and approval of an annual operating plan and budget for the upcoming fiscal year. This was known as the executive budget session. The key parameters set at this time were sales projections, profit targets, and plans for controllable marketing expenses. Capital investment requirements would also be discussed, if relevant. Approval for particular investment projects, however, was normally handled on a case-by-case basis throughout the year, with final approval frequently following a review by the board of directors. Step 4 involved a less formal monitoring of performance against budget.

Although corporate management indicated an openness to alternative approaches to formal planning and reporting procedures between the Operating Committee and the divisions, only Ellis LA/FE had introduced innovations, all based on the functioning of the CP-R system. Prior to each quarterly review meeting and drawing on the preparation for it, Ellis LA/FE submitted a planning and review book to top management that encompassed a rolling four-quarter plan, spanning two fiscal years. Lake and other corporate officers had an open invitation to attend the quarterly meetings. The preparation prior to the fourth quarter meeting also served as the basis for the submission of the division's executive budget proposal for the upcoming fiscal year.

3. The management personnel appraisal and promotion process. This was a regular, yearly process whereby managers evaluated all their direct reports and discussed with them their strengths and weaknesses. Relevant information was then passed up to successive levels of management along with recommendations for training, promotions, salary increases, and participation in the incentive compensation plan, which consisted of both a cash bonus and a stock option plan based on corporate and division profit performance. Salary, promotion, and incentive recommendations were reviewed by committees

at the division level (with participation by the executive vice president) and corporate level, depending on the manager's rank. The recommendations of the division general manager and the executive vice president carried a lot of weight.

Project Alpha

Mexico was the largest operating entity within LA/FE, and had concentrated traditionally on proprietary drugs. In 1979 it entered the nutrition field with the acquisition of NutriMilk, a well-established brand of powdered milk supplement with an existing distribution network. Consisting mainly of powdered milk, chocolate, and sugar, NutriMilk provided nutritional reinforcement as well as flavoring. It took several years to modernize the production facilities, improve the formula to suit changing tastes and meet several competitive entities, and develop the management capacity to deal with this new market. One of the main stumbling blocks was the absence of a reliable source of supply for high-quality chocolate that would make it possible to upgrade the product. This was achieved in 1981 with the acquisition of the Lopez Candy Company, one of Ellis's major chocolate suppliers. Now local management faced a new set of challenges. Not only did it have to proceed with the upgrading and expansion of NutriMilk, but it also had to learn to manage the specialty candy business into which it had entered. It took several more years for both tasks to be accomplished.

When Walter Barnes became managing director in Mexico in 1989, one of his early concerns was to strengthen the NutriMilk segment of the business. It seemed risky to have such an important segment relying on only one product that already dominated its market with a 50 percent market share, and that was under considerable competitive pressure. Secondly, the traditional proprietary drug business continued to be price controlled, offering negative prospects for improved profitability. Additional entries into the nutrition field appeared to be worth serious consideration.

After consultation with division headquarters, Barnes commissioned a study of potential entries for the Mexican nutritional product market. The study was carried out by the marketing research department in Mexico with assistance from a New York consulting firm in 1990 to 1991. The study took an exhaustive look at food items sold in grocery stores in Mexico, the United States, and Canada to identify categories of consumer needs for which solutions were sought through processed foods sold in food stores. The surveys were carried out with panels of Mexican housewives to learn their underlying concerns regarding each class of needs. Out of this emerged a slate of product concepts for development and testing. These were screened for feasibility as products for Ellis Mexico.

At a divisional management meeting in August of 1991, the results of the study were presented along with a final slate of potential new products for development and market testing. The slate was approved, as was an overall new product development program. A target was set to test market at least one new product from the slate each year. Product Alpha was the first new item on the slate.

Mirza Rao was assigned in October of 1992 to become director of Ellis's newly established Nutrition Division, responsible for the ongoing NutriMilk business and the new nutritional product development program. He already had a track record of successful development and introduction of new products with Ellis International's Indian subsidiary.

A philosophy major at Harvard College, Rao had decided after graduation to look for opportunities in business management that would allow him to return to India, use his creative energies, and still have time for personal development as a thinker and writer. He found the opportunity with WI, which he joined in 1978. In 1991, Rao was offered the choice of joining the division's Health Care Products marketing department to work on new product development, or to take the job in Mexico.

"I decided to go to Mexico," Rao said, "because I wanted to be close to the market, where the action is. I wanted to have responsibility for all the facets of product development, testing, and launching. I like to have control over my piece of the business and to be judged by the results I achieve. It allows me to exercise my creative energies. I guess I have an entrepreneurial spirit."

Alpha was Rao's first challenge in this new position. The product was aimed at a felt need of the Mexican mother for a quick, easy, yet nourishing beverage for use on hectic school days. Over the next 18 months Rao worked intensively with a technical group in the NutriMilk plant to develop a suitable product. He also enlisted the help of the marketing research department to carry out extensive product concept research with potential users. During this period there was little interaction with headquarters staff other than routine communication of progress and occasional inputs from the division research and development director on issues of product quality.

No formal Work Program was drawn up. Nonetheless, Ellis Mexico did have extensive internal plans and schedules including a PERT-type plan for Alpha. Since it was a totally new product with which the HQ staff had no familiarity, there were no PMG-1 and PMG-2. Barnes and Rao considered Alpha a nondivisional product like NutriMilk for which they were responsible.

In January of 1993, Rao contracted with a Mexico City advertising agency to start developing material for use in the first market tests later that year. He had another contractor develop an innovative container for Alpha.

With the time approaching to make initial commitments for market testing, it was necessary to obtain overall division management approval of the project's current status and direction. A meeting for this purpose was planned for early May. In preparation for this meeting, the PMGs 3, 4, 5, 6, 7, and 8 were completed in late April and sent to headquarters personnel for their review.

By separating the PMG into various documents, the CP-R system made it possible to assign different work roles to various individuals for each piece. While PMGs 1 and 2 were primarily the work of headquarters staff, the remaining parts required

substantial collaboration between headquarters and field. The Approver role for the PMG-3 was assigned to the regional managing director, with the Prime Mover, Concurrers, and Contributors coming from the local staff. The PMGs 4 and 5, which were key strategy documents, required the approval of the division president and the concurrence of several headquarters directors, as well as overseas unit functional managers. PMGs 6, 7, and 8, which usually were prepared after 4 and 5 had been approved, usually could be approved by the division assistant general manager with concurrence only from the headquarters director with specific functional expertise in each case.

With the Alpha PMG, however, because all six parts arrived at the same time, the package was reviewed as a unit by all the potential Concurrers and Approvers. Barbara March, as Prime Mover for the overall Development Products program, became the focal point for the review at HQ.

In studying the PMG documents on Product Alpha, March was surprised to see it classified as a nondivisional product. Nonetheless she felt that an excellent job had been done in the area of product concept research, product development in the lab, and assessment of market potential. Reactions from other headquarters departments were similarly supportive, with a few technical suggestions for improvement. The material on marketing strategy and advertising, however, was very spotty and failed to take full advantage of the marketing research.

During the next several weeks, Rao made three trips to division headquarters in the hope of getting the necessary approvals to proceed with a test market launch of Alpha. After the first meeting in May, Patrick O'Brian approved the Alpha program and the PMG-4 in principle. It was agreed that Mexico would undertake several technical improvements having to do with packaging, labeling, and product quality, as well as obtain some additional information on potential users. O'Brian also asked Rao to review PMGs 5 through 8 with March after the meeting, since extensive comment had been made about their adequacy. At this point, a Work Program was prepared (see Exhibit 7).

EXHIBIT 7 Alpha Work Program

OBJECTIVE/STANDARD:

Test market and evaluate Alpha leading to a decision to introduce nationally.

Major Steps	Person or Unit	Outputs	Start Date	End Date	*	Comments
1. Wilton approval of project	MR	1. Minutes of May 8 meeting.		05/93	*	1. Completed
2. Order packaging molds, raw and packaging materials	RB	2. a. Approval of preliminary molds. b. Receipt of all materials necessary for initial production.	R7/93 R8/93	R9/93 R10/93	*	2. B. Glass will be required to approve preliminary molds
3. Obtain advertising approval	MR AQ	3. Approved commercials for air. a) MC-1 approval b) Storyboard approval c) Pretesting/SSA d) Approval to produce	R6/93	R2/93 R7/93 R8/93 R10/93 R10/93	*	
4. Manufacturing booklet	SH/WRG	4. Red Book issued.	R8/93	R9/93	*	4. D. Jones to issue
5. Product ready	APS	5. Pipeline stock plus first two months expected consumer takeoff of finished stock in warehouse.	Rt-135	Rt-15	*	5. **Contingent on approval** of MO-2 (test market proposal) or separate approval to buy material and packaging inventories
6. Production of marketing communication materials	MR	6. Commercials in can. Promotion/display materials in warehouse. Media space booked. Sales force briefing/training.	Rt-75 Rt-60 Rt-30 Rt-5	Rt-15 Rt-15 Rt-30 Rt-1	*	(Note: In the date columns O stands for original and R stands for revised)
7. Test market distribution		7. Pipeline horizontal and vertical distribution objectives and promotion/display objectives achieved or surpassed.	Rt	Rt+21 Rt+56	*	MR = Rao / RB = Mexico Materials Manager / AQ = Mexico Nutritional Division Product Manager
8. Month x evaluation of test market	MR	8. Implement month x reaction program.	O 1/w R1/x	O 30/w R 30/x	*	WRG = Division Manufacturing Director
9. Month y evaluation of test market	MR WB	9. Monthly reaction program. Order balance of equipment.	O 1/x R 1/y	O 30/x R 30/y	*	APS = Mexico Manufacturing Director
10. Month z evaluation of text market	MR WB	10. TMM approval to go national, expand text market, or recycle.	O 1/y R 1/z	O 30/y R 30/z	*	HB = Mexico Nutritional Division Sales Manager / t = Test market starting date

Work Program	Prime Mover M. Rao — Approver W. Barnes	Business Segment or Department — Nutritional	Alpha Project	Date Initiated—5/93 — Last Revision—8/93	CP-R WP	Page
Corp/Country Mexico						

(In preparation for mid-August Inventory Review Meeting.)

For the first time, Rao became aware that an MC-1 (a CP-R document designed to provide an advertising agency with guidance for developing advertising material) would be required, and that for Development Products the MC-1 had to be approved by the division president and concurred with by Assistant General Manager Steve Polk, Barbara March, and the marketing communications director.

In June, Rao returned with a draft MC-1 and a package of advertising material that he wished to use in the test launch. He needed various concurrences and approval from headquarters management in order to proceed. Barbara March and the marketing communications director had previously reviewed the material and made some suggestions for improvement. When Rao met with Patrick O'Brian for approval, he found that O'Brian thought basic changes in the market positioning of Alpha, implicit in the advertising copy, would be necessary. He suggested that Rao return to Mexico and revise the PMG-5, PMG-6, and MC-1 in line with their discussion. He should then submit the MC-1 to headquarters for approval which, O'Brian promised, would be forthcoming within 48 hours. To assure a quick turnaround, he delegated the Approver role jointly to Polk and March.

Rao was crushed. He told O'Brian that he felt let down by the whole system. How could it be that after getting professional inputs from the agency in Mexico, approval in principle of the PMG, and comments about the advertising copy from headquarters staff that had been incorporated into the material, a major flaw should come out in a meeting with the division president? And with every passing day the project was falling further behind schedule.

Upon returning to Mexico, Rao revised the MC-1 and sent it to division HQ in early July. A week later he received a request from Barbara March to come to the United States for a meeting to get the MC-1 approved. In late July that meeting

took place. The PMG-5, PMG-6, and MC-1 were jointly rewritten. Then all Concurrers and the Approvers initialed the MC-1 document. Rao returned to Mexico to have the agency prepare storyboards for TV ads. He had instructions to return to headquarters with these for approval in late August.

Prior to his departure for the mid-August quarterly review meeting, Walter Barnes, who had been away for six weeks at a management education program, had a long discussion with Rao about the Alpha project.

Barnes: "Mirza was very unhappy. He had worked for a year and a half getting Alpha off the ground. He had been successful in getting our Mexican R&D, marketing research, manufacturing, and other staff departments involved and excited. They were all committed to a tightly programmed project schedule and had produced truly innovative top-quality results. We were convinced that we had identified a project with very significant potential.

"After moving along so well, however, we are now running into trouble. While the difficulties focus on Alpha, it is really the entire nutritional new product program that is at stake. The establishment of such a program had been attempted without success ever since the acquisition of NutriMilk in 1979. I had taken a different approach from my predecessors and, after four years of work with the entire Mexican organization and with the full knowledge of division management, appeared to be achieving results.

"To succeed, however, our people need to be free to take risks, to move quickly, to be entrepreneurial, and to feel that they will be judged on their results. The way the CP-R process is being applied is making this extremely difficult.

"I hope at the quarterly meeting we can work out some way of maintaining our present momentum and of providing the freedom and flexibility we need to ensure the continued progress of our whole nutritional new product program."

Case 2–2

AMERICHEM: THE GAYLORD
DIVISION (A)

"Well, all hell broke loose this morning. What do I have to do this afternoon to pull my group together and get some agreement?" Spencer Brown asked himself. As general manager of Americhem's Gaylord Division, Brown had spent the best part of the last day and a half with his immediate subordinates trying to get consensus on next year's operating budget. After a rough morning, he had used lunch as an opportunity to get away and plan how he could resolve the issues that were blocking progress.

In the past, budgeting had been straightforward: The previous year's budget was adjusted according to the changes that Brown and his department managers agreed would be necessary. This year, however, the Gaylord Division had been asked to employ a new budgeting process, Priority Resource Budgeting (PRB), as part of Americhem's effort to improve the management of overhead costs. The new process had proved to be far more time-consuming and complicated than the old.

During the past several months, Brown's department managers had worked with their subordinates to identify explicitly the tasks for which they were responsible and to attach specific estimates of benefits and costs to each task or activity. Each manager had then met with his or her key subordinates to rank the tasks ("increments," in PRB terms) from highest priority to lowest. The primary goal of this effort was to give priority to overhead activities that supported the unit's tactical and strategic business plans. A second important goal was to control the level of overhead expenditures.

Based on meetings with each of his department managers to discuss their rankings, Brown believed that the process was achieving these two goals.

PRB had required reams of paper and a substantial commitment of time, but until today, notwithstanding a certain amount of grumbling and confusion, the effort appeared to have gone smoothly.

Brown was now in the middle of his division ranking meeting. The goals of the meeting were the same as the departmental level, but the task was more complex. While rank increments within departments had often required that difficult decisions be made, the commonalties among the functional activities facilitated choices and trade-offs. Trying to decide whether the next $300,000 should be spent on Sales or R&D was altogether different. This interfunctional ranking seemed to Brown to produce an atmosphere of competition. Managers behaved as if they were in a zero-sum game, and Brown was worried that the conflict would undermine his efforts over the past two years to develop a spirit of teamwork in his group.

"I've never seen Louise Mercier so angry," he reflected, "and her Commodities group produced three-quarters of last year's cash flow. And Sales really has me stumped. What is the right level of support for that function? I guess we are wrestling with some issues we should have confronted before, so things aren't all bad. But I'm sure of one thing—if we can't pull together on this budget, it's going to be a tough year."

Company Background

Americhem's headquarters were located in a campuslike setting on the outskirts of Pittsburgh,

---

This case was prepared by David A. Garvin.

Copyright © 1996 by the President and Fellows of Harvard College. Harvard Business School case 396-189.

Pennsylvania, not far from where Charles M. Gaylord founded the company in 1916. In 1993, Americhem's sales were $5 billion. Net income before taxes was $576 million. Over 30,000 employees staffed its 175 plants and 135 offices around the world. Exhibit 1 shows recent financial results.

Americhem's widely diversified line of chemical products included chemical intermediates (petrochemicals, process chemicals, etc.), industrial chemicals (detergents and phosphates, rubber chemicals, plasticizers, etc.), plastics and resins, textiles (man-made fibers), agricultural chemicals, and industrial process controls. To a large extent, Americhem sold its products to other industries rather than to end users.

Management Style

In 1987 Peter J. Lane joined Americhem as president. Lane, age 50, had spent his entire career at Procter & Gamble, and his arrival from the outside broke with a long-standing Americhem tradition to grow its own leaders. His arrival signaled a new approach to management and, especially, an increased emphasis on marketing.

From the start, Lane saw a need to develop a new administrative structure with which to formulate and implement changes. By 1989, such a structure began to emerge, and with it a distinctive management style. Later Lane was to write: "The Americhem Management Style is the process by which we define what we want to accomplish and the framework in which we pursue our Corporate Objectives."

The process by which the management style was implemented was as follows (see Exhibit 2 for a flow chart showing implementation steps). Top management set corporate objectives and policies. Given these statements, Americhem's senior operating managers produced explicit statements of strategy ("Direction Papers"). Operating companies and similar units then produced "Summary Long-Range Plans." Next, individual managers identified the results they must achieve (the Management by Results program) to support the operational plans. The budgeting process was then supposed to develop explicit statements of organizational goals and resource commitments for a one-year period.

In the early 1990s Lane and other senior managers became increasingly concerned with the weakness of the link between business strategies and the budgets for Marketing, Administration, and Technology (MAT) expenses and for

EXHIBIT 1   Americhem Financial Results ($ millions)

	1993	*1992*	*1991*	*1990*	*1989*	*1988*	*1987*
Sales	5,109	4,595	4,270	3,625	3,498	2,225	1,939
Operating income	632	610	668	547	550	216	191
Net income	303	276	366	306	323	122	116
Total assets	5,036	4,350	3,959	3,451	2,938	2,237	2,012
Long-term debt	1,224	1,031	915	845	587	576	454
Shareowners' equity	2,579	2,401	2,253	1,977	1,755	1,294	1,205
Net income as a % of:							
Net sales	6.0%	6.0%	8.6%	8.4%	9.2%	5.5%	6.0%
Average shareowners' equity	12.2	11.9	17.3	16.4	20.0	9.7	9.8
Average total assets	6.3	6.6	9.9	9.6	11.8	5.6	5.0

EXHIBIT 2   Schematic of Americhem's Management Style

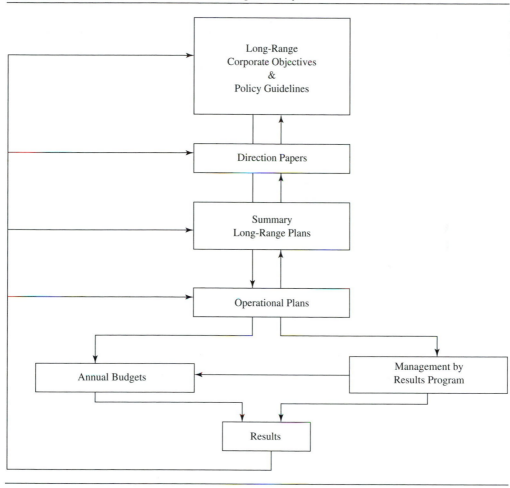

Factory Indirect Expense (FIE). Specifically, Lane said:

> As we continue to extend the entire planning process, it is important for Americhem to ensure that its total MAT expenses are both optimally allocated to support the various business strategies of the company and held to a level consistent with the planned overall financial results of the corporation.[1]

After investigating a variety of budgeting systems, it was decided that zero-based budgeting (ZBB) offered the most potential. In 1993, Priority Resource Budgeting (PRB),[2] a form of ZBB modified to fit Americhem's particular needs, was tested in several Americhem units. PRB was introduced throughout two Americhem companies in 1994, including the Americhem Commodity Chemicals

---

[1] *In 1993, MAT expenses for Americhem totaled $643 million. This amount represented almost 14.7 percent of total operating costs for the year.*

[2] *See the Appendix for a description of the Priority Resource Budgeting (PRB) system.*

EXHIBIT 3 Corporate Organization Structure, 1993

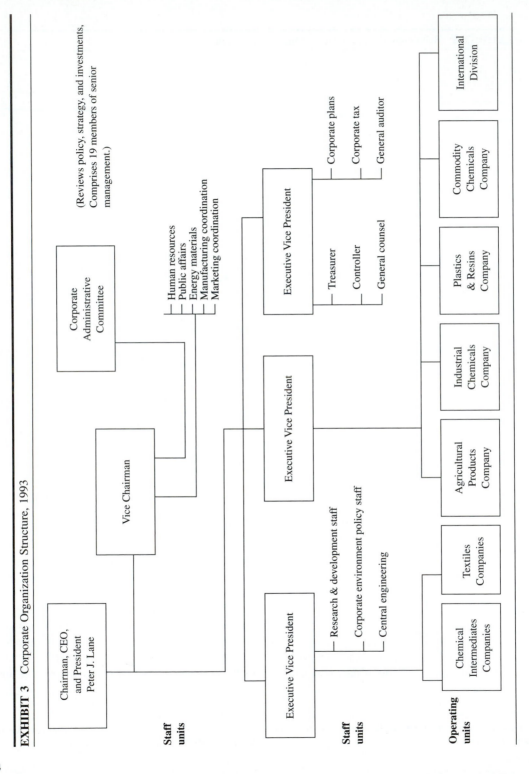

Chairman, CEO, and President Peter J. Lane

Corporate Administrative Committee

(Reviews policy, strategy, and investments. Comprises 19 members of senior management.)

Vice Chairman

Human resources
Public affairs
Energy materials
Manufacturing coordination
Marketing coordination

Executive Vice President

Research & development staff
Corporate environment policy staff
Central engineering

Executive Vice President

Executive Vice President

Treasurer
Controller
General counsel

Corporate plans
Corporate tax
General auditor

Staff units

Staff units

Operating units

Chemical Intermediates Companies

Textiles Companies

Agricultural Products Company

Industrial Chemicals Company

Plastics & Resins Company

Commodity Chemicals Company

International Division

EXHIBIT 4   Commodity Chemical Company Organizational Structure

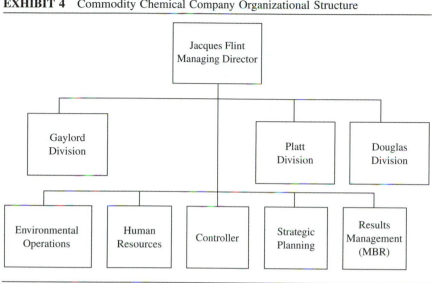

Company[3] (Exhibit 3 shows the corporate organizational structure).

The Gaylord Division

The Gaylord Division was one of the three operating divisions that made up the Americhem Commodity Chemicals Company. (See Exhibit 4 for an organization chart.) For most of its history, the Gaylord Division's product line had been dominated by six successful commodity chemicals for the food processing and related industries. Management of these products had been divided between two departments, each of which had responsibility for three of the major commodity items as well as a number of minor related commodity and consumer products. In 1985, Spencer Brown and Jack McKnight were the department heads of these units.

Market analysis during the mid-1980s had shown that four of the six commodity products were in the "mature" stage of their product life cycle and the other two were in "late growth." While the profit picture was quite good, Gaylord management con-fronted the prospect of little, if any, further growth from its major products.

Jim Applebaum, then the general manager of Gaylord, had responded by increasing the division's support of several of its newer products and by stepping up new product development efforts. One of his first moves was to place the promising oil additive chemical products into a newly created department. Jack McKnight, who had championed his relatively new line, left his department to head up the new unit. In 1990, Applebaum decided to separate the faster growing consumer chemicals from the slower growing commodity chemicals. As a result of the reorganization, Spencer Brown's department was given responsibility for all commodity chemicals, and Frank Baldwin (who stepped in when McKnight moved to oil additives) was given responsibility for all consumer chemicals.

In May 1992, Applebaum was promoted to managing director of the Commodity Chemical Company.[4] In turn, Brown became general manager

---

[3]*Americhem was organized into major business units, each of which was called a company.*

[4]*Applebaum was seriously injured months later as a result of an accident and elected to retire early from Americhem. He was replaced by Jacques Flint, general manager of the Platt Division.*

EXHIBIT 5   Gaylord Division Organizational Structure

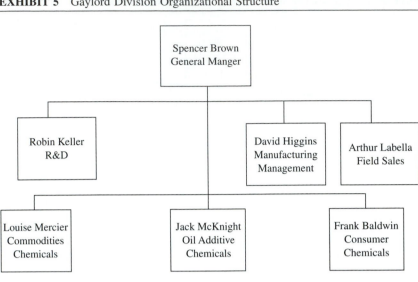

---

of Gaylord, and Mercier took charge of the Commodity Chemicals Department.

In 1994, Gaylord's performance was projected to be as follows:

Department	Sales (millions)	Net Pretax Income (millions)	Growth Rate
Commodity Chemicals	$600	$90	Slow
Consumer Chemicals	80	9	Rapid
Oil Additive Chemicals	220	60	Medium

The structure of the organization managed by Brown in 1994 was essentially identical to that which he took over in 1992. (Exhibit 5 contains an organization chart for the Gaylord Division.)

The Gaylord Division Ranking

"In an hour we begin again," thought Brown. "I'd better figure out how to make sense from the confusion we generated this morning. When this is all over, I'm going to have to spend a quiet weekend sorting out all I've seen of PRB."

One-on-One Meetings

"The seeds for what has been happening in this ranking meeting were planted in the one-on-one review sessions I held with each of my managers over a week ago,"[5] Brown reflected. (Exhibit 6 contains background information on each of the key managers in the Gaylord Division.)

Robin Keller's was the easiest and most informative session. As soon as he knew I was committed to doing some basic research, he loosened up. I liked the results of his R&D ranking meeting in that they fit our strategy. But I could see some potential problems coming from the big shift in research effort from Commodity Chemicals to Consumer Chemicals. I expected a backlash on that from Louise Mercier, and we sure got it.

---

[5]*The "one-on-one" review meetings were held between a ranking manager and each of his or her decision unit managers prior to the ranking meeting. According to the Americhem Priority Resource Budgeting Manual (1993): "This meeting is not a decision making meeting but rather an informational meeting."*

EXHIBIT 6   Biographies of Participants at Gaylord's PRB Ranking Meeting

Spencer Brown   Age 41, had worked at Americhem for 18 years. His first job had been as field salesman, but he was soon transferred into a product department where he worked for Jim Applebaum. He became a department head when Applebaum moved up to the division general manager post. In 1992 he replaced Applebaum as general manager of Gaylord. Brown was a reasonable man with a low-key management style. He had worked hard to build team spirit among managers.

Robin Keller   Age 45, had been at Americhem for over 20 years, the entire time in R&D. His staff now numbered over 60 and along with most of them he shared an enthusiasm for basic research. He believed that most of Americhem's R&D dollars had to be spent on immediately commercializable research, but as he told his people: "We do commercial stuff because it pays the bills, but it's basic research that keeps us intellectually alive and secures the future of this company."

David Higgins   Age 57, had spent his career in manufacturing at Americhem. Seven plant managers, and through them several thousand people, reported to him. Only his divisional headquarters staff was being ranked at this meeting; all the others would be ranked within their own plants. Higgins was widely respected as a hard-nosed guy who got things done.

Frank Baldwin   Age 35, had joined Americhem in manufacturing in 1982. Four years later he moved to field sales, then to the marketing staff. He became a product department head in 1988. Baldwin believed strongly that Gaylord's growth would have to come from Consumer Products.

Jack McKnight   Age 39, had joined Americhem in the late 1970s as an engineer. After three years in a plant, he had taken a leave of absence to go to a well-known midwestern business school. On his return he had progressed rapidly and was one of the two product department heads when Applebaum became Gaylord's general manager. When Applebaum created the Oil Additive Chemicals department, he put McKnight in charge of it.

Louise Mercier   Age 37, had been at Americhem for 13 years. When Brown was promoted to general manager, Mercier took over the Commodity Chemicals department. She was ambitious for her area and hoped that she could appeal for support to Brown. She was well liked and respected by her subordinates.

Arthur Labella   Age 35, was new to his job as manager of Gaylord's field sales. Only two months before he had headed up the Central Region Sales Office, where he had worked for almost 13 years. He had made his reputation as a salesman, and his skills as an administrator were not yet fully tested.

Susan Roscoe   Age 29, was a first-level manager in Americhem's Chemical Commodities Company's Controllers department. This was her first time as a PRB analyst, and she was unsure what to think of it. On the one hand she wanted the exposure; on the other hand she was concerned about making mistakes or antagonizing anyone.

Louise is doing a good job with Commodity Chemicals, and her PRB analysis showed it. Still, I don't think she can grow and resents all the attention Frank Baldwin is getting with Consumer. Competent but defensive is the way I'd characterize her behavior in our one-on-one meeting. She knew she wasn't going to get as much R&D as she wanted.

Arthur Labella was disappointing. His analysis was not so hot. He said his salesmen were all busy selling, and there was no time to fill out the forms. I must admit, though, I have a tough time defining a sales increment myself.

The others were about as I expected. Frank Baldwin was well prepared and aggressive. He intends to grow and he can make a good case for it with Consumer. Jack McKnight was confident and protective. Too confident, maybe; they needed *more* resources. I'm not sure they checked to see which areas are fat, and some are, for sure. David Higgins, on the other hand, was a little discouraged. He didn't see that PRB made any sense for Manufacturing, and I think he still feels that way.

When I think back on it, everyone I talked to gave me signals about what was likely to happen during this Division ranking meeting. At least next year I'll try to make better use of that information.

The Division Ranking Meeting: First Day
Brown's thoughts turned to the ranking meeting.

Yesterday morning the ranking had seemed mechanical, easy—almost trivial. The thresholds reviewed in the one-on-one meetings were accepted without debate, except that Labella hadn't studied all the other guys' work and that slowed things down a bit. David got a laugh when he said, "Hell, Arthur, you're in the big league now. You've got to read this stuff *before* you come to meetings."

Ranking the items just after the threshold was no real problem, although during the later afternoon there were a few disagreements. As could be anticipated, most differences of opinion centered on the question of relative priorities of untried growth products versus proven and profitable mature products. Agreement was reached amicably in each case. Exhibit 7 contains the final page of the Gaylord Division's PRB ranking table as it appeared at the end of the first day. It shows that 82 increments

had been ranked with cumulative expenses at 88 percent of the current level and headcount at 85 percent of the current level.

When the meeting broke up around four in the afternoon, Brown was confident that while the next day would bring some difficult issues, the group would continue to work well together to resolve them. "In retrospect," he mused, "I can see why those disagreements yesterday afternoon were so easily resolved. We were still well below what everyone figured to be the minimum funding level."

The Division Ranking Meeting: Second Day
Trouble had started early in the morning. Brown remembered one exchange almost word for word. Louise Mercier, defending her interest, had thrown up her hand like a traffic cop to confront Keller on the ranking of the R&D increments. (Exhibit 8 shows the R&D ranking table.)

"Wait a minute Robin, your next four increments all involve basic research aimed at Consumer products."

"Well that's where the future is, Louise."

"But we're in the present and won't ever reach the future unless we pay our bills," Mercier said adamantly. "There's no support for my stuff!"

"Calm down. If we want to get to the future, we have to start now. Besides, we have applications research and production service for Commodity Chemicals in the threshold."

"But, that's a tiny bit. Hell, my products pay the salaries around here, and we deserve a fair shake. I want those increments that have my stuff in them ranked now, before we spend all we've got on a future we're not sure exists."

At that point Frank Baldwin broke in. "Louise, demand in your markets isn't growing, and competition will soon start to drive your margins down. I know you are producing more of the cash generated by Gaylord, but we ought to use that cash to support the best opportunities we've got, and right now those opportunities are in Consumer. Besides, when you consider . . ."

Mercier interrupted, "That's bull! Our demand continues to grow and our competition won't

EXHIBIT 7 Gaylord Division Ranking Table After the First Day of the Ranking Meeting

Priority Resource Budgeting Ranking Table

Ranking Level: *Gaylord Division*

Rank	Increment Number	Decision Unit Name	Incremental		Cumulative		1994		% of 1994		Notes
			Expense ($K)	Headcount	Expense ($K)	Headcount	Expense ($)	Headcount	Expense	Headcount	
77	2 of 4	Manufacturing management	98	2	9,793	95			82	77	Better liaison with plants. Faster A.R. analysis.
78	1 of 1	AZ-42 cost reduction (R&D)	385	3.5	10,178	98.5	(Current commitments to decision increments were to be indicated in these columns. Since decision increments were being used for the first time, these data were not available for inclusion.)		82	80	Attempt 2¢/lb. cost reduction.
79	5 of 10	East region (field sales)	85	1.5	10,263	100			86	81	Open office in N. Carolina
80	2 of 5	R&D mgmt.	49	1	10,312	101			86	82	Statistical analyses.
81	2 of 4	Consumer products	150	2	10,462	103			87	84	Develop new markets for A2 products.
82	3 of 4	Consumer products	112	1	10,574	104			88	85	Full development of all identified market areas. Advertising research.

This was how Gaylord's ranking looked at the end of the first day.

EXHIBIT 8 R&D Ranking Table Showing Increments at Point of Debate Between Mercier and Baldwin

Priority Resource Budgeting Ranking Table

Ranking Level: R&D Director

Rank	Increment Number	Decision Unit Name	Incremental		Cumulative		1994		% of 1994		Notes
			Expense ($K)	Headcount	Expense ($K)	Headcount	Expense ($)	Headcount	Expense	Headcount	
54	3 of 5	R&D mgmt.	22	1	4,162	52			78	75	Statistical analyses.
55	2 of 5	AZ-42 liquid (Chemical Commodities)	115	2.5	4,277	54.5			80	79	Liquid applications research (high temperature).
56	3 of 4	S.P.P.-29 (Consumer)	195	1.5	4,472	56	*(See*		84	81	Process development.
57	4 of 4	S.P.P.-29 (Consumer)	85	.5	4,557	56.5	*Explanation*		85	82	Process development.
58	3 of 5	Food products Preservatives (Consumer)	115	2	4,672	58.5	*on* *Exhibit 7.)*		87	85	New process research.
59	1 of 3	NII-42 High Density (Consumer)	120	1.5	4,792	60			90	87	Manufacturing yield improvement.
60	1 of 2	ALPHA-12 (Commodities)	180	2	4,972	62			93	90	Basic research on use as paint base.

This was how Keller's ranking table looked when Mercier complained that the next four increments (#56 through #59) were for Baldwin's products.

change all that much. The fact of the matter is, Commodity Chemicals continues to be the mainstay of this division, and we would be crazy to weaken it. Process improvements, and that means R&D, and hard-driving marketing are what it will take to keep this cash cow producing."

Brown recalled that he had interrupted at that point to get the facts straight. He had asked Robin Keller exactly how much applications research and production support for Commodities was in the budget so far. Keller confirmed that production support was equal to 100 percent of the level expended during the past year. "I don't think we can change that since all our production is sold in advance and we have to be able to deliver," he said. But applications research had been cut to 30 percent of the current level for Commodities. For Oil Additives Chemicals, production support was at 120 percent and applications research at 140 percent. Consumer was at 140 percent and 100 percent respectively. Keller though that more should be spent for Consumer applications research.

Brown wondered whether getting the facts helped, though. Mercier had just sat there without saying a word. Looking for a way to calm the situation down, Brown had turned—mistakenly as it turned out—to David Higgins.

"Tell me, David, what about you? What kind of manufacturing support do you have in the budget for Louise? Is it enough to see that all of her stuff is out the door on time?"

"Sure, just as long as I have my eight people.[6] Frankly, Spence, I think this whole thing is dumb. We know how to run our business. I sure as hell know how I run my end of it. This is just another system trying to tell us what to do, and you know, I told that guy, that PRB, ABC, alphabet soup guy that was supposed to help me with this, 'I only have one increment, eight people, and 10 years on the job has taught me that eight is the right number.'

_____

[6] *Higgins's staff at headquarters consisted of eight people. The manufacturing line personnel in the plants were not included in these deliberations.*

But no, he made me play games, and now I have four levels or increments or whatever they're called, and who knows or cares what's in them? You want the plants to produce on time and at spec? I need eight guys, no more, no less. And no matter how many increments or whatever you cut that into, it adds up the same. I can't guarantee anything until I get *all* my people." (Exhibit 9 shows Higgins's PRB analysis.)

I was flustered a bit by that, Brown remembered. "You mean you can't operate with less then eight?"

"I mean I can't say what will happen with less than eight. It all depends on the risk you want to take. Four may be enough, or two, or none if you're lucky."

That was the first time I got angry, Brown reflected. "Well, why isn't your threshold eight people? What are you fooling around with less for?"

"Don't ask me. I tried to do the right thing and make it right. Ask her," David said, and pointed at Susan Roscoe, the PRB coordinator. "It was my PRB analyst who said I couldn't have eight in my threshold."

"Wait a minute, David," replied a much on-the-spot Roscoe. "I wasn't at your sessions when you did your original analysis, but I suspect the guy who worked with you said that the threshold could not be equal to the current level. That's a basic assumption in PRB. You have just told us how to view your department: The major issue is *risk*. How willing is Gaylord to risk a production delay or quality control problem? For what products? Which customers? What are the costs of a delay?"

"We can't take those risks and keep our customers. How much risk do you say we should take, Sue?" countered David.

"You have to make that decision," Roscoe replied. 'My job here is to facilitate the process, not to make operating or budgeting decisions. You have to make that decision, and you have made it, year after year. All the system does is help you attach different prices to different levels of risk. The choice is yours."

Higgins smiled ironically. "You say that like it's easy."

EXHIBIT 9 Summary of Higgins's Analysis

PRIORITY RESOURCE BUDGETING DECISION UNIT SUMMARY

1) Decision Unit Name: Cost Cent. # Manufacturing Management #0100	2) Division/Department Gaylord/MCC	3) Decision Unit Manager David Higgins	4) Date 8/1/94

5) Purpose of Decision Unit

Manage the utility and service functions of the Gaylord Division plants and manage the manufacture of Gaylord's commodities, oil additives, and consumer products to meet the agreed to unit costs and volumes.

6) What Does Your Unit Do and What Resources Are Used to Do It?

Eight people. *Director of Manufacturing* is department manager. He supervises those below him and is responsible for overall planning; *Four Managers, Manufacturing* each assigned to one or more products, follows up on all manufacturing problems, coordinates capital appropriation requests, provides technical assistance and expertise when required and coordinates with division R&D; *Two Manufacturing Service Managers* for Utilities and Service at plant locations and coordination of Division Function; and *one assistant.*

7) Decision Unit Results to Be Worked Towards in 1994.

A. Improve production yields 10% in S.PP.-29.

B. Improve COGS in Alpha-12 by 5%.

C. Implement $1.5 million of cost reduction programs.

D. Implement rehabilitation of existing facilities to meet safety and environmental needs.

8) What Will Be Done at the Threshold Level?

Maintain major administrative activities for plants.

- Manage only most profitable products in division
- Minimal planning and control of all other products
- Generally treat plants as a "wasting asset"

Requires:
  One Director Manufacturing
  One Manager Manufacturing
  One Assistant

9) Why Are These Activities Essential?

- Need to keep plants operating at economic levels.
- This level of effort would result in problems in production scheduling, lower yields, and higher COGS.

Unit Res. Sup.	People	% 1994	Expense	% 1994
Incremental				
	3	38	225	50

EXHIBIT 9 *(concluded)*

12) Incr. No.	13) What will be done at this Increment and what Resources are needed?	14) Why should this Increment be funded?	15) Unit Res. Supp.	16) What Incremental Resources are needed?		17) What Comulative Resources are needed?			
				People	Expense	People	% 1993	Expense	% 1993
2 of 4	Reallocate plant management to pick up limited planning and control for all products. Begin low level of cost reduction programs (.5 million) Requires: Two managers	Ensure that all product areas are "covered" from manufacturing planning/control. Bring yield and COGS down to planned level.		2	98	5	63	323	72
3 of 4	Cover all plants and product areas. Allow for coordination of capital projects, full cost reduction programs, and limited implementation of rehabilitation program. Requires: Two managers	Achieve planned increases in yield, improvements in COGS, and cost reduction programs.	A B C	2	108	7	88	431	96
4 of 4	Full implementation of rehabilitation program. Additional cost reduction opportunities (.5 million) Requires: One manager	Meet government imposed deadlines on plant rehabilitation.	D	1	49	8	100	480	106
	ESTIMATED EXPENSE 1994 (Basis: Six-month Act.)					8	100	450	100

"I don't mean it to sound easy," Roscoe said, looking around the room.

Mercier spoke up, "I think we should give David all of his people right now. All these management systems sound fine, but we know what's going to happen if the plants back up. We need the same amount of production as last year, and his staff worked full time then."

Nodding his head, McKnight called out, "I agree with Louise—let David have his people next."

Brown moved to get closure. "I think that's right. Anyone disagree? . . . No? then David, we'll accept all your other increments now."

Relaxing, Higgins responded, "Good! That finishes my part. Can I get back to work now, Spence?"

"No I want you involved in the rest of the ranking. A lot of the decisions we still have to make could indirectly affect your department."

Brown wondered whether he had moved for closure too soon. Higgins's impassioned complaint had interrupted the flow of the meeting, and Brown had wanted to return to the question of how much research support to devote to Commodity Chemicals.

Mercier raised the point immediately. "We still haven't answered the question we began with. I still think I should get more support from R&D."

Brown could picture himself nodding. "Robin, where is the rest of Louise's support?"

"Spread across my last eight increments, numbers 67 to 74." (Exhibit 10 shows the final page of the R&D ranking.)

"OK, Louise," Brown said as he turned to examine the display that explained what was in each of those increments, "if you could have two of those, which would they be?"

"I'll need three. Number 67 is the area where we have the best opportunity, but 67 alone doesn't do much for us. Increments 68 and 71 will give that project the punch it needs to produce some applications we can take to the market."

McKnight broke in, "Remember Spence, we haven't yet funded any of those new Oil Additives projects I spoke to you about, and . . ."

Mercier interrupted. "We have already ranked three of your exploratory research projects, Jack.

The increments you have left look like long shots to me, and my projects have pretty clear near-term benefits."

"These new projects have a lot of potential," McKnight countered, "and I think the results we've gotten in my group over the last five years show that investments in R&D for our business pay off."

Higgins spoke up. "Look why don't we give Louise one of her increments, then Jack one of his, then Louise and so on?"

Mercier responded before anyone could reply. "But aren't we supposed to rank each increment with the idea that it really is the most important thing available, and not simply trade around? My projects are critical and should go in the budget now!"

Everyone started speaking at once. After some 15 minutes of spirited argument, Brown intervened. "Look, we're getting nowhere on this one. Let's move on to something else for awhile and come back to this later."

The group made good progress on several items until Jack McKnight got upset. At the time, the group was discussing advertising, and the debate was whether Oil Additive Chemicals' increment should come before Consumer Chemicals.

"Right now I've got 90 percent of current advertising expense in the budget," McKnight said. "Rates will go up at least 15 percent and if we take my next increment I'll be just short of my current level in advertising purchasing power. If we take Consumer's increment, Frank will be at 160 percent of current. I don't even understand why we're wasting time talking about it."

"Maybe it's time to start cutting your advertising," Brown explained. "You've been spending at high levels, but you dominate the market now and you keep telling me you get terrific word-of-mouth. You haven't convinced me that this advertising increment will have much effect on either your share or profitability."

"I'm the one who needs the advertising," Frank Baldwin interrupted. "Consumer is right where you were a few years ago. We are at 'take-off.' We have terrific products in a growth market, and we have

EXHIBIT 10 R&D Ranking Table—Final Page

Priority Resource Budgeting Ranking Table

Ranking Level: R&D Director

Rank	Increment Number	Decision Unit Name	Incremental Expense ($K)	Incremental Headcount	Cumulative Expense ($K)	Cumulative Headcount	1994 Expense ($)	1994 Headcount	% of 1994 Expense	% of 1994 Headcount	Notes
65	4 of 5	R&D mgmt.	39	1	5,325	67.5			99	98	Budgeting and financial assistance
66	5 of 5	R&D mgmt.	22	1	5,347	68.5			100	99	Additional statistical analysis
67	3 of 5	AZ–42 liquid	115	2.5	5,462	71			102	103	Liquid applications research
68	4 of 5	AZ–42 liquid	230	2.5	5,692	73.5	(See Explanation		105	107	High altitude applications
69	3 of 3	SUR food preservative	85	1	5,777	74.5	on		108	108	New freezing applications
70	1 of 2	SUR cost reduction	185	1.5	5,962	76	Exhibit 7.)		111	110	Achieve 1¢/100 lb. by 1997
71	5 of 5	AZ–42 liquid	98	1.5	6,060	77.5			113	112	Low temperature applications
72	2 of 2	SUR cost reduction	75	.5	6,135	78			114	113	Achieve 1¢/100 lb. by 1997
73	5 of 5	pV-12	105	1	6,240	79			116	114	Continue environmental hazard tests to fail-safe level
74	3 of 3	LAPA	300	2	6,540	81			122	117	New fertilizer applications

This was the last page of Robin Keller's table. It expressed the priorities of Gaylord's R&D Department. Increments 67 through 74 were all for Louise Mercier's products.

215

to get out there and establish a dominant position. Right now, getting more awareness and supporting our distributors is critical."

McKnight looked straight at Brown. "If our ad budget gets cut, I can't promise the profits we've delivered in the past. We've been damn successful, and our advertising has been an important part of our marketing program. It doesn't make sense to change a successful strategy."

Brown wasn't sure whether he was grateful that Labella interrupted at this point, or whether it would have been better if they had resolved the ad question.

"Here we are talking about advertising and we don't even have enough guys in the field to take orders. Right now the budget only gives me skeleton crews in three sales offices. We don't have anyone out traveling around."

"You mean we haven't ranked your whole staff yet?" Mercier asked in amazement.

"No."

Mercier sat straight, exasperated. "That means that the whole ranking is screwed up! What are we supposed to do now?"

Brown broke in, "Art, if you were going to add someone to those ranked so far, what office would you do it in?"

"There's no way to answer that, Spence. We may sell in the East, but then again the East could be slow and all our sales come from the West or Central. There's no way to tell."

Mercier chimed in, "We've just never gotten a handle on how to judge the marginal utility of a salesperson. There's no useful information."

"What you mean," said Baldwin, "is that we don't know what information is useful."

Labella replied, with a look that said he had been through all this before, "Whichever, we don't have it. We know we need to add salespeople, and that means we need to add them everywhere."

That comment led to an extended discussion about how many salespeople were needed. The discussion produced lots of ideas but no resolution. Eventually everyone agreed that the Gaylord sales force could not be cut, and that probably Labella should be given budget for two new salespeople to be added where necessary.

Then came the issue of where the sales force should fit in the ranking. Should it simply be added now, or should it be inserted among increments ranked earlier in the meeting? The group decided to put it in earlier, but after 20 minutes of discussion still had not decided where.

"This is a mess," Mercier protested. "There's no way to compare Arthur's need for salespeople with my need for more R&D and for more guys on my commercial staff. How are we supposed to compare one against the other? They're apples and oranges."

"I don't think there's an easy way," Brown replied.

"I don't want an easy way . . . just a way!" Mercier was pushing.

"But you know, Louise," said Baldwin, "this is the first time we've sat down together and really talked about all our departments in this much detail."

"How is the talk helping?" asked Mercier.

"That's a good question, Louise," Brown said. "Why don't all of you try to answer it over lunch, and let's meet again at 1:30."

As Brown finished his own lunch he began to formulate a plan for resolving the issues that remained open.

The Priority Resource Budgeting (PRB Concept)

How do you plan your vacation?

Do you say: "Last year, we went to Florida and spent $2,000. Let's add 3 percent for inflation, and go!"

Or should you think: "Should we go on vacation, or use the money and time for something else? What other expenditures do we have coming up? How much money do we have to spend for a vacation? Where should we go? Should we fly or drive? Should we camp or stay at a motel?

The second approach, of course, makes more sense.

Priority Resource Budgeting (PRB) encourages the same kind of approach. PRB asks us to question the costs themselves. Why are we spending the money? What are we getting in return? How can we better spend the money? PRB involves cost/benefit trade-offs throughout the organization.

HOW PRB WORKS

1. Identify "Decision Units." A Decision Unit is the smallest meaningful group of people and/or other resource devoted to achieve a common significant business purpose. It can be a traditional cost center, a program, or a group of activities. Typical Decision Units include between 5 and 15 people and a dollar budget of about $150,000 to $400,000.

2. Analyze each Decision Unit. Each manager is asked to analyze the Decision Unit(s) for which he or she is responsible. Answers to the following seven specific questions guide this analysis.

EXHIBIT A–1   Decision Unit Analysis

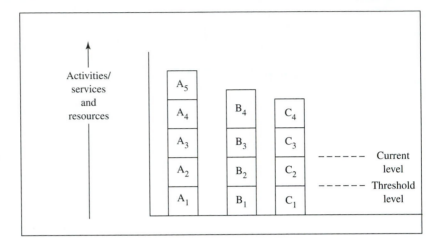

You, as Manager A, have developed your increments. Managers B and C have done the same.

You all have established threshold and current levels, and additional increments.

Q.1. What is the purpose (goal) of the Decision Unit?

Q.2. What Decision Unit results (special accomplishments) are to be worked toward next year?

Q.3. What does the Unit do (activities), and what resources are used to do it?

Q.4. What alternative methods for achieving the purpose are feasible?

Q.5. What is the minimal level of service the Unit could provide and still remain viable; why are those services essential? In PRB language, this is defined as the "threshold level."

Q.6. What additional increments of service can be provided?[1]

Q.7. Why should these additional increments be funded?

3. Rank in order of priority the Decision Unit increments obtained from the analysis in Step 2. The first ranking actually occurs at the Decision Unit level when the manager arranges his or her increments in order of their importance (Exhibit A–1). The next ranking occurs at the organizational level immediately above. This ranking involves the manager, peers, and their immediate supervisor. Together, these people rank all their increments—based on the objectives of the group and the organization (Exhibit A–2). This process continues all the way up the organization, and is portrayed graphically in Exhibit A–3.

---

[1]*Think of increments as the building blocks of resources (either money or people) that are added to achieve more completely the Unit's purpose and results. Each increment you add should be able to stand alone. Increment Two (for example) could be the addition of two people. The activities and services they provide will be above and beyond the first threshold limit. And if the two people were not added, the services and activities of the threshold limit would still be performed. Continue the same logic with Increment Three, Four, and so on.*

EXHIBIT A–2   Decision Unit Ranking

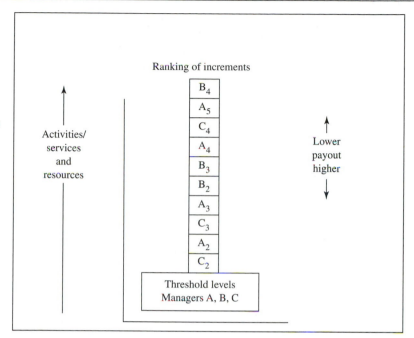

This next step is "ranking." This is where your increments (after the threshold level) are compared with others—in terms of payout on the investment of resources. At ranking sessions with your peers and supervisor, you will rank all your increments.

4. Prepare the organization's formal budget, based on the decisions made in Step 3. The final product of the preceding meetings and analyses is a ranking table for the entire organization. Subsequent to the final ranking meeting, that ranking manager studies the resulting ranking table, makes any required adjustments, decides which increments should and which should not be funded, and draws a "funding line" on the table that indicates the increments that have been approved, those that have not, and costs of each.[2] The ranking table thus is a record of all the decisions that have been made in the Priority Resource Budgeting process (Exhibit A–4). Not only does it show what will and will not be funded in the upcoming year, it also ranks activities in priority so that adjustments during the year can be made more easily.

5. The final budget, although prepared in a vastly different fashion from traditional budgets, is similar in format to the end product of the traditional approach. The cost breakdown (e.g., salaries, bonuses, travel) feed directly to the company's existing budgeting and control system.

---

[2]*While the finding line was "drawn" or set by the managing director of each Americhem company, each divisional general manager would indicate a recommended funding level for his or her unit at the conclusion of the divisional ranking.*

EXHIBIT A–3   Ranking Process Summary

ORGANIZATION LEVEL   ACTION

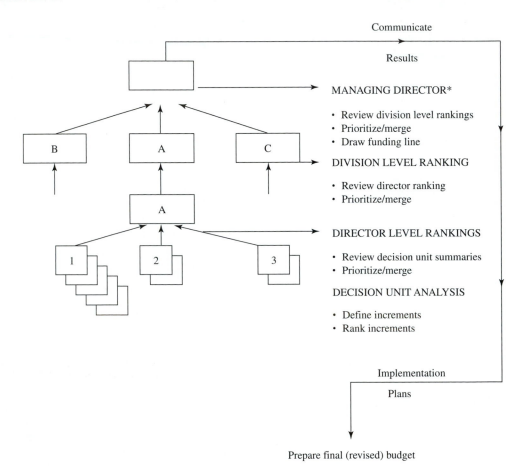

Communicate

Results

MANAGING DIRECTOR*

- Review division level rankings
- Prioritize/merge
- Draw funding line

DIVISION LEVEL RANKING

- Review director ranking
- Prioritize/merge

DIRECTOR LEVEL RANKINGS

- Review decision unit summaries
- Prioritize/merge

DECISION UNIT ANALYSIS

- Define increments
- Rank increments

Implementation

Plans

Prepare final (revised) budget

*Corporate management reviews the budget.

EXHIBIT A–4 Funding the Increments

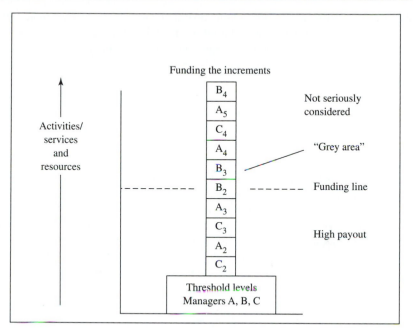

As the supervisor looks at the ranking of increments, the "normal" breakout would look something like the diagram. Beyond the threshold limits, there are some areas where the payout is high. At the top of the tower there might be some increments which are not likely to merit serious consideration. In between lies the "grey area," where the desirability of the increment is arguable. The funding line typically falls somewhere in the grey area.

Funding the increments

B_4
A_5 Not seriously considered
C_4
A_4 "Grey area"
B_3
B_2 ------- Funding line
A_3
C_3 High payout
A_2
C_2

Activities/services and resources

Threshold levels
Managers A, B, C

Case 2–3

WESTINGHOUSE ELECTRIC CORPORATION: AUTOMATING THE CAPITAL BUDGETING PROCESS (A)

When Tom Moser received the 1988 Capital Review Committee's (CRC's) voting results and recommendations for the Power Systems Division of the Westinghouse Energy Systems Business Unit (ESBU), he wasn't surprised. Moser, manager of computer systems support and himself a member of ESBU's 1988 CRC, had helped present his division's project proposals to the committee. One project in particular had polarized the views of project presenters and committee members. The Power Systems Division (PSD) wanted funding for the project, which would establish the division's reputation in a new, potentially profitable area. But without full support from the CRC, the division had some formidable selling to do.

This case was prepared by Mary Addonizio and Nicole Wishart under the direction of Lynda Applegate and Julie H. Hertenstein.

Company Background

Westinghouse Electric Corporation operated in diverse international, technology-based markets. It served industrial, construction, and electric utility markets and was a leading supplier of defense electronic equipment. Westinghouse was also involved in television and radio broadcasting, financial services, transport refrigeration, community development, and beverage bottling.

This wide array of businesses resulted from years of diversification. In the late 1960s and early 1970s, Westinghouse had acquired disparate businesses, including a mail-order house, a watchmaker, and a low-income housing developer, to complement its heavy manufacturing operations. Following these moves, traditionally strong businesses were neglected and profits stalled. In the late 1970s and early 1980s, Chairman R.E. Kirby and his successor, Douglas D. Danforth, restructured and refocused the company: They streamlined operations and cut costs to increase profitability. Using shareholder value-based planning, a methodology that focused on discounted equity cash flows, they determined the value of strategic plans for a business, analyzed entire businesses or business segments, and divested appropriately.

In January 1988, John C. Marous succeeded Danforth as chairman. Paul E. Lego was appointed president and named to be Marous's successor when Marous retired in three years. As managers under Danforth, Marous and Lego had worked closely with him to revitalize the company. In 1987, sales were approximately $10.7 billion and return on equity was 22.9 percent (see Exhibit 1). Marous and Lego were confident that Westinghouse could achieve 8.5 percent annual revenue growth while sustaining 18 percent to 21 percent return on equity. They planned to accomplish this with a threefold strategy: Pay close attention to productivity and quality; eliminate unprofitable business segments or divisions; and build new businesses, either by nurturing promising technologies or by making small, relevant acquisitions. The company's Productivity and Quality Center coordinated efforts to measure and improve efficiency in the office and the factory.

Impressive 6 percent annual increases in Westinghouse's white-collar productivity since the early 1980s had prompted managers from Japan to visit this center and study its methods.

In January 1988, the corporation was reorganized to serve its main markets more effectively. Operating units were aligned according to the seven groups shown in Exhibit 2.

Energy Systems Business Unit

ESBU, located within the Energy and Utility Systems Group, was a worldwide leader in energy technology. Its goal was to provide customers with high-technology, energy-related products and services. It developed, marketed, and managed power generation projects—primarily nuclear, municipal waste, and combustion turbine. It designed, manufactured, and serviced nuclear plant components and provided nuclear power plants with extensive services geared to increase plant availability and cover the lifetime operation of a completed plant. ESBU comprised six divisions (see Exhibit 3).

Given the corporate emphasis on value-based planning and division profitability, current and future projects had to be framed within the company's and the business unit's strategies. The capital planning process was a critical mechanism both for integrating corporate and business unit strategies and activities and for assuring that capital resources were allocated in the most effective manner.

Evolution of the Capital Planning Process within ESBU

Capital planning had changed considerably within ESBU since 1982, when capital investment planning, which had reported to Facilities, was shifted to the Strategic Resources Group. This shift was intended to emphasize capital as a strategic resource. As part of the capital planning process, each division prepared an annual capital plan, called a Facilities Investment Plan (FIP), that contained project proposals and requests for capital. Divisions submitted their plans to Tom Caye, senior planning engineer and capital coordinator from 1980 to

EXHIBIT 1   Condensed Consolidated Financial Statements (in millions of dollars except per share data)

Balance Sheet (December 31)	1987	1986
Cash	228.7	163.1
Marketable securities	1,206.1	434.4
Customer receivables	1,947.9	1,905.2
Inventories	1,237.5	1,161.6
Other assets	5,332.9	4,8017.5
Total assets	**9,953.1**	**8,481.8**
Short-term debt	1,535.7	596.9
Accounts payable	724.9	646.1
Other current liabilities	2,609.9	2,953.4
Long-term debt	830.2	518.2
Other noncurrent liabilities	654.9	734.0
Total liabilities	**6,355.6**	**5,448.6**
Minority interest	20.9	23.6
Total common stockholders' equity	3,576.6	3,009.6
Total liabilities and stockholders' equity	**9,953.1**	**8,481.8**

Statement of Income (year ended December 31)	1987	1986
Sales and operating revenues	10,679.0	10,731.0
Cost of sales	(7,820.9)	(7,771.2)
Marketing, administration, and general expenses	(1,603.0)	(1,718.0)
Depreciation and amortization	(318.0)	(371.0)
Gain from sale of Group W Cable	—	651.2
Unusual items	—	(790.0)
Equity in income of affiliates	148.5	111.1
Other income, net	112.5	103.8
Interest expense	(126.1)	(145.9)
Income before income taxes and minority interest	**1,072.0**	**801.0**
Income taxes	333.4	(129.0)
Minority interest	.3	(1.2)
Net income	**738.9**	**670.8**

Five Year Summary of Selected Financial and Statistical Data (in millions of dollars except per share amounts)

	1987	1986	1985	1984	1983
Sales and operating revenues	10,679.0	10,731.0	10,700.2	10,264.5	9,532.6
Net income	738.9	670.8	605.3	535.9	449.0
Return on average equity	22.9%	20.7%	16.0%	15.1%	13.8%
Primary earning per share	5.12	4.42	3.52	3.04	2.54
Dividends per share	1.64	1.35	1.15	.975	.90

EXHIBIT 2 Organization Chart after 1988 Restructuring

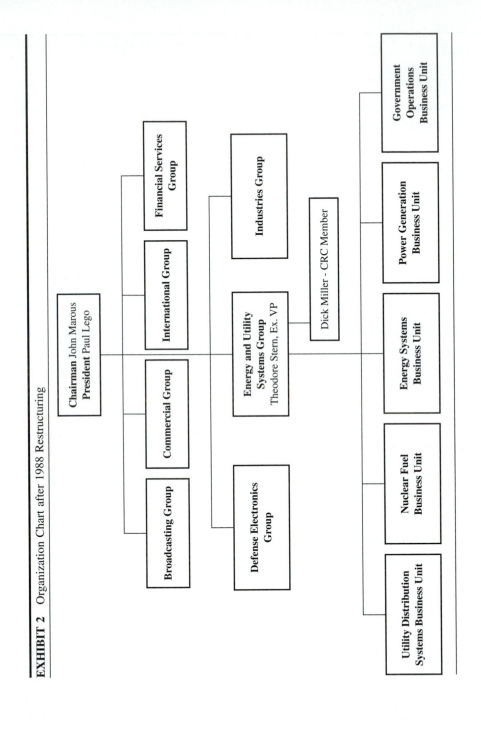

EXHIBIT 3 Energy Systems Business Unit Organization Chart

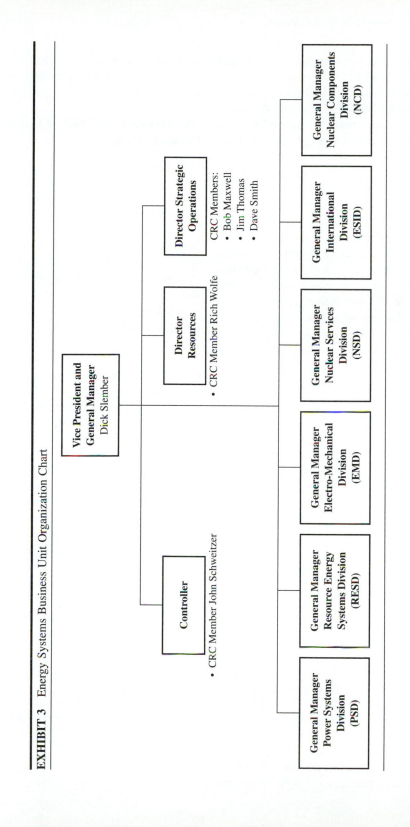

1984. Before 1982, Caye collected the plans and sent capital totals to ESBU's controller.

With the move toward value-based planning, Caye initiated the CRC in 1982 to review divisions' investment plans and ensure compatibility with company and business unit strategy. Each division sent a representative to present its plan to the review committee and answer questions about quality and strategic implications of proposed investments. The CRC provided support, recommendations on aggregate appropriations for divisions, and feedback for divisions and business unit management but did not allocate funds to specific projects. Decisions about specific projects were made by the division general managers and a corporate committee called the Appropriations Review Board (ARB).

In 1984, Jim Thomas, senior planning engineer, succeeded Caye as ESBU's capital coordinator. By then, the CRC reviewed more than 200 division projects during a two-day meeting. Thomas and his boss, Frank Arany, manager of strategic planning, fine-tuned the meeting format by developing six criteria for the committee to use when evaluating proposals: strategy, quality, risk, return, implementation, and technology (see Exhibit 4).

During his first year as capital coordinator, Thomas gave CRC members paper forms on which they manually scored every project on each criterion. He intended to analyze the data using a spreadsheet software package in order to provide summary results for the committee. This plan did not work. CRC members sometimes wrote illegibly, left scores or project identifications blank, or wrote comments instead of numeric scores. This meant that Thomas could not sort the data or calculate averages, and the promised reports were not produced.

Thomas decided to automate the scoring process for the following year and obtained barcode terminals and voting software. Members first used the software to evaluate projects at the 1985 CRC meeting. (See Exhibit 5 for an explanation of the process and a sample scoring sheet.) Because members were forced to score each criterion numerically, the problem of missing or illegible data was eliminated. In addition, CRC members received immediate feedback on a project's average scores. They were enthusiastic about the technology and continued using it at subsequent CRC meetings.

An Overview of ESBU's Capital Planning Process

Following development of preliminary capital spending and appropriations guidelines for the divisions, each division prepared and presented its investment plan to the CRC annually. The CRC evaluated and provided feedback on individual projects; it also recommended the next year's capital spending[1] and appropriation[2] limits for each division to ESBU and division general managers. The divisions, having considered the CRC's feedback, selected projects to submit to the ARB, which met monthly to approve individual projects. Exhibit 6 summarizes this process.

Generating Capital Spending and Appropriation Guidelines

In July of each year, the capital planning process began with the development of spending and appropriation estimates by each division. Divisions sent their estimates, along with a one-line description of each project, to Thomas, who sent revised projections and totals to the ESBU controller. Using historical, current, and forecasted data, the ESBU controller generated spending and appropriation guidelines for each division and returned these to Thomas, who evaluated the controller's guidelines, often noting that divisions' estimates were higher, and forwarded them to divisions and to CRC members. Divisions used these guidelines when preparing FIPs, and the CRC used them when evaluating the plans.

---

[1] *"Capital spending" refers to actual cash expenditures in each of the next two or three years.*

[2] *"Appropriation" refers to funds that have been allocated to a business unit for a particular purpose. When funds are appropriated, the exact timing of spending may not be defined. For example, even though $4 million had been appropriated in 1988 for a new building, depending on how long it took to secure and prepare a site and negotiate with a contractor, spending for construction might not start until 1990 or 1991.*

EXHIBIT 4   Capital Review Committee Project Evaluation Criteria

Strategy	**Consistency with ESBU Strategic Objectives**
	Are projects supporting division and business unit objectives (strategic, business, etc.) with a long-range focus?
	Are the proposed projects all that is needed (capital or other funds) to support business unit objectives and financial performance?
Quality	**Satisfying Customer Needs and Improving Productivity**
	Is the project helping to meet requirements, reduce/eliminate errors, and "do it right the first time"?
	Will the project improve productivity? Will the project make operations more effective and efficient? Will division processes be improved?
	Will customer satisfaction result?
Risks	**A Certain Amount of Risk Is Appropriate. Innovative Projects Are Appropriate Risks.**
	Is the amount of risk appropriate? It may be appropriate to find a high-risk project if it is highly innovative or if potential for large payoff exists.
	Do you think the project has a good probability of success?
Return	**Financial Benefit to Shareholders**
	What rate of return do you think will be realized? Is it enough for the risk involved?
	Do you feel the pay-off time is acceptable?
Implementation	**Adequate Resources to Make It Happen**
	Is there clear division commitment to the project? Will other necessary resources (personnel, budget, space, time) be made available?
	Does the division have command of *all* resources needed to implement properly?
	Is the project only the tip of the iceberg (first step of a larger commitment)?
	Is the timing right for proper implementation? Too early? Too late?
	Can this project be deferred without affecting the division or the business unit?
Technology	**Proper Technology Used to Implement the Project**
	Assuming the purpose of the project is good, is the proper technology (nature, key, base, leading, etc.) being used to implement the project's objective?

Source: Westinghouse Corporation

Preparation of the Facilities Investment Plans

Also in July of each year, Thomas sent each division a floppy disk containing Lotus spreadsheets that were a template for the FIP forms. (See Exhibit 7 for an overview of the FIP documentation.) During July and August, divisions prepared their investment plans. Capital coordinators within each division ensured that the plan covered all capital investment needed to address strategic objectives, support growth called for in the financial plan, and pursue cost-cutting opportunities. Divisions prioritized and assigned projects to categories and classes based upon their justification (see Exhibit 8). They also summarized their new appropriations and spending requests (see Exhibit 9). In September, division representatives presented their FIPs to the CRC.

The Capital Review Committee

The CRC was a 12-member, ad hoc planning committee consisting primarily of staff and line representatives from ESBU. Division general managers chose representatives who had detailed knowledge of

---

EXHIBIT 5   Automated Voting Process

---

1. Each CRC member was given a barcode terminal and an individualized scoring sheet.
2. CRC members scanned the name symbol to assign the terminals at the beginning of each day.
3. Division and project identification were entered from a master terminal before projects were presented.
4. CRC members rated projects while the projects were being presented. To rate a project, CRC members scanned each of the six criteria and a score for each criterion. Scores ranged from 1 (poor) to 4 (excellent).
5. CRC members could change scores for a specific project, until they scanned "Done," by rescanning the criteria and entering new scores.
6. The system tracked the active terminals. When the last voter had scanned "Done," the average scores for the project, by criterion, appeared on all active terminals immediately.
7. If CRC members left the room, they scanned "Exit" to deactivate the terminals.

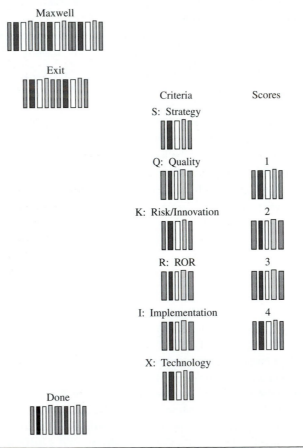

Scoring Sheet (reduced)
Energy Systems
Capital Review Committee
General Menu

EXHIBIT 6 Overview of the 1989 ESBU Capital Budgeting Process

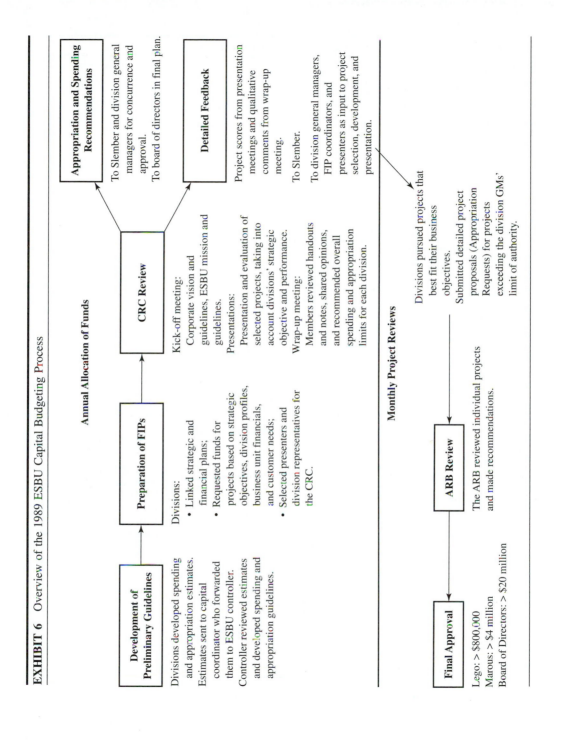

Annual Allocation of Funds

Development of Preliminary Guidelines

Divisions developed spending and appropriation estimates.
Estimates sent to capital coordinator who forwarded them to ESBU controller.
Controller reviewed estimates and developed spending and appropriation guidelines.

Preparation of FIPs

Divisions:
• Linked strategic and financial plans;
• Requested funds for projects based on strategic objectives, division profiles, business unit financials, and customer needs;
• Selected presenters and division representatives for the CRC.

CRC Review

Kick-off meeting:
Corporate vision and guidelines, ESBU mission and guidelines.
Presentations:
Presentation and evaluation of selected projects, taking into account divisions' strategic objective and performance.
Wrap-up meeting:
Members reviewed handouts and notes, shared opinions, and recommended overall spending and appropriation limits for each division.

Appropriation and Spending Recommendations

To Slember and division general managers for concurrence and approval.
To board of directors in final plan.

Detailed Feedback

Project scores from presentation meetings and qualitative comments from wrap-up meeting.

To Slember.

To division general managers, FIP coordinators, and presenters as input to project selection, development, and presentation.

Monthly Project Reviews

Divisions pursued projects that best fit their business objectives.
Submitted detailed project proposals (Appropriation Requests) for projects exceeding the division GMs' limit of authority.

ARB Review

The ARB reviewed individual projects and made recommendations.

Final Approval

Lego: > $800,000
Marous: > $4 million
Board of Directors: > $20 million

EXHIBIT 7 Overview of ESBU's Capital Planning Documentation

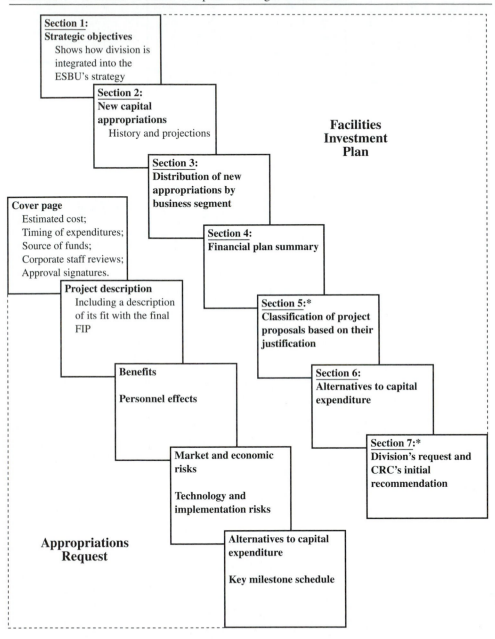

Section 1:
Strategic objectives
Shows how division is integrated into the ESBU's strategy

Section 2:
New capital appropriations
History and projections

Section 3:
Distribution of new appropriations by business segment

Section 4:
Financial plan summary

Section 5:*
Classification of project proposals based on their justification

Section 6:
Alternatives to capital expenditure

Section 7:*
Division's request and CRC's initial recommendation

Facilities Investment Plan

Cover page
Estimated cost;
Timing of expenditures;
Source of funds;
Corporate staff reviews;
Approval signatures.

Project description
Including a description of its fit with the final FIP

Benefits

Personnel effects

Market and economic risks

Technology and implementation risks

Alternatives to capital expenditure

Key milestone schedule

Appropriations Request

*See Exhibits 8 and 9 for expanded section.

EXHIBIT 8 FIP Section 5 Division Distribution of 1989 Projects (capital in thousands of dollars)

Project Number	Project Title	PRI	Total Capital Funding	Prior Year's Spending	1989 Spending	1989 Spending by Project Class				ROR	Strategic Objective from Section 1
						1	2	3	4		
Mandatory Projects:											
Prior year projects with 1989 spending of 100K or more											
7227	XYZ Project	M1	500	200	300	300				80%	Produce new products
8277	PQR Project	M2	1,500	1,100	500		500			20%	Improve product quality
	Total		**2,000**	**1,300**	**800**	**300**	**500**	**0**	**0**		
Total prior year, <100K spending		M	655	300	300	100	100	100		N/A	N/A
1989 projects with 1989 spending of 100K or more											
9101	Pump Project	M1	250	N/A	150	150				33%	Produce new products
9455	Building Project	M2	440	N/A	440				440	N/A	Maintenance
	Total		**690**	**0**	**590**	**150**	**0**	**0**	**440**		
Additional 1989 projects with appropriation of 100K or more											
9111	SWT Project	M1	750	N/A	50	50				34%	Reduce operating costs
	Total		**750**	**0**	**50**	**50**	**0**	**0**	**0**		
Remaining mandatory 1989 projects		M	565	N/A	565	250	130	170	15	N/A	N/A
Subtotal for priority M:		N/A	4,660	1,500	2,305	850	730	270	455	N/A	N/A

Sales Dependent Projects have the same format as the Mandatory Section.

Prudent Projects have the same format as the Mandatory Section.

Other Projects have the same format as the Mandatory Section.

(continued)

EXHIBIT 8   *(concluded)*

Instructions: FIP Section 5 Project Classification Criteria

Use the following categories to prioritize new and carry-over capital projects:

Mandatory

M1: Required to stay in business.

M2: Required to meet current contracts.

M3: Safety/regulatory requirement.

M4: Complete prior-year project, foolish to stop now.

Sales-Dependent

SD1: Expect contract by end of 1989, investment essential during 1989.

SD2: Expect contract during 1989, investment essential during 1989 to prepare for contract execution.

SD3: Expect contract with low stand-alone ROR, but other reasons (pull through sales, etc.) justify 1989 investment.

Prudent

P1: Excellent technology development, high return potential.

P2: Excellent cost reduction potential.

P3: Excellent quality improvement.

P4: Regulatory change imminent, may become mandatory.

P5: Small investment now versus large, mandatory one later.

Other

O1: Blue-collar productivity improvement.

O2: White-collar productivity improvement.

O3: Meet strategic goals but not covered by the criteria above.

O4: Other.

In the 1989 Spending the Project Class column, classify capital dollars to be spent in 1989 as one of the following:

Class	Definition
1	New volume, project justified by incremental sales.
2	Product improvement, project justified by incremental sales.
3	Cost reduction, project will reduce cost of product(s).
4	Other maintenance or regulatory objective.

---

the division's business. Thomas encouraged general managers to consider the CRC's need for line representation when choosing their representatives. Other CRC members were from staff positions at the business unit level and came with solid financial, information systems, and strategic planning backgrounds. A representative from Corporate and a representative from Energy & Utility Systems Group were also on the committee. (See Exhibits 10 and 11 for the 1988 CRC members.)

The CRC recommended aggregate capital spending and appropriation targets for each division. It did so by reviewing and evaluating each division's strategies, financial performance, and specific capital projects. The process in 1988 involved three stages: (1) a kick-off meeting to

EXHIBIT 9   FIP Section 7 CRC Initial Recommendations

CRC Member	Division

New Appropriations

Division Request:	CRC Member's Recommendation:
Mandatory: _____	
Sales-Dependent: _____	Required: _____
Prudent: _____	Contingency: _____
Other: _____	Total: _____
Total: 0	

1989 Spending

Division Request:	CRC Member's Recommendation:
Mandatory: _____	
Sales-Dependent: _____	Required: _____
Prudent: _____	Contingency: _____
Other: _____	Total: _____
Total: 0	

Instructions to FIP Coordinators: Fill in the column on the left and hand this out with your presentation. After your division's presentation, CRC members will fill out the column on the right.

review the CRC's mission and process, (2) two days of presentations, called the micro process, where divisions presented project proposals that CRC members evaluated using the automated voting technology, and (3) a wrap-up session, called the macro process, at which the CRC finalized its recommendations for division spending and appropriation limits.

1988 CRC Meetings

The Kick-Off   During the 1988 kick-off meeting, which began at noon on September 13, CRC members discussed the corporate perspective on capital and clarified their own mission. Helm Hansen, director of corporate planning and investment services, provided the link between ESBU and corporate headquarters. He outlined several guidelines for committee members:

No reasonable requests for capital made by business units with a track record will be turned down. There is capital to fund projects aimed at growth, where we see high sales. Although it's likely that Westinghouse will achieve its profit objectives, we're uneasy about the sales objectives.

This committee should focus on how well a division's proposals fit with the business unit's strategies. A division may come up with something new in biology, but how does it fit with energy-related business? Don't go too far afield.

EXHIBIT 10   Members of the 1988 Capital Review Committee and Appropriations Review Board

1988 Ad Hoc Capital Review Committee	*Overlapping Members*	*Appropriations Review Board*
Bob Maxwell Manager, Business Development ESBU, Strategic Operations	*Jim Thomas* Senior Planning Engineer, ESBU Strategic Operations	*P. G. DeHuff* Consultant to Ted Stern, Retired General Manager
Helm Hansen Director, Westinghouse Corporate Planning and Investment Services	*Dick Miller* Director, Energy and Utility Systems Information Systems	*Bill Whitehead* Manager, Specialty Metals Plant, Nuclear Fuel Business List
Tom Moser Manager, Computer Systems, Support, SDS	*Tom Caye* Senior Engineer, NSD	*Dick Atkins* Manager, Energy Systems Business Unit
Rick Wolfe Manager, Facilities ESBU Resource Function	*John Schweitzer* Manager, ESBU Financial Planning	
Bill Diehl Manager Cost Control and Analysis, RESD		
Don Pease Manager, Manufacturing, EMD		
Frank Sloss Program Manager, State Products, NCD		
Dave Smith Manager, Technology Development, ESBU Strategic Operations		

Members who were on the CRC in prior years:

> Jim Thomas
> Dick Miller
> Don Pease
> John Schweitzer
> Frank Sloss
> Dave Smith
> Tom Caye

EXHIBIT 11   CRC Seating Diagram

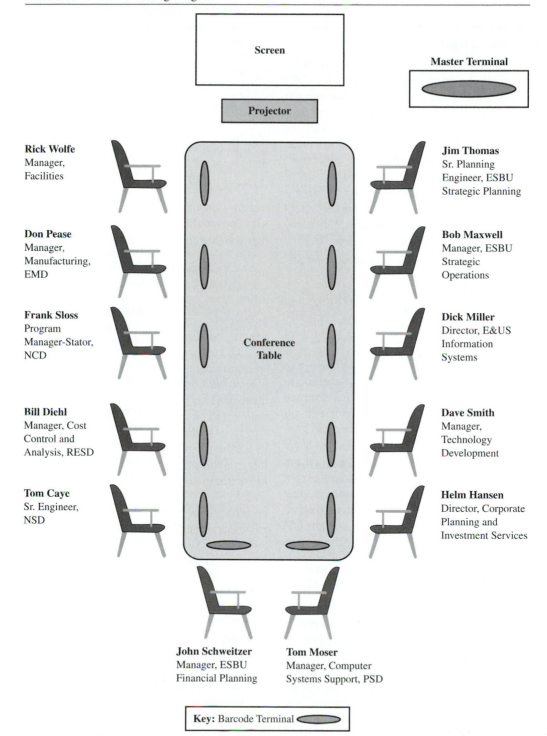

Arany offered the following guidelines from the business unit's perspective:

Since we have no reliable model for determining optimum business unit spending, the CRC should (1) evaluate proposals to determine the amount of capital required to maintain each division, and (2) put discretionary funds toward "good" projects. Good projects are those with strong financial performance and credible market projections supported by documentation on market returns, past and future market share, competitors' responses, sensitivity analyses on rates of return, and information about investment alternatives.

CRC members should use information about one division to help another, thus creating synergies. For example, equipment, technology, and space might be loaned by one division to another, or employees from one division might work in another temporarily. If two divisions have similar problems or are confronting similar issues, committee members should put the divisions in touch so they can learn from each other.

CRC members were encouraged to focus attention on areas key to Westinghouse's future strategy. Arany offered the following guidelines:

Corporate sees the nuclear divisions as key in government markets. New nuclear plants will come back, though it won't happen overnight, and Westinghouse will continue to position itself as the minimal cost provider. Sales to government will grow through quality initiatives, new products, innovation, and cost controls. The unit also has waste-to-energy projects that are in a high-growth portfolio, and new development in energy-related fields is being encouraged.

Members were informed that if growth projections looked good, some divisions should be encouraged to increase capital spending. They were also told to discourage the "solid gold syndrome" that had developed in ESBU. The business unit had a reputation for buying only the best equipment even though acceptable, less-costly alternatives were available. Bob Maxwell, ESBU's manager of business development and chairperson of the CRC, stated:

Some presenters may request capital for stress evaluations for waste-to-energy plants. These engineers are used to the rigor of nuclear plant engineering and may unnecessarily apply the same rigor to waste-to-energy plants.

Thomas encouraged committee members to take a shareholder perspective and make decisions in the best interest of the company. He explained the automated voting system, which would be used at the upcoming presentation meetings, and stressed that voting was not secret:

Although we don't announce scores during a presentation, we do distribute results, with CRC members' names, to presenters, division general managers, and other CRC members after the presentation meetings. Presenters can see how their projects rated against other projects and consider how they might improve future presentations. They can also follow up on high or low scores and ask scorers to explain why they gave a particular score to a project. To this end, we encourage CRC members to be candid and give presenters good feedback.

Presentation Meetings   ESBU's six divisions and three support groups itemized about 220 projects in the FIPs they presented to the CRC on September 19 and 20. Typically, three or four people represented a division; one presented while others provided detailed technical information or answered pointed strategic questions. Presentations included an overview of the division's investment programs and their relationships to division strategy, followed by a discussion of selected projects. According to Thomas, "One way we manage to cover so many projects is that we don't give the same amount of attention and effort to each of them. We spend more time on the ones that are complicated, critical, or unique." Thus, while CRC members merely skimmed the FIPs on projects where the need or value was obvious, they discussed other projects for as long as it took to clarify important issues. (These discussions ranged from 2 to 20 minutes.) Presenters and CRC members appeared relaxed although they did not hesitate to ask questions, express opinions, or voice concerns as approximately 100 projects were discussed and voted on. Division representatives on the CRC supported presenters from their division, answering questions and clarifying aspects of proposals.

During a division's presentation, Thomas entered the project identification number at the master terminal for each project discussed, and CRC members rated the project on each of the six criteria. Members typically discussed a project before voting, but sometimes individuals voted while a project was still being presented. Voters could change their scores throughout the presentation. Errors, such as scanning "Done" before scoring all criteria, caused the terminal to beep.

After the last person voted on a project, average scores appeared on each terminal, providing immediate feedback on the group's evaluation of the project. Members could compare their own votes to the group's averages. Thomas decided not to give project scores to presenters until the presentation meetings were over on the grounds that presenters, who would discuss several projects, could be discouraged by poor scores early on.

As each division completed its presentation, Thomas reminded CRC members to each make a preliminary allocation for the division while the presentation was fresh in their minds. CRC members jotted down their preliminary allocation recommendations in the right column of their copies of FIP Section 7 (see Exhibit 9); division coordinators had previously summarized the division's request for funds in the left column. CRC members were not held to their preliminary allocations; rather the allocations provided an input to the wrap-up meeting discussion.

Following the second day's presentations, Maxwell directed the committee's attention to the upcoming wrap-up meeting, where they would move from considering individual projects to considering each division as a whole. Maxwell stressed, "We entered this process to answer the question, 'What should we be spending?' This is still the question."

Wrap-Up Meeting   During the 1988 wrap-up on September 26, CRC members reviewed information from the presentations and expressed opinions; their goal was to recommend total appropriation and spending amounts for each division. Division general

managers, not CRC members, would ultimately decide which projects to pursue. Thomas explained:

> Division managers are the experts; they understand the strategic objectives, division priorities, customer needs, and business unit financials at a much deeper level. It is up to them to decide which projects are appropriate and necessary to do business. The project presentations help the CRC determine how much money to allocate to each division *as a whole.* But, the CRC's evaluation of projects also provides useful feedback and information for the divisions.

Thomas distributed voting results at the wrap-up meeting. Each member's scores for each project were clearly identified and various summaries and analyses of these data were prepared. Moser explained why the committee felt it was necessary to disclose voters' identities at this stage:

> Anonymity during the voting process is important because it prevents someone else's judgment from affecting one's own. After all the scores are in, however, it's important to know how each committee member rated a project. This gives us a chance to identify and discuss differences in opinions. Finding out why an individual voted the way he or she did provides insight into project weaknesses or strengths.

Thomas also produced a summary spreadsheet showing each division's request for appropriations and spending, the ESBU controller's recommended totals for each division, and the CRC's preliminary totals for each division. These last amounts were an average of the amounts each CRC member had recommended at the end of a division's presentation.

The group compared its own preliminary recommendations for each division with the amounts the controller had given at the beginning of the capital planning process. Thomas explained:

> This sets the direction for the wrap-up meeting. If committee averages are way over controller limits, I call the controller before the meeting begins, and we explore the reasons behind the difference. If additional capital is not easily available, CRC members will need to revise their recommendations during the wrap-up meeting. If additional capital could be made available, the CRC may recommend the higher

amount. In 1988, the committee's averages were fairly close to the controller's.

Using their preliminary averages as a starting point, CRC members discussed divisions one at a time. They examined the scores for a division; reviewed FIPs, handouts, and their own handwritten notes from the presentation meetings; and then backed away from details to share opinions and concerns. Thomas illustrated the process using PSD:

> I wrote our preliminary appropriation and spending numbers for PSD on the flip chart at the front of the room and asked for comments. The members reviewed their personal notes on the division, then Helm Hansen voiced his concern about one project's high risk of exposure to liability. We decided to decrease the recommended amounts for this division. For some divisions, we raised the recommended allocation based on our discussions.

Discussion revolved around each division's strategic goals and objectives, which projects could be deferred or accelerated, and which were too risky. Thomas wrote members' comments on the flip chart. (These became a major part of the feedback distributed to divisions at the end of the meeting.) CRC members commented on many things. They alerted divisions to potential problems, such as "You may encounter unforeseen technical problems when implementing this new technology." Or, "The customer must commit more money up front before you start building that plant." Or, "The market for [a new business] is not as large as projected."

The committee determined new appropriation and spending totals for each division, then added these amounts to arrive at the total capital allocation recommendations for ESBU. But, divisions requiring more money, perhaps due to unforeseen events that arose during the year, could still justify this during the informal midyear review. In this process, Thomas reviewed the divisions' monthly status reports, then called divisions to determine their midyear perspective on capital spending. For example, he might say, "You requested $140,000, we gave you $100,000, and you've spent $60,000 to date. How much do you think you'll spend by year-end?"

Feedback from the CRC

The CRC provided two types of feedback: (1) aggregate appropriation and spending recommendations needed for ESBU's financial plan and (2) detailed evaluations of division capital programs and specific projects.

The appropriation and spending recommendations were forwarded to Dr. Slember, ESBU vice president and general manager. He endorsed them, forwarded them to division general managers for their concurrence, then approved them for inclusion in ESBU's financial plan to be submitted for approval by the board of directors in January 1989. Following Slember's approval, divisions were instructed to update their FIPs consistent with the spending and appropriation limits.

Detailed results, including both qualitative comments and project scores, were distributed to FIP coordinators and presenters. Division general managers and Slember had received detailed results as backup information earlier when appropriation and spending limits were being finalized. Division managers and staff could use this feedback to aid project selection, identify problems to address during project development, and shape project presentations when submitting specific proposals to the ARB throughout the following year.

Appropriations Review Board

Theodore Stern, executive vice president of the Energy and Utility Systems Group, appointed ARB members, including Chairman P. G. DeHuff, a retired Westinghouse general manager, who acted as quality control watchdog and challenged many of the divisions' assumptions about their projects. Other board members represented a variety of businesses and disciplines; several were also CRC members (see Exhibit 10).

The ARB met monthly to review divisions' appropriation requests and to provide project management advisory services for all Energy and Utility Systems business units. An appropriation request was a detailed description of one project (see Exhibit 7 for its contents). Appropriation requests were sent to ARB members one week before the monthly meeting.

The ARB reviewed projects in risk categories B, C, or D,[3] or if they exceeded $100,000 for capital and expenses. Division general managers could approve projects outside these constraints. To ensure, however, that managers did not subdivide projects into smaller units to avoid ARB review, unreviewed small projects could not exceed 20 percent of a division's budget.

The ARB reviewed about 20 new project submissions each month. It also performed a post mortem of one prior-approved project every month to determine how money had been spent and whether milestones and market projections had been met. ARB members typically discussed projects and made decisions without presentations by divisions. Nevertheless, for large expenditures, the ARB asked the divisions to send a representative, or if technical questions arose, they made a conference call to division staff.

The ARB provided feedback to business unit general managers before sending its recommendations to Stern, who approved projects requiring less than $800,000. Paul Lego reviewed projects up to $4 million. Marous and Lego together approved projects up to $20 million, and any project greater than $20 million required approval from the board of directors.[4]

Thomas discussed the link between the CRC and the ARB:

> No direct link exists between the duties of the CRC and those of the ARB; however when a project reappears, overlapping members inform the ARB of CRC concerns. During CRC discussions, we advise divisions on how they might modify projects before presenting to the ARB. We're trying to create stronger links and continually improve the entire process.

Evaluation of the Capital Budgeting Process

Hansen described ESBU's capital budgeting process as "thorough and well-disciplined." He continued:

---

[3] *Projects in risk category A involved an existing product or technology, an existing facility, and an existing market. Projects in risk category B had one of the above new; in risk category C had two of the above new; and in risk category D had all three new.*

[4] *The approval limits have been disguised.*

This process does a good job of setting priorities among the diverse segments of the business unit. At the corporate level, we view the data coming out of the process as valid, and we use the CRC's recommended totals, which we weigh against the needs of other business units, to arrive at an appropriate corporate total.

When asked whether the divisions viewed the capital planning process as a fair way to allocate funds, Arany responded:

> When you're allocating funds you always have people who feel that it's not fair, whatever you do. To build acceptance, we thoroughly explained the process to division general managers and we gave them the right to select their representatives on the committee. The general managers also have the right to appeal to the business unit's vice president. So far they've not used that right of appeal. I think they accept the CRC's recommendations.

Caye, who had initiated the CRC, had moved to the Nuclear Services Division in 1984. He was a member of both the CRC and the ARB and was FIP coordinator for his division. He offered his assessment of the capital budgeting process:

> The strength of the process lies in its ability to achieve synergy and improve communication across ESBU divisions. If divisions are going in different directions we can explore the reasons. Have they spoken to each other? Is each aware of what the other is doing? Are their different approaches appropriate because their needs and applications differ, or is a single direction better for both divisions?

He continued, commenting on the technology used at CRC meetings:

> The barcode technology facilitated data collection during presentations and allowed us to express opinions, summarize group decisions, and get fast feedback. Having results at the wrap-up meeting allowed the group to see if there was consensus. If not, we could focus on outlying projects and question people who gave widely different scores so that we could understand their different perspectives.
>
> The technology allowed us to manipulate data, evaluate them from different perspectives, reconcile them, and report to management in a timely manner.

The feedback sends a real message to division managers. If a project received low scores, then the division will give it more thought; perhaps it wasn't presented well, or perhaps the project was flawed. Division staff may stick with the project but improve its presentation for the ARB, or they may drop it. As FIP coordinator for my division, I can attest that divisions put more effort into capital investment because they know the committee will review the projects in detail and give written feedback.

Bob Monley, technical services manager, presented the Electro-Mechanical Division's (EMD's) projects. He described how he used the voting results and qualitative comments from the CRC sessions:

I looked for low scores. These may indicate that I was not prepared on a particular point or that the project has more inherent weaknesses than we anticipated. The feedback from the CRC definitely affects the way we present a project to the ARB. We either incorporate the CRC's comments or we consider reducing the project's scope or dropping it altogether.

Fred Holler, EMD's FIP coordinator, gave further insight into his division's perspective on the CRC's feedback:

The consensus is that the information we receive has gotten better because it is more detailed. The feedback forces us to look deeper into each project. Our project concepts are planned years before they are presented to the CRC. We maintain three- and five-year plans with about $15 million to $20 million in planned capital involved. We prioritize projects at the division level. We know what the CRC will ask, so we look at our own projects and weed them out beforehand. We have a good idea of what we can get, though we never get everything we want.

Moser described PSD's response to the CRC's feedback on one controversial project:

We looked doubly hard at the project to determine if it was something we wanted to pursue. Because of the CRC's review, the controller became heavily involved in the decision. We decided to submit the project to the ARB despite its poor scores, and it was funded. The detailed feedback from the CRC really helped us address the ARB's concerns.

Caye, however, felt that, even with the aid of barcode terminals, the material covered in two days was overwhelming: "Toward the end of each day I became fatigued, and found it increasingly difficult to provide good, honest, critical evaluation."

Thomas agreed that the presentation meetings were tiring, but felt that overall the process was effective:

Toward the end of each day, you can tell that it's wearing on the committee members. The technology provides some discipline to help us get through the process. It forces us to evaluate each project against those six criteria. The criteria establish a common ground from which to evaluate projects and divisions. We must pay attention and get our questions answered so that we can appropriately evaluate the projects. The ability to link scores with each CRC member forces them to vote and be ready to stand behind their votes, which increases accountability. All of this reduces bias, involves all members, and strengthens the group's ownership of the decision.

Effective capital budget planning is critical if Westinghouse is going to accomplish its strategies. I believe the technology helps us make better decisions in this critical area. We feel it has been well worth the $35,000 investment.

Arany concurred with Thomas about the value of the technology:

Most companies don't get such specific feedback from their capital budgeting process. What is all this feedback worth? I don't know. We can't quantify the return on investment. Because CRC members realize that their scores will be available to presenters and general managers, they do a better job of listening, asking questions, and generally trying to understand how the division will spend money.

Summary

Thomas pondered new ways to use technology and automation in group decision making. He stated, "We're concerned with finding ways to support our strategic planning process and to improve the link with our financial planning process." He also expressed interest in how technology might be used in the more creative stages of decision making. But his immediate attention turned to 1989. What changes could be made to improve the capital planning process for the upcoming year?

Case 2–4

PETERSON INDUSTRIES: LOUIS FRIEDMAN

In August 1993, Louis Friedman, president and chief operating officer of Peterson Industries, reflected on the decision-making process at Peterson:

> In the last few years I think we've seen a real change in the way decisions get made at Peterson. In the past, there was a very gentlemanly process, due in part to the Rosegrant family influence and the chairman's temperament. He preferred one-on-one relationships. Decisions were a private matter between manager and subordinate, and managers had great discretion over what was done in their own departments. But with the internationalization of the company, decisions have become much more complex. Also, young managers won't tolerate being shut out of decisions—they leave if it happens—so there's been a shift to more analytical decisions. More people are involved and there's more controversy.
>
> Resource allocation decisions seem to be the biggest bones of contention. Peterson's operating management is decentralized, but capital funds and engineers from our central pool are divided up through a resource allocation process which attempts to rank the various development projects proposed by the divisions according to their potential value to the corporation as a whole. With the international scope of our business and our complex reporting relationships, resource allocation decisions are conceptually difficult and potentially divisive. Managing the process becomes a challenge in itself. The basic problem is how to get mature people through the posturing to the real issue of achievement.

Background

Peterson Industries was recognized as a leading producer of products made from specialty plastics and related materials. Peterson also produced a limited line of medical instruments, devices, and special peripheral materials. The company's reputation, growth, and profitability were based on technological innovation and manufacturing capabilities. It had a remarkable history of inventing products using plastic materials with superior technical qualities such as heat resistance, chemical stability, mechanical strength, or light transparency.

Many of these products were invented to order at the request of original equipment manufacturers (OEMs). The development process usually began in the Technical Staffs Division—a staff research and development unit under the purview of Dr. Roger Caldwell, vice chairman of the board and chief technical officer. Once the basic technology was developed, the Engineering and Production Division (E&P)—a central pool of Peterson's top engineers—took primary responsibility for applying the technology to specific products and manufacturing processes. E&P engineers worked closely with the line organization units responsible for producing and marketing the new product. Ideally, this development sequence resulted in the introduction of a new product with high growth potential and a strong market position protected by patents, manufacturing expertise, and heavy capital investment in the production process.

Peterson's ability to apply its technological superiority in plastic to the development of useful products was reflected in its long record of growth and profitability. However, the company's dependence on cyclical OEM customers and the sporadic nature of research breakthroughs had caused its financial performance to vary (see Exhibit 1). Peterson's vulnerability to economic downturns became a serious problem in 1990, when the recession made it necessary for the company to lay off about 10 percent of all salaried employees—including a similar

This case was prepared by David A. Garvin.

Copyright © 1996 by the President and Fellows of Harvard College. Harvard Business School case 396-182.

EXHIBIT 1 Peterson Industries' Financial Performance

Net Sales in Millions

92	$1,119.6
91	1,025.9
90	939.0
89	1,051.0
88	945.8
87	714.6
86	603.4
85	609.3
84	540.8
83	479.1

Net Income in Millions

92	$92.1
91	83.7
90	31.1
89	48.1
88	70.4
87	54.3
86	34.0
85	43.9
84	54.8
83	49.3

Stockholders' Equity in Millions

92	$666.4
91	600.5
90	542.3
89	535.7
88	511.0
87	458.7
86	428.1
85	416.5
84	388.5
83	352.8

Consolidated Statements of Income	1992	1991	1990	1989	1988
Net sales	$1,119,630	$1,025,905	$938,959	$1,050,962	$945,785
Cost of sales	762,424	701,647	708,455	797,528	656,746
	$ 357,206	$ 324,258	$ 230,504	$ 253,434	$ 289,039
Selling, general and administrative expenses	$ 187,756	$ 166,773	$ 151,819	$ 160,925	$ 146,300
Research and development expenses	54,812	48,857	42,285	37,628	35,172
	$ 242,568	$ 215,630	$ 194,104	$ 198,553	$ 181,472
Income from operations	$ 114,638	$ 108,628	$ 36,400	$ 54,881	$ 107,567
Royalty, interest and dividend income	20,572	18,038	11,317	15,272	19,066
Interest expense	(18,465)	(19,704)	(21,802)	(19,571)	(15,193)
Other income (deductions), net	7,611	3,745	(5,211)	(1,611)	(7,542)
Taxes on income	(53,201)	(51,874)	(7,723)	(19,182)	(50,076)
Income before minority interest and equity earnings	$ 71,155	$ 58,833	$ 12,981	$ 29,789	$ 53,822
Minority interest in (earnings) loss of subsidiaries	(1,174)	(595)	2,617	1,832	(1,258)
Equity in earnings of associated companies	22,102	25,475	15,539	16,504	178,818
Net income	$ 92,083	$ 83,713	$ 31,137	$ 48,125	$ 70,382
Per Share of Common Stock					
Net income	$ 5.20	$ 4.74	$ 1.76	$ 2.73	$ 4.00
Dividends	$ 1.56	$ 1.50	$ 1.40	$ 1.40	$ 1.40
Average shares outstanding (thousands)	17,696	17,648	17,635	17,601	17,573

proportion of its 600 executive-payroll employees—as part of a general reduction in workforce. This was the most severe cutback of executive and salaried personnel in the company's history, and it was an extremely painful step for Peterson.

In spite of its size and international scope, the company resembled a small-town firm in many ways. The chairman, Joshua Rosegrant, Jr., and vice chairman, Larry Rosegrant, were fifth-generation descendants of Peterson's founders. The Rosegrant family still controlled over 30 percent of the voting common stock, and the company was the dominant employer in the small Wisconsin town of Greenville. People from the several divisions saw each other frequently on Peterson's premises, on the streets of Greenville, and on social occasions. Business matters were discussed face to face. Personal relationships were informal; even top officers were addressed on a first-name basis. In a sense, the corporation operated like a family. Employment security was always an implicit assumption for managers who made a career commitment to the company. In the words of one manager, the 1990 layoffs left an "invisible scar" on the company psyche. Avoiding a repetition of this experience was still an important factor in management thinking in 1993.

Peterson's Management Structure

Peterson's line management organization was influenced by its historical development as a multinational corporation. In the early phases of its expansion into foreign markets, Peterson relied on exports. Products were developed and manufactured in the United States and sold in other countries through overseas sales offices. As the international market became more important, the company set up an international division and began to acquire and build foreign manufacturing facilities. In 1993, Peterson initiated a major restructuring of its organization under the rubric of internationalization. The objectives of restructuring were to eliminate the sharp split between domestic and foreign operations (the two sides sometimes competed for the same business), and to enable a rationalization of production and marketing decisions on a worldwide basis. This restructuring was carried out at the same time as the major layoff in 1990.

Peterson's 1993 organizational structure is illustrated in Exhibit 2. Line management of the company's business units was based on a matrix concept of shared responsibility. One side of the matrix consisted of the company's worldwide product divisions. Management responsibilities along this dimension included strategy formulation, technological development, and resource allocation. The time horizon for typical decisions was intermediate to long term. The other dimension of the matrix was based on geographic markets. Area managers were responsible for Peterson's assets in each geographic region, for day-to-day operations, and for relations with host countries. The North American area for each of the product divisions was under the direct control of the worldwide product division managers. Decision making in the areas focused on shorter-term management problems. In practice, of course, the two dimensions of responsibility often overlapped. Major investments, acquisitions, or marketing decisions required the cooperation of both product division managers and area managers. Peterson's chairman, Joshua Rosegrant, stressed that "part of a manager's job is to live with ambiguity. We look to Peterson's managers not only to watch over and direct their specific areas of responsibility, but also not to become so driven by strict organizational lines that they are unable to share with each other and the chairman the total responsibility for the corporation, with its close, intertwining relationships."

The company's organization was also complicated by what Friedman called "an ongoing ambiguity in the company's top management structure." Friedman had responsibility for assets and day-to-day operations in North America. He also had worldwide business responsibility for the seven product line divisions and for budgeting and resource allocation. Larry Rosegrant, vice chairman and chief international officer, was responsible for assets and operations outside North America. Thus, while Friedman had clear responsibility for domestic business, he and

EXHIBIT 2 Organization Chart

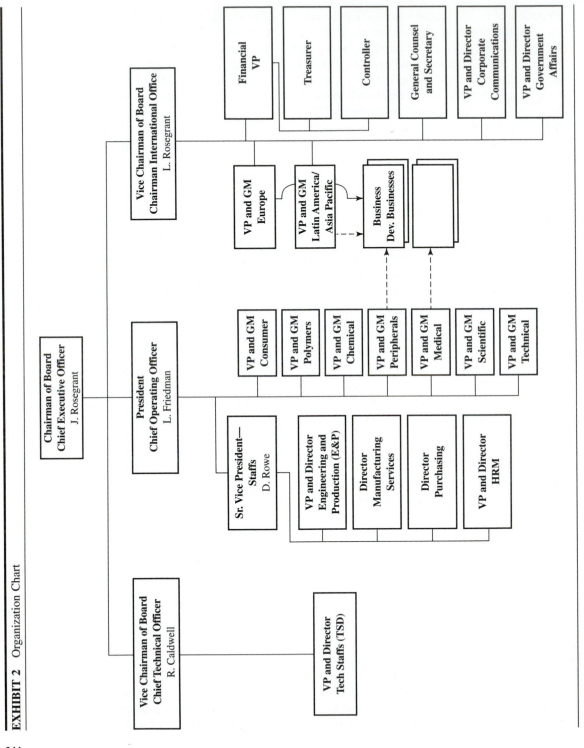

Rosegrant shared responsibility for the company's international development.

The line organization was supported by two centralized staff development units: the Technical Staffs Division (basic and applied R&D and product development), and the Engineering and Production Division (product and process engineering). The development process was coordinated by two committees: the Business Development Committee and the Resource Allocation Committee. The Business Development Committee's role was to help identify opportunities for new products or new markets that were well suited to Peterson's technical capabilities, and to make sure these opportunities were fully explored by the appropriate organizational units. The Resource Allocation Committee (which one officer called "an exclusive club for accountants") was responsible for recommending priorities and funding levels for development projects. These two committees were originally formed as a single unit. However, it was found that the critical stance of committee members with control responsibilities tended to stifle the initiative, creativity, enthusiasm, and effectiveness of members whose primary goals were to stimulate and exploit new technologies and market opportunities.

To help clarify the ambiguities in management roles, Peterson made extensive use of decision structure charts (see Exhibit 3 for a sample chart). Deborah Rowe, the company's senior vice president of staffs, commented:

> This organization is based on management processes rather than on structure. A major part of my job is being the management process engineer. We reviewed the recurring decisions on a business-by-business basis and got agreement on how they should be made. Each decision process is different. The decision grids cover management roles all the way up to the chairman's level. About a third of the process job was defining the roles of Lou Friedman and Larry Rosegrant. The other two-thirds of the time was spent on the areas and product divisions.

Commenting on the decision grids, Friedman said: "Shared responsibility is easy to say and hard to do! Developing the charts helped us work out the details. I don't have to refer to the grids very often any more, but I keep a copy in my computer."

Strategic Planning and Resource Allocation

Peterson's strategic planning process was based on a business unit classification that roughly followed the operating organization structure. The company was divided into seven product line divisions, 20 business groups, 60 businesses, and 130 geographic subdivisions of business. Each unit prepared two basic documents: Business Strategies and Resource Requests. Business Strategies (see Exhibit 4) included a narrative explanation of the proposed strategy; a planning matrix that positioned the business according to the maturity of the market and the business's competitive strength; and a long-range forecast of financial performance indicators such as sales, profit margins, turnover, and return on assets. Resource Requests for capital funds and E&P engineers were prepared for each capital project (see Exhibit 5). The Business Strategies and Resource Requests were reviewed and prioritized by both geographic area and worldwide business managers for submission to corporate management.

At the corporate level, the review process was coordinated by the Resource Allocation Committee, headed by Deborah Rowe. The committee's job was to recommend priorities for capital funding and assignment of E&P engineers to Friedman and L. Rosegrant. The committee was composed of the financial vice president, the controller, the director of strategic planning, the director of E&P, and the director of the Technical Staffs Division.

The company's strategic planner, who reported to the financial vice president, described his role as "keeping the process on a strategic level so we don't get lost in the numbers." One way this was accomplished was to rank each business according to its strategic role and importance. The categories used to determine rank were super-thrust, thrust, emphasis, reposition, sustain, and selective. These rankings were used as one criterion for setting resource allocation priorities. The new

EXHIBIT 3 Top Management Decision Structure

Legend

D - Decides TC - Technical Concurrence
A - Approves C - Concurs
R - Recommends I - Initiates
BC - Business Concurrence IP - Inputs

Column groups: **Operating Units** | **Corporate Staff Units** | **Executive Management** | **CDC** | **CMC** | **CEO** | **Boards of Directors**

D. DEPLOYING CORPORATE RESOURCES	C.S. Division Manager	Overseas Division Manager	Worldwide Business Manager	Managing Director Overseas Subsidiary	Area Manager	Staff Division Manager	Finance and Planning	Engineering and Production	Technical Staffs	Purchasing	Manufacturing Services	Industrial Relations	HR Development	Legal	Public Relations	Government Affairs	Senior Vice President—Staff	Vice Chairman—RC	Vice Chairman—LR	President	CDC	CMC	CEO	Overseas Subsidiary Boards	CIC Board	CGW Board
Capital																										
1. Establish annual capital budget																										
a. Determine level of annual investment							R												R	B		D	A	C^*		G
b. Determine allocation levels by major category—e.g., legally required, cost reduction	R_1		R_1	R_1	R_1		R_1	R_1	R_1								R_2	R_2	D	D		A				
c. Rank major capital projects greater than $100,000	R_1		R_1	R_1	R_1		R_2	R_2	R_2								R_2	R_2	D	D		A				
d. Rank projects under $100,000 for																										
—Legally required	R_1		R_1	R_1	R_1		R_2	R_2	R_2								R_2	R_2	D	D						
—Cost reduction	R_1		R_1	R_1	R_1		R_2	R_2	R_2								R_2	R_2	D	D						
—Maintaining existing business	R_1		R_1	R_1	R_1		R_2	R_2	R_2								R_2	R_2	D	D						
—Expanding existing business	R_1		R_1	R_1	R_1		R_2	R_2									R_2	R_2	D	D						
e. Decide on overall Capital budget																			D	D		A	A	C^*		C

*As appropriate

EXHIBIT 4   Division Business Strategy Summary

DIVISION BUSINESS STRATEGY SUMMARY

1993 PLAN - SCHEDULE A-1
FORM: 12/1992

Division
Business _____

Worldwide, or
Geographic Area,
or Subsidiary _____

Date Prepared
or Modified _____

STAGE OF MARKET LIFE CYCLE

	Embryonic	Growth	Mature	Aging
Strong				
Favorable				
Equal				
Weak				

COMPETITIVE STRENGTH

FINANCIAL DATA

	1992 Actual	1993 Forecast	1997 Estimate
Sales $000	_____	_____	_____
O.E. $000	_____	_____	_____
D.O.M. $000	_____	_____	_____
D.O.M. %	_____	_____	_____
Sales/Net Assets	_____	_____	_____
ROA %	_____	_____	_____

STRATEGY SUMMARY:

MEASUREMENT AND GOAL:

MAJOR RESOURCES REQUIRED/WORKING CAPITAL CHANGES:

COMPETITIVE POSITION:

THREATS/RISKS/OPPORTUNITIES:

SIGNIFICANT CHANGES FROM 1992 STRATEGY:

---

polymerization technology, for example, was a super-thrust business. The resulting materials from this technology were used in a wide range of computer- and telecommunication-related products. One of Peterson's most dynamic new technologies, this business opened a pilot facility in 1992 and doubled its capacity twice that year to meet rising demand. "It's a resource hog," said Friedman. "It chews up engineering talent, especially our key process engineers. But you can't allocate resources to a business like that on the basis of internal rate-of-return calculations. It's a major strategic decision—either we're in the business or not—and we're in it. The main question we ask is whether they can use more engineers or capital funds than they've requested."

EXHIBIT 5   Capital and E&P Engineering Resource Requests

Capital and E&P Engineering Resource Requests	1993 Plan—Schedule C-2	Form: 12/

Division_____   Plant/Entity_____   Date Prepared_____

A. TYPE OF REQUEST: Project>$100M; or   <$100M (Individual or Sum of Projects)

B. PROJECT NAME_____   CONTACT PERSON_____

C. CLASS OF REQUEST   1. Legal Req'd   4. Maint. Bus.   7. Energy Independence

(circle one)   2. Cost Reduc.   5. Develop. Bus.   8. Energy Conservation

3. Exp. Exist. Bus.   6. Other

D. BUSINESS AFFECTED & PERCENT ALLOC.

Business,	%	Business,	%	Business,	%
1. _____	____	2. _____	____	3. _____	___

E. Was project in last year's submission?   Yes, or   No   If Yes, Project No. _____
If no, is E&P Div. working on project now?   Yes, or   No   If Yes, E&P Project No. _____
Is A/R approved for this project?   Yes, or   No   If Yes, Bulletin No. _____

RESOURCES REQUESTED:

	TOTAL PROJECT	1993 SPENDING BUDGET	1993 SPENDING FORECAST	1994 REQUEST	1995 ESTIMATE
1. Property, Plant and Equip.	_____	_____	_____	_____	_____
2. Specialty Chemicals	_____	_____	_____	_____	_____
3. Total Project Capital	_____	_____	_____	_____	_____
4. E&P Div. Man-Yrs. (Estimate)	_____	_____	_____	_____	_____
5. CGW Capital Requested	_____	_____	_____	_____	_____

G. DESCRIPTION AND SUMMARY JUSTIFICATION OF PROJECT:

H. RANK: PLANT/ENTITY____out of____; DIVISION/AREA____out of____; W-W BUS.____out of____

COMPLETE FOLLOWING INFO. IF TOTAL <u>PROJECT</u> REQUIRES >$1MM CAPITAL OR >2 E&P MAN YEARS <u>AND</u> FOR <u>ALL EXPANSION</u> AND ENERGY CONSERVATION PROJECTS OVER $100M

I. ECONOMICS OF PROJECT:
   1. Internal Rate of Return (DCF)_____%
   2. Time Horizon used for DCF_____years
   3. NPV of Cash Flows at 20% $_____
   4. Payback_____years

J. DESIRED KEY MILESTONE SCHEDULE:
   1. A/R Approval_____
   2. Start Engineering_____
   3. Start Construction_____
   4. Project Complete_____

K. CONFIDENCE IN ECONOMIC ESTIMATES (check one)   L. PROBABILITY OF OCCURRENCE:_____

Solid Backup   Reasonable   Guess

DO NOT FILL IN

Legal Req'd _____	Energy _____	For Tk. Repair _____	Non-Producing _____
E&P _____	Corporate _____	Strategic Fit _____	Tech Feas. _____

The Engineering and Production Division played a pivotal role in reviewing the Resource Requests. Jake Carlton, director of E&P, said:

> In the early phases of developing the resource allocation process, the emphasis was on capital funds. Estimates of the number of E&P engineers required were included in the project description, but these were usually inaccurate. Even the capital estimates were wrong, since they were prepared without engineering input, and the total number of engineers estimated as required in the approved projects didn't jibe with the schedules or availability of E&P engineers. But my guys are the scarce resource. In 1991, we had good solid projects that would have required 50 percent more engineers than were available. In 1992, this figure was 75 percent, and this year the requests were double what we could assign. So now, the Resource Requests are submitted to us, and we recommend our own priorities based on engineering practicality, ROI (return on investment), ROE (return on engineering dollars), and strategic category. In fact, the engineering ranking is becoming dominant. Our fixed commitments, prior year projects, and contract obligations are so large that the new project options are pretty narrow.

The role of the controller was to manage the process from a budgeting standpoint. Decisions made about strategies and resources during the resource allocation process provided the bases for the annual capital and operating budgets used for management control. The controller's office reviewed the plans and requests to see that proposed expenditures were properly classified under corporate guidelines, and to supervise the consolidation of the plans at the corporate level. The analytical emphasis was on making sure that everyone involved understood the budgetary and financial implications of the resource allocation options.

Based on the analyses of its various members, the Resource Allocation Committee listed the proposed projects by priority and recommended a total capital funding level and engineering head-count ceiling for the coming year to Lou Friedman and Larry Rosegrant. This recommendation was also sent to division managers for their review and comment. The resource allocation process culminated in a three-day resource allocation meeting attended by division and area managers, staff officers, and the two top managers. Staff recommendations were discussed, and managers whose projects were not slated for funding were given a chance to present their cases to the group. The final decisions about total resource and project allocations were made by Friedman and L. Rosegrant at the end of the meeting.

Performance Measurements and Rewards

Management control at Peterson was based on the annual operating budget. As one division manager described it:

> We just take the three-year plan and translate the 1993 numbers into a budget using the latest projections about the economic environment—inflation, exchange rates, and so forth. It's the plan that yields the operating budget. Nothing goes in the budget without first being in the plan. People will try to put things into the budget to give you what they think you want in the way of operating performance, but the results don't usually correspond unless they've been thought through in the planning process.

Performance was measured by using profit centers for all line organization units down to the plant level. Profit itself was measured in terms of gross margin, operating margin, and contributed margin, as shown in the abbreviated format below:

Sales revenue	xxx
Manufacturing cost	xxx
Gross margin	xx
Selling and administrative expenses	xx
Operating margin	xx
Corporate expenses (assigned)	xx
Contributed margin	xx

At the divisional level, performance was measured primarily on the basis of variance from the budgeted divisional operating margin (DOM). Other profit measures were budgeted and reported, as were standard financial ratios such as return on assets (ROA), but most attention focused on the DOM.

This emphasis was reflected in Peterson's executive compensation system. Top management traditionally relied on operating margin as the key performance variable when reviewing salary increases for all of its managers—including division managers—although the review was broad enough to encompass other areas of performance as well. In calculating bonuses for managers below the officer level, the formula gave half-weight to operating margin variance and half-weight to Individual Performance Factors (IPF)—a series of personal objectives much like a Management-By-Objectives system. For many managers, however, the most important IPF was to meet the DOM budget. (See Exhibit 6 for an example of a bonus calculation.)i

The overall emphasis on operating margin was modified in several ways. Annual bonuses for corporate officers, including division managers, were based on corporate profits only. Payments were made from a pool of funds equal to 5 percent of corporate additional profits, defined as net income in excess of 8 percent of capital invested. Except in particularly bad years (such as 1990), the pool usually exceeded the sum of individual bonus entitlements.

Peterson's compensation system also included an Employee Equity Participation Program. This program had three parts: an equity purchase plan, a stock option plan, and an incentive stock plan. The equity purchase plan permitted about 500 of Peterson's managers and professionals to buy Peterson stock at book value up to an annual ceiling of 10 percent to 20 percent of the buyer's salary, depending on position level. The buyer was prohibited from reselling the shares to anyone other than Peterson, but could resell them to the corporation, at book value at the time of resale, upon retirement or termination of employment.

The stock option plan granted participants the option to buy shares of Peterson common stock for up to 10 years at the market price on the day the option was granted. Over the last four years, each officer received options to buy an average of 2,500 shares under this plan. However, the depressed price of Peterson's stock in recent years had significantly reduced the value of these options as a form of compensation.

The incentive stock plan, originally established in 1989, was designed to give Peterson's top officers a significant equity position in the company through grants of stock. About 36,000 shares had been distributed in the three years since the plan was approved. Under this original plan, each participant received an ownership amount of stock in proportion to the level of the participant's position. Individual performance was not a factor. Stock ownership was vested in the employee over a four-year period.

EXHIBIT 6   Pro Forma Bonus Calculation

A. Par calculation

Base salary	$180,000
Bonus class	× 35%
Bonus at par	$ 63,000

B. Performance measurement

1. Division operating margin

Budget	$50 million
Actual	$52 million
Variance	$2 million
Variance	(favorable)
	4% (favorable)

2. Individual performance factors

Over/under achievement	8% over

3. Aggregate performance

4% + 8% =	12% (favorable)

C. Earned bonus calculation

Bonus at par	$63,000
Plus performance	+ 12%
Earned bonus	$70,560

Top Management Goals

In spite of its technological capabilities and financial strength, Peterson's top managers were not satisfied with the company's performance. According to Lou Friedman:

> We're making a 12.5 percent return on investment, but we should be making 15 percent. We develop plans calling for improved performance each year, but somehow it doesn't happen. The chairman has set a target of reaching 15 percent ROI by the year 2000, and he has divided up the problem among me, Larry Rosegrant, and Ted Caldwell. Ted is supposed to help with a new big technology push. Larry is to

do it through acquisitions and external investments. My job is to find ways to get there with our present portfolio of businesses.

As part of the drive to close the profit gap, Peterson instituted a revised incentive stock plan in April 1993. (Exhibit 7 shows how the new incentive plan fits into the overall compensation system.) The principal new element in this plan was that stock awards were to be paid only to the extent that certain predetermined, long-term, individually tailored performance goals (among them a 15 percent ROI) were met by 1997. The plan included the company's key profit center and new business managers. It was

---

EXHIBIT 7   Personal Financial Impact Long-Term Incentive Plan

The plan in this example represents approximately 14% of total compensation over a four-year period, given the following assumptions:

- Base salary = $180,000
- Raises = $10,000 at end of 1st, 2nd, 3rd years
- Bonus (A/C) at 35%

$$\text{Payout} = 2 \text{ years at } 100\%$$
$$1 \text{ year at } 75\%$$
$$1 \text{ year at } 50\%$$

- Previously granted incentive stock = 1,400 shares to be vested
- Stock options   (1) 10,000 shares at $40 weighted average

    (2) Potential gain of $20/share = $200,000

Total Four-Year Compensation[a]

Salary $720,000 plus   (51%)

	Short Term	Long Term
Individual	Salary Changes $60,000 (4%)	Incentive stock plan $200,000 (14%)
Corporate	Bonus[b] $218,750 (16%)	Stock options $200,000 (14%)

= 1,398,750 (100%) Total Compensation

[a]Estimated (all percentages rounded)
[b]Bonus calculation:
$ 63,000 1st year at $180,000 paid at 100%
$ 66,500 2nd year at $190,000 paid at 100%
$ 52,500 3rd year at $200,000 paid at 75%
$ 36,750 4th year at $210,000 paid at 50%
$218,750

expected to be worth from $120,000 to $400,000 in the 1993 value of the stock to each participant, depending on base salary and achievements. Friedman commented on the revised plan:

> People don't do extraordinary things for money, but it sure improves their hearing. The first time around, the plan was explained to the participants by a compensation expert, but the division managers didn't hear the emphasis on the long-range performance aspects. The second time I explained it. I said that this time we were serious, that we were going to do what we said, and that I knew it because there was a lot of money riding on it. The first reaction to the stock plan was that it would be divisive, but I pointed out that most of the compensation was really tied to corporate performance. If the corporation isn't doing well in 1997, then the stock will be priced low and the grant won't be worth as much. Interestingly, the division managers want Larry and me to be able to override the formula with subjective judgments about whether they've been helpful members of the team.

Friedman also saw the resource allocation process as a key tool for improving performance over the long run:

> One reason we instituted this process was to improve the way we were using our critical resources, which are capital funds and engineers from E&P. In the past, there wasn't much of a process for allocating engineers. The E&P people worked out their own priorities and schedules with each division. The resource allocation process has been difficult for them. They can still effectively veto a project on technical grounds, but they no longer decide what to work on by themselves. Until we developed the resource allocation process, we never had a good handle on what they were doing!
>
> The process is also useful as a way of getting people to think about strategy in concrete terms. Traditionally, the budget has been taken as the serious performance measurement tool. The division managers usually filter out the more outrageous stuff in the strategic plans they get from their business, but they're not as rigorous as with the budget. I'm trying to get the same kind of hard-nosed thinking about strategy. The overriding question at the big resource allocation meeting, which included the division managers, was not just "how are we going to allocate resources?" but "how are we going to get to 15 percent ROI by

1997?" The incentive stock plan gives us a reason to think about that, and the resource allocation process ties that thinking into here-and-now decisions.

> I think perhaps the most important reason for having the big meeting at the end of the process is to gain commitment. The compensation system won't do it alone. It's a matter of managerial team building. I want the division managers to see the process from the corporate point of view as well as their own. That's the only way they'll really internalize these goals we're setting. No more "we/they." When good projects get turned down, it's important for the manager involved to accept the decision as best for the corporation, rather than simply as a rejection of an idea he or she believes in and has worked hard on. You can't just say it—they've got to see all the projects they're competing with and understand how tight the resource constraints are in relation. And they've got to feel the process is fair. You give managers the chance to make their individual pitch to justify the project not only to me but to their peers as well. And if the project gets cut, well, at least that manager went down fighting.

> But the way you handle the meeting is critical. Last year we listed all the projects by priority and opened it up for discussion. We went way down below the cutoff points we'd set for capital funding and head count. It took a long time for people to realize how narrow our options were. And having to reject so many projects after they were discussed in the meeting caused a lot of pain. This year Larry and I reviewed the staff recommendations in detail first, closed down some options, and held some one-on-one meetings with managers whose projects were cut or rejected. We made some compromises, but when people went into the meeting they knew what to expect. Things went much more smoothly than last year.

Two Proposals from Peripherals

Friedman continued:

> The Sam Kells incident is a good example of how it worked this year—not earth-shaking, but interesting. Sam Kells is the head of the Peripherals Division, which he manages on a worldwide basis. He had two proposed projects, each requiring about six engineers. He did a good deal of politicking before the resource allocation meeting. I first heard about the projects in the Business Development Committee (which I chair) and we were very enthusiastic. But

the peripheral components part of Sam's division, where the project came from, is a "sustain" business, so the projects didn't rank very high on the Resource Allocation Committee's list of priorities. As a side issue, it's interesting to note that Pierre Le Goff, who originated the projects, is the only key guy at his level who's not an American. When the division was internationalized he was brought from France to the United States as head of Kells's product and planning unit. He's first rate—he knows the technology, he's creative, aggressive—just what we want. Anyway, I got together with Kells before the meeting and cautioned him that he would only get six engineers in total for the two projects. So even though he made an impassioned plea for those two projects at the resource allocation meeting, he was prepared to lose. He could see how tight the engineering constraint was. The other managers also got on him about what a resource hog new polymerization technology is, which is one of his businesses. And it helped that fewer people were making special appeals this year.

Commenting on the decision, Sam Kells, vice president and general manager of the Peripherals Division, said:

The rejection of those projects may not have been an earth-shaking issue to the company, but I assure you it was earth-shaking to me. In the resource allocation meeting, the question put to me was "If you get half the engineers you need, couldn't you stretch the projects out over time and do them both?" The answer is that neither one can be delayed since both are related to the economic cycle. The molded parts project is designed to develop a proprietary process to lower the cost of molded plastics so we can build volume profitably with Hewlett-Packard. It's a highly competitive business; cost reduction and volume are the keys to profit. But the time to go for volume is now, when demand is growing. If we wait, we may get hit with an economic downturn that will make it all the harder. The same applies to the precision plastic project. There we're entering an existing market, which is very tough to do in this business if demand is soft, so we've got to move.

The problem with the decision to give us only six engineers is not that there is no money to go outside, but that we need trained people with some

stake in the project, some continuity of involvement. I want E&P to feel some responsibility for the project. I need their competence over the long run. But with E&P, you've got to get them to buy in early, to get them on the board. Actually, I'm pleased that at least we got the six engineers from E&P. The plan now is to divide them up between the two projects and use them to supervise outside engineers or the division's own people who can do the work. The six are enough so that E&P will own the projects.

One problem, of course, is that this way the money may have to come out of operating expenses. The operating budget gets put together based on what happens at the resource allocation meeting. We may raise the question about who pays for the outside consulting engineers. If Peripherals pays, it comes out of our divisional operating margin. If E&P pays, it will get charged back to us, but as a corporate expense below the DOM line.

As for the Peripherals Division's strategic role, Kells said:

I'm not sure whether we're a "sustain" or "emphasis" business—I think "emphasis" better describes it. I think it should be remembered that in the book the chairman put together this year (an overview of Peterson's management philosophy, mission, organization, and key objectives), he identified peripheral components as one of three profitable businesses that should be supported to make sure they stay profitable. We have a reputation for good estimates of what a project is going to cost and for getting results. That's why we're usually successful in getting resources. Lou Friedman used to be the Peripherals Division manager and he knows this. He's very open about the way he manages the managers of this company. The strategy is clearly understood, and he runs a simple, open process.

Interviewed about the two projects, Elizabeth Jenkins, assistant controller, commented first on the accounting issue raised by Kells, and then on the resource allocation process as a whole:

No, they can't charge the outside engineers to E&P. E&P pays only for *major* cost reduction projects—the precision plastic project doesn't qualify. And for new products like the precision plastic components, the engineering expense comes out of the division's operating margin. Sam Kells will have to pay for the engineers he hires out of his operating budget.

But the real issue isn't who pays—it's what gets done. Look, the idea behind the resource allocation process was to limit the capital dollars spent on development to projects with real payoff—the ones that represent the future of the company. Peripherals is a good business, but with only $90 million a year in sales and a mature product's growth potential, it isn't Peterson's future. We don't want to spend all the cash we can find, and we don't want to get caught in another 1990 situation again. One of the big issues for this company is how to deal with this drive to expand head count, not only in E&P, but operating people as well. It's a result of the push for better return; people respond by proposing all kinds of new projects. There's been a steady increase in head count—especially staff—since 1990, but there hasn't been an equivalent increase in performance. We ought to have learned after 1990 not to hire unless we're sure we've got a permanent job. The resource allocation process is supposed to help us limit the rate of growth of these development projects to what's profitable and manageable in the long run. But I'm not exactly thrilled with the result—the process is too mushy. Take these two projects from Peripherals. They asked for 12 engineers from the E&P pool. That's their opening bid—it's almost certainly more than they needed. They got six, which is probably less than they wanted, although they did pretty well considering their position. But look what they're going to do! They bootstrap the project with outside engineers, charge it to operating expense, and go ahead as they planned. So how have we allocated any resources? How have we limited the dollars spent for development? What has the process really accomplished?

One big problem is the one-shot nature of the process—there's only one major resource allocation meeting per year, and that's where all the decisions are supposed to be made. This just invites people to ask for everything they think they might get around to. Pretending we know how these projects are going to progress and what we'll be doing 18 months out is ridiculous. Halfway through the year you find that only 30 percent of the budget has been spent, even though people were screaming about how tight the allocations were. People come in high to be safe

and to establish a negotiating position. When they see how tight the constraints are, they come in even higher. We wind up having to raise the capital budget authorization from $120 million to $134million, and we still don't really know where we are.

I'd like to see two things. First, there should be top-level determination of firm limits on capital resources and E&P head count. The limits should be based on our long-run sustainable growth, and they shouldn't be subject to a lot of horse trading at the resource allocation meeting. Second, there should be more frequent allocation and reviews, say, every quarter. We should allocate the resources on the basis of rough estimates, and then track the capital funds and E&P man-years actually used. Based on the progress of the development portfolio, the allocation could be adjusted to give more to the projects that move and less to those with problems. That way, your decision making is based on more recent estimates of cost, schedule, and market potential. And if managers know they can come in with new proposals whenever they are ready, they feel less pressure to play games with the process.

Pierre Le Goff, product and planning manager for the Peripherals Division, was the originator and prime mover of the two projects:

Frankly, I was pretty frustrated. I go through all these meetings—here, look, we even put together a chronology on the precision plastic project (Exhibit 8)—and we made good presentations. A big part of my job is communicating with top management. They have to judge so many proposals; I want my projects to be clearly understood and easy to remember. So I put a lot of time into the presentations. And the response was, "These are good projects." Corporate management was very enthusiastic. But then I get to the resource allocation meeting—when dollars get involved—and the whole thing is called into question. I think they're saying yes to a lot of projects that add up to more than they can spend. The lack of coordination causes wasted time and expense. You spend time and money, maybe hire some staff, and then . . .

Now I look at the resource allocation meeting as the final decision. There you've got everybody together in the same room; everybody signs off. Those numbers go into the budget. You've got to have a final word somewhere. Still, the only

EXHIBIT 8 Chronology for Precision Plastic Project

Prepared by P. Le Goff for Resource Allocation Committee, 7/1/93

2/14/92	• CMC review of Peripherals business strategy
	- Outlined product development strategy
	- Proposed precision plastic project
3/10/92	• CMC approved "aggressively going after precision plastic opportunity"
5/23/92	• 1992 three-year plan strategy summary
	- Key decision: business plan to enter precision plastic market in the United States and Europe by 12/92. P. Le Goff
6/15/92	• Reorganized division product development
	- Product extensions
	- Product renewals: Le Goff (plus TSD and E&P)
1/16/93	• Division completed major market study to confirm and segment market
2/22/93	• Division reviewed project proposal and pro-forma A/R, made final decision to proceed
3/17/93	• Presented project to BDC
3/20/93	• "BDC considers precision plastic to be a good project deserving of corporate support"
3/29/93	• Technical request accepted by TSD
	- Project leader at TSD appointed
4/3/93	• Project leader at Peripherals appointed
4/20/93	• 1993 three-year plan
5/12/93	• Reviewed again with BDC in division BDC review

CMC—Corporate Management Committee (J. Rosegrant, L. Rosegrant, L. Friedman, R. Caldwell)
TSD—Technical Staffs Division
E&P—Engineering and Production Division
BDC—Business Development Committee

numbers taken seriously are next year's. There's a broad strategy, a three-year plan, but they just ask for the '94 numbers in the resource allocation process, so I've still got no commitment for '95 or '96. It doesn't make me feel very secure. I guess it's a question of personal confidence. If I do OK the first year, then everything will be all right.

Just to show you what happens, I asked for 12 engineering man-years from E&P for 1994. I got six to share between the two projects, but I got the Tech Staff R&D resources three months ago. You don't go through the resource allocation process for them—it's a matter of lobbying, keeping good relationships with the Tech Staff people. The guy I needed was appointed even before I wrote the technical request. The first time I knew they'd started was when I got some financial reports showing charges to the networks project.

As far as the engineering goes, I wasn't convinced that the E&P people were the most competent for the job anyway. Outside engineering houses can do the work, but I need E&P management skills and cooperation. The strategy is to get them involved initially, use off-the-shelf technology to enter the market, and improve after we get in. But you have to get E&P on board initially—it's much more difficult later on. Now that they're in, I'm over the biggest hump. The job now is to show some solid progress and build top management's confidence in these projects.

Decision-Making Processes

OVERVIEW

A vast mythology has grown up around decision making. Mention the phrase to managers and they typically conjure up images of a solitary executive holed up in an office or a senior team sitting pensively around the conference table. The executives are poring over memos and charts while struggling with a difficult, bet-the-company choice. Success requires a series of complex calculations and a careful weighting of pros and cons—a combination of rigorous analysis and large doses of judgment. And, as if these challenges weren't enough, the usual scenario includes intense time pressures and a looming deadline.

The reality of organizational decision making is quite different. Studies show that even the most senior general managers make relatively few policy decisions on their own.[1] Decision making is simply not a solo affair. Nor is it the exclusive province of a small, elite group. Especially when issues are large—a major investment, perhaps, or the choice of a new technology—the process normally involves large numbers of people, extending well beyond the senior team, and a multitude of interactions.[2] Seldom is the decision made in a single meeting. In fact, the precise time that a decision is "made" is surprisingly hard to identify. According to an auto company executive:

---

[1]H. Edward Wrapp, "Good Managers Don't Make Policy Decisions," *Harvard Business Review* 62 (July–August 1984), pp. 8–21.

[2]Yair Aharoni, *The Foreign Investment Decision Process* (Boston: Division of Research, Graduate School of Business Administration, Harvard University, 1966), and Robert A. Burgelman, "A Process Model of Internal Corporate Venturing in the Diversified Major Firm," *Administrative Science Quarterly* 28 (1983), pp. 223–244.

It is often difficult to say who decided something and when—or even who originated a decision . . . I frequently don't know when a decision is made in General Motors. I don't remember being in a committee meeting when things came to a vote. Usually someone will simply summarize a developing position. Everyone either nods or states his particular terms of consensus.[3]

The associated process is frequently lengthy and drawn out. A study of over 150 strategic decisions found an average duration—from first proposal to final decision outcome—of over 12 months. The shortest decision took a month, while the longest took four years.[4] In most cases, choices are based only partly on rational analysis. The tools and techniques of systematic problem solving so popular in business schools are seldom used.[5] Instead, politics and power play central roles, and bargaining is often essential to produce solutions that appeal to diverse interests.[6]

What are we to make of these findings? They suggest that many managers hold an idealized, inaccurate view of decision making. Many have failed to grasp a basic truth: decision making is a process. Like strategy development and resource allocation, it extends over time, has multiple stages, and involves large numbers of people spread throughout the organization. Highly placed individuals or teams, who play such central roles in the heroic model of decision making so dear to managers, have only limited impact in the real world of organizations. And social and political concerns, rather than rationality and formal analysis, often determine the final choice.

But that does not mean that decision making cannot be studied or improved. Here again, a process lens has much to offer, for it helps distinguish effective from ineffective approaches. Some decision-making processes, for example, are fast and efficient; others are slow and cumbersome. Some decision-making processes balance creativity and discipline; others give undue weight to one or the other. Some decision-making processes ensure that diverse options and points of view are explored before a solution is reached; others move mindlessly to closure after reviewing a single proposal. Each of these differences can be traced to an aspect of process design or process leadership that is discussed in this module.

---

[3]James Brian Quinn, *Strategies for Change: Logical Incrementalism* (Homewood, IL: Richard D. Irwin, 1980), p. 134.

[4]David J. Hickson et al., *Top Decisions* (San Francisco: Jossey Bass, 1986), pp. 100–101.

[5]According to a study of decision making in nearly 80 service organizations: "Nothing remotely resembling the normative methods described in the literature was carried out. Not even hybrid variations were observed. Either managers have little knowledge of these methods of find them naive." See Paul C. Nutt, "Types of Organizational Decision Processes," *Administrative Science Quarterly* 29 (1984), p. 446.

[6]Kathleen M. Eisenhardt and Mark J. Zbaracki, "Strategic Decision Making," *Strategic Management Journal* 13 (1992), pp. 17–37, and Jeffrey Pfeffer and Gerald R. Salancik, "Organizational Decision Making as a Political Process: The Case of a University Budget," *Administrative Science Quarterly* 19 (1974) pp. 135–151.

OUTLINE

The first class in the module, "British Steel Corporation: The Korf Contract" includes a case, a video, and a "Note on Process Observation." In 1975, managers at British Steel were struggling with a major investment decision: Should they purchase one or two direct reduction plants, to be installed at Hunterston, a major port in Scotland? These plants, which used a new technology, would produce pelletized iron for use in the company's blast furnaces. The decision hinged on a number of factors, including a calculation of anticipated iron needs, the projected demand for steel, purchase costs, the flexibility of the new plants, and political concerns.

Surprisingly, British Steel allowed a BBC camera crew to observe and document the ensuing decision-making process. Managers at multiple levels, from low-ranking analysts to the company's managing director and board, were filmed over several months as they went about their business, running calculations, crafting memos, participating in meetings, lobbying, negotiating, and making the final decision. The resulting video provides a unique, behind-the-scenes picture of corporate decision making, a "warts and all" view that even today retains its relevance.

The video is notable in three respects. First, it clearly shows decision making to be a process rather than an event. A wide range of players can be seen contributing as analysis is prepared, alternatives are considered, and the process cycles through multiple stages and iterations. Information and advice flow both vertically and horizontally, across hierarchical levels as well as across functional groups.

Second, the video shows two distinctive approaches to decision making—the analytical/rational and the social/political—that are an integral part of almost any choice process. The former involves the application of rigorous reasoning and quantitative methods to identify a preferred option or alternative; it is closely related to the normative techniques taught in modern-day finance and management science classes. The latter involves extensive negotiation, bargaining, and selling; it views organizations as "coalitions of competing interests" in which "decisions follow the desires and subsequent choices of the most powerful people."[7] These two approaches often coexist uneasily, and power usually triumphs. In fact, at British Steel the decision appears to have been almost preordained, dictated in large part by the managing director's enthusiasm for direct reduction plants.[8]

Finally, the video provides an opportunity to practice skills in process observation. The accompanying note describes several critical elements of group process: participation, influence, climate, acceptance, and functioning. Together,

---

[7]Eisenhardt and Zbaracki, "Strategic Decision Making," p. 23.

[8]Such processes, in which "the forms of decision making must be proceeded with even though it is apparent to some or all of those involved that the decision has already been made," have been called "quasi-decision making." Fully one-third of decision making appears to take this form. See David J. Hickson, "Decision-Making at the Top of Organizations," *Annual Review of Sociology* 13 (1987), p. 175.

they determine the effectiveness of a group. The note also offers a number of litmus tests and warning signs indicating potential problems, as well as helpful interventions. They apply not only to decision making, but also to virtually any process that involves meetings and personal interactions. All of these elements are on display at British Steel and can be decoded and discussed.

The second class in the module features two academic articles, "Strategic Decision Processes in High Velocity Environments: Four Cases in the Microcomputer Industry" and "Making Fast Decisions in High-Velocity Environments." They provide a sharp contrast to British Steel and show decision making in a completely different context. The steel industry is slow moving and reasonably predictable; the key uncertainties are the level of demand and the production levels of competitors. The microcomputer industry, by contrast, is characterized by rapid, hard-to-anticipate changes; the uncertainties are so large that "almost nothing is given or easily determined."[9] Products, technologies, and customer needs are almost impossible to foresee with any precision, making adaptability and rapid response essential.

The associated decision-making processes have a number of distinctive features. All are designed for speed. Managers draw heavily on real-time operating data; generate multiple, simultaneous alternatives; rely on experienced, trusted counselors for advice; come to a decision using a modified consensus approach (in which the senior team tries to reach collective agreement but, if it cannot, empowers the CEO make the choice); and delegate implementation to functional leaders. There are, however, still a number of parallels to British Steel. Even in high-velocity environments, decision making remains a process that unfolds over time, involves a large number of people, and passes through several distinct stages. Both analytical/rational and social/political modes are present, and conflict and bargaining continue to play key roles.

The third class in the module, the "Decision-Making Exercise," provides an opportunity to experience and evaluate three alternative approaches to decision making: consensus, dialectical inquiry, and devil's advocacy.[10] The consensus method requires that members of a decision-making group meet together and engage in a free exchange of ideas, discuss proposals in an open, constructive manner, and strive to reach consensus, with all team members accepting the final decision. The dialectical inquiry method requires that members of a decision-making group first divide into subgroups of equal size. The two subgroups develop opposing sets of assumptions and recommendations, meet together to debate their

---

[9]In technical terms, the distinction is between uncertainty and ambiguity (also called "great uncertainty"). See Henry Mintzberg, Duru Raisinghani, and André Théorêt, "The Structure of 'Unstructured' Decision Processes," *Administrative Science Quarterly* 21 (1976), pp. 250–251, and Sven Ove Hansson, "Decision Making under Great Uncertainty," *Philosophy of the Social Sciences* 26 (1996), pp. 369–386, for further discussion.

[10]David M. Schweiger, William R. Sandberg, and James W. Ragan, "Group Approaches for Improving Strategic Decision Making: A Comparative Analysis of Dialectical Inquiry, Devil's Advocacy, and Consensus," *Academy of Management Journal* 29 (1986), pp. 51–71.

points of view, and then settle on a single proposal. The devil's advocacy method also requires the formation of subgroups of equal size. But in this case, one subgroup develops a set of assumptions and recommendations while the other develops a logical, plausible critique. The two groups then meet together and try to settle on a single proposal.

All members of the class first participate in a consensus process. They then evaluate their experiences using a simple survey form. Next, all members of the class engage in either dialectical inquiry or devil's advocacy; again, they evaluate their experiences using the same set of survey questions. Class discussion revolves around a comparison of these experiences and the strengths and weaknesses of the three methods. Of special interest are the amount and types of conflict the methods generate, the levels of satisfaction and acceptance they produce, and their likely impacts on decision quality and effective, speedy implementation.

The next class in the module combines two readings, "A Thousand Days" and "Thirteen Days," that are excerpts from books of the same titles. Each describes the deliberations of a task force convened by President John F. Kennedy. The first task force, widely considered to be an example of flawed decision making, planned the Bay of Pigs invasion. The second task force, usually regarded as a success story, planned a response to the Cuban Missile Crisis. Surprisingly, the two groups had many of the same members. Both were also led by President Kennedy. Success and failure cannot be traced to the cast of characters, but must be rooted in features of the decision-making process.

Several factors played a role: the context and conditions surrounding each process, the process design, group dynamics, and Kennedy's approach to leadership. Context includes the level of urgency and crisis, the time available for discussion, and the experience of participants. Process design includes the means of dialogue—the way that debates were conducted and whether consensus, dialectical inquiry, or devil's advocacy techniques were used—as well as the roles assigned to participants. Group dynamics includes the implicit rules of the game, especially the norms governing information handling, communication, and conflict resolution. Leadership includes Kennedy's level of personal involvement and participation, the form and timing of his interventions, and the guidelines he provided to each group.

The last case in the module, "Decision Making at the Top: The All-Star Sports Catalog Division," provides a counterpoint to the Kennedy cases. Unlike the Bay of Pigs and Cuban Missile Crisis task forces, which were ad hoc groups assembled for the sole purpose of responding to the issue at hand, the decision-making body in All-Star Sports is an established senior management team. It is a standing group that meets weekly to discuss the strategic and operating issues facing a single division. The agenda varies over time and includes both problems and opportunities. Perhaps most important, group dynamics are based on ongoing relationships, since the members of the team will continue to meet and work together for months and perhaps years.

All-Star Sports provides an opportunity to evaluate a senior management team's decision-making process using many of the criteria that have already been introduced. Again, there are issues of context, process design, group dynamics, and leadership. The division's strategy, for example, is evolving; does that require a new approach to decision making? Subgroups are used at various stages to provide analysis and generate preliminary recommendations; are they a help or a hindrance? The division president dislikes confrontation; how do his preferences shape behavior? Overall, the process has many favorable characteristics, including high levels of analysis, limited politics, and active participation. But there is only limited constructive conflict, and decisions tend to be revisited multiple times because of a lack of buy-in and commitment. Do the strengths of the process outweigh the weaknesses, or should it be redesigned? If so, in what ways?

THEMES

Phases of Decision Making

Virtually all studies of decision making divide the process into distinct phases or stages.[11] Although the number of stages varies, the descriptions are remarkably similar. In most cases, the first step is problem formulation. An opportunity or issue arises and is deemed worthy of further discussion; the problem is framed and supporting analysis is prepared. The second step is the development of alternatives. Again, supporting analysis is required, this time to generate a set of potential solutions. The final step is selection, in which one approach is chosen from the menu of possibilities. All of these stages can be seen in British Steel, the Kennedy task forces, and All-Star Sports.

Early researchers viewed these steps as sequential. They expected them to occur in order and always in the same, predictable fashion. But that conclusion was soon questioned and disproved—even for individuals. People apparently find it very difficult to keep the stages of decision making separate and distinct. According to a classic study:

> We believe that human beings cannot gather information without in some way simultaneously developing alternatives. They cannot avoid evaluating these alternatives immediately, and in doing this they are forced to a decision. This is a package of operations, and the succession of these packages over time constitutes the total decision-making process.[12]

What is true of individuals is equally true of organizations and groups. Neither follows a simple sequence of steps when making decisions. Instead, they combine

---

[11]For representative examples, see Herbert Simon, *The New Science of Managerial Decision* (New York: Harper and Row, 1960); Mintzberg, Raisinghani, and Théorêt, "The Structure of 'Unstructured' Decision Processes"; and Nutt, "Types of Organizational Decision Processes."

[12]Eberhard Witte, "Field Research on Complex Decision-Making Processes—The Phase Theorem," *International Studies in Management and Organization* 2 (1972), p. 180.

activities, skip stages, and recycle multiple times. The precise approach taken depends on the content and complexity of the decision at hand.[13]

Even so, the three stages provide a valuable analytical framework, for they help pinpoint strengths and weaknesses in decision making. Many managers, for example, move too quickly to the later stages of the process; they do not spend enough time framing the problem properly.[14] The group planning the Bay of Pigs invasion clearly made this mistake. Alternative generation is often given short shrift; once a single option has been identified, many groups believe the evaluation process should begin. Consensus processes frequently suffer from this problem, while dialectical inquiry and devil's advocacy techniques are designed to overcome it. Slow, cumbersome processes keep the three stages relatively separate and discrete; more effective processes try to overlap steps and integrate upstream and downstream stages. British Steel suffered from the problem of unrelated stages, while the rapid decision makers in the microcomputer industry overcame it with seamless linkages. Finally, as All-Star Sports makes clear, the choice of participants in each stage—and whether the same people are involved throughout the process—has a powerful impact on both decision quality and decision acceptance.

Conflict and Politics

Both conflict and politics are common in decision making. They come in several varieties and may be healthy or unhealthy, desirable or dysfunctional. Conflict, for example, may be either task related or emotional.[15] Task-related (cognitive) conflict involves debates over ideas—disagreements about underlying assumptions, analysis, and the criteria that go into making a choice. Emotional (affective) conflict involves personal frictions—acrimonious debate, disparaging comments, and hostile criticism aimed at the individual rather than the substance of the issue at hand. Both forms of conflict can be seen in every class in the module, although the distinction between the two is clearest in the "Decision-Making Exercise" and "A Thousand Days" and "Thirteen Days."

---

[13]Marshall Scott Poole, "Decision Development in Small Groups I: A Comparison of Two Models," *Communication Monographs* 48 (1981), pp. 1–24; Poole, "Decision Development in Small Groups II: A Study of Multiple Sequences in Decision Making," *Communication Monographs* 50 (1983), pp. 206–232; and Poole, "Decision Development in Small Groups III: A Multiple Sequence Model of Group Decision Development," *Communication Monographs* 50 (1983), pp. 321–341.

[14]J. Edward Russo and Paul J. H. Schoemaker, *Decision Traps* (New York: Simon and Schuster, 1989), pp. 212–214.

[15]Allen C. Amason, "Distinguishing the Effects of Functional and Dysfunctional Conflict on Strategic Decision Making: Resolving a Paradox for Top Management Teams," *Academy of Management Journal* 39 (1996), pp. 123–148, and Karen A. Jehn, "Enhancing Effectiveness: An Investigation of Advantages and Disadvantages of Value-Based Intragroup Conflict," *International Journal of Conflict Management* 5 (1994), pp. 223–238.

In general, task-related conflict is desirable; it is what scholars have in mind when they urge management teams to "have a good fight."[16] Debates of this sort are invaluable for vetting assumptions, generating deeper insights, and carefully weighing alternatives. Emotional conflict, in contrast, is usually unhealthy; it leads to warring factions, isolated camps, and divisiveness. Disagreements of this sort impede effective implementation as well as a group's ability to work smoothly and harmoniously in the future.

Political behavior, in the sense of behind-the-scenes maneuvering and jockeying for position, is frequently associated with conflict. But the two need not move together. Only when power is unequally distributed among members of the decision-making group—as at British Steel and the Bay of Pigs task force—do the two tend to be associated. Then, conflict goes underground. Debate is suppressed, either consciously or unconsciously, and individuals try to get their preferred positions supported by backroom lobbying and covert political behavior. By contrast, when conflict is open and competing positions are fully aired—as the rapid decision makers in the microcomputer industry and the Cuban Missile Crisis task force—there is likely to be little in the way of backroom politics.[17]

These varied forms of conflict and politics combine to create two very different modes of decision making: advocacy (persuasion) and inquiry (problem solving).[18] They appear in several classes, especially the comparison of the Bay of Pigs and Cuban Missile Crisis task forces. In the advocacy mode, competing special interest groups present their own points of view as forcibly as possible. Participants believe that "my solution is the best solution"; they do not attend carefully to competing arguments, but strive only to enhance the likelihood that their preferred recommendation will be adopted. Information is presented selectively to buttress one's arguments, and backroom politics and behind-the-scenes maneuvering are common. Conflict can be intense and is only resolved through a battle of wills—what scholars call "bargaining and forcing."[19] The implicit assumption is that the desired solution will emerge from a test of strength among competing interests.

In the inquiry mode, participants strive for rational problem solving. There is a sense of shared purpose and sincere concern for the problem at hand; the goal is to find the best solution, not to have the group adopt one's preferred point of

[16]Kathleen M. Eisenhardt, Jean L. Kahwajy, and L. J. Bourgeois, III, "How Management Teams Can Have a Good Fight," *Harvard Business Review* 75 (July–August 1997), pp. 77–85.

[17]Kathleen M. Eisenhardt and L. J. Bourgeois, III, "Politics of Strategic Decision Making in High-Velocity Environments: Toward a Midrange Theory," *Academy of Management Journal* 31 (1988), pp. 737–770.

[18]Norman R. Maier, "Assets and Liabilities in Group Problem Solving: The Need for an Integrative Function," *Psychological Review* 74 (1967), p. 244.

[19]James Ware, "Problem Solving and Conflict Resolution in Groups," in John J. Gabarro, ed., *Managing People and Organizations* (Boston: Harvard Business School Publications, 1992), pp. 263–278.

view. Information is widely shared, multiple alternatives are considered, and each alternative is evaluated on its merits. Conflict is healthy and is resolved by confronting the group's differences and seeking ways to resolve disagreements amicably. For this reason, backroom politics are largely absent. The implicit assumption is that the desired solution will emerge from a test of strength among competing ideas, not from competition among advocates.

Problems and Pathologies

Unfortunately, even the best-designed decision-making processes are likely to experience problems. These problems are difficult to eliminate completely; they arise from deeply rooted patterns of thought and action that subtly bias the reasoning of both individuals and groups. Here, awareness is the first line of defense, for it improves the odds that difficulties will be recognized and countermeasures will be taken.

At the individual level, problems arise because people are flawed statisticians.[20] They do a poor job applying probabilistic reasoning and estimating cause and effect. They are extremely susceptible to vivid memories and experiences, drawing on them heavily even when they are not representative. They suffer from "confirmatory bias," viewing new information through the filter of preconceived theories and beliefs. They are far too confident in the validity of their estimates and assumptions, and seldom generate a wide enough range of alternatives. Several of these biases appear in "British Steel," the "Decision-Making Exercise," and "A Thousand Days" and "Thirteen Days."

At the group level, problems arise because of in-group pressures.[21] Most people want to be accepted as members of groups, especially those that are cohesive and have high status. Often, their identity and self-esteem depend on it. They therefore strive for unanimity and agreement in decision making, playing down their differences and disputes. Minority views are frequently ignored in the process, even though they contribute greatly to more robust analysis and higher

---

[20]For a general introduction, see Max Bazerman, *Judgment in Managerial Decision Making*, 4th ed. (New York: John Wiley, 1998), esp. chap. 2. For more on vividness, see Amos Tversky and Daniel Kahneman, "Judgment under Uncertainty: Heuristics and Biases," *Science* 185 (1974), pp. 1127–1128. For more on confirmatory bias, see Rohit Deshpande and Gerald Zaltman, "Factors Affecting the Use of Market Research Information: A Path Analysis," *Journal of Marketing Research* 19 (1982), pp. 14–31. For more on overconfidence, see Hillel J. Einhorn and Robin M. Hogarth, "Confidence in Judgment: Persistence of the Illusion of Validity," *Psychological Review* 85 (1978), pp. 395–416.

[21]For discussions of in-group pressures and the dangers of groupthink, see Irving L. Janis, *Victims of Groupthink* (Boston: Houghton Mifflin, 1972). For more on the importance of minority views, see Charlan Jeanne Nemeth, "Differential Contributions of Majority and Minority Influence," *Psychological Review* 93 (1986), pp. 23–32.

quality recommendations. Occasionally, members engage in "groupthink," a collective process of rationalization and discounting of warnings, in which the desire to belong overrides critical thinking and thoughtful analysis. Many of these group pathologies can be seen in the microcomputer industry's slow decision makers and the Bay of Pigs task force.

Guidelines for Improved Decision Making

By now it should be clear that decision making is a complex, difficult-to-manage activity. The steps in the process vary in order and duration, conflict and politics can easily become dysfunctional, and biases and pathologies often get in the way of precise, disciplined reasoning. Nevertheless, the odds of success can be sharply improved by following a few simple guidelines. They fall into two broad categories: improvements in process design and better process leadership.

Effective decision-making processes start with well-chosen groups. They should be of manageable size, neither so small that real debate is difficult nor so large that full inclusion is impossible. Between five and seven members is ideal.[22] Homogenous groups tend to work together better because they have fewer interpersonal problems.[23] But to avoid narrowness and parochial views, the process should be designed to encourage a diversity of opinions and positions. Minority views are especially important, and participants should be selected, in part, for their iconoclasm and willingness to speak up.

Some method of generating multiple alternatives, options, or scenarios is essential. The goal is to ensure that there is first "divergence"—the consideration of many possibilities—before the group moves to "convergence"—the choice of a single option or solution.[24] Here, dialectical inquiry and devil's advocacy processes are extremely helpful, as is the occasional introduction of new members to the group. Subgroups can also be used to flesh out positions and inject differing perspectives, especially if they draw upon brainstorming, role playing, and other creativity techniques.

Not surprisingly, the most effective decision-making processes keep task-related (cognitive) conflict high while minimizing emotional (affective) conflict. They do so, in part, by having clear rules of engagement. Among the most important guidelines: Participants should strive to be critical of ideas, not of

[22]Robert F. Bales, "In Conference," *Harvard Business Review* 32 (March–April 1954), pp. 44–50.

[23]Katherine Y. Williams and Charles A. O'Reilly, III, "Demography and Diversity: A Review of 40 Years of Research," in B. M. Staw and L. L. Cummings, eds., *Research in Organizational Behavior* 20 (Greenwich, CT: JAI Press, 1978), pp. 77–140.

[24]Dorothy Leonard and Walter Swap, *When Sparks Fly* (Boston: Harvard Business School Press, 1999), esp. chap. 3.

people. Minority views should be encouraged. All participants should feel that their opinions and positions have been recognized and considered, even if they were not formally adopted. The latter requirement, known as "fair process" or "procedural justice," is especially important for ensuring cooperation, buy-in, and trouble-free implementation.[25]

Most decision-making processes, of course, require leadership. Otherwise, they can easily derail. Here, the most powerful advice is also the simplest: Leaders should shape the process, not dictate the solution.[26] They should separate their role as participants—team members who offer analysis and opinions—from their role as decision makers and arbiters—the final authority who "calls the question" and makes the choice. They should listen attentively to others, especially those representing minority viewpoints, in order to build commitment and trust.[27] They should avoid stating their personal preferences too early, when they are likely to exert undue influence over others. They should ask probing, disconfirming questions to ensure that the group does not converge too early on an easy, obvious solution. And they should encourage "second-chance meetings," in which decisions are revisited a final time to ensure that earlier thinking was sound.[28]

Decision making, after all, is a process that flourishes only under the proper circumstances. Debates and divergent views are essential, but they must not come at the expense of group harmony and a willingness to move forward together. The leader's role is to cultivate and protect this delicate balance between comfort and contentiousness. David Hume, the Scottish philosopher, made much the same point over 200 years ago, when he observed that "truth springs from arguments amongst friends."[29]

---

[25]W. Chan Kim and Renée Mauborgne, "Procedural Justice, Strategic Decision Making, and the Knowledge Economy," *Strategic Management Journal* 19 (1998), pp. 323–338.

[26]David A. Nadler, "Managing the Team at the Top," *Strategy & Business* (Winter 1996), pp. 42–51.

[27]M. Audrey Korsgaard, David M. Schweiger, and Harry J. Sapienza, "Building Commitment, Attachment, and Trust in Strategic Decision-Making Teams: The Role of Procedural Justice," *Academy of Management Journal* 38 (1995), pp. 60–84.

[28]Janis, *Victims of Groupthink,* pp. 218–219.

[29]Quoted in Charles Handy, *The Age of Unreason* (Boston: Harvard Business School Press, 1989), p. 67.

Case 3–1

BRITISH STEEL CORPORATION: THE KORF CONTRACT

In early 1975 many of the top managers of the British Steel Corporation (BSC) were deciding whether to invest in one or two direct reduction plants at Hunterston.[1] The design under consideration was being offered by Korf, a West German manufacturer of process equipment for the steel industry. In mid-1974 Korf submitted a bid to build one 400,000-metric-ton (annual capacity) plant for £26 million. The company later tendered a second option to build two plants for £43 million, resulting in twice the capacity. The savings offered by the latter bid had reopened the discussion, but Korf's bid was to expire on February 15, 1975.

The decision hinged on a critical calculation called the *Fe balance*—the amount of iron required, given the anticipated demand for steel. The Fe balance was calculated as the sum of iron provided by blast furnaces, scrap, and other sources (such as direct reduction). Preliminary calculations showed that in 1979–1980, the first year the Hunterston plant would be in operation, there would be a requirement for iron pellets produced by direct reduction. In that year, about two-thirds of the iron requirements would be met by scrap. In following years, however, it appeared that the direct reduction capacity might be superfluous, in light of proposed increases in blast furnace capacity.

Cost was another critical factor. BSC estimated that pelletized iron from one new direct reduction plant would cost £63 per metric ton; from two new plants, the cost would fall to £58 per metric ton. Iron from blast furnaces cost £56 per metric ton. Many other factors were involved: long-term development of iron processing; cost and future availability of natural gas for direct reduction, versus the cost of coal for the blast furnaces; possible export of surplus pelletized iron; Korf's strong order-book position; and the advantage of having a source of iron not tied to blast furnaces or coal.

Background

After World War II, a Labour government was elected in Britain that nationalized several basic industries (coal, transport, utilities), including the steel industry in 1949. The Conservatives were returned to power in 1951 and carried out an election promise to denationalize steel. The period of state ownership had been short enough so that it was possible to denationalize steel under more or less the previous company structure. The Labour Party gave notice that, if and when it was returned to power, it would renationalize steel. By the end of the 1950s, political trends of voter's intentions began to give weight to that threat. Faced with the specter of the "juggernaut of state control,"[2] the industry campaigned heavily to remain private. Otherwise, it was felt, "no industry will be safe from the

---

[1] *Direct reduction is a process by which pelletized iron is produced from ore and fed directly into the basic oxygen and electric arc furnaces to produce crude steel. Iron for steel making is supplied by blast furnaces (pig iron), by processes like direct reduction, and by the scrap market.*

[2] Steel Times, *June 24, 1966.*

This case was prepared by John Stengrevics under the direction of John. P. Cotter.

TABLE A   Combined Results of the 14 Nationalized Steel Companies, 1958–1967 (£ millions, except ratios)

	1958	*1959*	*1960*	*1961*	*1962*	*1963*	*1964*	*1965*	*1966*	*1967*
Trading profits before depreciation[1]	138	143	181	148	115	114	148	145	115	93
Trading profits after depreciation	108	109	141	104	67	59	87	80	47	23
Capital employed[2]	624	696	750	840	1,010	1,238	1,189	1,194	1,230	1,228
Ratio of profits after depreciation to capital employed	17.3%	15.7%	18.8%	12.4%	6.6%	4.8%	7.3%	6.7%	3.8%	1.9%

[1]Before interest and taxes, other than interest on bank overdrafts which, where not shown separately on the accounts, has been estimated.
[2]Capital employed relates to start of the financial year and comprises share capital, reserves, and long-term borrowings.

Source: British Steel Corporation annual report, 1967.

possibility of takeover, and no industry will be safe from being in competition with a nationalized corporation not subject to the normal financial disciplines and having the power of the public purse behind it."[3] Steel would be the third major industry nationalized since the war.

In 1967 over the opposition of the Iron and Steel Board, which represented the interests of the private steel producers much as the AMA represents the interests of U.S. medical professionals, the British steel industry was again nationalized, this time permanently. The tenor of the opposition can be inferred from a comment in *British Steel* a few years later: "As those who were involved at the time will remember, the nationalization of the steel industry evoked more emotion than probably any other political issue."

Holders of securities in the 14 private companies that produced more than a total of 475,000 metric tons of steel in 1964 (1 metric ton = 1.102 tons or 2,200 lbs.) were awarded government stock equivalent to the stock exchange values of their securities. This represented about 90 percent of U.K. crude steel production at the time (private firms

accounted for the great majority of specialty steels). These securities were then vested in the BSC, which reported to the secretary of state for trade and industry, who in turn reported to Parliament.

In 1967 the 14 nationalized companies included 41 steel producing works, of which 50 percent had a capacity under 0.5M metric ton per year. About 10 percent of total steel output was produced in works with a capacity of 3M to 4M metric tons per year. (Economic size of a crude steel plant in the industry at that time was about 4M metric tons per year and appeared to be rising.) Selected financial data on the nationalized companies from 1958 to 1967 are shown in Table A; the effect of threatened renationalization can be seen in the lackluster performance and low capital growth in the 1960s.

A committee formed by the British government to study the issue of nationalization had recommended that, as a matter of policy, capacity follow demand as closely as possible. This represented a reversal of the industry's policy, which was to provide some margin for peak demand, and it probably reflected the fact that in 1967 there was a massive world steel surplus. Two members of this committee were appointed to the BSC: Lord

[3]Steel Times, *July 22, 1966.*

FIGURE A   Partial Organization Chart, 1969

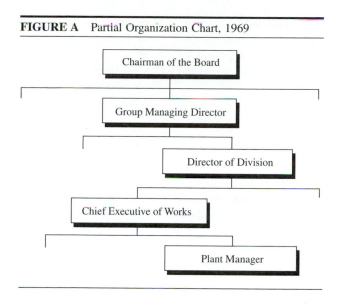

Melchett (who had a career in the Royal Navy after graduating from Eton) was named chairman in April 1967, and Dr. H. Montague "Monty" Finniston (Ph.D., Royal College of Science and Technology, Glasgow) was named deputy chairman.

"Profitability is the criterion for organization policy" was the headline of the first issue of *British Steel* in April 1968. Lord Melchett also noted: "The object will be to make the most economic use of large and highly capitalized resources, and to do it quickly enough to convince customers, the industry itself, and the world at large that the immense opportunities inherent in this huge and complex merger have been fully grasped." There were about 260,000 people employed at that time in the nationalized industry.

Corporation Chronology

1968–1969

Lord Melchett and the board of the BSC first organized the industry into four groups based on geography, product links, technology, and economic considerations. These groups would not compete in price but could compete with one

another in cost, service, quality, and productivity. There were clear lines of authority from the board to the works, as the partial organization chart illustrates (see Figure A).

Shortly thereafter Monty Finniston was appointed head of a new planning division at BSC. With him was John Grieve-Smith, who had joined BSC in June 1968 after some years as head of the Iron and Steel Board's economics division. Their objective for planning in the British steel industry may be inferred from the following: "The BSC does not intend, however, to make the mistake which has given the concept of planning such a bad name in recent years. Its 'plan' will not consist of a hard-and-fast, ex cathedra pronouncement imbued with a built-in determination to foresee the future. On the contrary, it will consist of a number of carefully weighed alternatives, flexible and malleable enough to accommodate unpredictable shifts in circumstances."[4]

As part of this objective, a computer model was designed for use at BSC's head office to prepare

---

[4]British Steel, *April 1968.*

short-term forecasts of steel demand (see Figure B). As the designers pointed out: "A final forecast will be the result of a subjective appraisal of several forecasts based on different projected assumptions."

Based on the first development plan for the nationalized industry, it was predicted that demand for BSC steel in five years would be 20 percent above 1968 capacity, or 30M to 34M metric tons per year. "It also became clear that a policy of concentrating investment on the more favourably located of the existing major works would yield a far higher return than investment in any greenfield site."[5]

1970–1971

In November 1969 Monty Finniston was appointed to chair a reorganization committee, which led to six product divisions by early 1970. Herbert Morley, a Yorkshireman with a reputation for toughness, was appointed managing director of one of these product divisions (general steels) in the same year. During this period there was a world shortage of steel, and the BSC works were plagued by serious unofficial strikes and labor disputes that exacerbated the shortage. Since nationalization, a Steel Committee, consisting of the unions represented in the industry under the Trades Union Congress (TUC), had been working with the BSC on industrial policy. These unions, most of which would be found in a single works, are listed in Figure C.[6]

It was expected that, as a result of the first development plan, BSC would invest £150 million to £175 million each year from 1970 through 1975 to upgrade and improve existing works and to construct new ones. Because many works were too far from major transportation terminals to be economical, in the spring of 1970 BSC announced tentative plans for a deep-water terminal at Hunterston on the coast of Scotland below Glasgow. Figure D illustrates the sites of the major works.

John Grieve-Smith in a 1971 article, "Planning for Profitability," explained the BSC strategy for investment:

> The corporation not only has to plan on a national scale, but like any other large commercial organization, it has to consider the development strategies first and foremost in the context of profitability.
>
> Much greater emphasis has had to be put on the economic and financial aspects of planning and on the need to look at the effects of development not merely in terms of the individual works, but the production and marketing system of the corporation as a whole.
>
> There are two types of planning decisions involved here. One is to shut down old plant. The other is to build new plant. In both cases the relevant costs are those which could be avoided if the plant were shut down or not built.
>
> The object will be to minimize overall production and transport costs.

A great many jobs were involved in these decisions. As stated in an article earlier that year: "There are areas of Britain where not only is BSC the major employer of labour but where the community depends for its very existence on iron and steel making."[7]

1972–1973

A third reorganization of BSC in early 1972 placed Lord Melchett as chairman of the corporate office and Finniston as chief executive of the operating organization (the six product divisions). Lionel Pugh, who had been director-in-charge of the Product Coordinating Division of BSC since 1968, was appointed a full-time member of the board of BSC for a five-year term.

---

[5]T. R. Craig, *"Steel in Scotland,"* British Steel, *May 1969.*
[6]British Steel, *Winter 1976–77.*

[7]*Kenneth Robinson, "The Role of Social Policy in British Steel,"* British Steel, *March 1971.*

FIGURE B   Model of U.K. Steel Consumption

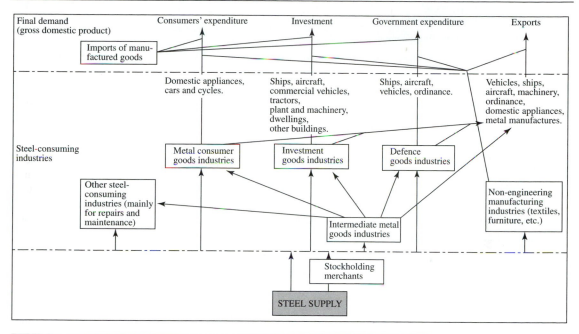

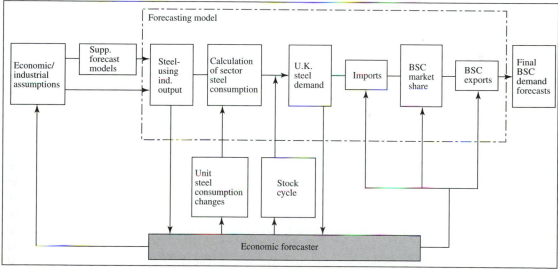

Source: "Demand Forecasting in the Short Term," *British Steel,* November 1969.

FIGURE C   Unions Represented in BSC

Iron and Steel Trades Confederation

National Union of Blast Furnacemen

Transport and General Workers' Union (including its Association of Clerical, Technical and Supervisory Staffs—ACTSS)

General and Municipal Workers' Union (including its Managerial, Administrative, Technical and Supervisory Association—MATSA)

National Craftsmen's Coordinating Committee made up of:

    Amalgamated Union of Engineering and Foundry Workers—Foundry Section

    Amalgamated Union of Engineering and Foundry Workers—Engineering Section

    Amalgamated Union of Engineering and Foundry Workers—TASS (Technical Administrative and Supervisory Section)

    Amalgamated Society of Boilermakers, Shipwrights, Blacksmiths and Structural Workers

    Electrical, Electronic, Telecommunications, and Plumbing Trades Union

    Electrical, Electronic, Telecommunications, and Plumbing Trades Union—Plumbing Section

    British Roll Turners' Trade Society

    Electrical Engineering Staff Association—EESA

    National Union of Sheet Metal Workers

    Coppersmiths, Heating and Domestic Engineers

    Association of Patternmakers and Allied Crafts

    Union of Construction, Allied Trades, and Technicians—Wood Section

    Union of Construction, Allied Trades, and Technicians—Building Section

---

U.K. consumption of steel had grown at about 2 percent per year over the past five years, and U.K. industry productivity in 1972 was the lowest of the five major steel producing countries, as shown in Figure E.

Many of the works were using outdated technology and were more heavily staffed than demand or technology warranted. Rather than attempt to update small works, a more promising approach appeared to be replacement of blast furnaces by direct reduction. Direct reduction would offer BSC flexibility on sources, as well as additional capacity. Direct reduction was fast becoming one of the technologies of choice for ironmaking in smaller, newly constructed plants worldwide.

In January 1973 it was announced that a direct reduction plant, probably at Hunterston (site of the deep-water terminal), would be built and that 4.5M metric tons of steel per year would be produced in Scotland. That same year the BSC's second development plan was published. The strategy outlined in this plan is summarized below:

1. The development strategy is based upon a future of bulk steel production using the basic oxygen process at large integrated steelworks that have access to a deep-water ore terminal.
2. Production will be concentrated at five such existing works—Port Talbot, Llanwern, Lackenby, Scunthorpe, and Ravenscraig.

FIGURE D   Location of Main Iron and Steel Works

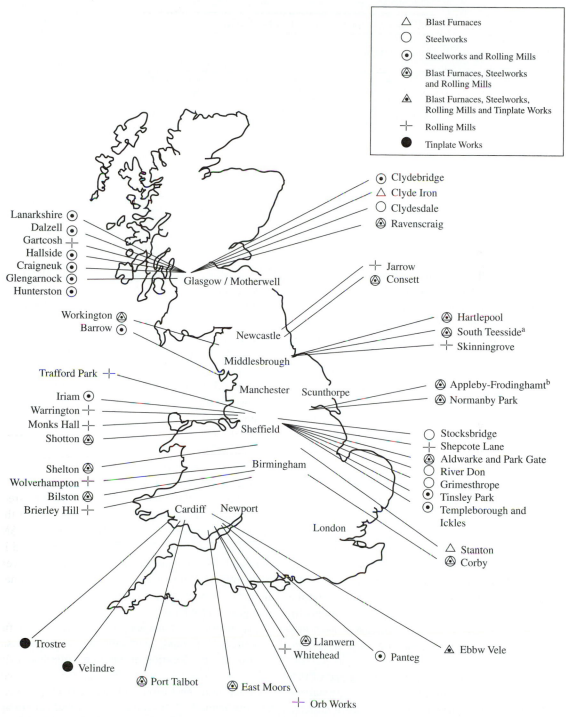

a. South Teesside includes Redcar, Lackenby, Cleveland, Cargo Fleet, and Ayrton.
b. Appleby-Frodingham includes Redbourn Works and the Anchor Project.

Source: British Steel Corporation files.

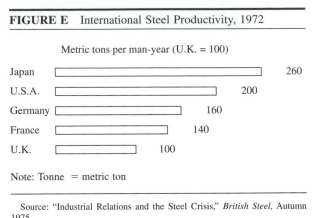

FIGURE E   International Steel Productivity, 1972

Metric tons per man-year (U.K. = 100)

Japan   260
U.S.A.   200
Germany   160
France   140
U.K.   100

Note: Tonne = metric ton

Source: "Industrial Relations and the Steel Crisis," *British Steel*, Autumn 1975.

3. The cost of the program will be £3,000 million over the next 10 years—the highest ever sustained level of investment in the industry.
4. Steelmaking at other centers will eventually be phased out. All open hearth furnaces will be closed by the end of the decade.
5. While the strategy should more than double labor productivity, it will bring about a reduction in manpower of about 50,000.
6. More than half the funds for the development strategy will be met, the corporation estimates, from its own resources. The remainder will be financed from public funds.
7. The government and the corporation are pursuing policies designed to tackle the problems created by plant closures.

The secretary of state for trade and industry at the time, the Right Honorable Peter Walker, M.P., acknowledged that "Of great concern to everybody is the loss of job opportunities in the steel industry over the next decade." (Manpower changes in the steel industry compared with the earlier nationalized coal and rail industries are shown in Figure F.)

John Grieve-Smith described the choice of the above strategy in terms similar to his explanation of the first development plan four years earlier:

1. Forecasting steel demand in the United Kingdom depends on the rate of growth of the economy as a whole . . . and the intensity with which steel is used.
2. A dozen or so carefully chosen strategies were formulated at a special two-day meeting of managing directors. These were designed (a) to include all the main schemes regarded worthy of consideration, and (b) to combine them into a number of strategies covering four different levels of capacity in the range of 28 to 36 million tons, which the BSC has agreed to examine.
3. The forecasts of profits and capital expenditures over the next 10 years together with the residual value of the plant in 1982 enabled the profitability of each strategy to be ranked according to its net present value in 1972 at various rates of discount.
4. In addition to the evaluation of the relative profitability of different strategies described here, the corporation examined in detail . . . the social and regional problems involved, . . . the effect on the balance of payments and the call on national resources, . . . [and] economic and social factors affecting the location of any new complex.

Concerning geographic location, Herbert Morley commented: "Looking at the national economy

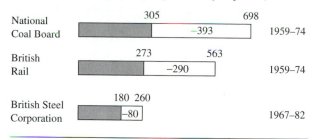

FIGURE F   Manpower Changes in Nationalized Industries

Totals in 000's of employees (comparable 15-year periods)

National Coal Board	305 → 698, −393	1959–74
British Rail	273 → 563, −290	1959–74
British Steel Corporation	180 260, −80	1967–82

Source: "Industrial Relations and the Steel Crisis," *British Steel*, Autumn 1975.

as a whole, I think there is too much emphasis on London and I would like to see more of the total business pyramid in the regions, including Wales, Scotland, and the north of England."

Lord Melchett, who had been ill when he took over as chairman of the BSC, died in late spring 1973. Monty Finniston—described in the BSC portrait article as "blunt," "sharp," "insomniac," "remarkable scientific career"—was appointed as Melchett's successor. At a salary of £27,750, Finniston was the highest paid person in the British government.

1974–1975

Some industrial and political leaders in Scotland gave steel a central regenerative role. Other commentators were less optimistic: "Too often in its hisotry, Scotland has been misled by a recurring dream of greatness." All agreed that "no domestic issue in Scotland has generated as much controversy in recent years as has the discussion of BSC's plans for steelmaking in Scotland."[8]

Steel could take on the same role in Scottish Nationalist party plans for devolution of that nation (partial self-government) as had discovery of North Sea oil. In early 1973 Scottish Nationalists had claimed that development of oil by a devolved Scotland would be far more profitable. By March of 1974, after the election of Harold Wilson, there were seven Scottish Nationalists in the House of Commons and talk by that party of "independence for Scotland by 1980." Indeed, Scottish Labour M.P.s were distributing pamphlets entitled "Scottish Labour and Devolution."[9]

A key project in BSC's development plan was the Hunterston complex—a deep-water terminal and direct reduction facility. By this time, "it [was] clearly no longer a question of whether Hunterston [would] be fully developed as a significant steelmaking center, but when?"[10]

In early January 1975, many of the managers believed that two direct reduction plants should be built; however, Jon Martin, a member of the planning division, pressed for a comparative analysis. Working on this analysis were Jon Martin, senior planner, and Peter Evans, manager of development planning. Their analysis would be reviewed by John Grieve-Smith, director of planning, who

[8]*Chris Bauer, "The Future of Steel in Scotland," British Steel, Autumn 1974.*

[9]The Economist, *March 9, 1974.*
[10]*Bauer, "Future of Steel in Scotland."*

would discuss the recommendations with Ron Atkin, director of project engineering (and BSC's chief negotiator with Korf), and Herbert Morley, then managing director of planning and capital development.

Morley would advise Monty Finniston, and the analysis and final recommendations would be submitted to the policy committee (chairman and two deputy chairmen, as well as seven full-time executive board members). The policy committee would make the decision on the Korf contract at its meeting on February 11, 1975. The board's role would be to decide whether or not to ratify the policy committee's action; however, the board would not meet until after the deadline had passed. (Exhibit 1 lists selected data on the U.K. economy, 1969–1974. Exhibit 2 lists selected data on the iron and steel industry over the same years. Exhibit 3 presents U.S. steel production for comparison.)

EXHIBIT 1   Selected Economic Statistics

	1951	*1961*	*1969*	*1974*
Population (000s)				
England and Wales	43,815	46,196	48,540	49,159
Scotland	5,102	5,184	4,209	5,217
Unemployment Rates				
Great Britain			2.3%	2.6%
Scotland			3.6%	4.0%
Number work stoppages				
(metals, engineering, shipbuilding, vehicles)			1,430	1,321
Total work stoppages			3,116	2,922
Number people involved in stoppages (metals, etc.)			750,000	733,000
Total people involved			1,656,000	1,622,000
Total days lost (metals, etc.)			3,739,000	5,837,000
Total days lost			6,925,000	14,845,000
Number strikes >50 days (all industries)			14	11
Number trade unions			565	507
Number members			10.5M	11.8M
BPO (£ millions)			+471	−3,374
GNP (£ millions at market prices)			47,071	84,307
Net national product (£ millions)			36,246	67,193
Index of retail prices (1962 = 100)			131.8	208.2
Index of salaries (1970 = 100)			—	177.5
% increase salaries (1973–1974)			—	17.8%

Source: *Annual Abstract of Statistics,* 1981 edition, General Statistical Office, London.

EXHIBIT 2 Selected Iron and Steel Industry Statistics (metric tons in 000s)

	1969	1970	1971	1972	1973	1974
Total Supply (ingot equivalent)	29,981	30,591	27,609	28,256	30,924	28,629
Home sources						
Total	27,176	27,755	24,926	24,704	27,065	23,314
Crude steel production	26,822	28,291	24,153	25,293	26,594	22,323
Reusable material[a]	224	242	181	160	149	100
Producers' stock changes[b]	+130	−778	+592	−749	+322	+891
Imported[c]						
Total	2,805	2,836	2,683	3,552	3,859	5,215
Ingots	435	197	18	3	19	18
Semifinished	703	993	465	372	131	150
Finished	1,667	1,646	2,200	3,177	3,709	5,047
Distribution of Supply (ingot equivalent)						
Exports[c]	5,013	5,240	6,382	6,037	5,604	4,323
Supply for home use	24,968	25,351	21,227	22,219	25,320	24,306
Estimated home consumption[d]	24,240	24,497	22,379	22,212	24,142	23,193
Net Deliveries (actual tonnage)[e]	22,017	22,389	20,628	21,182	23,330	21,536
Exports[c]	3,700	3,839	4,705	4,439	4,030	3,116
Supply for home use	18,317	18,550	15,923	16,743	19,300	18,420
Stocks (end of period, actual tonnage)						
Producers						
Ingots and semifinished steel	1,468	1,911	1,427	1,888	1,687	1,093
Finished steel[f]	1,352	1,408	1,510	1,672	1,600	1,392
Consumers[g]	3,760	4,149	3,470	3,438	4,440	4,960
Merchants[g]	641	876	715	727	582	872
Steel Furnaces (number in existence at end of period)[h]						
Total	657	622	610	562	546	535
Open hearth	181	167	137	124	107	97
Oxygen converters	25	24	27	28	30	25
Electric	434	414	426	392	391	396
Stock and tropenas	17	17	20	18	18	17
Production of Crude Steel (000s tonnes)						
Total by process	26,822	28,291	24,153	25,293	26,594	22,323
Open hearth	14,172	13,370	10,175	9,357	8,453	6,189
Oxygen converters	7,661	9,368	9,582	10,990	12,814	10,846
Electric	4,937	5,514	4,361	4,910	5,293	5,258
Stock and tropenas	52	39	35	36	34	31
Total by cast method						
Cast to ingot	25,836	27,211	23,253	24,325	25,275	20,646
Continuously cast[i]	470	485	386	522	811	1,126
Steel for castings	515	596	514	446	507	551

(*continued*)

EXHIBIT 2 (*concluded*)

	1969	1970	1971	1972	1973	1974
Total by quality						
Nonalloy steel	24,702	26,130	22,455	23,422	24,371	20,233
Alloy steel[j]	2,120	2,161	1,698	1,871	2,223	2,090

a. Mainly old rails for rerolling.
b. Steel industry stocks of ingots, semifinished, and finished steel.
c. Based on statistics as shown in "Overseas Trade Statistics of the U.K."
d. After allowing for changes in consumers' and merchants' stocks.
e. Finished steel, including that produced in the U.K. from imported ingots and semifinished steel, and secondhand materials; excluding deliveries of all material for conversion within the industry.
f. Excluding stocks of tubes, pipes, forgings, and steel castings.
g. Finished steel produced in the U.K. and imported. Wire is excluded and replaced by the material for its manufacture.
h. Includes steel furnaces at steel foundries.
i. Product weight of continuously cast semimanufacturers.
j. Any steel containing, by weight, at least 0.5% silicon, or 1.6% manganese, or 0.3% of chromium or nickel, or 0.1% tungsten or vanadium, or 0.08% molybdenum.

Source: U.K. Iron and Steel Statistics Bureau.

EXHIBIT 3   U.S. Raw Steel Production

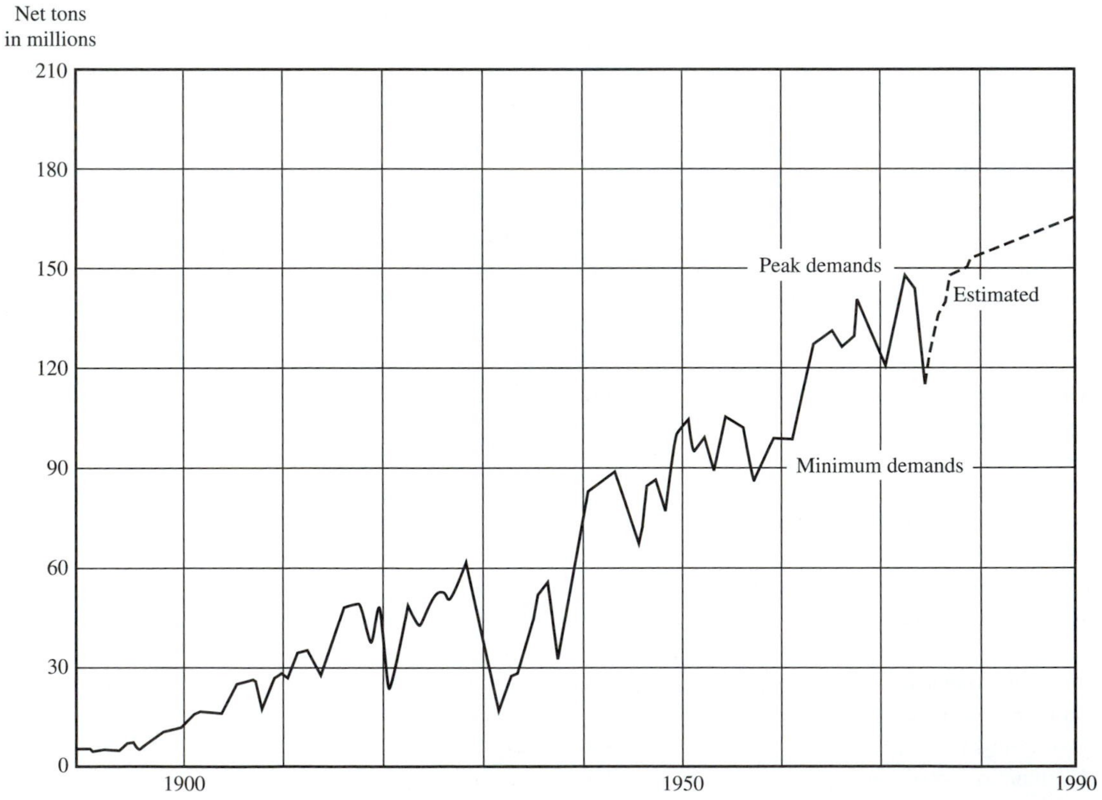

Source: Richard L. Deily, *Steel Plants U.S.A.: 1960–1980,* Institute for Iron and Steel Studies, New Jersey.

Case 3–2

NOTE ON PROCESS OBSERVATION

"A camel is a horse put together by a committee" is a saying frequently applied to group decision making. What is it that makes so many groups inefficient, slow, and frustrating, instead of effectively combining the insights and expertise of its members? To some extent the answer may be found in the formal group design. Perhaps the people chosen were not the ones who should have been included in such a group, or perhaps the group's goal was simply unattainable. More often, however, the difficulties encountered have less to do with content of task issues than with the *group process,* or how the group is going about achieving its formal task.

Each group member is a unique individual, bringing certain expectations, assumptions, and feelings to the group, not only about his or her own role but also about the roles of other members in the group. As a result of these expectations certain interrelationships develop. These patterns may become either beneficial or detrimental to the group's purpose. Spotting detrimental patterns is the first key to understanding and improving the functioning of any group, but often these patterns are hard to identify because you cannot read each person's mind. For instance, how do you know that everyone understands what the agenda is, or that person X understands it but is likely to deviate from it if possible, or whether person X has the leverage to change the agenda if he or she wants to? While you cannot see inside others' minds, you can develop a greater awareness of what is and what is not likely to happen in a group, and of what the group is or is not capable of doing at a given meeting by being attentive to what is happening among group members.

Being able to observe and understand a group's process is important for two reasons. First, it enables you to understand what is taking place covertly as well as overtly in the group's behavior. Second, it can provide you with insights into what you and others can do to make the group's interactions more productive.

Listed below are seven aspects of group behavior that can furnish valuable clues on how effectively a group functions. It is unlikely that all of these will be relevant to your concerns at a given point in time, or that you can attend to them all simultaneously. The more adept you are at observing and assessing them, however, the more likely it is that you will spot potential difficulties early and act on them to improve the group's effectiveness.

Participation

Participation—who participates, how often, when, and to what effect—is the easiest aspect of group process to observe. Typically, people who are higher in status, more knowledgeable, or simply more talkative by nature tend to participate more actively. Those who are newer, lower in status, uninformed, or who are not inclined to express their feelings and ideas verbally, generally speak less frequently. Even in groups composed of people of equal status and competence, some people will speak more than others; this variation is to be expected and is not necessarily a sign of an ineffective group. When large disparities exist among the contributions of individual members, however, it is

This case was prepared by Anne Harlan under the direction of John J. Garbarro.

usually a clue that the process is not effective—particularly when individuals or coalitions dominate the group's discussion.

There are many reasons why unequal participation can reduce a group's effectiveness. Low participators often have good ideas to offer but are reluctant to do so, or they cannot contribute their ideas because they are squeezed out by high participators who dominate the meeting. This imbalance can be a potential problem when we consider that those ideas receiving the most attention inevitably become the ones that are most seriously considered when it is time to make a decision. Considerable research shows that the most frequently stated ideas tend to be adopted by the group, regardless of their quality. Maier calls this the *valence effect*[1] and it is one of the reasons why groups often make poor decisions. Thus, large imbalances in participation can result in potentially good ideas being underrepresented in the discussion, or perhaps not even expressed.

Another negative consequence of uneven participation, understood through common sense as well as research, is that low participators are likely to tune out, lose commitment to the task, or become frustrated and angry—especially if they have tried to get into the discussion but have been ignored or cut off by high participators. These negative attitudes result not only in poorer quality decisions but also in less commitment to implementing the group's decision.

Several factors contribute to uneven participation. One is that people who have the most at stake in a given issue (and may therefore be the least objective) are more motivated to participate than others who may have better ideas to offer. Another is that different people have different internal standards on which they judge whether or not an idea they have is worth offering to the group. Thus, people with higher internal standards may be less likely to contribute than those with lower internal standards, with negative consequences for the quality of the group's discussion.

A marked change in a person's participation during a meeting is also a clue that something important may be going on. If a person suddenly becomes silent or withdraws during part of a meeting, it could suggest a number of possibilities (depending on the person's nonverbal behavior). For example, it might simply mean that the person has temporarily withdrawn to mull over the comments of a prior speaker. It may also be that the person has tuned out, or it may be a sign of hostility or frustration. Whatever the case, it could be a sign that something is not right.

Some questions to consider in observing participation include the following:

1. Who are the high participators? Why? To what effect?
2. Who are the low participators? Why? To what effect?
3. Are there any shift in participators, such as an active participator suddenly becoming silent? Do you see any reason for this in the group's interaction, such as a criticism from a higher-status person or a shift in topic? Is it a sign of withdrawal?
4. How are silent people treated? Is their silence taken by others to mean consent? Disagreement? Disinterest? Why do you think they are silent?
5. Who talks to whom? Who responds to whom? Do participation patterns reflect coalitions that are impeding or controlling the discussion? Are the interaction patterns consistently excluding certain people who need to be supported or brought into the discussion?
6. Who keeps the discussion going? How is this accomplished? Why does the group leader want the discussion to continue in such a vein?

Interventions.   There are a number of simple and unobtrusive process interventions that you can make, either as a group leader or group member, to

---

[1]*Norman R. F. Maier, "Assets and Liabilities in Group Problem Solving: The Need for an Integrative Function,"* Psychological Review *74, no. 4 (July 1967), pp. 239–248.*

bring about a better balance in participation. These interventions are particularly important if you think that potentially valuable minority views are not getting their share of time, that certain people have not had a chance to develop their ideas fully, or that some group members seem out of the discussion. One intervention is to try to *clarify* a point that someone had made earlier that seemed to fall through the cracks—going back to that person's point by saying something like "Tom, let me see if I understood what you said a moment ago." A related technique is simply to *reinforce* a prior point by asking the person to elaborate on it—"Sue, I was interested in what you were saying earlier; can you elaborate on it?" Similarly, a very direct technique for bringing out silent people is to simply *query* them—"Mary, you haven't said a word during this discussion; what are your ideas on it?" or to make a comment as direct as "We've heard a lot from the marketing people, but very little from production scheduling. What do you guys think about the problem?"

Influence

Influence and participation are not the same thing. Some people may speak very little, yet capture the attention of the whole group when they do speak. Others may talk frequently but go unheard. Influence, like participation, is often a function of status, experience, competence, and to some degree personality. It is normal for some people to have more influence on a group's process than others, and this fact is not necessarily a sign that a group is ineffective. However, when one individual or subgroup has so much influence on a discussion that others' ideas are rejected out of hand, it is usually a clue that the group's effectiveness will suffer and that the discussion will fail to probe alternatives. This imbalance is particularly dangerous when minority views are systematically squelched without adequate exploration.

An asymmetry in influence can have a number of negative consequences on a group's effectiveness. As we have already noted, it can result in the suppression of potentially valuable minority views, it can contribute to imbalanced participation, and it will inevitably result in hostility and lack of commitment by group members who feel that they have been left out. As with participation, considerable research on group behavior and alienation shows that the more influence people feel they have had on a group's discussion, the more committed they are likely to be to its decisions, regardless of whether their own point of view has been adopted by the group.

One way of checking relative influence is to watch the reactions of the other group members. Someone who has influence is not only likely to have others listening attentively but is also less likely to be interrupted or challenged by the others. He or she may also be physically seated at or near the head of the table or near the center of a subgroup.

Struggles for influence and leadership often characterize the early stages of a group's life, especially in temporary groups such as task forces, project teams, or committees. To some extent these struggles occur in most groups, although usually in a mild, covert fashion. Vying for leadership can become a problem, however, when it disrupts the group's ability to deal with the task at hand. The disruption occurs when being dominant is an important need for those who are vying for leadership. Under these circumstances, the competition gets played out in a sub-rosa fashion with one person disagreeing with the other because of his or her need to establish dominance, regardless of the relative merits of the other's arguments. The hidden agenda then becomes scoring points rather than working on the problem. Often two people engaged in such a power struggle are not even aware of their hidden motives and genuinely think that they are arguing about the problem at hand.

In assessing influence patterns within a group, you may find the following questions useful:

1. Which members are listened to when they speak? What ideas are they expressing?

2. Which members are ignored when they speak? Why? What are their ideas? Is the group losing valuable inputs simply because some are not being heard?
3. Are there any shifts in influence? Who shifts? Why?
4. Is there any rivalry within the group? Are there struggles among individuals or subgroups for leadership?
5. Who interrupts whom? Does this reflect relative power within the group?
6. Are minority views consistently ignored regardless of possible merit?

Interventions.   If you observe that the opinions of an individual or subgroup of people appear to be unduly influencing a group's progress, there are several brief interventions that can be made to open up the discussion. One strategy is simply to *support or reinforce* the views of minority members—"I think there is some merit to what Jane was saying earlier and I'd like to elaborate on it," or "I think that we're not giving enough thought to Jane and Sam's position and I think we should explore it further before dropping it." Another intervention is to actually *point out* that the opinions of certain people are dominating the discussion—"Mary, you've made your point quite forcefully and clearly, but I'd also like to hear the other side of the question before we go further." Similarly, another technique is to ask the group to *open up* the discussion—"So far we've spent a lot of time talking about Jane and Bill's proposal, but I'd like to hear some differing opinions," or "The managers seem to agree strongly on what needs to be done, but I'd like to hear more about what the customer representatives think are the problems."

Group Climate

Members bring with them many assumptions of how groups ought to function generally and how their particular group should function. Frequently, these expectations of assumptions will be quite different from one member to another. One person may feel that the way for a group to work effectively is to be strictly business—no socializing and with tight leader control over the group. Others may feel that the only way a group can work creatively is to give each person equal time for suggestions, get together informally, and use relatively loose leadership. After group members have tested each others' assumptions early on in the group, a climate or atmosphere becomes established that may or may not facilitate effective group functioning. Different group climates are effective in different situations; what is good for one situation is not necessarily good for another.

For example, if the problem to be solved is one that demands a creative, new solution and the collaboration of a number of different experts (such as on a task force problem), then a climate of openness in which everyone has an equal opportunity to participate will be most effective. In other situations, however, a more competitive or structured group climate might encourage a higher quality solution, especially if expertise is not distributed equally among all group members. To gauge a group's climate you should observe the following:

1. Do people prefer to keep the discussion on a friendly, congenial basis? Do people prefer conflict and disagreement?
2. Do people seem involved and interested? Is the atmosphere one of work? Play? Competition? Avoidance?
3. Is there any attempt to suppress conflict or unpleasant feelings by avoiding tough issues?

For most task groups an unstructured, laissez-faire, or conflict-free climate is not effective: Important issues and conflicts are not explored sufficiently, and the quality of the group's work is sacrificed for the maintenance of friendly and smooth relations. Conversely, a highly structured climate can impede effective problem solving because members do not allow each other enough freedom to explore alternatives or consider creative solutions. A highly competitive climate can also be dysfunctional; competition can get in the way of thoughtful deliberation and exchange, resulting in failure to build on other people's ideas.

Interventions. Intervening to alter a group's climate is more difficult than the previous interventions described. It can be done, however, by reinforcing and supporting desirable behavior, as well as by raising the issue directly. Where a group is smoothing over and avoiding important problems, for example, a useful intervention would be, "We seem to have a lot of agreement, but I wonder if we have really tackled some of the tougher underlying issues." When a group seems to be tied up by its own structure, often a comment as simple as the following will suffice: "I think that maybe we're looking at the problem too narrowly, and it might be useful to discuss whether we should also consider *X*, which isn't on the agenda but seems to have relevance to what we're talking about."

Membership

A major concern for group members is their degree of acceptance or inclusion in the group. Different patterns of interaction may develop in the group, providing clues to the degree and kind of membership:

1. Is there any subgrouping? Sometimes two or three members may consistently agree and support each other or consistently disagree and oppose one another.
2. Do some people seem to be outside the group? Do other members seem to be insiders? How are outsiders treated?
3. Do some members move physically in and out of the group—for example, lean forward or backward in their chairs, or move their chairs in and out? Under what conditions do they come in or move out?

The problem of in-groups and out-groups is closely related to the earlier discussion of influence within the group. The interventions described earlier are also useful for bringing in marginal members—for example, supporting, querying, and opening up the discussion.

Feelings

During any group discussion, feelings are frequently generated by interactions among members. These feelings, however, are seldom talked about. Observers may have to make guesses based on tone of voice, facial expressions, gestures, and other nonverbal cues.

1. What signs of feelings (anger, irritation, frustration, warmth, affection, excitement, boredom, defensiveness, competitiveness, etc.) do you observe in group members?
2. Are group members overly nice or polite to each other? Are only positive feelings expressed? Do members agree with each other too readily? What happens when members disagree?
3. Do you see norms operating about participation or the kinds of questions that are allowed (e.g., "If I talk, you must talk")? Do members feel free to probe each other about their feelings? Do questions tend to be restricted to intellectual topics or events outside of the group?

Most groups in business develop norms that only allow for the expression of positive feelings or feelings of disagreement, but not for anger. The problem with suppressing strong negative feelings is that they usually resurface later. For example, a person who is angry about what someone said earlier in the meeting gets back at that person later in the discussion by disagreeing or by criticizing his or her idea regardless of the idea's merit. The person's hidden motive becomes getting even and he or she will do so by resisting ideas, being stubborn, or derailing the discussion. This retaliation is usually disguised in terms of substantive issues and often has an element of irrationality to it. It is often more effective to bring out the person's anger in the first place and deal with it then.

Task Functions

In order for any group to function adequately and make maximum progress on the task at hand, certain task functions must be carried out. First of all, there must be *initiation*—the problem or goals must be stated, time limits laid out, and some agenda agreed upon. This function most frequently falls to the leader, but may be taken on by other group members. Next, there must be both *opinion* and *information seeking* and *giving* on various issues related to the task. One of the major problems affecting group decisions and commitments is that groups tend to spend insufficient time on these phases. *Clarifying* and *elaborating* are vital not only for effective communication but also for creative solutions. *Summarizing* includes a review of ideas to be followed by *consensus testing*—making sure all the ideas are on the table and that the group is ready to enter into an evaluation of the various ideas produced. The most effective groups follow this order rather than the more common procedure of evaluating each idea or alternative as it is discussed. Different group members may take on these task functions, but each must be covered.

1. Are suggestions made as to the best way to proceed or tackle the problem?
2. Is there a summary of what has been covered? How effectively is this done? Who does it?
3. Is there any giving or asking for information, opinions, feelings, feedback, or searching for alternatives?
4. Is the group kept on target? Are topic jumping and going off on tangents prevented or discouraged?
5. Are all the ideas out before evaluation begins? What happens if someone begins to evaluate an idea as soon as it is produced?

Maintenance Functions

Groups cannot function effectively if cohesion is low or if relationships among group members become strained. In the life of any group, there will be periods of conflict, dissenting views, and misunderstandings. It is the purpose of maintenance functions to rebuild damaged relations and bring harmony back to the group. Without these processes occurring, group members can become alienated, resulting in the group's losing valuable resources.

Two maintenance activities that can serve to prevent these kinds of problems are *gate keeping,* which insures that members wanting to make a contribution are given the opportunity to do so; and *encouraging,* which helps create a climate of acceptance.

Compromising and *harmonizing* are two other activities that have limited usefulness in the actual task accomplishment, but they are sometimes useful in repairing strained relations.

When the level of conflict in a group is so high that effective communication is impaired, it is often useful for the group to suspend the task discussion and examine its own processes in order to define and attempt to solve the conflicts. The following questions will focus attention on a group's maintenance functions:

1. Are group members encouraged to enter into the discussion?
2. How well do members get their ideas across? Are some members preoccupied and not listening? Are there any attempts by group members to help others clarify their ideas?
3. How are ideas rejected? How do members react when their ideas are rejected?
4. Are conflicts among group members ignored or dealt with in some way?

Process Observation and Feedback

This note has covered seven important aspects of group process that can influence a group's effectiveness. The interventions suggested are relatively simple and can be made naturally and unobtrusively during the normal progress of a meeting. The more people in a group skilled at making process observations, the greater the likelihood that the group will not bog down, waste valuable time, or make poor decisions. For this reason an increasing number of U.S. and foreign firms have developed norms that encourage open discussions of group process. In many companies, meetings are ended with a brief feedback session on the group's process, during which the meeting's effectiveness is critiqued by the group members.

It is not necessary, however, to be in such a firm or to use terms such as *process feedback* to contribute to a group's effectiveness. Most of the ideas presented in this note are based on common sense; practicing them does not require using the terms described here. The underlying ideas described here are more important than the specific labels, such as task and maintenance functions, applied to them.

Case 3–3

STRATEGIC DECISION PROCESSES IN HIGH VELOCITY ENVIRONMENTS: FOUR CASES IN THE MICROCOMPUTER INDUSTRY

**L. J. Bourgeois, III, and
Kathleen M. Eisenhardt**

*Darden School, University of Virginia; Department of
Industrial Engineering and Engineering Management,
Stanford University*

How do executives make strategic decisions in industries where the rate of technological and competitive change is so extreme that market information is often unavailable or obsolete, where strategic windows are opening and shutting quickly, and where the cost of error is involuntary exit? How do top management teams divide the decision-making responsibility? And how is risk of strategic error mitigated? What we report here is a set of hypotheses induced from a field investigation of four microcomputer firms, where we studied how each of the top management teams went about making major decisions. Our goal was to extend prior work on strategic decision making to what we term high velocity environments. Our results consist of a set of paradoxes which the successful firms resolve and the unsuccessful firms do not. We found an imperative to make major decisions carefully, but to decide quickly; to have a powerful, decisive CEO and a simultaneously powerful top management team; to seek risk and innovation, but to execute a safe, incremental implementation. Despite the apparent paradox, effective firms do all of these simultaneously. These paradoxes are presented in the form of propositions and testable hypotheses.

Many approaches to developing strategy rely on processing industry information as part of the strategy development process (e.g., Hofer and Schendel 1978; Porter 1980), and numerous studies on strategic processes have been conducted in settings where market data were plentiful enough to permit such analyses. For example, Fredrickson (1984) studied paints and forestry; Miles and Snow (1978), book publishing and hospitals; Jemison (1981), food processing and banks.

However, there are other industries where the rate of change is so extreme that information is often of questionable accuracy and is quickly obsolete. The question addressed by this study is: How do executives make strategic decisions in conditions at this extreme, conditions which we term high velocity environments? By high velocity environments we mean those in which there is rapid and discontinuous change in demand, competitors, technology and/or regulation, such that information is often inaccurate, unavailable, or obsolete.[1]

The microcomputer industry is one such industry. At the time we started our study (1984), it had an unusually high rate of change. The industry did not exist seven years previously (Apple was founded in 1977) and the dominant player (IBM) had been in

---

[1] *In high velocity environments there is continuous "dynamism" (Dess and Beard 1984), or "volatility" (Bourgeois 1985), but these are overlaid by sharp and discontinuous change (Meyer 1982; Sutton et al. 1986). Using this definition, microcomputers, airlines, and banking are high velocity industries. In contrast, although they score high on dynamism and volatility indexes (Dess and Beard 1984; Bourgeois 1985), cyclical industries such as forest products and machine tools are not.*

---

the market for only three years. Technological substitution was a frequent occurrence. Between 1980 and 1985, the UNIX and DOS operating systems supplanted CP/M; 16 and 32 bit microprocessors replaced the standard 8 bit; and the 64K RAM, the Winchester disk drive, and numerous computer architectures such as RISC emerged (Bell 1984, 1986).

Growth rates were explosive. The home computer segment grew by 805 percent in 1982 while the U.S. educational segment grew by 325 percent. Projections made in 1984 were for a "slowing" of demand to a compound annual growth rate of 29 percent (Creative Strategies International 1983). Firms continuously entered and exited the industry, and their relative competitive positions fluctuated constantly. In order of decreasing size, the leading firms in 1983 were Texas Instruments, Commodore, Sinclair/Times, Atari, Apple, and IBM. By 1984, only IBM and Apple were still major players, Sinclair no longer existed, and TI had exited the business. With these discontinuities in technology and competition and these extremes of growth, the information available for strategy was often of dubious quality (Future Computing, Inc., personal communication, 1985).

Strategic decision making is problematic in this kind of environment not only because change is so dramatic, but also because it is difficult to predict the significance of a change as it is occurring (Sutton, Eisenhardt, and Jucker 1986). As a result, it is particularly easy to make poor strategic judgments. A traditional way to avoid strategic errors is to simply wait to see how events unfold, or to imitate others (Bourgeois and Eisenhardt 1987). However, in this environment, the "wait and see" and "me too" decision strategies may also result in failure, as competitive positions change and windows of opportunity close. The dilemma of strategic decision making in this environment is that it is easy to make a mistake by acting too soon, but equally ineffective to delay decision making or to copy others. So, how do decision makers cope?

Based on our field investigation of four microcomputer firms, we induced several hypotheses. We discovered a series of paradoxes that successful firms resolve and unsuccessful firms do not: We found an imperative (1) to make strategic decisions carefully, but quickly; (2) to have a powerful, decisive chief executive officer (CEO) and a simultaneously powerful top management team; and (3) to seek risk while executing a safe, incremental implementation. The empirical derivation of these paradoxes is the subject of this article.

Background

There are two predominant views on how executive teams should make key decisions (Mintzberg 1973; Bourgeois 1980; Fredrickson and Mitchell 1984). The "rational-comprehensive" approach assumes that top management can agree on goal priorities, search thoroughly for alternatives, and then integrate the optimal choice into existing strategy (Fredrickson and Mitchell 1984). The alternative approach is based on "political incrementalism," in which there is no necessary *a priori* goal consensus (Lindblom 1959; Quinn 1978), search is problemistic and constrained (Cyert and March 1963), and choice is either satisficing (Simon 1957) or delayed (Quinn 1980). Under this approach, strategy is made piecemeal, adaptively, and in small increments, rather than comprehensively and in large, purposeful chunks.

The contrasts between these two approaches suggest several perspectives that might be taken when investigating strategic decision processes in high velocity environments. For example, the Rational Actor model (Allison 1971) suggests that strategic success depends on careful analysis and planning before action is taken. This suggests a picture of a contemplative, deliberative group of managers. In his book on "groupthink," Janis (1982) argues that extensive consideration of goals and a wide range of alternatives is a prerequisite to sound decision making. George (1980) describes superior decision making among U.S. presidents and their advisors in terms of the rational model. As all three studies focus on crisis and time-constrained decision making, one might conclude that "rational" processes are appropriate for high velocity environments.

However, many authors criticize this model as unrealistic, particularly in rapidly changing environments with their lack of information or time to process it. Both cognitive and resource limits force us to abandon comprehensive, rational analysis (Simon 1957; Cyert and March 1963). At best, viability of the rational model is seen as contingent upon a stable environment and bureaucratic organization (Mintzberg 1973), a view supported empirically by Fredrickson and Mitchell (1984). Further, Fredrickson's subsequent research suggested that incremental processes should be used in unstable environments (Fredrickson 1984). If we generalize from this literature, we might expect incrementalism to be more effective in high velocity industries.

Our dilemma is that the literature cited could suggest either approach—rational or incremental—as appropriate for high velocity environments.

Another set of questions revolves around the role of the CEO. Should the CEO act as "commander" by dictating strategy; as a consensus-builder who involves the entire team in making strategic decisions; or as a premise-setter who stands back after articulating general guidelines, letting the top management team make strategy (Bourgeois and Brodwin 1984; Mintzberg and McHugh 1985; Mintzberg 1987)? It is often suggested in both the strategic management and group dynamics literatures that decisions should be a product of management team involvement and consensus (Bourgeois 1980; Leavitt 1951; Bavelas 1951), and that firms with consensus CEOs will be more successful, particularly under conditions of high uncertainty. In its treatment of how organizations should be structured, the environmental contingencies literature also supports the idea that firms should be less centralized and mechanistic under conditions of high uncertainty and change (Burns and Stalker 1961; Lawrence and Lorsch 1967). However, building consensus takes time, and conditions of high velocity suggest a continual crisis orientation, a condition conducive to centralized, CEO dominated decision making (Mintzberg 1979).

The dilemma, again, is that while the literature on decision making and organization design is suggestive of general research questions, it is a problematic source of hypotheses because it supports a variety of conflicting predictions. Moreover, few field studies of actual corporate strategic decision making have been conducted in high velocity environments. This led us to pursue the inductive, case study approach described next.

Research Method

Research Design

We chose to study the dynamics of strategic decisions in their natural setting by investigating four microcomputer firms. Our design was what Yin (1984) has termed "embedded multiple case" design. *Embedded* design denotes several units of analysis. We conducted our investigation at three levels: (1) the firm (its strategy and performance); (2) the top management team (personalities within and interactions among the group); and (3) the strategic decision (tracing a recent decision). While an embedded design is complex, it provides greater richness and multiple perspectives in explaining behavior.

Multiple case design allows a "replication" logic (Yin 1984)—that is, the logic of treating a series of cases as a series of experiments in which each case study serves to confirm or disconfirm the inferences drawn from previous ones. While a multiple case design is more demanding than a single case, it permits induction of more reliable models.[2]

Data Gathering

In each firm, we traced the making of a recent strategic decision through documents, extensive interviews with *every* top management executive, and,

_____

[2]*A major challenge in case study research is to ensure that data collection and analysis meet tests of reliability, construct validity, and external and internal validity (Yin 1984). We promoted reliability by (1) using a case study protocol in which all firms and all informants were subjected to the same sequence of entry and exit procedures and interview questions (see "Data Gathering" section), and (2) by creating similarly organized case databases for each firm we visited. Construct validity was enhanced by using the multiple sources of evidence described, and by establishing a chain of evidence as we concluded each interview. External validity was dealt with by the multiple case research design itself, whereby all cases were firms from the same industry and relatively similar in size and age. Finally, we addressed internal validity by the "pattern matching" data analysis method described (Yin 1984).*

occasionally, observation of decision-making meetings. After asking CEOs to identify two or three recent or ongoing major decisions, we would select one with the following characteristics: It should (1) involve strategic repositioning or redirection of the firm; (2) have high stakes, that is, outcomes that the executives believe will significantly affect the firm's performance; (3) involve as many of the functions of the firm as possible; and (4) the decision should be considered representative of "major" decisions taken by the firm. The decisions we studied included entering a new product market, altering a firm's established identity, betting the firm on a totally new product, and going public. (These decisions will be described fully in the next section.)

By tracing the decision from the perspective of *every* participant, using a standard set of interview questions, we were able to construct what we call "stories" about each of the decisions. The questions were oriented towards developing a timeline for the decision (e.g., Neustadt and May 1987). The questions concentrated on facts and events, rather than on respondents' interpretations, using standard courtroom interrogation (e.g., "What did you do? When? Who said what to whom?"), and were pretested with executives who teach part-time at Stanford. (The full interview protocol is available from the authors.)

Each interview was conducted in tandem (two investigators), with one investigator primarily responsible for the interview and the other responsible for taking notes and filling in gaps in the questioning. Immediately after the interview, the investigators recorded and cross-checked facts, as well as their impressions. We followed several rules for within-case analysis (Yin 1984). The "24-hour rule" required that detailed interview notes and impressions were completed within one day of the interview. A second rule was to include all data. The third rule was to add our own impressions, but to separate them from the respondent's story. In addition, we asked ourselves open-ended questions ("What did we learn?" "How does this compare to prior interviews?") to generate richer impressions. Finally, when available, archival data documenting the decision were also collected.

Our combination of methods and tandem interviewing addresses some of the criticisms of relying upon executives' recollections (Huber and Power 1985). Although we studied only one decision per firm, previous researchers have indicated that a firm tends to make consequential, strategic decisions in an observably consistent manner (Fredrickson and Mitchell 1984; Miles and Snow 1978). That is, although individual strategic decisions might differ in substance, executive teams will follow a consistent pattern across decisions, patterns that persist even as individual positions in the team experience turnover (Weick 1979).

In addition to tracing a strategic decision in each company, we obtained extensive qualitative and quantitative data from each executive, including descriptions of their colleagues and their interactions, as well as descriptions of decision-making sessions in terms of climate, conflicts, consensus, and so forth.[3] This provided us a sense of the top management team culture.

Data Analysis and Presentation

Unlike positivist research, there is no accepted general model for communicating interpretive

---

[3]*We also obtained questionnaire data from each executive. We measured goals, interaction patterns, political behavior, and power. The power question consisted of a matrix in which key decision areas were listed down one side of the sheet and the executive titles were listed across the top. After indicating how important (0–10) each decision area was to the long-run health of their firm, executives were asked to assign scores to each manager on each decision in terms of how much influence that manager had on each decision. This item was introduced during the interview by stating that although most managers have titles that indicate their functional responsibility, many executive teams operate with managers influencing decisions in areas that are not strictly under their titular control.*

Power scores for each executive were computed by taking the mean of scores assigned to the executive by every other respondent. Two steps were taken: First, individual influence scores were multiplied by decision importance rating. Second, a mean power score for each person on each decision was computed. Decisions were then grouped according to functional area (e.g., marketing strategies and new product introductions were grouped under "marketing"), and a mean computed. (These scores appear later in Tables 2 through 5.)

research. Similarly, few guidelines exist for conducting the inductive process central to interpretive research (Hudson and Ozanne 1986). We used the following approach: Having collected both qualitative and quantitative data from each firm, each author independently analyzed one or the other data type. In effect, we treated them as separate studies. For each firm, one author calculated group-level scores of conflict, consensus, power, coalition formation, and so forth. He or she then analyzed these data for patterns. The other author combined the qualitative responses into narratives. Profiles for each executive were developed from the descriptions given by each member of the top management team, with traits mentioned by more than one executive included in the narrative. For example, Don (CEO of Alpha Computers) was described as "extremely bright" by all of his colleagues, and "very impatient" and "caring" by three of four. These traits were included in Don's profile, whereas other traits that were mentioned by only one person (e.g., "large ego") were dropped. This approach was also used to profile the decision climate and style.

Decision "stories" were developed by combining the accounts of each executive into a timeline beginning with decision initiation. We included all events mentioned. In each story, there was agreement around the critical issues of when the decision began, when it was made, and how it was made. Again, using Alpha as an example, the executives all agreed that the impetus for the decision was a board meeting with the corporate officers, that the CEO made the decision alone, and that he did so just before the annual May planning conference. Also, all Alpha executives (including the President) agreed that the decision was unpopular. Although they were few, conflicts in the stories were preserved. These usually concerned one person's assumptions about another person's motives or opinions, and not observable actions and events. For example, as reported in the Alpha story, the Vice President of Sales perceived that the Vice President of R&D supported the decision when, in fact, he did not.

Once each of us developed preliminary hypotheses from our respective data sets, we exchanged analyses. We then posted our stories, profiles, and tabulations on the walls around a small meeting room, and searched for patterns in the data.

The search for patterns was assisted by (1) taking pairs of firms and listing similarities and differences between each pair, and (2) by categorizing the firms on a variety of dimensions: public versus privately held; founder-run versus professional management; size; first versus second product generation; and so forth. Although it was not our intention to be normative, one variable that sorted *both* the quantitative *and* qualitative data into consistent patterns was a crude measure of performance.

We assessed performance by (1) market acceptance of each company's major product (order backlog), (2) CEO's numerical self-report of company "effectiveness" (0–10 scale) compared to ratings given to competitors, and (3) sales and profitability. In all cases, market success (as judged by recent revenue growth) paralleled CEO self-ratings. Recognizing the tentativeness of conclusions regarding "performance" with such a small sample and before an industry shakeout has run its course, we nevertheless were able to draw some inferences regarding strategic decision behavior of effective firms in this environment.

Although space prevents our providing "thick descriptions" of each case (McClintock et al. 1979), we will describe the four firms, their strategies, executives, and decision dynamics, set within the context of a recent strategic decision.

Four Companies and Their Strategic Decisions

The Alpha Company: Should We Be IBM-Compatible?

The Alpha Company manufactures a broad line of microcomputers and related software for financial applications. The firm has a nationwide direct sales force and is privately held.

The President of Alpha is seen as dominating decision making within the firm. He is described as extremely bright (perhaps brilliant), very impatient, and yet a caring, nice person. Because of his pervasive influence over all decision areas, the prevailing attitude regarding major decisions at Alpha can be described as "Let Don (the president) do it— he will anyway." This is consistent with the fairly relaxed atmosphere we observed and the resignation to presidential domination we heard so often.

Communication centers around the president, who imparts information to the top management executives individually. In frustration, the VPs set up Friday afternoon "outlaw staff meetings" among themselves to share information and to get around Don's preference for conducting business in one-on-one settings. Also apparent among Alpha executives are stable coalitions between the VPs of Sales and Operations, who are relatively new to the firm, and the VPs of R&D and Finance, who have been with Alpha for many years.

The strategic decision we traced was: Should Alpha expand product compatibility to IBM computers? The issue first surfaced at an off-site planning conference in May 1983. Several board members and the VP of Marketing expressed interest in tapping the large IBM market. Alpha was not doing as well financially as hoped and some thought that the move to IBM, with its large installed base, would help. The issue brought much argument. The result of the meeting was that Don, personally and alone, investigated the relevant technical problems and market potential.

The president became knowledgeable especially about the technical and market issues. However, he did not attempt to gain information from his functional VPs about issues such as resource availability in R&D, nor did he explore other alternatives. In early 1984, he developed a plan by which the firm would expand its product line to IBM. Prior to announcing his decision in a group setting, Don solicited—and thought he had gained—individual support for the plan. To his surprise, the rest of the officers (except the VP of Marketing) opposed the plan when he presented it to the group. Their objection was that the move to IBM would require far more R&D resources than the firm had. They also objected to Don's dominating manner on this issue and in general. However, the Marketing VP strongly backed the switch to IBM. His strident support of the move to IBM served as a rally point for the opposition of others. (The Marketing VP was a "hot shot MBA" with prestige consulting firm experience, but the others, including Don, had little regard for him, primarily due to his constant need to collect and analyze information beyond the time when a decision was needed.) The decision stayed in limbo for several months. Since Don scheduled few group meetings, several of the other VPs used the time to lobby directly with him. Although the R&D and Sales VPs were the major opponents of Don's plan, they were unaware of each other's opinion and thus made no attempt to form an alliance.

The annual May planning conference forced the final decision. The president thought that he needed to give the company focus and direction at that meeting. He chose not to move to IBM except for one PC-related product. The decision was made solely by the president. One VP described the decision as "pushed down our throats," and as still representing too much of a commitment to IBM. All of the VPs were unhappy with the decision. However, they expressed relief in having a renewed sense of focus and that Don did back down somewhat in his thrust towards IBM. The Marketing VP (like many of his predecessors in that position) was let go and has not been replaced.

The Alpha decision was made over a relatively long time although few options were actually considered. The president dominated the decision from beginning to end. He formulated the problem, gathered the facts, and made the choice. As Don said: "I made the final decision on my own, despite opposition from most everyone. I decided 'the hell with it, let's go with the PC interface.'" Natural alliances that might have formed around this decision (e.g., VP Sales and VP R&D) cut across traditional coalition boundaries and did not occur. Rather, each VP used the familiar pattern of one-on-one influence attempts with the president, and each VP was unaware of the opinions of the other VPs. The stable coalitions blocked information flow within the group. In the end, the president just decided and the decision was unpopular.

Alpha's performance has not measured up to the president's expectations. Alpha carries a strong balance sheet, but its growth has been declining and profitability has dropped steadily over the past four years from 17 percent to 6 percent. In both market tests (growth) and CEO self-rating, Alpha was the lowest performer in our sample.

First Corporation: Do We Need a New Name?

The First Corporation is a manufacturer of super-micro computers for professionals. The firm has always oriented its products towards the sophisticated user. Thus, the firm sells directly to OEMs and systems integrators.

The chairman and CEO is the founder of First. He is seen as both brilliant and volatile. As described by one VP, "Geoff is sometimes like a gun that goes off, but you never know in what direction he will fire." The 51-year-old president and COO plays a complementary role to that of the chairman. He appears to mediate the relationship between the chairman and the rest of the officers. Several respondents referred to him as "Pop," describing him as controlled, organized—characteristics opposite to those of the chairman. Several of the officers pass ideas through Pop rather than meeting with Geoff directly.

First executives place a premium on being decisive and "getting on with it," and (as in Alpha) criticize their big-corporation-oriented VP Sales for excessive deliberativeness. As Pop said: "The VP Sales has to have all his facts in before anything can be done." By contrast, "I got ahead at First because I act." As in Alpha, First has stable coalitions—between the VPs of Finance and Operations (school friends) and between the president and chairman. Also as in Alpha, the chief executive dominates every decision.

The ambience at group meetings was described to us as "violent" and frustrating. Several of the officers view meetings with the chairman with great trepidation, and claim that the meetings are good for small issues, but that major issues are avoided as Geoff goes off on tangents. Most are reluctant to disagree with Geoff in front of a group for fear of being dressed down, but some are willing to do

so "one-on-one." As in Alpha, the officers now hold regular meetings without the chairman in order to get important issues resolved, as well as to avoid his mercurial outbursts. The dominant attitude at First is: "It's pretty wild around here—I hope that Pop can keep us together."

The focal strategic decision at First was: Should the established name of the firm be changed? There had been a long-standing dislike of the firm's name by the officers. The issue had first surfaced 20 months previously when a study concluded that the name was difficult to remember and hard to spell. Some officers just did not like it: as one VP told us, "The name is dumb." However, the final impetus for the decision was not its unpopularity nor the study, but a letter received in summer 1984. In it, the attorneys for another company charged First with service mark infringement upon their name. Only a few months earlier, First had problems with a client who confused them with a bankrupt company with a similar name. Although the service mark infringement charge did not have a strong legal basis, it stimulated the chairman and president to sit down in early September and examine the benefit, costs, and risks of a name change (the cost was estimated to be about 5 to 10 percent of annual sales). They reportedly decided to change the name at this meeting, but most officers believe that the chairman had decided to change before this. Later, several VPs, the president, and the chairman lined up meetings with three name change consultants to select a new name. The first consultant was dismissed for personal style reasons; the second appealed to Geoff, so the third was canceled. Many names were discussed and everyone offered opinions. The chairman chose his own favored option and placed the president in charge of the implementation. The time from the initial consultant's study to final choice took about 20 months.

All of the officers, including Pop, opposed the chairman's decision to change the name at this time. Name recognition is a very valuable asset for small firms in the industry, and First had a strong name. The officers feared the loss of marketplace name recognition at the crucial time during which the firm was switching from one type of computer to another. Only the Finance VP made an effort to change the chairman's mind. However, as the president said, "This is not a democratic company."

First's latest product line has met with only modest enthusiasm from the market. Financial performance has been steady, but unspectacular. Although its profitability is greater than Alpha's, First is a mediocre performer in terms of sales growth and CEO self-report.

First's decision process has some similarities to Alpha's. The decision was dominated by the chairman and there was complete opposition to the decision among the VPs. As at Alpha, identifiable political coalitions and outlaw staff meetings emerged in defense against a decision process that was dominated by the CEO. Despite the important impact of the decision, there was almost negligible discussion among the VPs themselves or the VPs with the chairman and the president. A name change was the only alternative considered, and it was not extensively analyzed. Also, executives who were described as analytically oriented (VPs of Marketing and Sales at Alpha and First, respectively) were the least appreciated in each firm and were let go. In other words, both the constrained decision process itself and the short careers of analytical executives indicate a low value placed on "rational" or comprehensive decision processes in these two firms. Finally, both decisions were made over a relatively long time period—12 months at Alpha, 20 months at First.

Whereas Alpha and First shared some similarities in their decision processes and management styles, these were distinctively different from those at Maverick and Zap.

Maverick Computer Company: What Is Our New Business Strategy?

The Maverick Computer Company manufactures networked microcomputer systems for small business. Maverick systems are marketed worldwide through value added resellers, and Maverick has recently emerged with an exciting product. As one VP told us, Maverick's distinctive competence was expertise in its management team. Bill, the current president of Maverick, was described as "very competitive, very strong, a master strategist." All of the VPs had experience at large computer firms and were relatively new to Maverick. The president did a "housecleaning" of the prior management and personally hired each of the new VPs as part of the strategy formation process.

There is a very high level of agreement on policy issues among Maverick executives. As one executive put it, "everyone is working on one common thing—to make that machine the best thing in the market." Despite the high level of agreement, there is also relatively active challenging of each other's positions on policy. Unlike at First however, the policy challenges do not occur in the open forum of exasperating group meetings. According to our informants, the Maverick executives tended to disagree with each other "off-line" in private, usually after group meetings adjourned. There was a concerted effort by Maverick executives to maintain a team congeniality in group forums and to avoid challenges that may appear to "assign blame." In concert with this, Bill is known to push for consensus on decisions. The feeling at Maverick is one of a committed team. The dominant decision climate is "Analyze, get consensus, do it."

The focal strategic decision at Maverick was: What is our new business strategy? As a glamor start-up in the late 70s, Maverick was expected to have several years of dynamic growth followed by a public offering that would allow all involved to become wealthy. It didn't happen. Sales went flat, the company managers panicked, and they narrowed the focus of the product. Maverick ended up with an obsolete product in a small market.

Venture capitalists get impatient in scenarios like this. They removed the founders and hired Bill, the current president, to develop a new business plan and a new management team. Bill took charge of both. He quickly instituted weekend planning meetings. As the executives describe the process, it was classic rational strategic planning: (1) analyze the competition, (2) identify the firm's strengths and weaknesses, (3) identify a target market, (4) understand user requirements, and (5) develop a product strategy. Although we initially interpreted this description as retrospective rationalizing on the part of the president (our first interview at Maverick), we found all respondents independently providing similar accounts.

At the same time, the president systematically assembled a new management team of experienced professionals, several of whom had worked together before. The implementation of the strategy was worked out as each functional executive was brought on board.

The group met each weekend over a three-month period. As one officer described it:

> People automatically bought into the plan because the meetings were held outside the normal work time and the group itself actually developed the plan. Bill directed us to the end, but we made the decisions. At each step of the way, Bill would achieve consensus before moving on.

The output of the decision was the business plan for the new "Pineapple" line of networked microcomputers. The pressure to reach a final decision came from the venture capitalists. Maverick executives used three meetings with most company managers to finalize the plan. The decision ended with a companywide meeting of all employees.

The resulting plan was risky. It called for a leap to an unproven microprocessor technology, adoption of an improved operating system, and a non-IBM-compatible system architecture. Nonetheless, all of top management supported the decision and each had a clear understanding of his role in implementation.

Several points are apparent from the Maverick decision. One is that Maverick executives used a highly rational decision-making process and a highly participative one. They analyzed many alternatives in detail. Our interviews with these executives became tutorials on the alternatives available in the microcomputer business in finance, marketing, and so on. The Pineapple decision took a relatively short time (three months), and had high management support. Execution of the decision, however, is being carried out over an extended period, with functional strategies being decided by each VP in a sequential manner. For example, the distribution channel was chosen by the Sales VP several months after the extent of vertical integration was decided by the Manufacturing VP.

Although Maverick had been a mediocre performer prior to Pineapple, its current performance can be characterized as a turnaround: Orders for the Pineapple are strong and accelerating. The CEO rated Maverick's performance as superior to that of his main competitors.

Zap Computers: Should We Go Public?

Zap manufactures supermicro computers for professionals. (First and Zap are competitors.) The firm sells directly to a small number of large OEMs and universities. Zap's key business problem is maintaining its market position through technology as major computer firms enter Zap's niche.

The president of Zap is very young and nontechnical. He holds an MBA from a prestige program, and is regarded as bright, people-oriented, and a consensus style manager. The top management team has been assembled during the past three years and includes seasoned veterans from a variety of corporations. The Sales and Engineering VPs apparently give "fatherly counsel" to the president on an informal basis, and the president uses them as sounding boards and as a proxy for experience. There are no identifiable coalitions among Zap managers. Coalitions, when they arise, are decision specific. One VP describes their meetings as "very vocal. We all bring our own ideas. The meetings are constructive. We scream a lot, then laugh, then resolve the issue."

Zap executives are driven. There is an air of breathlessness in the executive suite that is characterized by bursts of energy, rapid communications, and short sentences. There is a no-time-for-BS orientation among Zap executives, who place a premium on getting consensus and acting in "real time." Communication is often by electronic mail.

The focal strategic decision at Zap was: Should the firm go public? Going public—eventually— has always been part of Zap's game plan. However, Zap managers did not begin to focus on this issue until May 1984 (three years after initial financing), when they observed potential cash flow problems during their budgeting process for fiscal 1985. Zap managers, especially the president, pay close, even daily, attention to key performance indicators such as bookings and the status of important development projects.

With his finance background, the president spearheaded this decision. He discussed it over the course of the summer with board members and several of the experienced VPs on an informal basis. The president used his staff meetings to outline the status of the decision, but not really to discuss it. The officers used the staff meeting to question the president on the status of the decision. Although most stood to gain substantial financial rewards, there were mixed feelings about the timing of a stock offering. One VP, an Osborne veteran, wanted to do it immediately. Both the Engineering VP and the treasurer wanted to remain private, as going public would have profound effects: Revenues and earnings would have to be smoothed for reporting purposes (Wall Street punishes volatility), which would constrain manufacturing, sales, and R&D operations and reduce flexibility throughout. The distinguishing feature at Zap is that everyone knew the positions of others and every one backed the president.

In late summer on an airplane trip, the president and the Sales and Engineering VPs came up with an alternative to going public. The alternative was to seek out either a major supplier or customer to buy a significant piece of the firm. This was the so-called "strategic alliance" option. The president used the Sales and Engineering VPs to clarify his ideas in subsequent meetings. He laid out a calendar, convinced the board, and negotiated a deal with a major customer in rapid succession. During the fall the deal was consummated on schedule. The firm still plans to go public, but has structured the going public decision on a quarter-to-quarter basis—depending upon specific earnings, market, and competitive results. In other words, the decision is programmed to occur, given some key contingencies and specific triggers. In the eventuality that the triggers are encountered, each officer has been

given a set of tasks to manage so that Zap could go public very rapidly if that were appropriate.

Zap's decision was triggered by the formal budgeting system, not by external events. The president considered a relatively wide range of options for Zap's projected cash flow problems—including additional venture capital financing and bank loans. He also analyzed the quantitative as well as intangible factors. As he told us: "We tend to over-MBA it around here." The final decision was made quickly and was well-supported and understood by the top management team.

Zap's performance has been spectacular, with growth fluctuating from 25 percent to 100 percent *per quarter.* Zap is considered to be a star in the industry. Right now, Zap has sold more computers than it can make.

Zap's decision process has some similarities to Maverick's. The decision was analyzed extensively and several alternatives were considered. The CEOs of both firms appeared to apply "rational" or business textbook analysis to their decisions. Second, both decisions were innovative—Maverick's technology leapfrog and Zap's discovery of what is currently termed a "strategic alliance" were both bold. Third, both decisions were taken over a relatively short time period, three months. Fourth, the execution of both decisions was delayed until either the appropriate functional VP could formulate his own strategy (Maverick) or until certain performance thresholds were crossed (Zap). Finally, both decisions were fully supported by relatively apolitical top management teams. A summary of these similarities, as well as those between Alpha and First, is given in Exhibit 1.

Propositions and Hypotheses

The decision to enter a new product market (Alpha), alter a firm's identity (First), leapfrog a technology (Maverick), and postpone relinquishing control to public stockholders (Zap), were all critical decisions that had major impact on the firms. The patterns we observed across these decisions allowed us to draw inferences regarding strategic

EXHIBIT 1   Summary of Four Firms' Decisions

	Alpha	*First*	*Maverick*	*Zap*
Decision	Expansion of product compatibility to IBM	Change of company name during time of new product line intro	New machine based on technology leapfrog to unproven microprocessor	Timing of going public and use of "strategic alliance" for funding
Impetus	Performance below aspirations	Consultant study, then name infringement lawsuit	New CEO with turnaround mission	Cash budget
Number of executives interviewed	5	6	6	7
Extent of search for alternatives	Constrained	Constrained	Wide	Wide
Type of analysis	Problemistic, Satisficing	Problemistic, Satisficing	Comprehensive, "rational"	Comprehensive, "rational"
Duration	12 months	20 months	3 months	3 months
Implementation	Dictated by CEO	Dictated by CEO	VPs decide, in sequence	VPs decide, based on triggers
Power	Strong CEO, Weak VPs	Strong CEO, Weak VPs	Strong CEO and Strong VPs	Strong CEO and Strong VPs
Political behavior	Stable coalitions Outlaw staff meetings	Stable coalitions Mercurial Outlaw staff meetings	Coalitions form around issues Polite conflict off-line	Coalitions around issues No time for politics
Performance	Declining	Mediocre	Taking off	Stellar

processes in high-velocity environments. Here, we present five general propositions, each of which summarizes a set of inferences as a theme. We then develop each proposition into specific hypotheses.

PROPOSITION 1.   *In high-velocity environments, effective firms use rational decision making processes.*

Earlier, we cited research suggesting that high-performing firms in fast-paced environments would use incremental approaches to strategic decision making (e.g., Cyert and March 1963; Mintzberg 1973; Fredrickson and Mitchell, 1984).

The argument was that, in conditions of instability and information scarcity, strategists would be unable to engage in the structured deliberation and analysis implied in formal strategic planning. Instead, they must react adaptively, dealing with competitive situations only as they arise and with information only as it becomes available.

The picture that emerges from our data is quite different. That is, as the speed of environmental change accelerates, effective executives deal with their extremely uncertain world by structuring it. This is done by employing a thorough, analytic process. In our study, both Maverick and Zap searched well beyond a single alternative and used computational analyses in their evaluation of strategies. The information gathering by Maverick was a classic textbook strategic planning effort. Maverick executives (1) analyzed their industry, (2) conducted a competitor analysis, (3) identified the firm's strengths and weaknesses, (4) identified the target market, and (5) developed the strategy. Similarly, Zap's president often commented that, perhaps, they "over MBA" the organization, from creating a business plan and hitting every target, to measuring every possible activity and performance indicator. The going public decision arose from the formal planning system and was the result of a careful analysis of alternative financing plans. In more formal terms:

H1.1. In high-velocity environments, the more analytic the strategic decision-making process, the better the performance of the firm.

Our argument has a parallel in psychoanalytic prescription, where persons stressed by a fast, disordered, and unstable personal environment are advised to "put their world in order" through a rational process of identifying goals and setting priorities, collecting information, and generating and evaluating alternatives, in order to gain a sense of control (deBoard 1978). Similarly, high velocity environments force executives to structure their cognitive maps and to form their theories regarding which strategies will succeed, as well as to cope psychologically with the instability.

The difference between our results and those of Fredrickson and Mitchell (1984) may be due, in part, to our differing methods (theirs was a scenario-based field study in the forest products industry). Another explanation may be that the computer industry may have a higher velocity than forest products, which, in turn, creates enhanced pressures for a more rational approach. Applying the Dess and Beard (1984) definition of "dynamism," which is based on aggregate industry demand figures, it appears that the instability of the forest products industry is caused largely by cyclical demand for a commodity product rather than by the more extreme instability of discontinuous change in the micro-

computer industry. Possibly, then, rational-analytic processes may be most appropriate at the extremes of industry stability (stable paints, high velocity microcomputers), while incremental processes are more appropriate at the midrange of instability (e.g., unstable forest products).

As alluded to in our literature review, some authors juxtapose the behavioral theory of the firm as a major alternative to normative "rational" decision models (Cyert and March 1963; Bower 1970; Allison 1971). Our data also indicate that the behavioral model does indeed describe strategic decision-making behavior. However, in this environment it characterizes the behavior of poor performers. Both Alpha and First examined a constrained set of options without much reliance on analytic detail. In classic satisficing behavior, Alpha considered only two alternatives (IBM compatibility or not), and stopped gathering information when the president was satisfied with whatever amount he had collected at a point in time. In First, there was no search at all undertaken for alternatives to a name change. In fact, although three consulting firms were contacted, a satisficing search pattern was evidenced. First's CEO rejected the first firm for emotional reasons and accepted the second firm because it "looked reasonable," causing the cancellation of any consideration for the third firm. Thus,

H1.2. In high velocity environments, the more comprehensive the search for strategic alternatives, the better the performance of the firm.

Finally, the firms also differed in the extent to which the senior executives could articulate their companies' goals. In First, there was no particular strategic goal involved, just the chairman's opportunistic reaction to a questionable lawsuit. By contrast, executives mentioned Maverick's goal as the "Best damn machine on the market." Zap's goal was the "largest possible war chest" with the fewest possible strings attached. In each firm, more than one executive volunteered the goal without our prompting. Note that both of these goals are proactive, reaching ("best," and "largest"), whereas First and Alpha were both *reacting* to negative stimuli (a lawsuit and declining profits, respectively) and did not articulate goals, let alone positive ones. In times of rapid change, people need an anchor for their actions, and clear, explicit goals provide this. Thus,

H1.3. In high velocity environments, the clearer and more explicitly articulated the institutional goal, the better the performance of the firm.

PROPOSITION 2. *In high velocity environments, effective firms try new things.*

The "threat-rigidity" hypothesis in organization theory suggests that under conditions of environmentally induced stress, firms will exhibit a tendency toward well-learned or habitual responses (Staw, Sandelands, and Dutton 1981). This is due, in part, to executives' tendency to centralize authority and tighten internal control when faced with environmental change or turbulence (Bourgeois, McAllister, and Mitchell 1978), which in turn leads to "rigidity" in response. These habitual, or rigid, responses will be maladaptive if the environment is undergoing radical change (Gladstein and Reilly 1985).

One form of environmental "threat" is severe time pressure associated with decision making (Gladstein and Reilly 1985)—a condition characteristic of the microcomputer industry. Under these circumstances, the "natural" response of executives is to centralize authority and to continue previous strategies, not to pursue new strategies or innovative alternatives. In Cyert and March (1963) terms, firms engage in problemistic search—that is, they search for solutions to problems in the neighborhood of old solutions before searching for untested ones.

The evidence from this study suggests that the effective firms are able to resist the rigidity response and to experiment—sometimes at high risk—with their environments. For example, Zap pioneered the concept of strategic alliance, in which a much larger external partner is sought as an alternative to traditional external financing. Similarly, Maverick pioneered a new technology in the Pineapple. In contrast, lower-performing Alpha followed an imitation strategy by examining an alternative—IBM compatibility—already prevalent in the industry.

H2.1. In high velocity environments, the more innovative and risky the set of strategic alternatives examined and chosen, the better the performance of the firm.

Taken together, Propositions 1 and 2 seem to present something of a paradox. Effective firms act rationally, but seek innovation and risk. Several authors suggest that rational and analytical planning often suffocates innovation and creativity (Weick 1979; Peters and Waterman 1982; Mintzberg and Waters 1982). How are these reconciled? One answer lies in Proposition 3.

PROPOSITION 3. *In high velocity environments, effective firms make strategic decisions quickly.*

What we found seems counterintuitive. Essentially, in high velocity environments, the need for rational planning seems critical, in that it sets a general direction for the firm and allows the top management team and the rest of the organization to focus on execution, or, at least, on watching for decision threshold triggers (see Proposition 4 below). In both Maverick and Zap we found the president taking *and announcing* a dramatic decision with execution involving the adaptation and sometimes reformulation of strategy by the rest of the top management team as events occurred and new information was available to the firm. This contrasts with Quinn's (1978, 1980) conclusion that effective CEOs make major strategic decisions privately and subsequently reveal these decisions over a possibly long period of time as subordinates expose "corridors of indifference" through their own proposals. Quinn's model probably holds in very large corporations in more mature industries (his sample included Chrysler, GM, Xerox). However, our data indicate that a high velocity environment leaves no room for this wait-and-nurture strategy.

H3.1. In high velocity environments, the shorter the time frame in which strategic decisions are made, the better the performance of the firm.

The key to resolving the paradox of rational planning versus innovation (Propositions 1 and 2) is the relationship of time to decision and implementation. Effective executives make decisions rapidly. For example, the CEOs of Zap and Maverick made major, strategic decisions in less than three months. Each had a tight cycle of analysis, planning, and decision making. Zap was characterized by an atmosphere of breathless pace and intense focus. Maverick executives dedicated their three months to developing a new strategy. By contrast, the decision at Alpha (the lowest performer) lasted 12 months, while First took 20 months from initial sensing to final decision. The more effective firms use a short, focused and intensive planning process in which an often bold, overall decision is set. This short, intensive process may well induce a kind of "risky shift" in the decision making that encourages innovation. But this also presents another paradox: How can firms do careful, rational planning (Proposition 1), which suggests time invested in search and analysis, yet act boldly (Proposition 2) and swiftly (Proposition 3)?

PROPOSITION 4. *In high velocity environments, effective firms build in decision execution triggers.*

Effective firms appear to put structure onto a stream of unstructured decisions. The CEO makes an initial, decisive choice, but also lays out subsequent decisions to be triggered by a schedule, milestone, or event. Zap would go public only after certain quarterly results were attained; the going-public decision would be postponed whenever strategic alliances (financial infusions from corporate partners) could be found. The Maverick CEO had set in place a grand strategy and had programmed the recruiting of top functional managers and the critical decisions in those functions. In both cases, the execution decisions were to be postponed until the appropriate managerial resources could be focused on them. By contrast, neither Alpha nor First used decision triggers, although their decisions were amenable to them.

H4.1. In high velocity environments, the greater the articulation of implementation triggers at the time a strategic decision is taken, the better the performance of the firm.

Execution triggers allow firms to keep implementation options open as long as possible without diverting management attention from other activities. Execution triggers help to control the risk of innovative decisions made quickly. What emerges is a model of swift and rational planning with adaptive execution. Analytical thinking orders a fast-moving world (Proposition 1), and provides a psychological coping mechanism. Threshold-triggered execution decisions prevent premature commitments to irretrievable action (this proposition), which provides a behavioral adaptation mechanism. The former provides order, the latter prevents error. Certainty is attained at a meta, or intellectual level; while uncertainty is maintained at the action, or behavioral level. In high velocity environments, the latter allows the pieces of a strategy to be changed as the environment or the requirements of the situation change.

PROPOSITION 5. *In high velocity environments, effective firms vest power to implement strategy in the top management team.*

Vroom and Yetton's (1973) model of effective decision making links fast decisions with autocratic leadership. So it was not surprising that, in this fast-paced environment, all four of the decisions we studied were made by the CEO. Although there was a fair degree of consultation with the top management team in Maverick and Zap, the CEO was always in charge, and acted as something of a "dictator." Moreover, in all firms the decisiveness provided a "let's get on with it" attitude on the part of the top management team, accompanied by a sense of relief and focus. So, although the CEO seemed to be dictatorial on occasion, the top management team saw some benefits in this.

What differs across firms was the extent to which execution of the decision was put squarely in the hands of the functional vice presidents. In Maverick and Zap, the execution triggers described above were identified and planned for by the functional executives, not the CEO. For example, Maverick's VP Software chose the Pineapple's operating system, the VP Marketing decided on the distribution

EXHIBIT 2   Alpha Power Matrix

	President	VP Sales	VP Finance	VP Ops	VP R&D
Marketing	8.8**	6.7	4.7	2.7	4.1
R&D	8.0**	3.8	3.7	2.9	5.6
Finance	4.2**	2.0	3.6	2.1	1.5
Operations	4.8**	2.0	2.7	3.3	2.9
Organization	7.1**	4.7	4.6	2.8	3.6
Total Power	6.6	3.8	3.9	2.8	3.5

Conclusion: CEO (president) is the most powerful executive in every decision area, with functional VPs being second-most powerful in their respective fields.
** = highest power score in top management team on each decision area.

channel, and the VP Manufacturing decided the extent of vertical integration. Thus,

H5.1.   In high velocity environments, the greater the delegation of execution triggers the top management team, the better the performance of the firm.

This conclusion is further supported by our quantitative data on power distribution within the executive teams. As shown in the power matrixes given in Exhibits 2 and 3, Alpha and First (the low performers) centralized *all* policy-level decision making in the CEO. (Footnote 3 explains how we computed power scores.) By contrast, Maverick and Zap exhibit power patterns in which the CEO is frequently only the second most powerful executive on several decisions. The greatest power over a

functional area generally resides in the functional vice president (see Exhibits 4 and 5).

The picture captured by our power matrixes shows an empowered group of senior executives among the high performers, and an emasculated top management team among the low performers. In formal terms,

H5.2.   In high velocity environments, the more the power to make functional strategy decisions is delegated to the functional executives, the better the performance of the firm.

Thus, while we see the autocratic decision pattern suggested by Vroom and Yetton (1973) for fast-paced decisions, we also see the decentralized pattern of decision authority advocated by contingency

EXHIBIT 3   First Power Matrix

	Chairman	VP Sales	VP Finance	VP Ops	President
Marketing	8.1**	6.3	3.4	3.2	3.3
R&D	8.5**	6.0	1.7	1.3	2.0
Finance	3.0**	1.2	3.0	1.4	1.9
Operations	3.4**	0.7	2.3	2.6	1.5
Organization	5.2**	1.2	3.2	1.1	3.4
Total Power	5.6	3.1	2.7	1.9	2.4

Conclusion: CEO (chairman) is most powerful executive in every decision area.
** = highest power score in top management team on each decision area.

EXHIBIT 4   Maverick Power Matrix

	President	VP Sales	VP Finance	VP Manuf	VP Engr
Marketing	9.7**	8.7	6.0	5.5	8.0
R&D	8.7	7.5	4.8	7.2	9.7**
Finance	7.8**(tie)	2.8	7.8**(tie)	3.5	3.4
Operations	5.0	2.0	4.7	5.7**	4.9
Organization	8.4**	5.1	6.2	4.2	3.8
Total Power	7.9	5.3	5.9	5.2	6.0

Conclusion: except for Sales VP, functional VPs are the most powerful in decision areas associated with their major function.
** = highest power score in top management team on each decision area.

theorists (Burns and Stalker 1961; Lawrence and Lorsch 1967) for highly uncertain environments. The effective firms are able to operate with both patterns of decision making simultaneously.

As exhibited by the less effective firms, one consequence of keeping power from the top management executives is compensating behavior: Alpha and First seemed more inclined to either engage in behind-the-scene political behavior through stable coalitions (Alpha), or to vent emotions in psychologically destructive ways (First's "gun about to go off"). Also, both top management teams formed "outlaw meetings" to circumvent their CEOs' power-centralizing tendencies, exhibiting clear self-preserving political actions.

H5.3.   In high velocity environments, the greater the power centralization in the chief executive, the greater the level of political behavior among the top management team.

But in high velocity environments, political behavior is associated with poor performance. Thus,

H5.4.   In high velocity environments, the greater the political behavior among the top management team, the poorer the performance of the firm.

Taken together, Propositions 4 and 5 have similarities to the logical incremental model proposed by Quinn (1978, 1980), in which the details of a strategy become known to the organization (and to the CEO) as events unfold. The primary difference in our conclusions lies in the locus of control over the details. In Quinn's model, the CEO is always the master, but a master of subtlety. The CEO is tentative, suggesting partial solutions, opportunistically

EXHIBIT 5   Zap Power Matrix

	President	VP Sales	VP Finance	VP Ops	VP Engr
Marketing	5.9	7.8**	3.4	4.1	7.5
R&D	5.7	5.5	3.2	3.7	9.2**
Finance	5.1**	2.1	4.1	2.7	3.5
Operations	5.7	3.5	4.2	7.1**	5.4
Organizations	5.6**	2.8	2.6	2.6	4.9
Total Power	5.6	4.3	3.5	4.0	6.1

Conclusion: except for Finance, functional VPs are the most powerful in their respective fields.
** = highest power score in top management team on each decision area.

broadening support, awaiting the emergence of champions. The formal commitment to a strategy and its announcement come as the *last* action in his model (see 1980, Diagram 3, p. 104). By contrast, our data suggest that formal commitment and explicit announcement are made *early* by the CEO (Proposition 3), but the details of execution *follow from* this rather than *build toward* it. Our effective CEOs make a strong and clearly articulated strategic choice early on. And, the locus of authority for implementation decisions is delegated to the functional vice presidents, not retained by the CEO. The effective CEOs "let go" of their strategies after the major decision has been made.

Conclusion

We began this paper with the question: How to executives make strategic decisions in high velocity environments? Many scholars of decision making have focused their efforts on large corporations in stable environments (e.g., Quinn 1980; Mintzberg and Waters 1982) or on nonprofit organizations (Pfeffer and Salancik 1974; March and Olsen 1976; Mintzberg and McHugh 1985). But the constraints faced by business firms in high velocity environments are different. Strategic decision making is difficult in this environment because mistakes and delays are costly. Once behind, it is difficult to catch up. Imitation is often not viable either, as it implies both waiting and jumping into an occupied niche. Thus, this environment puts a premium on high-quality, fast, and innovative decisions.

Several of our propositions focus on the quality of decision making. For example, rational analysis serves this function (Proposition 1), as do decentralizing power to functional VPs (Proposition 5) and establishing decision threshold triggers (Proposition 4). Rational analysis improves the initial quality of the decision, while decentralized power and decision triggers foster quality through flexibility to changing circumstances. At the same time, delays are avoided through the CEO's willingness to be decisive and to move quickly (Proposition 3). Innovativeness is achieved by experimentation in the face of threat

(Proposition 2), and by keeping the strategic decision cycle short, intense, and focused (Proposition 3).

The overall lessons are a series of apparent paradoxes: Plan carefully and analytically, but move quickly and boldly. CEOs should be decisive, but also delegate. Choose and articulate an overall strategy quickly, but put it in place only as it becomes necessary. Although some authors have described trade-offs between decision quality versus speed versus implementation (Vroom and Yetton 1973; Janis 1982), such trade-offs are less accessible to managers in high velocity environments. Rather, these executives must attain all three simultaneously.

We offer these paradoxes as propositions and hypotheses induced from our data. As presently constituted, these propositions and hypotheses are at least one step short of theory formation. At minimum, they are what Merton (1957) and Wallace (1971) refer to as empirical generalizations—they summarize observed uniformities of relationships between variables. At best, they suggest a rudimentary model of strategic decision making in high velocity environments, a model we have summarized in Exhibit 6.

The fast-moving nature of the microcomputer environment presents the firms in this industry with unique challenges. Given the recent trend toward technological discontinuity, deregulation, and global competition, it is possible that other industries will soon be facing similar rates of change. To the extent that our results are valid and can be supported by the data from our next research phase, we think that a normative theory of strategic decision making in high velocity environments can be built.[4]

———————

[4]*Support for this research was provided in part by the Strategic Management Program, Stanford Graduate School of Business, and by the Sponsors of the Colgate Darden Graduate School of Business Administration. We would like to thank our graduate assistants, Teresa Lant, Anita Callahan, and Dave Ellison, for their invaluable help as well as the executives of Alpha, First, Maverick and Zap computer companies. We would also like to thank Dave Anderson, Arie Lewin, and our three anonymous reviewers for their helpful comments.*

EXHIBIT 6   A Model of Strategic Decision Making in High Velocity Environments

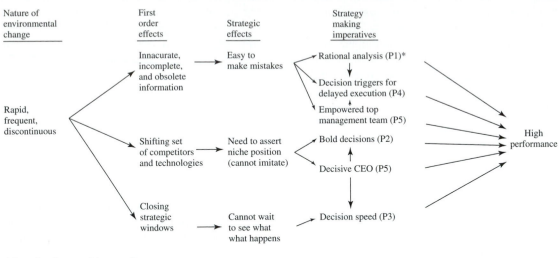

*Associated proposition number

References

Allison, Graham T. *Essence of Decision: Explaining the Cuban Missile Crisis.* Boston: Little, Brown, 1971.

Bavelas, Alex. "Communication Patterns in Task Oriented Groups," in Daniel Lerner and Harold Lasswell (eds.), *The Policy Sciences.* Stanford, CA: Stanford University Press, 1951.

Bell, C. Gordon. "The Mini and Micro Industries." *IEEE Trans. Comput.* (October 1984).

———. "RISC: Back to the Future." *Datamation* (June 1, 1986).

Bourgeois, L. J. "Performance and Consensus." *Strategic Management J.* 1, 3 (July–September 1980), pp. 227–248.

———. "Strategic Goals, Environmental Uncertainty, and Economic Performance in Volatile Environments." *Acad. Management J.* 28, 3 (September 1985), pp. 548–573.

———, D. W. McAllister, and T. R. Mitchell. "The Effects of Different Organizational Environments upon Decisions about Organization Design." *Acad. Management J.* 21, 3 (September 1978), pp. 508–514.

———, and David R. Brodwin. "Strategy Implementation: Five Approaches to an Elusive Phenomenon." *Strategic Management J.* 5, 3 (July 1984), pp. 241–264.

———, and Kathleen M. Eisenhardt. "Strategic Decision Processes in Silicon Valley: The Anatomy of a 'Living Dead.'" *California Management Rev.* 30, 1 (Fall 1987), pp. 143–159.

Bower, Joseph. *Managing the Resource Allocation Process.* Boston: Division of Research, Graduate School of Business Administration, 1970.

Burns, T., and G. Stalker. *The Management of Innovation.* London: Tavistock, 1961.

Creative Strategies International. *The Microcomputer Industry.* Private industry research report, August 1983.

Cyert, Richard M., and J. G. March. *A Behavioral Theory of the Firm.* Englewood Cliffs, NJ: Prentice-Hall, 1963.

deBoard, Robert. *The Psychoanalysis of Organizations.* London: Tavistock, 1978.

Dess, Gregory D., and Donald W. Beard. "Dimension of Organizational Task Environments." *Admin. Sci. Quart.* 29 (1984), pp. 52–73.

Fredrickson, James W. "The Comprehensiveness of Strategic Decision Processes: Extension, Observations, Future Directions." *Acad. Management J.* 27, 3 (September 1984), pp. 445–466.

———, and Terence R. Mitchell. "Strategic Decision Processes: Comprehensiveness and Performance in an Industry with an Unstable Environment." *Acad. Management J.* 27, 2 (June 1984), pp. 399–423.

George, Alexander L. *Presidential Decision Making in Foreign Policy.* Boulder, CO: Westview Press, 1980.

Gladstein, Deborah L., and Nora P. Reilly. "Group Decision Making Under Threat: The Tycoon Game." *Acad. Management J.* 28, 3 (September 1985), pp. 613–627.

Hofer, Charles W., and Dan Schendel. *Strategy Formulation: Analytical Concepts.* St. Paul: West Publishing Co., 1978.

Huber, George P., and Daniel J. Power. "Retrospective Reports of Strategic-Level Managers: Guidelines for Increasing Their Accuracy." *Strategic Management J.* 6, 2 (June 1985), pp. 171–180.

Hudson, Laurel, A., and J. L. Ozanne. "The Role of Guiding Assumption in Research: In Search of Method." Working Paper, University of Virginia, November 1986.

Janis, Irving L. *Victims of Groupthink.* Rev. ed. Boston: Houghton Mifflin, 1982.

Jemison, David B. "Organizational versus Environmental Sources of Influence in Strategic Decision Making." *Strategic Management J.* 2, 1 (January–March 1981), pp. 77–89.

Lawrence, Paul, and Jay Lorsch. *Organization and Environment.* Boston: Harvard Business School, Division of Research, 1967.

Leavitt, Harold J. "Some Effects of Certain Communication Patterns in Group Performance." *J. Abnormal and Social Psychology* 46 (1951).

Lindblom, Charles E. "The Science of 'Muddling Through.'" *Public Administration Rev.* 19 (1959), pp. 79–88.

March, James G., and Johan P. Olsen. *Ambiguity and Choice in Organization.* Bergen, Norway: Universitetsforlaget, 1976.

McClintock, Charles C., Diane Brannon, and Steven Maynard-Moody. "Applying the Logic of Sample Surveys to Qualitative Case Studies: The Case Cluster Method." *Admin. Sci. Quart.* 24, 4 (December 1979), pp. 612–629.

Merton, Robert K. *Social Theory and Social Structure.* Rev. and enlarged ed. Glencoe, IL: The Free Press, 1957.

Meyer, Alan D. "Adapting to Environmental Jolts." *Admin. Sci. Quart.* 27 (December 1982), pp. 515–537.

Miles, Raymond E., and Charles C. Snow. *Organizational Strategy, Structure, and Process.* New York: McGraw-Hill, 1978.

Mintzberg, Henry. "Strategy-Making in Three Modes." *California Management Rev.* 15, 2 (Winter 1973), pp. 44–53.

———. "Organizational Power and Goals: A Skeletal Theory." In Dan E. Schendel and Charles W. Hofer (eds.), *Strategic Management: A New View of Business Policy and Planning.* Boston: Little, Brown and Company, 1979, pp. 64–80.

———. "Crafting Strategy." *Harvard Business Rev.* 87, 4 (July–August 1987), pp. 66–75.

———, and James A. Waters. "Tracking Strategy in an Entrepreneurial Firm." *Acad. Management J.* 25, 3 (September 1982), pp. 465–499.

———, and Alexandra McHugh. "Strategy Formation in an Adhocracy." *Admin. Sci. Quart.* 30 (1985), pp. 160–197.

Neustadt, Richard E., and Ernest R. May. *Thinking in Time.* New York: The Free Press, 1986.

Peters, Thomas J., and Robert H. Waterman, Jr. *In Search of Excellence.* New York: Harper & Row, 1982.

Pfeffer, Jeffrey, and Gerald R. Salancik. "Organizational Decision Making as a Political Process: The Case of a University Budget." *Admin. Sci. Quart.* 19, 2 (June 1974), pp. 135–151.

Porter, Michael E. *Competitive Strategy.* New York: The Free Press, 1980.

Quinn, James Brian. "Strategic Change: 'Logical Incrementalism.'" *Sloan Management Rev.* 20, 1 (Fall 1978), pp. 7–21.

———. *Strategies for Change.* Homewood, IL: Dow Jones-Irwin, 1980.

Simon, Herbert A. *Administrative Behavior.* New York: The Free Press, 1957.

Staw, B. M., L. E. Sandelands, and J. E. Dutton. "Threat-Rigidity Effects in Organizational Behavior: A Multi-Level Analysis." *Admin. Sci. Quart.* 26 (1981), pp. 501–524.

Sutton, Robert, Kathleen Eisenhardt, and James Jucker. "Managing Organizational Decline: Lessons from Atari." *Organizational Dynamics* (Spring 1986).

Vroom, Victor H., and Phillip Yetton. *Leadership and Decision Making.* Pittsburgh, PA: University of Pittsburgh Press, 1973.

Wallace, Walter L. *The Logic of Science in Sociology.* Chicago: Aldine-Atherton, 1971.

Weick, Karl E. *The Social Psychology of Organizing.* 2nd ed. Reading, MA: Addison-Wesley, 1979.

Yin, Robert K. *Case Study Research: Design and Methods.* Beverly Hills: Sage, 1984.

Case 3–4

MAKING FAST STRATEGIC DECISIONS IN HIGH-VELOCITY ENVIRONMENTS

Kathleen M. Eisenhardt

Stanford University

How do executive teams make rapid decisions in the high-velocity microcomputer industry? This inductive study of eight microcomputer firms led to propositions exploring that question. Fast decision makers use more, not less, information than do slow decision makers. The former also develop more, not fewer, alternatives, and use a two-tiered advice process. Conflict resolution and integration among strategic decisions and tactical plans are also critical to the pace of decision making. Finally, fast decisions based on this pattern of behaviors lead to superior performance.

In October 1984, Gavilan Computer filed for bankruptcy protection under Chapter 11. Despite a $31 million stake from venture capitalists, Gavilan experienced delays and indecision that ultimately cost the firm its early technical and market advantages. The firm's leading-edge technology became a "me too" one and competitors flooded its empty market niche. As the firm died, one executive mourned: "We missed the window" (Hof, 1984).

This story is not unusual in fast-paced settings like the microcomputer industry. The tumult of technical change places a premium on rapid decision making. Yet, although decision speed seems to affect firm performance in such environments (Bourgeois & Eisenhardt, 1988) and is a key characteristic differentiating strategic decisions (Hickson et al., 1986), there has been little research on fast strategic decision making.

This article explores the speed of strategic decision making. In an earlier study (Bourgeois & Eisenhardt, 1988), my colleague and I linked fast strategic decision making to effective firm performance. In a second study on politics (Eisenhardt & Bourgeois, 1988), we noted that politics seemed to slow decision making. However, neither study addressed *how* executives decide quickly. The present study extends the previous work by exploring how executive teams actually make fast decisions.

This article is organized around two research questions: (1) How are fast strategic decisions made? and (2) How does decision speed link to performance? The setting is the high-velocity microcomputer industry. In a high-velocity environment, changes in demand, competition, and technology are so rapid and discontinuous that information is often inaccurate, unavailable, or obsolete (Bourgeois & Eisenhardt, 1988). During this research (1984–85), the microcomputer industry underwent substantial technological changes, such as the introduction of the UNIX operating system, 64K RAM memory, and RISC computer architecture, as well as substantial competitive change, such as the entry of IBM, the decline of Texas Instruments, and double-digit demand growth (Bell, 1984).

The results reported here are a set of propositions challenging traditional views of strategic decision making. The evidence suggests that fast

Academy of Management Journal by Kathleen M. Eisenhardt. Copyright 1989 by Academy of Management Journal. *Reproduced with permission of* Academy of Management Journal *in the format Textbook via Copyright Clearance Center.*

decision makers use more, not less, information, than do slow decision makers. They also develop more, not fewer, alternatives. In contrast to current literature, this study found that centralized decision making is not necessarily fast, but a layered advice process, emphasizing input from experienced counselors, is fast. The findings also indicate that conflict resolution is critical to decision speed, but conflict per se is not. Finally, integration among strategic decisions and between decisions and tactical plans speeds, not slows, decision making. Such integration helps decision makers cope with the anxiety of high-stakes decision making. Overall, fast decision making allows decision makers to keep pace with change and is linked to strong performance. A pattern of emotional, political, and cognitive processes that are related to rapid closure of major decisions emerged from this research. The empirical grounding of those ideas is the subject of this article.

Background

There are several perspectives on how rapid strategic decisions are achieved. One research stream emphasizes the idea that a high level of comprehensiveness[1] slows the strategic decision process. According to this perspective, consideration of few alternatives, obtaining input from few sources, and limited analysis lead to quick decisions (Mintzberg, 1973; Nutt, 1976). For example, Fredrickson and Mitchell (1984) argued that a process that is less comprehensive speeds decisions. Similarly, Schweiger, Sandberg, and Ragan (1986) noted that extensive analysis in dialectical inquiry is likely to slow the pace of decision making. Janis (1982) indicated that, although a rational process may be superior, it also lengthens decision making.

---

[1] *"Comprehensiveness is a measure of rationality and refers to the extent to which organizations attempt to be exhaustive or inclusive in the making or integrating of decisions" (Fredrickson & Mitchell, 1984, p. 399).*

A second view has emphasized that limited participation and centralized power speed decision making. For example, Vroom and Yetton (1973) advocated autocratic decision making when speed is essential. Powerful leaders can make rapid, unilateral choices. Similarly, March and Olsen (1976) argued that involvement by many decision makers lengthens the decision process. Finally, Staw, Sandelands, and Dutton (1981) indicated that power centralization is the most natural response to highly uncertain situations like high-velocity environments.

A third view is that limited conflict speeds decisions. The argument here is that conflict triggers interruptions in the decision process, which then slow the pace. For example, Mintzberg, Raisinghani, and Théorêt (1976) found that disagreements created decision interruptions, which in turn delayed the decision process in a study of 25 major decisions. Similarly, another study (Hickson et al., 1986) found that opposition, especially by powerful factions, slowed the pace of decision in a study of British organizations.

Although these views vary in detail, none deals with two key realities. First, how do decision makers overcome anxiety and gain the confidence to decide? As George (1980) noted, many individuals find it difficult to make big decisions in the face of high uncertainty. Yet such uncertainty is typical of strategic decisions, especially in high-velocity environments. So how do decision makers overcome their natural proclivity to procrastinate, especially when information is limited? Second, how do decision makers maintain decision quality while moving quickly? The existing views rest on the assumption that fast decisions are achieved through a less thorough strategic decision-making process involving limited information, analysis, participation, and conflict. However, as Bourgeois and Eisenhardt (1988) noted, there is pressure for both a rapid and high-quality decision process, especially in high-velocity environments. Is the snap decision process described by existing views realistic?

These questions suggest that extant views may inaccurately describe how executives make rapid

TABLE 1 Descriptions of Microcomputer Firms

Firm	Number of Employees	Number of Informants
Zap	500	7
Forefront	90	7
Promise	185	6
Triumph	150	7
Omicron	192	9
Neutron	200	7
Alpha	50	5
Presidential	462	5

decisions. This observation, coupled with the limited research base on fast strategic decision making, led to the inductive research described in this paper.

Methods

The study used a multiple case design that allowed a replication logic, that is, a series of cases is treated as a series of experiments, each case serving to confirm or disconfirm the inferences drawn from the others (Yin, 1984). Table 1 describes the eight microcomputer firms studied.

The study also employed an embedded design, that is, multiple levels of analysis, focusing on each firm at three levels: (1) top management team, (2) strategic decision, and (3) firm performance. Although an embedded design is complex, it permits induction of rich and reliable models (Yin, 1984).

Data Sources

Members of the research group conducted interviews with every member of the top management team of each firm, including CEOs and their immediate subordinates. The teams typically included the CEO and the heads of such major functions as sales, finance, and engineering.

There were four data sources: (1) initial CEO interviews, (2) semistructured interviews with each member of a firm's top management team,

(3) questionnaires completed by each member of the team, and (4) secondary sources.

CEO Interviews. An entry interview, using a semistructured format, was conducted with the CEO of each firm. The interview began by asking the CEO to describe the firm's competitive strategy. The CEO was then asked to describe the distinctive competencies of the firm, major competitors, and their performance. Each CEO then identified several recent or ongoing major decisions. The decision or decisions to study in depth in subsequent interviews with each member of the top management team were then chosen. The choices were based on criteria similar to those other researchers have used for defining strategic decisions (Hickson et al., 1986; Mintzberg, Raisighani, & Théorêt, 1976).[2] To be chosen, a decision had to (1) involve strategic positioning, (2) have high stakes, (3) involve as many

---

[2]*Ideally, many strategic decisions would have been studied in each firm. However, doing so was almost impossible because strategic decisions are infrequent events. The approach here was to triangulate insights from one or two decisions with evidence on the overall approach to strategic decision making within the firm. The validity of this approach is enhanced by previous research indicating that firms make decisions in a consistent pattern (Fredrickson & Iaquinto, 1987; Miles & Snow, 1978; Nystrom & Starbuck, 1984), even when the top management team experiences turnover in individual positions (Weick, 1979).*

of the functions of the firm as possible, and (4) be considered representative of the process by which major decisions are made at the firm.[3]

Top Manager Interviews.   After the initial CEO interview, semistructured interviews with every executive in the top management team, including the CEO, were conducted. The interview consisted of 16 open-ended questions. Following the methods of inductive research, these questions were supplemented with ones that seemed fruitful to pursue during the interview. The interviews were typically from 90 minutes to two hours long but occasionally took as long as four hours.

The interview began with a request for a description of the firm's competitive strategy. Each executive then described the functional strategy of his or her area, other members of the top management team, the frequency and nature of interaction with each other member of the team, and routine decision-making meetings. Thus, a general view of the strategic decision process within the firm emerged.

In the second portion of the interview, the story of each strategic decision identified in the CEO entry interview was traced. This yielded a view of specific decision processes within the firm. The perspective of every member of the top management team was traced using standard interview questions. The questions concentrated on facts and events, rather than on respondents' interpretations, through the use of courtroom procedure (e.g., When did this first become an issue? What did you do? When?).

Two investigators conducted each interview with one responsible for the interview and the other for taking notes. Immediately after the interview, the investigators cross-checked facts and impressions. Several rules were followed. The "24-hour rule" required that detailed interview notes and impressions be completed within one day of the interview.

A second rule was to include all data, regardless of their apparent importance at the time of the interview. A third rule was to end the interview notes with ongoing impressions of each company.

The combination of multiple informants, courtroom-style questioning, and tandem interviewing addresses some previous criticisms of research relying on executives' recollections (Schwenk, 1985). Moreover, previous research (Huber, 1985; Mintzberg et al., 1976) has indicated high temporal stability in executives' recollection of important decisions, especially for major recent decisions.

Questionnaires.   Quantitative data were gathered from questionnaires. The questions focused on variables, such as conflict and power, suggested by prior research on decision making (e.g. Mintzberg, Raisinghani & Théorêt, 1976; Pfeffer, 1981). The Appendix describes the questions and their administration.

Secondary Source and Other Data.   Industry reports and internal documents were examined as available. Informal observations were made, and data were collected on office locations, team demographics, and financial performance before and after the study. Finally, observations of a day-long strategy-making session in one firm and a weekly executive staff meeting in another were conducted.

Data Analysis

The data were analyzed as follows. For the quantitative data, team level scores of conflict and power were calculated and analyzed for patterns. The qualitative responses were combined using profiles of the decision climates and of each executive from the descriptions each member of the top management teams had given. Traits mentioned by more than one executive were included in the profiles. For example, three of his four colleagues described the president of Alpha as "impatient."[4] This trait was included in his profile, but other traits mentioned by only one person were dropped.

---

[3]*One decision was studied in depth at every firm except Omicron and Triumph. In those two firms, two decisions fit the selection criteria; both were subsequently studied to provide more solid empirical grounding for the propositions.*

[4]*The names used to identify the firms studied are pseudonyms.*

Decision stories were developed by combining the accounts of each executive into a time line that included all events. There was typically high agreement among respondents around the critical issues of when a decision began, when the decision was made, and how it was made. Again using Alpha as an example, the executives all agreed that the impetus for the decision studied was a specific board meeting, that the CEO made the decision alone, and that he did so just before the annual planning conference. Although they were few, conflicting reports were preserved in the stories. These usually concerned one person's assumptions about another's motives or opinions, not observable actions and events.

Once preliminary analyses had been developed from the respective data sets, I combined the analyses and induced propositions using methods for building theory from case studies (Eisenhardt, 1989; Glaser & Strauss, 1967). The search for propositions was assisted by selecting pairs of firms and listing similarities and differences between each pair and by categorizing firms according to variables of interest, such as the presence or absence of a counselor to the CEO. From these lists and comparisons, I induced tentative propositions. After the development of these tentative propositions, each case was revisited to see if the data confirmed the proposed relationship, and if they did, to use the cases to improve understanding of the underlying dynamics. After many iterations between data and propositions, I used existing literature to sharpen the insights yielded by the inductive process. What emerged were propositions linking information, alternatives, advice, conflict resolution, and integration with decision speed and performance. As in deductive research, the propositions fit the evidence but did not perfectly explain the cases (Sutton & Callahan, 1987).

How Are Fast Strategic Decisions Made?

Speed, Planning, and Real-Time Information

Prior research has suggested that comprehensiveness slows the strategic decision-making process (Fredrickson & Mitchell, 1984). Consideration of few alternatives, obtaining inputs from few sources of expertise, and limited analysis shorten the strategic decision process (Janis, 1982; Mintzberg, Raisinghani, & Théorêt, 1976; Nutt, 1976). This perspective implies that the greater the use of information, the slower the strategic decision process.

The data from this research indicate a different view. Executive teams making fast decisions used extensive information—often more information than the slower decision makers used. However, that information was not forecasted information. Rather, it was *real-time information,* especially on a firm's competitive environment and operations. Real-time information is defined as information about a firm's operations or environment for which there is little or no time lag between occurrence and reporting. In formal terms,

Proposition 1: The greater the use of real-time information, the greater the speed of the strategic decision process.

Table 2 summarizes this study's evidence on the speed of decision making. I assessed the overall speed of decision making from interview and story data. These qualitative assessments were corroborated with measurement of the duration of each strategic decision studied. Following prior research (Hickson et al., 1986; Mintzberg, Raisinghani, & Théorêt, 1976). I measured duration using the beginning and end times for each decision, with starting time indicated by the first reference to a deliberate action such as scheduling a meeting or seeking information and ending time indicated by the time at which a commitment to act was made.

As Table 2 indicates, there was high variation in the speed of decision making. The first four firms listed—Zap, Forefront, Promise, and Triumph—made the decisions that were studied in less than four months, and substantial evidence from the interviews and stories corroborated that such a fast pace was typical. For example, most Promise executives mentioned without prompting that they made decisions "quickly," and their making a

TABLE 2   Speed of Strategic Decision Making

Firm	Examples*	Decisions and Key Questions	Decision Durations in Months
Zap	"We try to be the first." (VP, engineering) "If we get bogged down, he [CEO] kicks ass." (VP, marketing) "The worst decision is no decision at all." (CEO)	Alliance: Should we form a strategic alliance or go public?	3
Forefront	"We're aggressive. We make things happen." (Director of marketing) "Big opportunities go by if you don't act quickly." (VP, sales)	New product: Should we develop a new product?	2
Promise	"I like quick decisions." (CEO) "We make decisions fast." (VP, systems development)	Strategy: Do we need a new strategic direction?	4
Triumph	"Decision making at Triumph is much faster." (VP, finance)	Strategy: Do we need a new strategic direction?	1.5
	"He [CEO] listens, makes up his mind, and does it. He's made the decision process shorter." (VP, sales) "Do something, don't just sit around worrying." (CEO)	New product: What should our next product be?	1.5
Omicron	"Slow moving." (VP, manufacturing) "There was a frustrating amount of decorum. Consensus was very important." (VP, sales)	Strategy: Do we need a new strategic direction?	12
		Strategy: What should our new strategy be?	6
	"We did what we intended, but took longer than we should have." (CEO)		
Neutron	"We were late." (VP, finance)	Alliance: Should we form a strategic alliance?	12
Alpha	"We never did anything concentrated . . . no particular dedicated time . . . things kind of evolved." (VP, sales) "We were kind of casting around."	New product: Should we develop an IBM-compatible product?	12
Presidential	"Presidential was unfocused. We weren't concentrated." (EVP) "Lots of arguments—no decisions." (VP, manufacturing) "There was no structure . . . nothing got accomplished." (VP, R&D) "Nothing happened . . . It was so hard to get ideas through." (EVP)	New product: Should we develop a new product?	18

*VP = vice president; EVP = executive vice president

decision on strategic direction in four months is consistent with the data. Throughout this article, those four firms are referred to as fast. The second four firms—Omicron, Neutron, Alpha, and Presidential—spent at least 6 months, and typically more than 12 months, making the decisions that were studied, and the qualitative evidence (see Table 2) corroborated that this slower pace was typical. Thus, I refer to those firms as slow.

Table 3 summarizes the evidence for the use of real-time information, which was assessed by (1) executive responses to interview questions regarding the regular review of performance measures and targets, (2) a count of the number of meetings regularly scheduled to review current operations, (3) the presence of a vice president (VP) of finance—typically the key provider of real-time information in firms like those studied—and (4) the orientation of a firm's CEO toward information. Executives' preferences for various communication media and the use of real-time information in the making of the strategic decisions studied in each firm were also noted.

The data shown in Tables 2 and 3 indicate that fast strategic decision making is associated with extensive use of real-time information. Executives making fast decisions routinely paid close attention to quantitative indicators such as daily and weekly tracking of bookings, scrap, inventory, cash flow, engineering milestones, and competitors' moves. They preferred these operational indicators to more refined accounting data such as profit. These executives averaged 2.5 regularly scheduled operations meetings per week and indicated a preference for real-time communication via face-to-face conversation or electronic mail rather than through time-delayed media like memos.

The Zap case illustrates the linkage between the use of real-time information and decision speed. Zap executives claimed to "measure everything." Without prompting, the CEO described exact targets for gross margin and expenses for R&D, sales, and administration. Executives reviewed bookings daily. Engineering schedules were reviewed weekly. The VP of finance ran a computer model of firm operations weekly. The VP of marketing monitored the environment continuously. As she told us, "I keep an eye on the market [and] funnel the information back." The R&D VP told us that he monitored the technology "grapevine" through his extensive network of friends. Monthly, the executive team reviewed a wide range of quantitative indicators, including revenue per employee, margins, backlog, scrap, cash, and inventory. This is a much more comprehensive set of indicators than the teams making the slower decisions used. Zap's CEO told us: "We have very strong controls. We over-MBA it." Zap executives also reported interacting continually through face-to-face communication and electronic mail. They avoided memos. For example, one executive described her communication with the CEO and several other VPs as "constant." Finally, the decision to forge a strategic alliance that was studied was triggered by the team's cash projection model, which predicted an upcoming cash shortfall. Zap executives made this decision in three months. A Zap executive claimed: "The worst decision is no decision at all."

The Triumph case also indicates the link between use of real-time information and rapid strategic decisions. For example, the first employee hired by the current CEO was a database manager whose job was to track new-product development projects, the lifeblood of microcomputer firms. Firm members described the CEO as "quantitative," and he claimed to "have lists for everything." Interviewees described the weekly staff meetings at Triumph as "a must." One executive said, "No one travels on Mondays." My own visit revealed that the Monday meetings were intense. The day began with a four-hour meeting that "[covered] what's happening this week—what's happening with sales, engineering schedules, and releases." In the afternoon, Triumph executives attended quality assurance and new-product progress meetings. The executives also conducted regular "round table" forums at which lower-level employees gave feedback to senior executives. Triumph executives made the decision on whether to redirect their strategy in six weeks and

TABLE 3   Real-Time Information

Firm	Vice President for Finance?	Routine Quantitative Targets and Measures	Number of Weekly Operations Meetings	CEO's Information Orientation	Examples
Zap	Yes	Cash Bookings Scrap Inventory Margins Revenue/employee Plus others	3	"Numbers guy"	"We have very strong controls. We over-MBA it . . . We measure everything." (CEO)
Forefront	Yes	Bookings Backlog Billings Receivables Customer service Plus others	2	"Short-term focused"	"Any company that is faced with long development can't know how things will evolve. You can only monitor the outside world and direct the evolving strategy at what you see." (VP, finance)
Promise	Yes	Cash Bookings Inventory Cost Plus others	2	"Numbers guy" "Very action-oriented" "Pragmatic"	"We have the constant pulse of how the company is doing." (VP, finance)
Triumph	Yes	Cash Bookings Engineering milestones Sales Quality assurance Plus others	3	"Quantitative" "Focused"	"I keep lists for everything." (CEO)
Omicron	Yes, but an engineer who was "weak" on finance	None mentioned	2	"Visionary" "Detached"	"Our business plan calls for certain business levels, but nothing specific . . . My own [targets] are subjective." (CEO)
Neutron	Yes	None mentioned	1	"Visionary"	"My role is to critique from a detached point of view . . . I protect funds and assets for the board and investors." (VP, finance)
Alpha	Yes	Sales Profit	1	"Always racing"	"We were not getting a lot of information." (VP, manufacturing)
Presidential	No	Sales Profit Gross margin	0	"Visionary" "Detached"	"Management by rambling conversation." (VP, manufacturing)

also made a major product decision in six weeks. One executive advised: "Do something, don't just worry about decisions."

In contrast, there was little mention of real-time information from the teams making the slower decisions. What was mentioned suggested that such information was not particularly germane to their decision processes. For example, the Omicron CEO was asked to describe any quantified targets that he used to track performance. He answered that he did not use quantified targets, saying "My own goals are subjective . . . Integrity is key for me." The VP of finance was an engineer, described as weak in financial matters. Omicron executives pondered whether to change their strategic direction for a year and then spent six more months deciding what their new strategic direction would be. The VP of manufacturing summarized: "We're slow-moving."

The evidence on real-time information use for the other teams making slow decisions is consistent with that at Omicron. For example, Alpha had no weekly operations meetings until several VPs insisted that they were necessary. Presidential had neither weekly operations meetings nor a VP of finance. Firm members described the CEO of Presidential as a "visionary" and as "a little detached from day-to-day operations," and described his key VP as "unfocused." At Neutron, no one mentioned real-time data, although there were stories of largesse such as trips to Hawaii for star design engineers and of the top management team's lack of interest in conserving cash. In these firms, the descriptions indicated that decision making was typically slow, and the durations of the strategic decision processes studied averaged 14 months, compared with 2.8 months at the fast firms.

Why does the use of real-time information quicken the pace of the strategic decision process? One reason may be that such information speeds issue identification, allowing executives to spot problems and opportunities sooner (Dutton & Jackson, 1988). For example, the rationale for the round table forums with lower-level staff at Triumph was "to avoid sudden, surprising, and bad information."

A second reason is more subtle. The literature on artificial intelligence indicates that intuition relies on patterns developed through continual exposure to actual situations (Hayes, 1981; Simon, 1987). If so, executives who attend to real-time information are actually developing their intuition. Aided by intuition, they can react quickly and accurately to changing stimuli in their firm or its environment. Although the data are limited, the CEOs who relied most heavily on real-time information were also most frequently described as being intuitive. For example, the CEO at Zap was known as a "numbers" person and claimed to "over-MBA it," yet he was also the CEO most strongly described as "intuitive," as "a lateral thinker," and as having "the best sense of everything in business"—despite his being the least experienced CEO in the study.

Finally, constant attention to real-time information may allow executive teams to gain experience in responding as a group. The frequent review of real-time information may develop the social routines people need to respond rapidly when pressing situations arise.

Why do the present results fail to support the view that information slows strategic decision making (Fredrickson & Mitchell, 1984; George, 1980; Nutt, 1976)? One reason is that this view does not distinguish planning information from real-time information on competitive environments and firm performance. However, executives do make that distinction. The CEO at Promise said: "I'm a numbers guy, but I'm not heavy on analysis." Zap executives used computer models but called them "pretty elementary." On the other hand, several teams making slow decisions fit the image of information-users as bureaucratic planners (Quinn, 1980). For example, Omicron executives spent about six months developing a forecast of technical trends. Thus, it appears that real-time information, which gives executives intimate knowledge of their business, may speed decision making, but planning information, which attempts to predict the future, does not.

Speed, Timing, and Number of Alternatives

Fredrickson and Mitchell described a comprehensive decision-making process as one that includes being "exhaustive in the generation and evaluation of alternatives" (1984: 402). However, as they and others (Janis, 1982; Vroom & Yetton, 1973) have noted, multiple alternatives are likely to slow the strategic decision process.

In contrast, the data here suggest that faster decision making was associated with more, not fewer, alternatives. Moreover, the sequencing of alternatives was crucial to the pace. Rapid decisions were characterized by simultaneous consideration of multiple alternatives, and the slower decisions were characterized by sequential consideration of fewer alternatives. In formal terms,

Proposition 2: The greater the number of alternatives considered simultaneously, the greater the speed of the strategic decision process.

The overall propensity of a team to use multiple simultaneous alternatives was assessed from the interview and story data. The number of alternatives was quantitatively measured in each decision by recording each unique alternative mentioned by every respondent. I also determined the timing of initiation and discarding of alternatives. Simultaneous alternatives were options that executives considered during at least partially overlapping time periods. Sequential alternatives were considered at times that did not overlap.

As Table 4 indicates, the data suggest that considering multiple simultaneous alternatives was associated with fast decisions. For example, Zap executives typically generated "multiple scenarios." The alliance decision, in which Zap executives considered bank loans, going public, and additional venture capital, in addition to the strategic alliance option, corroborates that finding. Within the strategic alliance option, Zap executives also negotiated simultaneously with several potential alliance partners.

Another example is the decision on strategic redirection at Triumph. The decision makers maintained multiple options, including sale of the firm's proprietary technology, liquidation, a new strategic direction, and tactical changes in the existing strategy, during the decision-making process. Moreover, firm informants described Harry, the CEO of Triumph, as typically retaining multiple options. One executive said, "Harry can live with a lot of ambiguity, a wide range of options . . . Harry likes to have a larger set of options than most people do. He can carry many in his head at once. He thinks it's better if you can work a multiple array of possibilities instead of just a couple."

Several Promise executives claimed that team members usually generated multiple alternatives. One VP described the tactics as follows: (1) proposing a sincere alternative, (2) supporting someone else's alternative even when actually opposing it, and (3) proposing an insincere alternative, one that the proposer did not actually support. The purpose of these tactics was to "aerate" different options.

In contrast, the slower teams usually considered few alternatives and searched for a new alternative only when an old one was no longer feasible. For example, the Alpha top management team considered only one new product option for almost a year. During that time, the CEO worked alone. When the CEO finally made a formal presentation of his alternative, the entire team opposed it. Only then did Alpha executives consider a second alternative. Similarly, the Neutron team moved to an alliance only when in-house product development plans were so delayed as to require an external product source.

Why do the results fail to support the view that consideration of multiple alternatives is time consuming (Fredrickson & Mitchell, 1984; Lindblom, 1959)? One reason is that alternatives are difficult to assess in isolation. For example, it is difficult to buy a car without looking at several cars. As studies of dialectical inquiry and multiple options have indicated (e.g., Anderson, 1983; Schweiger, Sandberg, & Ragan, 1986; Schwenk, 1983), the reason is that the process of comparing alternatives helps decision makers to ascertain the alternatives' strengths and weaknesses and

---

TABLE 4   Alternatives

Firm	Decision	Number of Alternatives	Alternatives	Timing
Zap	Alliance	4	Alliance Public offering Bank loans Venture capital	Simultaneous
Forefront	New product	3	New product Extension of existing product Status quo	Simultaneous
Promise	Strategy	3	Status quo Major strategic shift into new markets and products Minor strategic shift to capitalize on sales opportunities	Simultaneous
Triumph	Strategy	4	Refine current strategy Sell firm's technology Liquidate firm Major strategic shift	Simultaneous
	New product	2	Low-end product Moderate to high-end product	Simultaneous
Omicron	Strategy	2	Major strategic shift Better management of sales and manufacturing	Simultaneous
	Strategy	2	Major strategic shift in distribution Major strategic shift in product and market	Simultaneous
Neutron	Alliance	2	In-house development Alliance	Sequential
Alpha	New product	2	IBM-compatible product Interface product	Sequential
Presidential	New product	2	VLSI[a] product with U.S. partner Licensed product with Japanese partner	Sequential

[a]VLSI = very large scale integrated circuit

---

builds decision makers' confidence that the most viable alternatives have been considered. As one Promise executive stated, "This [considering multiple alternatives] forces us into hypothesis-testing mode."

Second, having simultaneous alternatives reduces the escalation of commitment to any one option (Staw, 1981). Decision makers who pursue multiple options have a lower psychological stake in any one alternative and thus can quickly shift between options if they receive negative information on any alternative. Thus, decision makers who pursue multiple options are less likely to become psychologically trapped and can quickly act on negative information.

Third, simultaneous alternatives provide a fallback position. If one alternative fails, executives can quickly shift to a new one. For example, Zap executives simultaneously pursued negotiation with multiple possible strategic alliance partners, going public, and obtaining bank loans and venture capital. When the "first-choice" alliance partner left the negotiations, the president quickly cut a deal with the second choice. If that deal had failed, the firm had a backup line of credit and was poised to go public. The entire decision process was consummated in three months. In contrast, sequential consideration of alternatives provides no such ready fallback positions. For example, Presidential executives explored one product option for nine months. When that option collapsed, the team had nothing to fall back on, and the decision was delayed another five months while the team searched for a new option.

Finally, the view that multiple alternatives are time consuming does not distinguish between the number of alternatives considered and the depth of analysis. The slow teams spent a great deal of time—but often on only one alternative. For example, Alpha and Presidential executives spent nine months working on single alternatives. In contrast, the fast teams pursued several alternatives, analyzed quickly. According to laboratory studies (e.g., Payne, Bettman, & Johnson, 1988), such a breadth-not-depth decision-making strategy is highly efficient in situations in which time pressure is high.

Speed, Power, and the Role of the Counselor

In addition to the cognitive factors discussed above, political factors may also influence the pace of decisions (Mintzberg, Raisinghani, & Théorêt, 1976; Vroom & Yetton, 1973). For example, Hickson and his colleagues (1986) found that resistance by influential people was a leading cause of delay in making strategic decisions in a sample of British organizations. Alternatively, when few executives are involved, a decision process can be rapid. For example, Vroom and Yetton (1973) advocated autocratic decision making in situations in which speed is essential. From that perspective, centralized power should quicken decision making.

In contrast, the data indicated no pattern linking decision speed to either qualitative or quantitative indicators of power centralization. Some autocrats were fast, but others were slow.[5] However, the process whereby CEOs gathered advice was important. The teams making faster decisions had a two-tier advice process. Their CEOs sought counsel from all members of the top management team, but they focused on obtaining advice from one or two of the firm's most experienced executives, whom I termed "counselors." In contrast, the CEOs whose teams made slow decisions either had no counselor or had a less experienced executive in the counselor role. In formal terms,

Proposition 3: The greater the use of experienced counselors, the greater the speed of the strategic decision process.

Table 5 summarizes the data on counselors. An executive was designated a counselor when (1) team executives explicitly identified the individual as a counselor, adviser, or confidante to the CEO, (2) the description of the interaction between the CEO and the focal executive indicated a companywide, rather than a functional, range of topics, and (3) there was story evidence of the CEO's seeking the counsel of the focal executive in the strategic decision studied. Table 5 also delineates each counselor in terms of age, experience, and personality descriptions provided by other executives.

Every team making rapid strategic decisions had at least one experienced counselor. For example,

---

[5]*Quantitative measures are explained in the Appendix; data are available from the author.*

TABLE 5 Characteristics of Counselors

Firm[a]	Counselors	Evidence[b]	Examples	Age	Description	Experience
Zap	VP, sales	I, S	"I talk a lot with the strongest managers—Bob who knows the outside world, and Jim, who is the best manager." (CEO)	55	"Experienced" "Solid guy"	20 years in the industry. Key sales executive for two prominent firms.
	VP, engineering	I, S		46	"Outstanding" "Savvy"	15 years in the industry. Senior general manager at a top firm.
Forefront	VP, sales	I, S	"My confidante . . . When I talk with Joe, it's often about company issues." (CEO)	48	"Extremely street savvy" "Senior guy" "Doer"	Sales executive in the industry for 15 years. Worked for CEO previously.
Promise	VP, marketing	I	"I talk with Jim about a broader range of issues." (CEO)	39	"Intelligent" "Far-thinking" "Renaissance man"	Cofounder with 12 years in the industry. Worked for CEO previously.
Triumph	Consultant	I, S2	"I offer advice and help and work with Harry on whatever he thinks is important." (consultant)	55	"Very experienced" "First-class manager" "High level of contacts"	Past CEO of two companies. Sits on several boards. Worked with CEO previously.
Omicron	VP, corporate development	I, S1, S2	"I come up with ideas and Jon reacts." (CEO)	33	"Hates to manage" "Quiet" "Bright"	Cofounder. Old friend of CEO. Nonmanager.
	VP, strategic planning	I, S1, S2	"I bounce ideas off Ken." (CEO)	32	"Young, bright" "Loyal"	First-line manufacturing manager.

[a] There was no counselor at Alpha, Presidential, or Neutron.
[b] I = Strong support from interviews, based on evidence from multiple individuals. S = Strong support from stories, based on evidence from multiple individuals. 1 = the first decision studied in a firm and 2 = the second decision.

the CEO at Forefront described the VP of sales as his "confidante." He described their interaction as "more general than just sales," adding "When I talk with Joe it's often about company issues." In the decision studied, this VP triggered the decision by alerting the CEO to a major competitor's entry into the market. He then advised the CEO regarding competitive responses and served as a sounding board for the CEO's ideas.

Frequently, the oldest and most experienced executives filled the counselor role. For example, the counselors at Zap were 10 to 20 years older than most other team members. One counselor, the sales VP, had worked in the microcomputer industry since its inception and had top-level experience at two prominent firms. The other, the VP of engineering, had worked for 15 years at a major computer firm, where he had been a senior general manager. Zap's CEO said: "I seek the advice of Bob [sales], the most knowledgeable about the market, and Jim [engineering], the best manager." Often, counselors were well known to the CEO. For example, at Forefront, Promise, and Triumph, the CEO and counselor had previously worked together. Finally, the counselors frequently were on a career plateau, with their aspirations centering on personal interest. As the VP for sales at Forefront claimed, "I'm not in it for the money. It's fun to build an organization again."

Triumph is a particularly telling illustration. When the CEO joined the firm, no one on the existing team fit the profile of an older, experienced executive. What did the CEO do? He hired a consultant, whom he had known for about 15 years, to fill the counselor role. The 55-year-old consultant had been a CEO, had extensive industry contacts, and had served on several boards. His colleagues described him as "very experienced" and "a first-class manager." Firm informants credited the individual with playing a critical role in developing alternatives in the new-product decision that was studied and with being a sounding board for several executives besides the CEO.

In contrast, the slow teams either did not have counselors (Alpha, Neutron, and Presidential) or

had less experienced executives filling the role (Omicron). For example, one counselor at Omicron was the VP of strategic planning. At 32, he was the youngest executive on the team. His colleagues described him as "bright," but "young." The other counselor, VP for corporate development, was described as "afraid of managing."

Why does an experienced counselor speed decision making? One reason is that the counselor hastens the development of alternatives, providing a quick sounding board for ideas. Also, since counselors are often long-time associates of a CEO and are people whose career aspirations have been met, they are likely to be particularly trustworthy, enabling executives to be very open. Finally, experienced counselors are likely to provide very useful advice.

Second, an experienced counselor can help a team deal with the ambiguity of high-stakes decision making in fast-paced environments. As George noted, "In the face of uncertainty embedded in complex issues executives often find it difficult to act" (1980:37). An experienced confidante can help overcome such barriers by sharing the decision-making effort and relating the decision to past experience. Confidence in a choice is likely to improve when the issues have been discussed with an experienced confidante.

Overall, the results fail to support the view that centralized power accelerates the pace of decision making (Vroom & Yetton, 1973). One reason is that this view neglects the effects of procrastination. People delay because of anxiety, inadequate information, and lack of time. These barriers to decision afflict autocrats as much as collegial executives. In fact, power centralization may exacerbate such barriers by isolating a CEO and creating an information-restrictive political culture (Eisenhardt & Bourgeois, 1988). For example, Alpha's autocratic CEO characteristically worked alone on the new-product decision. Since he worked without help, was burdened with his other duties, and was functioning in the context of a highly political team (Eisenhardt & Bourgeois, 1988), the decision process dragged on for a year.

Thus, power centralization may give a CEO the authority to decide but does not overcome the formidable information and psychological barriers to decision.

Speed, Conflict, and Resolution

Several authors (Hickson et al., 1986; Mintzberg, Raisinghani, & Théorêt, 1976) have argued that conflict influences the length of a decision process. For example, Mintzberg and his colleagues found that conflict created interruptions in the process. Therefore, from this perspective, increasing conflict slows the pace of strategic decisions.

The data indicated no pattern linking decision speed to either the general level of conflict within a team or conflict on the decision studied.[6] However, conflict resolution was crucial. The fast teams actively dealt with conflict, with decision makers resolving it on their own. In contrast, conflict resolution was problematic for the teams making slow decisions. They tended to delay until external events forced a choice. In formal terms,

Proposition 4: The greater the use of active conflict resolution, the greater the speed of the strategic decision process.

Table 6 summarizes the teams' approaches to conflict resolution. I assessed conflict resolution from interview responses indicating each team's usual approach and story data indicating the specific approach taken in the decision studied. Close attention was paid to whether the process was an active one in which decision makers resolved the conflict on their own or a passive one in which decision makers delayed the resolution of conflict until deadlines approached, opponents of an alternative left the team, or external events eliminated competing alternatives.

Every team making fast decisions took an active approach to conflict. In fact, all the fast teams used

the *same* process, termed "consensus with qualification" by a Promise VP. Consensus with qualification is a two-step process. First, a team attempts to reach consensus by involving everyone. If agreement occurs, the choice is made. However, if consensus is not forthcoming, the CEO and, often, the relevant VP make the choice, guided by input from the entire team. Zap's VP for engineering described the process as follows: "Most of the time we reach consensus, but if not, Randy [the CEO] makes the choice."

Forefront's new-product decision illustrates consensus with qualification. The decision generated significant disagreement. Several executives argued that a new product would divert engineering resources from a more innovative one currently in design. Others argued that a new product was necessary to counter the moves of an important competitor. Still others argued that a simple extension of an existing product was the appropriate choice. The team held a series of meetings, and the final decision was made at one such meeting. One VP described the decision as a push for consensus, followed by the CEO's decision. Not all the VPs agreed with the choice. However, as the CEO told us: "The functional heads do the talking . . . I pull the trigger."

In contrast, conflict resolution was problematic in the slow teams. Sometimes, the teams waited for consensus. That behavior was typical at Presidential, where the executives agreed that "we did everything by consensus." Not surprisingly then, Presidential executives sought consensus on the new-product decision that was studied. For a year, debate dragged on over whether they should develop the product with a U.S. partner. A decision was finally reached when several VPs who opposed that proposal left the firm, and that option was the only one still available.

Sometimes, the slow teams waited for deadlines. For example, a deadline—the annual meeting—triggered the Alpha decision. With the meeting less than a month away, the top management

---

[6]*Quantitative measures are in the Appendix; data are available from the author.*

TABLE 6   Conflict Resolution[a]

Firm	Active Consensus with Qualification	Passive		Examples
		Deadlines	Consensus	
Zap	I, S			"It's very open . . . We're successful most of the time in building consensus. Otherwise Randy [CEO] makes the choice." (VP, engineering)
Forefront	I, S			"The functional heads do the talking . . . then I pull the trigger." (CEO)
Promise	I, S			"Quick decisions involving as many people as possible." (CEO)
Triumph	I, S2			"Harry [CEO] just said something like 'this is what I've heard and it makes sense.'" "'We will do . . .' Harry sensed when everyone had said enough and all the points were out." (consultant)
Omicron		S2	I, S1	"Snap decisions where consensus is appropriate and vice versa." (VP, finance)
Neutron	S			
Alpha	S			"Don [CEO] will bring up topics over and over till decisions go his way." (VP, manufacturing)
Presidential			I, S	"We found that operating by consensus essentially gave everyone veto power . . . Nothing got accomplished." (VP, R&D)

[a]I = Strong support from interviews, based on evidence from multiple individuals. S = Strong support from stories, based on evidence from multiple individuals. 1 = the first decision studied in a firm and 2 = the second decision.

team rejected the CEO's first alternative of developing an IBM-compatible product. Team members believed that such a product would stretch R&D and sales resources too thin. Frustrated by this rejection and facing an impending deadline, the CEO came up with a new alternative. Without consultation, he made the choice himself. As he stated, "I said 'to hell with it' and shoved it down their throats."

Omicron executives oscillated between consensus and snap decisions in the face of deadlines. For example, in the first Omicron decision, the team waited for about a year for consensus to emerge. It did emerge only after the VP of marketing, the main opponent of the decision that was finally made, left the firm. The second Omicron decision was triggered by a deadline. The board of directors pressured the team to articulate a strategic direction. The CEO stopped consensus-style meetings, and then met alone with several VPs. Soon after this, he chose a strategic direction on his own. As he described: "One night, I went home after Andy [VP for strategic planning] had been really high on his idea. I slept on it and canned it. I pursued my idea." The CEO's choice was a recent idea that he had never discussed within the firm. One VP claimed: "[We] make snap decisions where developing consensus over time is appropriate and vice versa."

Why is consensus with qualification rapid? One reason is that it copes actively with the conflict common to strategic decisions. It does not involve waiting for outside events, such as executives leaving or deadlines arriving, to trigger decision. Second, it is popular with executives. Most executives want to be involved, but are not anxious to make choices, except in their own areas. For example, one VP at Zap claimed: "I'm happy just to bring it [her views on the alliance] up." This satisfaction limits time-consuming political activity (Eisenhardt & Bourgeois, 1988).

In contrast, other approaches to conflict resolution are often slow. Consensus takes time to develop and may never be achieved since many strategic decisions involve executives who hold honest differences of opinion. Although on occasion a team may reach consensus rapidly, more frequently consensual conflict resolution results in the situation described by a Presidential executive: "We found that operating by consensus essentially gave everyone veto power. There was no structure. No product would ever get out that way. Nothing got accomplished." In fact, many executives dislike the consensual approach. Typical were the comments of an Omicron VP: "I wanted Bill [the CEO] to dictate and not to waste time in meetings to bring consensus. I had more pressing problems to worry about." Waiting for deadlines is also slow because many strategic decisions do not have them. Deadlines, if they occur at all, may arise only after a long period of time, and so many strategic decisions can be postponed indefinitely.

The results have similarities with extant literature. As Gersick's (1988) work would predict, the slow teams accelerated their decision processes in the face of deadlines. However, they did not shift to the process used by fast decision-making teams. Rather, they shifted to the noncomprehensive decision process many authors have described (e.g., Fredrickson & Mitchell, 1984; Lindblom, 1959). For example, the CEO at Alpha made a snap decision to develop an interface product that no one had seriously analyzed. Similarly, the CEO at Omicron chose a strategy that involved major shifts in engineering and marketing but never discussed it within the firm. In those cases, the executives speeded up the process by making snap choices. Although others have described such a noncomprehensive process as fast (Fredrickson & Mitchell, 1984), the evidence here suggests that the approach was embedded in a slow decision process. Thus, noncomprehensive describes the way that slow teams accelerate.

Speed, Fragments, and Decision Integration

The final critical difference between teams making fast and slow strategic decisions lies in the web of relationships among those decisions. The evidence indicates that fast teams attempted to integrate strategic decisions with one another and with tactical plans. In contrast, the teams making slower decisions treated decisions as discrete and even disconnected events. In formal terms,

Proposition 5: The greater the integration among decisions, the greater the speed of the strategic decision process.

Decision integration was assessed using qualitative evidence for teams' usual approaches to decision integration and stories of the specific decisions. Decisions were examined in relation to their integration with past and current strategic decisions and tactical plans like budgets and engineering schedules.

The teams making fast decisions more completely integrated those decisions with other major decisions and with tactical plans. For example, Triumph executives claimed that when they made a major decision, they also developed plans to manage the worst-case outcome. One VP termed this practice "knowing your way out of each decision." During the time of the strategic redirection decision studied, the team members integrated their choice of strategy with a new-product decision, tactical plans for execution, and a worst-case plan to sell firm technology.

The decision began with the arrival of a new CEO. According to firm executives, the CEO spent about two weeks conferring with people throughout the firm. Gradually, he shifted the team's attention to articulation of alternative paths for the firm, including the sale of technology, liquidation, a new strategic direction, and tactical changes to the existing strategy. In the process of developing and choosing among these alternatives, the executives also decided the specifications for a new product, scheduled the timing of three new-product releases, and rebudgeted the entire firm for the coming year. At the end of six weeks, a new strategic direction was set, a new product choice was made, and tactical plans in the form of detailed budgets and engineering schedules were complete.

Similarly, the Zap alliance decision was integrated with other decisions. Although Zap executives chose an alliance to solve their short-term cash problems, they simultaneously addressed future cash needs by planning an initial public offering. The executives made tactical plans for each functional area and set milestones whose arrival would trigger the public offering. Thus, after three months, Zap executives emerged with a plan that coordinated the short-term decision to form an alliance with the long-term decision to make a public offering, tactical plans to execute a public offering, and contingency plans to obtain backup bank credit.

In contrast, the slow teams made decisions in fragments, with little concern for how decisions related to each other or to tactical plans. For example, Presidential executives struggled for over a year deciding whether to develop a new product. Only after the product decision was made did they consider how to integrate the product into their existing product lines. Presidential executives were still trying to decide after a year of deliberation. As one executive said, "We don't have a strategy of what to do with the [product] yet." Because of the delay, the new product still had not produced revenue.

Similarly, Omicron executives reported that they enjoyed thinking about strategic decisions in the abstract, "on a blank sheet of paper." Their approach to the strategic redirection decisions corroborates this view. Omicron executives spent about a year deciding whether to change strategy without any serious consideration of what the new strategy should be. Having made the decision to switch, they then spent another six months choosing the new strategic direction. Specific product choices still had to be made, and as this research concluded, tactical plans, such as changes in engineering priorities and budgets, had not been made. It is striking that, as described above, Triumph executives made a similar decision—and chose a new product, scheduled three product releases, and rebudgeted the firm—in six weeks, compared to the 18 months spent at Omicron on the initial decision.

Why is greater decision integration associated with faster decision making? One reason is that decision integration helps executives to analyze the viability of an alternative more quickly. Second, it helps them to cope with the ambiguity of high-stakes decision making. As the literature on active coping suggests (Gal & Lazarus, 1975), development of concrete ties with other major decisions and decision details may alleviate the anxiety that can plague executives as they face high-stakes decisions. The process of developing specific plans may give executives a better understanding of alternatives and provide feelings of competence and control (Langer, 1975). These in turn produce the confidence to act. Also, such integration may limit discontinuities between decisions. In contrast, lack of decision integration keeps decision making at an abstract level, where anxiety can loom large.

The data, especially those from the slow teams, support this interpretation. For example, one Omicron executive said, "We don't have the confidence to know how to do it [set strategic direction]." Another summarized the prevailing view: "Maybe we saw too much mystery. Maybe we needed more gut. You don't know any more even though you wait."

Why do the results fail to support previous views of decision integration as slow (Fredrickson & Mitchell, 1984; Quinn, 1980)? One reason is that prior research has neglected the effects of concrete planning on actively coping with uncertainty. Second, the prior views were predicated on the idea that executives achieve integration through complex formal planning systems. For example, Quinn noted: "The planning activity often tended to become a bureaucratized, rigid, and costly paper-shuffling exercise" (1980:2). However, the fast decision teams did not integrate decisions using complex systems involving a wide range of integration techniques, consultation with outsiders, or large expenses (Fredrickson & Mitchell, 1984). Rather, they maintained mental maps of how decisions fit together and supplemented those maps with brief plans and action-oriented, operational documents such as budgets and engineering schedules. For example, Promise executives summarized their strategic direction with a three-page statement. Overall, the fast decision-making teams simultaneously kept in mind multiple decisions. In contrast, the slow teams were linear thinkers, treating each decision as a discrete event.

How Does Strategic Decision Speed Link to Performance?

The second research question was: How does the speed of strategic decision relate to performance? Firm performance was assessed by (1) CEOs' numerical self-reports of company effectiveness (0 to 10 scale), (2) a comparison of that rating to ratings CEOs gave to competitors, and (3) sales growth and profitability figures before and after the study. At the decision level, I assessed performance by whether team executives supported a decision after the fact, made similar decisions later, and implemented the decision. Table 7 summarizes these data.

The data support the proposition that faster decision making is associated with better performance. Admittedly, the evidence is tenuous, because performance can depend upon many factors, including those described in earlier studies (Bourgeois & Eisenhardt, 1988; Eisenhardt & Bourgeois, 1988). Also, fast decision making using a different style than shown in these cases might lead to different results. For example, snap decision making by an impulsive CEO might lead to fatal errors. However, the proposition is presented because the performance differences were substantial and the data strongly suggested underlying dynamics that support the relationship. In formal terms,

Proposition 6: The greater the speed of the strategic decision process, the greater the performance in high-velocity environments.

For example, Zap's performance has been spectacular, with sales growing at 25 to 100 percent

TABLE 7 Performance

Firm	Decision Performance	1984 Sales[a]	1983–84 Sales Trend	1984 After-Tax Return on Sales[b]	Examples	1985 Performance[c]
Zap	"I'm happy with the decision." (VP, sales)	50,000	Up	8%	"Right on the money." (VP, sales)	Strong: 50 percent sales increase, initial public offering.
Forefront	"So far, I like what I see." (VP, sales)	30,000	Up	9	"We are right on plan." (president)	Strong: Initial public offering.
Promise	"Yes, I'm happy with the decision. Our strategy is now better articulated." (VP, software)	1,000	Up	−1,280	"Struggling to be great." (VP, finance)	Promising: 500 percent sales increase, losses trimmed.
Triumph	"Sure, I'm happy with the decision. It worked well." (VP, finance)	10,000	Up	−33	"The slope is in the right direction. We have a shot at being a remarkable company." (CEO)	Promising: 50 percent sales increase, break-even profits, initial public offering announced.
Omicron	"I wish it had been done in half the time. Sooner." (VP, corporate development) "Time is passing by." (VP, human relations)	30,000	Flat	−9	"It's put up or shut up time." (VP, human relations)	Turnaround: New CEO hired, 50 percent sales increase, profitability up to 5.9 percent.
Neutron	"We were late." (VP, finance)	30,000	Flat	−31	"Puberty has been rough." (VP, marketing)	Dead: Chapter 11.
Alpha	"The decision was used as a means of group focus." (VP, manufacturing)	10,000	Down	−1	"Disappointing." (VP, operations)	Mixed: Sales dropped 1 percent, profitability up to 3.5 percent.
Presidential	"The only problem was that the decision took too long to make." (EVP)	50,000	Flat	−20	"We didn't bring the technology to market as we should have." (EVP)	Down: Sales dropped 30 percent, continued to lose money.

[a] The sales figures are × $1,000 and rounded to preserve anonymity.
[b] After-tax profits ÷ sales.
[c] This is post-study performance.

per quarter. Zap executives considered the alliance decision to have been successful and have since executed other similar decisions. Forefront's executives also positively evaluated their decision. One stated: "So far, I like what I see." Another said: "The verdict so far is favorable." Forefront has been a strong performer, with sales tripling and after-tax profits running at 9 percent during the year after the study. Similarly, the Triumph and Promise executives assessed their decisions positively. For example, one VP at Promise said, "Yes, I'm happy with the decision. Our strategy is now better articulated." Another at Triumph said, "Sure, I'm happy with the decision. It worked well." At the time of the study, both firms were struggling. Promise was an early venture just getting started, and Triumph had recently replaced its CEO. Since the study, sales at Promise have soared 500 percent, and Triumph has become one of only two survivors in its niche and has announced plans to go public.

By contrast, slow decision making was associated with poor performance. For example, Presidential executives viewed their new product decision as good, but too slow. As one VP told us: "The only problem was that it took too long to make the decision." Another said: "Our products were too late and they were too expensive." As the firm fell behind its competitors, sales tumbled 30 percent in the year after this study, and the firm continued to lose money. The delay at Neutron proved costly as well. The market opportunity was missed, and the firm went bankrupt a year after the study. At Alpha, the executives expressed relief that the CEO's original alternative was shelved. However, the firm continued to drift, with stagnant sales and profits.

Omicron is an interesting case because there was a performance turnaround. During this study, the firm experienced flat sales and mounting losses. Omicron executives attributed much of the problem to the slow decision making of the CEO. As one VP said: "Bill's procrastination caused the problem." But Bill was replaced and, although the data are limited, the new CEO appeared to change the decision process. One VP reported: "Jim [the new CEO] has a different style; he pays more attention to the numbers." Another claimed: "He is not caught in analysis paralysis." Jim was also described by the same adjectives that were used to describe the CEOs of the fast decision teams—"decisive," "operations-focused," "hands-on," and "instinctive." He described others as either fast, indicating approval, or slow, indicating disapproval. Although Jim made several changes that seemed to improve firm performance (Eisenhardt & Bourgeois, 1988), the team agreed that he was "accelerating the decision process." Consistent with the proposition linking decision speed and performance. Omicron attained a 50 percent sales increase and became profitable during Jim's first year as CEO.

Why is slow decision making problematic? One reason may be learning. Executives learn by making decisions, but if they make few decisions, as slow decision makers do, they learn very little. So they are likely to make mistakes. A second reason is that, in fast-paced environments, opportunities move quickly, and once a firm is behind, it is difficult to catch up. The qualitative data were particularly supportive of this point. For example, a Presidential VP said: "We tried to use consensus, but it gave everybody veto power and we ended up doing a random walk. Our products were too late and they were too expensive." Presidential still has not caught its competitors. Neutron executives echoed this view. For example, the VP of finance observed: "The big players [customers and distributors] were already corralled by the competition. We were late." The firm never regained its early momentum and went bankrupt.

In contrast, the strong performers reiterated the importance of keeping pace with the environment. A Promise VP said: "You have to keep up with the train." Zap executives claimed: "If you don't innovate, someone else will." Their CEO argued that the best management training was playing video games, to hone fast decision-making skills. The sales VP at Forefront said: "You've got to catch the big opportunities." An executive at Triumph advised: "Do something, don't just sit around worrying about decisions." This quote may summarize such ideas best: "No advantage is long-term because our industry isn't static. The only competitive advantage is in moving quickly" (VP of finance, Promise).

Toward a Model of the Speed of Strategic Decision Making

This research explored the speed of strategic decision making in a high-velocity environment. Such environments are particularly challenging because information is poor, mistakes are costly, and recovery from missed opportunities is difficult. The findings are a set of propositions depicted in Figure 1. They are organized around three mediating processes.

Several of the propositions focus on how executives making fast decisions accelerate their cognitive processing. For example, these executives immerse themselves in real-time information on their environment and firm operations (Proposition 1). The result is a deep personal knowledge of the enterprise that allows them to access and interpret information rapidly when major decisions arise. In contrast, the slow executives have a less firm grasp on their business. So, when strategic decisions occur, they grope about, try to plan, and have trouble focusing on key information. The executives making fast decisions also use tactics to accelerate analysis of information and alternatives during the decision process. For example, they examine several alternatives simultaneously (Proposition 2). The comparison process speeds their analysis of the strengths and weaknesses of the options. They also gather advice from everyone but focus their attention on the most experienced executives, who are likely to have the most useful advice (Proposition 3). Finally, they integrate key decisions and tactical planning within the decision

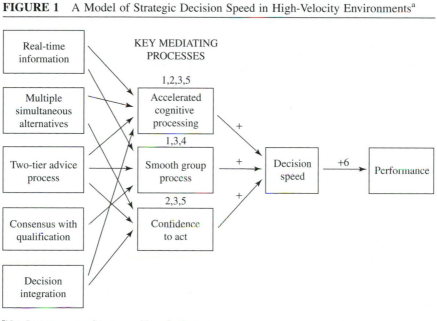

FIGURE 1   A Model of Strategic Decision Speed in High-Velocity Environments[a]

[a]Numbers correspond to propositions in the text.

process (Proposition 5). Doing so quickens executives' assessment of the viability of alternatives. Overall, the executives making fast decisions accelerate their cognitive processing by using efficient problem-solving strategies that maximize information and analysis within time constraints (Hayes, 1981; Payne, Bettman, & Johnson, 1988). These strategies are neither comprehensive nor noncomprehensive, but rather a mix of both.

Second, several of the propositions describe how executives making fast strategic decisions create a smooth group process. For example, constant perusal of real-time information allows executives to rehearse their performance routines with one another (Proposition 1). The result is a team conditioned to work together successfully in turbulent situations. Similarly, although the consensus-with-qualification approach emphasizes the roles of executives in their own areas, it also rests on participation by the entire team (Proposition 4). The data suggest that executives favor this approach. They want a voice but do not necessarily want to make choices, except in their own arenas. Finally, the fast teams use a two-tier advice process (Proposition 3). This advice process emphasizes the role of counselors, but all are consulted and can participate if they choose. In sum, the fast decision makers create a smooth group process through rehearsal and participation. In particular, these behaviors yield fast decisions because they combine participation and decisiveness in a way that is popular with executives.

Several propositions also converge on the importance of confidence in high-stakes decision making. Anxiety can cripple decision makers in such situations (George, 1980). The teams making fast decisions engage in behaviors to cope with this anxiety and build confidence. One tactic is to rely on the counsel of experienced executives, who impart confidence and a sense of stability (Proposition 3). A second tactic is to seek multiple alternatives (Proposition 2). Doing so gives decision makers the confidence that they have sur-

veyed most of the likely options, leaving "no stone unturned." Most important, the fast executives tie together strategic decisions and concrete operating plans (Proposition 5). This attention to day-to-day detail and linkage across major decisions gives a sense of mastery and control that imparts the confidence to act and creates a structure within which action is possible (Gal & Lazarus, 1975; Langer, 1975).

Finally, the findings corroborate an earlier study by Bourgeois and Eisenhardt (1988) linking fast decision making with effective performance (Proposition 6). The findings suggest a configuration of cognitive, political, and emotional processes that is associated with rapid closure on major decisions.

This article began by describing the extant views of fast strategic decision making: That is, strategic decision making is fast when it is more centralized, less comprehensive, and less conflictual. The results fail to support these views. Rather, the findings here suggest that comprehensiveness is not a single construct. Consistent with laboratory studies of decision making under time pressure (Payne, Bettman, & Johnson, 1988), the results suggest that fast decision makers try to be efficient in their use of time. So, they are comprehensive in some ways, but not in others. For example, they seek advice from the best sources but not from everyone, and they develop multiple alternatives but analyze them quickly in comparison. "Noncomprehensive" better describes how slow teams accelerate. The results also differ from the view (Hickson et al., 1986; Mintzberg, Raisinghani, & Théorêt, 1976) that conflict is an important determinant of pace. One reason may be that those authors focused on situations where conflict slowed the pace but not on equally conflictual situations in which conflict was resolved. Thus, they could not observe the essential role of conflict resolution in determining decision speed (Gersick, 1989; Tjosvold, 1985). Finally the centralization view (e.g., Vroom & Yetton, 1973) neglects that autocrats become bogged down by inadequate information, excessive workloads, and anxiety as much as, and perhaps more than, others do.

Conclusions Emerging from a Research Program

This work is part of a larger research program on strategic decision making in high-velocity environments. The initial article (Bourgeois & Eisenhardt, 1988) identified some attributes of successful decision making in this setting. A subsequent article on politics explored one of those attributes: the relationship between a decisive CEO and a powerful executive team (Eisenhardt & Bourgeois, 1988). The present article explores a second attribute: fast strategic decision making. The results link fast decisions to several factors, including the use of real-time information, multiple alternatives, counselors, consensus with qualification, and decision integration.

From this research program, a perspective is beginning to take shape that challenges some traditional thinking about strategic decision making. This emergent view places crucial importance on *top management teams*. Others (Hickson et al., 1986; Mintzberg, Raisinghani, & Théorêt, 1976) have argued that decision characteristics are paramount. The view here is that, although decision characteristics are important, there are recurring interaction patterns among executives that also profoundly influence strategic decision making and, ultimately, firm performance.

Second, this view emphasizes a *complex perspective on cognition*. A rational versus incremental paradigm has dominated the literature on strategic decision making, with the rational model often cast as a straw man (Anderson, 1983; Cyert & March, 1963; Lindblom, 1959; Quinn, 1980). The results of this research program suggest the limitations of that dichotomy. People are boundedly rational but are also capable of engaging in sensible problem-solving strategies to help compensate for their limitations. In this view, interesting research questions center on problem-solving strategies, and results from the artificial intelligence literature may be particularly relevant.

Finally, the emergent perspective highlights *emotion* as integral to high-stakes decision making. The politics article (Eisenhardt & Bourgeois, 1988) indicated that intense emotions such as frustration, distrust, and loyalty shaped organizational politics. Similarly, the present article identifies confidence and anxiety as key factors influencing the pace of decision closure. Thus, the view emerging from this research program is that emotion is critical for understanding strategic decision making.

The current article and the overall research program address the process of strategic decision making, especially in fast-paced, technology-driven environments. The microcomputer industry is admittedly an extreme situation, a setting that places an extraordinary premium on fast, high-quality decision making. However, if the ideas presented here survive empirical tests, they offer lessons for all organizations as they face an increasingly turbulent world.

References

Anderson, P. "Decision Making by Objection and the Cuban Missile Crisis." *Administrative Science Quarterly* 28 (1983), pp. 201–222.

Astley, W. G. *Sources of Power in Organizational Life.* Unpublished doctoral dissertation, University of Washington, Seattle, 1978.

Bell, C. G. "The Mini and Micro Industries." *IEEE Transactions on Computing* 17 (October 1984), pp. 14–29.

Bourgeois, L. J. "Performance and Consensus." *Strategic Management Journal* 1 (1980), pp. 227–248.

Bourgeois, L. J., and Eisenhardt, K. "Strategic Decision Processes in Silicon Valley: The Anatomy of 'Living Dead.'" *California Management Review* 30 (1987), pp. 143–159.

Bourgeois, L. J., and Eisenhardt, K. "Strategic Decision Processes in High Velocity Environments: Four Cases in the Microcomputer Industry." *Management Science* 34 (1988), pp. 816–835.

Dutton. J., and Jackson, S. "Discerning Threats and Opportunities." *Administrative Science Quarterly* 33 (1988), pp. 370–387.

Eisenhardt, K. "Building Theories from Case Study Research." *Academy of Management Review* 14 (1989), in press.

Eisenhardt, K., and Bourgeois, L. J. "Politics of Strategic Decision Making in High-Velocity Environments: Toward a Midrange Theory." *Academy of Management Journal* 31 (1988), pp. 737–770.

Eisenhardt, K., and Bourgeois, L. J. "Charting Strategic Decisions: Profile of an Industry Star." In M. Van Glinow and S. Mohrmann (eds.). *Managing Complexity in High Technology Organizations, Systems, and People.* New York: Oxford University Press, 1989.

Fredrickson. J., and Iaquinto, A. "Incremental Change, Its Correlates, and the Comprehensiveness of Strategic Decision Processes." *Academy of Management Proceedings* (1987), pp. 26–30.

Fredrickson, J., and Mitchell, T. "Strategic Decision Processes: Comprehensiveness and Performance in an Industry with an Unstable Environment." *Academy of Management Journal* 27 (1984), pp. 399–423.

Gal, R., and Lazarus, R. "The Role of Activity in Anticipating and Confronting Stressful Situations." *Journal of Human Stress* 2 (1975), pp. 4–20.

George, A. *Presidential Decision Making in Foreign Policy.* Boulder, CO: Westview Press, 1980.

Gersick, C. "Time and Transition in Work Teams: Toward a New Model of Group Development." *Academy of Management Journal* 31 (1988), pp. 9–41.

Gersick, C. "Marking Time: Predictable Transitions in Task Groups." *Academy of Management Journal* 32 (1989), pp. 274–309.

Glaser, B., and Strauss, A. *The Discovery of Grounded Theory: Strategies for Qualitative Research.* London: Wiedenfeld and Nicholson, 1967.

Hayes, J. *The Complete Problem Solvers.* Philadelphia: Franklin Institute Press, 1981.

Hickson, D., Butler, R., Cray, D. Mallory., G., and Wilson, D. *Top Decisions: Strategic Decision Making in Organizations.* San Francisco: Jossey-Bass, 1986.

Hof, R. "Why Once-Ambitious Computer Firm Quit." *Peninsula Times Tribune,* September 29, 1984, p. B1.

Huber, G. "Temporal Stability and Response-Order Biases in Participant Descriptions of Organizational Decisions." *Academy of Management Journal* 28 (1985), pp. 943–950.

Janis, I. *Victims of Groupthink* (rev. ed.). Boston: Houghton-Mifflin, 1982.

Langer, E. "The Illusion of Control." *Journal of Personality and Social Psychology* 32 (1975), pp. 311–328.

Lindblom, C. "The Science of 'Muddling Through.'" *Public Administration Review* 19 (1959), pp. 79–88.

March, J., and Olsen, J. *Ambiguity and Choice in Organizations.* Bergen, Norway: Universitetsforlaget, 1976.

Miles, R., and Snow, C. *Organizational Strategy, Structure, and Process.* New York: Mc-Graw-Hill, 1978.

Mintzberg, H. "Strategy Making in Three Modes." *California Management Review* 16 (1973), pp. 44–53.

Mintzberg, H., Raisinghani, D., and Théorêt, A. "The Structure of "Unstructured" Decision Processes." *Administrative Science Quarterly* 21 (1976), pp. 246–275.

Nutt, P. "Models for Decision-Making in Organizations and Some Contextual Variables Which Stipulate Optimal Use." *Academy of Management Review* 1 (1976), pp. 147–158.

Nystrom, P., and Starbuck, W. "To Avoid Organizational Crises, Unlearn." *Organizational Dynamics* 12 (Spring, 1984), pp. 53–65.

Payne, J., Bettman, J., and Johnson, E. "Adaptive Strategy Selection in Decision Making." *Journal of Experimental Psychology* 14 (1988), pp. 534–552.

Pfeffer, J. *Power in Organizations.* Marshfield, MA: Pitman, 1981.

Quinn, J. B. *Strategies for Change: Logical Incrementalism.* Homewood, IL: Dow-Jones-Irwin, 1980.

Schweiger, D., Sandberg, W., and Ragan, J. "Group Approaches for Improving Strategic Decision Making: A Comparative Analysis of Dialectical Inquiry, Devil's Advocacy, and Consensus." *Academy of Management Journal* 29 (1986), pp. 51–71.

Schwenk, C. "Laboratory Research on Ill-Structured Decision Aids: The Case of Dialectical Inquiry." *Decision Sciences* 14 (1983), pp. 140–144.

Schwenk, C. "The Use of Participant Recollection in the Modeling of Organizational Decision Processes." *Academy of Management Review* 10 (1985), pp. 496–503.

Simon, H. "Making Management Decisions: The Role of Intuition and Emotion." *Academy of Management Executive* 1 (1987), pp. 57–64.

Staw, B. "The Escalation of Commitment to a Course of Action." *Academy of Management Review* 6 (1981), pp. 577–587.

Staw, B., Sandelands, L., and Dutton, J. "Threat-Rigidity Effects in Organizational Behavior: A Multilevel Analysis." *Administrative Science Quarterly* 26 (1981), pp. 501–524.

Sutton, R., and Callahan, A. "The Stigma of Bankruptcy: Spoiled Organizational Image and its Management." *Academy of Management Journal* 30 (1987), pp. 405–436.

Tjosvold, D. "Implications of Controversy Research for Management." *Journal of Management* 11 (1985), pp. 21–37.

Vroom, V., and Yetton, P. *Leadership and Decision Making.* Pittsburgh, PA: University of Pittsburgh Press, 1973.

Weick, K. *The Social Psychology of Organizing* (2nd ed.). Reading. MA: Addison-Wesley, 1979.

Yin, R. *Case Study Research: Design and Methods.* Beverly Hills: Sage, 1984.

Appendix

Quantitative Measures

Goal Conflict (Bourgeois, 1980). The goal question consisted of a list of 10 organizational goals, introduced by the following instruction: "In the space provided, indicate how important each of these goals is to your firm" (0–10 scale). The goals included long-term profitability, growth, innovation, stock price, company prestige, and community service. Each top management team's standard deviation on each of the goal items was summed.

Policy conflict (Bourgeois, 1980). The questionnaire contained a matrix in which 12 key decision areas ran down one side of the paper and executive titles ran across the top. The text read: "Here is a list of various decision areas which may be of strategic importance to your firm. Please indicate how important each of these decision areas is to the long run health of your firm"

(0 = not at all important, 10 = extremely important). Decision areas were marketing strategies and product pricing, R&D project selection, expansion of production capacity, major financings, and restructuring the organization. The team standard deviation on each of the items was summed.

Interpersonal disagreement (Astley, 1978). Conflict was also measured in terms of interpersonal disagreement. In order to obtain interpersonal disagreement scores for each top management team, each executive was asked to evaluate the frequency of disagreement with each other specific member of the team. The text read: "How often during the process of deliberating, debating, and making policy decisions, have you found yourself in open disagreement with the suggestions or proposals of each of these individuals?" (0 = never, 10 = constantly). The mean score for each executive and then the overall mean for the team were computed.

Power (Astley, 1978). Using the same key-decision-area matrix described above, we asked executives to assign scores to each manager on each decision in terms of how much influence that manager had on the decision (0 = no influence, 10 = very great deal of influence). The text read: "Now, for the same list of decision areas (excepting those scored 0 or 1), indicate how much influence you think each manager has in making decisions concerning that decision area. If the manager has a very great deal of influence over the decision area, give a rating of 10; no influence would score 0; and so on." Computing mean scores that the other respondents assigned to an executive involved three steps: a mean power score for each person on each decision; a mean score for each decision area (R&D, marketing, finance, manufacturing, and organization); and an overall mean.

Case 3–5

DECISION-MAKING EXERCISE (A)

Please read these instructions carefully. They describe the **consensus** method of group decision making. You must utilize this process to develop recommendations for Cyrus Maher, CEO of Waterway Industries (see the following case, "Growing Pains"). *Please remember that this entire exercise must be completed in one hour.*

The consensus method requires the group to engage in a free exchange of ideas and opinions. Everyone contributes to the discussion by presenting logical arguments. The group ultimately develops a set of recommendations that all individuals find acceptable.

Please follow the key steps and process guidelines[1] outlined below:

Key Steps

1. Read "Growing Pains" carefully. Please do not discuss this reading with any other class member.
2. Meet with your assigned group to discuss the case. Each individual should have the opportunity to present their ideas to the other group members. Individuals must support their recommendations with explicitly stated assumptions, facts, and data.
3. The group discusses everyone's arguments in an open and constructive manner.
4. The group strives to achieve consensus, meaning that each member can accept a single set of assumptions and recommendations. This does not mean that everyone must be completely satisfied with the final decision. However, each individual should believe that the assumptions and recommendations comprise a logical and

plausible course of action for Cyrus Maher, CEO of Waterway Industries.
5. Please record the group's final recommendations as well as the supporting assumptions, facts, and data on the Final Recommendations Form (Exhibit 1).
6. Please individually complete the Student Survey (Exhibit 2).

Process Guidelines

- Explain your assumptions and recommendations in a clear and logical manner. Your should attempt to convince others of the merits of your position. However, you should also consider and recognize the merits of others' ideas. Give others ample opportunity to make their case.
- Attempt to avoid treating disagreements as a win–lose proposition. Look for ways to seek common ground or to move beyond the area of disagreement.
- Be quite flexible, but do not change your mind simply to avoid conflict with others.
- Avoid using techniques such as majority voting or coin tosses to resolve disputes. Move the discussion forward by calling for new information, new ideas, and the like.
- Remember that differences of opinion naturally occur in a group decision-making process. Often, these differences can enhance the group's final recommendations.
- Don't be fooled by initial agreement among group members. Make sure that the agreement actually stems from a common rationale.

---

[1]Adapted from Schweiger, Sandberg, and Ragan, "Group Approaches for Improving Strategic Decision Making," Academy of Management Journal 29, no. 1 (1986), pp. 51–71.

This case was prepared by Michael Roberto under the direction of David A. Garvin.

EXHIBIT 1   Final Recommendations Form

<u>Recommendations:</u>

1.

2.

3.

4.

<u>Assumptions:</u>

1.

2.

3.

4.

5.

6.

7.

8.

9.

10.

<u>Key Facts/Data:</u>

1.

2.

3.

4.

5.

6.

7.

8.

9.

10.

EXHIBIT 2   Student Survey

TEAM # _____

Instructions:

Please fill in your team number now. Then mark your responses to the survey using the 1–7 scale shown to the right of each question. 1 represents the response "a very low level" or "very little." 7 represents the response "a very high level" or "a great deal." The entire range of responses is as follows:

1 = very low level/very little   3 = moderately low   5 = moderately high   7 = very high level/great deal
2 = low   4 = moderate   6 = high

Please do not discuss these questions with any other group or class member.

	1 = very low					7 = very high	
1. Rate the quality of the recommendations that the group ultimately made concerning this business situation.	1	2	3	4	5	6	7
2. Rate the quality of the final list of assumptions.	1	2	3	4	5	6	7
3. How many disagreements over different ideas about this decision were there?	1	2	3	4	5	6	7
4. How many differences about the content of this decision did the group have to work through?	1	2	3	4	5	6	7
5. How much personal friction surfaced within the group during the decision-making process?	1	2	3	4	5	6	7
6. How many personality clashes became evident during the decision-making process?	1	2	3	4	5	6	7
7. How much did the group decision-making process make you critically reevaluate the assumptions and recommendations that you initially supported?	1	2	3	4	5	6	7
8. How much did the group decision-making process uncover valid assumptions and recommendations that you and/or others did not initially consider?	1	2	3	4	5	6	7
9. How much did you enjoy working with this group on today's exercise?	1	2	3	4	5	6	7
10. How satisfied are you with the group's final assumptions and recommendations?	1	2	3	4	5	6	7
11. How comfortable would you feel implementing this decision along with other members of this group?	1	2	3	4	5	6	7
12. How welcome did you feel to express opinions freely and to openly disagree with other group members?	1	2	3	4	5	6	7
13. To what extent did the group discourage dissent in the face of an emerging majority opinion?	1	2	3	4	5	6	7
14. To what extent did a leader emerge during the decision-making process?	1	2	3	4	5	6	7

Thank you very much for offering thoughtful responses to this survey.

Note: Questions 1–10 adapted from the following sources:
Schweiger, Sandberg, and Ragan, "Group Approaches for Improving Strategic Decision Making," *Academy of Management Journal* 29, no. 1 (1986), pp. 51–71.
Amason, "Distinguishing the Effects of Functional and Dysfunctional Conflict on Strategic Decision Making," *Academy of Management Journal* 39, no. 1 (1996), pp. 123–148.

Case 3–6

GROWING PAINS

Robert D. Nicoson

"I'm challenged and motivated where I am, and I like the company. You know that. But I've got to say I'm interested in the opportunity you're describing because of the money and the equity position. For those reasons alone, it's tough to pass by. Let me think about it some more and call you in the morning. Thanks, Les."

That was the extent of the conversation Cyrus Maher, CEO of Waterway Industries, overheard when he came around the corner just outside of Lee Carter's office. She must have been talking with Les Finch, Maher thought. Here's trouble.

Of course, it didn't necessarily mean anything, Maher told himself as he passed the office, waving to Carter. Finch, a well-connected marketing consultant, had been the matchmaker between Carter and Waterway Industries to begin with. With the company in the fourth quarter of its best year ever, he certainly wouldn't be encouraging her to leave. Would he?

Maher got a cup of coffee in the company's first floor kitchenette and deliberately took the long way back to his office, through the design room. As always, the atmosphere was upbeat, but these days he also thought he could detect a sense of purpose that had never before been a part of Waterway's organization.

Founded in 1963 in Lake Placid, New York, Waterway had started out as a small, high-quality canoe maker. Over the years, it had built a good reputation all through the Northeast and had acquired a base of customers in the Pacific Northwest as well. By 1982, Waterway was comfortably ensconced in the canoe market nationwide, and it had maintained a steady growth right up until 1990. Then, at the insistence of a friend who was the head of a major dealer and expedition company, Maher had decided to venture into kayaks. His friend had said that kayaks were the next big trend and that Maher would be a fool not to sign on.

Maher had done some checking and found the prospects promising. So by the end of 1992, Waterway had begun selling its own line of compact, inexpensive, high-impact plastic kayaks. Within one quarter, Maher had known that the move had been a smart one. Almost all of Waterway's existing canoe customers—mostly wholesalers who then sold to liveries and sporting goods stores—had placed sizable kayak orders. A number of private-label entities had also inquired about Waterway, and Maher was considering producing private-label kayaks for those companies on a limited basis.

For the most part, the staff had adjusted easily to the company's faster pace. The expanded business hadn't changed Waterway's informal work style, and people seemed to appreciate that. Maher knew that most of his employees were avid outdoor types who viewed their jobs as a means to an end, and he respected that perspective. On days when the weather was particularly good, he knew that the building would be pretty empty by 4 P.M. But he also knew that his employees liked their jobs. Work was always completed on time, and people were outspoken with new ideas and with suggestions for improving current designs and processes. There was no mistaking the genuine camaraderie.

Maher walked through the design room, stopping to talk with one of the two designers and to admire the latest drawings. Then he headed for the administrative suite. His thoughts returned to the company's recent history. Until 1990, Waterway's sales and revenues had increased with the market, and Maher hadn't been motivated to push any harder. But when he had decided to venture into kayaking, he also had thought he should gear up marketing—get ready for the big trend if it came. Until then, there had never been a formal, structured marketing department at Waterway. He had thought it was time. That's why he had hired Lee Carter.

Carter had gotten her MBA when she was 31. To do so, she had left a fast-track position in sales at Waterway's major competitor in the canoe market to devote her full attention to her studies. Finch, who was something of a mentor for Carter, had told her that she would hit the ceiling too early in her career if she didn't have the credentials to compete in her field.

In her final term at business school, which had included a full course load plus a demanding internship with the Small Business Administration, Carter had interviewed with Waterway. Finch had called to introduce her, but once Maher had met her and she had begun to outline the ways in which she could improve the company's sales and marketing efforts, Maher had needed no other references. He had thought from the start that Carter might be the right person to nurture the company's interest in the growing kayaking business and to run with it if the sport's popularity really took off.

When it had, he was proved right. True, the market was extremely favorable, but Carter had brought in more orders than even Maher had thought possible. Fortunately, the company had been able to keep up by contracting with other manufacturing companies for more product. Waterway had been extremely effective in keeping inventory in line with customer demand.

Maher was impressed with Carter's performance. From day one, she had been completely focused. She traveled constantly—worked so hard that she barely had time to get to know the staff. She came in on weekends to catch up with paperwork. Along with two of her direct reports, she had even missed the annual Waterway picnic; the three had been on the road, nailing down a large order. It was a dedication—a level of energy—that Maher had never seen before, and he liked what it said about his company.

Back in his office, Maher found that he couldn't concentrate on the product development report in front of him. That bit of conversation he had overheard outside Carter's office was troubling.

He certainly knew about the lucrative packages that were being offered in the sporting goods industry—even in Waterway's niche. He'd even heard that some sales managers were commanding a quarter of a million dollars or more. He had read enough of the annual reports of his publicly traded competitors to know that larger organizations created all sorts of elaborate systems—supplemental retirement packages, golden handcuffs, stock options, deferred compensation arrangements—to hold on to their top performers.

Maher wanted to recognize Carter's contribution. She had been extremely successful in opening new sales channels, and she was personally responsible for 40 percent of the company's sales for the last two years. Before Carter, the majority of sales had come through the independent reps and distributors. The sales network had grown informally, and Maher had never really tracked it or thought much about building a sales force or developing a formal distribution plan. Those were areas he wanted Carter to concentrate on as director of marketing, but right now she really had her hands full because business was booming.

He thought about the rest of the company. Waterway employed 45 people. Turnover was low; there was hardly ever any grumbling from the ranks. Recently, though, both of his designers had approached him—independently of each other—to request salary adjustments. They had been looking for equity in the company—a cut of the profits if their designs did well. Maher had rejected the proposals but had given the more senior of the two a modest raise and an extra week's vacation and had increased the bonuses of both. They had seemed happy with their new arrangements.

Then there was his former CFO, Chris Papadopoulos, who had left last year to take a position with a power boat manufacturer in Florida. Papadopoulos had twice requested that Maher redesign his compensation package to include equity, and because Maher hadn't been persuaded, Papadopoulos had left for a better job. Waterway's current CFO seemed perfectly content with a base salary and bonus.

The phone rang, jolting Maher out of his thoughts. It was Pat Mason, his assistant, reminding him that his flight to the Watergear Association meeting in Seattle would leave in three hours and that he had things to do before he left.

What Is Fair Pay?

Upon arrival at SeaTac Airport, Maher met up with Bryce Holmes, president of Emerald Rafting. Holmes had been a trusted colleague since Maher had entered the business. The two ran into each other frequently at industry and trade shows and tried to get together for a meal at association meetings whenever they could. They took a cab to a seafood restaurant near the Bainbridge Island ferry landing. As always, the conversation centered on the industry.

"Let me ask you this," Maher said, as the waiter served his salmon in white wine and caper sauce. "Do you think that we have to pay our new marketing people more than the industry standard? I mean, when is too much, too much? And who determines the standard anyway? I'd hate to think I would lose a really great marketing manager, but I don't know what to do."

Holmes nodded. "It's tough, because in today's business climate, marketers aren't loyal to one particular industry. Your marketing person would probably be just as happy working in the health club field or for a top-of-the-line jewelry company.

Or in speedboats, for that matter. Or at a phone company. God help you if she gets an offer from the telecommunications industry. The skill is transferable—people go where the money is. And you, my friend, have a reputation for a tight wallet."

He said it with a smile, but Maher still grimaced in response. He mentally reviewed his payroll. Professional staffers received a salary and a year-end bonus—10 percent to 15 percent of their pay. The controller made $65,000. The office administration manager was pulling $39,000. One designer received $48,000; the other $53,000. Maher himself took $150,000 annually, with a bonus if the company had a good year. And he was paying Carter $51,000 plus a yearly bonus of between $15,000 and $19,000, to make up for not paying a commission on her sales.

"I know the business could stand to pay more," Maher said, "but I don't want to get into the habit of paying now for results down the road. Too many people have gotten into trouble that way."

Holmes held up a warning hand. "I'm just telling you," he said, "that this is something we're all struggling with. I don't want to have to increase compensation costs for the people who seem satisfied now, either. You take someone who is making 60K a year, and you bump them to 85 with a package deal because they get wind of another offer, and what do you have? Not someone who is satisfied, that's for sure. You have someone who doesn't trust you anymore because they thought you were being fair at 60 and evidently you weren't. So now they think they can't trust you at 85. You see what I'm getting at?"

Holmes continued. "We're actually thinking of outsourcing marketing and sales. I'd guess that our pay scales aren't much higher than yours, and it seems that all we've been doing for the last two years is training employees for other companies. And although I shouldn't say this, my friend, I feel that I have to: The rumor mill says that Lee Carter is being tempted to leave Waterway even as we speak."

Maher nodded. "I know that. But, frankly, I'm not sure what to do about it."

More Money, More Growth?

Back in Lake Placid the following Tuesday, Maher had an appointment with Kate Travis, head of the commercial lending department at CenterTrust. Waterway had been doing its banking with Center-Trust for years. Travis showed Maher into her office and got out the company file.

"It looks as though kayaking really did take off," she said, studying the most recent report. "Based on your interim financials, you seem to be on target with your projections. Now, as I understand it, this additional line of credit would be to cover you for accounts receivable, is that correct?"

Maher nodded. "The sales are even better than we had anticipated," he said. "We're outsourcing to a certain extent, but we would also like to gear up production in-house. The increased credit would also give me a chance to look at the forest instead of the trees, if you will."

Travis took notes as they spoke. "Tell me a little bit about your sales," she asked. "What enabled you to do this well? Sales seem to be ahead of your projections."

"In a word, Lee Carter. She's our new marketing department, to put it simply. She's the best hiring decision I've ever made. The market has been agreeable, of course, but without Carter, we wouldn't have been able to take advantage of it."

"I did note that your operating expenses are higher than you had anticipated. Travel and entertainment, in particular."

"A natural outgrowth of our new marketing strategy," Maher said.

Travis continued. "You're also paying out more commissions to your reps and distributors than you ever have before. Now, I know that you have limited your exposure on some costs by outsourcing the manufacturing of certain boat models, but I really think . . ."

"We've also used consultants and temporary employees to handle short-term back-office and accounting support."

"Yes. I wonder if there isn't some more you can do along those lines before reaching for additional credit. Have you analyzed the increase in your sales and marketing costs?"

The two spoke for more than a half an hour, then Travis closed the meeting. "I'll get back in touch with you," she said.

Late that afternoon, Maher tried to finish up the short speech he was planning to deliver at the local Rotary meeting that evening. He couldn't concentrate. His conversation with Travis had raised some doubts in his mind about redesigning Carter's compensation package. With the new line of credit, would he be spreading himself too thin? Suppose he offered Carter a commission arrangement. That might keep her from taking any of those offers being waved in her face right now. But she *would* leave when the kayak boom eventually played out—unless by then Waterway was already pursuing the next hot product market. At the moment, Maher had no idea what that product would be. Chasing fad markets hadn't ever been part of his plan, and although his foray into kayaks was working well for the time being, he had never thought until now that the cutting edge was where he wanted Waterway to be.

Should Maher give his star performer star rewards—or risk her leaving?

Six Experts Weigh Human Resource Strategies

James McCann, 1-800-Flowers.[1]   Top executives usually don't have the luxury of a clear vision of the future, and Cyrus Maher is no exception. He may not realize it right now, but Maher is at a moment of truth as far as Waterway Industries is concerned. Whatever decisions he makes in the next few days will determine the kind of company he'll be governing over the long term.

Frankly, it's a wonderful position to be in. Maher may decide that he wants to run a sleepy little company—that he doesn't want any more pressure,

---

[1]*James McCann is the founder and president of 1-800-FLOWERS, based in Westbury, New York.*

doesn't want the gun to his head all the time—and that's fine. Or he may decide that he wants to go forward and grow aggressively. That's fine, too. Maher is a lucky man. In some industries, he wouldn't have such choices. The market would demand that he grow the company, sell it, or fold. Here, it is largely up to him what happens to his career and to his company.

But Maher does not have unlimited time in which to make his decision. In fact, if he doesn't act soon, his inaction, his employees, and the market will decide the future course of Waterways for him. He is doing the right things—asking colleagues and friends what they think of his strategy, management style, and market position—but he needs to do the right things a little faster, with a decision point in mind.

Going forward is a little scarier than going backward, but I suspect that Maher wouldn't be happy if Waterways returned to the sleepy little company it once was. So for the purposes of discussion, let's say that he decides to grow the company. In such a scenario, the most important thing for him to keep in mind is that he is, first and foremost, a cultural engineer. Every action he takes will affect the culture of the company, and it's up to him to create and maintain the kind of culture he wants to have.

Take his compensation plan—the most immediate critical item he must face once he commits to moving ahead. The kind of pay plans that most people considered normal in the past—base salaries with annual step increases in pay across the board—don't exist anymore. We're part of a new entrepreneurial environment, and the old rules don't apply. It is increasingly more acceptable to receive equity as part of a compensation package, depending on your level. And that equity is often in lieu of more generous cash compensation. It's also socially acceptable—and increasingly common—to be a hired gun, a specialist brought in at a higher rate for a single purpose. Maher needs to address this new environment when he makes a decision about Lee Carter's arrangement. But that doesn't mean he needs to create the same kind of compensation package for all his other employees.

Maher should take what I call the "Neon Deion" approach (after star National Football League player Deion Sanders). Jerry Jones, owner of the Dallas Cowboys, knows that his core team members are important, and he values them. But he also makes them understand that in order for the organization to be successful, he has to buy one extra ingredient, the hired gun, the star cornerback. He has to make two points clear: first, that he knows that the extra ingredient costs more because of market demands; second, that paying the extra money for Sanders doesn't mean he doesn't value the core.

Maher has to develop an understanding of what his people want. Carter and the two designers may want equity in the company, but that doesn't mean that everyone is going to want it. What good is equity if you want to buy a house and you need a mortgage?

I'd like to see Waterway take the cafeteria approach to compensation—at least until the company settles into its new pace. That is, I'd like to see Maher offering a variety of options to his employees. He can pay a base salary—as set by industry and community standards. And then he can offer extras based on how the company does. Those extras can take the form of equity or cash, depending on what individual employees value more highly.

Regardless of whether Maher decides to grow Waterway or take it gradually back down to the kind of company it used to be, he must talk to Carter as soon as he has made the decision. In fact, that's another reason for deciding fast. Carter will be coming to talk to him sooner rather than later, and if he beats her to the punch, he'll be in a much better position to get some honest feedback and support from her.

Maher should realize that Carter, being on the road almost all the time, is probably suffering from the road warrior blues. When people are working tremendously hard and traveling constantly, they can feel euphoric. At 1-800-FLOWERS, we feel that way during the flower holidays—our busiest times. But when the rush is over, it is normal to be exhausted and a little blue. When Carter is at her home office, she may be thinking, "Am I really appreciated? Does anyone care that I work so hard?" If she is unable to answer those questions with a yes, it is only a matter of time before she accepts an offer from another company.

Maher needs to get to her before that happens and show her that he is willing to create the kind of social structure that she needs in order to feel accepted—whether she is the key to Waterway's growth or simply a good marketing executive riding a trend. If she's too busy to attend the company picnic, he needs to find another way for the company to get to know her better. She needs to know that the company is cheering for her, not resentful of her or simply ignorant of her activities. She'll be able to help Maher figure this out; it's pretty clear that she likes the company and would prefer to stay there. But if he doesn't let her know that he understands her position and wants to make everything work out, she will accept another offer.

Right now, Waterway is on the verge of enjoying its 15 minutes of fame. My own company is in the middle of that 15 minutes, and although I can tell you that it is tremendously exciting, it is not impressive in and of itself. What will impress *me* is if I'm still being tapped for speaking and writing engagements in 10 years—if 1-800-FLOWERS has created a culture that maintains the excitement and commitment we currently have. Maher should strive for similar goals. He's in a good position now, but regardless of the path he chooses, what matters is the foundation he creates for the future.

Kay Henry, Mad River Canoe.[2] Maher needs Carter at the moment for one very simple reason: He doesn't have anyone to replace her. From a long-term perspective, he is unlikely to keep Carter. His business is more about lifestyle choice and a love of the product than it is about money, and Carter doesn't seem to be in love with the lifestyle or the products that Waterway can offer. But for the short term, I think Maher will be able to hold her if he

changes her compensation package, perhaps by offering her a commission arrangement.

Carter is the only semblance of organized marketing that Waterway has ever seen. Maher should take advantage of her energy while she's there. But he shouldn't let her continue to focus solely on sales. Her performance has been great, but what he really needs is for her to build a marketing department and work on a marketing strategy. I'm amazed that the company has gotten this far without a formal marketing plan; it certainly won't be able to get much further without one. Too much has happened too fast for the company to continue to play marketing by ear.

Before Carter develops a marketing plan, however, Maher should really do some hard thinking about where he wants the company to go. If he does want to pursue other trendy product lines, he may have to bring in a partner or give employees a stake in the company. That would be a big change for him, but to be honest, I don't think that he has the stamina to lead the company into aggressive growth by himself. He just doesn't seem to be the type; I certainly can't picture him missing a company picnic! For that reason, I think he should also consider pulling back and taking the company small again. Is growth what he really wants, or is he just fascinated by something new that won't make him happy over the long term?

He should work closely with Carter as she builds the marketing department. If she builds a team that suits her and then leaves to pursue a fast-paced career in software sales, he may find himself at odds with the personalities she has assembled. Right now, Carter's energetic style is intriguing. But if it simply isn't Maher, then he will have a hard time living and working with it over time.

For now, I don't think that Maher should worry too much about giving equity stakes to his employees across the board. Offering his designers a royalty arrangement is probably a good idea, but equity stakes would be a big jump for him, and they might not crack up to be all that the employees think they should be. Waterway is not an unusual example of a small, focused sporting goods

---

[2]*Kay Henry is the president of Mad River Canoe, a company based in Waitsfield, Vermont.*

company. Employees don't have to be part of the business by owning stock. They are a part of the business because they enjoy the lifestyle it offers them and because they take pride in the kinds of products they make—and the kinds of experiences that the products make possible for customers.

What Maher needs to do is to remind his employees of that fact. They have an excellent culture right now. They have benefits that other, fast-paced companies cannot offer. If equity offerings are tied up with growing the company, then the culture will inevitably change—and fast.

Of course, Maher may eventually decide to offer equity anyway, but in a different context. Over the next few years, he should be thinking about retiring. With the exception of Carter (who is a star, but probably not a good fit), he seems to have assembled a group of people who are not only bright but also devoted to the water-sports business. If he gets these people to invest in the company and to take it forward with a clear vision in mind, he will have left a legacy to be proud of.

Myra Hart, Staples.[3]   For Maher, trying to resolve salary, bonus, equity, and profit-sharing issues without testing his own assumptions about Waterway would rank somewhere between foolhardy and disastrous. First, he needs to review his company's history and think hard about his goals.

When he began the business in 1963, Maher had a set of product, profitability, and personal lifestyle objectives. Building a quality canoe was most likely a choice that grew out of a love of canoeing, a unique knowledge of the requisite performance criteria, and a vision of design and manufacturing processes that could deliver a superior product. It took him nearly 20 years to build Waterway's brand franchise, and once he achieved that, he let the industry set the pace of the company's growth. He was not particularly aggressive in the canoe market, nor did he explore related opportunities. He

---

[3]*Myra Hart is a founder of Staples, based in Framingham, Massachusetts, and an assistant professor at the Harvard Business School in Boston, Massachusetts.*

seemed content with business as usual and time left over for play.

What changed? How much of his 1990 expansion into kayaks was a conscious decision to seek new opportunity? How much was prompted by a perceived slackening in canoes? Was he becoming bored with the status quo or simply responding to a dealer's request? Did he have any idea of the challenges that he might face if the business experienced a serious change of pace?

If Maher is satisfied that growth was—and still is—the right decision, then he needs to go on to the next set of questions: Was the choice of the kayak business the best way to achieve growth? How well is it working? The kayak line seemed logical at the time he first considered it, and four years later, the strategy seems to have proved its value. But does Maher have a clear understanding of how kayak sales may be affecting his canoe business? Is there synergy between the product lines, or does the fact that sales are being made to the same customer base suggest that there may be some erosion of the canoe sales? How many new outlets have been added to the Waterway roster? At what cost? How healthy are the margins?

Has Maher considered any nonfinancial costs brought about by the introduction of the kayak line? If Carter is personally capturing 40 percent of the new sales, is she crowding out the existing sales network, possibly eroding their interest in the canoe line or driving up the sales commission they demand for handling the smaller accounts?

What about the manufacturing side of the business? So far, Maher has dealt with increased demand by outsourcing some of the production, but he is currently thinking about expanding Waterway's capacity and taking on some private-label manufacturing. Further, he is looking ahead to the day when the kayak business slackens and wondering what the next hot product will be. Can he really have thought through the ramifications of increased fixed costs and contract manufacturing when he is unsure of future demand?

If, after a careful analysis, Maher finds that he is still committed to continuing his growth strategy, he needs to review how well the organization has adapted to growth to date and where it is showing signs of stress. There are some indicators that the implicit work/play contract may be changing and, with it, the perception that the compensation is fair. The designers may believe that they are contributing more to the company's bottom line now and that they should share in the profits. Whether they have expanded their skill sets or have simply found themselves in more demand in a more competitive industry, some Waterway employees believe that they are worth more now. It may be that they have better information and are making comparisons across the industry but are not accounting for some of the perks that they still get. Maher needs to do some homework to understand what is behind the requests for compensation adjustments.

If he concludes that some change in the Waterway compensation package is appropriate, Maher needs to consider the organizational implications. Changes made as an exception for one member of the staff will be perceived as inequitable and eventually will be divisive. Maher seems to know this, but he also seems unsure of which alternative— higher base pay, commissions, equity across the board—he should pursue. His employees' proposals to increase base pay and to participate in equity ownership are merely their approximations of fair compensation and of how to participate in the business's growth. The suggestions need not be taken literally.

I would advise Maher to think twice before offering equity to anyone. Although often considered a panacea for aligning employees' and owners' interests, it may fall far short of Waterway employees' expectations and cause substantial headaches for Maher.

Since Maher has not given any indication that he is considering a sale of the business in either the public or private markets, there is no obvious way for an employee to extract equity value from the company at will. And even if Maher were to offer equity, a growth strategy would demand reinvestment in the company rather than distribution of profits to shareholders. His employees would prob-

ably be frustrated with their lack of liquidity and the long delay in sharing profits.

For his part, Maher might be equally frustrated by the challenges of sharing ownership in his privately held company. Among those challenges would be setting and adjusting prices or valuation for shares to be distributed. If Maher opts to set up a stock repurchase plan for departing employees, he may actually provide an incentive to leave rather than to stay. He could also be very frustrated by having minority shareholders who want a voice in decision making. On a more technical note, if Waterway is a Subchapter S Corporation, Maher will be forced to choose between limiting the number of shareholders to 35 or changing the legal form of the organization.

A profit-sharing plan for the existing private company can achieve the goals of the employees more simply and will allow them to reap rewards as they are earned. Some form of bonus plan that recognizes and rewards individual achievements can be coupled with profit sharing to provide a blended compensation package. As for base pay, Maher needs to look at trends in his industry and be sure that the package he is offering is equitable. He should consider all the benefits Waterway provides, including time off for kayaking and canoeing as well as more tangible benefits. Finally, he needs to factor cost-of-living adjustments into his plan. Waterway is still a small business in an upstate New York community that appears to draw primarily on the local population for its employees. It does not appear that base pay is far off the mark, but there is a need to provide incentives and rewards for employees willing and able to make the changes that growth demands.

When Maher is comfortable with the appropriate salary and benefit ranges for the various positions, he should run through the financial implications for the business. Once he has done his own reality check on the anticipated adjustment, he should involve his employees in the process. Allowing key employees to consider acceptable options and make recommendations may be enormously helpful. (Actually, although the issue of succession planning wasn't mentioned in the case study, Maher better be thinking hard about that, too. If he has been with the company since the early 1960s, he should be thinking about when and how he plans to retire. Is there a likely successor currently working for Waterway? If so, shouldn't that person have input into the decisions Maher is facing?)

Maher needs to weigh whether or not Lee Carter should be at the top of the list of Waterway's key employees. Carter was brought in to manage marketing, but so far, she seems to have spent very little time building a marketing organization. She has fallen back on her old skills as a salesperson and has spent the majority of her time on the road. In fact, she and her two assistants have not spent much time acclimating to the existing Waterway culture, let alone trying to develop new systems. Carter would probably be far more effective if she got off the road at least two or three days a week and began working on marketing plans and sales force management.

Carter's loss to another organization, whether to a direct competitor or to a company in another industry, would have an immediate impact on Waterway's sales. However, the relationships with the wholesalers are in place, and there is a network of independent sales reps who could service most of her accounts if she left. (As an aside, my own instinct would have been to talk with Carter and let her know that I had inadvertently overheard her conversation. Such a course would have had the advantage of allowing me to assess the intensity of the immediate threat and to determine how much urgency was required. It would certainly have provided some valuable information and probably would have bought me some time if Carter wasn't actually planning to leave. But such action doesn't seem to fit in with Maher's personal style.)

Maher has done a lot of thinking and has talked with trusted colleagues and advisors. With a review of his objectives, an understanding of current strengths and weaknesses, a clearer picture of where he wants to take Waterway, and a realistic appraisal of his current staff, he'll be ready to make some decisions. Then he can sit down with Carter and find out how and where she wants to fit in.

Ronald Rudolph and Bruce Schlegel, 3Com. [4]

Maher has gotten himself into a potential no-win situation because he lacks a clear business strategy. A company's business strategy should drive its compensation plan, and in the absence of either, Maher has been forced to react emotionally and inconsistently to employees' demands. He has already lost at least one senior manager that we know of, and he runs a great risk of having more key people lured away to greener pastures. Unfortunately, Maher's situation will only get worse if he chooses to pursue new markets and accelerated growth—unless he gets a handle on exactly what he wants the new Waterway to look like and makes a couple of important decisions accordingly.

The successful compensation and rewards techniques that Maher used in the past, when Waterway was enjoying steady but modest growth, are less successful in a fast-growth environment. It's no surprise that the traditional Waterway employee, who treasures the informality and camaraderie of the organization, is demanding to share in the tangible rewards of the more successful company. And the kinds of new employees that Waterway may need for future success—people with special advanced business skills, who may not necessarily share a love of the outdoors or a passion for Waterway's products—are certainly not going to be happy with outmoded compensation offerings.

If Maher wants to pursue Waterway's opportunity for accelerated growth, he needs a formal compensation philosophy and strategy—based on his business plan—to serve as an anchor for making compensation decisions in the new environment. Having said that, we should point out that Maher is not necessarily faced with an all-or-nothing scenario. He does not have to change his company's culture completely in order to succeed. Answering the following questions may help him figure out what needs to change and what needs to stay the same.

---

[4]*Ronald Rudolph is the director of human resources at 3Com Corporation in Santa Clara, California, and Bruce Schlegel is the director of compensation and benefits there.*

Where does Maher want to position the company in the market? One option would be to adopt a market-priced philosophy to let the marketplace determine the value of a particular set of skills. The market may value design skills in the new or so-called fad product areas much more highly than it does those related to older products. With a market-priced philosophy and a stated business goal of expanding quickly into new markets with cutting-edge products, Waterway would compensate at or above the competition to get and retain top design talent. Another option would be to price jobs under competitive rates, with the stated goal of attracting and retaining talented people who value a flexible work environment that encourages outdoor pursuits.

How should noncash compensation and rewards fit into Waterway's business strategy? Noncash rewards are a key component of a successful compensation strategy regardless of whether Maher sets pay at or below the market rate. But they are especially critical if he goes with the latter approach. If a high-growth company decides to pay below market rate, it must reward employees in some other tangible way for their contributions to company success. Profit sharing is one alternative. Another, easier way to keep people committed and use no cash (bankers love this!) is to offer equity. Performance-based equity sharing is an effective way of rewarding and retaining key employees. But there are other options as well, including recognition awards (cash or in kind) and personal development accounts for training and development programs (in addition to tuition reimbursement programs). Whatever they are, they should support the business plan, be consistent with the compensation philosophy, create an effective economic partnership between employee and employer, and take into consideration the competition's offerings and the broader external job market.

Which skills must be retained internally, and which can be outsourced? Are creating proprietary product designs and innovating to allow rapid penetration into new markets the competencies that the company must nurture for growth consistent with the business plan? Are people with these abilities more or less likely to value the intangibles of Waterway's environment than, say, sales-oriented people, who may be more motivated by cash compensation tied directly to sales? Maher is impressed with Carter's performance; but in his current situation, he should put his energy into assessing the distribution strategy in the context of an aggressive business plan rather than react too quickly to the possibility of losing one lone ranger, albeit a highly successful marketing person. Perhaps sales, marketing, and distribution ability could be more efficiently and effectively outsourced than developed and managed in-house.

Those questions raise issues that are central to any compensation strategy, and Waterway needs a strategy—fast. The new strategy doesn't necessarily have to include higher wages or be inconsistent with Waterway's superior work environment, the value of which should not be underestimated. Such an environment can continue to be a key employee motivator and contribute immeasurably to loyalty, high morale, and productivity. In fact, behavioral scientists have shown repeatedly that people are not motivated directly by pay but that pay becomes a dissatisfier when other elements of the satisfaction formula are lacking or out of kilter. But if Maher stays on the same growth path without adjusting his strategy, that superior environment is going to erode anyway. The only way Maher is going to get out of his current predicament is to define his new business goals clearly and then define a compensation philosophy and strategy that explicitly supports those goals.

Alan Johnson, Johnson Associates.[5]   Overhearing Carter's conversation with Les Finch was the best thing that could have happened to Maher and perhaps to Waterway Industries. Not only did it get Maher thinking about what Carter has meant to the company's phenomenal growth, it gave him a much-needed reason to consider the importance and needs of Waterway's other employees. Waterway needs Carter—at least in the short term. So any intellectual discussion of whether or not Maher should

---

[5]*Alan Johnson is the managing director of Johnson Associates, a New York–based consulting firm specializing in compensation issues.*

rethink her compensation arrangement is pointless. From a business standpoint, Maher has only one reasonable choice. Otherwise, Waterway's kayak business will sink and employee morale will suffer.

Granted, Maher doesn't seem to have a clear sense of what he intends to do with his business. But changing Carter's compensation arrangement will buy him some time to make those important strategic decisions. By pacifying Carter now, he can maintain his marketing and sales engine. He can then maximize the kayak boom and use that time to consider whether he wants to continue to grow the company. If he decides that the kayak boom will be the end and that he wants Waterway to return to its former state, he can wind down the marketing effort and phase out his part-timers and his outsourcing arrangements over a two- or three-year period. Maher isn't a snap-to-it kind of guy. It took him two or three years to get fully invested in the kayak market; there's no reason why he can't take the same amount of time to phase out of it.

As a short-term incentive, Maher should offer Carter a stay-put bonus or phantom shares in the business, contingent on a commitment for a given period of time. Then if Maher decides to pursue an aggressive growth strategy, he can offer her a three-to-five-year performance-based cash incentive plan. Her annual incentive might be based on her sales volume and on her ability to control marketing costs as a percentage of sales. In either case, he should ensure that Carter's base salary is competitive by checking it against available market data and running it past other marketing people he knows. (He can also check any one of a number of annually published salary surveys.) If her salary is not competitive, then an immediate adjustment is in order.

Maher also needs to consider other key employees. Regardless of the business strategy he eventually settles on, an equity arrangement for other senior staff will help focus the company; it will also provide a retention incentive. He may be concerned about such a move, but he should think about it this way: Would he rather own 100 percent of a little or 80 percent of a lot? If Maher doesn't give up some equity, he may find himself with

much less of a company than he had to begin with—in terms of size and quality of life. Maher is the one who started the company on its current path. To put the brakes on without any consideration for the change it has already undergone would be disastrous.

Once he has given his top managers equity in the company, Maher should solicit their advice about whether and how Waterway should grow. Most of Waterway's senior managers will probably be on the same wavelength. They joined Waterway because of its culture and its business, not because it was a big moneymaker. But different perspectives—such as Carter's—can help Maher grow the company, take it public, or shrink it in a healthy, well-rounded way.

Throughout all of this, Maher must communicate with his other employees. I'm sure that there are rumors going around right now that the company culture is going to change. If Maher is holding Carter up as an example of a great employee, his other staff members are probably wondering how they can keep up or whether they even want to. Maher needs to allay their fears, but he also needs to let them know what he is thinking about. If, along with the management team, he decides to pursue a growth strategy—even a modest one—he should let his employees know exactly what that will mean for them. If he institutes a companywide bonus plan, he needs to be candid about what that means for Waterway's culture. If he expects people to put in longer hours, he has to say so. And if they express concerns, he must be ready to respond.

For example, if one of his employees says, "Look, I know the workday ends at 5, but I always pick up my children from day care at 4," Maher needs to be prepared to react honestly. I suspect that he will be able to say that he is committed to managing the new company expectations in a fair way. He may explain that the push for more hours will be a seasonal kind of thing or that if people want to leave at 4 P.M., he expects them to put in more hours at another time. If Maher promises no surprises and keeps that promise, he'll also keep the loyalty and respect of his staff, without which Waterway would sink.

Case 3–7

DECISION-MAKING EXERCISE (B)

Please read these instructions carefully. They describe a group decision-making process called the **dialectical inquiry** method. You must utilize this process to develop recommendations for Bruce Reid, CEO of Blake Memorial Hospital (see Case 3–9, "The Case of the Unhealthy Hospital"). *Please remember that this entire exercise must be completed in one hour*.

In this process, your group divides into two equal-sized subgroups. The subgroups develop alternative sets of assumptions and recommendations. Then the two subgroups meet and debate these alternatives. The debate initially focuses on the assumptions that underlie each subgroup's argument. After reaching agreement on a set of assumptions, the groups discuss their recommendations and agree on a final set of recommendations.

Please follow the key steps[1] outlined below:

Key Steps
1. Read "The Case of the Unhealthy Hospital" carefully. Please do not discuss this reading with any other class member.
2. Assign one subgroup (Subgroup #1) to develop their assumptions and recommendations. Assign the other subgroup (Subgroup #2) to await this initial decision and to then build an opposing alternative. At this point, both subgroups should find separate physical locations in which to work.
3. Subgroup #1 should discuss the case and develop a set of recommendations for the Blake Memorial Hospital CEO. You should carefully construct a supporting argument with an explicit list of assumptions, facts, and data. When com-

plete, record your results on the Subgroup #1 Recommendations Form (Exhibit 1). Please take no longer than 15 minutes to complete Step #3.
4. While waiting for Subgroup #1, the others should discuss the case amongst themselves, but not with any others in the class.
5. The two subgroups come together. Subgroup #1 provides a brief oral presentation of their decision to the other subgroup along with a copy of their Recommendations Form. This presentation should describe the key recommendations and the major elements of the supporting argument.
6. The subgroups separate again. Subgroup #2 develops a reasonable set of opposing recommendations. You should buttress this decision with a logical supporting argument. Explicitly identify the key assumptions, facts, and data that underlie your argument. Record the results on the Subgroup #2 Recommendations Form (Exhibit 2). Please take no longer than 15 minutes to complete Step #6.
7. Subgroup #2 now presents their decision and provides the others a copy of their Recommendations Form.
8. The subgroups then debate the two alternatives. During this debate, you should carefully analyze both subgroups' assumptions. Through the discussion and group interaction, seek agreement on a final list of assumptions. This final list may comprise some original assumptions, some revisions, and perhaps a few altogether new assumptions that surface during the debate.

---

[1]Adapted from Schweiger, Sandberg, and Ragan, "Group Approaches for Improving Strategic Decision Making," Academy of Management Journal *29, no. 1 (1986), pp. 51–71.*

This case was prepared by Michael Roberto under the direction of David A. Garvin.

EXHIBIT 1   Subgroup #1 Recommendations Form

<u>Recommendations:</u>

1.

2.

3.

4.

<u>Assumptions:</u>

1.

2.

3.

4.

5.

6.

7.

8.

9.

10.

<u>Key Facts/Data:</u>

1.

2.

3.

4.

5.

6.

7.

8.

9.

10.

---

9. From this final list of assumptions, the entire group should develop a set of recommendations. Again, this process may involve considerable debate. When you finalize your decision, record your results on the Final Recommendations Form (Exhibit 3).

10. Please individually complete the Student Survey (Exhibit 4).

EXHIBIT 2   Subgroup #2 Recommendations Form

<u>Recommendations:</u>

1.

2.

3.

4.

<u>Assumptions:</u>

1.

2.

3.

4.

5.

6.

7.

8.

9.

10.

<u>Key Facts/Data:</u>

1.

2.

3.

4.

5.

6.

7.

8.

9.

10.

EXHIBIT 3   Final Recommendations Form

Recommendations:

1.

2.

3.

4.

Assumptions:

1.

2.

3.

4.

5.

6.

7.

8.

9.

10.

Key Facts/Data:

1.

2.

3.

4.

5.

6.

7.

8.

9.

10.

EXHIBIT 4   Student Survey

TEAM # _____

<u>**Instructions:**</u>

Please fill in your team number now. Then mark your responses to the survey using the 1–7 scale shown to the right of each question. 1 represents the response "a very low level" or "very little." 7 represents the response "a very high level" or "a great deal." The entire range of responses is as follows:

1 = very low level/very little	3 = moderately low	5 = moderately high	7 = very high level/great deal
2 = low	4 = moderate	6 = high	

Please do not discuss these questions with any other group or class member.

	1 = very low					7 = very high	
1. Rate the quality of the recommendations that the group ultimately made concerning this business situation.	1	2	3	4	5	6	7
2. Rate the quality of the final list of assumptions.	1	2	3	4	5	6	7
3. How many disagreements over different ideas about this decision were there?	1	2	3	4	5	6	7
4. How many differences about the content of this decision did the group have to work through?	1	2	3	4	5	6	7
5. How much personal friction surfaced within the group during the decision-making process?	1	2	3	4	5	6	7
6. How many personality clashes became evident during the decision-making process?	1	2	3	4	5	6	7
7. How much did the group decision-making process make you critically reevaluate the assumptions and recommendations that you initially supported?	1	2	3	4	5	6	7
8. How much did the group decision-making process uncover valid assumptions and recommendations that you and/or others did not initially consider?	1	2	3	4	5	6	7
9. How much did you enjoy working with this group on today's exercise?	1	2	3	4	5	6	7
10. How satisfied are you with the group's final assumptions and recommendations?	1	2	3	4	5	6	7
11. How comfortable would you feel implementing this decision along with other members of this group?	1	2	3	4	5	6	7
12. How welcome did you feel to express opinions freely and to openly disagree with other group members?	1	2	3	4	5	6	7
13. To what extent did the group discourage dissent in the face of an emerging majority opinion?	1	2	3	4	5	6	7
14. To what extent did a leader emerge during the decision-making process?	1	2	3	4	5	6	7

Thank you very much for offering thoughtful responses to this survey.

Note: Questions 1–10 adapted from the following sources:
Schweiger, Sandberg, and Ragan, "Group Approaches for Improving Strategic Decision Making," *Academy of Management Journal* 29, no. 1 (1986), pp. 51–71.
Amason, "Distinguishing the Effects of Functional and Dysfunctional Conflict on Strategic Decision Making," *Academy of Management Journal* 39, no. 1 (1996), pp. 123–148.

Case 3–8

DECISION-MAKING EXERCISE (C)

Please read these instructions carefully. They describe a group decision-making process called the **devil's advocacy** method. You must utilize this process to develop recommendations for Bruce Reid, CEO of Blake Memorial Hospital (see the following case, "The Case of the Unhealthy Hospital"). *Please remember that this entire exercise must be completed in one hour.*

In this process, your group divides into two equal-sized subgroups. One subgroup develops a set of recommendations. The other subgroup plays the devil's advocate, carefully probing all elements of their argument. Through a systematic, repeated exchange of ideas and critiques, the entire group arrives at a final set of recommendations.

Please follow the key steps[1] outlined below:

Key Steps

1. Read "The Case of the Unhealthy Hospital" carefully. Please do not discuss the case with any other group or class member.
2. Assign one subgroup (Subgroup #1) to develop their assumptions and recommendations. Assign the other subgroup (Subgroup #2) to play the role of the devil's advocate. At this point, both subgroups should find separate physical locations in which to work.
3. Subgroup #1 should discuss the case and develop a set of recommendations for the Blake Memorial CEO. You should carefully construct a supporting argument with an explicit list of assumptions, facts, and data. When complete,

record your results on the Subgroup #1 Recommendations Form (Exhibit 1). Please take no longer than 15 minutes to complete Step #3.
4. Meanwhile, Subgroup #2 may discuss the case amongst themselves, but not with any other members of the class.
5. The two groups come together. Subgroup #1 provides the others with a copy of their Recommendations Form. In addition, Subgroup #1 makes a brief oral presentation of their recommendations and supporting argument.
6. The two subgroups separate again. The devil's advocates develop a logical, plausible critique of the others' recommendations. This critique should explicitly identify problems with the assumptions, facts, and data that underlie Subgroup #1's decision. You should build a logical argument as to why the Blake Memorial CEO should not accept the others' recommendations. When you finish, complete the Subgroup #2 Critique Form (Exhibit 2). Please take no longer than 15 minutes to complete Step #6.
7. The two subgroups come together. The devil's advocacy group provides the others a copy of their Critique Form and briefly explains its main points.
8. The two subgroups now remain together and work towards an agreement. Subgroup #1 revises its decision in light of the valid criticisms raised by the others. As they do so, Subgroup #2 should examine the revised recommendations and offer additional, reasonable critiques.

---

[1]Adapted from Schweiger, Sandberg, and Ragan, "Group Approaches for Improving Strategic Decision Making," *Academy of Management Journal* 29, no. 1 (1986), pp. 51–71.

This case was prepared by Michael Roberto under the direction of David A. Garvin.

Copyright © 1996 by the President and Fellows of Harvard College. Harvard Business School Case 397-033.

EXHIBIT 1   Subgroup #1 Recommendations Form

Recommendations:

1.

2.

3.

4.

Assumptions:

1.

2.

3.

4.

5.

6.

7.

8.

9.

10.

Key Facts/Data:

1.

2.

3.

4.

5.

6.

7.

8.

9.

10.

EXHIBIT 2   Subgroup #2 Critique Form

What assumptions do you find invalid or irrelevant to the decision?

What key facts/data do you find invalid or irrelevant to the decision?

Please briefly describe your argument as to why the other group's recommendations are problematic.

This revision/critique/revision cycle should continue until both subgroups can agree on a final set of recommendations that provides a logical, reasonable course of action for the Blake Memorial CEO.

9. Record the ultimate decision and supporting assumptions, facts, and data on the Final Recommendations Form (Exhibit 3).

10. Please individually complete the Student Survey (Exhibit 4).

EXHIBIT 3   Final Recommendations Form

Recommendations:

1.

2.

3.

4.

Assumptions:

1.

2.

3.

4.

5.

6.

7.

8.

9.

10.

Key Facts/Data:

1.

2.

3.

4.

5.

6.

7.

8.

9.

10.

EXHIBIT 4 Student Survey

TEAM # _____

Instructions:

Please fill in your team number now. Then mark your responses to the survey using the 1–7 scale shown to the right of each question. 1 represents the response "a very low level" or "very little." 7 represents the response "a very high level" or "a great deal." The entire range of responses is as follows:

1 = very low level/very little	3 = moderately low	5 = moderately high 7 = very high level/great deal
2 = low	4 = moderate	6 = high

Please do not discuss these questions with any other group or class member.

	1 = very low					7 = very high	
1. Rate the quality of the recommendations that the group ultimately made concerning this business situation.	1	2	3	4	5	6	7
2. Rate the quality of the final list of assumptions.	1	2	3	4	5	6	7
3. How many disagreements over different ideas about this decision were there?	1	2	3	4	5	6	7
4. How many differences about the content of this decision did the group have to work through?	1	2	3	4	5	6	7
5. How much personal friction surfaced within the group during the decision-making process?	1	2	3	4	5	6	7
6. How many personality clashes became evident during the decision-making process?	1	2	3	4	5	6	7
7. How much did the group decision-making process make you critically reevaluate the assumptions and recommendations that you initially supported?	1	2	3	4	5	6	7
8. How much did the group decision-making process uncover valid assumptions and recommendations that you and/or others did not initially consider?	1	2	3	4	5	6	7
9. How much did you enjoy working with this group on today's exercise?	1	2	3	4	5	6	7
10. How satisfied are you with the group's final assumptions and recommendations?	1	2	3	4	5	6	7
11. How comfortable would you feel implementing this decision along with other members of this group?	1	2	3	4	5	6	7
12. How welcome did you feel to express opinions freely and to openly disagree with other group members?	1	2	3	4	5	6	7
13. To what extent did the group discourage dissent in the face of an emerging majority opinion?	1	2	3	4	5	6	7
14. To what extent did a leader emerge during the decision-making process?	1	2	3	4	5	6	7

Thank you very much for offering thoughtful responses to this survey.

Note: Questions 1–10 adapted from the following sources:
Schweiger, Sandberg, and Ragan, "Group Approaches for Improving Strategic Decision Making," *Academy of Management Journal* 29, no. 1 (1986), pp. 51–71.
Amason, "Distinguishing the Effects of Functional and Dysfunctional Conflict on Strategic Decision Making," *Academy of Management Journal* 39, no. 1 (1996), pp. 123–148.

Case 3–9

THE CASE OF THE UNHEALTHY HOSPITAL

Anthony R. Kovner

Bruce Reid, Blake Memorial Hospital's new CEO, rubbed his eyes and looked again at the 1992 budget worksheet. The more he played with the figures, the more pessimistic he became. Blake Memorial's financial health was not good; it suffered from rising costs, static revenue, and declining quality of care. When the board hired Reid six months ago, the mandate had been clear: Improve the quality of care and set the financial house in order.

Reid had less than a week to finalize his $70 million budget for approval by the hospital's board. As he considered his choices, one issue, the future of six off-site clinics, commanded special attention. Reid's predecessor had set up the clinics five years earlier to provide primary health care to residents of Marksville's poorer neighborhoods; they were generally considered a model of community-based care. But while providing a valuable service for the city's poor, the clinics also diverted funds away from Blake Memorial's in-house services, many of which were underfunded.

As he worked on the budget, Reid's thoughts drifted back to his first visit to the Lorris housing project in early March, just two weeks into his tenure as CEO.

The clinic was not much to look at. A small graffiti-covered sign in the courtyard pointed the way to the basement entrance of an aging six-story apartment building. Reid pulled open the heavy metal door and entered the small waiting room. Two of the seven chairs were occupied. In one, a pregnant teenage girl listened to a Walkman and tapped her foot. In the other, a man in his mid-30s

sat with his eyes closed, resting his head against the wall.

Reid had come alone and unannounced. He wanted to see the clinic without the fanfare of an official visit and to meet Dr. Renée Dawson, who had been the clinic's family practitioner since 1986.

The meeting had to be brief, Dawson apologized, because the nurse had not yet arrived and she had patients to see. As they marched down to her office, she filled Reid in on the waiting patients: the girl was 14 years old, in for a routine prenatal checkup, and the man, a crack addict recently diagnosed as HIV positive, was in for a follow-up visit and blood tests.

On his hurried tour, Reid noted the dilapidated condition of the cramped facility. The paint was peeling everywhere, and in one examining room, he had to step around a bucket strategically placed to catch a drip from a leaking overhead pipe. After 15 years as a university hospital administrator, Reid felt unprepared for this kind of medicine.

The conditions were appalling, he told Dawson, and were contrary to the image of the high-quality medical care he wanted Blake Memorial to project. When he asked her how she put up with it, Dawson just stared at him. "What are my options?" she finally asked.

Reid looked again at the clinic figures from last year: collectively they cost $1.1 million to operate,

Reprinted by permission of Harvard Business Review. From "The Case of the Unhealthy Hospital" by Anthony R. Kovner, Sept./Oct. 1991. Copyright © 1991 by Harvard Business School Publishing.

at a loss of $256,000. What Blake needed, Reid told himself, were fewer services that sapped resources and more revenue-generating services, or at least services that would make the hospital more competitive. The clinics were most definitely a drain.

Of course, there was a surfeit of "competitive" projects in search of funding. Blake needed to expand its neonatal ward; the chief of surgery wanted another operating theater; the chief of radiology was demanding an MRI unit; the business office wanted to upgrade its computer system; and the emergency department desperately needed another full-time physician. And that was just scratching the surface.

Without some of these investments, Blake's ability to attract paying patients and top-grade doctors would deteriorate. As it was, the hospital's location on the poorer, east side of Marksville was a strike against it. Blake had a high percentage of Medicaid patients, but the payments were never sufficient to cover costs. The result was an ever-rising annual operating loss.

Reid was constantly reminded of the hospital's uncompetitive position by his chief of surgery, Dr. Winston Lee. "If Blake wants more paying patients—and, for that matter, good department chiefs—it at least has to keep up with St. Barnabas," Lee had warned Reid a few days ago.

Lee complained that St. Barnabas, the only other acute-care hospital in Marksville, had both superior facilities and better technology. Its financial condition was better than Blake's, in part because it was located on the west side of the city, in a more affluent neighborhood. St. Barnabas had also been more savvy in its business ventures: It owned a 50 percent share in an MRI unit operated by a private medical practice. The unit was reportedly generating revenue, and St. Barnabas had plans for other such investments, Lee had said.

While Reid agreed that Blake needed more high-technology services, he was also concerned about duplication of service; the population of the greater Marksville area, including suburban and rural residents, was about 700,000. But when he questioned Richard Tuttle, St. Barnabas's CEO, about the possibility of joint ventures, he received a very cold response. "Competition is the only way to survive," Tuttle had said.

Tuttle's actions were consistent with his words. Two months ago, St. Barnabas allegedly had offered financial incentives to some of Marksville's physicians in exchange for patient referrals. While the rumor had never been substantiated, it had left a bad taste in Reid's mouth.

Reid knew he could either borrow or cut costs. But the hospital's ability to borrow was limited due to an already high debt burden. His only real alternative, therefore, was to cut costs.

Reid dug out the list of possible cuts from the pile of papers on his desk. At the top of the page was the heading "internal cuts" and halfway down was the heading "external cuts" (see Exhibit 1). Each item had a dollar value next to it representing the estimated annual savings.

Reid reasoned that the internal cuts would help Blake become a leaner organization. With 1,400 full-time equivalent employees and 350 beds, there was room for some cost cutting. Reid's previous hospital had 400 beds and only 1,300 FTE employees. But Reid recognized that cutting personnel could affect Blake's quality of care. As it was, patient perception of Blake's quality had been slipping during the last few years, according to the monthly public relations office survey. And quality was an issue that the board was particularly sensitive to these days. Eliminating the clinics, on

---

EXHIBIT 1   Possible Cuts

Internal Cuts

Cut 2% nursing staff: $340,000

Cut 2% support and ancillary staff: $290,000

Cut maximum 3% from business office staff: $50,000

Freeze all wages and salaries at 1991 level: $1.5 million

Eliminate weekly in-house clinics: $100,000

External Cuts

Eliminate all off-site clinics: $256,000

the other hand, would not compromise Blake's internal operations.

Everyone knew the clinics would never generate a profit for Blake. In fact, the annual loss was expected to continue to climb. Part of the reason was rising costs, but another factor was the city of Marksville's ballooning budget deficit. The city contributed $100,000 to the program and provided the space in the housing projects free of charge. But Reid had heard from two city councilmen that funding would likely be cut in 1992. Less city money and a higher net loss for the clinic program would only add to the strain on Blake's internal services.

Reid had to weigh this strain against the political consequence of closing the clinics. He was well aware of the possible ramifications from his regular dealings with Clara Bryant, the recently appointed commissioner of Marksville's health services. Bryant repeatedly argued that the clinics were an essential service for Marksville's low-income residents.

"You know how the mayor feels about the clinics," Bryant had said at a recent breakfast meeting. "He was a strong supporter when they first opened. He fought hard in City Hall to get Blake Memorial the funding. Closing the clinics would be a personal blow to him."

Reid understood the significance of Bryant's veiled threat. If he closed the clinics, he would lose an ally in the mayor's office, which could jeopardize Blake's access to city funds in the future—or have even worse consequences. Reid had heard through the City Hall rumor mill that Bryant had privately threatened to refer Blake to Marksville's chief counsel for a tax status review if he closed the clinics. He took this seriously; he knew of a handful of hospitals facing similar actions from their local governments.

When Reid tried to explain to Bryant that closing the clinics would improve Blake's financial condition, which, in turn, would lead to better quality of care for all patients, her response had been unsympathetic: "You don't measure the community's health on an income statement."

Bryant was not the only clinic supporter Reid had to reckon with. Dr. Susan Russell, Blake's director of clinics, was equally vocal about the responsibility of the hospital to the community. In a recent senior staff meeting, Reid sat stunned while Dr. Winston Lee, Blake's high-tech champion, exchanged barbs with Russell.

Lee had argued that the off-site clinics competed against the weekly in-house clinics that Blake offered under- and uninsured patients. He proposed closing the off-site clinics.

The four in-house clinics—surgery, pediatrics, gynecology, and internal medicine—cost Blake $200,000 a year in physician fees alone, Lee said. And because Medicaid was not adequately covering the costs of these services, the hospital lost about $100,000 a year from the in-house clinics. What's more, in-house clinic visits were down 10 percent so far this year. A choice had to be made, Lee concluded, and the reasonable choice was to eliminate the off-site clinics and bolster services within the hospital's four walls. "Instead of clinics, we should have a shuttle bus from the projects to the hospital," he proposed.

Russell's reaction had been almost violent. "Most of the clinics' patients wouldn't come to the hospital even if there was a bus running every five minutes," she snapped back. "I'm talking about pregnant teenage girls who need someone in their community they recognize and trust, not some nameless doctor in a big unfamiliar hospital."

Russell's ideas about what a hospital should be were radical, Reid thought. But, he had to admit, they did have a certain logic. She espoused an entirely new way of delivering health care that involved the mobilization of many of Blake's services. "A hospital is not a building, it's a service. And wherever the service is most needed, that is where the hospital should be," she had said.

In Blake's case, that meant funding more neighborhood clinics, not cutting back on them. Russell spoke of creating a network of neighborhood-based preventive health care centers for all of East Marksville's communities, including both the low-income housing projects and the pockets of middle-income neighborhoods. Besides improving health care, the network would act as an inpatient referral system for hospital services.

Lee had rolled his eyes at the suggestion. But Reid had not been so quick to dismiss Russell's ideas. If a clinic network could tap the paying public and generate more inpatient business, it might be worth looking into, he thought. And, besides, St. Barnabas wasn't doing anything like this.

At the end of the staff meeting, Reid asked Russell to give him some data on the performance of the clinics. He requested numbers of inpatient referrals, birth-weight data, and the number of patients seen per month by type of visit—routine, substance abuse, prenatal, pediatric, violence-related injury, HIV.

Russell's report had arrived the previous day, and Reid was flipping through the results. He had hoped it would provide some answers; instead, it only raised more questions.

The number of prenatal visits had been declining for 16 months. This was significant because prenatal care accounted for over 60 percent of the clinics' business. But other types of visits were holding steady. In fact, substance abusers had been coming in record numbers since the clinics began participating in the mayor's needle exchange program three months ago.

Russell placed the blame for the prenatal decline squarely on the city. "Two years ago, Marksville cut funding for prenatal outreach and advocacy programs to low-income communities. Without supplementary outreach, pregnant women are less inclined to visit the clinics," she wrote.

The birth-weight data were inconclusive. There was no difference between birth weights for clinic patients and birth weights for nonclinic patients from similar backgrounds. In fact, average birth weights in 1989 were actually lower among clinic patients. Russell had concluded that the clinic program was too new to produce meaningful improvements.

On the positive side, inpatient referrals from the clinics had risen in the last few years, but Russell's

comments about the reasons for the rise were speculative at best. HIV-related illnesses and violence-related injuries were a large part of the increase but so were early detection of ailments such as cataracts and cancer. Reid made a note to ask for a follow-up study on this.

He put the report down and stared out his window. Blake had a responsibility to serve the uninsured. But it also had a responsibility to remain viable and self-sustaining. Which was the stronger force? It came down to finding the best way to provide high-quality care to the community and saving the hospital from financial difficulties. The consequences of his decision ranged from another year of status quo management to totally redefining the role of the hospital in the community. He had less than a week to decide.

What should Reid cut, and what should he keep?

Experts in Health Care and Public Service Discuss His Options

Dan Pellegrini.[1]   Blake Memorial's long-term viability is at risk. Reid must make substantial cuts immediately, and eventually the hospital must relocate.

I see Bruce Reid making the following presentation to Blake Memorial's board of directors.

Six months ago, I came to this hospital because of the challenge it offered. Blake certainly hasn't disappointed me: It has rising costs, a healthy operating deficit, a high percentage of Medicaid low-scale reimbursement, forceful physician demands, potential physician defection, and a poor location and reputation.

In its current state, Blake's long-term viability is at risk. While we must immediately address the

---

[1]*Dan Pellegrini is a judge of the Commonwealth Court of Pennsylvania. Previously, he was city solicitor of Pittsburgh, Pennsylvania, where he negotiated a landmark settlement of Presbyterian-University Hospital's tax-exempt status. The case resulted in the hospital having to pay the city of Pittsburgh $11.4 million for 10 years of municipal services.*

operating deficit, the core issue is the hospital's long-term direction. While I believe that we can solve the immediate financial crisis, the board must decide Blake's future so that an orderly planning process can begin.

I recommend eliminating 260 staff positions immediately, bringing staffing more in line with my former hospital. I see no reason why we cannot achieve comparable quality of care at that level of staffing, assuming that effective management procedures are put in place. I am confident that our management is capable of doing this. I calculate that such personnel reductions will save close to $5.9 million, rather than the $2 million originally forecast. I do not know the net inpatient revenues that the clinics generate, so I cannot make a recommendation about closing the clinics, but if we do, I expect little opposition from the city. The appalling conditions of the city-supplied facilities and the funding reduction make me believe the city is no longer committed to the clinics.

The cuts I am suggesting will generate sufficient working capital to examine available options. But over time, serving the same patient population—with its high proportion of Medicaid patients—will eat away at the surplus generated from these personnel reductions. Because of our present location and negative image, Blake cannot hope to change its patient mix.

As I see it, the hospital has two options. One is to gradually abandon this neighborhood. Blake could open free-standing care centers in a more affluent suburb of Marksville, in conjunction with our staff doctors. At the same time, I recommend construction of a minihospital in this neighborhood, with an emergency room, an operating room to perform same-day surgery, a neonatal unit, and a sufficient number of inpatient beds to handle uncomplicated matters from the emergency room, surgical center, and obstetrics.

We could open a physicians' office near the minihospital, which eventually should generate a good profit, primarily because of higher insurance reimbursement rates that come with serving a more affluent population. Such a relocation would satisfy our admitting physicians, who would receive both higher reimbursements and the newest and best technology.

Initially, both the care centers and the minihospital would feed more serious cases to Blake's current location, helping to increase margins. But through phased expansion, the entire operation eventually would relocate to the suburban site. We could then convert the old hospital to a nursing home or other specialized center, depending on what is more advantageous from a reimbursement perspective. Blake's name would be changed to reflect our more upscale image. Quite simply, this strategy is to out-St. Barnabas St. Barnabas.

The alternative is not as dynamic, but it is one that I am obliged to put forth because you are directors of a nonprofit institution. As with other hospitals, when Blake was established as a nonprofit, it was chartered to carry out a societal need not served by either government or for-profit enterprises. We were created to serve the medical needs of the community, especially those who could not receive such care elsewhere.

If we opt to move from this neighborhood, we will be abandoning that societal mission for a more financially sound and technically advanced hospital. Instead of seeking insured reimbursements, we could look to serve our present patients' needs, knowing that in the present reimbursement climate our financial position will always be precarious.

If we decide to stay in our present location, we will need to cut costs ruthlessly and accept serviceable rather than cutting-edge technology. We will provide adequate and otherwise unavailable medical care to a section of the population that has no other options. Inevitably, this will result in the defection of a significant number of primary admitting physicians, with an attendant loss of profitability from insured patient referrals. In five to seven years, rather than celebrating the opening of a new hospital, we will, in all likelihood, be wondering how to keep the existing hospital open.

The only justification for staying put is that we are meeting a societal need for which we were created and which no one else is meeting, certainly not St. Barnabas.

If you choose the option of continuing to serve the same patient population, I will, for the good of my career, be forced to submit my resignation. I could not, with a clear conscience, remain committed to a hospital that knowingly courts financial insolvency. My peers would think of me as a social worker, not a bottom-line manager. I await your decision.

Ellen Schall.[2]   The solution lies outside Blake and in the community as a whole.

To paraphrase Sister Irene, CEO of Daughters of Charity National Health System, Bruce Reid is caught in the margin-mission trap. He imagines he has to choose between fiscal survivability of the hospital and meeting community needs. He sees only unappealing options—closing clinics, cutting staff, freezing salaries. Framed in such narrow terms, the decision is as simple as it is hopeless; Reid will no doubt make the cuts. But, instead, with creative leadership and a willingness to reach out, Reid can develop a service mission that also meets the concerns of margin.

The mission will best be developed not by Reid alone but in cooperation with his staff and in conversations with the community. Reid should lead this process and authorize the contributions of others.

Reid may have a willing ally in Clara Bryant, Marksville's commissioner of health services, and he should focus on bringing her into the decision-making process. He needs to lower his guard and make use of Bryant's leverage and insight. He can use his decision not to close the clinics—at least not for now—to build cooperation and get her to help search for a long-term solution.

_____
[2]*Ellen Schall is president of the National Center for Health Education, a private nonprofit organization located in New York City. From 1983 to 1990, she was commissioner of the New York City Department of Juvenile Justice.*

That solution lies outside the confines of the institution. Working in concert with the community, Reid must begin the difficult process of identifying the unmet health care needs of Marksville's underserved residents and then explore and introduce innovative solutions.

The New York City Department of Correction faced a related challenge in the early 1980s when I served as deputy commissioner. Like many correction departments across the country, New York City had enormous overcrowding problems in its jails. But narrowly defining our options—that is, by including only choices over which we had control—got us nowhere in solving the long-term problem. We searched for beds much the way Reid is searching for ways to cut costs: alone, with bad choices, inadequate information and resources, and increasing frustration.

With the problem approaching crisis proportions, we started to reach out for help. We convened monthly meetings of all the actors in the criminal justice system—the judges, prosecutors, police, the defense bar, probation, the pretrial service agencies, the mayor's office of criminal justice—most of whom had a much more direct influence on the jail population and many of whom had definite ideas about what was wrong and what needed to be done.

By involving them and getting wider ownership of the problems, we got better solutions. Judges gave priority to cases where the defendant was incarcerated, probation hired typists to speed up preparation of presentencing reports, and the police changed their booking procedures so people who had been arrested saw a judge more quickly. The changes freed up hundreds of jail beds.

My experience with solving the problems of jail overcrowding involved only the public sector. In health care, as in many other fields, the reach needs to be broader. Reid needs to include both the public and the private sectors in his coalition: not just the hospital and city hall but the business community, social advocacy agencies, community-based self-help organizations, and the medical community. He must charge the group with creating solutions that go beyond the routine—new ways of solving old problems.

The Marksville coalition does not need to begin from ground zero. Many communities have struggled with similar problems and have found innovative solutions. Reid needs to call on all the networks of his coalition members to make sure his group begins with a good understanding of what has been tried already. He could also take advantage of groups such as the National Civic League, which maintains an index by subject matter of local solutions to pressing urban problems, or the Ford Foundation–Kennedy School of Government Innovations Award program, a repository of innovative approaches to pressing state and local concerns. Two interesting models come to mind.

- In Montgomery County, Maryland, the local health department and the local medical society formed a partnership to treat high-risk indigent women patients who were spurned by local hospitals due in part to the high cost of obstetric malpractice insurance. Three of the four hospitals had stopped providing obstetrical care to these patients. With both the health department and the medical society pushing, all four agreed to an equitable patient distribution plan, and private obstetricians agreed to serve as part-time health department employees during labor and delivery. The doctors are paid by the county and covered by the county's self-insurance program.
- In Fairfax County, Virginia, the Medical Care for Children Project tackled a significant unmet need: Before 1986, there was no comprehensive and consistent countywide medical or dental care available for children of the working poor. The project persuaded private medical providers—HMOs, physicians and dentists, pharmacies and laboratories—to provide services at 50 percent of actual cost or less. Business leaders were invited to contribute funds, and the county paid administrative costs and subsidized the cost of care.

There is no easy blueprint to offer Reid, but there are workable alternatives. Changing the way a community defines and meets its health care problems is tough and complicated work that requires imagination and encourages creativity and persistence. Reid will ultimately have to chart his own course, but he will be more likely to succeed if he reaches out beyond the four walls of Blake Memorial.

Keith F. Safian.[3]   Reid needs a market-niche strategy if he expects to turn the clinics around and eventually expand them.

I know what Bruce Reid is up against. After trying for over a year to turn around an evening clinic in a low-income community, I was forced to replace it with a bus service to the hospital a few miles away. Under the circumstances, closing the clinic seemed to be the only rational solution. In retrospect, however, it was less than optimal. I know now that Bruce Reid has other options that he should pursue. On all fronts—political, social, and economical—an expanded network of clinics is Blake's best long-term strategy.

First, closing a clinic is a serious blow to the community it serves. When I closed the evening clinic and provided bus service in its place, I was surprised to see patient visits fall off so precipitously, especially among adult males. Some patients went to a local daytime clinic run by the county, but many others simply opted not to seek early treatment for health problems.

While the closure of my clinic was painful, it was not a public relations disaster for the hospital. From the outset, the county government was aware of the financial problems we faced and participated in developing the interim solution. When it became clear that the clinic would always lose money, government participants helped make the final decision to close the clinic. Consequently, negative publicity was deflected from the hospital.

Unfortunately, the financial benefits were modest. The clinic was losing $50,000 a year, but the

---

[3]*Keith F. Safian is president and CEO of Phelps Memorial Hospital Center, a 215-bed acute care hospital in North Tarrytown, New York. A fellow of the American College of Healthcare Executives, he has worked as an administrator in voluntary and public hospitals for the past 18 years.*

eventual savings amounted to only $15,000. As it turned out, $35,000 of the loss was overhead that had to be redistributed to other cost centers.

Reid can learn from this. First, he should not underestimate the value of cultivating a strong relationship with local government. His current relationship with Bryant is neither supportive nor trusting. He should address this immediately. Even though Blake is financially responsible for the clinics, Reid should work toward establishing a partnership with Marksville City Hall in general and with Clara Bryant in particular. He should open the clinics' books for public scrutiny and let Bryant participate in long-term planning to restructure the clinics.

On the social front, Reid needs to accept that the clinics are necessary for the reasons Dr. Susan Russell gives. The shuttle bus service that Dr. Winston Lee suggests could never serve the community in the same way. Neighborhood clinics provide an important social function as well as a medical need, especially in low-income communities. They give residents a sense of ownership and self-determination that they cannot find in a large hospital-based clinic. At a local clinic I was involved with, the indigent community sponsored a successful fund-raising event.

Economically, it is possible for Reid to turn the clinics around so they continue to generate crucial inpatient referrals and still run efficiently. He needs to think in terms of a market-niche strategy because Blake will never be in a position to compete head-to-head with St. Barnabas. It makes sense to think in terms of extending the reach of the clinics to include low- and middle-income communities in other Marksville neighborhoods, as well as in the surrounding suburban and rural areas. This reach would give Blake the coverage it needs for more inpatient referrals and give it a near monopoly on the services it can operate economically.

Blake Memorial—and Blake Memorial alone—is responsible for serving the health care needs of East Marksville's low-income community in the absence of a publicly funded city or county hospital. If Reid closes the clinics, the city would be justified in canceling Blake's grants and other support.

Reid's best bet is to deal with the immediate financial problems through belt tightening—balancing staffing and patient volumes—while concurrently developing a longer-term plan to expand the clinic system and make it more cost-effective.

He needs to take decisive action now to ensure that the clinics become revenue generators for Blake as quickly as possible. First, he should evaluate the clinics' productivity. He should limit clinic hours by consolidating sessions and by cutting staff positions accordingly. Other short-term measures can be taken: Centralize record keeping, assist more patients to enroll in Medicaid, increase charges to sliding-fee patients, add clinics staffed with social workers or other lower-cost providers, and phase out one or two clinics that lose too much money.

Reid's dilemma is fundamentally about balancing short-term financial constraints against long-term strategic goals. It is a problem faced by virtually all hospital administrators in this era of cost containment. Without imaginative and bold leadership, however, the outcomes will be stopgap at best.

By publicly committing himself to creating a clinic network as the centerpiece of a long-term strategy to rejuvenate Blake Memorial, Reid will satisfy the board of directors, the city government, and the community.

Jane Delgado.[4]   Instead of playing with figures and becoming pessimistic, Reid should take charge. He must frame an effective strategy that treats the clinics as a resource, not a cost.

Bruce Reid must act swiftly and decisively to define the goals of Blake Memorial. He has already spent too many months playing with figures and becoming pessimistic, rather than taking charge and reframing the hospital's long-term strategy. He has to rethink the framework on which the hospital operates. His challenge is to develop a new understanding of whom the hospital will serve,

---

[4]*Jane Delgado is CEO of the National Coalition of Hispanic Health and Human Services Organizations in Washington, D.C.*

change how the clinics operate without incurring unreasonable costs, and develop more tailored analyses of the hospital's operation.

Whom the hospital will serve.   As it stands, Blake serves only the east side of Marksville, comprised primarily of low-income residents. St. Barnabas, on the west side of the city, serves the more affluent communities. Reid's primary objective must be to broaden the hospital's base to include more paying patients, while continuing to serve the local low-income communities adequately. To do so, he must redefine the hospital's niche and rethink the competitive relationship between Blake and St. Barnabas.

Fundamentally, Blake cannot and should not try to compete with St. Barnabas as they differ in both market and mission. Reid should break out of a narrow comparative analysis and attempt to assess Blake's mission *independently*. He can then more precisely determine the community's needs and create the appropriate services for satisfying those needs.

How the clinics should operate.   The clinics play a crucial role in developing Blake's mission. Reid must embrace Dr. Susan Russell's prescription for creating locally based preventive health care centers for the entire Marksville metropolitan area, regardless of income or geographic location. Such a network would be both politically correct and financially lucrative. A clinic network would provide a different approach to delivering care: Blake would provide "high-touch" health care, while St. Barnabas would focus on "high-tech" care. Financially, a more extensive clinic system would enable Blake to expand its patient base, increase revenues, and reduce its losses.

A careful analysis would quickly reveal that the clinic system as it is run now is both mismanaged and underutilized. To correct this, Reid needs to think of the clinics as an extension of the hospital, rather than as an optional appendage. This calls for positioning them as part of a cooperative system rather than as a peripheral cost center that drains resources.

The clinics must become the point of entry into the Blake system. Once patients—both paying and nonpaying—have entered the clinic system, Blake benefits by providing many of the routine follow-up services either at the clinics or within the four walls of the hospital. For those services involving high-technology diagnostics or treatment, the patient would be referred to St. Barnabas.

An important first step in implementing the new strategy is to renovate the existing clinics. Above all, this is an opportunity for Reid to build relationships with local community and political groups and to ensure community ownership of the clinics.

Developing analyses for operation.   Of course, none of this is possible unless Reid rethinks his role as administrator. He must recognize that he is no longer at a university-based hospital where research takes precedence over service. Improving the "quality of service" at Blake is central to his mission and goes far beyond counting beds and comparing numbers of employees. Reid needs to look beyond gross figures and identify the types of patients Blake serves and the types of employees necessary to satisfy those needs.

Reid must analyze the cost and revenue of the different categories of health professionals and services at Blake. The megacomparisons on which he previously relied will not give him enough information. Moreover, in the analyses of potential cuts, he must try to project future trends in both client population and reimbursement strategies.

At the same time, Reid must avoid the use of across-the-board cuts as they are unfair and generally seen as a sign of weakness. Decisions must be based on the actual care that's needed. For example, it may be inequitable to cut 2 percent from a department that has three physicians and 2 percent from a department that has 20 physicians.

Finally, Reid must be prepared for the inevitable loss of staff that occurs when there is a change in how an organization conducts business. Some will welcome the new relationship with the community, others will be appalled. The work will be in discerning staff allegiances and building an agenda for those who remain. I suspect that Winston Lee, the chief of surgery, would be one of the first to leave Blake.

The financial viability of the hospital depends on Reid's ability to make fundamental changes in the institution's mission. Those members of staff who cannot accept these changes will have no choice but to leave. In the long run, this will be best for Blake Memorial and for the community it serves.

***Bernard Lachner.*[5]**   Reid cannot and should not solve all of Marksville's social and health needs. His job is to run an economically healthy hospital.

Bruce Reid should close the clinics. He doesn't have to apologize for doing his job. He wasn't hired—nor does the hospital have the available resources—to solve all Marksville's social and health needs. Blake Memorial's mission in the community is to provide acute inpatient and some outpatient care within its four walls, and it can only succeed in this role if it is economically healthy.

It may sound callous, but Reid would be doing the community a service by closing the off-site clinics. If nothing else, such a bold move would bring the issue to a head and mobilize Marksville's political and community leaders to search for an alternative solution—one owned and operated by the public sector.

Above all, Reid must lead Blake by defining a clear role for the hospital. While an off-site clinic system is a noble pursuit, it must be discontinued because of poor financial return. Unlike the 1980s, when it was fashionable and financially feasible for hospitals to assume an interest in and responsibility for a broad range of community, social, and health needs, the 1990s call for a leaner approach. Instead of offering nonrevenue-generating services, private hospitals like Blake should return to the basics of serving specific acute health care needs.

Reid should argue that it is a mistake to make Blake the hub for the coordination, provision, and financing of the community's social and health needs. In the era of inadequate Medicaid coverage for the uninsured, such a business philosophy by a private hospital is an inappropriate use of resources. Clearly defined agencies established by the city, state, and federal governments have these responsibilities.

Reid should fight for the best in-house acute care services he can afford, in line with what is appropriate for the community's needs. For example, if demographic projections indicate that the child population in East Marksville will grow over the next few years, then upgrading Blake's neonatal wing would be appropriate. At the same time, Reid needs to evaluate other internal services with an eye to eliminating as much waste as possible. If, for instance, a patient stays in the hospital over the weekend because the physical therapy department is closed, then something must be done to reform the way those services are delivered, possibly keeping a physical therapist on call on Saturdays and Sundays, for example.

Of course, Reid should play a pivotal role in leading the transition to a publicly run clinic system. His first step is to convene a meeting with Clara Bryant, Marksville's commissioner of health services, and Richard Tuttle, CEO of St. Barnabas Hospital. If Tuttle is unwilling to meet with Reid, he should make sure that another member of St. Barnabas's administration or board of directors is present—preferably someone more sympathetic to the needs of low-income neighborhoods. Ideally, the meeting would lay the groundwork for transferring responsibility for the clinics from Blake to the city government. Reid should make it clear that Blake would relinquish control of the clinics and both Blake and St. Barnabas would participate in planning them. Both hospitals should be involved because both will draw on the clinics for their patient referrals. Also, it is only right that such an important public health care service receives input from all parties.

---

[5]*Bernard Lachner is vice chairman and CEO of the Evanston Hospital Corporation, which operates privately run acute care facilities in Evanston and Glenview, Illinois.*

Blake's present financial problem typifies the bankrupt policies of government at all levels. For the last decade, the federal government has passed the cost of health care along to the states, which passed it along to the cities, which, in turn, passed it along to the hospitals and the communities they serve. In addition, the cost shifting has raised the expense of health care to the insured—both businesses and individuals—which now must pay for the uninsured.

As a consequence, hospital emergency rooms and outpatient clinics have become the repositories for a variety of underfunded and ill-fated government programs. The stress on the system is exacerbated by the needs of uninsured mental health patients released from facilities and an increasing number of homeless people, all victims of poverty, poor education, and crime.

Reid is in a position to turn the tide on the buck passing and put the responsibility back on the government's shoulders. It will take courage and strong leadership to fashion a response, but maybe this time a more equitable and humane solution to the health care needs of communities like Marksville can be devised.

Case 3–10

A THOUSAND DAYS

Kennedy and His Cuban Inheritance

The Eisenhower administration thus bequeathed the new President a force of Cuban exiles under American training in Guatemala, a committee of Cuban politicians under American control in Florida and a plan to employ the exiles in an invasion of their homeland and to install the committee on Cuban soil as the provisional government of a free Cuba.

On January 22, two days after the inauguration, Allen Dulles and General Lemnitzer exposed the project to leading members of the new administration, among them Dean Rusk, Robert McNamara, and Robert Kennedy. Speaking for the Joint Chiefs, Lemnitzer tried to renew discussion of alternatives ranging from minimum to maximum United States involvement. Six days later President Kennedy convened his first White House meeting on the plan. He was wary and reserved in his reaction. After listening for a long time, he instructed the Defense Department to take a hard look at CIA's military conception and the State Department to prepare a program for the isolation and containment of Cuba through the OAS. In the meantime, CIA was to continue what it had been doing. The ground rule against overt United States participation was still to prevail.

The Joint Chiefs, after brooding over CIA's Trinidad plan for a week, pronounced favorably on the chances of initial military success. The JCS evaluation was, however, a peculiar and ambiguous document. At one point it said categorically, in what would seem an implicit rejection of the Anzio model, that ultimate success would depend on either a sizable uprising inside the island or sizable support from outside. Then later, without restating these alternative conditions for victory, the document concluded that the existing plan, if executed in time, stood a "fair" chance of ultimate success. Even if it did not immediately attain all its goals, the JCS remarked philosophically, it

---

would still contribute to the eventual overthrow of the regime.

There was plainly a logical gap between the statement that the plan would work if one or another condition were fulfilled and the statement that the plan would work anyway. One cannot know whether this gap resulted from sloppiness in analysis or from a conviction, conscious or unconscious, that once the invasion were launched, either internal uprising or external support would follow, and, if not the first, then the second—that, in short, once the United States government embarked on this enterprise, it could not risk the disaster of failure. Certainly this conviction permeated the thinking of the exiles themselves as well as of the United States officers in Guatemala. Since some, at least, of the Joint Chiefs had always been skeptical of the CIA ground rule, that conviction may well have lurked in the back of their minds too.

Late in February the Chiefs sent an inspection team to the Guatemala base. In a new report in early March, they dropped the point about external support and hinged victory on the capacity of the assault to produce anti-Castro action behind the lines. From the viewpoint of the Joint Chiefs, then, the Cuban resistance was indispensable to success. They could see no other way—short of United States intervention—by which an invasion force of a thousand Cubans, no matter how well trained and equipped nor how stout their morale, could conceivably overcome the 200,000 men of Castro's army and militia.

The pace of events was quickening. Robert Alejos, the Guatemalan planter whose *finca* had been sheltering the Brigade, arrived in Washington in early March with a letter from President Ydígoras to President Kennedy. Ydígoras wrote that the presence of the Cubans was a mounting embarrassment and that he must request assurances that they depart by the end of April. For its part, the CIA reported that the Cubans themselves were clamoring to move; the spirit of the Brigade had reached its peak, and further postponement would risk demoralization. Moreover, the rainy season was about to begin, the ground would turn into

volcanic mud, and training would have to stop. And there was another potent reason for going ahead: Castro, the CIA said, was about to receive jet airplanes from the Soviet Union along with Cuban pilots trained in Czechoslovakia to fly them; once the MIGs arrived, an amphibious landing would turn into a slaughter. After June 1, it would take the United States Marines and Air Force to overthrow Castro. If a purely Cuban invasion were ever to take place, it had to take place in the next few weeks.

By mid-March the President was confronted, in effect, with a now-or-never choice.

Cuba in the Cabinet Room

On March 11, about a week after my return from Latin America, I was summoned to a meeting with the President in the Cabinet Room. An intimidating group sat around the table—the Secretary of State, the Secretary of Defense, the director of the Central Intelligence Agency, three Joint Chiefs resplendent in uniforms and decorations, the Assistant Secretary of State for Inter-American Affairs, the chairman of the Latin American Task Force and appropriate assistants and bottle-washers. I shrank into a chair at the far end of the table and listened in silence.

I had first heard of the Cuban operation in early February; indeed, the day before leaving for Buenos Aires I had sent the President a memorandum about it. The idea sounded plausible enough, the memorandum suggested, if one excluded everything but Cuba itself; but, as soon as the focus was enlarged to include the rest of the hemisphere and the rest of the world, arguments *against* the decision gained strength. Above all, "this would be your first dramatic foreign policy initiative. At one stroke you would dissipate all the extraordinary good will which has been rising toward the new Administration through the world. It would fix a malevolent image of the new Administration in the minds of millions."

It was apparent now a month later that matters were still very much in flux. No final decision had yet been taken on whether the invasion should go forward at all and, if so, whether Trinidad should be the landing point. It fell to Allen Dulles and Richard M. Bissell, Jr., as the originators of the project, to make the main arguments for action.

I had known both men for more than 15 years and held them both in high respect. As an OSS intelligence officer in London and Paris during the war, I had admired the coolness and proficiency of Dulles's work in Bern; and, meeting him from time to time in the years after the war, I had come greatly to enjoy his company. Years in the intelligence business had no doubt given him a capacity for ruthlessness; but he was urbane, courtly and honorable, almost wholly devoid of the intellectual rigidity and personal self-righteousness of his brother. During the McCarthy years, when John Foster Dulles regularly threw innocent State Department officials to the wolves, Allen Dulles just as regularly protected CIA officers unjustly denounced on the Hill.

Richard Bissell, whom I had known as an economist in the Marshall Plan before he turned to intelligence work and became CIA's deputy director for operations, was a man of high character and remarkable intellectual gifts. His mind was swift and penetrating, and he had an unsurpassed talent for lucid analysis and fluent exposition. A few years before he had conceived and fought through the plan of U-2 flights over the Soviet Union; and, though this led to trouble in 1960, it still remained perhaps the greatest intelligence coup since the war. He had committed himself for the past year to the Cuban project with equal intensity. Yet he recognized the strength of his commitment and, with characteristic honesty, warned us to discount his bias. Nonetheless, we all listened transfixed—in this meeting and other meetings that followed— fascinated by the workings of this superbly clear, organized, and articulate intelligence, while Bissell, pointer in hand, would explain how the invasion would work or discourse on the relative merits of alternative landing sites.

Both Dulles and Bissell were at a disadvantage in having to persuade a skeptical new administration about the virtues of a proposal nurtured in the hospitable bosom of a previous government—a proposal on which they had personally worked for a long time and in which their organization had a heavy vested interest. This cast them in the role less of analysts than of advocates, and it led them to accept progressive modifications so long as the expedition in some form remained; perhaps they too unconsciously supposed that, once the operation began to unfold, it would not be permitted to fail.

The determination to keep the scheme alive sprang in part, I believe, from the embarrassments of calling it off. As Dulles said at the March 11 meeting, "Don't forget that we have a disposal problem. If we have to take these men out of Guatemala, we will have to transfer them to the United States, and we can't have them wandering around the country telling everyone what they have been doing." What could one do with "this asset" if not send it on to Cuba? If transfer to the United States was out, demobilization on the spot would create even greater difficulties. The Cubans themselves were determined to go back to their homeland, and they might well forcibly resist efforts to take away their arms and equipment. Moreover, even if the Brigade were successfully disbanded, its members would disperse, disappointed and resentful, all over Latin America. They would tell where they had been and what they had been doing, thereby exposing CIA operations. And they would explain how the United States, having prepared an expedition against Castro, had then lost its nerve. This could only result, Dulles kept emphasizing, in discrediting Washington, disheartening Latin American opponents of Castro and encouraging the *Fidelistas* in their attack on democratic regimes, like that of Betancourt in Venezuela. Disbandment might thus produce pro-Castro revolutions all around the Caribbean. For all these reasons, CIA argued, instead of turning the Cubans loose, we must find some means for putting them back into Cuba "on their own."

The contingency had thus become a reality: Having created the Brigade as an option, the CIA now presented its use against Cuba as a necessity. Nor did Dulles's arguments lack force. Confronted by them, Kennedy tentatively agreed that the simplest thing, after all, might be to let the Cubans go where they yearned to go—to Cuba. Then he tried to turn the meeting toward a consideration of how this could be done with the least political risk. The first step was to form a more liberal and representative exile organization, and this the President directed should be done as soon as possible.

Bissell then renewed the case for the Trinidad plan. Kennedy questioned it as "too spectacular." He did not want a big amphibious invasion in the manner of the Second World War; he wanted a "quiet" landing, preferably at night. And he insisted that the plans be drawn on the basis of *no United States military intervention*—a stipulation to which no one at the table made objection. Thomas Mann seconded these points, stressing the probability of anti-American reactions in Latin America and the United Nations if the American hand were not well concealed. He was especially worried that the air strikes would give the show away unless they could seem plausibly to come from bases on Cuban soil; and the Trinidad airstrip could not take B-26s. The President concluded the meeting by defining the issue with his usual crispness. The trouble with the operation, he said, was that the smaller the political risk, the greater the military risk, and vice versa. The problem was to see whether the two risks could be brought into reasonable balance.

For the next three days the CIA planners canvassed alternative landing sites, coming up with three new possibilities, of which the most likely was about 100 miles west of Trinidad in the Zapata area around Cochinos Bay—the Bay of Pigs. The Joint Chiefs, examining these recommendations on March 14, agreed that Zapata, with its airstrip and the natural defense provided by its swamps, seemed the best of the three but added softly that they still preferred Trinidad. When we met again in the Cabinet Room on March 15, Bissell outlined the Zapata plan. The President, listening somberly, suggested some changes, mostly intended to "reduce the noise level"—such as making sure that the invasion ships would be unloaded before dawn.

He then authorized CIA to continue on the assumption that the invasion would occur. But he repeated his decision against any form of United States military intervention and added carefully and categorically that he was reserving his final decision on the plan itself. The expedition, he said, must be laid on in a way that would make it possible for him to call it off as late as 24 hours before D-day.

We all in the White House considered uprisings behind the lines essential to the success of the operation; so too did the Joint Chiefs of Staff; and so, we thought, did the CIA. It was only later that I learned about the Anzio concept; it certainly did not come across clearly in the White House meetings. And it was much later that Allen Dulles wrote: "Much of the American press assumed at the time that this action was predicated on a mistaken intelligence estimate to the effect that a landing would touch off a widespread and successful popular revolt in Cuba . . . I know of no estimate that a spontaneous uprising of the unarmed population of Cuba would be touched off by the landing."* This statement plainly reflected the CIA notion that the invasion would win by attrition rather than by rebellion. It also, strictly construed, was accurate enough in itself—if due attention is paid to such key words as "spontaneous," "unarmed" and "landing." Obviously no one expected the invasion to galvanize the unarmed and unorganized into rising against Castro at the moment of disembarkation. But the invasion plan, as understood by the President and the Joint Chiefs, did assume that the successful *occupation* of an enlarged beachhead area would rather soon incite *organized* uprisings by *armed* members of the Cuban resistance.

Dulles and Bissell themselves reinforced this impression. When questioned early in April about the prospects of internal resistance, instead of discounting it, which seems to have been their view, they claimed that over 2,500 persons presently

_____

Allen W. Dulles, The Craft of Intelligence *(New York, 1963), p. 169.*

belonged to resistance organizations, that 20,000 more were sympathizers, and that the Brigade, once established on the island, could expect the active support of, at the very least, a quarter of the Cuban people. They backed up such sanguine estimates by citing requests from contacts in Cuba for arms drops and assurances that a specified number of men stood ready to fight when the signal was given.

My experience in OSS during the Second World War left me with a sad skepticism about such messages. Too often the senders inflated their strength, whether out of hope or despair, or because they wanted guns, ammunition, and radios to sell on the black market. Recalling disappointment and miscalculation then, one could not find the CIA assurances satisfying. But mine was a special experience; and the estimates coming, as we all supposed, with the Agency's full authority behind them, impressed most of those around the table. Again it appeared only later that the Intelligence Branch of CIA had never been officially apprised of the Cuban expedition and that CIA's elaborate national estimates procedure was never directed to the question whether an invasion would trigger other uprisings. Robert Amory, Jr., the able deputy director for intelligence, himself a veteran of amphibious landings in the Second World War, was not informed at any point about any aspect of the operation. The same men, in short, both planned the operation and judged its chances of success. Nor was anyone at State, in intelligence jargon, "witting" below Tom Mann, which meant that the men on the Cuban desk, who received the daily flow of information from the island, were not asked to comment on the feasibility of the venture. The "need-to-know" standard—that is, that no one should be told about a project unless it becomes operationally necessary—thus had the idiotic effect of excluding much of the expertise of government at a time when every alert newspaperman knew something was afoot.

The talk with Newman strengthened misgivings about CIA's estimates. He said that, though anti-Castro sentiment had markedly increased since his last visit the year before, Castro still roused intense enthusiasm and faith, especially among the young and among those who had benefited from the social changes of the revolution. These two groups, Newman added, constituted a considerable part of the population. Even a sizable middle group, now disillusioned about Castro, would not be likely to respond with enthusiasm to an invasion backed by the United States because we were so thoroughly identified in their minds with Batista. As much as many Cubans detested the present situation, they still preferred it to a restoration of the old order. "We must understand that from the viewpoint of many Cubans, including anti-Castro Cubans, we come into the ring with exceedingly dirty hands."

Approach to a Decision

The meetings in the Cabinet Room were now taking place every three or four days. The President, it seemed to me, was growing steadily more skeptical as his hard questioning exposed one problem after another in the plans. Moreover, the situation in Laos was at a point of crisis. Kennedy feared that, if the Cuban invasion went forward, it might prejudice chances of agreement with the Soviet Union over Laos; Ambassador Thompson's cables from Moscow reported Khrushchev's unusual preoccupation with Cuba. On the other hand, if we did in the end have to send American troops to Laos to fight communism on the other side of the world, we could hardly ignore communism 90 miles off Florida. Laos and Cuba were tied up with each other, though it was hard to know how one would affect the other. But after the March 29 meeting I noted: "The final decision will have to be made on April 4. I have the impression that the tide is flowing against the project."

Dulles and Bissell, convinced that if the Cubans were ever to be sent against Castro they had to go now, sure that the Brigade could accomplish its mission, and nagged by the disposal problem, now redoubled their efforts at persuasion. Dulles told Kennedy that he felt much more confident about success than he had ever been in the case of Guatemala. CIA concentrated particularly in the meetings on trying to show that, even if the expedition failed, the cost would not be excessive. Obviously no one could believe any longer that the adventure would not be attributed to the United States—news stories described the recruitment effort in Miami every day—but somehow the idea took hold around the cabinet table that this would not much matter so long as United States soldiers did not take part in the actual fighting. If the operation were truly "Cubanized," it would hopefully appear as part of the traditional ebb and flow of revolution and counterrevolution in the Caribbean.

Moreover, if worst came to worst and the invaders were beaten on the beaches, then, Dulles and Bissell said, they could easily "melt away" into the mountains. This might have been true at Trinidad, which lay near the foothills of the Escambray, and it was more true of the Bay of Pigs than of the other two alternative sites proposed in mid-March. But the CIA exposition was less than candid both in implying that the Brigade had undergone guerrilla training (which had substantially ended five months earlier, before most of the Cubans had arrived in Guatemala) and in suggesting the existence of an easy escape hatch. I don't think we fully realized that the Escambray Mountains lay 80 miles from the Bay of Pigs, across a hopeless tangle of swamps and jungles. And no one knew (until Haynes Johnson interviewed the survivors) that the CIA agents in Guatemala were saying nothing to the Cubans about this last resort of flight to the hills, apparently fearing to lower their morale. "We were never told about this," San Román said later. "What we were told was, 'If you fail *we* will go in.' "*

Our meetings were taking place in a curious atmosphere of assumed consensus. The CIA representatives dominated the discussion. The Joint Chiefs seemed to be going contentedly along. They met four times as a body after March 15 to review the Bay of Pigs project as it evolved; and, while their preference for Trinidad was on the record and

they never formally approved the new plan, they at no time opposed it. Their collaboration with CIA in refining the scheme gave the White House the impression of their wholehearted support. Robert McNamara, who was absorbed in the endless task of trying to seize control of the Pentagon, accepted the judgment of the Chiefs on the military aspects of the plan, understood the CIA to be saying that invasion would shortly produce a revolt against Castro, and supposed in any case that the new administration was following a well-established policy developed by its predecessors. Dean Rusk listened inscrutably through the discussions, confining himself to gentle warnings about possible excesses. When he went to the SEATO conference in late March and Chester Bowles as Acting Secretary sat in his place, Bowles was horrified by what he heard but reluctant to speak out in his chief's absence. On March 31 he gave Rusk a strong memorandum opposing the invasion and asked to be permitted, if Rusk disagreed, to carry the case to the President. Rusk reassured Bowles, leaving him with the impression that the project was being whittled down into a guerrilla infiltration, and filed the memorandum away.

In the meantime, Senator Fulbright had grown increasingly concerned over the newspaper stories forecasting an invasion. The President was planning to spend Easter weekend in Palm Beach and, learning that Fulbright also was going to Florida, invited him to travel on the plane. On March 29 Fulbright, with the assistance of Pat Holt, a member of the Foreign Relations Committee staff, wrote a memorandum that he gave Kennedy the next day.

There were two possible policies toward Cuba, Fulbright argued: overthrow, or toleration and isolation. The first would violate the spirit and probably the letter of the OAS charter, hemisphere treaties, and our own federal legislation. If successful, it "would be denounced from the Rio Grande to Patagonia as an example of imperialism." It would cause trouble in the United Nations. It would commit us to the heavy responsibility of making a success of post-Castro Cuba. If it seemed to be failing, we might be tempted to use our own armed

---

*Haynes Johnson, The Bay of Pigs *(New York, 1964 [Dell edition]), p. 67.*

force; and if we did this, "even under the paper cover of legitimacy, we would have undone the work of 30 years in trying to live down earlier interventions."

> To give this activity even covert support is of a piece with the hypocrisy and cynicism for which the United States is constantly denouncing the Soviet Union in the United Nations and elsewhere. This point will not be lost on the rest of the world—nor on our own consciences.

Instead, Fulbright urged a policy of containment. The Alliance for Progress provided a solid basis for insulating the rest of the hemisphere from Castro. As for the Cuban exiles, an imaginative approach could find a more productive use of their talents than invading their homeland. Remember always, Fulbright concluded, "The Castro regime is a thorn in the flesh; but it is not a dagger in the heart."

It was a brilliant memorandum. Yet the President returned from Palm Beach more militant than when he had left. But he did ask Fulbright to attend the climactic meeting on April 4. This meeting was held at the State Department in a small conference room beside Rusk's office. After the usual routine—pervasive expositions by the CIA, mild disclaimers by Rusk and penetrating questions by the President—Kennedy started asking people around the table what they thought. Fulbright, speaking in an emphatic and incredulous way, denounced the whole idea. The operation, he said, was wildly out of proportion to the threat. It would compromise our moral position in the world and make it impossible for us to protest treaty violations by the Communists. He gave a brave, old-fashioned American speech, honorable, sensible and strong; and he left everyone in the room, except me and perhaps the President, wholly unmoved.

Kennedy continued around the table. McNamara said that he favored the operation. Mann said that he would have opposed it at the start, but, now that it had gone so far, it should be carried through. Berle wanted the men to be put into Cuba but did not insist on a major production. Kennedy once again wanted to know what could be done in the way of quiet infiltration as against the beachhead assault.

The meeting fell into discussion before the round of the table was completed. Soon it broke up.

In the months after the Bay of Pigs I bitterly reproached myself for having kept so silent during those crucial discussions in the Cabinet Room, though my feelings of guilt were tempered by the knowledge that a course of objection would have accomplished little save to gain me a name as a nuisance. I can only explain my failure to do more than raise a few timid questions by reporting that one's impulse to blow the whistle on this nonsense was simply undone by the circumstances of the discussion.

It is one thing for a Special Assistant to talk frankly in private to a President at his request and another for a college professor, fresh to the government, to interpose his unassisted judgment in open meeting against that of such august figures as the Secretaries of State and Defense and the Joint Chiefs of Staff, each speaking with the full weight of his institution behind him. Moreover, the advocates of the adventure had a rhetorical advantage. They could strike virile poses and talk of tangible things—fire power, air strikes, landing craft, and so on. To oppose the plan, one had to invoke intangibles—the moral position of the United States, the reputation of the President, the response of the United Nations, "world public opinion" and other such odious concepts. These matters were as much the institutional concern of the State Department as military hardware was of Defense. But, just as the members of the White House staff who sat in the Cabinet Room failed in their job of protecting the President, so the representatives of the State Department failed in defending the diplomatic interests of the nation. I could not help feeling that the desire to prove to the CIA and the Joint Chiefs that they were not soft-headed idealists but were really tough guys, too, influenced State's representatives at the cabinet table.

The President's Decision

More than once I left the meetings in the Cabinet Room fearful that only two of the regulars present were against the operation; but, since I thought the President was the other, I kept hoping that he would avail himself of his own escape clause and cancel the plan. His response to my first memorandum was oblique. He said, "You know, I've reserved the right to stop this thing up to 24 hours before the landing. In the meantime, I'm trying to make some sense out of it. We'll just have to see." But he too began to become a prisoner of events. After another meeting on April 6, I noted: "We seem now destined to go ahead on a quasi-minimum basis—a large-scale infiltration (hopefully) rather than an invasion." This change reflected the now buoyant CIA emphasis on the ease of escaping from the beaches into the hills. By this time we were offered a sort of all-purpose operation guaranteed to work, win or lose. If it failed of its maximum hope—a mass uprising leading to the overthrow of the regime—it would at least attain its minimum objective—supply and reinforcement for the guerrillas already on the island.

The next morning Dick Goodwin and I met for breakfast in the White House Mess to consider whether it would be worth making one more try to reverse the drift. Though Dick had not attended the Cuba sessions, we had talked constantly about the problem. Later that morning before departing for an economic conference in Latin America he went to see Rusk. When Goodwin expressed strong doubts about the Cuban operation, Rusk finally said, "Maybe we've been oversold on the fact that we can't say no to this." Afterward Goodwin urged me to send Rusk a copy of my memorandum to the President and follow it up by a personal visit. I arranged to see Rusk the next morning.

When I set forth my own doubts on Saturday, the Secretary listened quietly and somewhat mournfully. Finally he said he had for some time been wanting to draw a balance sheet on the project, that he planned to do it over the weekend and would try to talk with the President on Monday. He reverted to a suggestion with which he had startled the Joint Chiefs during one of the meetings. This was that the operation fan out from Guantánamo with the prospect of retreating to the base in case of failure. He re-

marked, "It is interesting to observe the Pentagon people. They are perfectly willing to put the President's head on the block, but they recoil from the idea of doing anything which might risk Guantánamo."

I don't know whether Rusk ever drew his balance sheet, but probably by that Saturday morning the President had already made up his mind. When Goodwin dropped into his office Friday afternoon to say goodbye, Kennedy, striding over to the French windows opening to the lawn, recalled Goodwin's fiery campaign statement and said ironically, "Well, Dick, we're about to put your Cuban policy into action." I saw the President myself later that same afternoon and noted afterward: "It is apparent that he has made his decision and is not likely now to reverse it."

Why had he decided to go ahead? So far as the operation itself was concerned, he felt, as he told me that afternoon, that he had successfully pared it down from a grandiose amphibious assault to a mass infiltration. Accepting the CIA assurances about the escape hatch, he supposed that the cost, both military and political, of failure was now reduced to a tolerable level. He added, "If we have to get rid of these 800 men, it is much better to dump them in Cuba than in the United States, especially if that is where they want to go"—a remark that suggested how much Dulles's insistence on the disposal problem had influenced the decision, as well as how greatly Kennedy was himself moved by the commitment of the Cuban patriots. He was particularly impressed by the fact that three members of the Cuban Revolutionary Council had sons in the Brigade; the exile leaders themselves obviously believed that the expedition would succeed. As the decision presented itself to him, he had to choose whether to disband a group of brave and idealistic Cubans, already trained and equipped, who wanted very much to return to Cuba on their own, or to permit them to go ahead. The President saw no obligation to protect the Castro regime from democratic Cubans and decided that, if the Cubans wished to make the try on the categorical understanding that there would be no direct United States military support, he would help them do so. If the expedition succeeded, the overthrow of Castro would greatly strengthen democratic prospects in the hemisphere; if he called it off, he would forever be haunted by the feeling that his scruples had preserved Castro in power.

More generally, the decision resulted from the fact that he had been in office only 77 days. He had not had the time or opportunity to test the inherited instrumentalities of government. He could not know which of his advisers were competent and which were not. For their part, they did not know him or each other well enough to raise hard questions with force and candor. Moreover, the massed and caparisoned authority of his senior officials in the realm of foreign policy and defense was unanimous for going ahead. The director of the Central Intelligence Agency advocated the adventure; the Joint Chiefs of Staff and the Secretary of Defense approved its military aspects, the Secretary of State its political aspects. They all spoke with the sacerdotal prerogative of men vested with a unique understanding of arcane matters. "If someone comes in to tell me this or that about the minimum wage bill," Kennedy said to me later, "I have no hesitation in overruling them. But you always assume that the military and intelligence people have some secret skill not available to ordinary mortals." The only opposition came from Fulbright and myself (he knew nothing of Bowles's memorandum to Rusk, nor did he know that Edward R. Murrow, the new director of the United States Information Agency, who had learned about the operation from a *New York Times* reporter early in April, was also deeply opposed), and this did not bulk large against the united voice of institutional authority. Had one senior adviser opposed the adventure, I believe that Kennedy would have canceled it. Not one spoke against it.

One further factor no doubt influenced him: the enormous confidence in his own luck. Everything had broken right for him since 1956. He had won the nomination and the election against all the odds in the book. Everyone around him thought he had the Midas touch and could not lose. Despite himself, even this dispassionate and skeptical man may have been affected by the soaring euphoria of the new day.

On the following Tuesday the Robert Kennedys gave a party to celebrate Ethel's birthday. It was a large, lively, uproarious affair, overrun by guests, skits, children, and dogs. In the midst of the gaiety Robert Kennedy drew me aside. He said, "I hear you don't think much of this business." He asked why and listened without expression as I gave my reasons. Finally he said, "You may be right or you may be wrong, but the President has made his mind up. Don't push it any further. Now is the time for everyone to help him all they can."

Case 3–11

THIRTEEN DAYS

"Tuesday Morning, October 16, 1962 . . . "

On Tuesday morning, October 16, 1962, shortly after 9 o'clock, President Kennedy called and asked me to come to the White House. He said only that we were facing great trouble. Shortly afterward, in his office, he told me that a U-2 had just finished a photographic mission and that the Intelligence Community had become convinced that Russia was placing missiles and atomic weapons in Cuba.

From Thirteen Days: A Memoir of the Cuban Missile Crisis *by Robert F. Kennedy. Copyright © 1968 by McCall Corporation. Used by permission of W. W. Norton & Company, Inc.*

That was the beginning of the Cuban missile crisis—a confrontation between the two giant atomic nations, the United States and the Union of Soviet Socialist Republics, which brought the world to the abyss of nuclear destruction and the end of mankind. From that moment in President Kennedy's office until Sunday morning, October 28, that was my life—and for Americans and Russians, for the whole world, it was their life as well.

At 11:45 that same morning, in the Cabinet Room, a formal presentation was made by the Central Intelligence Agency to a number of high officials of the government. Photographs were shown to us. Experts arrived with their charts and their pointers and told us that if we looked carefully, we could see there was a missile base being constructed in a field near San Cristobal, Cuba. I, for one, had to take their word for it. I examined the pictures carefully, and what I saw appeared to be no more than the clearing of a field for a farm or the basement of a house. I was relieved to hear later that this was the same reaction of virtually everyone at the meeting including President Kennedy. Even a few days later, when more work had taken place on the site, he remarked that it looked like a football field.

The dominant feeling at the meeting was stunned surprise. No one had expected or anticipated that the Russians would deploy surface-to-surface ballistic missiles in Cuba. I thought back to my meeting with Soviet Ambassador Anatoly Dobrynin in my office some weeks before. He came to tell me that the Russians were prepared to sign an atmospheric-test-ban treaty if we could make certain agreements on underground testing. I told him I would transmit this message and the accompanying documents to President Kennedy.

I told him we were deeply concerned within the Administration about the amount of military equipment being sent to Cuba. That very morning, I had met on this subject with the President and the Secretaries of State and Defense. There was some evidence that, in addition to the surface-to-air missile (SAM) sites that were being erected, the Russians, under the guise of a fishing village, were constructing a large naval shipyard and a base for submarines. This was all being watched carefully—through agents within Cuba who were reporting the military buildup in a limited but frequently important way, through the questioning of refugees who were screened and processed as they arrived in Florida, and through U-2 flights.

It was election time. The autumn days of September and October were filled with charges and countercharges. Republicans "viewing with alarm" were claiming the United States was not taking the necessary steps to protect our security. Some, such as Senator Homer E. Capehart of Indiana, were suggesting that we take military action against Cuba.

I told Ambassador Dobrynin of President Kennedy's deep concern about what was happening. He told me I should not be concerned, for he was instructed by Soviet Chairman Nikita S. Khrushchev to assure President Kennedy that there would be no ground-to-ground missiles or offensive weapons placed in Cuba. Further, he said, I could assure the President that this military buildup was not of any significance and that Khrushchev would do nothing to disrupt the relationship of our two countries during this period prior to the election. Chairman Khrushchev, he said, liked President Kennedy and did not wish to embarrass him.

I pointed out that I felt he had a very strange way of showing his admiration; that what the Russians had been doing in Cuba was a matter of the deepest concern to the United States; and that his protestations of friendship meant little alongside the military activities in the Caribbean. I told him we were watching the buildup carefully and that he should know it would be of the gravest consequence if the Soviet Union placed missiles in Cuba. That would never happen, he assured me, and left.

I reported the conversation to President Kennedy, Secretary of State Dean Rusk, and Secretary of Defense Robert McNamara, and relayed my own skepticism, and suggested that it might be advisable to issue a statement making it un-equivocally clear that the United States would not tolerate the introduction of offensive surface-to-surface missiles, or offensive weapons of any kind, into Cuba.

That same afternoon, September 4, from a draft prepared by Nicholas Katzenbach, the Deputy Attorney General, and myself, the President issued exactly this kind of warning and pointed out the serious consequences that would result from such a step.

A week later, on September 11, Moscow disclaimed publicly any intention of taking such action and stated that there was no need for nuclear missiles to be transferred to any country outside the Soviet Union, including Cuba.

During this same period of time, an important official in the Soviet Embassy, returning from Moscow, brought me a personal message from Khrushchev to President Kennedy, stating that he wanted the President to be assured that under no circumstances would surface-to-surface missiles be sent to Cuba.

Now, as the representatives of the CIA explained the U-2 photographs that morning, Tuesday, October 16, we realized that it had all been lies, one gigantic fabric of lies. The Russians were putting missiles in Cuba, and they had been shipping them there and beginning the construction of the sites at the same time those various private and public assurances were being forwarded by Chairman Khrushchev to President Kennedy.

Thus, the dominant feeling was one of shocked incredulity. We had been deceived by Khrushchev, but we had also fooled ourselves. No official within the government had ever suggested to President Kennedy that the Russian buildup in Cuba would include missiles. On a number of occasions, the President had asked for a specific evaluation on what the Intelligence Community felt to be the implications for the United States of that buildup. The Intelligence Community, in its National Estimate of the future course of events, had advised him—on each of the four occasions in 1962 when they furnished him with official reports on Cuba and the Caribbean—that the Russians would not make offensive weapons available to Cuba. The last estimate before our meeting of the 16th of October was dated the 19th of September, and it advised the President that without reservation the United States Intelligence Board, after considerable discussion and examination, had concluded that the Soviet Union would not make Cuba a strategic base. It pointed out that the Soviet Union had not taken this kind of step with any of its satellites in the past and would feel the risk of retaliation from the United States to be too great to take the risk in this case.

We heard later, in a postmortem study, that reports had come from agents within Cuba indicating the presence of missiles in September of 1962. Most of the reports were false; some were the result of confusion by untrained observers between surface-to-air missiles and surface-to-surface missiles. Several reports, however, turned out to be accurate—one from a former employee at the Hilton Hotel in Havana, who believed a missile installation was being constructed near San Cristobal, and another from someone who overheard Premier Fidel Castro's pilot talking in a boastful and intoxicated way one evening about the nuclear missiles that were going to be furnished Cuba by Russia.

But before these reports were given substance, they had to be checked and rechecked. They were not even considered substantial enough to pass on to the President or other high officials within the government.

The same group that met that first morning in the Cabinet Room met almost continuously through the next 12 days and almost daily for some six weeks thereafter. Others in the group, which was later to be called the "Ex Comm" (the Executive Committee of the National Security Council), included Secretary of State Dean Rusk; Secretary of Defense Robert McNamara; Director of the Central Intelligence Agency John McCone; Secretary of the Treasury Douglas Dillon;

President Kennedy's adviser on national-security affairs, McGeorge Bundy; Presidential Counsel Ted Sorensen; Under Secretary of State George Ball; Deputy Under Secretary of State U. Alexis Johnson; General Maxwell Taylor, Chairman of the Joint Chiefs of Staff; Edward Martin, Assistant Secretary of State for Latin America; originally, Chip Bohlen, who, after the first day, left to become Ambassador to France and was succeeded by Llewellyn Thompson as the adviser on Russian affairs; Roswell Gilpatric, Deputy Secretary of Defense; Paul Nitze, Assistant Secretary of Defense; and, intermittently at various meetings, Vice-President Lyndon B. Johnson; Adlai Stevenson, Ambassador to the United Nations; Ken O'-Donnell, Special Assistant to the President; and Don Wilson, who was Deputy Director of the United States Information Agency. This was the group that met, talked, argued, and fought together during that crucial period of time. From this group came the recommendations from which President Kennedy was ultimately to select his course of action.

They were men of the highest intelligence, industrious, courageous, and dedicated to their country's well-being. It is no reflection on them that none was consistent in his opinion from the very beginning to the very end. That kind of open, unfettered mind was essential. For some there were only small changes, perhaps varieties of a single idea. For others there were continuous changes of opinion each day; some, because of the pressure of events, even appeared to lose their judgment and stability.

The general feeling in the beginning was that some form of action was required. There were those, although they were a small minority, who felt the missiles did not alter the balance of power and therefore necessitated no action. Most felt, at that stage, that an air strike against the missile sites could be the only course. Listening to the proposals, I passed a note to the President: "I now know how Tojo felt when he was planning Pearl Harbor."

"The President . . . knew he would have to act"

After the meeting in the Cabinet Room, I walked back to the Mansion with the President. It would be difficult; the stakes were high—of the highest and most substantial kind—but he knew he would have to act. The United States could not accept what the Russians had done. What that action would be was still to be determined. But he was convinced from the beginning that he would have to do something. To keep the discussions from being inhibited and because he did not want to arouse attention, he decided not to attend all the meetings of our committee. This was wise. Personalities change when the President is present, and frequently even strong men make recommendations on the basis of what they believe the President wishes to hear. He instructed our group to come forward with recommendations for one course or possibly several alternative courses of action.

It was during the afternoon and evening of that first day, Tuesday, that we began to discuss the idea of a quarantine or blockade. Secretary McNamara, by Wednesday, became the blockade's strongest advocate. He argued that it was limited pressure, which could be increased as the circumstances warranted. Further, it was dramatic and forceful pressure, which would be understood yet, most importantly, still leave us in control of events. Later he reinforced his position by reporting that a surprise air strike against the missile bases alone—a surgical air strike, as it came to be called—was militarily impractical in the view of the Joint Chiefs of Staff, that any such military action would have to include all military installations in Cuba, eventually leading to an invasion. Perhaps we would come to that, he argued. Perhaps that course of action would turn out to be inevitable. "But let's not start with that course," if by chance that kind of confrontation with Cuba, and of necessity with the Soviet Union, could be avoided.

Those who argued for the military strike instead of a blockade pointed out that a blockade would not in fact remove the missiles and would not even stop the work from going ahead on the missile sites themselves. The missiles were already in Cuba, and all we would be doing with a blockade would be "closing the door after the horse had left the barn." Further, they argued, we would be bringing about a confrontation with the Soviet Union by stopping their ships, when we should be concentrating on Cuba and Castro.

Their most forceful argument was that our installation of a blockade around Cuba invited the Russians to do the same to Berlin. If we demanded the removal of missiles from Cuba as the price for lifting our blockade, they would demand the removal of missiles surrounding the Soviet Union as the reciprocal act.

And so we argued, and so we disagreed—all dedicated, intelligent men, disagreeing and fighting about the future of their country, and of mankind. Meanwhile, time was slowly running out.

An examination of photography taken on Wednesday, the 17th of October, showed several other installations, with at least 16 and possibly 32 missiles of over a thousand-mile range. Our military experts advised that these missiles could be in operation within a week. The next day, Thursday, estimates by our Intelligence Community placed in Cuba missiles with an atomic-warhead potential of about one-half the current ICBM capacity of the entire Soviet Union. The photography having indicated that the missiles were being directed at certain American cities, the estimate was that within a few minutes of their being fired 80 million Americans would be dead.

The members of the Joint Chiefs of Staff were unanimous in calling for immediate military action. They forcefully presented their view that the blockade would not be effective. General Curtis LeMay, Air Force Chief of Staff, argued strongly with the President that a military attack was essential. When the President questioned what the response of the Russians might be General LeMay assured him there would be no reaction. President Kennedy was skeptical. "They, no more than we, can let these things go by without doing something. They can't after all their

statements, permit us to take out their missiles, kill a lot of Russians, and then do nothing. If they don't take action in Cuba, they certainly will in Berlin."

The President went on to say that he recognized the validity of the arguments made by the Joint Chiefs, the danger that more and more missiles would be placed in Cuba, and the likelihood, if we did nothing, that the Russians would move on Berlin and in other areas of the world, feeling the United States was completely impotent. Then it would be too late to do anything in Cuba, for by that time all their missiles would be operational.

General David M. Shoup, Commandant of the Marine Corps, summed up everyone's feelings: "You are in a pretty bad fix, Mr. President." The President answered quickly, "You are in it with me." Everyone laughed, and, with no final decision, the meeting adjourned.

Later, Secretary McNamara, although he told the President he disagreed with the Joint Chiefs and favored a blockade rather than an attack, informed him that the necessary planes, men, and ammunition were being deployed and that we could be ready to move with the necessary air bombardments on Tuesday, October 23, if that was to be the decision. The plans called for an initial attack, consisting of 500 sorties, striking all military targets, including the missile sites, airfields, ports, and gun emplacements.

I supported McNamara's position in favor of a blockade. This was not from a deep conviction that it would be a successful course of action, but a feeling that it had more flexibility and fewer liabilities than a military attack. Most importantly, like others, I could not accept the idea that the United States would rain bombs on Cuba, killing thousands and thousands of civilians in a surprise attack. Maybe the alternatives were not very palatable, but I simply did not see how we could accept that course of action for our country.

"A majority opinion . . . for a blockade . . ."

By Thursday night, there was a majority opinion in our group for a blockade. Our committee went from the State Department to the White House around 9:15 that night. In order to avoid the suspicion that would have ensued from the presence of a long line of limousines, we all went in my car—John McCone, Maxwell Taylor, the driver, and myself all crowded together in the front seat, and six others sitting in back.

We explained our recommendations to the President. At the beginning, the meeting seemed to proceed in an orderly and satisfactory way. However, as people talked, as the President raised probing questions, minds and opinions began to change again, and not only on small points. For some, it was from one extreme to another—supporting an air attack at the beginning of the meeting and, by the time we left the White House, supporting no action at all.

The President, not at all satisfied, sent us back to our deliberations. Because any other step would arouse suspicion, he returned to his regular schedule and his campaign speaking engagements.

The next morning, at our meeting at the State Department, there were sharp disagreements again. The strain and the hours without sleep were beginning to take their toll.

Finally we agreed on a procedure by which we felt we could give some intelligent recommendations to the President. We knew that time was running out and that delay was not possible. We split into groups to write up our respective recommendations, beginning with an outline of the President's speech to the nation and the whole course of action thereafter, trying to anticipate all possible contingencies and setting forth recommendations as to how to react to them.

In the early afternoon, we exchanged papers, each group dissected and criticized the other, and then the papers were returned to the original group to develop further answers. Gradually from all this came the outline of definitive plans. For the group that advocated the blockade, it was an outline of the legal basis for our action, an agenda for a meeting of the Organization of American States, recommendations for the role of the United Nations, the military procedures for stopping ships, and, finally, the circumstances under which military force might be used. For the group that advocated immediate military action, it was an outline of the areas to be attacked, a defense of our position in the United Nations, suggestions as to how to obtain support from Latin American countries, and a proposed communication to Khrushchev to convince him of the inadvisability of moving militarily against us in the Caribbean, Berlin, or elsewhere in the world.

During all these deliberations, we all spoke as equals. There was no rank, and, in fact, we did not even have a chairman. Dean Rusk—who, as Secretary of State, might have assumed that position—had other duties during this period of time and frequently could not attend our meetings. As a result, with the encouragement of McNamara, Bundy, and Ball, the conversations were completely uninhibited and unrestricted. Everyone had an equal opportunity to express himself and to be heard directly. It was a tremendously advantageous procedure that does not frequently occur within the executive branch of government, where rank is often so important.

"It was now up to one single man"

We met all day Friday and Friday night. Then again early Saturday morning we were back at the State Department. I talked to the President several times on Friday. He was hoping to be able to meet with us early enough to decide on a course of action and then broadcast it to the nation Sunday night. Saturday morning at 10 o'clock I called the President at the Blackstone Hotel in Chicago and told him we were ready to meet with him. It was now up to one single man. No committee was going to make this decision. He canceled his trip and returned to Washington.

As he was returning to Washington, our armed forces across the world were put on alert. Telephoning from our meeting in the State Department, Secretary McNamara ordered four tactical air squadrons placed at readiness for an air strike, in case the President decided to accept that recommendation.

The President arrived back at the White House at 1:40 P.M. and went for a swim. I sat on the side of the pool, and we talked. At 2:30 we walked up to the Oval Room.

The meeting went on until 10 minutes after five. Convened as a formal meeting of the National Security Council, it was a larger group of people who met, some of whom had not participated in the deliberations up to that time. Bob McNamara presented the arguments for the blockade; others presented the arguments for the military attack.

The President made his decision that afternoon in favor of the blockade. There was one final meeting the next morning, with General Walter C. Sweeney, Jr., Commander in Chief of the Tactical Air Command, who told the President that even a major surprise air attack could not be certain of destroying all the missile sites and nuclear weapons in Cuba. That ended the small, lingering doubt that might still have remained in his mind. It had worried him that a blockade would not remove the missiles—now it was clear that an attack could not accomplish that task completely, either.

The strongest argument against the all-out military attack, and one no one could answer to his satisfaction, was that a surprise attack would erode if not destroy the moral position of the United States throughout the world.

Adlai Stevenson had come from New York to attend the meeting Saturday afternoon, as he had attended several of the Ex Comm meetings. He had always been dubious about the air strike, but at the Saturday meeting he strongly advocated what he had only tentatively suggested to me a few days before—namely, that we make it clear to the Soviet Union that if it withdrew its missiles from Cuba, we would be willing to withdraw our missiles from Turkey and Italy and give up our naval base at Guantanamo Bay.

There was an extremely strong reaction from some of the participants to his suggestion, and several sharp exchanges followed. The President, although he rejected Stevenson's suggestion, pointed out that he had for a long period held reservations about the value of Jupiter missiles in Turkey and Italy and some time ago had asked the State Department to conduct negotiations for their removal; but now, he said, was not the appropriate time to suggest this action, and we could not abandon Guantanamo Bay under threat from the Russians.

Stevenson has since been criticized publicly for the position he took at this meeting. I think it should be emphasized that he was presenting a point of view from a different perspective than the others, one which was therefore important for the President to consider. Although I disagreed strongly with his recommendations, I thought he was courageous to make them, and I might add they made as much sense as some others considered during that period of time.

The President's speech was now scheduled for Monday evening. Under the direction of George Ball, Alex Johnson, and Ed Martin, a detailed hour-to-hour program was arranged to inform our allies, prepare for the meeting of the OAS, inform the ambassadors stationed in Washington, and prepare for them and others in written form the legal justification on which our action was predicated. More and more government officials were brought into the discussions, and finally word began to seep through to the press that a serious crisis was imminent. Through the personal intervention of the President with several newspapers, the only stories written Monday morning were reports that a major speech was to be given by the President and that the country faced a serious crisis.

During this same period, military preparations went forward. Missile crews were placed on maximum alert. Troops were moved into Florida and the southeastern part of the United States. Late Saturday night, the First Armored Division began to move out of Texas into Georgia, and five more divisions were placed on alert. The base at Guantanamo Bay was strengthened.

The Navy deployed 180 ships to the Caribbean. The Strategic Air Command was dispersed to civilian landing fields around the country to lessen its vulnerability in case of attack. The B-52 bomber force was ordered into the air fully loaded with atomic weapons. As one came down to land, another immediately took its place in the air.

An hour before the President's speech, Secretary Rusk called in Ambassador Dobrynin and told him of the speech. The newspapers reported that Dobrynin left the Secretary's office looking considerably shaken.

On that Monday afternoon, before his speech and after lunch with Jackie, the President held several meetings. At the first, he formally constituted our committee—which up until that time had been called "the group" or "war council"—under National Security Council Action Memorandum Number 196 as the Executive Committee of the National Security Council, "for the purpose of effective conduct of the operations of the executive branch in the current crisis." The President became the official chairman, and until further notice we were to meet with him every morning at 10:00 A.M.

Shortly thereafter, the President met with the members of the Cabinet and informed them for the first time of the crisis. Then, not long before the broadcast, he met with the leaders of Congress. This was the most difficult meeting. I did not attend, but I know from seeing him afterward that it was a tremendous strain.

Many Congressional leaders were sharp in their criticism. They felt that the President should take more forceful action, a military attack or invasion, and that the blockade was far too weak a response. Senator Richard B. Russell of Georgia said he could not live with himself if he did not say in the strongest possible terms how important it was that we act with greater strength than the President was contemplating.

Senator J. William Fulbright of Arkansas also strongly advised military action rather than such a weak step as the blockade. Others said they were skeptical but would remain publicly silent, only because it was such a dangerous hour for the country.

The President, after listening to the frequently emotional criticism, explained that he would take whatever steps were necessary to protect the security of the United States, but that he did not feel greater military action was warranted initially. Because it was possible that the matter could be resolved without a devastating war, he had decided on the course he had outlined. Perhaps in the end, he said, direct military action would be necessary, but that course should not be followed lightly. In the meantime, he assured them, he had taken measures to prepare our military forces and place them in a position to move.

He reminded them that once an attack began our adversaries could respond with a missile barrage from which many millions of Americans would be killed. That was a gamble he was not willing to take until he had finally and forcefully exhausted all other possibilities. He told them this was an extremely hazardous undertaking and that everyone should understand the risks involved.

He was upset by the time the meeting ended. When we discussed it later he was more philosophical, pointing out that the Congressional leaders' reaction to what we should do, although more militant than his, was much the same as our first reaction when we first heard about the missiles the previous Tuesday.

At 7 o'clock, he went on television to the nation to explain the situation in Cuba and the reasons for the quarantine. He was calm and confident that he had selected the right course.

Case 3–12

DECISION MAKING AT THE TOP: THE ALL-STAR SPORTS CATALOG DIVISION

Introduction

Don Barrett, president of the All-Star Sports Catalog Division (ASC), was preparing for a special meeting of his senior management staff on August 21, 1997. The purpose of the meeting was to review the findings from a consultant's study of the staff's strategic decision-making process. Barrett was certain that the consultant's recommendations would generate sharp differences of opinion within the group, but hoped that changes could be made to improve the organization's ability to identify and exploit the strengths of the division's different businesses. As Barrett had told the consultant: "The most challenging part for the group has been getting effective cross-functional communication and coordination."

Just before the meeting began, Barrett reviewed the study's recommendations. In his report, the consultant had outlined three alternatives for redesigning the group's decision-making process:

- Engage the entire staff in a more "team-oriented" approach to decision making.
- Formally establish a smaller "top management team," consisting of only three to four key staff members, to chart the division's strategic direction.
- Fine-tune the existing decision-making process by changing the group's rules and norms.

Company Background

Steve Archibald, a 1978 graduate of Harvard Business School, originated the idea of the high-volume, discount sporting goods superstore in 1987. He founded All-Star Sports later that year and opened the first store in Tampa, Florida, on June 15, 1988. The company expanded rapidly in those early years, and sales and profit growth continued in the mid-1990s. From 1993 to 1996, sales grew at a compound annual growth rate of 55 percent, earnings per share grew by 65 percent per year, and shareholders realized annual returns in excess of 35 percent. (See Exhibit 1 for more details on the firm's financial performance.)

As All-Star Sports grew, it created three divisions: U.S. Superstores, All-Star International, and ASC. As of September 1997, U.S. Superstores consisted of 450 retail stores located throughout the country, and All-Star International operated 60 stores in Canada, Mexico, and Brazil. ASC consisted of a group of catalog delivery businesses.

The All-Star Sports Catalog Division

Strategy

All-Star Sports initially entered the mail order catalog business in 1990 by creating All-Star Express. The business offered shoppers the convenience of free next-day delivery. All-Star Express grew very rapidly and profitably and achieved sales of $300 million in 1996.

In 1995, All-Star Sports decided to begin targeting schools, sports teams, and other organizations that purchased high volumes of both standard and customized sporting good products. The company, therefore, created the All-Star Sports Catalog Division. Don Barrett, the head of All-Star

---

This case was prepared by Michael Roberto under the direction of David A. Garvin.

EXHIBIT 1   All-Star Sports Inc. Financial Performance (dollars in thousands)

	1992	1993	1994	1995	1996
Income Statement Data					
Sales	$550,122	$845,546	$1,403,112	2,104,145	$3,148,708
Operating income	21,543	28,586	52,401	99,155	162,998
Net income	12,346	15,433	28,126	54,890	91,996
Earnings per share	.45	.53	.97	1.56	2.38
Balance Sheet Data					
Total assets	$287,110	$419,916	$ 707,890	961,456	$1,414,556
Total long-term debt, less current portion	63,353	79,288	174,786	235,845	309,234
Total stockholders' equity	134,390	185,578	269,334	418,012	600,378

Source: All-Star Sports 1996 Annual Report

Express at that time, became the president of the newly formed division. ASC initially consisted of All-Star Express and two acquired sporting good wholesalers—Jackson Sports and Hoffman's Team Apparel. These wholesalers also operated catalog delivery businesses. However, they traditionally served organizations such as schools, clubs, and athletic teams through long-term contractual relationships cultivated by commissioned sales forces. During the next two years, ASC acquired four other major regional sporting good wholesalers in order to build a national delivery network. By 1996, ASC reached nearly $800 million in sales. The acquisition integration process had entered its third stage by mid-1997. In the first stage, ASC had consolidated purchasing across the businesses in order to leverage All-Star Sports' buying power. In the second stage, ASC had developed common systems and merged administrative functions. Now, in the third stage, ASC was integrating the customer service and order fulfillment processes so that a common operating infrastructure would support all of the businesses.

As the industry consolidated during the past few years, success increasingly depended on achieving scale economies in purchasing and distribution and lowering the cost of providing crucial services to customers. As a result, ASC developed a strategy that sought to achieve the operating synergies across these delivery businesses, while appropriately serving the distinct customer needs of two key market segments. To that end, it created distinct sales and marketing units to serve the needs of the two customer segments—individual customers who valued home delivery of standard products (All-Star Express), and organizations that purchased large batches of standard and customized products (All-Star Team Advantage). A consolidated infrastructure of distribution, purchasing, merchandising, information systems, and administration supported these two sales and marketing channels.

Organization

As part of an effort to increase coordination and integration across the division, an organizational restructuring took place in early 1997. Prior to the reorganization, general managers—typically the former owners of acquired firms—still bore complete responsibility for individual wholesaler business units. ASC had retained these general managers in order to preserve customer relationships while learning about the wholesaler business. In early 1997, ASC shifted to a functional organizational structure. Barrett appointed vice presidents for each functional area and gave them responsibility for activities across all delivery businesses.

Incentives

All-Star Sports possessed a strong pay-for-performance system. The company believed that this system aligned the interests of managers and shareholders, motivated and rewarded high levels of performance, and recognized contributions to corporate success. This incentive system included an annual cash bonus as well as stock option grants for key managers. The cash bonus payout depended on four key performance measures: corporate earnings per share, business unit earnings, business unit sales, and customer service. In the past, the business unit portion of each ASC staff member's bonus depended on performance at his or her particular unit within ASC. However, at the beginning of 1997, Barrett announced that future bonuses for all division staff members would depend on total ASC earnings and sales.

The ASC Senior Management Team

Don Barrett

Don Barrett, a graduate of Harvard College and Harvard Business School, had worked for Nicholson's Supermarkets for over a decade before joining All-Star Sports as a regional vice president of store operations in 1989. Soon thereafter, he moved over to head up the All-Star Express business. Barrett had managed All-Star's delivery businesses since 1992 when annual sales equaled only $35 million. More recently, he had guided ASC through the wholesaler acquisition screening and integration processes. In addition to running ASC, Barrett served as a member of CEO Steve Archibald's management staff that oversaw the entire corporation.

Barrett was widely credited for making All-Star Express one of the corporation's most profitable businesses. He had done so by developing effective direct marketing strategies and by investing heavily in call center technology and employee development in order to improve both customer service and productivity. Barrett had also capitalized effectively on synergies with the retail division.

As the division expanded rapidly, Barrett continually sought to build consensus among his management team before moving forward. He set aggressive goals and expectations for the organization but actively sought managers' input on how to achieve those objectives. Moreover, Barrett encouraged managers to respect each other's opinions. As he put it: "I wanted to develop an atmosphere where I could push people, move the organization ahead . . . while letting people know that it's OK to disagree."

Staff members described Barrett as a good listener who was quite willing to accept differing opinions:

> Don is a great listener. He distills information and comments well. He listens and will back up if he needs to after a comment or suggestion that he makes. I think people are quite willing to challenge him.

Another staff member concurred, extolling Barrett's patience and his respect for people:

> We are quite willing to challenge him. That's because Don allows people to disagree . . . He never attacks you personally, never diminishes your importance, or anything like that. He is very patient, maybe exceedingly so. His respect for people is probably his best ability.

One vice president noted that Barrett freely delegated responsibility to those who had earned his trust: "He gives us freedom to do what we believe is right." Staff members valued Barrett's trust and loyalty:

> Don is definitely loyal, perhaps too much so, especially on personnel change issues.
> Loyalty can be a double-edged sword . . . I'm loyal to my people as well. This is OK. It's good to have loyalty to your people. But it can also cloud your judgment. You don't want a total lack of loyalty, however. Then you wouldn't want to work for those kinds of managers.

While he trusted his people, Barrett certainly scrutinized their positions on particular issues. Several managers described how Barrett tested people's thinking on issues:

> Don often states his position to create conversation rather than because it's what he definitely wants to do . . . He says stuff to get us thinking or moving in a particular direction.
>
> He tends to push back at you. He will say it's black if it's white just to push you, especially on issues that cost dollars.

Barrett described why he utilized this tactic:

> I tend to stake out extreme positions just to get a reaction from people and virtually always do get a reaction . . . I will put pressure on them, but it's OK to disagree . . . I want the team to know that I am flexible . . . I don't want people to be afraid to tell me bad news.

While Barrett encouraged managers to disagree with him, he did not like conflict among staff members during meetings. Staff members repeatedly described Barrett as "nonconfrontational":

> He just isn't comfortable with confrontation.
>
> The meeting is really not our place for tackling issues. Don likes things handled off-line if there is disagreement.
>
> Don's style is nonconfrontational . . . He encourages us to take such disagreements off-line.

In sum, managers described Barrett as a consensus-builder, not a "screamer or a yeller." As one manager stated, "Don seeks our input . . . Don allows us to come to a consensus as a team."

The Senior Management Team Members

Barrett personally assembled the current ASC management team, which consisted of 13 individuals including himself.[1] Barrett had purposefully tried to blend together a diverse team at ASC. He sought heterogeneity in backgrounds and experiences.

Moreover, Barrett explained that he had spent considerable time searching for individual executives who not only had the requisite skills to manage the business but who also fit well with the other management team members and with the company's culture and values. As he said, "I've hand-picked these folks as much for fit with our values and culture as for their personal abilities." These values included a bias for managerial and entrepreneurial action, an emphasis on analytical approaches to problem solving, and especially a strong focus on achieving financial performance targets. As Lynn McHale explained, everyone knew that they had to "make the numbers" to be successful at All-Star Sports.

Each staff member had achieved considerable individual success during his or her career and was still adapting to working with such a large, diverse group. For example, Henry Rice and Bill Hoffman, former owners of acquired firms, had spent their entire adult lives as entrepreneurs who built their own highly successful organizations before selling their firms to All-Star Sports. Others, such as Lynn McHale and Jim Maxwell, had enjoyed successful careers within All-Star Sports, having built All-Star Express from its days as a small start-up venture within the corporation. While some of the members, such as McHale and Maxwell, had worked together for nearly four years, the group as a whole had not been together for a long period of time. As one manager concluded, the staff consisted of highly capable individuals who don't yet "do the dance real well together."

The staff members not only had diverse backgrounds; they also approached problems quite differently. Five staff members had graduated from Harvard Business School and prided themselves on their analytical approach to decision making. Others, such as industry veterans Jay Evans and Bill Hoffman, tended to rely on instinct and experience to solve problems. They not only approached problems differently, but did so at quite different speeds. As Barrett said, some were "ready, aim, aim, aim, fire" types, and some

---

[1]*For profiles of each staff member, including each's position on the staff, see Exhibit 2.*

EXHIBIT 2 Individual Staff Member Profiles

Note that each individual worked at ASC headquarters in Tampa, Florida, and reported to Barrett unless otherwise noted.

Jim Maxwell, Senior Vice President, All-Star Express

Maxwell managed All-Star Express. He had spent 7 years in marketing at All-Star Sports, including the last $3\frac{1}{2}$ years working closely with McHale and Barrett at All-Star Express. He had an MBA from Harvard Business School, and had 18 years of experience in direct marketing.

Jay Evans, Senior Vice President, Team Sales

Evans joined All-Star Sports after a long career at Pro Apparel Inc. He brought 22 years of sporting good wholesale industry experience to the team. He had now spent $2\frac{1}{2}$ years at All-Star Sports, most recently as the head of all team/organization sales. Evans worked from the All-Star Team Advantage headquarters in Dallas, Texas.

Jill Johnson, Senior Vice President of Merchandising

Johnson recently rejoined the ASC management team after one year at the All-Star Sports business unit in Mexico. She had 10 years of experience in merchandising at All-Star Sports. After 7 years in merchandising in the retail division, she moved to ASC in 1994 to oversee the consolidation of purchasing and the blending of product lines across the acquired business units.

Henry Rice, Senior Vice President, Operations

Rice joined the company after selling his company, Jackson Sports, to All-Star Sports in early 1995. During the recent reorganization, Rice became the SVP in charge of ASC operations. Rice earned his MBA at the University of Michigan. His primary office was located in Lansing, Michigan.

Bill Hoffman, President, National Accounts

Hoffman joined ASC after he and his partners sold Hoffman's Team Apparel to All-Star Sports in a January 1995 stock swap arrangement. Hoffman had built his company into a $120 million sporting good wholesaler that exclusively served professional athletic teams that desired customized products and services. Hoffman now managed professional team sales and reported to Evans. Hoffman also worked from the Dallas, Texas, office.

Lynn McHale, Vice President of Customer Service

McHale had spent $6\frac{1}{2}$ years at All-Star Sports, the last 4 at ASC. Until recently, she managed the call centers and distribution centers at All-Star Express, working closely with Maxwell and Barrett. Now she managed customer service operations across all of the wholesale business units. McHale had recently begun reporting to Rice as a result of her new assignment. She had been recognized in the *Wall Street Journal* for her innovative employee development techniques. McHale was also a graduate of Harvard Business School.

Dan Hannah, Vice President, Human Resources

Hannah had spent 3 years at All-Star Sports in human resources, the last 2 on the ASC top management team. He had no previous industry experience, but had 9 years of experience in the area of human resources. He had initiated a major effort to improve training and development activities at ASC.

Bruce Ford, Acting VP, Information Systems

Ford had spent the past 2 years as a consultant to All-Star Sports. For the past four months, Ford had stepped in as the acting Vice President of Information Systems at ASC while the division searched for a permanent VP.

Jack Burleson, Vice President, Systems Migration

Burleson had spent over 8 years at All-Star Sports, primarily in distribution in the retail division. For the past 20 months, Burleson had worked at ASC to oversee the process of converting the wholesalers and All-Star

---

EXHIBIT 2   (*concluded*)

Express to common inventory control and distribution center management information systems. Burleson had 24 years of experience in the sporting goods industry.

Anne Lansford, Vice President, Finance

Lansford joined ASC two months ago after 12 years of experience in finance and strategic planning in other industries. Lansford earned her MBA from Harvard Business School.

Kate Walton, Director of Strategy and Integration

Walton joined All-Star Sports 1½ years ago after working in strategic planning at a major athletic footwear company. She is a 1994 graduate of Harvard Business School. Walton led the strategic planning process at ASC and oversaw the integration planning and implementation efforts.

Steve Cunningham, Manager of Budgets and Financial Analysis

Cunningham had spent 7 years at All-Star Sports, the last 2 at ASC. He joined the management team eight months ago on a temporary basis upon departure of the Vice President of Finance. He continued to participate in team meetings as the new Vice President of Finance, Anne Lansford, became acclimated to the company.

---

liked to "shoot from the hip." One vice president described the diversity in people's styles and perspectives:

> People have different backgrounds and philosophies about how to do business . . . We are really like a bunch of married people. We know everyone else's problems, personalities, and backgrounds. That's just part of how everyone approaches the business a little differently, but we all care about the company as a whole. Those who didn't care about others are not here anymore.

Managers had learned about each other mainly through one-on-one interactions. The group was very "efficiency oriented" and did not want to waste time in large meetings. Through this one-on-one interaction, individuals had worked to get to know each others' businesses. As Bill Hoffman noted, "Jim Maxwell and Lynn McHale have been interested and have cared about trying to understand our business." This learning process helped to overcome people's affiliations to the business units where they once had worked. Still, it was a slow and challenging process. One staff member described the natural loyalties that existed:

> Bill [Hoffman] and Henry [Rice] are clearly dedicated to their own businesses. Of course, you

would expect this from entrepreneurs who have built their own businesses from the ground up.

Dan Hannah noted that the group had not overcome territorial loyalties easily:

> I think for some time, we had a good amount of clinging to old loyalties, but that these have eroded with time and effort on the part of everyone.

[For more information regarding the staff, refer Exhibits 2–4. These exhibits provide short profiles of each staff member (Exhibit 2) as well as a summary of the demographic characteristics of the group (Exhibit 3). Exhibit 4 provides results from a group effectiveness survey conducted by the consultant.]

Overview of the Decision-Making Process

The ASC management team met each Monday for two hours. The group spent the first hour reviewing and discussing a variety of issues, including financial performance, integration milestones, and new market developments. This block of time provided an opportunity for staff members to share information and to update each other on key projects. Periodically, this block of time

EXHIBIT 3   Summary of ASC Management Team Demographic Characteristics

Individual Characteristic	Team Average	Standard Deviation	Maximum Value	Minimum Value
Age	42.7	10.0	61.0	30.0
Years on ASC management team	2.4	1.6	5.7	0.2
Years at ASC	2.5	1.4	5.7	0.2
Years at All-Star Sports	4.8	3.1	10.0	0.2
Years of industry experience (exc. All-Star Sports)	8.0	11.5	31.8	0.0
Years of experience in other industries	8.9	7.7	30.0	0.0

Characteristic	Percent of Team
Male	62%
From acquired firms	15
Bachelor's degree	100
MBA degree	46
Harvard MBA degree	38
Primary experience at All-Star Express	15
Primary experience at acquired wholesalers	46
Experience across both Express and wholesale	39

Source: Consultant's Final Report

included presentations from middle managers, aimed to update the senior team on particular projects, such as the division's employee-training initiative or the corporate communications plan. The second hour consisted of a more in-depth discussion of a particular topic such as the adoption of a new salesperson compensation plan. Decision making about key issues typically occurred during this block of time. Once per month, instead of the regular weekly staff meeting, the group met for three hours with CEO Steve Archibald. These meetings served as forums for updating corporate management on key projects or initiatives at ASC. (For staff member assessments of the format and agenda of the regular weekly meetings, refer to Exhibit 5.)

When asked to describe the group's decision-making process, staff members explained that they did not really make decisions as a group during these meetings:

> Look, real decisions don't happen in that group. . . . It's not a forum to break new ground. We do make decisions together, don't get me wrong, but not as a whole group.
>
> We tend to solve problems with others, but not necessarily in the whole group, in the meeting.

Staff members stressed, however, that Barrett did not make strategic decisions alone. Lynn McHale described this puzzle:

> It's not Don making the calls, but we're not a tightly knit decision-making group either.

Instead, the group engaged in a decision-making process that combined team interaction, subgroup discussions, and one-on-one meetings with Barrett.

EXHIBIT 4   Team Effectiveness Survey Results[a]

Team members completed the following survey questions concerning team effectiveness:

For each of the statements listed below, please respond using the following 1–7 scale:

1 = very inaccurate	4 = uncertain	7 = very accurate

1. *This management staff operates as an effective team whose members work well together.*
2. *Staff members perform most of their work individually. They do not work together closely as a group.*
3. *Certain staff members are not effective team players.*
4. *Staff members are capable of working effectively as members of a team.*
5. *Performance expectations frequently change for this management group.*
6. *Behavioral norms for group interaction are unclear.*
7. *The company's incentive system reinforces efforts to improve team effectiveness.*

Survey Question	Senior Faction[b] (> 3 years at ASC)	Junior Faction (< 3 years at ASC)	Difference (Absolute Value)	Score for D. Barrett	Score for Rest of Group	Difference (Absolute Value)
Group operates as a team	4.00	3.75	0.25	5.00	3.75	1.25
Members work individually, not together	2.60	4.00	1.40	3.00	3.50	0.50
Certain members are not team players	2.80	4.88	2.08	2.00	4.25	2.25
Members have team skills	5.80	4.50	1.30	6.00	4.92	1.08
Expectations change frequently	3.00	4.38	1.38	3.00	3.92	0.92
Standards of behavior unclear	2.40	3.63	1.23	2.00	3.25	1.25
Rewards reinforce team building	4.80	3.29	1.51	5.00	3.82	1.18

[a]Survey questions adapted from research methods utilized by Professor Richard Hackman, Department of Psychology, Harvard University.
[b]Senior Faction excludes Barrett for purposes of this analysis. His scores are shown separately.

Source: Consultant's Final Report

Stages of the Decision Process

The senior team's decision-making process consisted of five major stages. The following section describes these stages and explains how group members are involved at each stage. (See Exhibit 6 for a process flow diagram that illustrates the five stages with reference to a recent decision.)

Framing the Problem

The staff tended to structure or frame problems as a group. Typically, this occurred during the second

EXHIBIT 5   Survey Assessment of Meeting Agenda[a]

Team members responded to a survey regarding the agenda and format of their weekly staff meetings. For each category listed, they provided two numerical responses. First, they assessed the time spent on each topic, area of focus, or meeting format (1 = very little, 5 = a great deal). Second, they assessed the importance of each topic, area of focus, or meeting format (1 = not important, 5 = very important).

	Time Spent (1 = very little 5 = a great deal)	Importance (1 = not important 5 = very important)	Difference (Time spent less importance)
Agenda Topics			
Financial performance	3.3	4.7	(1.5)
Project updates	3.3	3.9	(0.6)
Division strategy	2.1	4.1	(2.0)
Resource allocation	1.7	3.3	(1.5)
Day-to-day operations	2.4	2.1	0.3
Administrative policies	2.4	2.4	0.0
Areas of Focus			
Internal operations	3.1	3.7	(0.6)
Competitors	1.4	3.2	(1.8)
Customers	1.5	4.1	(2.5)
Suppliers	1.5	2.6	(1.2)
Capital markets	1.3	2.0	(0.7)
Meeting Formats			
Staff member presentations	3.5	3.4	0.2
Presentations by nonstaff personnel	2.3	2.8	(0.5)
Group discussion	2.4	4.3	(1.9)

[a]Survey technique adapted from method utilized by Professor Jay Lorsch, Harvard Business School, in a study of boards of directors. See Jay Lorsch, *Pawns or Potentates* (Boston: Harvard Business School Press, 1989).

Source: Consultant's Final Report

one-hour block of time at staff meetings. During those discussions on a particular topic or initiative, staff members surfaced issues or problems that required further attention. Often, a manager requested the group's help on a problem in his or her area and pointed out the broad implications for the division as a whole. At this point, the staff members freely shared information regarding the issue and perhaps offered their opinions. For example, during a May 1997 meeting, Lynn McHale surfaced an issue regarding the organization's plans to integrate a wholesaler acquired in California. She expressed concern with the existing project schedule and explained the issues that threatened the current plan. Group members then discussed McHale's concerns and helped her identify the key issues that required additional investigation.

For most complex issues such as this, the group attempted to examine multiple courses of action. For that purpose, they selected a subgroup to

EXHIBIT 6   Decision-Making Process Flow Diagram

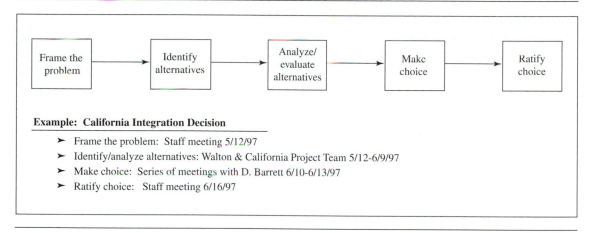

Example: California Integration Decision

➤ Frame the problem: Staff meeting 5/12/97
➤ Identify/analyze alternatives: Walton & California Project Team 5/12-6/9/97
➤ Make choice: Series of meetings with D. Barrett 6/10-6/13/97
➤ Ratify choice: Staff meeting 6/16/97

Source: Consultant's Final Report

identify alternatives and to perform analysis of competing options. The subgroup composition varied somewhat depending on the issues involved. Dan Hannah described this process: "We tend to surface the issue, then figure out who needs to get together to solve it, and work on the problem off-line."

Identifying Alternatives

Typically, subgroups consisted of two to four members of the senior team who had chosen to become involved based on their experience and the issue's relevancy to their functional area. As director of strategy, Kate Walton often served as the facilitator or coordinator in these subgroups. The subgroup then worked off-line to identify alternative courses of action. Managers discussed the issue with others in their own organizations and gathered input and feedback. Then the subgroup narrowed down the possible options. At this point, they decided which options warranted more extensive analysis prior to making a choice. Walton explained that "it was important to present Don with alternatives . . . rather than a simple go/no-go decision." There were differing opinions about the effectiveness of this stage of the process. One manager noted a tendency

for people "to make a case for their own area" during these subgroup meetings; Walton, by contrast, believed that this stage "worked better in small groups."

As an example, after the May 1997 meeting, Walton worked off-line, along with McHale and Bruce Ford, to identify and analyze several options for improving the California integration plan. She also consulted extensively with the middle managers on the California integration project team. By working with the subgroup in this fashion, Walton concluded that "the middle managers bought into the decision."

Analyzing Alternatives

Having narrowed down the options, the subgroup then performed extensive analysis of the remaining alternatives. In most cases, the subgroup went beyond qualitative comparison of the options and conducted quantitative cost/benefit analysis. After completing these analyses, the subgroup arrived at a tentative recommendation. As Walton explained the California integration decision, she stressed that "the idea is to present the pros and cons of each option, quantified when possible, with a risk assessment."

Making the Choice

Barrett then met with the subgroup, often in a series of meetings. He reviewed the analysis, discussed the subgroup's assumptions, and sometimes requested additional work. Finally, Barrett and the subgroup together selected a particular course of action. Lynn McHale emphasized that these subgroups served as the primary forum for making choices: "We tend to work in the smaller groups off-line to actually solve problems or make decisions." Kate Walton concurred:

> For the most part, there are not a lot of issues where the whole group is involved. Don does a lot of the decision making on a one-to-one basis or in small groups. The staff meeting is not a forum for decision making.

In the example of the California integration decision, the subgroup completed the analysis and arranged a meeting with Barrett. Walton and Ford met with Barrett several times to discuss the analysis and recommendations. Barrett expressed significant reservations and challenged several key assumptions. Ultimately, however, Barrett expressed his approval for the subgroup's recommendations.

Ratifying the Choice

Finally, the subgroup would present its recommendations to the staff at one of the weekly meetings. At that point, the staff either ratified the choice or expressed dissatisfaction with the recommendation. If the staff did not ratify the choice, then the subgroup collected feedback from the staff and "quickly took it off-line again." Walton described this aspect of the decision process:

> Someone goes away and investigates a problem, then comes back with a recommendation, and we say yeah or nay.

Barrett explained the purpose of this ratification stage of the decision process:

> On strategic decisions, we tend to deal with those off-line. Then we bring them to the group to get three things. One, for them to accept or reject.

Second, people can raise objections or offer improvements or changes. And third, we bring it to the staff to get their buy-in, to get everyone's commitment.

Jack Burleson explained that the ratification discussion often focused on implementation issues:

> The way it works is that some person makes a call, gets Don's backing, then presents the decision to the group. The discussion then centers on implementation of that decision and on discussing any pitfalls that come with that decision.

On the California decision, Walton presented the analysis and recommendations to the senior team at their June 16th weekly meeting. No one voiced any objections at that meeting, although some discussion ensued regarding the resources required to implement the recommended proposal. After this discussion, the group decided to move forward based on these recommendations.

Attributes of the Decision Process

The consulting study identified four key attributes of this decision-making process. The process was quite rational and analytical and relatively free of political behavior. In addition, team members were aligned with common goals, and they actively participated in group discussions. (For more information on these attributes, see Exhibits 7 and 8.)

Analytical

For most decisions, the ASC staff performed a thorough analysis prior to making a choice. As Walton put it: "We need to make informed decisions based on facts in the All-Star Sports organization." McHale concurred: "We are a very analytical company."

This meant that in order to obtain support on key decisions, individuals had to systematically demonstrate that the recommended alternative's benefits outweighed the costs. Staff members typically quantified costs, benefits, and risks as much as possible. Quantitative analysis was viewed as crucial, given the company's focus on financial targets. As

---

EXHIBIT 7   Survey Assessment of the Decision-Making Process

Team members also completed a survey that assessed the decision-making process along a variety of dimensions. In each case, team members utilized a 1–7 scale to record their responses. The questions are listed below:

Question	Mean	Standard Deviation	Maximum Value	Minimum Value
Does the group make decisions: 1 = too quickly 7 = too slowly	4.06	1.13	6.00	2.00
Does this group: 1 = engage in constructive debate 7 = smooth over certain issues	3.88	1.93	7.00	1.00
Does this group: 1 = primarily surface problems 7 = actually solve problems together	2.79	1.23	5.00	1.00
Does this group: 1 = engage in little political maneuvering 7 = engage in much political maneuvering	2.98	0.96	5.00	2.00
Does this group function: 1 = in an advisory capacity to D. Barrett 7 = as a decision-making body	3.38	1.56	6.00	1.00
Do team members: 1 = cling to old loyalties 7 = focus on what's best for All-Star Sports as a whole	4.16	1.10	6.00	2.00
Do people use meetings to: 1 = gain understanding of other functions, issues 7 = make a case for their own priorities	5.15	1.39	7.00	3.00
Do you feel that participation is: 1 = relatively equal 7 = relatively unequal/several people dominate	4.60	1.25	6.30	3.00
If D. Barrett states his position, is the group: 1 = willing to challenge him 7 = hesitant to do so	2.51	1.81	6.50	1.00
Does the group: 1 = achieve closure on issues during meetings 7 = allow issues to linger and resurface over time	4.93	1.35	7.00	2.10

Source: Consultant's Final Report

EXHIBIT 8   Team Member Participation During Meetings

This chart shows participation by group member, as observed by the consultant over the course of five meetings during May and June 1997. The chart does not list individuals' names to protect their privacy. Note that Don Barrett, who naturally spoke more than others, was not included in the data set. However, the data does include a strategic planner who attended most of the meetings during this period.

Participation by group member

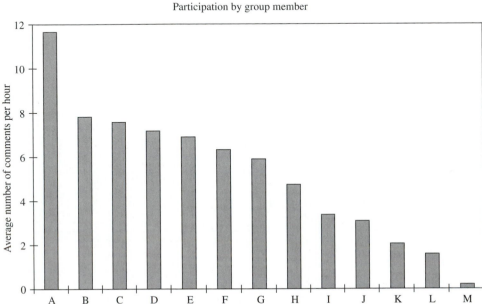

Source: Consultant's Final Report

Walton noted, "We are all over the numbers." The All-Star Sports culture encouraged this rational approach to choosing among alternatives, as opposed to a reliance on instincts and emotions. Barrett too emphasized the reliance on "fact-based decisions rather than emotional ones."

For example, Walton explained how she utilized a detailed cost/benefit analysis to overcome Barrett's early objections to her California integration proposal:

> It was a very analytical presentation . . . There was incremental benefit . . . but there were costs. So we factored in all sides of the equation. That was key. Break it down into steps. Get buy-in along the way. Be very analytical and methodical.

Aligned

The staff exhibited a high level of agreement with regard to the division's overall goals. Staff members felt that this consensus regarding their overall mission facilitated the decision-making process. For example, when asked to list the division's goals, 77 percent of the staff members reported the achievement of acquisition integration as a key strategic goal for 1997. Moreover, 85 percent reported "make the numbers" as a key objective at all points in time. As McHale stated:

> On this issue, we are very crisp and clear. We know our mission—it's to make the numbers, and thus, we do a good job working to achieve those goals.

Similarly, the group exhibited a high level of agreement when asked to describe the organization's strengths and weaknesses. For instance, 77 percent reported purchasing leverage or other synergies with the retail division as a key strategic strength of the ASC organization. An almost equal number cited brand equity as a key strategic strength.

Apolitical

The staff reported low levels of political behavior during the decision-making process. As Jim Maxwell said, "I think we are rather apolitical around here." Barrett concurred with Maxwell, stating, "I don't think that there is much political maneuvering within the group." Team members stressed that individuals did not attempt to trumpet their own successes at the expense of others, nor did they engage in extensive finger pointing. Individuals also typically did not attempt to diminish or exaggerate the role that others played in achieving success or failure.

When politics did surface, Barrett typically intervened. According to Rice, "There is a little [political behavior] by some folks, but Don quickly recognizes this kind of behavior and acts to reign it in." Barrett emphasized that he had avoided selecting "political animals" as members of the team.

Active Participation

Staff members wholeheartedly felt free to express their opinions during group meetings. They stressed that everyone had the opportunity to be heard. Barrett commented on the participation as follows: "I think we have a good active discussion, and people openly discuss the issues and offer their opinions." Bruce Ford summarized staff member perceptions concerning the discussion: "Everyone seems comfortable participating, not intimidated by others in the group."

Burleson added that "Don encourages everyone to talk" during meetings. In fact, the consultant's report stated that "20 percent of Barrett's comments attempt to solicit participation either from the group as a whole, or from specific individuals." Several managers noted, however, that inequality in participation persisted despite these efforts. Dan Hannah acknowledged this fact: "Some people do speak more than others, though I don't think it's to the point of dominating the meetings."

Concerns about the Decision Process

During the consultant's study, three major concerns emerged about the decision-making process. First, team members discerned a lack of adequate debate during group meetings. Second, they cited an inability to always achieve closure on discussions. Third, several team members expressed concern that the group did not achieve the required level of commitment or buy-in on key decisions.

Conflict

While staff members found Barrett extremely open to opposing views, they expressed concern at the lack of open debate during group meetings. One manager linked the absence of open debate to the fact that some staff members did not participate much during meetings:

> Of the 13 people, I would say that about 6 dominate the meetings. Others say very little . . . It would be useful to encourage folks to be more open. Someone may have opposing views that are valid, but they may not want to open up. We need to consider those views, get them on the table. We do not consider alternative views as frequently as we should. We should be willing to throw open discussions more often.

Another staff member made a distinction between the amount of discussion and the extent to which the group engaged in constructive debate:

> I think that there is a discussion, though I would argue that there is less confrontation than would be productive with this group. The group tends to quickly take issues off-line when conflict emerges. Perhaps the group ought to openly address these issues as a group.

Someone stressed that discussion ended when conflict emerged:

> The key is that the group and Don engage in a discussion only to the extent that it doesn't get to

the point where the discussion actually affects individuals. At the confrontation stage, we stop talking about it.

Maxwell pointed out the group's problem with debates:

There is a fair amount of discussion at weekly meetings, but we don't really have a good mechanism for resolving conflict when it does emerge.

Others explained how the group dealt with conflict:

The meeting is not a forum where we engage in debate. If there is disagreement, then we quickly tend to agree to take it off-line.

When asked to explain why the group quickly took disagreements off-line, a staff member offered the following explanation:

Two reasons. One, the size of the group. It's difficult to have a discussion with so many of us in the room, and also, it's not efficient to tie everyone's time up while a few of us hash out a disagreement. Two, Don's style is nonconfrontational, efficiency oriented. He's crisp. He encourages us to take such disagreements off-line.

Closure
On a second key point of concern, the group often found it difficult to achieve closure during the decision-making process. In other words, they either could not reach consensus on a choice, or they found themselves repeatedly circling back to the problem definition and alternative generation stages of the decision-making process.

Staff members attributed the lack of closure to the search for consensus on most decisions. This represented a dilemma for most of the vice presidents at ASC. On the one hand, they valued Barrett's efforts to build consensus within the group before moving forward. On the other hand, group discussion and the effort to build consensus sometimes did not yield closure on issues. Henry Rice found this lack of closure puzzling at times. As he said,

A conclusion is apparently reached, but we are not necessarily through with that issue. Something

prevents us from actually reaching a definitive conclusion on issues.

Barrett acknowledged that closure represented a problem for the group:

If people don't agree with a decision, then they tend to think they can keep bringing it up over and over and that this will lead to a change in the decision. That's not constructive.

One vice president contended that the search for consensus, while useful for numerous reasons, inevitably yielded a lack of closure at times:

The problem is that most decisions have to be consensus-built . . . Don is not confrontational. It's like sandbox fighting. He doesn't send one kid home if two are fighting. He says go find another sandbox and work it out. But in reality, people just want their positions heard. Then they really want a choice to be made.

To overcome the lack of closure, many staff members believed that the group must adopt some mechanism for making a transition from consensus building to choice. Several comments emphasized this focus on the need for some mechanism to close off discussion:

I think that we don't get a tie breaker when we need one. Sometimes someone needs to make a decision. We need action at the end of discussion.

Commitment
In a final area of concern, staff members disagreed over the amount of commitment and buy-in achieved during the decision-making process. Some individuals stressed that the subgroups worked effectively to achieve the necessary buy-in from people throughout the organization as the decision-making process unfolded. For example, Walton explained that one key to her successful California integration decision process was her ability to "get buy-in along the way" as she performed her analysis. As she put it, managers almost always "greased the skids" before taking a recommendation to a staff meeting.

Others concurred with this assessment. One manager noted that, during the ratification stage of the decision-making process, proponents of a particular position "can achieve support . . . [and] buy-in from others, and also we get a chance to approve the proposal." Barrett, too, emphasized that his consensus-building approach focused on achieving everyone's buy-in on a decision in order to facilitate implementation.

Some managers, however, believed that this type of decision-making process did not yield sufficient buy-in from all individuals. One vice president explained his concerns:

> Most of the thought process occurs individually or in small group meetings, rather than among the staff as a whole. By not talking as a full group, we don't get enough discussion of cross-functional issues and coordination.

Another vice president added:

> I'm concerned that we don't get full buy-in this way. I come from an organization where real calls were made in the room. There was healthy give and take. We knew what the ground rules were. That was to discuss and even argue about decisions. Then once we made them, we walked out of the room as a unified group. I'm not sure that's what happens here—I mean that we walk out of the room as a unified group . . . People don't invest heavily in what goes on in the room . . . The meeting is the wrong place to object, so people work around it.

The August 21st Meeting of the Senior Team

After reviewing the consultant's study once again, Barrett went off to his August 21st meeting with the senior team. As the meeting began, he welcomed the team members and the consultant who had performed the study. All participants had already reviewed the survey and interview data contained in the consultant's report. The ensuing discussion focused on the three concerns of conflict, closure, and commitment. Everyone agreed that the team had to address these issues in order to achieve the organization's objective of enhanced integration and to effectively implement otherwise sound decisions.

The team then turned to the three alternatives outlined in the consultant's report. Under the first option, the management group would conduct all stages of the decision-making process together as a single team. All subgroups and off-line meetings would be eliminated, with the goal of increasing commitment and closure. Moreover, since everyone would participate throughout the process, the expectation was that they would understand the rationale for particular choices and commit to their implementation. Team members would also come to better understand the links across the businesses by working together as a full group.

Still, there were concerns. One staff member noted a potential problem with this approach:

> The real problem is that the group is too large . . . There is definitely an inverse relationship between the group's size and the quality of the discussion . . . With such a large group, people are unwilling to engage in discussion.

The consultant explained that this concern had led him to develop a second option. Under this proposal, a small "top management team" consisting of only three to four key members of the current staff would be formed. This new group would bear responsibility for making all key strategic decisions for the division. A potential advantage of such a small group setting would be a better dialogue and a forum more conducive to constructive debate.

But, several team members expressed concerns with this option as well. They feared that the existence of a small, elite team might inhibit integration and commitment because key managers would be left out of the decision process. Their input generated a third option: The team ought to maintain the existing decision process, while fine-tuning it to overcome current weaknesses. After all, they argued, ASC had already achieved a remarkable record of success using this present strategic decision-making process. As one manager exclaimed: "Is this process really broken?"

Learning Processes

OVERVIEW

In today's economy, knowledge is increasingly the source of competitive success.[1] Intellectual capital has become the coin of the corporate realm as managers, from Singapore to Silicon Valley, struggle daily to create, leverage, and retain the very best ideas and insights. Competition requires it, as do continuous improvement programs. How else can companies create successful new products and services or achieve breakthroughs in quality, cost, and cycle time reduction? Without a continual flow of new ideas, the status quo is certain to remain unchanged.

For these reasons, it is hard to find a manager today who does not give at least lip service to the importance of building a learning organization. Unfortunately, their efforts have all too often been limited to sweeping rhetoric or attacks on prevailing norms. They have treated the problem as one of culture, not day-to-day practice. Predictably, these efforts have had little impact because they have failed to recognize a basic truth:

> Learning . . . is simply another organizational process, not all that different from strategy formulation, product development, or order fulfillment. Like other processes, it unfolds over time, has inputs and outputs, involves diverse departments and levels, and consists of interconnected activities and steps. And like other processes, it must be crafted and led.[2]

Benchmarking, for example, involves a concrete set of activities and steps, as do experimentation and intelligence gathering. All are learning processes that can be deployed with varying degrees of success, depending on how well their basic elements have been designed and integrated.

---

[1]Peter F. Drucker, *Post-Capitalist Society* (New York: HarperBusiness, 1993), chap. 1.
[2]David A. Garvin, *Learning in Action* (Boston: Harvard Business School Press, 2000), p. 190.

To begin, managers must develop an understanding of the stages that constitute every learning process.[3] These stages take different forms, depending upon the mode of learning, but are always present. Organizations first acquire knowledge, collecting the raw material that leads to further understanding. They then interpret the resulting facts, data, and opinions, giving them meaning by putting them in categories and frameworks. Next, they apply what they have learned, acting in new and different ways. Finally, for maximum impact they share these practices and ideas throughout the organization so that they are put to wider and wider use.

The first three of these stages fall broadly under the heading of "organizational learning," while the fourth is usually characterized as "knowledge management." Experts tend to apply these terms narrowly, assigning them to individual functions or departments. They view organizational learning as the responsibility of Human Resources (HR), and knowledge management as the province of Information Technology (IT). But the line dividing these categories is hazy, and both must ultimately become the purview of general managers if companies are to reap the greatest benefits. Otherwise, neither activity will ever become part and parcel of daily work.

OUTLINE

The first class in the module, "Building a Learning Organization," provides a broad introduction to the meaning, management, and measurement of organizational learning. It begins with a definition of learning organizations that is actionable and precise, then moves to describe a number of associated activities. Among those featured at length are systematic problem solving, experimentation with new approaches, learning from one's past experience and history, learning from the experiences and best practices of other companies, and transferring knowledge quickly and efficiently throughout the organization.

Each of these activities, it should be emphasized, is a process, with a well-defined sequence of steps that can be articulated, managed, and carried out more or less effectively. Most organizations, in fact, already conduct these activities to some degree, but with little conscious thought. They are learners, but by default rather than careful design. By contrast, the companies featured in the article— Boeing, British Petroleum, Chaparral Steel, Copeland, GE, PPG, and Xerox, among others—are far more thoughtful and disciplined about their learning processes. They have, as a result, achieved dramatic improvements in the amount of useful knowledge they are able to create and share.

But because managers are practical people, they are unlikely to accept these improvements on faith. The best companies have therefore developed innovative measurement systems to track learning and ensure that it is taking hold. The article describes a number of alternative approaches, including learning curves, experience curves, half-life curves, surveys of attitudes and new ways of thinking, and direct observations of behavior. Some of these techniques track changes

---

[3]Ibid., chap. 2.

in frameworks or "mental models," others track changes in behavior, and still others track changes in performance. But each, in its own way, honors that age-old maxim: "If you can't measure it, you can't manage it."

The second and possibly third classes in the module, "Types of Learning Processes," expand on these themes. They use videotapes to illustrate the stages of learning—acquiring, interpreting, and applying information—and how they unfold in four quite different processes. Depending on the tapes selected by the instructor, students will examine some subset of benchmarking, after action reviews, intelligence gathering, and experimentation. Each has distinctive strengths, weaknesses, and implementation challenges; in combination, they offer revealing comparisons.

The first video shows Mobil Oil's use of benchmarking to improve the speed and quality of customer service. It sent teams of employees to visit organizations far removed from gasoline retailing—the Ritz-Carlton Hotel chain, the Penske racing team, and Home Depot—and asked them to interpret the data they saw and then borrow creatively, using their insights as a springboard to devise creative new approaches to service station design.

The second video shows soldiers in the U.S. Army learning from their own successes and failures. The Army has institutionalized two closely related processes: learning from experience, in which soldiers conduct debriefings immediately after missions using a structured format called After Action Reviews (AARs); and learning from observation, in which teams of specialists, under the supervision of the Center for Army Lessons Learned (CALL), conduct real-time surveillance, identify emerging lessons, and relay them back to CALL headquarters for recording and rapid dissemination to others in the field.

The third video shows L.L. Bean, a successful direct mail marketer, learning by collecting, interpreting, and applying customer feedback. It has developed two complementary approaches: exploratory techniques, based on broad, open-ended questions that are designed to identify customers' unmet (and often unstated) needs; and descriptive techniques, based on targeted, focused questions that are designed to identify the strengths and weaknesses of competing products and the desired combination of features. The techniques are similar in that they both require skill at framing questions and listening attentively, but differ dramatically in the amount and nature of interpretation required.

The fourth video shows engineers at Allegheny Ludlum Steel learning through a process of shop-floor experimentation. They launch experiments by completing a simple form describing the associated steps, success measures, and responsible personnel, then actively manipulate variables to isolate cause-and-effect relationships. The process mimics the scientific method—a working hypothesis is framed, careful controls are put in place, detailed measures are used to capture before-and-after impacts, and multiple trials are required to ensure repeatability—but without the usual pristine laboratory conditions. Allegheny Ludlum shows how companies can conduct disciplined, systematic experiments even when they are operating in messy, real-world environments.

The final class in the module, "A Note on Knowledge Management," shifts the focus from knowledge creation to knowledge transfer and retention. Here, critical insights already exist, and the challenge is to spread them to others in the organization. Managers often assume that high-powered information technology is the secret to successful sharing. The reality, however, is that technology is at best a supplement and an enabler of the process.[4] It cannot replace face-to-face or personal interactions, and it must be accompanied by thoughtful efforts to identify, codify, and disseminate important insights. The note therefore describes the need for targeted knowledge strategies, well-designed knowledge collection processes, and supportive knowledge infrastructures.

New roles and responsibilities have emerged to meet these challenges, as have specialized knowledge management units; frequently, they include a chief knowledge officer and various kinds of knowledge managers. Their departments and jobs can be designed in various ways, and the note concludes with two contrasting examples: Arthur Andersen and Ernst & Young. Both are leading accounting and consulting firms, with a similar base of clients and tasks, yet they have structured their knowledge management activities quite differently.

THEMES

Building a Learning Organization

Learning organizations are skilled at generating new ideas *and* putting them into practice. This combination is surprisingly difficult to come by, and a number of obvious candidates fail the test. R&D laboratories, for example, routinely produce new ideas, while marketing departments regularly generate unexpected insights about customers. Relatively few, however, take the more difficult step of acting on what they have learned. As "Building a Learning Organization" makes clear, such changes in behavior are required if companies or departments are to qualify as full-fledged learning organizations.

To get these changes, managers must move simultaneously on three fronts. First, they must create supportive, stimulating environments. For most employees, learning is a risky business: it requires new skills and competencies, raising the possibility of errors, mistakes, and failed adjustments. Few employees will put themselves on the line unless they believe that the environment is "psychologically safe." Such settings have five distinguishing characteristics: "(1) opportunities for training and practice, (2) support and encouragement to overcome fear and shame associated with making errors, (3) coaching and rewards for efforts in the right direction, (4) norms that legitimize the making of errors, and (5) norms that reward innovative thinking and experimentation."[5] These conditions appear at many of the organizations featured in this module—Allegheny Ludlum, Chaparral Steel, GTE, L.L. Bean, and the U.S. Army—as well as in

---

[4]Nancy M. Dixon, *Common Knowledge* (Boston: Harvard Business School Press, 2000), pp. 3–5.

[5]Edgar H. Schein, "How Can Organizations Learn Faster? The Challenge of Entering the Green Room," *Sloan Management Review* 34 (Winter 1993), p. 89, and Amy Edmondson, "Psychological Safety and Learning Behavior in Work Teams," *Administrative Science Quarterly* 44 (1999), pp. 350–383.

the course's other case studies of American Express, Harvard Business School Publishing, Millipore, and others.

A supportive culture, however, is not enough. There must also be incentives that encourage—or at least do not discourage—learning. Allegheny Ludlum, for example, funds all experiments out of a separate account, removing their results from the accounting system used to evaluate operating managers. Ernst & Young bases consultants' compensation, in part, on their contributions to, development of, and use of the company's knowledge repository. Mobil Oil assigns dedicated teams to benchmarking projects and gives them the freedom to try out their most innovative ideas at pilot sites. In each of these cases, employees find that their self-interest is well aligned with the goal of furthering corporate learning.

Second, managers must install well-crafted learning processes. A supportive environment goes only so far: It provides the soil, but managers must plant the seeds and till the crops if they are to flourish and grow. This involves a number of associated tasks. Managers must oversee the design of intelligence gathering, experimentation, reflection, and review processes. They must install knowledge-sharing programs and systems. They must allocate the resources—both dollars and skilled personnel—required for success. And they must insist that these activities be pursued rigorously and systematically, applying the same standards that they use for other, more operationally oriented process improvement projects.

It is no coincidence that all of the learning processes featured in this module are carefully planned approaches developed under the guidance of senior executives. For example, both Allegheny Ludlum's system of experimentation and L.L. Bean's approach to customer inquiry are the products of thoughtful design, not chance. Each is also comprehensive, including a set of well-defined roles and responsibilities, simple but powerful tools and methodologies, an integrated sequence of activities, and carefully specified outputs and deliverables. These processes work well because they were designed well, with repeated improvements over time.

Third, managers need to encourage learning behaviors. Some forms of corporate behavior stifle learning, while others stimulate it. Information politics, for example, is a prominent barrier, with employees hoarding or filtering critical information in pursuit of their own self-interest.[6] When such behavior persists, learning is likely to be limited. Question asking, by contrast, normally fosters learning because it prompts dialogue and new ways of thinking. This is especially true when questions are broad and open-ended, as they are at L.L. Bean. Assumption testing serves a similar role: It gets people to puzzle over the roots of their opinions and the sources of prevailing views. It is all the more powerful when underlying data are subject to measurement and verification, as they are at Allegheny Ludlum. Reflection is the pause that refreshes: By providing a break in the action, it offers an opportunity to draw lessons from immediate past

---

[6]Thomas H. Davenport, Robert G. Eccles, and Laurence Prusak, "Information Politics," *Sloan Management Review* 34 (Fall 1992), pp. 53–65.

experience. When all participants engage in the exercise, as they do in the U.S. Army's After Action Reviews, the resulting cross talk is likely to be especially fertile and productive.

Leading Learning

Of course, one of the best ways for managers to encourage learning behaviors is to model them personally. Here, too, there are several essential steps. When working with others, managers should create opportunities for learning, cultivate the desired attitudes and tone, and then personally lead the ensuing discussions. When working individually, they should remain open to new perspectives, aware of their personal biases, immersed in unfiltered data, and humble rather than all knowing.[7]

As a first step, managers can create "learning forums—assignments, activities, and events whose primary purpose is to foster learning."[8] The possibilities are endless: get-togethers with customers to discuss proposed or existing products or services; benchmarking visits to best-in-class performers to learn new approaches; reviews of strategies, programs, and market trends to test underlying assumptions and plan for the future; periodic meetings to discuss the latest in competitive intelligence; and in-house audits to compare successful and less successful projects. These forums will seldom occur without managers' active involvement; they are often threatening and viewed as a diversion from "real work." But they can have an enormous impact on performance and future direction, providing managers take the lead and provide the necessary resources and support. Xerox '95, the strategic review discussed in the first module of the course, is a powerful example, as are L.L. Bean's meetings with field testers and Mobil Oil's benchmarking visits.

Tone matters as well. If employees see forums as searches for the guilty—efforts to find fault, rather than to fix a problem or take advantage of an opportunity—they will refuse to participate actively or openly. Managers therefore need to send clear signals about their intent, keeping finger-pointing to a minimum. They need to separate performance evaluations from learning, as the U.S. Army has done with After Action Reviews, and keep the focus on improvement and growth. This does not mean that challenge and debate should be absent. But discussions should be aimed squarely at issues and ideas, not the failings of individuals.

Managers must often lead these discussions personally. A variety of skills are necessary; most are closely akin to those of the very best teachers and facilitators. Managers must become more expert at asking questions that open up dialogue, like the product managers at L.L. Bean and benchmarking team

---

[7]Garvin, *Learning in Action,* chap. 6.
[8]Ibid., p. 191.

members at Mobil Oil. They must master the ability to frame and test hypotheses, like the metallurgists and operating managers at Allegheny Ludlum. They must become skilled at prompting self-examination, like the Army commanders who run After Action Reviews. And they must learn the art of teasing out and articulating best practices, like the knowledge managers at Arthur Andersen and Ernst & Young.

Equally important, they must continue to pursue their own learning and growth. Without managers who learn, there can be no learning organizations. Leaders must therefore strive to remain open to diverse, conflicting views; in fact, they must cultivate them if they are to broaden their horizons. Unhappy customers are an obvious resource, as are disagreements among direct reports. Both are surprisingly easy sources to tap. So too are side-by-side product comparisons and visits to unfamiliar environments, such as overseas markets or cutting-edge laboratories.

In these encounters, managers must remain sensitive to their personal biases. Like most people, they rely on deeply engrained patterns of thought and analysis that lead them to favor some interpretations over others.[9] They also tend to discount surprises and ignore contradictory information.[10] Without some countervailing influence, such as a strong minority position, unassailable data, or an obvious failure in the marketplace, these biases are difficult to overcome. At a minimum, managers need to be aware of the possibility of bias; they should also try to draw upon objective, apolitical information sources whenever possible. Both L.L. Bean and the U.S. Army use this approach with considerable success.

An equally powerful corrective technique is direct immersion in raw, unfiltered data. All too many managers are distressingly removed from the front lines. They base their decisions on reports, memos, and summary statistics, already massaged and aggregated, rather than first-hand, unprocessed information. By going to the source—suppliers, distributors, and customers, as well as their own laboratories, factories, and service centers—managers are much more likely to form accurate, undistorted pictures of the situation at hand.

Finally, if they hope to build learning organizations managers must cultivate an attitude of humility. Learning, after all, begins with the admission of ignorance; without gaps in one's knowledge, there would be nothing left to learn. By acknowledging that they do not have all the answers, managers are encouraging others to act in the same way. And by admitting that the best solutions often lie outside the executive suite, they are empowering others to put their own knowledge to work.

---

[9]See, for example, William H. Starbuck and Frances Milliken, "Executives' Perceptual Filters: What They Notice and How They Make Sense," in Donald C. Hambrick, ed., *The Executive Effect* (Greenwich, CT: JAI Press, 1988), pp. 35–65.

[10]Rohit Deshpande and Gerald Zaltman, "Factors Affecting the Use of Market Research Information: A Path Analysis," *Journal of Marketing Research* 19 (1982), pp. 14–31, and Rohit Deshpande and Gerald Zaltman, "A Comparison of Factors Affecting Researcher and Manager Perceptions of Market Research Use," *Journal of Marketing Research* 21 (1984), pp. 32–38.

Case 4–1

BUILDING A LEARNING ORGANIZATION

David A. Garvin

Continuous improvement programs are sprouting up all over as organizations strive to better themselves and gain an edge. The topic list is long and varied, and sometimes it seems as though a program a month is needed just to keep up. Unfortunately, failed programs far outnumber successes, and improvement rates remain distressingly low. Why? Because most companies have failed to grasp a basic truth. Continuous improvement requires a commitment to learning.

How, after all, can an organization improve without first learning something new? Solving a problem, introducing a product, and reengineering a process all require seeing the world in a new light and acting accordingly. In the absence of learning, companies—and individuals—simply repeat old practices. Change remains cosmetic, and improvements are either fortuitous or short-lived.

A few farsighted executives—Ray Stata of Analog Devices, Gordon Forward of Chaparral Steel, Paul Allaire of Xerox—have recognized the link between learning and continuous improvement and have begun to refocus their companies around it. Scholars too have jumped on the bandwagon, beating the drum for "learning organizations" and "knowledge-creating companies." In rapidly changing businesses like semiconductors and consumer electronics, these ideas are fast taking hold. Yet despite the encouraging signs, the topic in large part remains murky, confused, and difficult to penetrate.

Meaning, Management, and Measurement

Scholars are partly to blame. Their discussions of learning organizations have often been reverential and utopian, filled with near-mystical terminology. Paradise, they would have you believe, is just around the corner. Peter Senge, who popularized learning organizations in his book *The Fifth Discipline,* described them as places "where people continually expand their capacity to create the results they truly desire, where new and expansive patterns of thinking are nurtured, where collective aspiration is set free, and where people are continually learning how to learn together."[1] To achieve these ends, Senge suggested the use of five "component technologies": systems thinking, personal mastery, mental models, shared vision, and team learning. In a similar spirit, Ikujiro Nonaka characterized knowledge-creating companies as places where "inventing new knowledge is not a specialized activity . . . it is a way of behaving, indeed, a way of being, in which everyone is a knowledge worker."[2] Nonaka suggested that companies use metaphors and organizational redundancy to focus thinking, encourage dialogue, and make tacit, instinctively understood ideas explicit.

[1]*Peter M. Senge, The Fifth Discipline (New York: Doubleday, 1990), p. 1.*
[2]*Ikujiro Nonaka, "The Knowledge-Creating Company," Harvard Business Review, November–December 1991, p. 97.*

Sound idyllic? Absolutely. Desirable? Without question. But does it provide a framework for action? Hardly. The recommendations are far too abstract, and too many questions remain unanswered. How, for example, will managers know when their companies have become learning organizations? What concrete changes in behavior are required? What policies and programs must be in place? How do you get from here to there?

Most discussions of learning organizations finesse these issues. Their focus is high philosophy and grand themes, sweeping metaphors rather than the gritty details of practice. Three critical issues are left unresolved; yet each is essential for effective implementation. First is the question of *meaning*. We need a plausible, well-grounded definition of learning organizations; it must be actionable and easy to apply. Second is the question of *management*. We need clearer guidelines for practice, filled with operational advice rather than high aspirations. And third is the question of *measurement*. We need better tools for assessing an organization's rate and level of learning to ensure that gains have in fact been made.

Once these "three Ms" are addressed, managers will have a firmer foundation for launching learning organizations. Without this groundwork, progress is unlikely, and for the simplest of reasons. For learning to become a meaningful corporate goal, it must first be understood.

What Is a Learning Organization?

Surprisingly, a clear definition of learning has proved to be elusive over the years. Organizational theorists have studied learning for a long time; the accompanying quotations suggest that there is still considerable disagreement (see the insert "Definitions of Organizational Learning"). Most scholars view organizational learning as a process that unfolds over time and link it with knowledge acquisition and improved performance. But they differ on other important matters.

Some, for example, believe that behavioral change is required for learning; others insist that new ways of thinking are enough. Some cite information processing as the mechanism through which learning takes place; others propose shared insights, organizational routines, even memory.

Definitions of Organizational Learning

Scholars have proposed a variety of definitions of organizational learning. Here is a small sample:

Organizational learning means the process of improving actions through better knowledge and understanding.
C. Marlene Fiol and Marjorie A. Lyles "Organizational Learning," *Academy of Management Review,* October 1985.

An entity learns if, through its processing of information, the range of its potential behaviors is changed.
George P. Huber, "Organizational Learning: The Contributing Processes and the Literatures," *Organization Science,* February 1991.

Organizations are seen as learning by encoding inferences from history into routines that guide behavior.
Barbara Levitt and James G. March, "Organizational Learning," *American Review of Sociology* 14, 1988.

Organizational learning is a process of detecting and correcting error.
Chris Argyris, "Double Loop Learning in Organizations," *Harvard Business Review,* September–October 1977.

Organizational learning occurs through shared insights, knowledge, and mental models . . . [and] builds on past knowledge and experience—that is, on memory.
Ray Stata, "Organizational Learning—The Key to Management Innovation," *Sloan Management Review,* Spring 1989.

And some think that organizational learning is common, while others believe that flawed, self-serving interpretations are the norm.

How can we discern among this cacophony of voices yet build on earlier insights? As a first step, consider the following definition:

> *A learning organization is an organization skilled at creating, acquiring, and transferring knowledge, and at modifying its behavior to reflect new knowledge and insights.*

This definition begins with a simple truth: new ideas are essential if learning is to take place. Sometimes they are created de novo, through flashes of insight or creativity; at other times they arrive from outside the organization or are communicated by knowledgeable insiders. Whatever their source, these ideas are the trigger for organizational improvement. But they cannot by themselves create a learning organization. *Without accompanying changes in the way that work gets done, only the potential for improvement exists.*

This is a surprisingly stringent test for it rules out a number of obvious candidates for learning organizations. Many universities fail to qualify, as do many consulting firms. Even General Motors, despite its recent efforts to improve performance, is found wanting. All of these organizations have been effective at creating or acquiring new knowledge but notably less successful in applying that knowledge to their own activities. Total quality management, for example, is now taught at many business schools, yet the number using it to guide their own decision making is very small. Organizational consultants advise clients on social dynamics and small-group behavior but are notorious for their own infighting and factionalism. And GM, with a few exceptions (like Saturn and NUMMI), has had little success in revamping its manufacturing practices, even though its managers are experts on lean manufacturing, JIT production, and the requirements for improved quality of work life.

Organizations that do pass the definitional test—Honda, Corning, and General Electric come quickly to mind—have, by contrast, become adept at translating new knowledge into new ways of behaving. These companies actively manage the learning process to ensure that it occurs by design rather than by chance. Distinctive policies and practices are responsible for their success; they form the building blocks of learning organizations.

Building Blocks

Learning organizations are skilled at five main activities: systematic problem solving, experimentation with new approaches, learning from their own experience and past history, learning from the experiences and best practices of others, and transferring knowledge quickly and efficiently throughout the organization. Each is accompanied by a distinctive mind-set, tool kit, and pattern of behavior. Many companies practice these activities to some degree. But few are consistently successful because they rely largely on happenstance and isolated examples. By creating systems and processes that support these activities and integrate them into the fabric of daily operations, companies can manage their learning more effectively.

1. *Systematic problem solving.* This first activity rests heavily on the philosophy and methods of the quality movement. Its underlying ideas, now widely accepted, include:

- Relying on the scientific method, rather than guesswork, for diagnosing problems (what Deming calls the "Plan, Do, Check, Act" cycle, and others refer to as "hypothesis-generating, hypothesis-testing" techniques).
- Insisting on data, rather than assumptions, as background for decision making (what quality practitioners call "fact-based management").
- Using simple statistical tools (histograms, Pareto charts, correlations, cause-and-effect diagrams) to organize data and draw inferences.

Most training programs focus primarily on problem-solving techniques, using exercises and practical examples. These tools are relatively straightforward and easily communicated; the necessary mind-set, however, is more difficult to establish. Accuracy and precision are essential for

---

Xerox's Problem-Solving Process

Step	Question to Be Answered	Expansion/ Divergence	Contraction/ Convergence	What's Needed to Go to the Next Step
1. Identify and select problem	What do we want to change?	Lots of problems for consideration	One problem statement, one "desired state" agreed upon	Identification of the gap; "desired state" described in observable terms
2. Analyze problem	What's preventing us from reaching the "desired state"?	Lots of potential causes identified	Key cause(s) identified and verified	Key cause(s) documented and ranked
3. Generate potential solutions	How *could* we make the change?	Lots of ideas on how to solve the problem	Potential solutions clarified	Solution list
4. Select and plan the solution	What's the *best* way to do it?	Lots of criteria for evaluating potential solutions	Criteria to use for evaluating solution agreed upon	Plan for making and monitoring the change
		Lots of ideas on how to implement and evaluate the selected solution	Implementation and evaluation plans agreed upon	Measurement criteria to evaluate solution effectiveness
5. Implement the solution	Are we following the plan?		Implementation of agreed-upon contingency plans (if necessary)	Solution in place
6. Evaluate the solution	How well did it work?		Effectiveness of solution agreed upon	Verification that the problem is solved, or
			Continuing problems (if any) identified	Agreement to address continuing problems

---

learning. Employees must therefore become more disciplined in their thinking and more attentive to details. They must continually ask, "How do we know that's true?", recognizing that close enough is not good enough if real learning is to take place. They must push beyond obvious symptoms to assess underlying causes, often collecting evidence when conventional wisdom says it is unnecessary. Otherwise, the organization will remain a prisoner

of "gut facts" and sloppy reasoning, and learning will be stifled.

Xerox has mastered this approach on a company-wide scale. In 1983, senior managers launched the company's Leadership Through Quality initiative; since then, all employees have been trained in small-group activities and problem-solving techniques. Today a six-step process is used for virtually all decisions (see the insert "Xerox's Problem-Solving

Process"). Employees are provided with tools in four areas: generating ideas and collecting information (brainstorming, interviewing, surveying); reaching consensus (list reduction, rating forms, weighted voting); analyzing and displaying data (cause-and-effect diagrams, force-field analysis); and planning actions (flow charts, Gantt charts). They then practice these tools during training sessions that last several days. Training is presented in "family groups," members of the same department or business-unit team, and the tools are applied to real problems facing the group. The result of this process has been a common vocabulary and a consistent, companywide approach to problem solving. Once employees have been trained, they are expected to use the techniques at all meetings, and no topic is off-limits. When a high-level group was formed to review Xerox's organizational structure and suggest alternatives, it employed the very same process and tools.[3]

2. *Experimentation.* This activity involves the systematic searching for and testing of new knowledge. Using the scientific method is essential, and there are obvious parallels to systematic problem solving. But unlike problem solving, experimentation is usually motivated by opportunity and expanding horizons, not by current difficulties. It takes two main forms: ongoing programs and one-of-a-kind demonstration projects.

Ongoing programs normally involve a continuing series of small experiments, designed to produce incremental gains in knowledge. They are the mainstay of most continuous improvement programs and are especially common on the shop floor. Corning, for example, experiments continually with diverse raw materials and new formulations to increase yields and provide better grades of glass. Allegheny Ludlum, a specialty steelmaker, regularly examines new rolling methods and improved technologies to raise productivity and reduce costs.

[3] *Robert Howard, "The CEO as Organizational Architect: An Interview with Xerox's Paul Allaire,"* Harvard Business Review, *September–October 1992, p. 106.*

Successful ongoing programs share several characteristics. First, they work hard to ensure a steady flow of new ideas, even if they must be imported from outside the organization. Chaparral Steel sends its first-line supervisors on sabbaticals around the globe, where they visit academic and industry leaders, develop an understanding of new work practices and technologies, then bring what they've learned back to the company and apply it to daily operations. In large part as a result of these initiatives, Chaparral is one of the five lowest cost steel plants in the world. GE's Impact Program originally sent manufacturing managers to Japan to study factory innovations, such as quality circles and kanban cards, and then apply them in their own organizations; today Europe is the destination, and productivity improvement practices the target. The program is one reason GE has recorded productivity gains averaging nearly 5 percent over the last four years.

Successful ongoing programs also require an incentive system that favors risk taking. Employees must feel that the benefits of experimentation exceed the costs; otherwise, they will not participate. This creates a difficult challenge for managers, who are trapped between two perilous extremes. They must maintain accountability and control over experiments without stifling creativity by unduly penalizing employees for failures. Allegheny Ludlum has perfected this juggling act: It keeps expensive, high-impact experiments off the scorecard used to evaluate managers but requires prior approvals from four senior vice presidents. The result has been a history of productivity improvements annually averaging 7 percent to 8 percent.

Finally, ongoing programs need managers and employees who are trained in the skills required to perform and evaluate experiments. These skills are seldom intuitive and must usually be learned. They cover a broad sweep: statistical methods, like design of experiments, that efficiently compare a large number of alternatives; graphical techniques, like process analysis, that are essential for redesigning work flows; and creativity techniques, like storyboarding and role playing, that keep novel ideas flowing. The most effective training programs are tightly focused and feature a small set of techniques tailored to employees' needs. Training in design of experiments, for example, is useful for manufacturing engineers, while creativity techniques are well suited to development groups.

Demonstration projects are usually larger and more complex than ongoing experiments. They involve holistic, systemwide changes, introduced at a single site, and are often undertaken with the goal of developing new organizational capabilities. Because these projects represent a sharp break from the past, they are usually designed from scratch, using a "clean slate" approach. General Foods's Topeka plant, one of the first high-commitment work systems in this country, was a pioneering demonstration project initiated to introduce the idea of self-managing teams and high levels of worker autonomy; a more recent example, designed to rethink small-car development, manufacturing, and sales, is GM's Saturn Division.

Demonstration projects share a number of distinctive characteristics:

- They are usually the first projects to embody principles and approaches that the organization hopes to adopt later on a larger scale. For this reason, they are more transitional efforts than endpoints and involve considerable "learning by doing." Midcourse corrections are common.
- They implicitly establish policy guidelines and decision rules for later projects. Managers must therefore be sensitive to the precedents they are setting and must send strong signals if they expect to establish new norms.
- They often encounter severe tests of commitment from employees who wish to see whether the rules have, in fact, changed.
- They are normally developed by strong multifunctional teams reporting directly to senior management. (For projects targeting employee involvement or quality of work life, teams should be multilevel as well.)
- They tend to have only limited impact on the rest of the organization if they are not accompanied by explicit strategies for transferring learning.

All of these characteristics appeared in a demonstration project launched by Copeland Corporation, a highly successful compressor manufacturer, in the mid-1970s. Matt Diggs, then the new CEO, wanted to transform the company's approach to manufacturing. Previously, Copeland had machined and assembled all products in a single facility. Costs were high, and quality was marginal. The problem, Diggs felt, was too much complexity.

At the outset, Diggs assigned a small, multifunctional team the task of designing a "focused factory" dedicated to a narrow, newly developed product line. The team reported directly to Diggs and took three years to complete its work. Initially, the project budget was $10 million to $12 million; that figure was repeatedly revised as the team found, through experience and with Diggs's prodding, that it could achieve dramatic improvements. The final investment, a total of $30 million, yielded unanticipated breakthroughs in reliability testing, automatic tool adjustment, and programmable control. All were achieved through learning by doing.

The team set additional precedents during the plant's start-up and early operations. To dramatize the importance of quality, for example, the quality manager was appointed second-in-command, a significant move upward. The same reporting relationship was used at all subsequent plants. In addition, Diggs urged the plant manager to ramp up slowly to full production and resist all efforts to proliferate products. These instructions were unusual at Copeland, where the marketing department normally ruled. Both directives were quickly tested; management held firm, and the implications were felt throughout the organization. Manufacturing's stature improved, and the company as a whole recognized its competitive contribution. One observer commented, "Marketing had always run the company, so they couldn't believe it. The change was visible at the highest levels, and it went down hard."

Once the first focused factory was running smoothly—it seized 25 percent of the market in two years and held its edge in reliability for over a decade—Copeland built four more factories in quick succession. Diggs assigned members of the

Stages of Knowledge

Scholars have suggested that production and operating knowledge can be classified systematically by level or stage of understanding. At the lowest levels of manufacturing knowledge, little is known other than the characteristics of a good product. Production remains an art, and there are few clearly articulated standards or rules. An example would be Stradivarius violins. Experts agree that they produce vastly superior sound, but no one can specify precisely how they were manufactured because skilled artisans were responsible. By contrast, at the highest levels of manufacturing knowledge, all aspects of production are known and understood. All materials and processing variations are articulated and accounted for, with rules and procedures for every contingency. Here an example would be a "lights out," fully automated factory that operates for many hours without any human intervention.

In total, this framework specifies eight stages of knowledge. From lowest to highest they are:

1. Recognizing prototypes (what is a good product?).
2. Recognizing attributes within prototypes (ability to define some conditions under which process gives good output).
3. Discriminating among attributes (which attributes are important? Experts may differ about relevance of patterns; new operators are often trained through apprenticeships).
4. Measuring attributes (some key attributes are measured; measures may be qualitative and relative).
5. Locally controlling attributes (repeatable performance; process designed by expert, but technicians can perform it).
6. Recognizing and discriminating between contingencies (production process can be mechanized and monitored manually).
7. Controlling contingencies (process can be automated).
8. Understanding procedures and controlling contingencies (process is completely understood).

Adapted from Ramchandran Jaikumar and Roger Bohn, "The Development of Intelligent Systems for Industrial Use: A Conceptual Framework," *Research on Technological Innovation Management and Policy* 3 (1986), pp. 182–188.

---

initial project to each factory's design team to ensure that early learnings were not lost; these people later rotated into operating assignments. Today focused factories remain the cornerstone of Copeland's manufacturing strategy and a continuing source of its cost and quality advantages.

Whether they are demonstration projects like Copeland's or ongoing programs like Allegheny Ludlum's, all forms of experimentation seek the same end: moving from superficial knowledge to deep understanding. At its simplest, the distinction is between knowing how things are done and knowing why they occur. Knowing how is partial knowledge; it is rooted in norms of behavior, standards of practice, and settings of equipment. Knowing why is more fundamental; it captures underlying cause-and-effect relationships and accommodates exceptions, adaptations, and unforeseen events. The ability to control temperatures and pressures to align grains of silicon and form silicon steel is an example of knowing how; understanding the chemical and physical process that produces the alignment is knowing why.

Further distinctions are possible, as the insert "Stages of Knowledge" suggests. Operating knowledge can be arrayed in a hierarchy, moving from limited understanding and the ability to make few distinctions to more complete understanding in which all contingencies are anticipated and controlled. In this context, experimentation and problem solving foster learning by pushing organizations up the hierarchy, from lower to higher stages of knowledge.

3. *Learning from past experience.* Companies must review their successes and failures, assess them systematically, and record the lessons in a form that employees find open and accessible. One

expert has called this process the "Santayana Review," citing the famous philosopher George Santayana, who coined the phrase "Those who cannot remember the past are condemned to repeat it." Unfortunately, too many managers today are indifferent, even hostile, to the past, and by failing to reflect on it, they let valuable knowledge escape.

A study of more than 150 new products concluded that "the knowledge gained from failures [is] often instrumental in achieving subsequent successes . . . In the simplest terms, failure is the ultimate teacher."[4] IBM's 360 computer series, for example, one of the most popular and profitable ever built, was based on the technology of the failed Stretch computer that preceded it. In this case, as in many others, learning occurred by chance rather than by careful planning. A few companies, however, have established processes that require their managers to periodically think about the past and learn from their mistakes.

Boeing did so immediately after its difficulties with the 737 and 747 plane programs. Both planes were introduced with much fanfare and also with serious problems. To ensure that the problems were not repeated, senior managers commissioned a high-level employee group, called Project Homework, to compare the development processes of the 737 and 747 with those of the 707 and 727, two of the company's most profitable planes. The group was asked to develop a set of "lessons learned" that could be used on future projects. After working for three years, they produced hundreds of recommendations and an inch-thick booklet. Several members of the team were then transferred to the 757 and 767 start-ups, and guided by experience, they produced the most successful, error-free launches in Boeing's history.

Other companies have used a similar retrospective approach. Like Boeing, Xerox studied its product development process, examining three troubled products in an effort to understand why the company's new business initiatives failed so often. Arthur D. Little, the consulting company, focused on its past successes. Senior management invited ADL consultants from around the world to a two-day "jamboree," featuring booths and presentations documenting a wide range of the company's most successful practices, publications, and techniques. British Petroleum went even further and established the postproject appraisal unit to review major investment projects, write up case studies, and derive lessons for planners that were then incorporated into revisions of the company's planning guidelines. A five-person unit reported to the board of directors and reviewed six projects annually. The bulk of the time was spent in the field interviewing managers.[5] This type of review is now conducted regularly at the project level.

At the heart of this approach, one expert has observed, "is a mind-set that . . . enables companies to recognize the value of productive failure as contrasted with unproductive success. A productive failure is one that leads to insight, understanding, and thus an addition to the commonly held wisdom of the organization. An unproductive success occurs when something goes well, but nobody knows how or why."[6] IBM's legendary founder, Thomas Watson, Sr., apparently understood the distinction well. Company lore has it that a young manager, after losing $10 million in a risky venture, was called into Watson's office. The young man, thoroughly intimidated, began by saying, "I guess you want my resignation." Watson replied, "You can't be serious. We just spent $10 million educating you."

Fortunately, the learning process need not be so expensive. Case studies and postproject reviews like those of Xerox and British Petroleum can be performed with little cost other than managers' time. Companies can also enlist the help of faculty and students at local colleges or universities; they

---

[4]*Modesto A. Maidique and Billie Jo Zirger, "The New Product Learning Cycle,"* Research Policy *14, no. 6 (1985), pp. 299, 309.*

[5]*Frank R. Gulliver, "Post-Project Appraisals Pay,"* Harvard Business Review, *March–April 1987, p. 128.*
[6]*David Nadler, "Even Failures Can Be Productive,"* New York Times, *April 23, 1989, sec. 3, p. 3.*

bring fresh perspectives and view internships and case studies as opportunities to gain experience and increase their own learning. A few companies have established computerized data banks to speed up the learning process. At Paul Revere Life Insurance, management requires all problem-solving teams to complete short registration forms describing their proposed projects if they hope to qualify for the company's award program. The company then enters the forms into its computer system and can immediately retrieve a listing of other groups of people who have worked or are working on the topic, along with a contact person. Relevant experience is then just a telephone call away.

4. *Learning from others.* Of course, not all learning comes from reflection and self-analysis. Sometimes the most powerful insights come from looking outside one's immediate environment to gain a new perspective. Enlightened managers know that even companies in completely different businesses can be fertile sources of ideas and catalysts for creative thinking. At these organizations, enthusiastic borrowing is replacing the "not invented here" syndrome. Milliken calls the process SIS, for "Steal Ideas Shamelessly"; the broader term for it is benchmarking.

According to one expert, "benchmarking is an ongoing investigation and learning experience that ensures that best industry practices are uncovered, analyzed, adopted, and implemented."[7] The greatest benefits come from studying *practices,* the way that work gets done, rather than results, and from involving line managers in the process. Almost anything can be benchmarked. Xerox, the concept's creator, has applied it to billing, warehousing, and automated manufacturing. Milliken has been even more creative: In an inspired moment, it benchmarked Xerox's approach to benchmarking.

Unfortunately, there is still considerable confusion about the requirements for successful benchmarking.

---

[7]*Robert C. Camp,* Benchmarking: The Search for Industry Best Practices that Lead to Superior Performance *(Milwaukee: ASQC Quality Press, 1989), p. 12.*

Benchmarking is not "industrial tourism," a series of ad hoc visits to companies that have received favorable publicity or won quality awards. Rather, it is a disciplined process that begins with a thorough search to identify best-practice organizations, continues with careful study of one's own practices and performance, progresses through systematic site visits and interviews, and concludes with an analysis of results, development of recommendations, and implementation. While time consuming, the process need not be terribly expensive. AT&T's Benchmarking Group estimates that a moderate-sized project takes four to six months and incurs out-of-pocket costs of $20,000 (when personnel costs are included, the figure is three to four times higher).

Benchmarking is one way of gaining an outside perspective; another, equally fertile source of ideas is customers. Conversations with customers invariably stimulate learning; they are, after all, experts in what they do. Customers can provide up-to-date product information, competitive comparisons, insights into changing preferences, and immediate feedback about service and patterns of use. And companies need these insights at all levels, from the executive suite to the shop floor. At Motorola, members of the Operating and Policy Committee, including the CEO, meet personally and on a regular basis with customers. At Worthington Steel, all machine operators make periodic, unescorted trips to customers' factories to discuss their needs.

Sometimes customers can't articulate their needs or remember even the most recent problems they have had with a product or service. If that's the case, managers must observe them in action. Xerox employs a number of anthropologists at its Palo Alto Research Center to observe users of new document products in their offices. Digital Equipment has developed an interactive process called "contextual inquiry" that is used by software engineers to observe users of new technologies as they go about their work. Milliken has created "first-delivery teams" that accompany the first shipment of all products; team members follow the product through the customer's production process to see how it is used and then develop ideas for further improvement.

Whatever the source of outside ideas, learning will only occur in a receptive environment. Managers can't be defensive and must be open to criticism or bad news. This is a difficult challenge, but it is essential for success. Companies that approach customers assuming that "we must be right, they have to be wrong" or visit other organizations certain that "they can't teach us anything" seldom learn very much. Learning organizations, by contrast, cultivate the art of open, attentive listening.

5. *Transferring knowledge.* For learning to be more than a local affair, knowledge must spread quickly and efficiently throughout the organization. Ideas carry maximum impact when they are shared broadly rather than held in a few hands. A variety of mechanisms spur this process, including written, oral, and visual reports, site visits and tours, personnel rotation programs, education and training programs, and standardization programs. Each has distinctive strengths and weaknesses.

Reports and tours are by far the most popular mediums. Reports serve many purposes: They summarize findings, provide checklists of dos and don'ts, and describe important processes and events. They cover a multitude of topics, from benchmarking studies to accounting conventions to newly discovered marketing techniques. Today written reports are often supplemented by videotapes, which offer greater immediacy and fidelity.

Tours are an equally popular means of transferring knowledge, especially for large, multidivisional organizations with multiple sites. The most effective tours are tailored to different audiences and needs. To introduce its managers to the distinctive manufacturing practices of New United Motor Manufacturing Inc. (NUMMI), its joint venture with Toyota, General Motors developed a series of specialized tours. Some were geared to upper and middle managers, while others were aimed at lower ranks. Each tour described the policies, practices, and systems that were most relevant to that level of management.

Despite their popularity, reports and tours are relatively cumbersome ways of transferring knowledge. The gritty details that lie behind complex management concepts are difficult to communicate secondhand. Absorbing facts by reading them or seeing them demonstrated is one thing; experiencing them personally is quite another. As a leading cognitive scientist has observed, "It is very difficult to become knowledgeable in a passive way. Actively experiencing something is considerably more valuable than having it described."[8] For this reason, personnel rotation programs are one of the most powerful methods of transferring knowledge.

In many organizations, expertise is held locally: in a particularly skilled computer technician, perhaps, a savvy global brand manager, or a division head with a track record of successful joint ventures. Those in daily contact with these experts benefit enormously from their skills, but their field of influence is relatively narrow. Transferring them to different parts of the organization helps share the wealth. Transfers may be from division to division, department to department, or facility to facility; they may involve senior, middle, or first-level managers. A supervisor experienced in just-in-time production, for example, might move to another factory to apply the methods there, or a successful division manager might transfer to a lagging division to invigorate it with already proven ideas. The CEO of Time Life used the latter approach when he shifted the president of the company's music division, who had orchestrated several years of rapid growth and high profits through innovative marketing, to the presidency of the book division, where profits were flat because of continued reliance on traditional marketing concepts.

Line to staff transfers are another option. These are most effective when they allow experienced managers to distill what they have learned and diffuse it across the company in the form of new standards, policies, or training programs. Consider how PPG used just such a transfer to advance its human resource practices around the concept of high-commitment work systems. In 1986, PPG

---

[8]*Roger Schank, with Peter Childers,* The Creative Attitude *(New York: Macmillan, 1988), p. 9.*

constructed a new float-glass plant in Chehalis, Washington; it employed a radically new technology as well as innovations in human resource management that were developed by the plant manager and his staff. All workers were organized into small, self-managing teams with responsibility for work assignments, scheduling, problem solving and improvement, and peer review. After several years running the factory, the plant manager was promoted to director of human resources for the entire glass group. Drawing on his experiences at Chehalis, he developed a training program geared toward first-level supervisors that taught the behaviors needed to manage employees in a participative, self-managing environment.

As the PPG example suggests, education and training programs are powerful tools for transferring knowledge. But for maximum effectiveness, they must be linked explicitly to implementation. All too often, trainers assume that new knowledge will be applied without taking concrete steps to ensure that trainees actually follow through. Seldom do trainers provide opportunities for practice, and few programs consciously promote the application of their teachings after employees have returned to their jobs.

Xerox and GTE are exceptions. As noted earlier, when Xerox introduced problem-solving techniques to its employees in the 1980s, everyone, from the top to the bottom of the organization, was taught in small departmental or divisional groups led by their immediate superior. After an introduction to concepts and techniques, each group applied what they learned to a real-life work problem. In a similar spirit, GTE's Quality: The Competitive Edge program was offered to teams of business-unit presidents and the managers reporting to them. At the beginning of the three-day course, each team received a request from a company officer to prepare a complete quality plan for their unit, based on the course concepts, within 60 days. Discussion periods of two to three hours were set aside during the program so that teams could begin working on their plans. After the teams submitted their reports, the company officers studied them, and then the teams implemented them. This GTE program produced dramatic improvements in quality, including a recent semifinalist spot in the Baldrige Awards.

The GTE example suggests another important guideline: Knowledge is more likely to be transferred effectively when the right incentives are in place. If employees know that their plans will be evaluated and implemented—in other words, that their learning will be applied—progress is far more likely. At most companies, the status quo is well entrenched; only if managers and employees see new ideas as being in their own best interest will they accept them gracefully. AT&T has developed a creative approach that combines strong incentives with information sharing. Called the Chairman's Quality Award (CQA), it is an internal quality competition modeled on the Baldrige prize but with an important twist: Awards are given not only for absolute performance (using the same 1,000-point scoring system as Baldrige) but also for improvements in scoring from the previous year. Gold, silver, and bronze Improvement Awards are given to units that have improved their scores 200, 150, and 100 points, respectively. These awards provide the incentive for change. An accompanying Pockets of Excellence program simplifies knowledge transfer. Every year, it identifies every unit within the company that has scored at least 60 percent of the possible points in each award category and then publicizes the names of these units using written reports and electronic mail.

Measuring Learning

Managers have long known that "if you can't measure it, you can't manage it." This maxim is as true of learning as it is of any other corporate objective. Traditionally, the solution has been "learning curves" and "manufacturing progress functions." Both concepts date back to the discovery, during the 1920s and 1930s, that the costs of airframe manufacturing fell predictably with increases in cumulative volume. These increases were viewed as proxies for greater manufacturing knowledge, and most early studies examined their impact on the costs of direct labor. Later studies expanded the focus, looking at total manufacturing costs and the impact of experience in other industries, including shipbuilding, oil refining, and consumer electronics. Typically, learning rates were in the 80 percent to 85 percent range (meaning that with a doubling of cumulative production, costs fell to 80 percent to 85 percent of their previous level), although there was wide variation.

Firms like the Boston Consulting Group raised these ideas to a higher level in the 1970s. Drawing on the logic of learning curves, they argued that industries as a whole faced "experience curves," costs and prices that fell by predictable amounts as industries grew and their total production increased. With this observation, consultants suggested, came an iron law of competition. To enjoy the benefits of experience, companies would have to rapidly increase their production ahead of competitors to lower prices and gain market share.

Both learning and experience curves are still widely used, especially in the aerospace, defense, and electronics industries. Boeing, for instance, has established learning curves for every work station in its assembly plant; they assist in monitoring productivity, determining work flows and staffing levels, and setting prices and profit margins on new airplanes. Experience curves are common in semiconductors and consumer electronics, where they are used to forecast industry costs and prices.

For companies hoping to become learning organizations, however, these measures are incomplete. They focus on only a single measure of output (cost or price) and ignore learning that affects other competitive variables, like quality, delivery, or new product introductions. They suggest only one possible learning driver (total production volumes) and ignore both the possibility of learning in mature industries, where output is flat, and the possibility that learning might be driven by other sources, such as new technology or the challenge posed by competing products. Perhaps most important, they tell us little about the sources of learning or the levers of change.

Another measure has emerged in response to these concerns. Called the "half-life" curve, it was originally developed by Analog Devices, a leading semiconductor manufacturer, as a way of comparing internal improvement rates. A half-life curve measures the time it takes to achieve a 50 percent improvement in a specified performance measure. When represented graphically, the performance measure (defect rates, on-time delivery, time to market) is plotted on the vertical axis, using a logarithmic scale, and the time scale (days, months, years) is plotted horizontally. Steeper slopes then represent faster learning (see the insert "The Half-Life Curve" for an illustration).

The logic is straightforward. Companies, divisions, or departments that take less time to improve must be learning faster than their peers. In the long run, their short learning cycles will translate into superior performance. The 50 percent target is a measure of convenience; it was derived empirically from studies of successful improvement processes at a wide range of companies. Half-life curves are also flexible. Unlike learning and experience curves, they work on any output measure, and they are not confined to costs or prices. In addition, they are easy to operationalize, they provide a simple measuring stick, and they allow for ready comparison among groups.

Yet even half-life curves have an important weakness: They focus solely on results. Some types of knowledge take years to digest, with few visible changes in performance for long periods. Creating a total quality culture, for instance, or developing new approaches to product development are difficult systemic changes. Because of their long gestation periods, half-life curves or any other measures focused solely on results are unlikely to capture any short-run learning that has occurred. A more comprehensive framework is needed to track progress.

Organizational learning can usually be traced through three overlapping stages. The first step is cognitive. Members of the organization are exposed to new ideas, expand their knowledge, and begin to think differently. The second step is behavioral. Employees begin to internalize new insights and alter their behavior. And the third step

The Half-Life Curve

Analog Devices has used half-life curves to compare the performance of its divisions. Here monthly data on customer service are graphed for seven divisions. Division C is the clear winner: even though it started with a high proportion of late deliveries, its rapid learning rate led eventually to the best absolute performance. Divisions D, E, and G have been far less successful, with little or no improvement in on-time service over the period.

On-time customer service performance – Monthly data (August 1987 – July 1988)

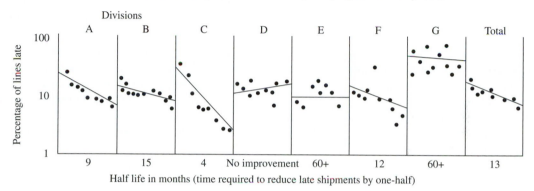

Source: Ray Stata, "Organizational Learning—The Key to Management Innovation," *Sloan Management Review* (Spring 1989), p. 72.

is performance improvement, with changes in behavior leading to measurable improvements in results: superior quality, better delivery, increased market share, or other tangible gains. Because cognitive and behavioral changes typically precede improvements in performance, a complete learning audit must include all three.

Surveys, questionnaries, and interviews are useful for this purpose. At the cognitive level, they would focus on attitudes and depth of understanding. Have employees truly understood the meaning of self-direction and teamwork, or are the terms still unclear? At PPG, a team of human resource experts periodically audits every manufacturing plant, including extensive interviews with shop-floor employees, to ensure that the concepts are well understood. Have new approaches to customer service been fully accepted? At its 1989 Worldwide Marketing Managers' Meeting, Ford presented participants with a series of hypothetical situations in which customer complaints were in conflict with short-term dealer or company profit goals and asked how they would respond. Surveys like these are the first step toward identifying changed attitudes and new ways of thinking.

To assess behavioral changes, surveys and questionnaires must be supplemented by direct observation. Here the proof is in the doing, and there is no substitute for seeing employees in action. Domino's Pizza uses "mystery shoppers" to assess managers' commitment to customer service at its individual stores; L.L. Bean places telephone orders with its own operators to assess service levels. Other companies invite outside consultants to visit, attend meetings, observe employees in action, and then report what they have learned. In many ways, this approach mirrors that of examiners for the Baldrige Award, who make several-day site visits to semifinalists to see whether the companies' deeds match the words on their applications.

Finally, a comprehensive learning audit also measures performance. Half-life curves or other performance measures are essential for ensuring that cognitive and behavioral changes have actually produced results. Without them, companies would lack a rationale for investing in learning and the assurance that learning was serving the organization's ends.

First Steps

Learning organizations are not built overnight. Most successful examples are the products of carefully cultivated attitudes, commitments, and management processes that have accrued slowly and steadily over time. Still, some changes can be made immediately. Any company that wishes to become a learning organization can begin by taking a few simple steps.

The first step is to foster an environment that is conductive to learning. There must be time for reflection and analysis, to think about strategic plans, dissect customer needs, assess current work systems, and invent new products. Learning is difficult when employees are harried or rushed; it tends to be driven out by the pressures of the moment. Only if top management explicitly frees up employees' time for the purpose does learning occur with any frequency. That time will be doubly productive if employees possess the skills to use it wisely. Training in brainstorming, problem solving, evaluating experiments, and other core learning skills is therefore essential.

Another powerful lever is to open up boundaries and stimulate the exchange of ideas. Boundaries inhibit the flow of information; they keep individuals and groups isolated and reinforce preconceptions. Opening up boundaries, with conferences, meetings, and project teams, which either cross organizational levels or link the company and its customers and suppliers, ensures a fresh flow of ideas and the chance to consider competing perspectives. General Electric CEO Jack Welch considers this to be such a powerful stimulant of change that he has made "boundarylessness" a cornerstone of the company's strategy for the 1990s.

Once managers have established a more supportive, open environment, they can create learning forums. These are programs or events designed with explicit learning goals in mind, and they can take a variety of forms: strategic reviews, which examine the changing competitive environment and the company's product portfolio, technology, and market positioning; systems audits, which review the health of large, cross-functional processes and delivery systems; internal benchmarking reports, which identify and compare best-in-class activities within the organization; study missions, which are dispatched to leading organizations around the world to better understand their performance and distinctive skills; and jamborees or symposiums, which bring together customers, suppliers, outside experts, or internal groups to share ideas and learn from one another. Each of these activities fosters learning by requiring employees to wrestle with new knowledge and consider its implications. Each can also be tailored to business needs. A consumer goods company, for example, might sponsor a study mission to Europe to learn more about distribution methods within the newly unified Common Market, while a high-technology company might launch a systems audit to review its new product development process.

Together these efforts help to eliminate barriers that impede learning and begin to move learning higher on the organizational agenda. They also suggest a subtle shift in focus, away from continuous improvement and toward a commitment to learning. Coupled with a better understanding of the "three Ms," the meaning, management, and measurement of learning, this shift provides a solid foundation for building learning organizations.

Case 4–2

TYPES OF LEARNING PROCESSES

Through learning, corporations can dramatically improve their performance. They can recognize and capitalize on new opportunities by better understanding customer needs. They can rectify problems, such as excess production costs and shipping errors, by tracing them to their source. They can install new technologies faster and more efficiently by experimenting continuously. As a leading CEO has remarked, in a world of widely available information and rapid emulation, learning "may well become the only sustainable competitive advantage."[1]

Learning is a process that occurs over time and must be repeated for maximum effectiveness. Like other processes, it has inputs and outputs. The primary inputs are time, resources, expertise, and skills, and the primary outputs are new knowledge and changes in behavior. Companies that excel at learning have institutionalized the associated processes. They come in many varieties and are distinguished by the sources and methods of obtaining and processing data. All, however, consist of the same basic stages.[2]

Stages of Learning

The first stage in any learning process is acquiring information. Data must be collected through search, scanning, observation, or interviews. Here, organizations face the challenge of determining which pieces of information to collect and how to obtain them. Next, organizations must interpret the information they have assembled, developing perspectives, conducting analyses, and arriving at a more complete understanding of what needs to be done. At this stage, they face the difficult task of grouping and organizing information to determine the underlying relationships (causal and otherwise) that are at work. Finally, organizations must apply their findings, modifying their behavior as needed. Here, they must choose which new activities to undertake and must implement these changes while gaining collective organizational support.

During each of these stages, companies have to contend with a host of impediments—what might be called "learning disabilities"—caused by organizational, climatic, and cognitive factors. Omissions, errors, and cognitive biases can disrupt the data collection process and result in inaccurate perceptions. For example, managers frequently ignore unfamiliar sources of information, downplay discordant data that clashes with pre-existing mind-sets, and only reluctantly share their findings internally. Interpretation often runs into similar problems as managers process data through frameworks that favor the status quo. Most managers are also imperfect statisticians who routinely misjudge frequencies and probabilities. For example, they often identify spurious relationships between variables, have a difficult time tracing causality, and confidently assert

---

[1]*Ray Stata, "Organizational Learning—The Key to Management Innovation,"* Sloan Management Review, *Fall 1989, p. 64.*

[2]*For a detailed discussion of the stages of learning and the associated learning processes, see David A. Garvin,* Learning in Action *(Boston: Harvard Business School Press, 2000).*

This case was prepared by Jeffrey Berger under the direction of David A. Garvin.

their beliefs based on the availability and vividness of information rather than its validity. Finally, many companies have difficulty applying and using knowledge. Risk-averse managers do not always act on their interpretations. They also face formidable barriers in convincing people to make changes in long-established patterns of behavior.

Types of Learning

These stages of learning and the associated disabilities play out in different ways, depending on the precise learning challenge. Four Harvard Business School videos depict different modes or types of learning. The first is *benchmarking,* which involves visiting other companies to identify, understand, and emulate their best practices. The second is *reflection,* in which managers and employees generate data through introspection and then review and act on their findings to sustain successes and eliminate failures. The third approach, *intelligence gathering,* requires companies to focus their attention on customers and competitors, collecting feedback and criticism in order to produce better products and services. The fourth mode of learning is *experimentation,* in which companies engage in trials or tests of different methods or techniques to identify underlying cause-and-effect relationships.

Each video displays one of these modes of learning in action and brings to light its challenges and opportunities. Each shows companies acquiring, interpreting, and applying knowledge. Each also describes the skills and success factors needed to harness the power of these techniques and suggests the conditions and settings in which each mode is best used.

The first video, *Benchmarking Outside of the Box,* shows how Mobil Oil used benchmarking to improve the speed and quality of customer service.[3] There are two broad approaches to benchmarking: copying other companies' processes exactly and adapting the processes of others to match one's own distinctive needs. Mobil followed the latter approach. It sent teams of employees to visit companies in three very different settings, all far removed from gasoline—the Ritz-Carlton Hotel chain, the Penske racing team, and Home Depot—to identify the secrets of their speedy operations and superior customer service. Team members borrowed creatively from each of these organizations, interpreting the data they collected and applying it to service stations. For example, members of the benchmarking team observed how the Penske pit crew used headsets to communicate; they developed a similar approach to link gas pumpers with counter clerks to improve service. Mobil next applied the knowledge it gained, launching a series of pilot tests at stations in the Orlando, Florida, area before considering a nationwide rollout.

The second video, *Putting the Learning Organization to Work: Learning after Doing,* focuses on reflection and features the U.S. Army's structured process for learning from its successes and failures.[4] It highlights two ways in which the Army learns from its own activities: through experience and observation. Effective learning from experience requires a systematic and immediate debriefing process, an atmosphere of candor in which even superiors can be openly critiqued, and skilled facilitation of discussions. The video focuses on the Army's use of After Action Reviews (AARs) immediately after exercises at its National Training Centers to show experiential learning in action. It also features AARs in the field, including footage from Haiti where soldiers employed a complex, multilevel review process to identify and distribute their findings both quickly and widely. Finally, the video shows the Army learning through observation. The Center for Army Lessons Learned (CALL) sends teams of specialists into battle to carry out real-time surveillance. It then captures

---

[3]*Harvard Business School video #6963A.*

[4]*Harvard Business School video #7099A.*

and records these lessons and disseminates them in the form of reports, videotapes, and training vignettes.

In the third video, *Redesigning Product/Service Development,* L.L. Bean learns by collecting, interpreting, and applying customer feedback.[5] Both exploratory and descriptive methods are used. The former involve broad, open-ended questions, while the latter involve targeted, focused questions. Both methods, however, require careful framing of questions to avoid bias, a conscientious selection of respondents to ensure representativeness and depth, and attentive listening to accurately capture concerns and unmet needs. In the video, an L.L. Bean team of product developers uses open-ended questions to interview experienced hunters and learn more about what they want in a hunting boot. The team then assembles its observations and insights, developing lessons by reasoning inductively. Members summarize, distill, and abstract the comments of different customers and then apply the pared-down list of requirements to brainstorm possible new designs. L.L. Bean also uses descriptive techniques to learn from its customers. In the video, a team literally goes for a hike with seasoned testers, who try out different parkas and footwear products made by Bean and its competitors. The next day, team members ask testers pointed, specific questions about the positives and negatives of each product and ask for their evaluations of perfor-

mance, durability, and features. Their responses are then interpreted and incorporated into revised product designs.

The fourth video, *Redoubling Shop-Floor Productivity,* focuses on Allegheny Ludlum Steel's system of shop-floor experimentation.[6] Allegheny Ludlum manipulates variables and conditions to tease out underlying cause-and-effect relationships and solve production problems. This approach mirrors the scientific method. Testers begin with a hypothesis in mind, ensure that critical measures are in place, and then manipulate one variable at a time to isolate the true cause. They use comparison groups and other controls to ensure valid results, and conduct multiple trials to ensure repeatability. After describing the system for launching experiments, which includes a simple, two-page form that contains a description of the purpose and plan of the experiment, a sign-off process to obtain approvals, and a system of incentives to encourage risk taking, the video then shows the process in action. A difficult-to-manufacture steel alloy has been transferred to a new annealing line, resulting in an unacceptable deterioration in quality. A team of Allegheny's metallurgists conducts an experiment to pinpoint the causes of the problem, moving from the shop floor to the laboratory and then back to the shop floor, as they isolate the critical variable, correct the deficiency, and then optimize the equipment settings to improve efficiency.

---

[5]*Harvard Business School video #8117A.*

[6]*Harvard Business School video #8109A.*

Case 4–3

A NOTE ON KNOWLEDGE MANAGEMENT

The management of intellectual capital has become a central theme in today's business literature and a commonly cited source of competitive advantage. Not surprisingly, a wide range of companies have launched initiatives to share their best ideas and management practices. A few have gone further, approaching knowledge management as a distinct and explicit process. This note examines that process in more detail, providing a description of its basic elements. Most examples are drawn from professional service firms. They have been at the forefront of thinking about how to manage knowledge because their own success depends heavily on developing, selling, and applying ideas. The note begins with an overview of knowledge management and then contrasts the approaches of two consulting firms, Arthur Andersen and Ernst & Young, that have been leaders in the field.

The Landscape of Knowledge Management

Behind the rise of knowledge management lies a simple fact: A surprising amount of corporate knowledge is the property of individuals, not the firm. All too often, when someone leaves an organization, their experience leaves with them. Even when people remain for long periods of time, a limited number of others may benefit from their ideas, mostly those with whom they work face to face. Nor do discoveries or successful practices in one part of an organization normally transfer easily,

if at all, to other parts. Because such knowledge is embedded and hard to extract—contained in practices, projects, processes, products, patents, and pieces of paper—employees frequently spend large amounts of time reinventing the wheel. They lose considerable productivity, and do not convert already established learnings into shared, organizational platforms. Clearly, there are enormous opportunities for improvement.

Knowledge Management Strategies

Knowledge management strategies set forth the criteria for choosing what knowledge a firm plans to pursue, and how it will go about capturing and sharing it. For obvious reasons, business needs are the starting point. A "company has to know the kind of value it intends to provide and to whom. Only then can it link its knowledge resources in a way that makes a difference . . ."[1] The focus is on providing answers to high-level "what," who," and "how" questions. Given a business's positioning, what sorts of knowledge are especially critical to support it? Who needs to have what information, and when do they need to know it? The knowledge requirements for a firm that competes as a low-cost producer of undifferentiated products, for example, are quite different from those of a firm that succeeds by generating a constant stream of new products for diverse applications. A strategic audit can identify these needs, as well as the current state of the firm's knowledge and its critical gaps. Choices then have to be made about how the required knowledge will

---

This case was prepared by Artemis March under the direction of David A. Garvin.

[1]*Brook Manville and Nathaniel Foote, "Strategy As If Knowledge Mattered,"* Fast Company, *April/May 1996, p. 66.*

be obtained. Alternatives include creating new knowledge through experimentation and research, sharing already available internal knowledge, and purchasing externally available information, ideas, or databases.

In addition, firms have to decide how they will execute their chosen knowledge management strategies. There are many possible approaches. The firm may begin with a planned, structured methodology, or allow its knowledge needs to emerge organically. It may assign responsibility for knowledge management throughout the existing organization, or develop specialized roles and organizational units to carry out the work. It may direct its initial efforts broadly or narrowly. Dow Chemical, for example, began by focusing solely on its 29,000 patents. By actively classifying, weeding, licensing, and investing in this portfolio, Dow developed a strategic approach to patents, as well as a blueprint for managing less tangible know-how such as trade secrets and technical expertise.[2]

In most cases, only a fraction of the available knowledge can be systematically captured and shared. Too much information exists already, and new knowledge is constantly being generated. Thus, when firms begin to think consciously about their knowledge management strategies, selectivity is crucial. The task is complicated by the fact that a considerable portion of corporate knowledge is tacit. Tacit knowledge includes all knowledge that has not yet been articulated or made explicit, or that is known at a nonverbal level and does not lend itself to being described or translated into formal, codified categories. As a leading philosopher has put it: "We can know more than we can tell."[3]

It is one thing, for example, to make available to consultants the best current thinking on reorganiz-ing a client's purchasing process and the five main benefits that are likely to result. It is another thing entirely to describe clearly when and how to bring up hard issues with managers, when to push to close a sale, and which benefits or arguments are likely to be most persuasive at a particular moment. The former type of knowledge is easy to communicate; the core concepts and ideas can be written down and then transmitted in discrete segments from one person to another. The latter type of knowledge is transmitted in a very different way—holistically, as a practice—usually through trial and error, apprenticeship, and skilled coaching, and often at a level below that of explicit language.[4] Tacit knowledge thus requires distinctive approaches if best practices are to be identified and communicated effectively.

Knowledge Management Processes

At the core of knowledge management lie four processes: generating, organizing, developing, and distributing content.

Generating. Generating content involves two tasks: identifying the desired content proactively, often before it is in finished form; and getting people to contribute ideas, either through online discussions or by submitting deliverables that have emerged from other work, such as client engagements. Both technological and cultural barriers make the process difficult. Groups and individuals have to learn how to submit material electronically, and in most cases, have to undergo a shift in mindset and culture, away from hoarding knowledge and toward sharing ideas. Giovanni Piazza, a developer of knowledge management systems at Ernst & Young, has described these challenges succinctly: "If people don't want to share, they are not going to do it even if you have the best technology in the world. People won't share if they don't see what's in it for them."

[2]*Rich Mullin, "Knowledge Management: A Cultural Evolution," Journal of Business Strategy, September/October 1996,* pp. 56–59.

[3]*Michael Polanyi,* The Tacit Dimension *(New York: Anchor Books, 1966),* p. 4.

[4]*Donald A. Schön,* Educating the Reflective Practitioner *(San Francisco: Jossey-Bass, 1987).*

Organizing.   Once information has been collected, it must be organized so that it can be represented and retrieved electronically. Knowledge-sharing systems or tools, including knowledge bases, navigational devices, user interfaces, and taxonomies, must be designed to facilitate this process. Proper positioning of material and linkages among the elements are critical; for this reason, knowledge bases are not synonymous with databases. The latter contain little more than fields of raw data, while the former are sensitive to context and relationship, making the material easier to access, interpret, and use. Knowledge bases can be further distinguished by their degree of "filtering." Unfiltered knowledge bases include those that archive documents directly, or that enable many-to-many communication without intervention by others. Filtered knowledge bases, by contrast, contain content that has been screened, distilled, and approved for use by recognized experts. Here, a critical task is continually refreshing the material, deleting and adding information to retain its currency. Avoiding obsolescence is a primary concern. According to John Peetz, chief knowledge officer of Ernst & Young: "A knowledge base without maintenance is worth nothing."

Developing.   Development activities involve the selection and further refinement of material to increase its value for users. In many cases, the line between organizing and developing material is difficult to draw; often, the two occur simultaneously. Both tasks are normally collaborative and draw upon the expertise and experience of practitioners. At a minimum, subject matter experts review and bless the work done by others, who may be researchers, writers, or editors specifically tasked with knowledge management responsibilities. Together, they produce a package of distilled material that has been certified as being important, represents the best ideas of its kind, and reflects the perspective of the firm's top experts in the area.

How to "chunk" material and divide it into meaningful categories is an area of increasing focus, especially as firms begin to develop "knowledge objects." A knowledge object is a module of information or knowledge that has been carved out of its original context for reuse in other settings. An example might be a framework for diagnosing quality problems, or a set of strategic concepts. A considerable literature has now developed in the area of intelligent agents and expert systems about how to construct valid knowledge objects. Wendi Bukowitz, a key developer of Arthur Andersen's Global Best Practices knowledge base, has described the challenge:

> I think the hardest thing to do is to know how to chunk material. The chunks must fit the context you are writing for—say, Process A—but must also be able to be decoupled and fit comfortably somewhere else, say, Process B. That's important for trying to build links between different processes. The way you have chunked and constructed your content will also affect your search mechanisms and tools, especially those that are more advanced.

Distributing.   Distribution refers to how people gain access to material. There are two primary objectives: making it easy for people to find what they are looking for, and encouraging the use and reuse of knowledge. Both training and reward systems play important roles. The most critical choice, however, is between "push" and "pull" systems. The former make material available by sending large masses of information out to users, while the latter wait until users call on the knowledge base to draw material out of it, often through detailed searches. Knowledge managers at both Arthur Andersen and Ernst & Young believe that pull systems are less desirable, largely because the typical consultant is too busy to spend time searching for specific data, frameworks, or tools. But they argue that push systems have flaws too because they contain a glut of information. Both firms are therefore working on "targeted push" systems that are sensitive to users' interests and even their current work context, and proactively deliver material that would be helpful and relevant. Because virtually every professional uses e-mail, tool developers are also working to achieve interoperability between e-mail and knowledge-sharing tools.

Knowledge Management Infrastructure

To carry out the above activities, companies need an appropriate infrastructure. This usually includes new organizational units and roles, as well as the development and enculturation of knowledge-sharing technologies and tools.

Organizational Units. *Specialized knowledge management units* often emerge, or older units expand their responsibilities, to establish, coordinate, and manage the technology and tools and to facilitate the capture, development, and distribution of knowledge. The work of these units is normally aimed at ensuring that common approaches are used and become institutionalized among users. Members interact frequently with IT about systems, user interfaces, and search tools, and with practice leaders and subject matter experts about content. *Communities of practice* are the acknowledged "owners" of content; they have responsibility for generating and developing the knowledge relevant to their work. At consulting firms, these communities may be organized around industries, functional expertise, or selected activities such as mergers and acquisitions. Oversight is often provided by senior management through some sort of *knowledge management steering committee.* Its responsibilities include developing or assessing knowledge strategies, setting knowledge investment levels and priorities, and establishing the scope of knowledge-sharing activities.

Roles and Responsibilities. Several roles have emerged to focus and drive the knowledge process. *Chief knowledge officers* or their equivalents (e.g., vice president of global intellectual assets) champion knowledge management activities, develop strategic approaches to knowledge, and build the knowledge management infrastructure at the firm level. *Knowledge managers* work as intermediaries and facilitators. Some focus on process issues, getting people to contribute ideas, developing structures for organizing information, and making sure that content owners carry out their responsibilities. Others work more directly on content, filtering and developing material that has been generated internally through client engagements or externally from published sources. The latter group draws heavily on the skills of librarians, information professionals, researchers, analysts, and writers, and includes such activities as searching, collecting, distilling, organizing, and packaging information.

Technology and Tools. Most experts in knowledge management agree that success requires much more than state-of-the-art information systems. Nevertheless, recent increases in the scope and volume of knowledge management activities rest, to a great extent, on technology developments that burst on the scene in the mid-90s. As Maryam Alavi, an expert in information systems and professor at the College of Business and Management, University of Maryland at College Park, has observed:

> First of all, you need three different technologies: database and database management systems to collect and hold enormous amounts of information, communications and messaging to retrieve and transmit material independent of location, and secure browsing that allows people to search databases remotely yet protect against unauthorized use. All three of those technologies must be seamlessly integrated on a large scale, and the end result must be robust. The integration and operation of all of those technologies has been greatly facilitated by Internet-based standards and architecture which allows different databases and platforms to work together.[5]

In 1997, it was possible to develop systems using either an Intranet or a groupware platform such as Lotus Notes. The most powerful argument in favor of an Intranet-based approach was that all the tools and information exist in one place and are linked together seamlessly. Those who work with Notes, however, claim several advantages: smoother integration with e-mail, better security, easier to manage databases, and easier to structure searches.

Increasingly, these and other system design issues have become a major concern for companies

---

[5]*Personal interview with case writer, April 8, 1997.*

pursuing knowledge management. Several difficulties remain. One is getting all of the required data in one location, so that it is accessible through a single search process. A second concern is data security—who should see what, when, and with what authorization. A third issue is how to get people to use these systems. Peggy Odem, knowledge management project director for the American Productivity and Quality Center, has described the dilemma:

> You can't add publishing to people's workload. It should not be another thing that they have tacked on to their existing responsibilities. You therefore need to understand how people work and what they need in terms of knowledge, access, and communication; then you design your system to meet those needs. In fact, you design it so that they can't do a good job without it, or can do their job even better and more easily because of it. Then you get the behavior you want.[6]

Challenges

Despite recent progress in developing knowledge management processes and systems, a number of critical challenges have yet to be resolved.

Role Clarification.   Within professional service firms, most knowledge managers support client-serving professionals. There are conflicting views about whether people in these roles should work part-time as knowledge managers while also doing client work, rotate in and out of full-time knowledge management roles, or commit to a knowledge management career track. Some experts argue against rotation, saying that consistency is essential to providing high-quality knowledge services; others believe that losing touch with clients is a far greater danger. There are similar debates over the need for a specialized corps of knowledge managers. Some see these skills as distinctive and hard to develop, while others see the tasks as simple extensions of day-to-day consulting activities.

Performance, Incentive, and Measurement Systems.   Many experts believe that changes in performance and incentive systems are essential to create a culture in which knowledge sharing is the norm. Measurement, however, remains problematic. Tracking is usually easier on the contribution side because an individual's contributions to knowledge bases or online discussions are readily observable, and names can be attached to specific pieces of material. Usage is more difficult to assess, especially when data can be accessed remotely. In particular, the number of "hits" on an entry in a knowledge base is only a fuzzy indicator of value; it says very little about how often or how well people are using an idea.

Tacit Knowledge: Capture and Transfer.   Tacit knowledge remains elusive, limiting the degree to which internal best practices can be articulated and shared. A recent research study found that most difficulties in transferring such practices are not, as conventionally assumed, due to motivational factors (an unwillingness to accept ideas "not invented here") but instead reflect knowledge barriers. Two of the primary constraints are recipients who lack the depth of experience or knowledge to make effective use of new ideas, and problems in identifying with precision the set of interrelated variables and activities that led to success and superior performance at the original site.[7]

Knowledge Management at Arthur Andersen

Andersen Worldwide was a global partnership consisting of two units, Arthur Andersen and Andersen Consulting. Arthur Andersen (hereafter, AA, Andersen, or the firm) was a $4.1 billion business with 50,000 employees divided among four service lines: audit, tax, financial consulting, and business consulting. Each professional belonged to

---

[6]*Telephone interview with case writer, April 8, 1997.*

[7]*Gabriel Szulanski, "Exploring Internal Stickiness: Impediments to the Transfer of Best Practice within the Firm,"* Strategic Management Journal *17 (Winter Special Issue, 1996), pp. 27–43.*

one of these service lines, and was also focused by geography and industry. The result was over 80 "communities of practice" (also called "groups") within the firm, each corresponding roughly to one of these matrixed units.

Overview. Andersen's approach to knowledge management distinguished between convergent and divergent processes. Each was supported by its own knowledge bases. Global Best Practices (GBP), a collection of highly distilled information on best business practices, was representative of the former, while AA Online, an organizational forum for sharing information and ideas using Lotus Notes as the platform, was representative of the latter. A new role of knowledge manager had emerged to oversee and build AA Online; it had evolved over time and was now well established. In the fall of 1995, the firm began offering knowledge management services to clients, and in early 1997 was planning to sell parts of GBP externally as "packaged knowledge." It had also begun to draw together its various knowledge-sharing tools and applications using an Intranet platform called AA KnowledgeSpace, and had assigned these and other knowledge-related products to a new organizational entity called AA Knowledge Enterprises.

Divergent and Convergent. AA had discovered that it needed both divergent and convergent processes for managing knowledge. Divergent systems were organizational forums to which anyone could post a question, idea, or document. There was no editing, and no assessment of quality before material was entered into the system. By contrast, the material that was entered into convergent systems had to be reviewed and approved by subject matter experts as being among the best of its kind— what Andersen consultants called "the 24-karat gold standard."

Not only were both systems considered essential, but they also had to be linked for maximum effectiveness. Convergent systems served to communicate what experts believed were the best insights, approaches, methodologies, and practices of the time; they ensured that far-flung professionals,

in offices around the world, were reading off the same page. Yet they came with an important limitation. Without a complementary divergent process, the material was likely to decay, becoming rigid and out of date. Divergence ensured that new ideas were introduced, making it possible to see what emerging ideas were hot and what unanticipated topics were attracting interest. Robert (Bob) Hiebeler, the AA partner in charge of developing GBP, observed:

> To get people to contribute their tacit knowledge, we have to ask them specific questions in a context, and provide a forum for them to have a conversation. That's the role of AA OnLine. Then we need a way to harvest the best ideas in that conversation and create packaged knowledge. In the GBP group, we monitor daily the questions being raised in our divergent systems by all practice areas. Our goal is to identify trends; sometimes, that generates proactive research.

AA OnLine: A Divergent System

AA OnLine (AAOL), developed in 1994, was one of the firm's most important organizational forums. It was one of several Notes-based, knowledge-sharing applications that had been created by the firm's IT organization. According to lead development manager Toby Bell, IT did little more than

> change the medium through which knowledge sharing took place. Our business consulting service line already had a person, Tina Schultz, whose primary responsibility was to gather and disseminate ideas and information. That's what a knowledge manager does, right? In fact, Tina knew a great deal about what knowledge managers can, might, and actually do, so we put her in charge of the whole AAOL application at the firm. Part of her job was to identify people in each Andersen community who might be responsible for the content, context, and classification of knowledge, and to then work with them.

Getting Started. Schultz, in effect, created the first de facto knowledge manager role at AA, working initially by phone and word of mouth. Material was collated in binders, and subsequently in several CD-ROMs that featured methodologies, tools, work plans, proposals, PowerPoint presentations, and other material that consultants had sent her because they thought it could be reused. But the main responsibility was to develop firmwide usage of AAOL. Most discussions arose from a real need: Someone had a proposal due and needed help, or was in the field and wanted ideas from others who had faced a similar situation. Taking advantage of these situations, Schultz brought 50 groups into the process, one at a time:

> For two years, almost all I did was help get this system into the culture of each service line. We did it group by group, not office by office. I did it that way so people would have other members of a community to talk to. We got a lot of flak for that from the offices, who thought they were the right units on which to build AAOL. But in an office, you have too many diverse interests, and no critical mass.

One of the critical obstacles Schultz faced was concern about security, especially in sensitive areas such as tax. This abated when participants were given the ability to mark an item as shareable or not beyond one's community of practice. "A big part of my job," Schultz observed, "was getting them comfortable with the idea that they could put limits on material and the controls would in fact work."

Elements of the System.　AAOL had three primary components: announcements, resources, and threaded discussions. *Announcements* were aimed at the group as a whole; they largely replaced paper memos, had a 30-day life cycle, and did not require a response. *Resources* were documents that had a longer life span and relatively high value. They were of two types. Individual postings were presented as food for thought; they were usually accompanied by an introductory statement saying, in effect, "Here is a work plan that worked well for us and we are proud of . . ." Group postings were presented by knowledge managers after thorough review by experts; they were accompanied by a statement saying, "Here is a work plan we are all going to use." Over time, the resources section of

AAOL had become the company's main repository for engagement deliverables. By 1997, nearly 30,000 items had been contributed, even though AA had relatively few incentives to actively encourage knowledge sharing, and no knowledge-sharing requirement in performance or promotion reviews. Finally, *threaded discussions* were interactive dialogues, using groupware, that began with an originating question or comment followed by a series of responses. All responses formed a thread that could be printed out by pushing a button ("show thread").

AAOL had three mechanisms for "escalating" content and giving it greater visibility. Individual users could ask for only those documents that matched their needs. Group voting was also available, with multiple users indicating the material they found to be especially helpful. Those items receiving high ratings showed up automatically on the screens of people entering the database for the first time, or those who used it infrequently. Usage was also tracked, and the resulting scores indicated the items receiving a large number of hits. Finally, a third method of escalating content was the promotion of material by knowledge managers. They could flag a document as especially valuable, much like a "cool site" on the Web pointed people toward a desirable location.

Knowledge Managers

At Andersen the term "knowledge manager" was applied in several different contexts. Two roles/contexts were particularly important: knowledge managers who facilitated the use of particular Lotus Notes applications, and knowledge managers who pulled together the best content for particular communities of practice. In addition, large offices began to appoint their own knowledge managers to help local consultants gather and share knowledge. The Atlanta office, for example, now had four people playing this role.

Applications-Centered Knowledge Managers. Some knowledge managers were attached to a Notes application, and worked with all service lines and communities of practice to facilitate its use. They were usually experienced line employees who had decided to shift their career to knowledge management and serve primarily in a support role. Schultz noted: "Rotation in and out doesn't work. There is not enough continuity, and it's not fair to users." These knowledge managers were located at different levels in the organization. Every Notes application had a knowledge manager at the firm level, and AAOL also had knowledge managers at the service line level. Because the number of knowledge tools was proliferating, technical qualifications were becoming more important in these roles. According to Schultz: "At a minimum, they have to understand what is being said in technical meetings about how applications are going to get built."

Community-Centered Knowledge Managers. About 25 knowledge managers had also emerged in the firm's industry groups and "Competency Centers," which were charged with thought leadership in specific fields of expertise. They, too, were line employees, but reported to a practice or industry leader. Their job was to pull together the best material (e.g., best presentations, articles, material from engagements) for their service line, and make it accessible to everyone in the community. One piece of their work was to manage the space in AAOL for their Competency Center; that included populating and refreshing their communities' AAOL knowledge bases.

For Business Consulting as a whole, a Knowledge Management Group (KMG) managed its Knowledge Space. Consisting of 10–12 people, including a small development team, and headed by Mark Stone, the KMG continually examined and developed new technologies to improve the technological side of Knowledge Space. They developed new knowledge bases to house content and new search tools and interfaces, and they ensured that Competency Centers were consistent in the way they packaged and codified content. Schultz described the relationship between her AAOL group and the KMG:

We provide AAOL as a tool for any group that wants to use it, and then support it. Mark Stone is therefore my client, and I am here to help him achieve his goals. AAOL is simply one of his tools. I am responsible for AAOL in every group, while Mark is responsible for AAOL plus all the other knowledge management tools that are used in Business Consulting.

Role Definition. To better define the role of knowledge manager, Schultz and Lisa Kelley, one of the service line knowledge managers for AAOL, had organized several internal symposia, forums, and training sessions. Kelley had also written a white paper in which she laid out the requirements for effectiveness in this new position. All knowledge managers, she argued, should be skilled in five areas. They should:

- *Know their community.* Knowledge managers needed to understand the business strategy and objectives of their community, be well linked with users and their needs, and ensure that members of the community were accurately represented in discussions.
- *Design the context.* Knowledge managers had to structure the categories that set the context for dialogue; this included creating an index, developing and refining the graphical user interface and screens, and organizing the presentation of views within AAOL.
- *Oversee the content.* Knowledge managers were responsible for loading the system with information that was highly detailed, robust, and relevant, and keeping it fresh.
- *Support the infrastructure.* Knowledge managers were expected to promote the tools of knowledge sharing, guide users, and help direct application developers in the continuous improvement of knowledge-sharing tools.
- *Enhance the sharing process.* Knowledge managers were expected to synthesize discussion threads and otherwise "mine the gold" in the mass of information that emerged from users. This could lead to new ideas, connections, and, potentially, new services. They were also

expected to stimulate the kind of interaction and sharing that pulled tacit knowledge out of individuals.[8]

GBP: A Convergent Knowledge Base

AA's convergent knowledge bases were designed to help practitioners sell and perform engagements. They included an engagement information system, a repository of tools and methodologies, and, most significantly, Global Best Practices (GBP).

Basic Elements. Global Best Practices was a knowledge base of highly distilled research concerning the most effective ways of performing particular processes. Its stated goal was to "obtain and share best practice information with our professionals worldwide to help clients improve their performance" and was open to all members of the firm, not just partners. GBP was based primarily on external, qualitative research drawn from secondary sources, rather than best practices that had emerged from client engagements. All material was organized using a process classification scheme that AA had codeveloped with the American Productivity and Quality Center.

The classification scheme, which was later adopted as a standard by the International Benchmarking Clearinghouse, organized virtually all of an enterprise's activities, irrespective of industry, into seven broad operating processes that directly impacted the customer, and six broad management and support processes that aided, directed, and supported the operating processes. These large processes were then further divided into 256 more specific processes. (See Exhibit 1 for the classification scheme.) Ruth Williams, one of the key developers for the project, noted: "We never intended to collect material on all 256 processes in the framework. Our initial focus was on areas, such as finance, that were meaningful for us because they represented a primary focus for our work. As the scope

of our consulting practice has grown, we've populated an increasingly broad range of processes."

For each of these processes, the GBP knowledge base included material in 10 categories, which appeared as icons on the first computer screen display. They included descriptions of best practices, how they could be achieved, examples of what best practice companies were doing in the area, world-class performance metrics, relevant AA engagement experience, diagnostic tools, and presentations that could be customized. Best practices were further described in several, more detailed subcategories, including benefits, approach, performance measures, roles and responsibilities, and expert commentary. The heart of this section, according to Bukowitz, was the approach to implementation, which was described in 3 to 10 pages of text for each process.

Development. GBP had been in continuous development since 1992. Originally, the GBP unit was a small skunkworks; eventually it grew to include 35 people, many of them writers and researchers on long-term contract to AA. The group conducted a massive amount of research on over 100 business processes, from which they distilled best practice information and trends. This information was then brought to subject matter experts within AA for review; with their input and suggestions, writers crafted the final package. Because of the pace of development, a new and expanded CD-ROM version of the database was released every few months; more recently, CD-ROMs had been replaced by an intranet version of the database.

Diagnostics. Andersen professionals used GBP primarily at the front end of engagements to assess situations and sell work. Diagnostic tools were especially useful for this purpose, and the GBP unit had built 13 such tools in recent years, using benchmarking data drawn from the field. Each consisted of a set of questions, as well as a database of answers already collected from clients or potential clients. Diagnostics were of two types: quantitative and qualitative. When a consultant used one of the quantitative tools, s/he collected hard, objective

---

[8]*Lisa Kelley, "The Role of the Knowledge Manager at Arthur Andersen," February 14, 1996.*

EXHIBIT 1   Process Classification Scheme—Overview

The Arthur Andersen Global Best Practices℠ knowledge base is driven by a unique Process Classification Scheme, which was developed in partnership with the International Benchmarking Clearinghouse.

By using a universal business language across all countries, global Arthur Andersen specialists contribute their experience on dozens of generic and industry-specific processes. We can compare your processes to the best in the business, regardless of industry or geographic location

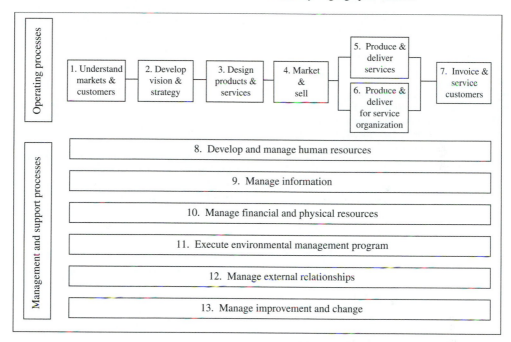

Operating Processes

1. Understand Markets and Customers

1.1 Determine customer needs and wants
- 1.1.1 Conduct qualitative assessments
  - 1.1.1.1 Conduct customer interviews
  - 1.1.1.2 Conduct focus groups
- 1.1.2 Conduct quantitative assessments
  - 1.1.2.1 Develop and implement surveys
- 1.1.3 Predict customer purchasing behavior
1.2 Measure customer satisfaction
- 1.2.1 Monitor satisfaction with products and services
- 1.2.2 Monitor satisfaction with complaint resolution
- 1.2.3 Monitor satisfaction with communication
1.3 Monitor changes in market or customer expectations
- 1.3.1 Determine weaknesses of product/service offerings
- 1.3.2 Identify new innovations that are meeting customer needs
- 1.3.3 Determine customer reactions to competitive offerings

2. Develop Vision and Strategy

2.1 Monitor the external environment
- 2.1.1 Analyze and understand competition
- 2.1.2 Identify economic trends
- 2.1.3 Identify political and regulatory issues
- 2.1.4 Assess new technology innovations
- 2.1.5 Understand demographics
- 2.1.6 Identify social and cultural changes
- 2.1.7 Understand ecological concerns
2.2 Define the business concept and organizational strategy
- 2.2.1 Select relevant markets
- 2.2.2 Develop long-term vision
- 2.2.3 Formulate business unit strategy
- 2.2.4 Develop overall mission statement
2.3 Design the organizational structure and relationships between organizational units
2.4 Develop and set organizational goals

(continued)

EXHIBIT 1   (*continued*)

3. Design Products and Services

3.1 Develop new products/service concept and plans
- 3.1.1 Translate customer wants and needs into product and/or service requirements
- 3.1.2 Plan and deploy quality targets
- 3.1.3 Plan and deploy cost targets
- 3.1.4 Develop product life cycle and development timing targets
- 3.1.5 Develop and integrate leading technology into product/service concept

3.2 Design, build, and evaluate prototype products or services
- 3.2.1 Develop product/service specifications
- 3.2.2 Conduct concurrent engineering
- 3.2.3 Implement value engineering
- 3.2.4 Document design specifications
- 3.2.5 Develop prototypes
- 3.2.6 Apply for patents

3.3 Refine existing products/services
- 3.3.1 Develop product/service enhancements
- 3.3.2 Eliminate quality/reliability problems
- 3.3.3 Eliminate outdated products/services

3.4 Test effectiveness of new or revised products or services

3.5 Prepare for production
- 3.5.1 Develop and test prototype production process
- 3.5.2 Design and obtain necessary material and equipment
- 3.5.3 Install and verify process or methodology

3.6 Manage the product/service development process

4. Market and Sell

4.1 Market products or services to relevant customer segments
- 4.1.1 Develop pricing strategy
- 4.1.2 Develop advertising strategy
- 4.1.3 Develop market messages to communicate benefits
- 4.1.4 Estimate advertising resource and capital requirements
- 4.1.5 Identify specific target customers and their needs
- 4.1.6 Develop sales forecast
- 4.1.7 Sell products or services
- 4.1.8 Negotiate terms

4.2 Process customer orders
- 4.2.1 Accept orders from customers
- 4.2.2 Enter orders into production and delivery process

5. Produce and Deliver Products and Services

5.1 Plan for and acquire necessary resources
- 5.1.1 Select and certify suppliers
- 5.1.2 Purchase capital goods
- 5.1.3 Purchase materials and supplies
- 5.1.4 Acquire appropriate technology

5.2 Convert resources or inputs into products

- 5.2.1 Develop and adjust production delivery process (for existing process)
- 5.2.2 Schedule production
- 5.2.3 Move materials and resources
- 5.2.4 Make product
- 5.2.5 Package product
- 5.2.6 Warehouse or store product
- 5.2.7 Stage products for delivery

5.3 Deliver products
- 5.3.1 Arrange product shipment
- 5.3.2 Deliver products to customers
- 5.3.3 Install product
- 5.3.4 Confirm specific service requirements for individual customers
- 5.3.5 Identify and schedule resources to meet service requirements
- 5.3.6 Provide the service to specific customers

5.4 Manage production and delivery process
- 5.4.1 Documents and monitor order status
- 5.4.2 Manage inventories
- 5.4.3 Assure product quality
- 5.4.4 Schedule and perform maintenance
- 5.4.5 Monitor environmental constraints

6. Produce and Deliver for Service Oriented Organizations

6.1 Plan for and acquire necessary resources
- 6.1.1 Select and certify suppliers
- 6.1.2 Purchase materials and supplies
- 6.1.3 Acquire appropriate technology

6.2 Develop human resource skills
- 6.2.1 Define skill requirements
- 6.2.2 Identify and implement training
- 6.2.3 Monitor and manage skill development

6.3 Deliver service to the customer
- 6.3.1 Confirm specific service requirements for individual customer
- 6.3.2 Identify and schedule resources to meet service requirements
- 6.3.3 Provide the service to specific customers

6.4 Ensure quality of service

7. Invoice and Service Customers

7.1 Bill the customer
- 7.1.1 Develop, deliver, and maintain customer billing
- 7.1.2 Invoice the customer
- 7.1.3 Respond to billing inquiries

7.2 Provide after-sales service
- 7.2.1 Provide post-sales service
- 7.2.2 Handle warranties and claims

7.3 Respond to customer inquiries
- 7.3.1 Respond to information requests
- 7.3.2 Manage customer complaints

EXHIBIT 1   (*continued*)

Management and Support Processes

8. Develop and Manage Human Resources

8.1 Create and manage human resource strategy
- 8.1.1 Identify organizational strategic demands
- 8.1.2 Determine human resource costs
- 8.1.3 Define human resource requirements
- 8.1.4 Define human resource's organizational role

8.2 Cascade strategy to work level
- 8.2.1 Analyze, design, or redesign work
- 8.2.2 Define and align work outputs and metrics
- 8.2.3 Define work competencies

8.3 Manage deployment or personnel
- 8.3.1 Plan and forecast workforce requirements
- 8.3.2 Develop succession and career plans
- 8.3.3 Recruit, select, and hire employees
- 8.3.4 Create and deploy teams
- 8.3.5 Relocate employees
- 8.3.6 Restructure and rightsize workforce
- 8.3.7 Manage employee retirement
- 8.3.8 Provide outplacement support

8.4 Develop and train employees
- 8.4.1 Align employee and organization development needs
- 8.4.2 Develop and manage training programs
- 8.4.3 Develop and manage employee orientation programs
- 8.4.4 Develop functional/process competencies
- 8.4.5 Develop management/leadership competencies
- 8.4.6 Develop team competencies

8.5 Manage employee performance, reward, and recognition
- 8.5.1 Define performance measures
- 8.5.2 Develop performance management approaches and feedback
- 8.5.3 Manage team performance
- 8.5.4 Evaluate work for market value and internal equity
- 8.5.5 Develop and manage base and variable compensation
- 8.5.6 Manage reward and recognition programs

8.6 Ensure employee well-being and satisfaction
- 8.6.1 Manage employee satisfaction
- 8.6.2 Develop and manage work/life support programs
- 8.6.3 Manage and administer employee benefits
- 8.6.4 Manage workplace health and safety
- 8.6.5 Manage internal communications
- 8.6.6 Manage and support workforce diversity

8.7 Ensure employee involvement

8.8 Manage labor management relationships
- 8.8.1 Manage collective bargaining process
- 8.8.2 Develop labor-management partnerships

8.9 Develop Human Resource Information Systems (HRIS)

9. Manage Information Resources

9.1 Plan for information resources management
- 9.1.1 Derive requirements from business strategies
- 9.1.2 Define enterprise system architectures
- 9.1.3 Plan and forecast information technologies and methodologies
- 9.1.4 Establish enterprise data standards
- 9.1.5 Establish quality standards and controls

9.2 Develop and deploy enterprise support systems
- 9.2.1 Conduct specific needs assessments
- 9.2.2 Select information technologies
- 9.2.3 Define data lifecycles
- 9.2.4 Develop enterprise support systems
- 9.2.5 Test, evaluate, and deploy enterprise support systems

9.3 Implement systems security and controls
- 9.3.1 Establish systems security strategies and levels
- 9.3.2 Test, evaluate, and deploy systems security and controls

9.4 Manage information storage and retrieval
- 9.4.1 Establish information repositories (databases)
- 9.4.2 Acquire and collect information
- 9.4.3 Store information
- 9.4.4 Modify and update information
- 9.4.5 Enable retrieval of information
- 9.4.6 Delete information

9.5 Manage facilities and network operations
- 9.5.1 Manage centralized facilities
- 9.5.2 Manage distributed facilities
- 9.5.3 Manage network operations

9.6 Manage information services
- 9.6.1 Manage libraries and information centers
- 9.6.2 Manage business records and documents

9.7 Facilitate information sharing and communication
- 9.7.1 Manage external communications systems
- 9.7.2 Manage internal communications systems
- 9.7.3 Prepare and distribute publications

9.8 Evaluate and audit information quality

10. Manage Financial and Physical Resources

10.1 Manage financial resources
- 10.1.1 Develop budgets
- 10.1.2 Manage resource allocation
- 10.1.3 Design capital structure
- 10.1.4 Manage cash flow
- 10.1.5 Manage financial risk

(*continued*)

EXHIBIT 1   *(concluded)*

10.2 Process finance and accounting transactions
- 10.2.1 Process accounts payable
- 10.2.2 Process payroll
- 10.2.3 Process accounts receivable, credit, and collections
- 10.2.4 Close the books
- 10.2.5 Process benefits and retiree information
- 10.2.6 Manage travel and entertainment expenses

10.3 Report information
- 10.3.1 Provide external financial information
- 10.3.2 Provide internal financial information

10.4 Conduct internal audits

10.5 Manage the tax function
- 10.5.1 Ensure tax compliance
- 10.5.2 Plan tax strategy
- 10.5.3 Employ effective technology
- 10.5.4 Manage tax controversies
- 10.5.5 Communicate tax issues to management
- 10.5.6 Manage tax administration

10.6 Manage physical resources
- 10.6.1 Manage capital planning
- 10.6.2 Acquire and redeploy fixed assets
- 10.6.3 Manage facilities
- 10.6.4 Manage physical risk

11. Execute Environmental Management Program

11.1 Formulate environmental management strategy

11.2 Ensure compliance with regulations

11.3 Train and educate employees

11.4 Implement pollution prevention program

11.5 Manage remediation efforts

11.6 Implement emergency response program

11.7 Manage government agency and public relations

11.8 Manage acquisition/divestiture environmental issues

11.9 Develop and manage environmental information system

11.10 Monitor environmental management program

12. Manage External Relationships

12.1 Communicate with shareholders

12.2 Manage government relationships

12.3 Build lender relationships

12.4 Develop public relations program

12.5 Interface with board of directors

12.6 Develop community relations

12.7 Manage legal and ethical issues

13. Manage Improvement and Change

13.1 Measure organizational performance
- 13.1.1 Create measurement systems
- 13.1.2 Measure product and service quality
- 13.1.3 Measure cost of quality
- 13.1.4 Measure costs
- 13.1.5 Measure cycle time
- 13.1.6 Measure productivity

13.2 Conduct quality assessments
- 13.2.1 Conduct quality assessments based on external criteria
- 13.2.2 Conduct quality assessments based on internal criteria

13.3 Benchmark performance
- 13.3.1 Develop benchmarking capabilities
- 13.3.2 Conduct process benchmarking
- 13.3.3 Conduct competitive benchmarking

13.4 Improve processes and systems
- 13.4.1 Create commitment for improvement
- 13.4.2 Implement continuous process improvement
- 13.4.3 Reengineer business processes and systems
- 13.4.4 Manage transition to change

13.5 Implement TQM
- 13.5.1 Create commitment for TQM
- 13.5.2 Design and implement TQM systems
- 13.5.3 Manage TQM lifecycle

Source: Arthur Andersen

information from the client—for example, how many invoices were processed in a given period of time. By entering these numbers into the tool, consultants could get a quick report on what quartile of performance the potential customer was in. Moreover, because the metrics were designed with best practices in mind, potential improvements were easy to identify. The consultant simply searched the GBP database to find approaches that leading companies were using to achieve their superior levels of performance.

Qualitative tools were based on more subjective assessments. The Knowledge Management Assessment Tool, for example, listed 24 emerging practices that companies were using to create, grow and share knowledge. Each item was accompanied by two 1–5 scales, one describing the extent to which the practice was in place; the other, its importance to the organization. Potential clients assessed themselves on these scales, and their responses were captured in a benchmarking database. Comparisons could then be made to the self-assessments of other organizations that had already submitted scores. As Hiebeler explained, both the quantitative and qualitative tools were designed to open the door to conversations about performance:

> What you're really trying to do is emotionally disturb your client—but in a positive way. You want them to become dissatisfied with their current performance, and reach forward to see how can they do better. GBP does not provide *the* answer to be plugged in. It provides insights that contribute to answers.

Knowledge Services and Products

By 1995, Andersen had begun offering knowledge management services, similar to the work it was doing for itself. A Knowledge Services Competency Center was formed to spearhead the effort. Members spent time with other AA consultants, helping them build their capability to sell and perform such work through training, or working side-by-side with them on engagements. In early 1997, AA was preparing to launch a new organizational entity, AA Knowledge Enterprises (AAKE), to sell knowledge products in the market. As part of that activity, Hiebeler was named Managing Director of Packaged Knowledge Products, and the GBP unit was folded under AAKE.

Knowledge Management at Ernst & Young

Ernst & Young International (EYI) was a global confederation of professional service organizations resulting from the 1989 merger of Ernst & Whinney and Arthur Young. Its U.S. subsidiary (hereafter, E&Y, Ernst & Young, or the firm) employed 25,000 people in three business units: tax, assurance and advisory services, and management consulting. In addition, the firm was made up of diverse practices (called "communities of interest") that focused on industries, service lines and business processes.

Overview

Ernst & Young spent about 6 percent of its consulting practice revenues on knowledge management and related technology. Its approach was based on the centralization and standardization of critical knowledge management processes, and it formalized roles and responsibilities for both the content and management of those processes (see Exhibit 2). This approach had emerged from strategic planning activities in 1992–93 when the firm, led by a new CEO and a new vice chairman of consulting, constructed a process model of itself. Five value-adding "mega-processes" were identified: sales, service delivery, people management, strategic services development, and knowledge management. Each process was subsequently mapped at several levels, and performance planning and evaluation was restructured around the five processes. Over the next few years, the firm installed a global infrastructure to support its new approach, making important changes in organization, technology, and culture. In 1996, it began selling knowledge management services directly to clients.

Organization and Roles

E&Y developed a multitiered governance structure for the knowledge process, vesting ownership in a chief knowledge officer and Center for Business Knowledge. It also defined roles for Knowledge Networks, which were affiliated with individual practice areas and communities of interest, and articulated the ways in which knowledge would be captured, encoded, stored, and deployed.

Governance. Each business unit formed a Knowledge Advisory Committee composed of 10–12 senior partners. Carl (Chris) Christensen, who chaired the committee for Consulting Services, described its activities: "We examine our approaches to creating, gathering, sharing, accessing, and using knowledge assets from the standpoint of our business needs. Are we getting the most value we can from our chosen knowledge strategies? Do they align with the business?"

The committees oversaw the Center for Business Knowledge, which collected and archived knowledge gained from engagements and outside sources. In addition, Consulting Services had established two other knowledge centers that were overseen by its Knowledge Advisory Committee: The Center

EXHIBIT 2   Ernst & Young's Framework for Knowledge Management

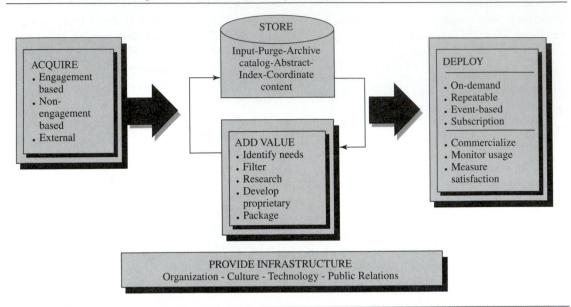

Source: Ernst & Young

for Business Innovation performed early-stage research and created new knowledge around emerging issues in technology and management; the Center for Business Transformation structured knowledge into methodologies and automated tools.

To ensure consistency across business units, a Knowledge Council was formed at the firm level; it set standards and policies for major decisions involving architecture and technology. The need for worldwide consistency led to a Global Knowledge Steering Group, which set knowledge management policies in such areas as client confidentiality and copyright conformance, and enforced the EYI belief that it must have common technology platforms, architectures, and taxonomies all over the world for everything from communicating by e-mail to the transmission of massive documents.

Chief Knowledge Officer.   John Peetz, a consulting partner who had been active in the firmwide

knowledge-charting process and had chaired Consulting Services' knowledge advisory committee before Christensen, was named chief knowledge officer (CKO) in May 1995. Peetz recalled: "All we knew was that we needed process ownership for knowledge management at the firm level if we were going to be a world-class provider of professional services to our clients." He set as a goal the building of a "true knowledge-sharing culture, one in which an individual will willingly rely on the work of another individual whom they have never met, and whose name they might not even be able to pronounce."

Peetz's primary focus was the development and operation of a firmwide infrastructure for knowledge management. In addition, he advised E&Y senior management on strategic matters having knowledge implications, helped the practice areas develop knowledge measurements appropriate to their businesses, and acted as a highly visible champion of knowledge sharing within the firm. He also educated clients, analysts, and the media about the company's knowledge management activities. In the latter role, he observed:

> We serve as a showcase and laboratory for what our clients might be doing for themselves in this area. But the primary external impact is to credentialize us as excellent service providers because of how we manage our own knowledge.

Center for Business Knowledge. The Center for Business Knowledge (CBK) was the implementation arm of the CKO's office. The CBK provided services and support to E&Y account teams, but did not usually work directly with clients. Instead, it designed, managed, and enforced the architecture and technology standards that enabled communities of interest to further develop and share the content they generated from client engagements. By mid-1997, the Center consisted of 165 employees, divided into several groups whose four directors reported to Peetz, and who worked together as a management team.

The Knowledge Services Group provided knowledge navigation services to professionals through its call center, conducted business research through a firmwide library system and 70 librarians who were distributed globally, and interpreted emerging trends and issues through its business analysts.

Responsibility for all the technology applications that supported knowledge sharing throughout the firm was vested in director Ralph Poole. Two CBK groups reported to him: the KnowledgeWeb Group, and the Repository Management Group. In addition, Poole had primary responsibility for managing knowledge sharing within the management consulting practice.

The KnowledgeWeb Group had designed and managed the firm's current knowledge management architecture, applications, navigational tools, and taxonomies. Members worked closely with software developers from IT, specifying design parameters for the KnowledgeWeb, which was the firm's knowledge management system. Laura Eisenmann, manager of group, explained: "We tell them the kinds of information we want to capture

from a document, how we want users to be able to find it, how that content should be presented, and whether there are security issues that need to be addressed."

The architecture of a new Web-based delivery system was being designed under the leadership of Giovanni Piazza. Piazza also managed the CBK large document repositories and databases in which content was held, and oversaw the systems that measured individuals' contributions, use, and development of knowledge.

The CBK's Network Support Group, under director Richard (Dick) Loehr, had day-to-day network program management responsibility for the CBK, and managed the daily interaction between knowledge process and content on a network-by-network basis. The key hands-on role was that of network coordinator. Coordinators reported to the CBK, and each one worked with a particular network (a group of senior practitioners, all belonging to a single practice area or community of interest), assisting them with CBK categories, formats, and search tools, helping them manage their content, and ensuring that the work was carried out in conformance with CBK process standards. Coordinators also made sure that their networks were connected to the rest of the firm, were receiving the information and research they needed, and were taking advantage of the learnings of others.

Knowledge Networks. Knowledge Networks consisted of a small number of senior members of a practice area or community of interest who were formally designated to lead the group's processes of acquiring, developing, and sharing knowledge. Each network "owned" its own knowledge base. Peetz explained the implications:

> Ownership means you fund it, maintain it, and make sure the content is fresh. You are responsible for quality, for the business case that says we need to have this information, and for continuing to provide the resources.

In 1997, there were 24 networks in Consulting Services, and over 80 networks in the firm as a whole. Each was composed of 6–12 people, mostly partners, who were recognized as having a high level of competency in a practice area. Each was led by a chairperson who drove the agenda, assembled people, assigned work, and was held accountable for what happened in the network. The other network members acted as a mini-board of directors, or steering group. According to Loehr:

> Their most important role is to think conceptually about what we are doing. They need to examine the knowledge base and ask, "Is it good enough? Where are the gaps? Where do we need more content, or more people to serve an emerging area? Where do we need to develop people faster, or share things more quickly?"

Another role, that of steward, had emerged as well. Stewards had hands-on responsibility for managing a network's knowledge base. They were of two types: network stewards and knowledge stewards. The former were typically senior consultants or managers who were responsible for oversight of the network's knowledge assets—its collection of best practices, innovative work examples, past client experiences, and the like. They knew where and when knowledge bases needed updating and who should be involved in the process, and they were authorized to add or delete material as necessary. Knowledge stewards, by contrast, were members of engagement teams who ensured that the content created by an engagement flowed back into CBK repositories. They also connected their teams with the relevant knowledge assests of the firm, and made sure they received the best materials currently available.

In practice, the line separating stewards and coordinators could not be drawn precisely. The intent, however, was clear. Stewards were on the service line payroll and had direct responsibility for content, while coordinators, for the most part, worked for the CBK and facilitated the processes of knowledge collection, sharing, and retrieval. Peetz, Poole, and Loehr all agreed that coordinators should not be overly involved with the details of content. As Loehr put it: "If we in the CBK start doing a lot of hands-on content work, we will start giving people the idea that it is our knowledge base to manage, not theirs."

Building a Knowledge-Sharing Culture

"Knowledge sharing is becoming a cultural norm at Ernst & Young, particularly in Consulting Services, the group I work with," noted Ellen LoPresti of Human Resources. The transition had begun in 1993, she observed, when "our business leadership focused on knowledge as a way to operationalize our strategy. They made a strategic decision to build knowledge into performance standards for everyone in the company."

These decisions seemed to have achieved the intended effect. Piazza, who had joined E&Y in 1996 after working at another organization that had resisted making a similar shift, observed: "Ernst & Young has made a transition to being an organization in which people *want* to share knowledge. Training is important to create the mind-set, and reward is important to transfer the mind-set to behavior." Piazza's view was shared by other managers at the firm, as well as by an independent newsletter, Emerson's *Professional Services Review,* that provided detailed coverage of the Big 6 accounting and consulting firms.[9]

Every member of E&Y was required to have objectives in all five process areas, and results were linked to incentive compensation. In the case of knowledge management, the initial emphasis on contributing and sharing knowledge soon expanded to include the development of new knowledge and the reuse of existing knowledge. This had required considerable work on how best to measure knowledge. The CBK collaborated with Human Resources and the service lines to develop measurements, leading the thinking process and providing the systems that made it possible to track knowledge contributions, development, and retrievals.

---

[9] *"Ernst & Young LLP: Setting the New Knowledge Sharing Standard,"* Emerson's Professional Services Review, *The Emerson Company, March/April 1997.*

Measurement was supplemented by self-reporting, particularly on the reuse of knowledge.

Consulting Services had taken the process even further by tying knowledge measurements to a competency model that was both linked to business strategy and part of a blueprint for moving toward a competency-based organizational structure. For each process, the model defined the key competencies required to deliver services in each service line, with finer distinctions based on an employee's level in the organization. A junior consultant, for example, was expected to be able to package what s/he had learned on an engagement, including archiving deliverables and writing abstracts to facilitate their retrieval. A senior manager, on the other hand, was held to a higher standard: demonstrating knowledge in front of a client. S/he had to be able to discuss new concepts and knowledge fluently and be able to shift client thinking in relevant areas. LoPresti observed: "Consulting services now uses the competency model to drive recruiting, the staffing of internal projects, individual performance planning and career management, and our training and development."

Technology and Architecture

The Ernst & Young KnowledgeWeb had a three-tier architecture. The actual content resided at the bottom level in repositories that were not filtered for content. Organization of this material was provided by the architecture's second tier in the form of "containers," knowledge bases, and navigational support systems. The first tier of the KnowledgeWeb, called the catalog, listed the various knowledge bases, described their content, and provided search tools and paths for users to find their way to the specific information they needed.

Containers.   Containers were standardized software applications for organizing, housing, and navigating through content. They provided templates for coding knowledge based on the nature and type of data or raw material. Container types included periodicals, discussion databases, document repositories, and descriptions of leading practices. Each type

had its own rules and standards, ensuring that all similar knowledge bases worked in the same way.

One goal in using containers was to house the majority of content in standard formats rather than customized applications. Poole explained: "We learned that we have to create an environment where everything has a common look and feel. We now manage that part of the process very tightly." A second reason for using containers, Eisenmann explained, was to "avoid redundant storage of content. We want to store each thing only once, yet have the flexibility to change how we access content. The architecture is like post-and-beam houses—a solid structure in which you can move the walls around."

Platforms.   The firm had two platforms for knowledge sharing—Lotus Notes and Web-based technologies. The KnowledgeWeb took advantage of the strengths of each technology—Lotus Notes in its ability to provide off-line access to content through a practitioner's hard disk, and Web technology with its ability to do large-scale searches and provide on-line access to large quantities of content. E&Y planned to continue to base its knowledge management infrastructure on both technologies until such time as their capabilities gradually merged.

The Process in Action

Submissions.   The raw material generated by an engagement team could be extensive—a stack of disks, as one partner described it. Documents included work plans, interim or final reports, analytical models, and PowerPoint presentations. Teams decided what material was valuable enough to retain. Before sending this information electronically to the CBK, the engagement team scrubbed it for client confidentiality, wrote an abstract, and filled out a "wrapper" that identified critical parameters (e.g., industry, business process, engagement director) so that it could be plugged into many possible search paths.

Escalation.   When professionals thought their material was particularly valuable and a good candidate for reuse, they could take a variety of steps to escalate its importance. For example, project teams or individuals could, in addition to submitting material to the CBK repositories, also send work products directly to their networks. A second approach to escalation was for the networks to target certain jobs or work products as important while they were in process. A third method was daily monitoring of the discussion databases for innovative ideas and emerging topics of interest, and then flagging those of special significance.

Packaging Information. One form of container for packaging engagement material was called PowerPacks. In it, networks published their most important filtered material, adhering to a standard template. Every PowerPack followed the same classification scheme and had the same navigational properties.

PowerPacks represented a synthesis by a network of the best material available on a particular topic. These syntheses were limited to 50 megabytes so that professionals could carry the information on the hard drive of their laptops. All PowerPacks were organized into eight, high-level categories: people, sales and marketing, leading practices, articles and research, learning resources, regulations and standards, service delivery, and network communications. The emphasis was usually on sales and marketing materials; these might include successful proposals, qualifications statements from clients, resumes, big-picture presentations that could be customized, market reports concerning the industry and competition, a few high-level solutions, and the best business case for doing this kind of work. PowerPacks were credited with being a major contributor to E&Y's recent reduction in proposal turnaround time from two to three weeks to two to three days.

Knowledge Objects. Another way of adding value was to pull nuggets of information out of their originating documents, creating "knowledge objects" that could be reused. New instructions were provided, together with descriptions of settings in which the objects could be applied. Examples included interview guides, analytical models, diagnostic approaches, work schedules, and benchmark data on processes or practices. By late 1996, the leadership of Consulting Services thought it so important to carve knowledge objects out of the 13,000 documents that it had accumulated in its repositories that each of its networks was asked to form teams of three to five senior people to create them. Each team was assigned a project manager with at least 10 years experience in his or her area, and drew on network members as well as other experts during the review process. Phase I of the Knowledge Object Repository (KOR) Project, as it came to be known, took place between November 1996 and January 1997, with each of the 19 teams working full-time on the project for five to eight weeks. During this period, they developed a total of 2,000 knowledge objects. At least half of these pertained to systems integration, including SAP implementation, which was a major focus of E&Y consulting activity. Before the teams disbanded, they were required to define a process for creating knowledge objects in their networks on an ongoing basis.

Knowledge Services and Products

By 1996, Ernst & Young was building a consulting capability to help clients with their knowledge management issues and had begun offering knowledge management consulting services to clients. Chris Christensen, who had long chaired the knowledge advisory committee in consulting services, assumed leadership of the new practice area, called Knowledge-Driven Business Consulting. In 1997, a second group was formalized to help the firm build new knowledge-based businesses outside of the core service business. One of these new businesses, for example, would distribute and redistribute basic content to the health care industry through the development and implementation of technology that connected the entire value chain.

Managerial Processes

OVERVIEW

Managing is often described as the art of getting things done. In most cases, this means "working with and through people," since little of substance is accomplished solo.[1] How, after all, do managers succeed in launching new products, generating complex reports, or solving pressing production problems? Not by working alone, but by drawing on an intricate web of relationships. Coordinated action is the key to success, and, in most organizations, the more complex the challenge the greater the number of required interactions.

In fact, when confronted with a problem a manager's first thoughts are normally about how to gain the support of critical people.[2] Buy-in and commitment are usually regarded as essential to moving forward. Why? Because, as Andy Grove, the CEO of Intel, has observed, a manager's output is no more—and no less—than the output of the people in his or her organization.[3] Mobilization and coordination are critical to success. It is for this reason that the interpersonal arts—communication, persuasion, negotiation, and selling—are so central to effective management, and why scholars have so often concluded that management is best viewed as a social process. "It is a *process* because it comprises a series of actions that lead to the accomplishment of objectives. It is a *social* process because these actions are principally concerned with relations between people."[4]

The challenges are especially daunting for general managers, who work high in the organization and are evaluated on the overall performance of their units.

---

[1]Leonard R. Sayles, *Managerial Behavior* (New York: McGraw-Hill, 1964), p. 35.

[2]Daniel J. Isenberg, "How Senior Managers Think," *Harvard Business Review* 62 (November–December 1984), pp. 82–83.

[3]Andrew S. Grove, *High Output Management* (New York: Random House, 1983), pp. 39–40.

[4]William H. Newman, Charles E. Summer, and E. Kirby Warren, *The Process of Management,* 3rd ed. (Englewood Cliffs, NJ: Prentice-Hall, 1972), p. 12. Italic in original.

They are generalists, not specialists, judged on profit and loss rather than the excellence of their individual functions or the success of isolated initiatives. Compared with other managers, they engage in activities of greater scale and scope, face far higher levels of ambiguity and uncertainty, and oversee individuals with broader and more diverse expertise and talents.[5] Their goal is integration and alignment, and they must be skilled at capturing and focusing the attention of large numbers of people, melding diverse perspectives, and harmonizing competing interests and claims.

How do effective general managers meet these challenges? Not, as conventional wisdom suggests, by thoughtful, reflective, systematic planning. Even the best general managers are surprisingly reactive; their days, rather than being orchestrated and tightly scripted, are normally fragmented and choppy. They engage in many brief, unscheduled meetings and encounters, not formally listed on the calendar. They draw heavily on conversations and personal interactions, preferring them to written reports and carefully argued memoranda. And they have a strong bias toward action, even in the face of limited and incomplete information.[6]

The result is a large "discrepancy between commonly held beliefs and expectations about what managers *should* be doing, what academics *think* they are doing, and what they *really* do."[7] All too often, the usual prescription—proactive planning and systematic, thoughtful analysis—does not square with the realities of organizational life. Unexpected events, unanticipated conflicts, and unscheduled crises arise and must be solved or responded to in real time, even as larger strategic needs are kept front and center. The best general managers therefore have a kind of bifocal vision: They are able "to remain focused on long-term objectives while staying flexible enough to solve day-to-day problems and recognize new opportunities."[8] As the cases in this module show, they do so by relying on a set of processes and skills that enable them to move their organizations steadily forward while simultaneously juggling diverse objectives and complex tradeoffs.

OUTLINE

The first case in the module, "Serengeti Eyewear: Entrepreneurship within Corning Inc.," features a small, extremely profitable division within a large, multibillion-dollar corporation. The division sells high-end sunglasses and has prospered with

---

[5]John P. Kotter, *The General Managers* (New York: Free Press, 1982), chap. 2.

[6]Henry Mintzberg, "The Manager's Job: Folklore and Fact," *Harvard Business Review* 54 (July–August 1975), pp. 49–61.

[7]Fred Luthans, Richard M. Hodgetts, and Stuart A. Rosenkrantz, *Real Managers* (Cambridge, MA: Ballinger, 1988), p. 27. Italic in original.

[8]Daniel J. Isenberg, "The Tactics of Strategic Opportunism," *Harvard Business Review* 66 (March–April 1985), p. 92.

a distinctive approach: It operates as a virtual, networked organization. Serengeti retains only a few core skills in-house, outsources such critical functions as design and manufacturing, and, despite having grown to $62 million in sales, has a staff of only 51 people. Now the senior team is facing a critical decision: whether to launch a new line of sunglasses, called Eclipse, that would place it in head-to-head competition with Ray Ban, the industry giant, at nearly 10 times its size. The choice is made doubly difficult by the increases in scale and scope that are certain to come with Eclipse. As a medium-priced, high-volume product, it will require fundamental changes in Serengeti's systems and processes, including greater operating discipline and formalized planning and delivery systems.

To date, Serengeti has succeeded with an informal approach that can be traced directly to Zaki Mustafa, the general manager, who has led the division for nearly a decade. Mustafa's approach to management combines several elements. He is extremely unstructured, focused on values and norms rather than formal systems or codified procedures. He is highly territorial, determined to run the division in his own way rather than according to corporate policies or rules. He is heavily qualitative and conceptual, convinced that his staff should "get the logic right" before massaging reams of numbers. And, perhaps most important, he is highly oriented toward people and their development, almost to the exclusion of other, generally accepted management tasks and responsibilities.

Mustafa's management processes illustrate the value (and risks) of spending the bulk of one's time on people and relationships. His calendar is filled with interactions, both inside and outside the organization. Mustafa meets routinely with a wide variety of customers. He travels globally to visit suppliers around the world. He stays in close touch with many of Corning's scientists and technologists. And he spends enormous amounts of time communicating with Serengeti's employees.

Here too his approach is distinctive. Mustafa discourages memos and regularly scheduled meetings. Instead, he manages by wandering around, dropping in on people in a seemingly random fashion. In these discussions he inquires about their needs and personal concerns, helps them with pending business decisions, and serves as a sounding board and adviser. He is, by his own admission, a "surrogate father," striving to remove barriers to achievement, improve self-esteem, and motivate the people in his organization. Such a developmental approach to management can be enormously powerful, but demands special skills and abilities. Success is by no means assured. In addition, this approach raises difficult ethical questions. Where, for example, should managers draw the line between employees' personal and professional lives? At what point does management end and intrusion begin?

The second case in the module, "The Soul of a New Machine," continues with many of these same themes. It consists of an excerpt from Tracy Kidder's Pulitzer Prize–winning book, describing the design and development of a new minicomputer by a small team of engineers at Data General. Like the Serengeti case, it allows for a discussion of managerial processes and their links to employee motivation and development, but from a very different perspective. Tom West, the leader of the minicomputer project, is in many ways the antithesis of Mustafa—distant and aloof rather than warm and engaged, sparing rather than effusive in praise, and often Machiavellian in his politicking and behind-the-scenes maneuvering. West has isolated the project team from the rest of the organization, kept its members uninformed and resource poor, and slowly but steadily ratcheted up the pressure to perform. His managerial processes are neither developmental nor supportive. Yet surprisingly, the young engineers on the project remain extraordinarily motivated and driven to succeed. Despite all odds, they eventually produce a new computer in record time. It quickly becomes a runaway hit and is embraced enthusiastically by the marketplace.

The case raises the question of what (if anything) West did to foster these results. How did he create such high levels of employee enthusiasm and commitment? How did he keep the project on track? How did he overcome the obstacles impeding progress? How did he deal with other key players, such as corporate management, staff and support groups, and peers at competing divisions? Here too there are a number of deeper, philosophical questions. West's actions have clearly been effective, but have they also been ethical? Has West, for example, exploited the engineers in ways that take unfair advantage of their youth and inexperience? Has he been duplicitous in his dealings with other managers at Data General? Or has he simply employed clever, innovative techniques that, despite the ensuing political friction and lack of organizational support, were useful for getting the job done?

Serengeti and "The Soul of a New Machine" offer another powerful contrast: between the jobs of general managers and the jobs of project managers. Both types of managers oversee multiple functions and diverse departments. Both take a holistic view of the challenge at hand and are responsible for integration and coordination. General managers like Mustafa, however, are charged with ongoing, continuing tasks that involve repeated interactions over an extended period, usually with the same set of players. Project managers like West, by contrast, are given time-limited assignments with changing groups of people. Team members devote themselves to projects for periods ranging from several days to several years; once the projects are completed, they disband and move on to other assignments. One issue raised by these cases is whether the processes used by West would also be effective in general management settings. Are they sustainable and repeatable? Could they, for example, be used in organizations like Serengeti that cultivate long-term, continuing relationships? Or are they only appropriate for one-time use?

The third class in the module, "Transition to General Management Website," expands on these themes by exploring the distinctive features of the general manager's job. Most managers follow a predictable progression as they climb the corporate ladder, moving from functional leadership (a position such as vice president of marketing, finance, or operations), to divisional leadership, with responsibility for an entire organization or unit, multiple functions, and a full P&L. The associated shift in tasks, skills, philosophy, and perspective is only dimly understood.[9] Newly minted general managers must usually develop a new set of abilities. They must learn to make decisions outside their areas of expertise (usually while relying on people who bring far more experience and knowledge to the table); to manage subordinates who were only recently peers; to meld specialized, often competing objectives into larger, integrated wholes; to make difficult, delicate tradeoffs in the absence of complete information; and to motivate, monitor, and direct large numbers of people simultaneously.

These needs are examined in "Transition to General Management Website," which contains a wide range of quotations and video clips, organized into categories for easy viewing, that were collected from a series of Web-based discussions between MBA students and recently appointed general managers. The site is divided into two broad sections: "The General Manager's Job," and "Managing the Transition." The former discusses the dilemmas associated with such key tasks as decision making, accessing/utilizing resources, balancing, communicating, interacting, integrating, monitoring, and transitioning. How, for example, do skilled practitioners handle the choice between delegating and deciding? When do they rely on analysis, and when on intuition? How do they deal with mistakes? These questions, as well as many others, are answered directly by newly minted general managers, who share their experiences and offer a number of practical guidelines.

The second part of the site focuses more explicitly on the tasks and challenges of the transition process. A functional manager has just been promoted to division president or CEO; what are some guidelines for how she or he should spend the first day, week, or month on the job? What early signals should she or he send? What are some predictable pitfalls and problems? How are they best avoided? What resources and supports are available to ease the transition? This portion of the site contains a wealth of practical information and career advice, presented in a simple, question-and-answer format. Because so many students head to entrepreneurial start-ups immediately after graduation, the site also contains a separate section discussing their distinctive challenges.

The next class in the module, "No Excuses Management," describes the management processes used by T.J. Rodgers, the CEO of Cypress Semiconductor, a chip manufacturer in Silicon Valley. Rodgers employs a heavily formalized approach to management that puts a premium on predictability, order, and control. He has installed a large number of IT systems—they are used for setting goals, allocating resources, hiring people, reviewing progress, and evaluating individual performance. Little is left to chance. Even at the most senior levels, managers have only limited discretion and are required to follow these systems. The entire organization, in fact, operates according to seven guiding principles—no secrets, no surprises, no politics, no distractions, no confusion,

---

[9]David B. Jemison, "The Role of the Division General Manager in Corporate Strategic Management," in Robert Lamb and Paul Shrivastava, eds., *Advances in Strategic Management,* vol. 3 (Greenwich, CT: JAI Press, 1985), pp. 164–166.

no waste, and no illusions—designed to encourage transparency and disciplined execution.[10]

This approach raises three fundamental questions. First, at what point does control become micromanaging? Rodgers personally oversees each of the company's systems and reviews their outputs daily. Has he taken critical decisions out of the hands of senior managers, or do they still retain the needed authority? Second, how do senior managers add value in Cypress's formalized, systems-driven environment? Managing, after all, is normally thought to involve large amounts of subjectivity and judgment. But when IT systems routinely provide critical insights and point out areas where intervention or remedial work is required, what remains for general managers to do? Where (if anywhere) is judgment required?

Finally, the case raises difficult questions about the application of a process perspective to managerial work. The notions of repeatability, discipline, and efficiency that lie at the heart of process thinking are widely accepted by managers today, who routinely apply them to product development, order fulfillment, and other operational processes. But when the same approach is applied to managerial work—which is exactly what Rodgers has done—it is often firmly resisted. Why? Do managerial processes have special qualities that make them unsuitable for codification and standardization? Is there something fundamentally different about these kinds of processes? Or are managers simply reacting defensively?

"Harvard Business School Publishing," the final case in the module, pulls together many of the preceding themes. It provides a rich, textured portrait of a new general manager as she takes charge, provides direction, and ultimately resurrects a faltering, unsettled organization. In 1994, Harvard Business School Publishing was only two years old. A collection of diverse, previously independent product lines, it was now operating as a separate, professionally managed subsidiary of Harvard Business School (HBS). The organization had gotten off to a rocky start under its first CEO, and Linda Doyle, an HBS insider, was soon brought in as her replacement.

On her arrival, Doyle faced serious problems: a confused mandate, an unclear strategy, a troubled relationship with the parent organization, a fragmented senior team, and employees who were unsure of their roles. The case describes her initial moves at some length—especially her first week and first six months on the job—to illustrate her skilled use of symbolism, her effectiveness at communication, and her sense of the levers and resources available to address these problems. The case then describes several of Doyle's most important strategic and organizational initiatives in the following two years. One of these efforts, the shift to centralized marketing, has led to sharp disagreements within the senior team. In particular, the vice president of sales, marketing, and operations, representing centralized marketing, and the head of *Harvard Business Review,* the leading

---

[10]T. J. Rodgers, with William Taylor and Rick Foreman, *No Excuses Management* (New York: Doubleday, 1993).

product group, are battling over a proposed new product. Doyle must decide how best to resolve the underlying issues of power, turf, and responsibility while still moving forward with her larger agenda.

Doyle's approach to management provides a nice contrast with T. J. Rodgers's. Her primary concerns are coordination and learning, while his are discipline and control. In fact, Doyle's goal is in many ways similar to Mustafa's: to unleash the power of the organization by taking a developmental approach. She is particularly concerned with developing the members of her senior team and overcoming their inability to work together productively. To that end, Doyle has developed and deployed a distinctive managerial style. She works as a teacher, shaping the environment, framing questions, and capitalizing on issues as they emerge in order to build understanding, gain buy-in, and move her agenda forward. Her goal is to create dialogue, and she does so by intervening in unproductive exchanges, coaching people privately, and creating a safe space for the discussion of hard issues. At the heart of this approach, which has considerable scholarly support, are efforts to influence behavior not only through direct interventions but also by shaping the environment in which decisions are made.[11]

THEMES

Core Processes

General managers seek to shape and direct the behavior of people in their organizations so that together they meet performance goals. The tactics they use are many and varied, and often appear to be an assortment of tasks with little underlying logic. Close study of effective managers, however, suggests that a small set of processes recurs repeatedly and is crucial to success. These processes provide coherence and organization; they unify what would otherwise be unrelated activities. Among the most important of these managerial processes are direction setting, negotiating and selling, and monitoring and control.[12]

Direction Setting.   Direction setting is the most widely recognized managerial activity. Experts agree that clear goals and targets are essential for organizational progress and that those in charge are responsible for their development. In most cases, the process begins with intensive data collection.[13] Newly appointed CEOs

---

[11]Doyle's approach fits well with the model of leadership proposed by Ronald Heifetz, who argues that the primary task of leaders is not making decisions but creating an environment and set of conditions in which people are better able to make decisions themselves. See Ronald Heifetz, *Leadership Without Easy Answers* (Cambridge: Harvard University Press, 1994).

[12]David A. Garvin, "The Processes of Organization and Management," *Sloan Management Review* 39 (Summer 1998), pp. 43–46.

[13]Gabarro, *The Dynamics of Taking Charge,* pp. 20–29, and Kotter, *The General Managers,* pp. 60–67.

or division presidents immerse themselves in their industries and organizations, seeking to understand their distinctive strengths, weaknesses, and challenges. Often, they meet individually with key employees, as Linda Doyle did with every member of her staff in her first week at Harvard Business School Publishing. Many also reach out to customers and suppliers, as did Zaki Mustafa as well as several of the managers represented on the Transition to General Management Website.

Once they have collected the necessary information, managers move to the next step of the process. They begin to craft and communicate a vision or sense of direction. This is a surprisingly difficult and mysterious task, requiring two distinct steps. First, managers must come up with a new concept, strategy, or business model. Here, the challenge is largely creative; at times, it requires "a spark of genius."[14] A good vision, after all, is distinctive; it often combines policies, products, and technologies in ways that were previously unimagined. The evolving vision at Harvard Business School Publishing is a good example, since it suggests a variety of innovative alliances and new product classes. But a good vision also makes sense to others, is easy to communicate, and is achievable with available resources and skills.[15] For these reasons, managers must eventually take a second step, translating their visions into tangible terms, including goals, strategies, and resource commitments that are actionable and implementable. Examples of this second step include Mustafa's description of the turnaround strategy at Serengeti and West's design goals for the new minicomputer at Data General.

Negotiating and Selling.   Once managers have set direction, negotiating and selling processes come into play. They are usually necessary to ensure buy-in and commitment. Visions, especially when they involve substantial change, seldom take root without concerted, disciplined efforts to alter perceptions and deepen understanding.[16]

There are several associated activities. To begin, leaders must often develop a shared language that communicates their new perspective. Evocative language and imagery are powerful forces; they shape underlying beliefs, give meaning to events, and encourage common, collective interpretations.[17] Linda Doyle clearly understood this well. Early in her tenure at Harvard Business School Publishing, she developed the Whirligig, a visual image of the organization she desired that conveyed dynamism, integration, and equality among product groups, and then used it to stimulate conversation among members of her senior team. Other

---

[14]Warren Bennis and Burt Nanus, *Leaders* (New York: Harper & Row, 1985), p. 103.

[15]Charles Handy, "The Language of Leadership," in Michael Syrett and Clare Hogg, eds., *Frontiers of Leadership: An Essential Reader* (Oxford: Blackwell, 1992), pp. 10–11.

[16]Donald C. Hambrick and Albert A. Cannella, "Strategy Implementation as Substance and Selling," *Academy of Management Executive* 3 (1989), pp. 278–285.

[17]Jeffrey Pfeffer, "Management as Symbolic Action: The Creation and Maintenance of Organizational Paradigms," in L.L. Cummings and B.M. Staw, eds., *Research in Organizational Behavior,* vol. 3 (Greenwich, CT: JAI Press, 1981), pp. 24–26.

managers use "rallying cries" and emotional appeals to unify the troops and gain commitment.[18] At Data General, for example, Tom West repeatedly urged his engineers forward by comparing their sparse funding and poor reputations with those of the competing North Carolina design team. Surpassing North Carolina soon became an important source of motivation.

At times, personal persuasion is necessary as well. Leaders must gain an understanding of employees' values, interests, anxieties, and desires and then frame or reframe problems in ways that are amenable to common, mutually acceptable solutions.[19] Here too one-on-one meetings are invaluable because they allow for in-depth probing and vigorous give-and-take.[20] T.J. Rodgers relied on this approach to convince departing employees to remain at Cypress Semiconductor, while Mustafa used it to encourage packers to attend Serengeti's companywide meetings.

Symbolism and storytelling are equally powerful tools. They tap into emotion as well as reason, and are often the decisive factors in determining whether or not an idea is accepted. According to scholars: "[T]he way an issue is presented (e.g., its drama and its succinctness) is vital for determining whether selling attempts will be successful."[21] It is for this reason that skilled managers so often tell personal stories, craft compelling metaphors, and create a visceral identification with their cause. Most recognize that they are competing for their organizations' attention and must mobilize people who are already inundated with countless other demands. Mustafa, West, Rodgers, and Doyle all provide examples of talented managers framing and presenting issues in ways that command attention and widespread support.

Monitoring and Control.   Once managers have obtained buy-in, they initiate action. Then, a third set of processes, focused on monitoring and control, becomes important. Managers use these processes to ensure that the organization is performing as planned. They are necessary because business environments are inherently unstable, with any number of unexpected shocks and disturbances. Competitors respond unpredictably, suppliers fail to deliver, machinery and equipment malfunction, and suddenly, even the best-laid plans are virtually useless. Oversight is needed to ensure that problems are quickly identified and corrective action is taken.

Effective managers therefore have a sixth sense; they know "how to spot trouble, how to know when things aren't going well" even before results are in.[22] To

---

[18]For more on rallying cries, see Gabarro, *The Dynamics of Taking Charge,* pp. 88–90.

[19]Leonard R. Sayles, *Leadership: Managing in Real Organizations,* 2nd ed. (New York: McGraw-Hill, 1989), p. 59.

[20]Jay A. Conger, "The Necessary Art of Persuasion," *Harvard Business Review* 79 (May–June 1998), pp. 88–89.

[21]Jane E. Dutton and Susan J. Ashford, "Selling Issues to Top Management," *Academy of Management Review* 18 (1993), p. 415.

[22]Sayles, *Managerial Behavior,* p. 43 and chap. 10.

that end, they rely on a variety of monitoring techniques. Both formal and informal processes may be used. T. J. Rodgers drew heavily on quantitative reports to flag discrepancies and identify unexpected variances, while Mustafa relied largely on personal intuition and a sense that things were not right with particular employees. Control systems play a complementary role: They shape behavior by establishing ground rules and guidelines. They also provide general managers with both the tools and rationale for interacting with and disciplining employees. At Cypress Semiconductor, Rodgers used IT and project management systems for this purpose; at Harvard Business School Publishing, Doyle used the employee evaluation system (PMP); and at Data General, West used informal norms and peer pressure.

Multiple Roles, Multiple Skills

Most scholars agree that general managers wear many hats. Often, they are described in terms of roles. The general manager is said to be playing interpersonal (figurehead, leader, liaison), informational (monitor, disseminator, spokesman), or decisional (entrepreneur, disturbance handler, resource allocator, negotiator) roles; to be serving as a vision setter, motivator, analyzer, or task master; or to be primarily a strategist, organization builder, or doer.[23] Clearly, these categories overlap, and many of the differences are semantic. Far more important, however, is the fact that effective general managers are willing and able to alternate among these roles. They are not wedded to a single, unvarying approach, but instead shift smoothly and flexibly among different ways of thinking and acting. In technical terms, they possess both cognitive and behavioral complexity.[24] Linda Doyle provides the best example in this module, although there are many similar observations on the Transition to General Management website.

As the website shows, the associated skills are equally diverse. Many, such as communication and decision making, have already been discussed. But several deserve further attention because they are so often overlooked. For example, many skilled general managers possess finely tuned intervention skills. They know when, where, and how to get involved in the work of others.[25] Even when delegation is the preferred strategy, senior managers must at times weigh in and

---

[23]See, respectively, Mintzberg, "The Manager's Job: Folklore and Fact," pp. 54–59; Stuart L. Hart and Robert L. Quinn, "Roles Executives Play: CEOs, Behavioral Complexity, and Firm Performance," *Human Relations* 46 (1993), pp. 543–574; and Joseph L. Bower et al., *Business Policy,* 8th ed. (Chicago: Richard D. Irwin, 1995), pp. 4–6.

[24]On cognitive complexity, see Craig Eric Schneier, "Measuring Cognitive Complexity: Developing Reliability, Validity, and Norm Tables for a Personality Instrument," *Educational and Psychological Measurement* 39 (1979), pp. 599–612. On behavioral complexity, see Hart and Quinn, "Roles Executives Play."

[25]For a broad discussion of intervention strategies, see Edgar H. Schein, *Process Consultation,* vol. II (Reading, MA: Addison-Wesley, 1987), chap. 10.

redirect the work of others. Here, they face several alternatives. Some, like West and Rodgers, intervene primarily on tasks and projects—their goal is to get the work out by removing obstacles and impediments. Others, like Mustafa, intervene primarily on personal matters—their goal is to build employees' skills and self-esteem. Still others, like Doyle, intervene primarily on social and group matters—their goal is to build better working relationships and a heightened sense of teamwork. None of these strategies is inherently superior, and each can be effective when deployed properly.

A second, often overlooked managerial skill is the ability to manage oneself. Everyone has foibles and weaknesses, and general managers are no exception. They too are likely to benefit from efforts to identify their personal limitations and blind spots and find ways of compensating for them. This is particularly true when difficult emotional issues are at stake, as they were at Data General and Harvard Business School Publishing, and employees need their leaders to provide a clear path and a steadying hand. In such situations, a particularly helpful hint comes from the Transition to General Management website. Several of the newly minted general managers benefited enormously from efforts to "get on the balcony" and gain a larger, dispassionate view of the situation, the key players, and emerging needs.[26] Such an objective, big picture view offers a much-needed counterpoint to the press of daily events and the all-too-common tendency for the urgent to drive out the important.

Shaping the Environment

Studies of work groups have found that leaders obtain superior performance not only through direct interventions, but also by shaping the environment in which the work gets done. According to a leading social scientist:

> [T]hose who create and lead work groups might most appropriately focus their efforts on the *creation of conditions* that support effective team performance. Rather than attempting to manage group behavior in real time, leaders might better spend their energies creating contexts that increase the likelihood . . . that teams will prosper.[27]

What is true of work groups appears to be equally true of organizations: Supportive, stimulating settings are often essential to success. Skilled general managers therefore devote considerable attention to shaping the environments in which people work. Some, like West and Mustafa, cultivate a sense of camaraderie and belonging by hiring complementary, like-minded people. Others, like Mustafa and Doyle, create a sense of shared destiny by fostering communal activities and open discussion. Still others, like Doyle and Rodgers,

---

[26]Also see Heifetz, *Leadership Without Easy Answers,* pp. 252–258.

[27]J. Richard Hackman, ed., *Groups That Work (and Those That Don't)* (San Francisco: Jossey-Bass, 1990), p. 9. Italic in original.

foster norms of improvement by installing detailed measurement systems and then routinizing feedback and performance reviews. In most cases, the more successful general managers are at establishing these conditions, the less they need to intervene in real time.

For similar reasons, skilled general managers try to free up employees by eliminating barriers that impede organizational accomplishment. These barriers take a variety of forms: restrictive policies and procedures, power struggles and political infighting, and second-guessing from above. All of the managers in this module paid special attention to removing, or at least minimizing, these constraints. Mustafa and West attended corporate meetings on behalf of their subordinates, fought off excessive oversight, eliminated unnecessary reviews, and battled personally to obtain required resources and staff support. Doyle met repeatedly with members of the HBS faculty and administration to ensure a warm reception for her managers' new initiatives; she also sent clear signals about the unacceptability of turf battles and internecine competition. Rodgers used the daily output of IT systems to identify managers who were overburdened and needed additional help.

The tone of these efforts matters as well. Superior performance requires a rare combination of conditions, a blending of opposites that must be carefully tended:

> The atmosphere must be one of challenge, skepticism, and doubt, so that easy, pat solutions are not accepted until they have been subjected to careful scrutiny. Participants must feel a sense of security, so that they can stretch themselves in new directions without fear of failure, and incentives must support experimentation and risk taking. A sense of fairness must prevail, with no group feeling that its ideas are getting short shrift. And the rules of engagement must encourage the sharing of knowledge.[28]

Mustafa and Doyle were successful on each of these fronts. They pushed employees to think hard about issues, provided safety nets and protection in the event of error or failure, and encouraged openness and collective responsibility. West and Rodgers, by contrast, met some of these conditions but not others. They were far more successful in provoking and challenging, far less effective in creating a sense of security and support. These contrasts provide a powerful lens for reflecting on one's own work experiences and the impact of the work environment on motivation and personal commitment.

---

[28]David A. Garvin, *Learning in Action* (Boston: Harvard Business School Press, 2000), p. 198.

Case 5–1

SERENGETI EYEWEAR: ENTREPRENEURSHIP WITHIN CORNING INC.

Finally alone in his office, Zaki Mustafa, vice president and general manager of Serengeti Eyewear, relaxed and collected his thoughts. He had spent all of May 12, 1993, gathering opinions from members of Serengeti's management team. On the face of it, the choice before them was simple enough: whether to launch a new line of sunglasses called Eclipse. But it seemed that everyone in the firm had a slightly different opinion of what should be done.

Mustafa and his team were determined to maintain the momentum that had made Serengeti one of the fastest-growing and most profitable businesses within Corning. The Eclipse decision, however, involved considerable risk. Because the new product line was aimed directly at the medium-priced market, it would put Serengeti on a collision course with Ray-Ban, the industry giant.

Company and Industry Background

Serengeti Eyewear specialized in premium, technology-oriented sunglasses aimed at the high end of the sunglasses market. It was a division of Corning Incorporated, a 120-year-old worldwide organization with 1992 sales of $3.7 billion, 40 plants, 44 offices, and 33 clinical-testing or life-science laboratories. Corning's core business was specialty glass and materials, but it also produced consumer housewares, laboratory services, and opto-electronics. Company brochures described technology as "the glue that binds the firm together."

Corning possessed a substantial research capability, with centers in the United States, Japan, and France employing some 1,500 scientists, engineers, and support staff. Over time, they had developed such breakthroughs as fiber-optic cables and laminated glass, as well as products sold under the firm's consumer brands of Corelle, Corning Ware, Pyrex, Revere Ware, Steuben, Visions, and Vycor. Like Corning's other divisions, Serengeti drew heavily on the research laboratories for new product ideas.

Serengeti sunglasses, for example, featured "spectral control," a technology that reduced the distracting effect of blue light on vision. Many also featured another Corning innovation—photochromic lenses that darkened in bright sunlight and lightened in lower light. Products were aimed at diverse audiences and uses. Serengeti's main product, Drivers, which accounted for 60 percent of the division's sales, was directed at automobile drivers. Other products targeted skiers, shooters, and sailors.

Analysts normally divided the $1.8 billion U.S. market for nonprescription sunglasses into four segments: low end, moderate, midrange, and high end. Low-end sunglasses were priced at less than $25 and accounted for 6 percent of industry dollar sales. They normally contained plastic or polycarbonate lenses and simple plastic frames, and appealed to buyers who valued appearance over performance. Moderate-priced products sold for $25–$49.99 and accounted for 18 percent of industry sales. In this category, lenses were still primarily plastic, but came with additional features, such as polarization and diverse frame styles. The midrange segment was the largest, accounting for 48 percent of industry sales. Midrange sunglasses

This case was prepared by Jonathan West under the direction of David A. Garvin.

were priced at $50–$74.99, allowed a choice between polycarbonate and ground-and-polished lenses, and were normally sold by department stores or specialists, such as sunglasses shops, optical stores, or sporting goods outlets. High-end sunglasses sold for $75 or more and accounted for 28 percent of industry sales. They came primarily with ground-and-polished lenses and often had optical quality frames, and were sold mainly by sunglasses shops and optical specialists, with smaller numbers offered by department stores and sporting goods outlets.

Within this market Serengeti faced several major competitors. (See Exhibit 1 for market shares in the $25 and up segments.) Ray-Ban, a division of optical-glasses maker Bausch and Lomb, was by far the most important. It was the goliath of the sunglasses industry with worldwide sales of over $500 million in 1992, and the only competitor to have built a strong and enduring brand image. Ray-Ban had long been identified with pilots and was featured in the popular movie *Top Gun*. It was slightly preferred by male buyers and competed strongly in all but the low end of the market. Oakley was a distant second to Ray-Ban, having recently emerged as the second-strongest brand in both the midrange and high-end segments. It had

developed a strong sports and athletic image and was preferred by men. Vuarnet, manufactured in France, enjoyed a European image. It sold better to women and had its roots in the ski industry. Designer and other brands accounted for the balance of the market and competed primarily on fashion and style.

The Early Years

Serengeti evolved from Corning Sunglass Products, a division launched in 1982. For many years Corning had sold eyeglass blanks to eyeglasses manufacturers. Then, in 1964, after the company's scientists invented photochromic glass, it became a major supplier of sunglass blanks as well. Corning Sunglass Products was created to capture a larger share of the profits from the downstream consumer business. Its strategy was to price slightly above the market, winning a premium for superior quality, while offering both low- and high-end sunglasses positioned as fashion accessories.

At the time, Corning had little experience in such businesses. It was more at home in scale-intensive markets, where it sold to original equipment manufacturers. Early signs for the new division were good, but after a year it began to sour. Manufacturing,

---

EXHIBIT 1   1993 U.S. Sunglasses Market Shares (units)

	Total Sunglasses Bought At:			
	$25–$49.99 %	$50–$74.99 %	$75+ %	All Categories, $25 and above
Ray-Ban	39	48	28	38
Oakley	8	16	16	13
Vuarnet	5	9	10	7
Serengeti	**3**[a]	**5**[a]	**14**	**7**
Designer	14	8	12	11
Other/Don't know	31	14	20	24

[a]Serengeti's sales at these price points reflect heavy discounting by retailers, usually for special promotions.

Source: Market research

quality, and distribution problems undermined Corning's reputation with consumers and retailers, while poor product positioning eroded sales. Substantial losses were incurred, and in June 1984 Corning's senior management discontinued one of the major product lines. A month later, they began to consider closing the entire venture, and in August 1984 decided to exit.

The Turnaround Years

Zaki Mustafa assumed control of Serengeti after he and a small group at Corning Sunglass Products disagreed with senior management's decision to close the division. They believed that the early stumbling reflected poor positioning and Corning's inexperience in consumer markets, not inherent flaws in the product or business. In fact, Mustafa, who was at the time the Sunglass Products operations manager, believed that the primary problem was an unwillingness to listen to customers. He later summed up the situation:

> Somewhat typical of an arrogant organization, we thought we could dictate to the market what we'd make and sell. It turned out that the market was controlling us, not the other way around.

In September 1984, in a private meeting with group president William Hudson, Mustafa argued that closure would be a mistake and asked for a second chance to make the business a success. Because he wanted to fundamentally reposition the division's products and approach, he requested full control, including independence from the rest of Corning's management structure. When Hudson asked why Corning should indulge his scheme, Mustafa responded that he could offer nothing more than his commitment—and that he was willing to bet his career on it. Three weeks later, he and his group were told that they had been given the chance to revive the sunglasses business.

They immediately developed both short- and long-term plans. Short-term, they focused on cutting costs and stabilizing the business. All low-end product lines were eliminated and their production

contracts ended. Any remaining inventory was sold, and physical facilities were consolidated under one roof. Serengeti thus became the first unit of Corning to move into its own building, apart from other divisions but in a neighboring town. And because Mustafa wanted to build a new organization that would meet the needs of customers by offering quality products, he decided to focus for the long term on the division's high-end product line, called Serengeti, and to rename the business Serengeti Eyewear.

Operationally, Mustafa put development of a core team of people, unswervingly committed to the business, as his top priority. To get them, he assembled the entire sunglasses staff and made an offer: "Anyone who wants to leave today can do so, and the company will find you another job at Corning. But if you stay for a year and then we have to shut down, we cannot guarantee that the company will relocate you."

The initial impact was predictable. Mustafa recalled:

> The best and brightest left straight away, and the company's staff fell from 135 people to 35. But those who stayed showed commitment to the cause. Most of them were novices, especially in marketing, but today they run the business.

Mustafa's second fundamental decision was to return to Corning's traditional strength in technology. He and his team felt that Serengeti sunglasses should be repositioned as high-tech, high-end, functional products, rather than fashion accessories. Whereas the old products had hidden the Corning name so as not to detract from their fashion image (and not to offend other sunglasses manufacturers, who continued to purchase sunglass blanks from Corning), all future products would prominently display the name to take advantage of the company's technology reputation. Products were also repositioned as male oriented. In the past, Serengeti had sold mainly to women because of its fashion focus. At the same time, the product line was reduced from 230 to 53 items to allow for more targeted marketing. Using this approach, the Serengeti line was relaunched in January 1985.

Word-of-mouth advertising was used aggressively in the early lean years. Mustafa and his staff donated hundreds of pairs of free sunglasses to opinion leaders in various high-profile sports and occupations: ski patrolmen, members of the U.S. Sailing Association, pilots, even state troopers. Their objective was to have the company's products seen in places where performance was paramount. At one time, booths were even established on ski slopes to allow skiers to take Serengetis for a "test-run."

As the new team struggled to rebuild the business, Mustafa continued to wrestle with Corning to maintain independence. To insulate his managers from what he regarded as Corning's time-consuming corporate style, he personally attended required corporate meetings in their place. Earlier, in 1985, when group management had attempted to install an "oversight committee" to guide Serengeti, Mustafa had walked out of the first meeting in frustration, declaring that he was too busy to waste his time at such gatherings. Fortunately, his dramatic gesture persuaded corporate management to give Serengeti the leeway he sought. The alternative, he recalled later, was probably an abrupt end to his career at Corning.

Eventually success came, but only after several difficult years. During this period, every substantial new order was viewed as a milestone, and each day ended with the entire staff gathered together in the packing and shipping department. Sales manager Hugh Ogle remembered the time:

> We began in a very negative position with retailers following the product withdrawals of a few years before, so we had to bend over backward to provide customer service. In the new building we were all together and could go into customer service to see orders coming in. That was good news and it kept us going. In fact, all the senior people would come in and pack orders themselves to ensure that every order was sent the next day.

As Sharon Stone, Serengeti's marketing manager, put it: "That was when we learned to serve customers and lost our arrogant attitude." But there was excitement, too, as Mustafa recalled:

> It was harrowing at the time. But somehow we never felt that much pressure. I used to go home so exhausted that I'd fall asleep in front of the TV still in my work clothes. I'd wake up, find that my wife had thrown a blanket over me, change clothes, and head back to work . . . But everybody who was in the business was there by choice. It was a story about how people can pull together and fight a war.

The Growth Years

Over a period of several years Serengeti's management team succeeded in resuscitating sales and then in scoring strong growth. Between 1985 and 1987 sales increased fourfold; at the same time gross margin grew nearly sixfold. Between 1987 and 1992 both sales and gross margin more than tripled. (See Exhibit 2 for additional financial information on sales, contribution, and ROE.) During this period Serengeti won a number of prestigious awards for technical and design excellence and was included on several "best products" lists. Growth was steady, except for a brief downturn in 1990. In order to meet aggressive sales goals the previous year, Serengeti sold into customers' warehouses ahead of final demand. When the expected demand failed to materialize, distributors and retailers were left with large inventories, depressing the next year's sales.

Growth was sustained by three main initiatives. First, Serengeti sales staff worked to restore and broaden their relationships with U.S. distributors and retailers. Because of the abrupt reversals of the early 1980s, many buyers remained suspicious that Serengeti would again switch its policy or product line without notice. A satisfied and complete U.S. distribution network therefore demanded considerable time and investment. International expansion soon followed. Between 1987 and 1993 Serengeti moved to increase its reach, first into Canada and then into Europe and Asia. During this period, Mustafa established a goal of eventually drawing a third of company sales from each of the three

EXHIBIT 2   Financial Summary ($ in millions)

	1985	1986	1987	1988	1989	1990	1991	1992
Sales	$5.0	$11.0	$19.0	$32.5	$45.0	$38.7	$52.3	$62.0
Contribution	−3.0	−0.9	2.5	4.7	7.9	3.4	9.6	10.1
ROE%[a]	−104%	−56%	−7%	10%	23%	−6%	39%	37%

[a]To compute the equity of its divisions, Corning used the following calculations:

Operating assets = Inventory + net fixed assets @ book value (including precious metals) + accounts receivable − accounts payable (12% of sales) ± goodwill

Corning assets = Operating assets − minority assets

Total equity = Operating equity (60% of Corning assets) + investment in equity companies − minority interest in equity

Source: Company records

regions of North America, Europe, and Asia. Finally, Serengeti expanded its product line by relying on further advances in technology. Between 1987 and 1993 several new products were added. Each drew on innovations developed in Corning's laboratories. Strata, a new high-end product in the $300 price bracket, was the most distinctive. Along with photochromic glass, blue-shift correction, and full ultraviolet (UV) protection, it featured a new system for polarizing light and reducing glare. All competitive glass polarizing systems required plastic laminates; Strata, by contrast, used a proprietary surfacing process, for which Serengeti held exclusive rights, that integrated a layer of polarizing glass directly onto the lens.

The idea and technology for Strata came from Corning's research laboratory in France. It was originally invented for another purpose, but its properties made it a natural for sunglasses. After hearing of the innovation through their research contacts, Mustafa and Ogle, then in operations, traveled to Geneva to meet Serge Renault, the scientist responsible, and learn more about the technology. They decided on the spot to go ahead with the product. The only problem was the high price Serengeti would have to charge because of Strata's complex manufacturing process.

Because few companies had ever tried to sell $300 sunglasses, Serengeti began cautiously with a "test launch." To limit exposure, 100 retail outlets were selected for a trial run. In one week seven Serengeti employees set up all necessary product displays and trained all store personnel in the special features of the product. After collecting feedback from customers, the test was quickly judged a success, and Strata began to sell steadily.

The concept of a test launch took hold at Serengeti and was used again to enter the European market. There, Serengeti chose to launch its products by selling for the first year only in Finland, a country somewhat outside the European mainstream but regarded as representative enough to provide cultural and institutional learnings. After a successful test launch, distribution was broadened to other parts of Europe.

Organization and Functions

Mustafa described the firm's organizational structure as "buckets to put people's tasks in, not watertight buckets, but buckets nonetheless." (See Exhibit 3 for an organization chart.) He added:

The organization chart is for people who need to see the world through those filters. We don't actually operate that way. People here often share and swap assignments, for example, when someone is out of town . . . In fact, if there's been any influence from me, it's to keep things informal and fluid. There's a formal and an informal organization, and if there's one thing I've tried to cultivate, it's to let the informal organization dominate.

EXHIBIT 3   Organization Chart

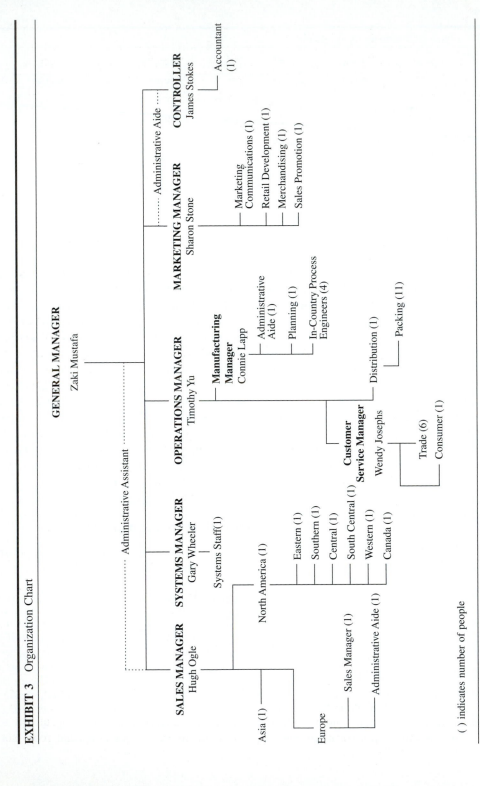

( ) indicates number of people

Source: Company records

Marketing

Serengeti's marketing revolved around technology. According to Stone, the strategy was straightforward: "We want to be on the leading edge of technology, and in the mainstream of fashion." To that end, marketing was responsible for the coordination of design projects, pricing, development and planning of new point-of-sale displays, advertising campaigns, and public relations. In each area, marketing focused on the special features of the company's technology: photochromic lenses, spectral control, ultraviolet protection, and polarization. Many advertisements, for example, included detailed descriptions of Serengeti's features, which other sunglass manufacturers normally avoided. (See Exhibit 4 for a sample advertisement.)

Marketing was also responsible for new product development, including incremental changes to the existing line (new frames, styles, colors, and lens shapes) and major additions such as Strata. But the actual design work was outsourced to Smart Design, a small design specialist in New York City that worked closely with Serengeti's marketing staff to draw up new fashion ideas. In fact, in its early years Serengeti had also leaned heavily on outside consultants for marketing and positioning advice. But unlike design, most of these functions had been gradually brought in-house. Stone believed that a rapidly shifting consumer market required managers who knew their customers intimately and built that understanding into every decision they made. Marketing staff therefore stayed in touch with trends by spending at least some time every few months selling sunglasses from behind the counters of different retail outlets.

In recent years Stone had been able to shift her own attention away from crisis management and toward the long term. She observed:

> In the beginning I didn't even know how to write a marketing plan. I was always absorbed by day-to-day tasks. Now I spend about 25 percent of my time with domestic customers, 25 percent with international customers, 25 percent training and developing my staff, and the rest on matters that simply come to the office. I'm in the field about half the time.

Sales

Because of Serengeti's distinctive positioning, sales staff approached their task somewhat differently than their counterparts at other companies. A technology message, they believed, required knowledgeable and informed retailers. Consequently, Serengeti sold primarily through optical shops and sunglass retail chains. Typically, Serengeti accounted for 25 percent to 30 percent of their total sunglass sales. Most sales were direct. However, distributors were used for selling to optical shops and retail chains with less than 15 stores; they accounted for less than 10 percent of sales. Fifteen national accounts were responsible for 80 percent of Serengeti's volume, and the total number of accounts was approximately 750. The leading accounts, like Sunglass Hut, Lenscrafters, and Pearle Vision, had hundreds of stores. Close relationships with these stores was considered a must, and Serengeti placed great emphasis on training retail assistants. According to Ogle, "We take every opportunity to stand up in front of our customers' people."

Serengeti's customer training program, for example, was longer and more detailed than those offered by competitors. Complete training of a client's staff might take up to 10 sessions, spread over two days. Sessions included slides, overheads, videos, technical manuals, and hands-on demonstrations of the technical performance of Serengeti products. The object was not only to acquaint customers with the company's products and encourage them to carry the line, but also to make the retailer's own staff as confident and skilled as possible in presenting the underlying technology story.

For similar reasons, sales staff invited different retailers to visit Serengeti headquarters every four to six weeks. Visitors came from diverse accounts and usually included the account's top executive, as well as members of his or her next layer of management. The aim was to help them learn as much as possible about the company's products, organization, and people, while at the same time allowing Serengeti management and employees to better understand their clients. New customers normally spent between one-half and a full day touring the facilities, visiting a special room set up

EXHIBIT 4   Serengeti Advertising

SERENGETI® DRIVERS.
The only driving glasses that shift gears automatically...

through fog...

through haze...

through glare.

Funny thing about other sunglasses that purport to be for driving: they're not. They can't help you drive any better than ordinary sunglasses.

Only SERENGETI DRIVERS from Corning Optics shift gears automatically, darkening in bright sun to slash glare and sharpen contrast. And lighten in overcast weather for exceptional vision.

Only SERENGETI DRIVERS have patented photochromic copper lenses, for a level of spectral performance not possible with copper-coated or dyed imitations. SERENGETI DRIVERS selectively filter out irritating blue light, for a brighter, virtually glare-free field of vision. They cut infrared and over 99% of all UV rays in sunlight.

Only SERENGETI DRIVERS with second-generation photochromic technology adjust so precisely to changing light and weather, you see razor-honed contrast and sharp detail, even in haze, fog or rain. Even on snow and ice.

If those other "driving" glasses don't promise any of this, it's no wonder: they can't.

SERENGETI DRIVERS. The only driving sunglasses worthy of the name.

SERENGETI® DRIVERS
By CORNING OPTICS

At better stores in the U.S. and Canada, or call 1-800-525-4001. In New York, call 1-800-648-4810.
Serengeti is a registered trademark of Corning Glass Works, Corning, N.Y. 14831

permanently with point-of-sale displays, and meeting with the entire Serengeti staff.

During these visits, both sides made substantial presentations about their objectives and ideas. One of the goals of the meetings, according to Ogle, was to "expose customers to our values." Discussions covered a broad range of topics and questions: What is your business? What does your company do? How do you do it? What does Serengeti do well? In what areas is Serengeti a benchmark for the industry? What does Serengeti need to improve upon? Ogle observed:

> We tell them not to be shy, that we really want to get better at meeting their needs. And they're not. The presentations can take as long as one and a half hours. And everybody in Serengeti who's here at the time attends, including the packers.

Partnership Programs, which helped customers set and then meet higher sales goals for the Serengeti products they sold, were another priority of the sales group. They began in 1989 when Serengeti was striving to double its own sales. To create a partnership, Ogle and Stone sat down with clients to establish joint sales goals, usually involving a substantial increase over previous years' performance. The two then worked with clients to determine how the targets would be met and how Serengeti could help through activities such as joint promotions.

Mustafa encouraged the sales staff to focus on long-term customer satisfaction rather than quick sales. In one instance he liked to cite, an airline pilot wanted to purchase top-of-the-line Stratas but had been dissuaded by Mustafa, who was himself a pilot. He knew that Strata's polarizing feature would make it difficult to read the instrument panel, and that the pilot would be better off with less-expensive Drivers.

Operations

Serengeti's manufacturing was unusual for a sunglasses company in that it was almost entirely outsourced. Timothy Yu, operations manager, explained that outsourcing allowed the company to go anywhere to obtain the highest-quality frames and parts while still maintaining maximum flexibility. Only lens blanks were manufactured internally, and that was done by Corning Incorporated, not Serengeti. Yu observed: "Our expertise is in the glass itself, so we said to ourselves early on, 'Let's play to our strength and not tie up capital in things we're not good at.'"

Manufacturing was conducted at sites around the world. Lens blanks were melted and shaped at a Corning plant in Harrodsburg, Kentucky; most grinding and polishing was done by subcontractors in Japan; frames and assembly were assigned to partners in Japan, Hong Kong, France, Italy, and the United States. Because of their technical complexity, Strata lenses were manufactured in France, close to the research facility where the concept originated. Serengeti purchased all of the sunglass blanks made by Corning.

Serengeti preferred to rely on existing suppliers bound by long-term contracts, rather than on competitive bidding. Contracts were terminated only in extreme circumstances. Typically, one or two sources were used for each item. Of Serengeti's 14 original suppliers, all but two were still with the company. Cost improvements were gained by careful negotiation, and the goal, according to Yu, was to ensure "a fair margin to both parties." If suppliers were not able to meet cost-reduction targets, Serengeti engineers provided manufacturing and technical assistance.

Serengeti's suppliers enjoyed a number of advantages. The usual practice in the optical business was for suppliers to be paid only after goods were received by the buyer; Serengeti, by contrast, paid when orders left the country. Information on forecasts and predicted demand was shared routinely. And if a supplier had to invest in new capacity to meet Serengeti's requirements, it was guaranteed orders for a certain period. Yu summarized the company's approach by saying, "We are very responsible buyers."

Serengeti did not have a separate quality assurance group, nor was there a single individual with responsibility for quality. In fact, there had been no formal quality improvement programs since 1985. Instead, much of the responsibility for quality rested with a network of country manufacturing managers (also called in-country process engineers) who reported directly to Connie Lapp, the manufacturing manager. These engineers were stationed in different regions of the world and worked on-site with suppliers on a daily basis. Their task was to advise suppliers of Serengeti's needs, assist with production problems, and ensure that standards were met. Manufacturers were not paid until inspection was completed and standards were verified. Inspection was carried out by in-country process engineers at the source plant, and again by packers in the company's single warehouse, located adjacent to the offices, where every pair of sunglasses was checked before shipment. While there were variations across the product line, total manufacturing costs for Serengeti sunglasses followed the trade average of one-seventh the product's suggested retail price.

Because Yu felt that formal manufacturing systems were more of a burden than a help, he preferred to use direct feedback from customers and country manufacturing managers (whom he regarded as "the best advance warning system for quality problems") to guide his department. Problems were fixed as they arose. In mid-1993 Yu was resisting pressure from Corning's corporate staff to institute new quality control programs, as well as a just-in-time system. He commented:

> Our goal is zero defects. We were practicing customer satisfaction before they [Corning] were even tracking it. We know what's right for the customer; we know what's right for the business; we just do it . . . Now the battle is around inventory. Because Corning is an original equipment maker, it doesn't need inventory. But Serengeti does because we must have product on hand to meet the needs of a cyclical fashion industry. Forecasts are always going to be unreliable. Yet we promise to ship within 24 hours.

Operations staff spent much of their time getting to know suppliers personally. As Yu put it: "At Serengeti we believe in face-to-face meetings. Over the phone doesn't cut it. I want to see the person's expression and body language." This philosophy resulted in considerable overseas travel. For example, in 1992 Yu made six trips to Asia and three to Europe, each lasting about a week. The Japan country manufacturing manager came to Corning twice

for similar periods, while his European counterpart came three times. Comparable, and occasionally more intensive, travel schedules were followed by Yu's predecessors as operations manager, Mustafa and Ogle. Mustafa had headed operations before taking the helm in the 1985 turnaround; at the time he had developed the concept of a supplier network. Ogle had followed Mustafa as operations manager before becoming sales manager; he estimated that in the mid-1980s he spent almost 90 percent of his time on the road.

Operations also included distribution and the customer service department, which handled orders, inquiries, and complaints from retailers and consumers. Mustafa gave the service staff clear guidelines for dealing with unhappy customers: "Make the decision as if you were the one with a broken pair of sunglasses." To ensure rapid response, all customer-service representatives were able to make on-the-spot decisions. Judgment calls were inevitable, and customers occasionally appealed decisions to higher levels of management. In such cases, Mustafa told the customer-service staff, he would always back them up, even if he disagreed with the decision.

Systems

Two people were responsible for maintaining and developing Serengeti's information technology, including systems for customer service, ordering, inventory management, and distribution control. Despite their small number, they had succeeded in radically transforming the company's information systems.

Between 1982 and 1992 Serengeti used a system that was supplied by Corning to all divisions. It had been developed in the late 1970s, and was based on an IBM mainframe and centralized data processing services. Unfortunately, the system allowed records to be accessed in only a limited number of ways. Because most of them were designed for Corning's commodity businesses, Mustafa felt that the approach was too rigid and slow to meet Serengeti's increasingly flexible requirements. In 1991 he called Gary Wheeler, then a systems manager at Corning's central information systems division, and invited him to rejoin Serengeti to upgrade its information technology. Wheeler had previously been with the Sunglasses division between 1982 and 1985. Mustafa gave him a clear mandate: to select hardware and software that was appropriate for Serengeti's special needs. Wheeler recalled:

> Zaki told me: "Put in a customer service system that is best for the business. Don't do what other people say; do what's best for *this* business. You can't be successful if you conform all the time." That created a real problem, because corporate information services had already made a substantial investment in a new replacement system that they wanted us to use. But it was still centralized, and we weren't sure that it would be best for our needs.

In fact, when Wheeler drew up a list of requirements for Serengeti's new system, he realized that it would have to meet the needs of four main groups: staff, customers, country manufacturing managers, and suppliers. At the bottom of the list were the requirements of Corning corporate, who wanted Serengeti connected to the company's electronic mail network but really needed only an occasional information update, not constant interaction.

After nine months of research, conversations with several other companies that had downsized their computer systems, and consideration of 15 alternative packages, Wheeler recommended that Serengeti move to a system of linked personal computers. The new system offered several features not found on the IBM: online help for all data fields, paperless entry, frequent updates, flexibility, and the ability to be used outside of Corning's usual hours, which was important for Serengeti's European and Asian suppliers. Moreover, the new system cost between $80,000 and $90,000 for both hardware and software, whereas the alternative proposed by the corporate information group would have cost $780,000.

Management Style

Mustafa believed that business should be based on shared values, and that rigid rules and procedures obstructed customer service and flexibility. He therefore cultivated an informal management style.

Philosophy and Values

Mustafa was fond of quoting snippets of homespun philosophy to his colleagues. These were fondly called "Zaki-isms" because they neatly summarized his beliefs about life and business (see Exhibit 5). For example, Mustafa argued that values should be the starting point in business:

> Motivation to service and quality are not conscious acts at all. They have to be a reflection of what you are, and what you yourself believe. The issue of compatibility of style and belief is very important, and I think that belief comes first. If it's not in you, I don't know how to cultivate it. You can't create the capacity to be quality oriented in people; you can only destroy it.

Mustafa worked hard to build an atmosphere of teamwork and mutual support at Serengeti. From the time he became general manager, he viewed team building as one of his major responsibilities. He always asked employees to put the team first and carefully selected personnel who would be at home in such an environment. Trust, Mustafa believed, was critical to creating an effective business team. He observed:

> We may not have the best and the brightest, but we all pull together. Don't worry about having the brightest people; worry about the team.
>
> Trust comes from interdependence, not independence. We've made a clear statement: "The individual is secondary to the organization."

Management at Serengeti did not merely espouse these values; they tried to live them. (See Exhibit 6 for excerpts from an employee climate survey.) A vital factor in Mustafa's assessment of a prospective employee's potential was the likelihood that he or she would become part of the team. He observed:

> There are some people who take great pride in excellent output of their own. Others take great pride in excellent output of the group. I'm always looking for people in the second category.

EXHIBIT 5   "What I Taught the Harvard Business School"

In 1992 Zaki Mustafa attended the Harvard Business School's Advanced Management Program. On his return, Technical Products Division staff organized a dinner and presented him with a book, "What I Taught the Harvard Business School," which contained a collection of "Zaki-isms." The following are excerpts:

On Boston:	There is no place like home. Home is where the heart is. Boston does not qualify.
Harvard Business School:	is where you go when you have a 50% ROE budget and you don't have any idea how to get there. or . . . when the five-year plan needs to be done.
Cases:	should have executive summaries so you don't have to read the stupid things.
Customers:	are where you go when there's a:

• staff meeting
• staff trip
• quality trip
• KRI discussion
• strategy setting meeting
• period review
• quarterly review

or . . .

• TO GET SALES

On Winning:	Winning isn't everything but it sure beats losing. Without victory there is no survival. Win without risk, triumph without glory.
On American Business:	. . . American business thrives on organizational change

• Restructuring
• Centralization
• Decentralization

But as long as American business rewards style over substance, its erosion is likely to continue.

On People:	I'd rather have terrifically talented people with no product than a terrific product with no people, because people can improvise.
On Caring:	Caring about issues means we see ourselves as forces for change and improvement.
The Radical Heart:	The **radical heart** keeps us focused on a vision of the future . . . on the opportunity, not the risk, of finding out what is possible.
	The **radical heart** wishes to be practical, but is willing to live on the frontier with its danger and is of the belief that human beings have only begun to reach their potential.

Prospective employees were therefore screened extremely carefully for fit with these values. As Ogle put it: "We check chemistry as well as resumes." The hiring-in process involved extensive interviews with managers throughout the company. One recent hire summarized the process by saying, "I didn't feel like I was being hired; I felt like I was being adopted."

Mustafa also believed that it was important to involve everyone in the business fully, from top management to warehouse personnel. He shared

EXHIBIT 6   Corning Employee Satisfaction Surveys

In January 1990 Corning conducted a wide-ranging Climate Survey to assess employees' views of the work environment. The following is a selection of the results for all divisions in the Technical Products group, including Serengeti:

	Total Tech Products	*Advanced*	*Materials*	*Optical*	*LA/AP*	*Serengeti*
Organizational Outcomes						
Overall effectiveness	84[a]	81	87	88	75	86
General satisfaction	67	55	75	79	50	76
Work satisfaction	79	77	88	82	68	79
Pay satisfaction	48	41	52	69	21	49
Working conditions	63	70	48	49	67	90
Training satisfaction	66	59	70	65	63	62
Benefits satisfaction	51	74	50	73	40	24[b]
Intent to stay	61	59	65	69	38	73
Job security	61	59	65	68	42	74
Organizational Culture						
Market sensitivity	66	51	61	74	64	78
Innovativeness	72	54	84	74	62	71
Capacity to act	57	41	56	68	46	65
Total quality[c]	65	62	69	74	68	46
Openness	65	55	66	58	61	65
Intergroup cooperation	54	43	53	60	45	65
Valuing diversity	67	51	81	69	63	60
Corning Values						
Total quality	72	61	67	73	67	89
Integrity	77	78	81	73	63	83
Performance	78	78	74	70	72	94
Leadership	65	52	45	73	58	92
Technology	74	65	64	80	63	94
Independence	79	64	79	87	66	94
The individual	61	48	57	63	39	78

[a] Percent of employees expressing favorable view.
[b] Serengeti was the only business to include corporate union group in its survey. Union benefits were negotiated at the corporate level, not the business level.
[c] Refers to the use and application of Corning's quality system, policies, and tools.

Source: Company records

virtually all information, including financial and performance data, with the entire staff. Yu commented on the company's norms of equality:

> Typical firms are like an army, with a caste system. We don't have that here. There is no reserved parking (except for visitors), no separate dining areas, no separate bathrooms. And everybody, including the packers, attends the annual sales meeting.

Mustafa believed that this approach should extend beyond working relationships. In 1985, at the end of his first year as general manager, he sent all hourly workers an invitation to the annual Christmas party. He recalled:

> None of them showed up. I was very disappointed and later asked them why they hadn't attended. It turned out that they thought my invitation wasn't serious, that it was merely a casual note. So the next year I visited each one personally to invite them. By the third year, we had full attendance.

Mustafa emphasized that building teamwork and trust was a two-way street: He had to trust employees if they were to trust him. He gave an example of what that approach meant for management: "When we moved into our own building, I was told that we needed a security system in the warehouse and packing area to prevent theft. I wouldn't do it." At the same time, he set demanding goals and expected high performance. Mustafa stressed self-reliance, and several Serengeti employees noted that he asked more of them than their previous bosses. Lapp observed:

> Working for Zaki is probably the most challenging thing you could do. Why? Because if you have a normal ego and ambition you often think to yourself, "So much achievement would be fine." But he thinks you could do so much more. He doesn't care about where you went to school, or anything like that: He goes right to your soul. And because of that, I've been able to achieve more.

To illustrate her point, Lapp described an occasion when she had expressed doubts to Mustafa about her ability to perform a new and more demanding job. He responded by asking her to write down 10 good things about herself and put the list on his desk by the next morning. She found the task almost impossible, and hoped he would forget. But

Mustafa kept asking. Finally, several weeks later she forced herself to write down everything she could think of, and gave him the list. She remembered what happened next:

> He threw it in the trash. I asked, "What are you doing? Aren't you going to look at the list?" He replied, "It doesn't matter what I think, it's what you put on the list that's important." That's what I got for all my agonizing and worrying about what he would think. But I could do a lot better list now.

Mustafa believed that an important part of his job was caring for his staff. He commented:

> I regard myself not just as a business manager, but as a surrogate father for our people. I say to our employees: "You worry about your work, I'll worry about you." I am a friend, and I do it because I get a lot of pleasure out of it.

Decision Making

Most decisions at Serengeti, even very important ones, were reached with a minimum of memos, reports, and formal meetings. Indeed, Serengeti had no scheduled meetings of any kind, other than with customers and suppliers. According to Mustafa: "If an individual thinks a meeting is needed, it happens. But seldom. I spend a good part of my day visiting people, chatting with them over coffee. That's how we usually make decisions."

Mustafa stressed that informality did not mean shooting from the hip, or working without the facts. At Serengeti large amounts of information were collected before reaching a conclusion. In this sense, Mustafa felt that Serengeti's decision-making style was different from that of many other entrepreneurial companies:

> We're actually very cautious and conservative in what we do. We think things through, and that requires a lot of information. Some businesses describe themselves as entrepreneurial, but they're really irresponsible. They operate by the seat of their pants, just a brief conversation or two, then move to a decision. We don't. A true entrepreneur takes a long-term view.

Not all information, however, was treated equally. Mustafa believed that quantitative information often took the place of managers developing "a sense about what's right." For this reason, he strove for numbers that were "directionally correct," while avoiding artificial precision and extensive documentation. He explained:

In this business we emphasize the ability to become comfortable with qualitative information. We have two principles: Always deal with the broad picture before getting into the details, and always get the rationale right before running the numbers. If there's one legacy I want to leave here, it's that people look at the broad picture first and do a logic check.

Unfortunately, the bureaucrats want documentation. You can give them perfect information, or, at the risk of accuracy, you can give them directionally correct information and save several days of work. But at no point in time, for any reason, have I ever misled people directionally.

James Stokes, Serengeti's controller, who had worked elsewhere in Corning, believed that Mustafa had a reputation within the company for being cavalier with numbers. But Stokes thought that he simply used them in a different way:

I don't accept the traditional view that Zaki is not interested in numbers, that he's not numbers oriented. What he's really interested in is directional analysis, rather than precise predictions. When numbers are relevant, he studies them exhaustively.

Mustafa recognized that the combination of informality, a team orientation, and his approach to numbers could weaken individual responsibility. He therefore insisted on strict accountability:

I always tell people: "Don't say to me, 'To the best of my knowledge,' 'As advised by,' 'To the best of my ability,' 'As I'm told,' or whatever. Either it is or it isn't. Check it out. Don't rely on a third party." Our presumption is that if you're going to make a decision, you need to have first-hand information, because we want first-hand ownership and results. Anything that smacks of covering your tracks, like approvals or memos, is frowned on.

Or as Stone jokingly summed up the culture: "If you don't meet results, we take out a gun and shoot you—but we're unhappy about it."

Running the Business

To achieve these ends, Mustafa estimated that he spent about a third of his time on the road. Of that, 40 percent was spent visiting customers, 40 percent visiting suppliers, and the balance visiting Serengeti employees in the field. His customer visits were primarily with small accounts, he observed, "because they need more reinforcement that we care about them." When not traveling, Mustafa usually arrived at the office between 7:00 and 7:15 and left between 6:30 and 7:00; he tried to be the first one in and the last out so that "things were never a rush." About 10 percent to 15 percent of his time was spent on matters that he handled himself, such as budgets, reviews of financial performance, and attendance at corporate meetings. Several hours each week were devoted to meeting with customers at Serengeti. The remaining time either was spent wandering around visiting with employees or was unscheduled free time.

Mustafa's employee visits were unstructured and seemingly random. Often, he simply arrived at the company cafeteria and sat down with whomever was there. At other times, he wandered the hallways, dropping in on people in their offices. Free time was even less programmed. Some was spent mulling over what he had heard on his visits—in his words, "letting the mind wander." As much as two hours a day was spent reading, usually newspapers and business journals from around the world. And some time was spent indulging his interests in flying, tennis, and other recreations. Mustafa strove for a balanced life and drew a sharp distinction between a hard worker and a workaholic. He commented: "Make sure you have some free time, and be comfortable with it. There's a busyness problem for many managers. A balanced life is possible, providing you don't take pride in a full calendar, lots of phone calls, and back-to-back meetings."

The New Product Line Decision

For several years Serengeti had been exploring the idea of a higher-volume product. Young people aged 18–24 were a special target because the company currently had no products aimed specifically at them. Yet as a group they represented 24 percent of all purchases in the $25–$49.99 price segment and 27 percent of purchases in the $50–$74.99 segment. Moreover, at the $75 price point there were few competitive offerings, and a leading sunglass chain had observed: "The first one who does something branded with this market wins." The proposed product line fit this niche. It had emerged in late 1992 from casual discussions between Lapp and a friend at Corning laboratories.

Lapp had raised the idea of developing a cheaper, fixed-tint lens; the scientist had responded by saying that he was working on "something better." He and his group had already created a test lens that blocked 100 percent of ultraviolet (UV) rays. (Most existing glass lenses met the national standard of 95 percent UVA protection; 100 percent UVA blockage, however, was technologically difficult for glass.) The new manufacturing process was likely to result in sunglasses with a suggested retail price of approximately $80. And while the lens was neither photochromic nor polarized, it was distinctive in an important respect. By operating at a point on the spectrum that scientists call "neutral C," it offered completely undistorted color.

The proposed new product, tentatively called Eclipse, would be positioned as "Earth-friendly." The technology, on which Serengeti would hold exclusive rights, would also be marketed slightly differently. Research suggested that young people were less interested in the traditional Serengeti technologies of photochromic lenses and spectral control, but were far more concerned that their sunglasses block 100 percent of UV rays. In addition, they seemed to like the idea of "natural color." Stone observed:

> The biggest challenge now is coming up with a technology story. We don't offer "me-too" products. So we need to find a scientist with imagination, just like we did with Drivers and Vermilion [another Serengeti product], to help us tell the story that explains why the lens is great. Our sales force needs one, and I feel comfortable that we can sell young people on performance. After all, they buy high-tech

sneakers and high-tech stereo equipment, and they're better at computers than we are. As long as you meet their primary needs of style and price, it'll be fine.

Bausch and Lomb, of course, was certain to react to Eclipse. At the moment, there was limited direct competition between the two companies, mostly between high-end Ray-Bans and discounted Drivers. Yet Bausch and Lomb had already decided, in response to competition, to raise its advertising budget from a reported $2.7 million in 1992 to $7 million in 1993. Stone predicted: "They will try to use price as a blocking tool, offering retailers heavy promotions and price specials on basic Ray-Bans like Wayfarers." But she added:

> If we test Eclipse at the largest retail chains, and they have had a hand in designing the product, they'll be much harder to move. Nobody wants to see their baby killed. That's why our retail chains, which have a one-third share of the high-end business, will play such a big role in the development of the new line.

Mustafa, however, remained concerned about the product's risks. He feared that "neutral C" might not provide a compelling sales advantage and that the company's technology reputation might be undermined as a result. Cannibalization was a worry as well. Drivers, Serengeti's leading seller, carried a list price of $130, but could be found discounted for substantially less. Mustafa feared that Eclipse might hurt its sales. Perhaps most troubling were the organizational implications. Would Serengeti's approach to business succeed in the medium-priced market? Or was it appropriate only for competition as a high-end specialist?

There was an even deeper concern. What would happen if the new line failed? Since 1985 Serengeti had earned considerable latitude from corporate management because of its continued growth and profitability. Mustafa knew he had the authority to make the Eclipse decision without seeking approval from Corning management. But would Serengeti be able to maintain its independence if it suffered a major financial reversal? The opportunity, Mustafa knew, was enormous, but was Eclipse worth the risk?

Case 5–2

THE SOUL OF A NEW MACHINE

Tracy Kidder

It had been painful for [Tom] West and for a number of engineers working with him at [Data General's headquarters in] Westborough, [Massachusetts] to watch DEC's VAX go to market, to hear it described as "a breakthrough," and not have a brand-new machine of their own to show off. It had been painful for them to read in the trade press of the VAX's growing success; VAX was beginning to look like one of those best-sellers that come along only once in a while. But by the fall of 1978 West had drawn around him a team of enthusiastic engineers and they were finally working on their own supermini, which they had nicknamed Eagle. A new computer, especially one of this class, does not get built in a month. Often it takes years to bring one to life. But it wasn't too late, West was saying. Not if they could build this computer in the record time of something like a year. This was at last "the right machine." This was "the answer to VAX." At times West fancied that this computer would become the source of Data General's continued ascent in the *Fortune 500*. "This is the second billion," he said. His doubts he did not share widely.

Some of the engineers closest to West suspected that if he weren't given a crisis to deal with once in a while, he would create one. To them he seemed so confident and happy in an emergency. But as for this big crisis in the little world of Westborough engineering, although West had made it his own, no one could say he had invented it.

Why had Data General failed to produce a rival to VAX? When trade journalists asked this question, Data General put on a bold face of course, and suggested in essence that all was proceeding according to plan. In fact, years before the appearance of VAX, Data General engineers had foreseen the advent of such machines. For about five years they had been trying to produce one of their own. But there had been problems. They had made some false starts, and the engineers involved had been arguing over who was going to produce this new machine and what it would be.

Matters proceeded so informally and with such speed that there would never be any way of telling afterward where all of the first technical solutions to the problem of making a 32-bit Eclipse came from. But it was West who gathered them together. Soon he began an in-house PR campaign that would not end for a long time.

Carl Alsing participated in the beginnings of West's proselytizing. Among other acts, Alsing gave the new, unbuilt machine the code name Eagle. Mostly, though, he observed. Alsing was by temperament a watcher, a moviegoer. He had been with West longer than anyone else in the Eclipse Group. He felt that he knew West and then again he felt that he didn't. West launching Eagle was to Alsing something worth watching. For example, the meeting West set up with the vice presidents of engineering and software. West took Alsing along. The way it looked to Alsing, West brought two proposals to the vice presidents. One of these was an obvious loser and the other was Eagle. "West's letting them pick Eagle," thought Alsing, and he smiled.

"West's never unprepared in any kind of meeting. He doesn't talk fast or raise his voice. He conveys—it's not enthusiasm exactly, it's the intensity of someone who's weathering a storm and showing us the way out. He's saying, 'Look, we gotta move this way.' Then once he gets the vice presidents to say it sounds good, Tom goes to some of the software people and some of his own people. 'The bosses are signed up for this,' he tells them. 'Can I get you signed up to do your part?' He goes around and hits people one at a time, gets 'em enthused. They say, 'Ahhh, it sounds like you're just gonna put a bag on the side of the Eclipse,' and Tom'll give 'em his little grin and say, 'It's more than that, we're really gonna build this fucker and it's gonna be fast as greased lightning.' He tells them, 'We're gonna do it by April.' That's less than a year away, but never mind. Tom's message is: 'Are you guys gonna do it or sit on your ass and complain?' It's a challenge he throws at them."

Alsing went on: "West brought us out of our depression into the honesty of pure work. He put new life into a lot of people's jobs, I think."

Not everyone associated with the Eclipse Group liked the looks of this proposed new machine. They thought it would be just a refinement of the Eclipse, which was itself a refinement of the NOVA. "A wart on a wart on a wart," one engineer said. "A bag on the side of the Eclipse." Some even said that it would be a "kludge," and this was the unkindest cut. *Kludge* is perhaps the most disdainful term in the computer engineer's vocabulary: It conjures up visions of a machine with wires hanging out of it, of things fastened together with adhesive tape.

So some engineers dropped out of the project right away. To the remainder and to new recruits, West preached whatever gospel seemed most likely to stir up enthusiasm. It would be an opportunity for them to "get a machine out the door with their names on it."

Rosemarie Seale, the group's main secretary, felt excitement in the air. She, for one, took West's exhortations to heart. She resolved to do whatever she could in order to keep bureaucratic and trivial affairs from distracting these youngsters on their crucial mission. Her spirit never flagged, but from time to time she did wonder why, if this project was so important to the company, so few people in other departments seemed to recognize the fact. Why, for instance, was it allowed that the mailroom be moved in the midst of the project, creating the risk that vital mail would be held up? To prevent that sort of small catastrophe, for several weeks she would go to the mailroom daily and sort through the mail herself. Likewise, why would the carpenters be allowed to come in during a particularly delicate phase of the Eagle project and totally remodel the Eclipse Group's office space?

The answer, one possible answer, was that West had two ways of describing Eagle. One way made it sound important and glorious; the other, like something routine. West explained:

> You gotta distinguish between the internal promotion to the actual workers and the promoting we did externally to other parts of the company. Outside the group I tried to low-key the thing. I tried to dull the impression that this was a competing product with North Carolina. I tried to sell it externally as not much of a threat. It was selling insurance; this would be there if something went wrong in North Carolina. It was just gonna be a fast, Eclipse-like machine. This was the only way it was gonna live. We had to get the resources quietly, without creating a big brouhaha, and it's difficult to get a lot of external cooperation under those circumstances.

Here's how it looked to West: The company could not afford to field two new big computers; Data General had made a large investment in North Carolina as a place where major computers would be built; and although the Eclipse Group's engineers had good technical reputations, North Carolina's had better ones. The game was fixed for North Carolina and all the support groups knew it.

So West started out by calling Eagle "insurance"— it would be there in case something went wrong down south. Thus he avoided an open fight and thus he could argue that the support groups should hedge their bets and put at least a little effort into this project, too. As for North Carolina's superior reputation, West never stopped suggesting to people around Westborough that their talents had been slighted. His message was: "Let's show 'em what we can do."

"West takes lemons and makes lemonade," observed Alsing.

Between the summer of 1978 and the fall of that year, West's team roughly doubled in size. To the dozen or so old hands—old in a relative sense—were added about a dozen neophytes, fresh from graduate schools of electrical engineering and computer science. These newcomers were known as "the kids." West was the boss, and he had a sort of adjutant—an architect of the electronic school—and two main lieutenants, each of whom had a sub-lieutenant or two. One lieutenant managed the crew that worked on the hardware, the machine's actual circuitry, and the members of this crew were called, and called themselves, "the Hardy Boys." The other main part of the team worked on micro-code, a synaptic language that would fuse the physical machine with the programs that would tell it what to do. To join this part of the group, which Alsing ran, was to become one of "the Microkids." There were also a draftsman and some technicians. The group's numbers changed from time to time, generally diminishing, as people dropped out. But usually they totaled about 30.

How was it to be one of "the kids"? You were in no danger of being fired, but you didn't know that, and besides, when you are brand-new in a job you want to make a good impression right from the start. So you set out to get to know your boss, as Hardy Boy Dave Epstein did. You walk into his office and say, "Hi, I'm Dave," and you begin to extend your hand. Epstein would never forget that experience: "West just sat there and stared at me. After a few seconds, I decided I'd better get out of there."

But where did the relish in their voices come from?

At the start of the project, a newcomer could expect to earn something like $20,000 a year, while a veteran such as Alsing might make a little more than $30,000—and those figures grew enormously at Data General and elsewhere over the next few years. But they received no extra pay for working overtime. The old hands had also received some stock options, but most seemed to view the prospect of stock as a mere sweetener, and most agreed with Ken Holberger, sublieutenant of Hardy Boys, who declared, "I don't work for money."

Some of the recruits said they liked the atmosphere. Microkid Dave Keating, for instance, had looked at other companies, where de facto dress codes were in force. He liked the "casual" look of the basement of Westborough. "The jeans and so on." Several talked about their "flexible hours." "No one keeps track of the hours we work," said Ken Holberger. He grinned. "That's not altruism on Data General's part. If anybody kept track, they'd have to pay us a hell of a lot more than they do." Yet it is a fact, not entirely lost on management consultants, that some people would rather work 12 hours a day of their own choosing than 8 that are prescribed. Provided, of course, that the work is interesting. That was the main thing.

A couple of the Microkids were chatting. They talked about the jobs they had turned down.

"At IBM we wouldn't have gotten on a project this good. They don't hand out projects like this to rookies."

"They don't hand out projects like this to rookies anywhere but Data General."

"I got an offer at IBM to work on a memory chip, to see what could be done about improving its performance. Here I got an offer to work on a major new machine, which was gonna be the backbone of company sales. I'd get to do *computer* design. It wasn't hard to make that choice."

There was, it appeared, a mysterious rite of initiation through which, in one way or another, almost every member of the team passed. The term that the old hands used for this rite—West invented the term, not the practice—was "signing up." By signing up for the project you agreed to do whatever was necessary for success. You agreed to forsake, if necessary, family, hobbies, and friends—if you had any of these left (and you might not if you had signed up too many times before). From a manager's point of view, the practical virtues of the ritual were manifold. Labor was no longer coerced. Labor volunteered. When you signed up you in effect declared, "I want to do this job and I'll give it my heart and soul." It cut another way. The vice president of engineering, Carl Carman, who knew the term, said much later on: "Sometimes I worry that I pushed too hard. I tried not to push any harder than I would on myself. That's why, by the way, you have to go through the sign-up. To be sure you're not conning anybody."

The rite was not accomplished with formal declarations, as a rule. Among the old hands, a statement such as "Yeah, I'll do that" could constitute the act of signing up, and often it was done tacitly—as when, without being ordered to do so, Alsing took on the role of chief recruiter.

The old hands knew the game and what they were getting into. The new recruits, however, presented some problems in this regard.

The demand for young computer engineers far exceeded the supply. The competition for them was fierce. What enticements could the Eclipse Group offer to the ones they wanted that companies such as IBM could not? Clearly, West and Alsing agreed, their strongest pitch would be the project itself. Alsing reasoned as follows: "Engineering school prepares you for big projects, and a lot of guys wind up as transformer designers. It's a terrible letdown, I think. They end up with some rote engineering job with some thoroughly known technology that's repetitive, where all you have to do is look up the answers in books." By contrast, Alsing knew, it was thought to be a fine thing in the fraternity of hardware engineers—in the local idiom, it was "the sexy job"—to be a builder of new computers, and the demand for opportunities to be a maker of new computers also exceeded the supply. West put it this way: "We had the best high-energy story to tell a college graduate. They'd all heard about VAX. Well, we were gonna build a 32-bit machine less expensive, faster and so on. You can sign a guy up to that any day of the year. And we got the best there was."

But the new recruits were going to be asked to work at a feverish pace almost at once. They'd have no time to learn the true meaning of signing up on their own. They had to be carefully selected and they had to be warned. Common decency and the fear of having to feel lingering guilt demanded that this be done.

"West's not a technical genius. He's perfect for making it all work. He's gotta move forward. He doesn't put off the tough problem, the way I do. He's fearless, he's a great politician, he's arbitrary, sometimes he's ruthless." Alsing laced his hands together so that his knuckles made an arch, on which he rested his chin. Why was West so obsessed about this machine? How would it all end? Sometimes, Alsing said, he felt he had joined up mainly to find out. He went on: "I screamed and hollered over NAND gates and microinstructions with the first Eclipse, but I'm too old to feel that way about computers now. This would be crashingly dull if I was doing it for someone else. West is interesting. He's the main reason why I do what I do."

From the start of Eagle, Alsing disengaged himself from much of the technical work on the machine. He was running the Microteam, but from a little distance. Eagle would contain more code than any Data General machine before it—as much code as Alsing had written in his entire career. Alsing could not write all of it, even if there were time. He simply could not generate the excitement he used to feel about gates and bits. Moreover, he believed that since he could not write all of the code, then he couldn't write any of it. These new kids, he saw, approached the job in a way he never had. They worked steadily, day after day, night after night. That was fortunate, for the sake of the team. Alsing admired their discipline. He believed that it exceeded his by far. So he left the writing of the code to half a dozen new recruits, and most of the supervision of their work to submanagers. West often said that they were playing a game, called getting a machine out the door of Data General with their names on it. What were the rules?

"There's a thing you learn at Data General, if you work here for any period of time," said West's lieutenant of hardware, Ed Rasala. "That nothing ever happens unless you push it." To at least some people upstairs, this condition took the name "competition for resources." As a strategy of management, it has a long lineage. *Throw down a challenge,* writes Dale Carnegie in that venerable bible of stratagems dressed up as homilies, *How to Win Friends and Influence People.*

In a sense, the competition between Eagle and North Carolina was institutionalized; each project lay in the domain of a different vice president. But that may have been accidental. West's boss, who was the vice president of engineering, Carl Carman, remarked that he had worked at IBM and that compared to competition among divisions there, rivalry among engineering teams at Data General resembled "Sunday school." Moreover, Carman said, in a company with a "mature product line" like Data General's, situations naturally occur in which not enough large new computers are needed for every team of computer builders to put one of its own out the door. "And yeah," Carman continued, "the competition is fostered." He said that de Castro liked to see a little competition stirred up among teams. Let them compete with their ideas for new products, and bad ideas, as well as the negative points of good ones, are likely to get identified inside the company and not out in the marketplace. That was the general strategy, Carman said. What it now meant downstairs, to the Eclipse Group, was that they not only had to invent their new computer but also had to struggle for the resources to build it. Resources meant, among other things, the active cooperation of such so-called support groups as Software. You had to persuade such groups that your idea had merit and would get out the door, or else you wouldn't get much help—and then your machine almost certainly *wouldn't* get out the door.

From the first rule—that you must compete for resources—it followed that if your group was vying with another for the right to get a new machine out the door, then you had to promise to finish yours sooner, or at least just as soon as the other team promised. West had said that the Eclipse Group would do EGO in a year. North Carolina had said, okay, they'd finish their machine in a year. In turn, West had said that Eagle would come to life in a year. West said he felt he had to pursue "what's-the-earliest-date-by-which-you-can't-prove-you-won't-be-finished" scheduling in this case. "We have to do it in a year to have any chance." But you felt obliged to set such a schedule anyway, in order to demonstrate to the ultimate bosses strong determination.

Promising to achieve a nearly impossible schedule was a way of signing up—the subject of the third rule, as I saw it. Signing up required, of course, that you fervently desire the right to build your machine and that you do whatever was necessary for success, including putting in lots of overtime, for no extra pay.

The fourth rule seemed to say that if the team succeeded, those who had signed up would get a reward. Not one in the group felt certain that stock options were promised in case of success. "But it sure as hell was suggested!" said one of the Microkids. All members of the team insisted that with or without the lure of gold, they would have worked hard. But for a while, at least, the implied promise did boost spirits, which were generally high anyway.

At last, by the fall of 1978, the preliminaries were complete. The kids had been hired, the general sign-up had been performed, the promises suggested, and the escape valve established. Then West turned up the steam.

You're a Microkid, like Jon Blau. You arrived that summer and now you've learned how to handle Trixie. Your immediate boss, Chuck Holland, has given you a good overall picture of the microcode to be written, and he's broken down the total job into several smaller ones and has offered you your choice. You've decided that you want to write the code for many of the arithmetic operations in Eagle's instruction set. You always liked math and feel that this will help you understand it in new, insightful ways. You've started working on your piece of the puzzle. You can see that it's a big job, but you know you can do it. Right now you're doing a lot of reading, to prepare yourself. Then one day you're sitting at your desk studying Booth's algorithm, a really nifty procedure for doing multiplication, when Alsing comes by and tells you, "There's a meeting."

You troop into a conference room with most of the other new hires, joking. Feeling a little nervous, and there waiting for you are the brass: the vice president of engineering, another lower-level but important executive, and West, sitting in a corner chewing on a toothpick. The speeches are brief. Listening intently, you hear all about the history of 32-bit superminis. These have been around a while, but sales are really picking up. DEC's starting to turn out VAXes like jelly beans, and the word is DEC'll probably introduce a new model of VAX in about nine months. No one's saying it's your fault, but Eagle's late, very late. It really must be designed and brought to life and be ready to go by April. Really. In just six months. That won't be easy, but the brass think you can do it. That's why you were hired—you're the cream of a very fine crop. Everything depends on you now, they say.

You feel good about yourself and what you're doing when you leave that meeting. You go right back to your desk, of course, and pick up Booth's algorithm. In a little while, though, you feel you need a break. You look around for another Microkid to share coffee with you. But everyone is working, assiduously, peering into manuals and cathode-ray tubes. You go back to your reading. Then suddenly, you feel it, like a little trickle of sweat down your back. "I've gotta hurry," you say to yourself. "I've gotta get this reading done and write my code. This is just one little detail. There's a hundred of these. I better get this little piece of code done today."

Practically the next time you look up, it's midnight, but you've done what you set out to do. You leave the basement thinking: "This is life. Accomplishment. Challenges. I'm in control of a crucial part of this big machine." You look back from your car at the blank, brick, monolithic back of Building 14A/B and say to yourself, "What a great place to work." Tomorrow you'll have to get to work on an instruction called FFAS. That shouldn't be too hard. When you wake up the next morning, however, FFAS is upon you. "Oh my God! FFAS. They need that code next week. I better hurry."

"The pressure," said Blau. "I felt it from inside of me."

In another cubicle, around this time, Dave Epstein of the Hardy Boys is dreaming up the circuits of a thing called the Microsequencer. Nothing else will work without this piece of hardware.

Some weeks ago, Ed Rasala asked Epstein, "How long will it take you?"

Epstein replied, "About two months."

"Two months?" Rasala said. "Oh, come on."

So Epstein told him, "Okay, six weeks."

Epstein felt as if he were writing his own death warrant. Six weeks didn't look like enough time, so he's been staying here half the night working on the thing, and it's gone faster than he thought it would. This has made him so happy that just a moment ago he went down the hall and told Rasala, "Hey, Ed, I think I'm gonna do it in four weeks."

"Oh, good," Rasala said.

Now, back in his cubicle, Epstein has just realized, "I just signed up to do it in four weeks."

Better hurry, Dave.

"I don't know if I'm complaining, though," says Epstein. "I don't think I am. I work well under pressure." Indeed, Epstein will finish on schedule and his design will turn out to be almost errorless.

But not everyone works well under such conditions. Not everyone thinks it is worth it. A couple of engineers have already dropped out. A few are less than happy. One Hardy Boy, Josh Rosen, looks around and can hardly believe what he sees. For example, Microkids and Hardy Boys are arguing. A Microkid wants the hardware to perform a certain function. A Hardy Boy tells him, "No way—I already did my design for microcode to do that." They make a deal: "I'll encode this for you, if you'll do this other function in hardware." "All right."

What a way to design a computer! "There's no grand design," thinks Rosen. "People are just reaching out in the dark, touching hands." Rosen is having some problems with his own piece of the design. He knows he can solve them, if he's just given the time. But the managers keep saying, "There's no time." Okay. Sure. It's a rush job. But this is ridiculous. No one seems to be in control; nothing's ever explained. Foul up, however, and the managers come at you from all sides.

"The whole management structure," said Rosen. "Anyone in Harvard Business School would have barfed."

West figured that the Eclipse Group had to show quick and constant progress in order to get the various arms of the company increasingly interested in helping out. For public relations, and maybe in order to keep the pressure on his crew, he made extravagant claims. He always pushed them one step ahead of themselves. Before Wallach finished specifying the architecture, West had the team designing the boards that would implement the architecture; before the engineers cleaned up their designs, West was ordering wire-wrapped, prototype boards; before the wire-wraps could possibly be made right, he was arranging for the making of printed-circuit boards; and long before anyone could know whether Eagle would become a functioning computer, West had the designers stand in front of a TV camera and describe their parts of the machine. The result of this last act of hubris was a videotaped extravaganza some 20 hours long. West planned to use it, when the right time came (if it ever did), as a tool for spreading the news of Eagle all around Westborough. "Pretty gutsy," he said, with a grin, nodding toward the shelf full of videocassettes.

West never passed up an opportunity to add flavor to the project. He helped to transform a dispute among engineers into a virtual War of the Roses. He created, as Rasala put it, a seemingly endless series of "brushfires," and got his staff charged up about putting them out. He was always finding romance and excitement in the seemingly ordinary. He welcomed a journalist to observe his team; and how it did delight him when one of the so-called kids remarked to me, "What we're doing must be important, if there's a writer covering it."

One evening West paused to say to me: "I'm flat out by definition. I'm a mess. It's terrible." A pause. "It's a lot of fun."

West established the rules for the design of Eagle and he made them stick. The team should use as little silicon as possible, a mere few thousand dollars' worth of chips. The CPU should fit on far fewer than VAX's 27 boards, and each major element of the CPU should fit on a single board. If they could fulfill those requirements, Eagle would be cheaper to build than VAX. On the other hand,

it had better run faster than VAX, by certain widely accepted standards. It should be capable of handling a host of terminals. A CPU is not a functioning computer system; Eagle also had to be compatible with existing lines of Data General peripherals as well as with Eclipse software . . . West espoused these principles of computer design: "There's a whole lot of things you've gotta do to make a successful product. The technological challenge is one thing, but you can win there and still have a disaster. You gotta give 'em guidelines so that if they follow them, they're gonna be a success. 'Do ABC and D without getting the color of the front bezel mixed up in it.'" Another precept was "No bells and whistles." And a third: "You tell a guy to do this and fit it all on one board, and I don't want to hear from him until he knows how to do it."

That fall West had put a new term in his vocabulary. It was *trust*. "Trust is risk, and risk avoidance is the name of the game in business," West said once, in praise of trust. He would bind his team with mutual trust, he had decided. When a person signed up to do a job for him, he would in turn trust that person to accomplish it; he wouldn't break it down into little pieces and make the task small, easy, and dull.

To Alsing, West still had that knack for making the ordinary seem special, and the way West said "Trust" made Alsing wonder whether either of them had ever heard the word before. But West prided himself on his skills at debugging, and, by repute, he excelled at it. He wanted to go into the lab and will the machine into life, Alsing thought. But if West barged in there now, he would be admitting that he didn't trust his team after all. So West was staying away from the lab and instead was banning laughter outside his door and throwing water pumps around. Most every day now West called Alsing into his office, closed the door, and asked, "What's really going on in the lab, Alsing?"

Wasn't all this excessive? If you set a preposterous schedule, don't you figure that it can slip a little? True, said Alsing, but not to the point. "If you say you're gonna do it in a year and you don't take it seriously, then it'll take three years. The game of crazy scheduling is in the category of games that you play on yourself, in order to get yourself to move."

It was a game in which new hands were always being dealt, a little like poker perhaps. West and his staff had created the deadline of April and, in the act, had agreed at least to pretend to take it seriously. Many months later, Carl Carman would say that no one upstairs believed they would finish Eagle that soon. Some evenings downstairs, West seemed to say the same thing. "We're gonna finish this sucker by April, Alsing," he'd say.

"Yeah, Tom. Sure we are," Alsing would reply. They'd smile at each other.

Sometimes, however, when, for instance, Alsing came in and told West that the Microteam would probably miss some intermediate deadline, West would say, "Come on, Alsing, this schedule's real."

Now, on an evening early in 1979, Carman brought West a piece of momentous news: North Carolina was going to miss their own deadline by a huge margin.

What did this mean? That the game of internal competition had essentially ended and the game of outlandish scheduling had begun in earnest? West had always maintained that Eagle was crucial to the company. Well, events were proving him right. But that was no cause for celebration. Meeting that preposterous deadline of April, when Eagle should be free of all bugs, was no longer merely desirable or just a matter of pride: It had become a corporate necessity.

West called himself "a mechanic"—one who could take the ideas of engineers technically brighter than he and make those ideas work; he thought he had spotted that quality in Rasala, too, and he had promoted it. West groomed Rasala as a leader of hardware teams. Eventually, he put Rasala in charge of the hardware for the biggest of the 16-bit Eclipses, the M/600. As often happened, the pace of that project became frenetic. It took a year of increasingly intense labor from Rasala, and when it ended he felt tired. He was looking around for something easy to do when West asked him to manage the development of Eagle's hardware. Rasala declined.

In his office, the door closed, West schemed. "How am I gonna get Rasala to sign up?" he asked Alsing.

Unlike Wallach, Rasala wasn't a student of advanced architectures. Rasala wasn't worried about Eagle's supposed inelegance; he was just tired. Offering him a chance for vengeance wouldn't work, because Rasala had been pounding out the M/600 during the EGO wars and he didn't have anything to feel vengeful about. Rasala was a hard one, West said. Bringing him to the signed-up condition was mainly a matter of persistence. West presented Eagle to him as a test of strength. Could they get this machine out the door on time? Again and again, he told Rasala that the company needed this machine desperately. Rasala never actually said, "I'll do it." One day, it seemed to him, he was just doing it.

For months afterward, he would come home at night and his wife would ask him, "How was your day?"

"It was terrible," Rasala would tell her. But as he went on describing the day's events, his wife noticed, he became increasingly excited.

"Maybe it's masochism," Rasala said. "But I guess the reason I do it fundamentally is that there's a certain satisfaction in building a machine like this, which is important to the company, which is on its way to becoming a billion-dollar company. There aren't that many opportunities in this world to be where the action is, making an impact." It struck him as paradoxical, all this energy and passion, both his own and that of the engineers around him, being expended for a decidedly commercial purpose. But that purpose wasn't his own. He had enjoyed his years at Raytheon; life had been pleasant there and he had been an easygoing fellow. Now, in the Eclipse Group, for several years in a row he had been working overtime without extra pay in an atmosphere that was decidedly not easygoing. Why had he made the switch to Data General and now signed up to work on Eagle?

Rasala said, "I was looking for"—he ticked the items off on his fingers—"opportunity, responsibility, visibility."

What did those words mean to him, though?

Rasala shrugged his shoulders. "I wanted to see what I was worth," he explained.

Months later, looking back, Rasala decided that when West took on people in other groups and "beat them up," as this sort of activity was called, he did so in a purposeful way, one that was usually "not so much mean as intimidating." In one fairly typical case, a support group missed a promised deadline. At a meeting, West questioned the group's leader. The leader said that he hadn't received a certain piece of equipment yet. West would not let the matter rest there. He wanted to know why it hadn't been shipped and what was being done about it. West was "always pushing," Rasala noticed. But the act, Rasala would come to believe, was never as dramatic as the language West used to describe either what he was going to do or what he had actually done. For a long time, however, Rasala took West's descriptions as a fairly literal model of how to contend, and when Rasala confronted a troublesome support group, he beat his fist on the table and shouted and made open threats. I saw him after one such encounter, returning to his cubicle. He was red. "I don't want to beat people up," he said, throwing his hands down. "I don't want to be a bad guy. I just want to get something done." He took some deep breaths, then proceeded to explain that it really wasn't the support group's fault. Eagle wasn't their machine, they couldn't be expected to work as diligently on it as the Eclipse Group.

To almost everything they touched, the Microteam attached their prefix. The office that four of them shared, sitting virtually knee to knee, had a sign on the door that said THE MICROPIT; the room in which they held their weekly meeting was the microconference room. They gave out microawards and Carl Alsing had his microporch. One of them owned a van, which became the microbus. That winter several of them would go out riding in it on Friday afternoons, when West held his own weekly meetings with his managers. Then, in the first warm days of spring, they created the outdoor microlounge, to which they now repaired on those Friday afternoons.

West remembered working on the prototype of the Eclipse. Most evenings the company's president, Ed de Castro himself, would appear in the lab, eating a Fudgsicle. The soft-spoken de Castro wouldn't say much. He'd ask a few questions, ones that seemed remarkably acute to West. The questions and the man's mere presence made West feel, again and again, "This project is really important."

Then one night, without any warning, de Castro said to him softly, "Got that fucking pig working yet?"

West was startled, then amused, and finally, though he could hardly explain it to himself, aroused. *No. But I will,* he wanted to say to de Castro.

For some time during the debugging of the first Eclipse, West was ill every morning before work— a psychological form of morning sickness, perhaps. But when the job was done and he went to the factory floor and saw a long file of brand-new Eclipses come gliding down a conveyor belt, some great delight, which he would describe as "almost a chemical change," came over him, and what he wanted most of all to do then was to do it all over again someday, only better.

To the observant Rosemarie, it seemed that West was always planning. She began to believe that he planned almost everything that happened during the season of Eagle. As time went on he seemed to grow skinnier and skinnier before her eyes, as if the job and all that planning were somehow consuming his flesh. Once in a while she would look into his office. He would be staring at some paper and wouldn't notice her standing in the doorway. She would watch for a moment. "Why is he doing this?" she wondered. "He belongs in the north woods somewhere, canoeing and fishing and appreciating nature. He doesn't belong here."

Long afterward, at a time when she found herself talking about West in the past tense—"Geez, I hate to talk about him in the past"—the question of West's motivation still had importance for her. Most people, she reasoned, do jobs because they are told to and might get fired if they don't obey.

But certainly West didn't have to drum up Eagle and waste away over it. Indeed, from her perspective, it really did seem as though the company didn't want the project undertaken at all. "So why is he doing it?" she asked.

"There's a big high in here somewhere for me that I don't fully understand," said West. "Some of it's a raw power-trip . . ."

"The reason why I work is because I win . . ."

"Realistically, I've got some stock in this company. I gotta help keep it afloat for a while."

Someone once suggested to West that he wanted to build Eagle out of love for chains and whips. West lay awake several nights worrying that it might be so.

"I'm sitting here burning myself up and doing it because I like it. You wouldn't have to pay me very much to do this," he said one night while he sat fretting, sick to his stomach over the slow progress of the debugging.

Later: "I'm trying to talk myself into quitting . . ."

"Not many people around here would admit to being in business," he said. And: "What makes this all possible is doing this and putting money on the bottom line and not having to go all the way with the capitalist system . . ."

"What makes it all possible is the kids."

When he talked about his reasons for wanting to build Eagle, West might have been trying to figure out how to get one of his lieutenants to sign up. He said he wished someone could explain his reasons to him. He said once, "de Castro knows what makes me go." He smiled. "The bastard."

He also said: "No one ever pats anybody on the back around here. If de Castro ever patted me on the back, I'd probably quit."

Holberger is married but has no children yet. He says he has more than enough money right now. He has also received some company stock. Stock options, he notes, blur issues of salary; "Data General turns people into capitalists," he says. Holberger likes the local atmosphere. The jeans, West's casual dress, remind him, he says, "that we're not at IBM." He likes not having to punch a time clock. But he knows that his freedom from company clocks doesn't stem from corporate altruism. "They don't want us to know how many hours we work. If we did, they'd have to pay us a lot more . . . But," Holberger says, "I don't work for money."

For the last two years, he has been involved in projects with the flavor of crisis about them. He worked on the M/600 with Rasala and went without a break into Eagle. He has been saying of late that he doesn't want to take on any more jobs like this one, but he's also been saying that he isn't sure he means it. "It's very challenging and very interesting," he says. "There's a lot of, uh, prestige, I would say. Perhaps I like some of the things I say I don't like. It's consuming. I don't know. Perhaps I don't like it. But jobs like this aren't real common. In other companies people with our experience aren't allowed to do this, I think." He wears a wry smile. "Of course, that's how Data General gets cheap labor." Holberger has noticed that there is almost no one in the basement involved in CPU design who is over 35. What happens to old CPU engineers? Holberger is 26 now, and though not exactly on his deathbed, he is curious about what a computer engineer does "afterward." Maybe, he says, efforts like this one can only be conducted by the very young.

"Like war," I suggest.

"Yeah, really," he says, laughing.

From the moment they started designing the computer, engineers were dropping out. The reasons varied, from the feeling that the machine would be a kludge to disappointment over positions in the group's pecking order. Some may have tired of the competition within the group, of what Ken Holberger called the peer pressure: "If I screw up this, then I'll be the only one, and I'm not gonna be the only one." Some may have had trouble keeping up with the others. A few did not participate in the group's social life, and some seemed to drift away from the project. Building Eagle wasn't the best of times for everyone.

Rosen came to the group in the middle of the summer of 1978 and went to work on the all-important ALU. He felt constrained to start designing right away, before he could really study the architectural spec—before, indeed, a complete spec existed. A few months later, in August, he decided that he had chosen to use the wrong sort of chips. He told Rasala he wanted to redesign the whole board. Rasala replied, "There isn't time." In effect, Rosen felt, Rasala was saying: "This'll probably work. Put a Band-Aid fix on it."

In December Rosen brought in a design that called for far more chips than it was supposed to contain. West assigned another engineer to examine Rosen's work—a necessary act from West's point of view, but a form of censure for Rosen. A while after that, Rosen underwent his review, a periodic ritual at Data General in which your boss evaluates your performance and sometimes gives you a raise. He was handed a report card less flattering than he was used to. It was the only unflattering one he had ever seen in his brief but distinguished career as a builder of computing equipment.

Rosen had come over from Data General's Special Systems Division, which produces equipment for customers' special needs. "I was *the* star at Special Systems," he said. "I got all the sexy jobs. I went to the Eclipse Group and I wasn't treated like a star." Ken Holberger, about the same age as Rosen and endowed with roughly the same amount of experience, occupied that position among the Hardy Boys, if anyone did. Clearly, Rasala considered Holberger to be the team's stellar designer. Rosen, by his own account, found himself competing with Holberger. He wanted to be "the driving force" behind Eagle's hardware. He was used to being in control of entire designs. Over at Special Systems, he had often felt free to pursue pure technical excellence. Three weeks after joining the Eclipse Group, he said to himself, "This is all wrong."

Data General recruited Rosen by promising him interesting work, and he got it. The first truly commercial product he designed was something known as a cluster controller, a kind of computer terminal, which he called Hydra. After it had been built and shipped, a small microcode error cropped up it, and

Rosen's boss sent him to California to make the repair. Out west, Rosen was ushered into a room and saw a dozen people using the machine that he had designed. The sight made him tremble. It took his breath away. He felt scared. "My God!" he thought. "Don't use one of those. Why don't you use a real terminal?" He felt thrilled. "That's something I designed. That's my machine. That's not Data General's. That's me.

"You don't get to see that very often," Rosen said. "But that's the biggest satisfaction of all."

He was only 22, and he had done it all—except that he had never helped to build a commercially important, big and brand-new computer. He expressed an interest in doing so, and the word got back to the Eclipse Group. They recruited him; he had fine credentials. Then, of course, everything went sour for him. But perhaps his personal catastrophe had started earlier. Maybe he volunteered for Eagle looking for a way out of a malaise already upon him. He thought that was probably the case.

Rosen said that when he first came to Data General a few years before Eagle, the staffer at Personnel told him, "We know how you fellows work, and we will remind you if you forget to take your vacations." But, he said, they never did remind him. Probably, it wouldn't have mattered if they had. He went to work at Special Systems, and in his first year there, he was assigned so many important, challenging projects that he not only forgot to take his vacation, he also failed to take a weekend off. What would obtain in the Eclipse Group also held at Special Systems. "There was no question of deadlines. You'd already missed it, whatever it was." He worked many 80-hour weeks—without extra pay, of course, but that wasn't the issue. "I had a lot of control over the things I did, and the price was a lot of pressure. If I spent only a 60-hour week, I felt intensely guilty."

He told himself that he was having the time of his life. During his second year at Special Systems, he began to remind himself of this with some regularity. "Josh," he would say to himself, "you're designing the sexy machines."

The dialogue with himself continued when he joined the Eclipse Group and began working on Eagle. "You've always revered the people who built the NOVA and the PDP-11. Now you're one of them. You're the guy you always wanted to be," he said in his mind.

"So why," he asked himself, "am I not happy?"

Many of the team, especially some of the Hardy Boys, said they felt comfortable around their division's vice president, Carl Carman. He visited the lab almost every morning and evening now. He asked them about their problems. He knew all their names. But most of them, when they ran into West in the hallways, got the feeling that their immediate boss did not know nearly so much about them. "He'll look off in another direction as he walks by, and you never see him smile." When West did speak to the masses, some felt afraid.

It seemed peculiar to some of the team. Here they were laboring mightily on the most crucial project in the company, and yet they lacked equipment, comforts, and all signs of recognition from their boss. Their project had number-one priority. Their vice president said so. Who among them could doubt that what they were doing was important to the company? The problem had to lie with West. "Why are some managers effective in getting resources and Tom isn't? That's my bitch," complained one member of the team.

"Sometimes even the pencil supply seems short," said another. "I can't help but think that someone wants us to run lean and mean because he thinks we work better that way. I don't know. Maybe Carman doesn't have the pull. Maybe Tom West only talks tough to people at his own level and below. Maybe he wants us to look lean and mean to impress other people above him."

When they had time on their hands to look up from the machine, some saw that they were building Eagle all by themselves, without any significant help from their leader. It was *their* project, theirs alone. West was just an office out of which came "disconnected inputs and outputs," said one Hardy Boy. He shrugged. It didn't matter. "West may be acting as a real good buffer between us and the rest of the company. Or maybe he's not doing anything."

Alsing listened, and sometimes he smiled. "When this is all over, there are gonna be 30 inventors of the Eagle machine," he predicted. "Tom's letting them believe that they invented it. It's cheaper than money."

West had put this project together, almost single-handedly. If West did nothing else, Alsing felt, Eagle would still in some ways be West's machine. But the idea that he was doing nothing else was crazy, although Alsing could understand why many on the team got that impression. Maybe they were supposed to. West had never sat down with him and Rasala and Steve Wallach and Rosemarie Seale and said: "We're gonna bury this team. They're not gonna see anything except the machine." But West had said, in a cautionary tone: "There's 30 guys out there who think it's their machine. I don't want that tampered with. It's very useful to me right now."

From time to time, Rasala and Alsing would tell some of their troops that West was acting as a buffer between them and the company bureaucrats, but the two managers didn't go into details. To do so would have violated West's unspoken orders—"an unspoken agreement," said Alsing, "that we won't pass on the garbage and the politics." They wished sometimes that the rest of the team could get a glimpse of West when some other manager dared to criticize the Eclipse Group or one of its members. West, notoriously, kept a double standard in such matters. He criticized other groups but would brook no criticism directed toward his own. He could carry this policy to absurd lengths, Rasala thought. Sometimes West would simply ignore criticism directed toward his team. Sometimes he would answer it with questions in this vein: "Are your people working 60-hour weeks?"

I can't imagine someone else running that show. Someone else might have smiled at them and said the right words, but not many bosses would have done as much as he did for them, letting them grow in their work, giving them a chance to really do something. Tom West gave the appearance of not caring for them, but he did the things that a person would do if he did care for them. Life is odd. Is it the words? Or the thing itself? I don't think those guys could've accepted a person keeping their minds down, but I don't think they know it yet. For a lot of them, you see, this was their first working experience. They never had a boss who kept them down. I have [but West:]

> He kept it inside him. He didn't go out and complain. Maybe he didn't pat people on the back, but he didn't complain either. He was very tired. He poured himself into it. I think he allowed all the complaints to be on himself. I think it was deliberate. My opinion is he wanted them to have someone to lay it all on, all their problems, so they could get rid of their frustrations and all their problems quicker and go on and do that thing that was desperately needed. I think he set himself out there as the bad guy, but bad guy is too strong. For people to grow up they need someone to lay their problems on. "You're the daddy." She laughed. Whether he did that or not deliberately, it had that effect.

Eagle was failing its Multiprogramming Reliability Test mysteriously. It was blowing away, crashing, going to never-never land, and falling off the end of the world after every four hours or so of smooth running.

"Machines somewhere in the agony of the last few bugs are very vulnerable," said Alsing. "The shouting starts about it. It'll never work, and so on. Managers and support groups start saying this. Hangers-on say, 'Gee, I thought you'd get it done a lot sooner.' That's when people start talking about redesigning the whole thing."

Alsing added, "Watch out for Tom now."

West sat in his office. "I'm thinking of throwing the kids out of the lab and going in there with Rasala and fix it. It's true. I don't understand all the details of that sucker, but I will, and I'll get it to work."

He called for Rasala one evening. "I want to go into the lab."

"Gimme a few more days," said Rasala.

On September 25 Rasala said, "As of this morning, Eagle ran Multiprogramming 12 hours overnight without failing."

Holberger said, "I know how West felt, but he couldn't have done a thing."

Back in his office West said: "It wasn't an empty threat. The game, of course, though, is that when I say I'm gonna go in there, they haul ass, because they assume it's gonna be some kind of trivial dumb thing."

A month after Gallifrey Eagle was rolled slowly down the corridor to Software, Ed Rasala and several of the Hardy Boys got together at the Cain Ridge Saloon and did some reminiscing disputatiously, as usual. At one point, Jim Guyer said: "We didn't get our commitment to this project from de Castro or Carman or West. We got it from within ourselves. Nobody told us we had to put extra effort into the project."

Ken Holberger burst out laughing.

Guyer raised his voice. "We got it from within *ourselves* to put extra effort in the project."

Laughing hard, Holberger managed to blurt out, "Their idea was piped into our minds!"

"The company didn't ask for this machine," cried Guyer. "We *gave* it to them. We created that design."

Others raised their voices. Quietly, Rasala said, "West created that design."

Rasala's big forearms rested on the table, surrounding a mug of beer. I thought perhaps I had not heard him right. He had always insisted that Eagle belonged equally to every member of the team. There was a whiff of heresy in the air.

"What did you say that West created?"

"Eagle," said Rasala.

By then the others had stopped arguing and turned toward Rasala, who was wearing one of his looks; it seemed to warn against contradiction.

"You mean West created the excitement."

"No," said Rasala, in a flat voice. "The machine."

"The opportunity," offered Holberger.

"The machine," said Rasala.

Then there was a moment during which everyone avoided everyone else's eyes, and the conversation resumed on another subject.

Case 5–3

TRANSITION TO GENERAL MANAGEMENT WEBSITE

Shifting from a functional manager to a general manager can be a daunting task, both personally and professionally. The Transition to General Management website, located at http://www.hbs.edu/gm, conveys these distinctive challenges by drawing on the insights and experiences of over 50 Harvard Business School graduates who recently made the shift.[1]

Functional managers administer an individual department or area such as marketing, operations, or finance. They possess specialized, in-depth knowledge and skills pertaining to their areas of expertise. In contrast, general managers possess broad, integrative skills. They are responsible for the overall performance of their units or organizations, measured by profit and loss, and oversee large, diverse constituencies of functional specialists, who frequently have more detailed knowledge than they do. Occasionally, as CEOs and group or sector heads, they oversee other general managers as well. But whatever the level, new general managers must quickly master a complex array of skills, attitudes, and behaviors. They must learn to make difficult decisions, often with incomplete information, communicate effectively on a broad range of issues, and gain the respect and trust of subordinates, superiors, and peers.

The Transition to General Management website provides a revealing look at how a large sample of newly minted general managers acclimated to their positions in diverse companies and industries. The material in the site was collected in 1996 and 1997 from a series of Web-based discussions between second-year MBA students at Harvard Business School and alumni who had recently become general managers. The site combines quotations and video clips to illustrate the often tumultuous transition to a general manager.

The General Manager's Job

The first section of the site dissects the general manager's job, dividing it into eight activities or responsibilities: integrating, balancing, decision making, interacting, communicating, utilizing resources, monitoring, and transitioning.

1. General managers must *integrate* the activities of functional managers to form coherent strategies and plans of action. They must set the context, coordinate departmental goals, motivate subordinates, and create and manage information flows in ways that fuse the various pieces of the unit into a seamless whole.
2. *Balancing* entails weighing the needs and wants of different organizational constituencies, making trade-offs, allocating time and other scarce resources, and deciding what to do and what to delegate.
3. *Decision making* is a central activity of general managers. To be effective, they must employ both intuition and rational problem solving. They must learn to recover quickly from poor choices. And they must learn to implement rapidly, obtaining buy-in from direct reports

---

[1]*The website contains both text and video materials. The entire text can be accessed over the Internet using standard browsers. For technical reasons, however, the video clips can only be screened over Harvard Business School's intranet.*

This case was prepared by Jeffrey Berger under the direction of David A. Garvin.

while empowering others to make their own decisions.

4. Listening, building relationships, conveying and gaining respect, and coaching are crucial components of *interacting* with subordinates, superiors, and peers. General managers must learn to be fair and consistent when managing up and evaluating down.

5. *Communicating* expectations about performance or vision can be difficult for new general managers, who are often unaccustomed to thinking strategically. A general manager must also talk to subordinates about sensitive topics that others avoid. In addition, communication skills are essential to managing external relationships, outside one's division and outside the company.

6. *Utilizing resources* covers such issues as working with a board of directors and drawing on the advice of trusted advisors, consultants, and outside experts.

7. General managers must have superior *monitoring* skills. They must develop quantitative metrics for assessing progress and tracking employee performance. In addition, they must create incentives that drive performance and support their unit's goals.

8. *Transitioning* to the job can be one of the most difficult tasks for new general managers. Individuals must learn to act as generalists rather than specialists, to hire and fire at the very highest levels, and to work with others who only recently were peers. These tasks frequently require adjustments in one's priorities and ways of working.

Managing the Transition

The second section of the site focuses heavily on the dynamics of shifting from functional to general management. It highlights the transition process and looks at the problem over time. This section is divided into five parts: managing yourself, managing your career, managing others, managing the organization, and managing start-ups.

1. *Managing yourself* can be very difficult. A new general manager must often change his or her approach and learn new behaviors, such as acting decisively and making difficult personnel changes. General managers must also learn to effectively manage their time in an environment where they are continually overloaded and can seldom do everything.

2. *Managing your career* describes a number of alternative routes to becoming a general manager. Some managers elect to climb the internal ladder through a variety of functional positions, while others begin in consulting or investment banking and then shift over to general management. Each approach has advantages and disadvantages.

3. *Managing others* is especially critical for general managers because their subordinates invariably have more knowledge of a particular specialty than they do. The general manager must learn to make subordinates feel comfortable by listening attentively and must learn when delegating tasks is appropriate and when it is not.

4. General managers operate under a myriad of formal and informal corporate systems. *Managing the organization* requires learning how these systems work, understanding the hierarchy, adjusting to sometimes elaborate controls, meshing with the corporate culture, and recognizing and confronting office politics.

5. *Managing start-ups* examines the general manager's role in a distinctive corporate setting. Start-ups present special issues and challenges, such as continual recruiting, managing growth, and balancing entrepreneurship with day-to-day oversight and control.

Together, these categories provide a detailed map of what was previously uncharted territory: the complex transition an individual makes when moving from functional to general management. The associated conflicts and changes, pressures and pleasures, are discussed at length by those who only a few years earlier sat in the same position as today's MBAs.

Format

The site is easy to navigate. Each major subsection can be reached from the initial page (see Exhibit 1). In addition, each subsection is further divided into categories arranged by topic (see Exhibit 2). By clicking on any of the headlines on the right side of the page, the user will instantly see either a verbatim quote from a general manager or an icon showing that a brief video clip is available. Users will need *Real Player* in order to view the video clips; it can be downloaded at no charge from the company's website. Users can also move to different subsections of the site at any time by simply clicking on a category in the index that appears on the left side of each page.

EXHIBIT 1   The Opening Page

The Transition to General Management

This site, which was developed for the MBA course *General Management: Processes and Action,* has three primary purposes: to provide an overview of **the general manager's job,** to describe some of the critical issues in **managing the transition** from functional positions to general management, and to provide a few "rules of the road" for helping new general managers work more effectively. *More . . .*

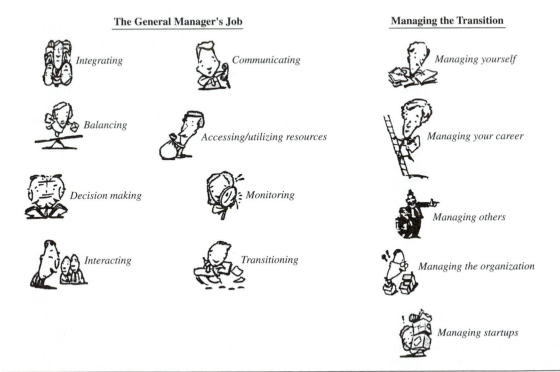

The General Manager's Job

Integrating

Communicating

Balancing

Accessing/utilizing resources

Decision making

Monitoring

Interacting

Transitioning

Managing the Transition

Managing yourself

Managing your career

Managing others

Managing the organization

Managing startups

EXHIBIT 2   An Example of the Indexing Structure

<u>The GM's Job</u>

  <u>Integrating</u>

  <u>Balancing</u>

  <u>Decision Making</u>

  <u>Interacting</u>

  <u>Communicating</u>

  <u>Accessing/Utilizing</u>

   <u>Resources</u>

  <u>Monitoring</u>

  <u>Transitioning</u>

<u>Managing the Transition</u>

  <u>Managing Yourself</u>

  <u>Managing Your Career</u>

  <u>Managing Others</u>

  <u>Managing the</u>
   <u>Organization</u>

  <u>Managing Start-ups</u>

The General Manager's Job
Communicating

Setting Expectations	• <u>Being clear</u> • <u>Mission vs. tasking</u> • <u>Soliciting feedback</u>
Communicating Your Vision	• <u>Articulating objectives</u> • <u>Talking openly</u> • <u>Focusing on communication</u> • <u>Relating strategy</u> • <u>Forming the vision</u>
Difficult Information	• <u>Sensitive information</u> • <u>The importance of candor</u> • <u>Implications for morale</u>
Email	• <u>Useful tool</u> • <u>Email culture</u> • <u>Blessing and curse</u>
External Contacts	• <u>Raising your profile</u> • <u>Having internal house in order</u> • <u>When to be "out there"</u> • <u>Importance of the external role</u> • <u>International expansion</u>

Case 5–4

NO EXCUSES MANAGEMENT

T.J. Rodgers

If everyone in our company made ordinary business decisions in a commonsense way, we would be unstoppable. It turns out that very few people, at our company or anywhere else, make ordinary business decisions in a commonsense way. Most companies don't fail for lack of talent or strategic vision. They fail for lack of execution—the mundane blocking and tackling that the great companies consistently do well and strive to do better.

At Cypress, our management systems track corporate, departmental, and individual performance so regularly and in such detail that no manager, including me, can plausibly claim to be in the

Reprinted by permission of Harvard Business Review. *From "No Excuses Management" by T.J. Rodgers, July/Aug. 1990. Copyright © 1990 by Harvard Business School Publishing.*

dark about critical problems. Our systems give managers the capacity to monitor what's happening at all levels of the organization, to anticipate problems or conflicts, to intervene when appropriate, and to identify best practices—without creating layers of bureaucracy that bog down decisions and sap morale.

Lots of companies espouse a "no surprises" philosophy. At Cypress, "no surprises" is a way of life. We operate in a treacherous and unforgiving business. An integrated circuit is the end result of a thousand multidisciplinary tasks; doing 999 of them right guarantees failure, not success. Last year, we shipped 159 different chips (56 of which were new in 1989) in seven distinct product categories using 26 different process-technology variations. This year, we plan to add another 50 products to our portfolio. Our watchwords are discipline, accountability, and relentless attention to detail—at every level of the organization.

How do we measure success at Cypress? By doing what we say we are going to do. We meet sales projections within a percentage point or two every quarter. We don't go over budget—ever. Our silicon wafer manufacturing plant in Round Rock, Texas, which now accounts for 70 percent of our sales, shipped its first revenue wafer eight months after ground breaking. That performance tied the industry record, which had been set in 1984 by our manufacturing facility in San Jose.

Some who learn about our systems raise the specter of Big Brother or use terms like "electronic treadmill." This is nonsense. Our management systems are not designed to punish or pressure; people put enough pressure on themselves without any help from me. The systems are designed to encourage collective thinking and to force each of us to face reality every day.

At Cypress, we collect information in such detail and share it so widely that the company is virtually transparent. This works against the political infighting and bureaucratic obfuscation that cripple so many organizations. People at Cypress disagree vigorously on many things; in our management meetings, people of any rank are free (and eager) to challenge senior executives. But we disagree over substance and the best ways to make the hardheaded trade-offs that are the essence of management. Nobody gets ahead by using information selectively to win internal battles.

Technological change drives the semiconductor industry, and several of our management systems help us make decisions about technology assessment and product development that are quite specific to our business. But most of our management systems (and certainly the most important ones) address the universal challenges of business—motivating people to perform effectively and allocating resources productively. To succeed over the long term, we have to do at least four things better than our competitors:

1. Hire outstanding people and hold on to them.
2. Encourage everyone in the organization to set challenging goals and meet them.
3. Allocate key resources (people, capital, operating expenses) so as to maximize productivity.
4. Reward people in ways that encourage superior performance rather than demotivate superior performers.

Before I describe several of our most important systems, let me make three points. First, I don't use the word *systems* loosely. Each one involves holding specific meetings, maintaining databases, submitting specific reports, and securing approvals. For example, managers grant raises by using a software package that takes them step by step through the required performance-evaluation procedure, recommends salary increases that they can modify within limits, and alerts them if their final decisions violate company policy. A few of our systems virtually run themselves. We've developed a set of computer applications that automatically shuts down a manufacturing operation if it detects that performance has violated a critical procedure. Dubbed "killer software" by our MIS group, these applications have inspired dramatic performance improvements in our factories, and we are transferring the concept to administrative functions such as order entry and accounts receivable.

Second, we don't confuse systems with bureaucratic planning. In our business (and, I suspect, most businesses), five-year plans, even one-year plans, are obsolete 60 seconds after they are written. So we have plans, but we don't become enslaved by them at an unrealistic level of precision. Our annual marketing forecasts are probably 95 percent accurate, with respect to total revenues for each of our product lines. For groups of products within each line, the plans may be 70 percent accurate. For individual products within groups, it's not that unusual to be off by 100 percent.

At the same time, we are absolute sticklers about meeting quarterly revenue and profit targets. Precisely because we understand that detailed long-term forecasts are so unreliable, we track product shipments and revenues on a *daily* basis, evaluate how they measure up against the plan, and identify what adjustments we have to make to meet the plan in the aggregate. We worry less about meeting product-by-product forecasts than about reacting instantaneously to unforeseen competitive developments.

Finally, top management cannot manage without a thorough mastery of the details of its business. To my mind, no CEO can claim to be in charge of the organization unless within 15 minutes—and I mean this literally—he or she can answer the following questions. What are the company's revenues per employee? How do the figures compare with the competition's? What are the revenue-per-employee figures for each of the company's leading product lines? What explains recent trends in each line? What is the average outgoing quality level in each product line? How many orders are delinquent? Which of the company's top 20 executives are standouts, which are low performers, and why? Which departments could recover from a major competitive shock, and which are vulnerable to change? What are the yields, costs, and cycle times at every manufacturing operation? What explains the company's stock market valuation relative to its competitors'?

By now, I suspect, readers are ready to protest: Isn't this a formula for "micromanagement" by the CEO? Won't top executives get lost in the thicket of details and lose sight of broader strategic

imperatives? Being in command of detail *doesn't* mean interfering where you don't belong. Collecting information, reviewing it regularly, and sharing it widely allows me to practice management by exception in the truest sense. So long as we stick to our systems, this organization virtually runs itself. I intervene only to solve problems and champion urgent projects.

How to Hire Outstanding People

Great people alone don't guarantee corporate success—but no company can succeed without them. Sounds like a truism, right? Yet how many companies are as scientific about hiring as they are about designing new products or perfecting the latest market research techniques? Hiring is one of the most bureaucratic, passive, and arbitrary parts of corporate life. The day we founded Cypress we understood that our greatest proprietary advantage would be to do a better job of hiring than the big companies against which we would compete. We think we've sustained that advantage.

Cypress now employs more than 1,400 people. Our philosophy of hiring (and the system that puts the philosophy into practice) hasn't changed much since we founded the company in 1982. I know the entire organization is implementing the system because no one can bring in a new employee, no matter the rank, without submitting a "hiring book" that documents the entire process and gives comprehensive results of interviews and reference checks. Until we reached 400 employees, I read every one of those books before we made a job offer. I now share that task with six other senior managers. In no more than 15 minutes, with no verbal communication whatsoever, one of us can determine whether or not a hiring manager has followed our procedures. When the system has been followed, we make the hire. When it hasn't, we don't.

Recently, for example, one of our vice presidents submitted a hiring book that violated a cardinal rule not to offer big raises to job candidates. His explanation was familiar: "At my old company, we had to give big raises to convince people to sign on." My response was unequivocal: "We've hired 1,400 people with this system. Is there any reason we can't hire number 1,401 the same way?" The vice president resubmitted the hiring book two weeks later, and it still contained an out-of-policy raise. To emphasize my point, I tracked down a big pair of scissors, cut the book in half, and mailed it back to him. He now does it right the first time.

The hiring book serves another purpose. When people don't work out, it helps us go back and evaluate what went wrong. Hiring the wrong people is a very expensive mistake. We give no raises to about 3 percent of our employees every year, a sign that they are low performers. This company would die if 3 percent of the products we shipped were defective. We strive for 100 percent quality in manufacturing; we have the same goal for hiring. In many cases, when an employee leaves because of poor performance, we send his or her manager the hiring book, ask how we might have spotted the problem earlier, and use the departure as an opportunity to improve our hiring procedures.

Three strongly held beliefs drive our hiring system. First, the only way to hire outstanding people is for managers themselves to find the people they need. Hiring, like most everything else in business, is an acquired skill. The more people you interview, evaluate, and select, the better you get at interviewing, evaluating, and selecting. Thus if 1 of my 12 direct reports (8 vice presidents and 4 subsidiary presidents) is authorized to hire a new manager, or 1 of our 72 managers is authorized to hire an individual contributor, it is up to *that manager,* not the human resource staff, to locate desirable candidates, prescreen them before they enter the formal evaluation process, and monitor the process as it unfolds. We make almost no use of executive recruiters. The human resource department plays a modest role in suggesting candidates but no role in evaluating them. Indeed, prospective employees don't see anyone in human resources until they report to work and fill out their insurance applications.

Most companies—and certainly most big companies—do just the opposite. Managers sit behind their desks and wait for personnel to parade candidates through their office. Of course, personnel is never as motivated as the hiring manager is to fill an open slot. As the hiring schedule falls behind, the manager grows increasingly desperate and makes an offer to the first warm body that meets rudimentary requirements. This approach guarantees that the quality of the company's work force will nicely (and disastrously) mirror the quality of the available labor pool. The organization drifts toward average.

In our system, managers have only themselves to blame if they can't fill open slots. After eight years, we have a good feel for the employment "hit rate." It takes 10 prescreen telephone interviews to find one person good enough to qualify for the formal evaluation process. We make offers to about 25 percent of the people who go through our evaluation, and about 85 percent of the people to whom we make offers accept. If our managers do their math, they quickly understand that quality hiring takes a lot of work. They'll need to make about 100 telephone calls to find two great people. By the way, if they don't fill their open slots by the end of the quarter, they lose the hiring requisition and have to justify the new position again.

Another weakness with most companies' passive approach to hiring is that executives lose touch with the job market. Regular interaction with the job market provides insights on marketplace dynamics. A few years ago, in a memo explaining our hiring system to a new top manager, I wrote down what I had learned as a result of my own job-related calls and interviews. For example, people didn't like Intel's 8 A.M. sign-in policy, which the company has since eliminated. Intel and National Semiconductor were paying 15 percent premiums to layout designers on the night shift while Cypress paid none. But most layout designers cared less about shift differentials than about the kinds of chips they were designing. The market value of plasma engineers ranged from $20,000 a year to $50,000 a year, with little variation of price with quality. The list could have gone on for several pages.

We have a second inviolate principle of hiring: We don't buy employees. This is uncommon in Silicon Valley, but it serves as an excellent screen. Someone who will join Cypress for a few percentage points more in salary or a better dental plan is not the kind of career-oriented person we want. Good people want to be paid fairly, in a way that reflects the organization's success over the long term. They are rarely concerned with earning an excessive amount of money relative to their peers. What drives them is the desire to win.

Until 1986, therefore, we had a very simple policy: A candidate who had received a raise from a previous employer within the last four months came to Cypress without a raise. We now offer an 8 percent prorated increase, but the basic premise holds. We do not bid for great talent; people with great talent come to Cypress because they want to win. Members of our team are rewarded with stock options and the highest percentage raises in the industry. Everyone at the company, from the receptionists to the CEO, participates in an aggressive stock-option program. (We recently repurchased 2 million shares to fund that option program.) As for raises, our formal policy is to survey the competition, calculate the average of the three companies that grant the highest raises and add one-half a percentage point or more to determine the Cypress raise budget.

We have a third principle: The interview and evaluation process should be tough, fair, and expeditious. Quality interviewing is the most important part of the hiring process—and something most managers are terrible at. We've developed several interview techniques to keep these sessions productive. (See the insert "The Science of Interviewing.") Although the interview and evaluation process is demanding, it need not take forever. There's no reason a manager can't prescreen a candidate by telephone, bring him or her in for two rounds of interviews, and make an offer within one week. We're not there yet; we meet the one-week target about 75 percent of the time. We also expect the hiring manager to be in *daily* contact with the candidate as the process unfolds.

Set Goals—Then Measure and Meet Them

All of Cypress's 1,400 employees have goals, which, in theory, makes them no different from employees at most other companies. What does make our people different is that every week they set their own goals, commit to achieving them by a specific date, enter them into a database, and report whether or not they completed prior goals. Cypress's computerized goal system is an important part of our managerial infrastructure. It is a detailed guide to the future and an objective record of the past. In any given week, some 6,000 goals in the database come due. Our ability to meet those goals ultimately determines our success or failure.

Most of the work in our company is organized by project rather than along strict functional lines. Members of a project team may be (and usually are) from different parts of the organization. Project managers need not be (and often aren't) the highest ranking member of the group. Likewise, the goal system is organized by project and function. In Monday project meetings, employees set short-term goals and rank them in priority order. Short-term goals take from one to six weeks to complete, and different employees have different numbers of goals. At the beginning of a typical week, for example, a member of our production-control staff initiated seven new goals in connection with three different projects. He said he would, among other things, report on progress with certain minicomputer problems (two weeks), monitor and report on quality rejection rates for certain products (three weeks), update killer software for the assembly department (two weeks), and assist a marketing executive with a forecasting software enhancement (four weeks).

On Monday night, the project goals are fed back into a central computer. On Tuesday mornings, functional managers receive a printout of their direct reports' new and pending project goals. These printouts are the basis of Tuesday afternoon meetings in which managers work with their people to anticipate overload and conflicting goals, sort out priorities, organize work, and make mutual commitments about what's going to get done. This is a critical step. The failure mode in our company (and I suspect in most growing companies) is that people overcommit themselves rather than establish unchallenging goals. By 5 P.M. Tuesday, the revised schedule is fed back into the central database.

This "two pass" system generates the work program that coordinates the mostly self-imposed

The Science of Interviewing

You can't hire quality people without a systematic approach to interviewing. Four basic rules guide our interview and evaluation process.

1. *Use the big guns.* If you want job prospects to know that you are serious, high-ranking executives should take the time to get involved in the interview process. At Cypress, all candidates for exempt positions, whether or not they are senior enough to report to vice presidents, interview with two vice presidents. I interview all candidates who would report to vice presidents as well as many important individual contributors who report to managers. This is the technique Jerry Sanders used on me when I was considering joining Advanced Micro Devices. The first day I walked in the door, the receptionist in a building of 2,000 people smiled and said, "Oh yes, Dr. Rodgers, Jerry is waiting for you." She took me right upstairs—no waiting in the lobby—and our session began. That's the way to communicate to job prospects how valuable they are.

2. *Make interviews tough and technically demanding—even for people you know you want.* We are a hard-charging company in a tough business and have a no-nonsense way of communicating. People should know that before they sign on. At the beginning of the evaluation process, candidates receive a form that lists the technical skills the position requires, with whom they'll be interviewing, and the questions they will be asked. This focuses the interviews and alerts the candidates to how rigorous the sessions will be.

After several "technical" interviews and the interviews with two vice presidents, candidates go through what we call the "pack of wolves" session. The applicant sits in a conference room where senior technical people pose difficult questions that the candidate does not know in advance. Some of the questions are virtually impossible to answer, and they come in rapid succession. When the candidate makes a mistake, the interviewers point it out and give the correct answer. The tone of this session is aggressive but not abusive. It is an excellent way to weed out qualified managers and engineers who can't take the pressures of our business.

3. *Interviews should lead to detailed assessments of strengths and weaknesses, not vague impressions.* Our interview evaluation forms include numerical scores (on a scale of zero to five) that mirror the technical qualifications on the requisition. Our people are tough graders. I also insist that the hiring vice president write an interview strategy before my session with a managerial candidate. That strategy highlights the specific strengths and weaknesses of the candidate, particular concerns he or she has expressed about the job or the company, and other critical issues. I'm not reluctant to share the numerical evaluations with a candidate, especially one who has been assessed as weak in a particular area. This candid feedback is usually a positive experience. Good people know their weaknesses and are eager to improve them.

4. *Check for cultural fit.* Most companies claim to do this, but few are very systematic. We probe work attitudes and career goals through a questionnaire that requires brief but direct answers to open-ended questions. The questionnaire forces candidates to be as specific as possible about hard-to-quantify issues that are addressed only obliquely, if at all, in most evaluation processes. Among the questions are: How is the morale in your company or department? Why? What do you expect Cypress has to offer you in the way of a work environment that your employer doesn't offer? What would your boss say is your best attribute? What would the "needs improvement" section of your performance review address? Can you describe your personal experience with a difficult boss, peer, or subordinate?

activities of every Cypress employee. It allows the organization to be project driven, which helps us emphasize speed and agility, as well as functionally accurate, which works against burnout and failure to execute. On Wednesday morning, our eight vice presidents receive goal printouts for their people and the people below them—another conflict-resolution mechanism.

In the early days of the company, until we hit about 100 employees, I read every employee's goals every week. I knew what every person in the company was doing on a week-to-week basis. That's not the role of the CEO in a company with more than 1,400 people, so my approach to the goal system has changed. Today my job is to anticipate problems, largely by sorting through the goal system looking for patterns. I use the system as a kind of organizational speedometer that not only tells me how fast we're traveling but also helps explain what's holding us back.

On Wednesday afternoons at my weekly staff meeting, I review various database reports with my vice presidents. We talk about what's going wrong and how to help managers who are running into problems. The following reports typically serve as the basis for discussion: progress with goals on critical projects; percentage of delinquent goals sorted by managers (their goals plus those of their subordinates); percentage of delinquent goals sorted by vice president (the percentage of pending goals that are delinquent for all people reporting up the chain of command to each vice president); all employees without goals (something I do not tolerate); all goals five or more weeks delinquent; and all employees with two or more delinquent goals, sorted by manager.

As we've refined the goal system and used it more extensively, I've developed some general principles. First, people are going to have goals they don't achieve on time; the key is to sense when a vice president or a manager is losing control of the operation. My rule of thumb is that vice presidents should not have delinquency rates above 20 percent, and managers should not let more than 30 percent of their goals become delinquent. When managers do have a delinquency problem, I usually intervene with a short note: "Your delinquency rate is running at 35 percent, what can I do to help?" I often get back requests for specific assistance. Part of my role is to hold people accountable. But it is also to identify problems before they become crises and to provide help in getting them fixed.

Second, people need positive feedback. Every month we issue a Completed Goal Report for every person in the company. The report lists all goals completed over the past four weeks as well as those that have yet to come due.

The completed goal report is also a valuable tool for performance evaluation. Like most companies, we use annual reviews to set salary increases. The trouble with annual reviews is that managers succumb to the "proximity effect." An employee who performs outstandingly for the first 10 months of the year but has a subpar 2 months just before the review is more likely to get a poor evaluation than is a colleague who had a lousy 10 months but did a great job in the 2 months just before the evaluation. At Cypress, the completed goal report triggers a performance minireview; every month managers read through their people's printouts and prepare brief, factual evaluations. At year-end, managers have a dozen such objective reviews to refresh their memories and fight the proximity effect.

It's important to note that the goal system does not require big investments in computer hardware and software. Indeed, we have no equipment dedicated exclusively to the goal system. We use personal computers and a DEC minicomputer that also handles the company's administrative tasks. The software is Lotus 1-2-3 and Paradox—two of the most common microcomputer applications. Much of the system still runs on "sneakernet"—people pass disks back and forth rather than use networking systems, although we are in the process of networking the entire company more effectively.

Indeed, I developed the goal system long before personal computers existed. It has its roots in management-by-objectives techniques I learned in the mid-1970s at American Microsystems (AMI), where I ran the random access memory (RAM) group.[1] Back then my hardware was a blackboard, and my software was chalk. In a typical year, we

---

[1] *Several of Cypress's systems are enhancements of best practices among our competitors or companies with which our executives have been affiliated. For example, the goal system traces its origins to management-by-objectives techniques I learned from former AMI chief executive Glenn Penisten, who brought them over from Texas Instruments. Our expense-control system draws on techniques practiced at Mostek.*

Individual Monthly Goal Report

Workweek	Date	Manager	Dept.	Project	Begin	End	Delinquent	Status	Who	Goal
8945	11/08/89	RF	310	OPLN	35	45		C	GB	DEFINE DIE KIT REQUEST QUEUE TIME; REQUEST SCREEN [DEV/PKG/GRADE]
8945	11/08/89	RF	310	OPLN	38	45		C	GB	KILLER FOR PURCHASING: SHUTDOWN PURCHASING IF RECEIPTS LATER THAN COMMIT
8945	11/08/89	RF	310	OPLN	40	44	45	C	GB	TURN ON KILLER SOFTWARE FOR "IQA"
8945	11/08/89	RF	310	OPLN	41	45		C	GB	ACTION REQUEST #3561: SCHEDULE FOR REMOTE ORDER ENTRY
8945	11/08/89	RF	310	OPLN	44	45		C	GB	IGNORE 7C34x DEVICES IN THE KILLER FOR SORT
8945	11/08/89	RF	310	OPLN	44	45		C	GB	PRINTOUT OF 3Q89 SHIPS FOR RF
8945	11/08/89	RF	310	OPLN	44	45		C	GB	PUBLISH WEEKLY MIS SUMMARY
8945	11/08/89	RF	310	OPLN	44	45		C	GB	VERIFY THAT FAB 2 SHIPREVIEW DATA IS UPDATED (NOT SINCE WW33)
8945	11/08/89	RF	310	OREN	44	45		C	GB	TRAIN MARKETING ON ED1 FORMS AND GETTING CUSTOMERS INTO SYSTEM

This excerpt lists all the goals one production-control staffer completed in workweek 45.
The entire report consisted of 49 completed and pending goals.

would develop as many as 10 new chips, and tracking each project became a nightmare. So I got a blackboard, wrote down everything that had to be done before each product could ship, and attached names and due dates to each task. My update routine was an eraser.

After I left for Advanced Micro Devices (AMD), where I was responsible for RAM manufacturing as well as design, it became a bit harder to keep score. So I covered my walls with blackboards, used masking tape to divide them into project panels, and transported the system from AMI. Once a week, my assistant would wheel in an electric typewriter, record the schedule, and send it out to the troops. If people in my organization wanted to know where things stood, all they had to do was come into my office and look at the blackboards.

The Cypress system is just an enhanced, electronic version of what I've been doing for 15 years. The computer record on each goal includes a description of the task, when the goal was set, when it is due, what priority it is, who has agreed to complete it, to what manager that person reports, and to what vice president the manager reports. We are now enhancing the system by recording long-term goals (which we call "strategic" goals) and all quality-oriented goals. Of course, recording that information means

I can sort by each of those fields and create special-exception reports. With a few keystrokes, I can check on the performance of any one of my vice presidents, see how a manager is relating to subordinates, or check on the progress of a particular project.

No one can accuse me of not "knowing the details" of my business. Yet I don't have to intervene where I don't belong or try to be in a hundred places at once. The goal system provides warnings when something goes wrong and offers instant access to data in any area that I am concerned about. I'm a big advocate of management by walking around, and I regularly block out time on my calendar to visit our facilities. The goal system lets me practice MBWA all the more effectively. By sorting through the database and following up with telephone calls, I can get up to speed on an operation before I arrive.

I don't want to give the impression that the goal system is strictly a support mechanism. It does give me the ammunition I need to cut through bureaucratic obfuscation. My access to the details means vice presidents and managers know they can't snow me. For example, we recently shafted a valued customer by delivering an emergency shipment of parts one day late. (I learned about the problem because every officer at Cypress is "godfather" to one strategic customer and I happened to be godfather to this customer.) I spent 15 minutes at my computer screen reviewing relevant goal reports and data from a few other systems. With a follow-up telephone call or two, I discovered what went wrong. Shipping was overloaded on the day the parts were scheduled to go out; the parts were not marked as a "JIT order," so they weren't shipped immediately. By the time the department shipped the parts, they were a day late. With another call, I learned that certain people in marketing did not understand the shipping department's priority system. I called the relevant people into my office and asked them to change our procedures so that the problem would never happen again.

Now think what might have happened without the goal system. After I learned about the problem, I would have called in the marketing manager, who would have made plausible excuses, produced nice-looking graphs showing a 99 percent on-time delivery performance—and blamed the jerks in shipping. Then I'd have called shipping, a manager there would have complained about having been overloaded, about how marketing always expects miracles, and the political infighting would have been hot and heavy. I would have been virtually powerless to cut through to the truth.

People at Cypress know I don't tolerate bureaucratic politics—it's one of the items on a very short list of what can get you fired. They also know I have the ability to peer down into the bowels of the organization, drag up relevant data, make a few telephone calls, and find out what really happened in any situation. The knowledge that I can call on so much detail so easily *means I seldom have to.* No vice president of manager wants to be in the awkward position where the CEO knows more about a situation than he or she does.

Allocate Resources for Maximum Productivity

Middle managers can be an organization's most enduring strength. They are more aware of the company's day-to-day business realities than any other group, and they are earnest, committed, and creative. Middle managers can also cause companies to grow fat and uncompetitive, not because they don't do their jobs, but because they think their jobs are the most important in the world and thus lose sight of the broader corporate imperative. I call this phenomenon middle management myopia. In organizations that suffer from this disease (and it afflicts the majority of large companies), middle managers clamor for resources while top managers are chartered to hold the line. Usually, top managers are forced to cave in because middle managers can call on so much more information and functional expertise. How can a senior executive turn down a request for resources (people, equipment, expenses) when a well-respected middle manager makes a plausible argument that the department will unravel without them—probably taking the company with it?

These "gun-to-the-head" stories are a staple of corporate life. If you don't think any good middle manager can come up with several of them, you are fooling yourself. Consider just two:

- From a financial manager: "We have $40 million of excess receivables on which we pay $140,000 of interest every year. I could get the receivables down to $20 million, but I need another clerk to do it. The basic problem is paperwork; sometimes our invoices don't match our customers' records, and we have to work the phones to get them to agree to pay. I know I told you seven clerks was enough. But if we hire one more at $30,000 a year, we can cut the uncollected receivables in half, saving us $70,000. It's foolish not to make the hire."
- From the engineering manager: "We generate annual revenues of $20 million with this particular chip. Our final-test yield is 90 percent, which means we're throwing away $2 million a year. If you let me hire two more engineers (they will cost us less than $100,000 a year combined), we can get yields up to 94 percent, saving $400,000—a four-month payback. It's foolish not to make the hires."

The moment senior executives buy into the tunnel vision of their middle managers, they've lost control of the company. If that happens, it's *not* the middle managers' fault; they're simply doing their jobs as they understand them. Our resource-allocation systems are designed to prevent middle management myopia by forcing collective thinking at all levels. Every quarter, based on our revenue projections, we establish total corporate allowances for new hires, capital investment, and operating expenses. We then allocate this overall target by departments and force critical trade-off decisions down to the middle management level. We get these people into the same room at the same time, with a computer model that allows us to conduct resource negotiations online, and cut the deals that would otherwise lead to memo wars and special pleading.

Our resource-allocation systems also address a second source of waste and inefficiency: the false confidence created by prosperity. The seeds of business failure are sown in good times, not bad. Economic reversals have a wonderful way of concentrating minds and encouraging groups to overcome long-standing differences. During times of prosperity, however, danger lurks everywhere. Growth masks waste, extravagance, and inefficiency. The moment growth slows, the accumulated sins of the past are revealed all the way to the bottom line.

At Cypress, our annual revenues have grown 40 percent or more per year since we founded the company in 1982. We're proud of that record, but we're even more proud of our consistent quarter-to-quarter profitability. Even in 1986, when the semiconductor industry was in the midst of a crippling downturn, we maintained industry-leading operating margins of 20 percent. And we did it on revenues of only $50 million.

This was no accident. The performance measures that drive the company adjust our thinking to control the prosperity illusion. Sure we want aggressive revenue growth. But we *demand* ever-increasing revenue per employee, ever-higher capital productivity (revenue dollars per dollar of undepreciated fixed assets), and ever-lower expense ratios. And we constantly check our performance against the best of our competition. The graphs in "Tracking Performance at Cypress" review our record on these measures.

Our system for controlling head count is one of the three most important systems we have at Cypress. Here's how it works. At the beginning of every quarter, we hold a head-count meeting for the entire company. Our eight vice presidents attend the meeting along with middle managers. Together we review the last quarter's total revenue, total head count, and revenue per employee. We then use forecast revenues to determine the allowable head count at the end of the quarter and thus the total number of requisitions we can afford to open in the new quarter. There are two things to keep in mind. First, we are almost always within 1 percent or 2 percent of forecast revenue—this is not a hypothetical exercise. Second, our target head count is based on continual improvement in revenue per employee. We expect this critical productivity measure to improve every quarter or, in difficult economic times, to hold the line.[2]

Thus, quickly and directly, everyone in the room (which means virtually everyone in the company with hiring authority) understands how many new employees will join Cypress over the next three months. This is not a negotiable figure. The negotiations start once we total up the vice presidents' head-count requests and start adjusting them to meet the new total.

The power of our system is that it presents the real trade-offs to everyone at the same time. Everyone in the room understands that we are playing a zero-sum game. A vice president who insists on all his or her requisitions understands (as does everyone else) that these slots come at the expense of other requests. Such stark trade-offs create incentives for everyone else to think creatively about solving that vice president's problems without hiring more people. In other words, I enlist many allies in my effort to hold the line on resources. Moreover, vice presidents who can't make the number

---

[2]*It's not always possible to improve corporate revenue per employee. When our Round Rock fab went on line, corporate productivity "dropped" until the plant began volume shipments. But we still insisted on continual improvement from the rest of the company, and we adjusted our quarterly figures to measure it.*

Tracking Performance at Cypress

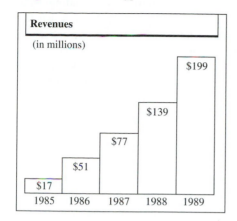

Revenues
(in millions)

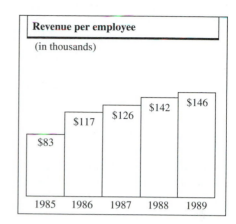

Revenue per employee
(in thousands)

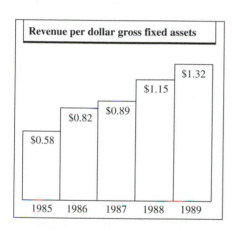

Revenue per dollar gross fixed assets

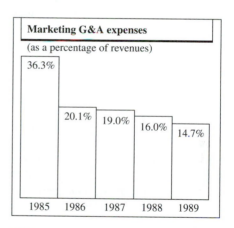

Marketing G&A expenses
(as a percentage of revenues)

of hires they want don't feel arbitrarily denied. Even if they're unhappy, they understand the logic behind the final decisions.

The negotiations are conducted in great detail—they're not for the faint of heart. Every department has a microperformance index that divides some useful measure of output by head count. These indexes, which we flash on the screen for everyone to see, become the basis of the trade-offs between departments. Let's say shipping and receiving has requested an additional clerk. We flash a graph that tracks the department's productivity index—line items shipped per week per clerk—and ask the

manager and vice president to justify the request. Or say the vice president of manufacturing needs 10 more operators in our San Jose fab. The group reviews weekly wafer output per employee per week, builds in further progress on this performance index, and weighs the vice president's request accordingly. In each negotiation, the group knows the number of requisitions we must eliminate to meet the corporate target, the productivity trends for each department making requests, and which departments won't be able to hire new people if other departments make all the hires they've requested.

Our system for allocating capital works much the same way. We track total revenues as a function of undepreciated capital, insist on continual improvement in the macroindex, approve overall corporate targets on this basis, and use the targets to drive capital spending down through the departments. In our capital-intensive business, having just enough capital just in time is even more important than controlling head count.

Our expense-control system goes one step farther. The CEO of any start-up company signs every purchase order for the first few years. This is a deadly efficient way to control spending. But there comes a time (at about $40 million of annual revenues for a semiconductor company) when the CEO faces a moment of truth: He or she can spend every waking minute signing purchase orders or develop a new approach. This is where the extravagance usually begins or where a new purchasing bureaucracy chokes off necessary expenditures and creates frustration throughout the company.

We've developed a system that gives senior management ironclad control of spending and that requires no more than five working days for a purchase order to be approved or sent back to the requester for cause. As with head count and capital, allowable expenses in a given quarter start from the top line. We project revenues, insist on improvement in the corporate expense-to-revenue ratio, and then allocate allowable purchases by function and department through real-time negotiation and adjustment.

Then comes a second critical step. We divide each manager's quarterly expenses by 13 and create a weekly budget that governs spending for the quarter. Of course, some spending comes in clumps; a manager may need to make one purchase that exceeds the weekly budget. That's allowed—so long as the manager has accrued enough "credit" in previous weeks so that the big purchase does not bump overall spending for the quarter off track.

This system is rigorous. It also works. If senior management controls the quarterly spending meter, and the meter determines how fast money flows into the corporate pipeline each week, we can't be surprised by what comes out at the end of 13 weeks.

Controlling the meter does not mean I abdicate my role in monitoring expenses. With few "emergency P.O." exceptions, the spending window at Cypress is open for two hours a week. Every Thursday from 8 A.M. to 10 A.M. we hold a purchase-order commit meeting with the vice presidents. They summarize the purchase orders that need my approval that week; I look for questionable expenditures and probe for extravagance. Even more important, the weekly meetings become a way of transferring best practices on spending throughout the organization. I invariably come out of them full of ideas about cost reduction that I immediately share with people who can benefit from them.

A visitor unfamiliar with our system could sit in on a purchase-order commit meeting and conclude that the CEO of this $200 million company still signs every purchase order above the petty cash limit. That visitor would be correct in the literal sense but dead wrong about how the system really works. Indeed, our approach to expense control has cascaded down through all four levels of the company, to a point where I don't worry about missing a purchase-order commit meeting. (I miss one out of three.) Vice presidents routinely take their weekly expense budgets and divide them appropriately among their managers to guide weekly budgets. In turn, managers take their weekly expenses and divide them appropriately among their subordinates, who take their weekly budgets and divide them among their contributors.

Today our expense-control system virtually runs itself. It drives us every week of every month of every quarter. It's no accident we have never exceeded a quarterly budget by more than 1 percent.

Take the Mystery Out of Performance Appraisal

Managers shouldn't expect outstanding performance unless they're prepared to reward outstanding performers. Yet evaluation and reward systems remain an organizational black hole for three reasons.

First, managers aren't very scientific about rating their people. They may be able to identify the real stars and the worst laggards, but the vast majority of people (who must still be ranked) get lost somewhere in the middle. Second, even it they evaluate people correctly, managers like to spread raises around evenly to keep the troops happy. This is a deadly policy that saps the morale of standouts who deserve more and sends the wrong signal to weak performers. Third, managers are totally incapable of distinguishing between "merit" and "equity" when awarding increases. Merit refers to that portion of a raise awarded for the quality of past performance. Equity refers to adjustments in that raise to more closely align salaries of equally ranked peers. Merit and equity both have a place in the incentive mix, but confusing the two makes for mushy logic, counterproductive results, and dissatisfied people.

Cypress is not immune to these problems; I'd say a third of our vice presidents still don't have a good feel for how to review performance and award raises. But I'm not too concerned about that.

Our focal-review system, one of the most efficient systems we've ever developed, controls the three big problems I just identified. Our managers follow the system because the only way to grant raises in the company is to use the series of computer templates that walks managers through a series of review-process steps and alerts them to violations against company policy.

As with all our resource-allocation systems, the focal-review system starts with policies at the top and forces middle management decisions to be consistent with that thinking. Senior management and the board of directors review our annual revenue forecasts, survey compensation trends among our competitors, and settle on a total corporate allowance for raises. The "raise budget" is not negotiable, and it drives raises throughout the company. If the corporate budget is 8 percent, then every department must meet a weighted-average salary increase of 8 percent. It's up to managers to distribute the 8 percent pool, which is where the focal-review system comes in.

How Cypress Awards Raises

| Employee | Rank | Merit Increase | | Current Salary | Equity Increase | | | Final Raise | New Salary |
		cREC%	iREC%		cEQ$	cAEQ%	iAEQ%		
BB	1	10.6%	12.0%	$53,400	$3,700	0.7%	0.7%	12.7%	$60,200
DD	2	9.7	10.4	59,800	(5,500)	−0.9	−0.9	9.5	62,859
FF	3	8.8	9.3	49,300	3,600	0.7	0.7	10.0	54,245
EE	4	7.9	8.1	50,300	100	0.0	0.0	8.1	54,383
CC	5	7.1	7.1	42,800	5,600	1.3	1.3	8.4	46,398
AA	6	6.2	6.9	53,400	(8,700)	−1.6	−1.6	5.3	56,217
GG	7	5.3	5.0	42,100	1,200	0.3	0.3	5.3	44,323
HH	8	4.4	3.0	41,100	0.00	0.0	0.0	3.0	42,335
Quality Checks		**Wt'd Avg:** 8.0%		$49,025				8.0%	$52,620

cREC% = Computer recommends   **iREC%** = Leader awards   **cEQ$** = Equity differential   **cAEQ%** = Computer recommends   **iAEQ%** = Leader recommends

This condensed report shows how a focal-group leader awards raises among eight SRAM product engineers. The ranking committee rated engineer DD higher than FF, so the group leader awarded DD a larger merit increase. However, the computer's equity analysis showed that DD was overpaid by $5,500 relative to his peers, while FF was underpaid by $3,600. As a result of equity adjustments, DD received a lower raise than FF.

What to Do When a Valued Employee Quits

February 24, 1988

TO: Vice Presidents and Managers
FROM: T.J. Rodgers

I have not been called on to save a valued employee for some time. Last week, I became involved in two such situations—both were successful—but my job was made more difficult because we did not follow some basic rules.

I realized I have never formally stated our policy on resignations. Here it is:

1. *React immediately.* That means within five minutes. Nothing takes priority over working with a valued employee who has resigned. Delays such as "I'll talk to you after our staff meeting" are unacceptable. Cancel the next activity you have scheduled.

This demonstrates to the employee that he or she takes precedence over daily activities. It also gives you the best chance of changing the employee's mind before he or she makes an irreversible decision.

2. *Keep the resignation quiet.* This is important for both parties. If other employees don't know about the resignation, the employee does not face the embarrassment of publicly changing his or her mind. The company also gets more latitude. In one recent case, the resignation was disclosed. After I convinced the employee to stay, there were multiple rumors (all untrue) that we had "bought back" the employee. Cypress does not negotiate the salaries of employees who have resigned. We may communicate information about upcoming raises and evergreen stock options if that information is available at the time.

3. *Tell your boss immediately and me within an hour.* There is no excuse for not informing me (and everyone in the chain of command between the individual and me) as soon as a resignation occurs. I expect instantaneous communication and can be interrupted in meetings, called out of meetings in outside locations, or called at home. (I am listed in the telephone directory.)

4. *Listen carefully to the employee.* Once a resignation has occurred and the proper people know, the employee's manager and vice president should sit down with the employee and listen carefully to the reasons behind the resignation. Any attempt to retain the employee will be severely impaired unless management listens to *exactly* what the employee says and accepts it. That message should then be transmitted up through the chain of command without any changes, even if it is unflattering to the manager involved.

You should also make an exact determination of the employee's options at the other company. Is he or she looking at a better job, more money, slower pace, faster pace, or fundamental career change? These issues will obviously be imperative in constructing an argument to change the employee's mind.

5. *Construct your arguments.* Once you've gathered accurate data, sit down with your vice president and put together a plan to convince the employee to stay. The only possibly effective argument is one that validly claims the employee's best interests are served by staying at Cypress. Once you and the vice president have formulated your employee-retention arguments, you may want me to become involved to help set the overall strategy. This strategy should be defined and refined on the very same day the employee resigns.

Typically, an employee will have quit because of a "push" of some sort involving long-standing frustration at Cypress and a "pull" from another company where the grass looks greener. In some cases, realism will dictate that we can't keep the employee. Ninety percent of the time, however, we can make a good argument that it is in the employee's best interest to stay at Cypress.

6. *Use all the horsepower at your disposal to win.* With a carefully constructed strategy, we can proceed to win back the employee. Think of what we've already done on day one. The employee got the message that quitting was a big deal because of our rapid reaction to the resignations. We reminded the employee that the company was truly interested in him or her because we took as long as needed *to listen* to what was wrong.

On the second day, the employee should get the message that quitting was a mistake, that the company knows it was a mistake, and that we will single-mindedly try to rectify that mistake. Cypress will accept only two answers to our proposal to stay: yes, or we'll talk about it some more.

On the second or third day, as we present our position, the employee should continue to understand that this is not business as usual. We will interrupt our schedules. If appropriate, we may meet over meals during off hours. If the employee's spouse is a major factor in the resignation, the spouse should be involved in the discussions. Bring in any level of management required to get the job done. If it takes the president (and it does in half the cases), then I have nothing more important to do than to sit down with the employee. Many middle managers mistakenly assume that I am too busy to interrupt my schedule to keep a good person in the company. Nothing is further from the truth.

7. *Solve the employee's problems.* If we correct the problems that caused the employee to start looking around, we will succeed more than 80 percent of the time in changing the employee's mind. Most often, resigning employees like Cypress, its benefits, and the people with whom they work. They usually, however, do not like some of the particulars of their jobs or their direct supervisors. Their resolve to leave is further strengthened because they have found jobs (typically) at companies that are poor seconds to Cypress but that appear to offer some relative benefits. By alleviating the root problem at Cypress, and by stressing the fundamental differences between us and the other company, we can usually persuade the employee to stay.

8. *Wipe out the competitor.* Two objectives are important here: to shut down them competitor so firmly that it will conduct no further negotiations with our employee, and to shut down the competitor in such a manner that it believes it has wasted its time trying to hire away from Cypress. The employee should call the competition and turn down the offer and, in doing so, make it clear that he or she does not want counteroffers and continuing negotiations.

A model response goes something like this: "There was no counteroffer, I just want to stay at Cypress. I think my long-term interests are served by being here. The same hour that I told my boss I was thinking about leaving, I had meetings with my boss, the vice president, and T.J. Rodgers. When they made the comparisons between my career at Cypress and at your company, it was clear that I made a mistake in thinking about leaving. I really do not want to take any time to come over to talk to you; my mind is made up. It would not be helpful to change your offer monetarily; I am fairly paid and have a good stock-option package. Money is not the issue."

9. *Prevent the next problem.* The last step in the process is really the first step: sit down, think about your people, try to anticipate where you might have a problem in the future, and fix it before it starts.

There are four stages to the process. Everyone at Cypress is part of a "focal group" (there are 132 groups in the company) composed of peers with comparable responsibilities. For example, all vice presidents are in one focal group, all weekend night-shift assembly operators are in another, all RAM circuit designers are in a third. The ranking committee for each focal group includes the members' supervisors as well as managers from other parts of the company in a position to judge each member's performance and service. The ranking committee for our shipping clerks might include representatives from sales or manufacturing. The ranking committee for a group of circuit designers might include representatives from marketing or manufacturing. Before evaluations take place, we post rosters of focal groups and ranking committees to allow people to question their assignments.

Much of the discussion in the ranking committee centers on the monthly reviews stemming from the goal system. This controls the proximity effect I've already discussed and provides an objective record of performance based on goals employees have set for themselves.

The ranking procedure helps control a second problem that undermines so many performance reviews; I call it the mayonnaise effect. Suppose you're running a food company that wants to enter the mayonnaise market. You can make your mayonnaise with olive oil, sunflower oil, or corn oil. You can use vinegar, lemon, both, or neither. You can emulsify with egg yolks, dry eggs, or whole eggs. You can use lots of salt or not much salt. If you put 10 different mayonnaise formulas on a table and ask people to rate each one, chances are pretty good they'll make some big errors. They'll probably recall their absolute favorites and the recipes that made them sick. But what about all the recipes in the middle? Are you confident your tasters will correctly rank formulas three through seven—none of which made a dramatic impression, but each of which has its unique qualities?

This same problem afflicts performance appraisal. It's not too hard to identify the two outstanding performers and the two laggards in a group of 10 employees. But to the people in the middle, there's a big difference between being ranked fourth and seventh—and managers can badly muff these rankings. That's why our system forces comparisons between pairs that leave little room for error. Consider a 10-person focal group with members A through J. The ranking committee's job is to review every possible two-employee comparison and determine who was the superior performer for the year: Has A performed better than B? Has A performed better than C? Has B performed better than C? And so on. The software records the outcome of each comparison and develops relative rankings as the basis for merit increases. No confusion, no mistakes, no mayonnaise effect.

These rankings become the basis of merit increases decided by the focal-group leader, the senior member of the ranking committee. (The focal-group leader alone is chartered to divide up

the raise budget once the rankings are completed.) And merit means merit. The software reviews the ranking committee's individual judgments and recommends appropriate merit increases. At this point in the process, no salaries have been disclosed—everything is expressed in percentages. The computer uses a pure and uncomplicated process to assign a certain percentage raise for a certain ranking. The leader can make adjustments to these recommendations, but the software checks to make sure the final numbers comply with several principles. There are 20 quality checks in all, including these:

- Monotonic distribution. Any group member ranked higher than another must receive a higher merit raise. This check prevents managers from taking money away from a top performer who happens to be highly paid and giving it to a weak performer.

- Forced differentiation. There must be a minimum spread (last year it was 8 percent) between the largest and smallest raises in the group. This check prevents the most common managerial cop-out, spreading raises evenly throughout the group.

- Reasonable adjustments. Although leaders are free to adjust the computer-generated recommendations, there are limits. This check works against clustering the majority of increases around one figure.

- Budgets. The average raise for the group cannot exceed the corporate target. This check emphasizes the point that giving big raises to people who deserve low raises hurts the entire group.

Only after they have awarded percentage increases based strictly on merit can managers make adjustments for salary inequities created by personal circumstances and historical accidents. Again, the software plays a central role. For each and every focal group, it generates a simple graph that compares the salaries of each group member (on the vertical axis) with merit rankings (on the horizontal axis). The graph also displays a trend line that describes the desired salary distribution for the department. We operate according to the general principle that the best performer in a department should earn at least 50 percent more than the worst performer in that department. Managers adjust raises up or down to move salaries closer to the trend line. Here too the system checks for mistakes and makes sure the overall increase stays within budget.

The power of our focal-review system is its simplicity. An easy-to-use software application (it runs on Lotus 1-2-3) rigorously applies a set of principles without usurping managerial discretion. It guides managers on a step-by-step journey through the evaluation and reward process, alerts them instantaneously when their decisions violate company policy, and guarantees that they stay within budget. The system also creates a paper trail that managers can use to explain to employees how raises were determined. We can tell each of our people how the ranking committee evaluated his or her performance ("You rated above average but not in the top 10 percent"), the percentage merit increase awarded by the focal-group leader, and how the manager adjusted the merit increase for equity. Most people will accept an outcome they are unhappy with so long as they understand the logic behind it.

As for senior management, the system becomes yet another tool for management by exception. In a single, effective two-hour meeting, I review the raise of every employee at Cypress by reviewing the printouts the system generates. I can compare an individual's raise with those granted to his or her peers, look at raise distributions in one group versus those in another, or compare this year's raises for an individual or group with raises from the last two years. Of course, I can also check to make sure the system has been followed. Any manager who submits a printout that violates our policy gets it back with a note to do it right—which means very few managers ever submit faulty printouts. The system is simple, effective, and consistent.

How Big Is Too Big?

It's natural to ask whether the systems I've described can work in companies much bigger than Cypress. I don't know. But I do know that if they

can't, then these companies are probably unmanageable. We respect the limitations of size. I am absolutely convinced that any small group of smart, dedicated, hard-working professionals can beat any large group of average professionals with superior resources. There comes a point in any organization's evolution when adding more people, more buildings, and more equipment reduces overall productivity.

I believe that point is somewhere in the neighborhood of $100 million in annual revenues for a semiconductor company. Which is why Cypress today is not one company with total revenues of $200 million but five distinct companies linked by a common strategy, vision, and management systems. We have chosen to fund our growth with a venture-capital model, seeding new ventures under the Cypress umbrella.

Our first start-up, Cypress Semiconductor (Texas), was the Round Rock wafer fab. Aspen Semiconductor was founded in 1987 to design and develop new categories of logic chips. Multichip Technology was founded in 1988 to combine multiple chips into memory subsystems. Ross Technology, our fourth new company, has delivered the industry's highest performance RISC microprocessor since it was formed in 1988.

These subsidiaries have true autonomy. But I do expect two major commitments. A subsidiary must use the management systems that have served Cypress so well. It must also send high-level managers (almost always the president) to a few key corporate meetings in which we track and coordinate activities across the subsidiaries.

We intend Cypress to be a billion-dollar enterprise before too long—without the waste, bureaucracy, and complacency that afflict so many large organizations. We'll achieve that goal by seeding new start-ups, dividing down successful businesses as they get too big to manage tightly, continuing to refine our management systems, and driving them down through our organization and its subsidiaries.

Author's note: I wish to acknowledge the role of MIS director Rick Foreman and his team in the design and implementation of our management systems.

Case 5–5

HARVARD BUSINESS SCHOOL PUBLISHING

In spring 1996, Linda Doyle was finishing her second year as president and CEO of the Harvard Business School Publishing Corporation (HBSP), a separate, wholly owned, nonprofit subsidiary of Harvard University. HBSP had been formed in 1992 from several distinct product groups; they included the *Harvard Business Review,* Harvard Business School Press, Harvard Business School Video, and Cases and Reprints. A primary goal of the consolidation was to improve editorial synergy among the groups, while better leveraging the HBS brand. After an early period of turmoil, HBSP had made considerable progress on these goals under Doyle's leadership.

Now, however, Doyle faced a dilemma. In recent months, she had introduced a centralized marketing organization, but the precise division of authority remained unclear. The problem had come to a head over the marketing of *Harvard Business Review* reprints, with Joel Hughes, vice president of sales, marketing, and operations, and Nan Stone, the editor of the *Review,* at odds over Hughes's proposal for a reprint-of-the-month program. Doyle was struggling to find a way to resolve the immediate conflict, while also clarifying the longer-term impact of the reorganization on managers' roles and responsibilities.

The Creation of HBSP

Harvard Business School had operated separate publishing entities since the 1920s, when the *Harvard Business Review* (HBR) was founded as a bimonthly journal for professional managers and a distribution function was established for cases. For most of HBR's existence, the editorial side was headed by a member of the faculty, who served for five to eight years, while the business side was overseen by a publisher. Both reported to the Dean. Cases, meanwhile, had been the mainstay of the School's curriculum from its earliest years; as demand rose, an order fulfillment function was established within the Division of Research. In the 1970s, a third business, Reprints, emerged; it included reprints of individual HBR articles as well as special collections that bundled articles into books.

By the mid-1980s, these groups were growing rapidly. While HBR remained separate, the editorial, production, and IT functions of the other two groups were consolidated in a Publications Division, housed within the Division of Research. Under its umbrella, the Harvard Business School Press was reestablished in 1984, with the intention of publishing the best thinking in business and management irrespective of its source. (In a prior incarnation, the Press had fallen into the role of a vanity press for HBS faculty and had been disbanded.) The Reprint business was variously divided and recombined, with softcover books going to the Press, and other parts of the business passing back and forth between HBR and Cases. A small number of video programs were also developed as a way of experimenting with the medium; all featured HBS faculty and were produced and directed by an outside firm.

The Dream of a Single Publishing Company
By 1990, the Publications Division had been physically consolidated at a location a half-mile from

---

This case was prepared by Artemis March under the direction of David A. Garvin.

the HBS campus. When HBR was included, HBS Publishing activities grossed $40 million and were clearly becoming too large and complex to be managed through a governance structure that the Dean described as a "bowl of spaghetti." A consulting firm was engaged to answer two questions: Is there an opportunity to grow the business? If so, how should it be organized? The consultants found the opportunity to be enormous, but suggested that success required a professional publishing organization, separate from the School and University. One reason was compensation. To recruit, hire, and reward people with the necessary talent and skills and gain credibility as a serious player in the publishing world, compensation and incentives would have to be competitive with those of commercial publishers and other media companies.

A steering committee was formed to explore, develop, and champion the concept, design a governance structure, and work through the difficult issues of creating a separate company and distancing it from HBS and the University. One of the members was William (Bill) Sahlman, a faculty member who was later named Senior Associate Dean and Director of Publication Activities, a new position that also included oversight of HBR. In a series of presentations, Sahlman laid out the dream. The Publishing Group would leverage world-class intellectual capital created at the School and elsewhere, making the best ideas accessible not only to managers attending Harvard's on-campus programs, but also those who remained at a distance. It would deliver these ideas in whatever form or medium was appropriate, and whenever the information was needed. In this way, the group would vastly expand the reach and impact of the School, at the same time responding to technological and economic forces that were shifting the locus of education away from campuses and into corporations and homes. As a consequence of these activities, Publishing would be able to increase its financial contribution to HBS, providing additional support for the School's substantial research and case development program.

Between 1990 and 1992, the steering committee, working with Publications managers, began shaping the organization and negotiating with assorted constituencies throughout the University. The new entity would combine HBR with the existing Publications Division, forming a separate, nonprofit corporation. This structure was unusual, but not without precedent. The Harvard Management Company, which handled the University's investments, was organized along the same lines. The Dean would be the corporation's sole shareholder; he, in turn, would appoint a Board of Directors consisting of HBS faculty, representatives of HBS departments such as External Relations, Executive Education, and the Division of Research, and members of the business community. Internally, Publishing would follow a corporate model, with a president and CEO at the top. The committee immediately launched a search for a publishing professional to fill these roles.

Yet many issues remained unresolved or ambiguous. Even as the board was forming in early 1993, there was little clarity about how it would operate. Sahlman was appointed board chairman but was still learning his new role. Nor was the mission completely clear. Publishing was expected to contribute both educationally and financially; various members of the HBS community assigned different weights to the two roles. The Dean, for example, spoke of education at HBS in terms of three legs of a stool (MBA, Executive Education, and Publishing), yet was known as a tough budgeting person who pressed for financial performance and contribution. Some board and faculty members felt that the primary goal of the new organization was to grow rapidly, increasing its financial contribution to the School and providing additional support for faculty research. Faculty took differing positions on whether they, as authors, should be free agents, able to sell their manuscripts or video projects to the highest bidder, or whether HBSP should have the right of first refusal since the School paid their salaries and funded their research. A few believed that the new organization existed primarily to publish the work of junior faculty.

Members of the staff faced additional uncertainties. While HBSP offered them career opportunities that did not previously exist, job titles, compensation, and benefits packages were still to be determined. With the cutover to the new organization, staff members knew their Harvard benefits and compensation would change, but until their custom-designed, market-based salary and compensation package was finally approved by the University in the fall of 1993, existing employees did not know exactly what they were giving up and what they would gain. During the same period, all outside recruits, including the new CEO, were hired as consultants rather than permanent employees, with neither long-term contracts nor benefits.

Breaking Away: 1992–1994

A tremendous amount of behind-the-scenes work was required to give birth to the new organization— or, as one manager put it, "to better define its bone structure and neural networks." HBSP's first president and CEO, Ruth McMullin, was recruited from a major publisher; she quickly established a new structure and operating philosophy. The functionally organized departments of the past, focused on cost control and embedded in a university environment, were replaced by a product-line organization. Each product line would have its own business manager, marketing strategy, and P&L, and would be supported by HR, IT, and financial systems developed expressly for Publishing, rather than relying on the University's existing systems. Under McMullin, the new organization also struggled to define and implement its complex and fuzzy mandate. It tilted in the direction of becoming a commercially competitive publishing organization and asserting its independence from HBS. In retrospect, Sahlman was philosophical about the ensuing difficulties:

> Ruth broke the ship away from the administrative structure of the School, and in the process, an us-versus-them environment developed on both sides. Frankly, to some degree, she had to do it.

> Things that worked for the School didn't work for Publishing.

For example, HBS thrived on ambiguity because it left considerable latitude for independent action by the faculty, who typically did not like to be told what to do. McMullin, on the other hand, put a premium on clarity. She was building a business and believed in clear objectives, roles, and responsibilities. Within HBSP, some welcomed McMullin's directness; others resisted her frontal approach to tough issues. Tensions were further exacerbated by several flawed hiring choices. These and other difficulties were reported and misreported in the press, producing considerable embarrassment for the School and deep and enduring wounds within many of the product groups, particularly HBR.

A Change at the Top

Sahlman was the first to suggest that Linda Doyle, then Associate Dean for Administration, might be the right person to heal the wounds:

> Linda was perfect for the job. She is a world-class people person; in fact, she is probably the single best people person I've ever seen. Linda's tough, but she's fair. She has a sense of humor, but also has high standards; she demands a lot of herself, but doesn't try to do all the work. She delegates and listens well, and can give real feedback. Plus she inspires confidence in those above and below her. She also turned out to be 100 percent fully qualified to craft and execute business strategy, and took about three days to figure out all the finance she ever needed to know.

As Associate Dean for Administration, Doyle had served as the School's chief operating officer and the Dean's "right arm" since 1989. She was especially involved with budgeting, planning, communications, staffing, and personnel issues. Often, her work involved delicate diplomacy and troubleshooting. According to several people, after the Dean said "yes" to someone, as he usually did, Doyle's job was to find a way to graciously tell them "no." Moreover, she was intimately familiar with HBSP. Doyle had been a member of the original Publications steering committee and was currently serving on HBSP's Board of Directors. Hillery Ballantyne, then director of human resources, recalled: "Linda had been our main contact at the School, and we had worked together in the trenches for several years." Doyle held a doctorate in English and had spent 20 years at HBS; during that period, she had taught Management Communications and also served as Director of Human Resources for support and administration.

Doyle's long history and prior relationships at the School at first created considerable trepidation at HBSP. But they were soon recognized as assets. One manager observed: "Linda knows the faculty, what they are doing, and what outside relationships they have. She brings deep institutional knowledge and the ability to leverage it. The School is now more willing to let go because they trust Linda, know we are listening, and won't go off the deep end."

There was broad consensus about Doyle's talents. She was described as having excellent interpersonal and communication skills, being flexible, open to change, and down to earth, and unwilling to play politics or pursue hidden agendas. She was also known as an excellent reader of people's personalities and a great cheerleader, but one who could be very, very tough when necessary. Her leadership style was more difficult for people to describe succinctly, for it was tailored to the particulars of the situation, the developmental needs of the organization, and people's capacity and readiness for change.

Doyle was viewed as especially skilled at creating space for open communication and synthesis from diverse, competing views. She used a variety of approaches, including interventions by outside consultants, to unfreeze perspectives, shift thinking, and create movement. When discussions heated up too quickly or threatened to become unproductive, Doyle often called a break,

then coached the individuals separately, helping them understand each other and find ways to communicate their own views more effectively. Employees cited her ability to hold multiple perspectives simultaneously, as well as her skill at finding fresh ways of approaching issues. One manager commented:

> Linda has a real gift—the ability to see everything from the vantage points of both Publishing and the School. Within the company, she helps us come at things from widely differing points of view. And she does it differently every time.

Another manager observed: "She schmoozes with every one of us, causing each of us to move a little from where we are, and work together in a more positive way."

Doyle seldom approached issues frontally, but preferred to orchestrate a slow, steady building process in which employees came to identify critical problems themselves and own them personally. She then built upon their insights when they arose in meetings or informal discussions. One manger observed: "Linda has a way of getting people to own up to the realities of the organization. She does it subtly, by the way she frames questions. As a result, the group moves forward, yet it doesn't feel like it's simply her idea, it becomes theirs as well." Another manager characterized Doyle's approach as "introducing concepts gradually," while a third spoke of "Linda's theme-building capacity. She will talk about the same topic at widely spaced intervals. The first time may be to get buy-in, the second time to get understanding, and the third time, perhaps three months later, to build momentum and instigate action."

Organization and Product Groups

The organization Doyle inherited had about 100 people, generated $48 million in revenues and $12 million in contribution, and was, despite its small size, extraordinarily complex. HBSP consisted of four main product groups, each with its own history and culture, editorial process, market focus,

---

EXHIBIT 1   Share of Revenues by Product Group, 1994

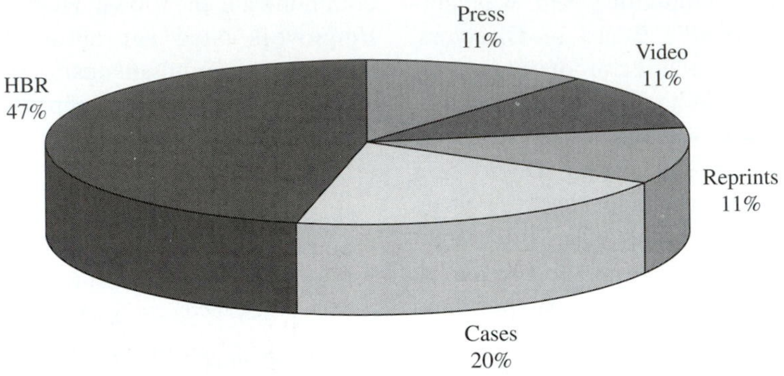

Source: HBSP

---

channels of distribution, and challenges. (See Exhibit 1.) Yet the product groups also shared certain similarities. All were in quest of the highest quality intellectual content, and all had an intense identification with the products they produced and ideas they nourished and shaped, often as silent partners with authors. They also faced related problems in the areas of author and content acquisition, relationship management, and maintaining a full product pipeline.

Harvard Business Review

According to Nan Stone, editorial chief since 1994, the *Harvard Business Review* was a "learning program, in the form of a bimonthly publication, for people who take the profession of management seriously." It was aimed at generalists rather than specialists, took a general management approach to topics of interest, and was distinguished by articles that tested leading-edge ideas against the realities of practice—why they mattered, how they affected decision making, and how they related to prevailing approaches. HBR's staff of professional editors believed that there were no more than a few hundred authors capable of generating the thought leadership and compelling insights that such articles required.

   Many articles published by the *Review* were actively solicited by editors and went through an elaborate editorial process. Ideas were first generated by editors' continual scanning of published research, examples of best practice, and conversations with managers, consultants, and faculty around the world; manuscripts then went through intensive development and rework that could take months. According to Stone, these activities—the scanning, evaluating, selecting, developing, and revising of content—were the soul of the *Review,* and were tightly linked to the concept of editorial integrity. She explained:

> Integrity starts with having a sense of the purpose of your publication. Then you do your best to be a responsible steward and honest broker of that purpose. You must understand the field well enough to know the problems managers face, the research that is pathbreaking, and the characteristics of a groundbreaking article. Independence is part of it too. An idea-driven organization like ours has lots of strong-minded people who want to create things their way, and don't respond well to being told what to do. For example, if HBR editors were told to publish something simply because HBS Press was doing a book on it, that would be viewed as the worst kind of breach of editorial integrity.

   HBR had stabilized under Stone, after several years of turmoil. In the early 1990s, there were personality clashes between editors and publishers, considerable management and staff turnover, and bruised relationships with authors because of uncertain and varying production cycles. HBR staff had virtually demanded that Stone, then working on HBS videos after many years at the *Review,* come back and take over as their editorial chief. Initially, she focused on developing staff, rebuilding the pipeline of articles, and smoothing production cycles; improvements in quality and morale soon followed. Now, however, HBR faced external threats. Revenues came from a base of 200,000 subscribers who were solicited by direct mail, and secondarily from advertising. It was becoming more expensive to acquire new subscribers. Moreover, subscription levels and advertising rates were intertwined. Two hundred thousand subscribers was a cutoff level for many advertisers; below it, many would buy space only on a spot basis or at a lower price per page.

Cases and Reprints

Cases were developed and written by faculty members and their research associates, with the financial support of the School's Division of Research. They were then produced, marketed, and distributed by HBSP's Case group. In 1994, the group, under director Judy Uhl, sold over 4.5 million cases and 2.5 million HBR reprints. Because of the School's overwhelming dominance in the field, the case business had long provided a significant stream of revenues and contribution.

Now, however, the group was facing growing threats from casebook publishers and new methods of electronic distribution. Most cases were sold through campus bookstores, and casebook publishers like Irwin had begun to bundle individual cases into books that stores could handle and sell more easily. At the same time, universities and copy shops were producing customized course modules and casebooks on demand. Electronic distribution was also coming quickly; it was likely to give smaller schools the same reach as HBS.

In response, Cases had become a more active and aggressive marketer. Uhl's strategy was aimed at the academic market and focused on increased adoption and distribution, coupled with greater targeting of materials. She and her staff had identified the critical points where HBSP could intervene to persuade professors to adopt the case method, increase their case use, or adopt new case materials. Interventions included case method seminars and videos, teaching notes, making the case catalog available electronically, and offering a periodic newsletter describing new material. Yet even if adoption increased, distribution problems had to be addressed. Uhl explained:

> We are constantly competing to get distribution channels to handle our material, customize it, and sell it to students. Part of our growth strategy is to develop better channel strategies—for example, mixing and matching the material, and actually delivering it like a book, or giving distributors electronic files so they can bundle the material quickly and easily.

Harvard Business School Press

Harvard Business School Press produced about 30 titles per year, including four theme-oriented collections of HBR articles and a few paperbacks from the backlist. Its offerings were quite diverse because the Press, unlike most other business publishers, participated in three distinct market segments: trade, professional, and scholarly. Each required different channel and pricing strategies. In all three, however, the Press's goals were the same. Carol Franco, director of the Press since late 1994, observed: "We want to be known for doing the best books, the ones that really influence the practice of management." To that end, Franco thought it essential to have at least four titles that sold an average of 50,000 copies in their first year:

> Those books make us credible and lift the whole boat. They also garner media attention and foreign rights, and help us get the next big book. I can't tell you what having *Competing for the Future*[1] did for us. We simply have to have books like that to be a player.

---

[1]Prahalad, C.K., and Gary Hamel, *Competing for the Future* (Boston, MA: Harvard Business School Publishing, 1994).

The Press's acquisition editors had a broad range of responsibilities. They were known for finding authors whose ideas were still being formulated, helping them develop their manuscripts, and giving high-quality feedback on work in progress. They also managed the peer review process that was essential for ensuring that manuscripts met the highest possible quality standards. Marketing and publicity were closely linked with these editorial responsibilities, and the groups worked hand in hand. Meetings with authors, positioning books, developing sales kits and presentations, and launching new publications were collaborative activities, as were the development of spring and fall sales projections and decisions about the allocation of promotional investments. Because the Press lacked a direct sales force, McGraw-Hill handled all sales and retail distribution.

Besides being the only HBSP business using retail channels, the Press was the only group that had to compete for authors. Competition had become increasingly intense in the past decade. Several large publishers, including Doubleday, Harper, and Random House, had established their own business divisions, and advances against royalties were skyrocketing. In this environment, success required large financial offers, as well as the ability to sign authors quickly, form relationships with top agents, and maintain a strong presence in multiple channels. Franco observed: "The Press was not set up to play by these rules. But we have to be willing and able to enter this new, riskier world to attract the authors we want."

Harvard Business School Video

HBS began experimenting with video in 1988, relying on an outside partner for most of the work. Its first product, featuring Michael Porter on strategy, was a big hit, but subsequent videos, which followed the same format of a professor lecturing to the camera interspersed with company visits and interviews, were less successful. In 1992, HBSP brought all of Video's editorial, marketing, and customer service activities in-house, and hired a group head, plus three program managers with comple-

mentary skills: William (Bill) Brennan, whose background was in public television; Kent Lineback, whose background was in marketing; and Nan Stone, whose background was in editing and production. Drawing from Brennan's experience and informal queries, they changed to a new format, shortening all videos to 30 minutes or less, and shifting to a documentary, storytelling approach. Subsequent products featured best practices in such areas as time-based competition, activity-based accounting, teams, and reengineering programs. Of the highly successful time-based competition video, Brennan noted that it had come "in the right place in the life cycle" of that idea. After Stone returned to HBR, Brennan and Lineback produced seven or eight programs a year in total.

The editorial process for videos involved four steps: conceiving and acquiring ideas, developing them in visual form, directing and producing the program, and filming and final production. The first two steps were managed in-house, while the third and fourth were subcontracted to documentary filmmakers, with Brennan and Lineback acting as executive producers. Program investment was high, running as much as $200,000–$400,000 for production and an equal amount for marketing. The Video group used direct mail to reach its target buyers, drawing heavily on the HBR subscriber list. As time went on, however, they came to recognize that senior managers were not the appropriate target market for videos because they were neither the primary users nor the gatekeepers. They therefore targeted with some success another group of users—managers who were charged with leading a corporate initiative and who had found videos useful for initiating and socializing the change. To better fit this market the format was further streamlined: All videos were limited to 20 minutes, and a single story was told. Managers were then provided with a users' guide and other materials to shape the subsequent discussion.

Despite the success of the new format and some individual video programs, the Video group had not yet found a way to make money consistently. Both market and technological uncertainties clouded efforts to define the group's future. Who, for example, were the users of business videos, and how exactly did they use them? How would the availability of video-on-demand through corporate networks affect the form and distribution of the group's current product—videocassettes that were marketed through direct mail and shown on VCRs? Would computer-based media render obsolete visual presentations that were not interactive? Ideas would still have to be acquired and developed into visual form, but what kind of products should Video offer and what kind of business should it become?

New Media

Prior to Doyle's arrival, HBS Publishing had begun exploring new technologies that did not fit the traditional product groups. Between September 1993 and March 1994, Cinny Little, while still holding a full-time job as editor of the Case collection, worked with a consultant to develop and test market the company's first interactive product using CD-ROM technology. Based on a book by Professor Linda Hill, previously published by HBS Press, the prototype allowed users to witness a number of management dilemmas, portrayed by professional actors, and then select from a menu of responses, see the chosen alternatives acted out, hear commentaries and short lectures by Hill, and view summaries of lessons learned. Little described the editorial process:

> We found that book content had to be completely redone for CD-ROM, but that it was possible to translate from one medium to another without trivializing the ideas. We also discovered that you can't create technology-based products in a vacuum. These new media require close relationships between authors, editors, designers, and software experts. In fact, creating a multimedia product is itself an interactive process in which a team collaborates to get the product's look, feel, interface, and content to work as an integrated whole.

Once the prototype was up and running, Little and her partner took it on the road, making presentations to management development professionals at over 100 companies. This was a first for HBSP, for no group had previously targeted the management development market. The response was favorable; a few months later, Hughes created the concept of corporate development partners who were enlisted to provide additional funding and further shape HBSP's multimedia projects. Doyle committed significant investment dollars to the project, and soon after her arrival the prototype was expanded into a full-fledged product, The Interactive Manager, and a fifth product group, New Media, was formed around it. Little was named director of the group. She described its strategy and positioning:

> We create interactive, multimedia products for management development; they are then
> site-licensed to mid- and large-sized companies. Our core competence is knowing how to deal with interactive content.

Services

In addition to the product groups, the organization Doyle inherited had several service departments, including production, information technology, marketing services (customer service and fulfillment), finance, and human resources and administration. The production department, for example, oversaw design and prepress operations for all products and marketing materials except HBR, while information technology built and operated a local-area network that supported Publishing's desktop activities, as well as the company's legacy system, which now ran in a UNIX environment.

Doyle's First Six Months

Initially, HBSP employees were uncertain about Doyle's appointment, and rumors began to circulate. One story was that she had come in temporarily, to quiet the place down and see that there were no more embarrassments to the School; when the Dean retired in a year or so, she too would disappear. Others thought that the appointment was a signal that HBS was giving up on the concept of a separate organization. As one manager put it: "We expected to be pulled back to the School, and that a lot of the separateness we had struggled to establish would vanish." Still others read the situation more favorably: "HBSP must be really important to the Dean if he's willing to send Linda over to work on it."

Week One

Doyle's immediate priority was to assess and stabilize the organization. She first met with every member of the staff in one-on-one meetings or in work groups, a process that took five days. Sahlman attended many of the meetings as well. The discussions were difficult, as Doyle recalled: "Some of the groups were downright hostile to both of us." Doyle directly addressed people's feelings, mistrust, and doubts; she did not ask them to believe what she said, but to observe what she did. On one matter, however, she was quite clear: Doyle stated explicitly that she would not be cleaning house, and would continue with the same management team. To ease the transition for the staff, McMullin stayed on for three weeks to help, a gesture that Doyle described as "gracious and extremely classy."

Stakes and Signals

Following her first week of intensive meetings, Doyle decided "it was time to get on with the work—big time and fast—because there was stuff roaring down the pike and we had to make some decisions." The operating plan and budget had to be developed for FY 95, which was just three months away. Doyle viewed the plan as an opportunity to begin to shape her vision for HBSP. She also committed to the Performance Management Process (PMP), which had been launched at the beginning of the year.

New Businesses. From the outset, Doyle was unequivocal about the importance of experimentation, risk taking, and new technologies to HBSP's future. James (Jim) Biolos, director of business development, recalled:

> Linda sent the message early on that this organization will not live and die on its existing product groups. She could have spent $50,000 rather than the $500,000 she did for New Media,

but she took the risk of a major commitment to an uncertain, undefined product for which there was not yet a market.

Doyle similarly affirmed HBSP's commitment to video, providing additional marketing dollars and silencing the critics who questioned HBSP's commitment to the medium. She personally appealed to Brennan and Lineback to stay; she knew that both were on the verge of leaving because of their widespread uncertainty about the future of video at HBSP.

Vision. Within three weeks of her arrival, Doyle developed a pictorial model, called the whirligig, that captured her vision of the company (Exhibit 2). She saw it as a device for bringing people together and helping them understand her vision of HBSP as a single company, rather than a collection of product groups. She commented: "We would never unleash the power of this organization unless, over time, we shared resources, gained editorial synergy, and developed marketing clout." Doyle's model helped attune people to her point of view, but she did not force it on anyone or use it as the basis for formal planning. Biolos recalled: "Linda used the model judiciously. She didn't show it at every meeting. She just threw it out every so often, and talked about the organization in these terms."

Performance Management Process. The Performance Management Process was a system of interconnected objectives, measurements, and evaluations designed to align individual, unit, and company goals. It went into effect on January 1, 1994, and covered all exempt employees. A critical feature was the performance-variable pay plan. Ballantyne explained:

> We wanted to leverage incentive compensation as a way to control fixed costs, and to encourage people to work on shared objectives. Professional development was also a major part of the system. We didn't want simply to attract people, but also to develop them so that they were able to take on ever-increasing and different challenges.

EXHIBIT 2 The Whirligig

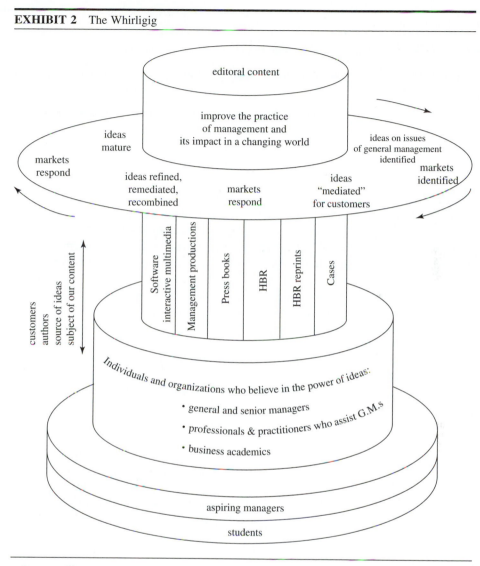

editoral content

improve the practice
of management and
its impact in a changing world

ideas
mature

ideas on issues
of general management
identified

markets
respond

ideas refined,
remediated,
recombined

markets
respond

ideas
"mediated"
for customers

markets
identified

Software
interactive multimedia

Management productions

Press books

HBR

HBR reprints

Cases

customers
authors
source of ideas
subject of our content

Individuals and organizations who believe in the power of ideas:

• general and senior managers

• professionals & practitioners who assist G.M.s

• business academics

aspiring managers

students

Source: HBSP

Many at HBSP hoped Doyle's arrival would scuttle the plan. Few University employees had ever received a performance review; a number of editors, in particular, felt that they were professional individuals and disliked the idea of having their compensation tied, in part, to performances other than their own. Doyle, however, had been the primary liaison between Publishing and the School for HR matters, was involved in PMP's development, and strongly supported the new process. She saw it as an important tool for "coaching senior managers on how to do development work with their people," and committed herself to staying on schedule. Within five months, she had learned the system, reviewed

---

EXHIBIT 3   Mission Statement

Our mission is to improve the practice of management and its impact in a changing world.

We collaborate to create products in the media that best serve our customers: individuals and organizations who believe in the power of ideas.

We will be distinguished by our access to ideas, authors and companies, and by the integrity, quality and relevance of what we produce.

Source: HBSP

everyone's goals, and assessed the company, the units, and all of her direct reports in forthright detail.

Her written evaluations were presented in clear, concrete prose, extensively illustrated with examples. They revealed Doyle's in-depth knowledge about how each individual worked, described patterns of behavior that needed to be addressed, and gave managers a clear sense of how and why she valued their contributions but why it was also important for them to set more aggressive goals, stretch in new directions, and develop additional skills. The reviews also sent a clear message about Doyle's priorities. Units or individuals that had achieved their success at the expense of others or commandeered more than their fair share of resources were marked down in the performance ratings.

Setting Strategic Direction

In the fall of 1994, Doyle launched a process to clarify HBSP's purpose, role, and mission. Concurrently, she was educating board members and HBS faculty about how Publishing was mapping out its territory, and producing a white paper that described the partnership in more detail. These efforts paved the way for the first round of HBSP's strategic planning process.

Mission Statement
To initiate the process, Doyle brought in a consultant to lead the company's first blue-sky brainstorming session. The consultant's opening question to the senior managers in attendance was broad and open-ended: "If HBSP were featured in *Fortune* magazine five years from now, what would the article say?" Soon, the group was analyzing the gap between their desired future and current position, as well as surfacing internal issues that were likely to impede or promote progress. Between meetings, senior managers spent several months collecting background information, crafting a written mission statement, and wrestling with difficult choices of wording and emphasis. (See Exhibit 3.)

For example, to find an approach that was acceptable to all groups they changed the wording of a critical section of the statement from "we collaborate to publish products that best serve our customers" to "we collaborate to create products in the media that best serve our customers." They also vigorously debated whom their target audience should be. Should HBSP produce products primarily for general managers, as they traditionally had, or should they reach out to middle managers and management developers? Finally, the group explored Publishing's relationship with the School, and the need to balance the School's educational and financial expectations with editorial independence. Stone reflected on both the process and outcome:

> We had been meeting for awhile as a management committee, but this was the first time we did real work together. As a result, we did a lot of listening and got to know one another's thinking processes. Because we had so little experience in common, it would have been easier in the short run if our mission statement had a neat hierarchy and clear decision rules. But that would have been too limiting over time. In the long run, the statement's openness is a real strength.

Millennium

In the course of these discussions, Doyle wrote an 11-page white paper, "Management Education at the End of the Millennium: The Role of Harvard Business School Publishing," that grew out of her and Sahlman's thinking about the growing gap between the School's traditional focus and Publishing's traditional offerings—a gap that competitors were rapidly trying to fill. (See Exhibit 4.) She positioned the two groups as complementary partners in a dramatically changing world of management education, where new skills and activities were required for success. (See Exhibit 5.) The paper was aimed at members of both communities, and the Dean subsequently circulated it to the entire faculty. Uhl commented on Doyle's vision and timing:

Linda has a clear point of view, which she expressed in her white paper. She sensed that Publishing was not on the same page as HBS and knew she needed to make a strong statement quickly. Otherwise, we would be foundering vis-à-vis our parent. Linda saw us as extending the reach of the School and being able to do things they can't. She offered the document to people here and at the School as a basis for discussion. She also had the Dean over to discuss it with the senior management team—that was a first.

Biolos added:

The boundary between the School and Publishing is very ambiguous, and Linda's white paper started to clarify where each group operates. At the same time, she was walking a fine line—clarifying, but without giving people enough to disagree with. The document says things that no one would dispute, yet still preserves maneuvering room.

EXHIBIT 4   Product/Service Gap

HBS
- On-campus programs
- Outstanding, diverse community of students
- Case-method teaching:
  —complex materials
  —outstanding facilitation
- World-class library resources
- How we teach is what we teach

HBSP
- Print materials
- Recently, videos
- Non-facilitated
- Self-selected
- Self-evaluated

Products:
Interactive multimedia
Teleseminars/distance learning
Simulations
Reference line
Newsletters

Services:
Alumni plus
List serves
WWW
Searchable electronic catalog
Groups or products, packaged as solutions

Source: HBSP

EXHIBIT 5   Excerpts from "Management Education at the End of the Millennium"

There is increasing pressure to ask for immediate payoffs from education, and substantially less inclination to spare a key employee for extended periods . . . All sorts of new entrants have plunged into this arena. Trade associations, large consulting and accounting firms, publishers, third-party packagers of faculty drawn from various institutions, the faculty themselves as part of their "outside activities" . . .

Desktop computing power . . . Networks . . . document management and transmission . . . [allow professors to] splice their own papers, reprints from magazines, sections of books, government documents, etc., into a tailored textbook . . . Little wonder that this arena is teeming with new entrants and new alliances attempting to capitalize on the new forms that are emerging. These new forms are also fundamentally changing the way people get information, how they use it, and how they learn . . . The extraordinary changes and new entrants bespeak a fundamental shift in the nature of education—where it happens, who provides it, in what form, to whom, for what price, and who gets the revenue . . . It is the university without walls, and the infrastructure required is entirely different from a university campus . . .

. . . It is also the case that universities are not well positioned to take advantage of the opportunities present in this bazaar . . . Entries into this field require a kind of focus and attention that is antithetical to most faculty . . .

. . . The School has done a number of things during the last decade that were both in response to and in anticipation of some of these changes . . . It established HBS Publishing as a free-standing entity that could also enter into that central space between its traditional competencies.

. . . Now, more than ever, it is critical for the faculty and the skilled professionals at HBSP to see themselves as working partners, with different skills, different tasks, but destined to succeed or fail together—for together, our goal must be to fundamentally remake management education.

Source: HBSP

Getting the Distance Right

Managing the relationship with the School was a complex and subtle process that Doyle likened to a continuous balancing act. The difficulty, she observed, was primarily in

> getting the distance right. It's a lot like having a pair of binoculars: The magnification you get depends on the end you're looking through. When you are looking from HBS, we at Publishing look really far away. But when you are looking from our side, the School seems awfully close. The challenge is to get people to understand what magnification to use, and when.

The Millennium paper was an important first step in this process. Another was coming up with a new approach for determining Publishing's financial contribution to the School. In the past, the Dean had simply told HBSP what contribution he expected the following year. This had resulted in planning and investment strategies that were developed through backward engineering: First, managers deducted the required contribution to the School; then, they allocated the remaining dollars to investment projects. Doyle thought it imperative that HBSP develop preliminary investment plans on the basis of its own strategic objectives, and that the board and the Dean be fully aware of the options Publishing was considering. Only then should a decision be made about HBSP's contribution to the School. To ensure cooperation, Doyle actively engaged the board in the new planning process, informed them of possible investment alternatives, and accepted their suggestions about priorities and timing. With the help of Ray Carvey, whom she hired as chief financial officer in January 1995, she then presented the board with an early version of the budget, including anticipated contribution.

Strategic Initiatives

Between December 1994 and March 1995, a broad spectrum of HBSP employees participated in a preliminary round of strategic planning. The process was viewed as a pragmatic exercise, not a full-scale strategic process; it built on the mission statement and the Millennium paper to identify assorted projects and opportunities that would provide growth over the next three years. As Jon Winder, who joined the company in January 1995 as vice president of business development and subsequently led the process, observed: "We were collecting fruit that were either lying on the ground or were readily discernible. At that point, it was unrealistic to do anything more."

Doyle, however, had a developmental agenda as well. She wished to create new ground rules, behaviors, and relationships, and chose this process as her starting point. Editorial and academic environments, she observed, attracted bright people who by temperament and training had a critical cast of mind, enjoyed finding holes in arguments, and were skilled at explaining why new ideas wouldn't work. Typically, they had little experience creating and developing proposals as a group. Doyle likened the situation when she arrived at HBSP to a "skeet shoot. Someone would yell, 'pull,' there would be a deafening blast, and the idea would be in pieces on the ground." She therefore established strict ground rules for the strategic initiatives exercise—no one was allowed to criticize an idea during the brainstorming process.

During the initial brainstorming, senior managers generated over 160 product and service ideas. They were then put on paper, voted on privately, and consolidated, simplified, and winnowed down to a list of potential initiatives. Each was then examined by a self-selected, cross-business group. In total, over 50 employees were involved in the process. Using the criteria of strategic importance and commercial opportunity, senior managers ultimately selected 14 projects for funding in FY 96. The range was quite broad, and included defensive actions, expansion opportunities, high-potential new businesses, and research initiatives for future

businesses. An example was Electronic Futures, which involved several projects aimed at developing more business through electronic distribution: establishing Web capability, putting product samples and marketing material on the Web, improving current CD-ROM versions of catalogs and backlists, and creating the ability to send targeted marketing to customers via e-mail. One of the most important outcomes of this round of strategic planning was that HBSP employees began to see, often for the first time, how the company was actually going to grow, and began to believe that it was possible to achieve ambitious goals. The collective bet was that an investment of $2 million in FY 96 would increase FY 98 contribution by as much as $7 million.

Organizational Development

During Doyle's first nine months, a few managers left because they fit poorly with Publishing's new priorities. There were also a number of promotions and new hires. Hughes and Ballantyne were promoted to vice president; Brennan and Lineback were made codirectors of Video, each with his own separate product line; Little was made editorial director (and later director) of New Media; Franco was named director of Harvard Business School Press; and Carvey and Winder were hired from outside. Doyle then established a senior management group consisting of the vice presidents, product group heads, and Jim Biolos as senior staff person. (See Exhibit 6.)

The four vice presidents were a diverse group, with broad mandates. Winder, a former McKinsey consultant and Disney vice president, described his charter as "how to use, expand, and enhance—rather than trade on or exploit—the HBS brand in order to extend our impact and increase our financial returns." Carvey, with a background in both for-profit and not-for-profit companies, had the charter of shifting the finance function from a reactive, gatekeeping role to a more proactive, business-building role where there was closer collaboration with the product groups. He also assisted

EXHIBIT 6 Partial Organization Chart, Summer 1995

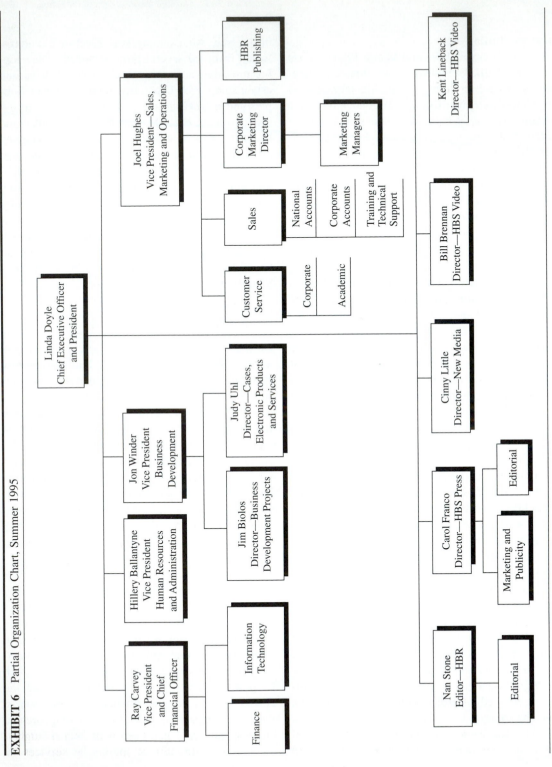

Source: HBSP

Doyle in managing HBSP's relationship with the School, especially its financial expectations. Like Winder and Carvey, Hughes had come to HBSP without prior publishing experience. He had formerly managed a $150 million division in a direct marketing organization and had spent 20 years building field sales organizations. Ballantyne, on the other hand, had spent several years in publishing companies as well as in retailing, and had managed a wide range of human resource functions; she was the only one of the four who had been with HBSP from its earliest days.

Doyle saw the development of a cohesive senior management group as a long-term process. Most of the vice presidents were new to publishing and academia, while the product group directors were relatively inexperienced as general managers. Early on, Doyle consciously used the word *group* to refer to the collective body rather than *team:* "I've told them explicitly that they are not yet a team, and I'm not going to use that word." The aspiration, however, was to develop a senior management *team* and, "if we do really well, to become HBSP's *leadership* team."

To that end, Doyle paid considerable attention to group process, especially during the group's earliest meetings. When necessary, she stopped overheated or nonproductive discussions and worked privately with people before they reengaged with one another. Her goal at the time was to counteract the "skeet shoot mentality" and create an environment in which "people could disagree without being disagreeable." One of the results, she later noted, was that "I pushed some stuff underground by not permitting certain kinds of interchanges."

The need for more candor arose clearly in feedback senior managers gave a consultant that Doyle, at Ballantyne's suggestion, had invited during the summer of 1995 to assess the organization's health and her leadership style. His report, which Doyle discussed with the group, found managers universally positive about the quality of HBSP's people and products, the lack of political infighting, and Doyle's interpersonal skills and impact on the organizational climate. But they also wanted more

strategic clarity and greater directiveness from Doyle. Some expressed skepticism about whether the high levels of cross-product collaboration and synergy she expected were even possible.

Doyle responded to the report in several ways. One was to hire a consultant to introduce Edward de Bono's "six thinking hats" to the organization. De Bono was a leading expert in creativity; he had developed the six thinking hats as a way of categorizing the types of comments people tended to make and the roles and positions they frequently took in discussions. (See Exhibit 7.) The goal was to help people vary their own thinking styles, become more receptive to different types of thinking, open up and broaden discussion, and give people permission to express feelings or make negative comments while softening their effect. Winder recalled: "After the six hats were introduced, people were freer in making comments. In fact, when the hats were initially described, the first thing someone said was a red-hat comment: 'I'm angry.' I'm not sure they would have been able to say that before." Doyle concurred: "I knew we had a serious breakthrough when someone said, 'This makes me angry,' and then shut up—and it was okay."

Doyle also shifted her approach to group meetings, working to create "a clearing where it is safe to talk about hard issues." By late 1995, considerable progress was evident. For example, on a 1-to-10 scale the group rated a difficult meeting to discuss the shift to centralized marketing an 8 on candor. Doyle summarized the current state of affairs:

> We have now reached the point where people can confront difficult issues without it becoming a skeet shoot. We are getting to the point where we can honestly engage one another on problem definition. But we have not yet gotten to the point where we have all the skills we need to constructively and collectively come up with solutions.

Centralized Marketing

The desire for marketing synergy had always been an integral part of the Publishing dream. Progress, however, had been slow. When Hughes was hired as director of marketing services in

---

EXHIBIT 7   The Six Thinking Hats

Edward de Bono's "six thinking hats" is a method for becoming aware of one's habitual way of thinking, and broadening it to include other approaches. The hats are used for role-playing; they help players describe their own and others' comments and classify them into one of six color-coded categories. When using this approach, people refer directly to the hats when making comments, not to their function. They might say, "I'm going to put on my yellow hat now," or "I'd like you to take off your black hat." The hats can therefore be used to legitimate emotions and intuitions as part of thinking, as well as to indicate when a thinker is switching from one mode to another.

The six hats, and the types of comments they represent, are as follows:

White Hat.   Neutral and factual. White hat comments use proven facts, or facts that are qualified. For example, "We usually get over half of our orders within three weeks of doing a mailing."

Red Hat.   Emotions, hunches, intuitions, and aesthetic judgments. For example, "I hate the idea," or "I think the client will love it." Red hat comments do not have to be explained or justified.

Yellow Hat.   Positive and constructive. Yellow hat thinking looks for the value in something, with the goal of opening up discussion or generating alternative approaches to a situation. It permits visions, dreams, and speculation, with the aim of making things work. For example, "Wait a minute. I think we could do something with that." When new ideas are being discussed, yellow hat comments should always precede black hat comments.

Black Hat.   Negative assessments. Black hat comments point out why an idea won't work, how it does not fit with past practice, the risks it poses, or errors in the thinking process. For example, "We don't have the editorial resources to take this on." Black hat ideas should not be used to cover up red hat feelings, which should be stated directly.

Green Hat.   Creativity, lateral thinking, new ideas, and new ways of looking at things. Ideally, listeners as well as the speaker put on their green hats to keep building the discussion and moving it forward, rather than stopping the momentum with judgment. For example, "Suppose we tried to do the project in a completely new way—with teams connected electronically."

Blue Hat.   Controls and organizes the thinking process itself. Blue hat thinking defines the problems, shapes the questions, and orchestrates the use of other hats. It makes summaries, conclusions, and may call for time out. For example, "Let's stop for a moment and see if we can resolve the disagreement between Mary and Fred."

Source: Adapted from Edward de Bono, *Six Thinking Hats* (Boston: Little, Brown and Company, 1985).

1992, he had successfully rationalized separate customer service and order fulfillment operations, forming a single service for the entire company. But he and McMullin had been unable to centralize other aspects of marketing and sales because of significant resistance from the product groups. Doyle did not even attempt to initiate serious discussions about centralizing marketing until she had been at HBSP for almost a year. She observed:

> Until people began to see the vision of what might be and could live it and breathe it, they were never

going to give up control. If I had forced the issue, I would just have driven them underground. What I had to do was lead the case discussion, so they would see the need for themselves and would begin to say things like, "We're never going to reach our goals with the marketing organization we now have." They had to be the ones to recognize that we had to reorganize to do what we want, because they were the ones who were going to have to give up so much.

Doyle framed the discussion by highlighting the advantages of coordination and specialized skills.

It made little sense, she argued, for smaller product groups to be served by a marketing generalist when several specialists, organized on a company-wide basis, could serve all groups more effectively. She also pointed out that customers were currently being bombarded by diverse marketing materials, created by individual product groups, with little or no connection to one another. A far preferable situation would be coordinated marketing that was more relevant to the customer, backed by internal sharing and analysis of customer information.

Some of the product groups, however, were still reluctant to give up control of their own marketing. One reason was cultural. As the consultant had noted, HBSP's culture was one in which resource ownership was regarded as preferable to resource sharing. A second reason was the P&L responsibilities carried by the product groups; with centralized marketing, product groups would still be held accountable for profitability, but would lack direct control of a critical function. Finally, some felt that fundamental differences among HBSP's products made the idea of centralized marketing unfeasible. There were real concerns about whether a centralized group would be able to understand the subtleties of each business deeply enough to position their products properly, without compromising quality or editorial integrity.

Reorganization

Doyle approached the redesign by first asking Hughes to think about the proper allocation of decision-making authority for various marketing activities, and to come up with a specific proposal that divided tasks between the product groups and centralized marketing. Hughes constructed a decision-making matrix; in it, he assigned a small x to those who had input rights to an activity (i.e., the right to be consulted and offer suggestions), and a big X to those who had decision rights (i.e., authority to make the final decision). (See Exhibit 8.) Hughes recalled: "The big X, little x chart went a long way towards getting agreement. We argued in the senior management group for a couple of hours and resolved the issues the following week, after

making some switches in the Xx's." At the time, Doyle reminded the group that the chart was a temporary solution; because HBSP was still evolving, no arrangement was fixed in stone, and responsibilities would undoubtedly change over time.

Hughes took the matrix as the basis for his FY 96 planning and budget proposals, as well as the design of a new marketing organization. Centralized marketing would have a corporate marketing director and five managers. Each manager would wear two hats, specializing in a particular area or activity (e.g., direct mail, database, creative), while also serving as the marketing manager for a single product group. In the latter role, marketing managers would work with the product heads to develop marketing and revenue plans for products; the overall business plan, however, would remain the responsibility of the product group head. Centralized marketing would also have a sales director overseeing three groups: national account representatives, corporate account sales and service, and technical training and support. A service director would oversee customer service representatives and fulfillment. Academic marketing for all products, originally slated to be part of the new organization, stayed with Uhl because of her responsibility for cases and her intimate understanding of that market. HBR's business people, however, would report to Hughes rather than to the CEO.

The impact of the reorganization varied by product group, with Harvard Business School Press and New Media at different ends of the spectrum. The Press's marketing organization was left largely intact, because marketing was so intertwined with editorial activities and the process of acquiring authors. Franco described the challenge ahead: "How can we maintain our current cohesion and ability to understand our authors and our books, while at the same time getting the reach and impact from authors' ideas that centralized marketing can provide?" The Press's publicity group assumed responsibility for all HBSP publicity, however, while their direct mail person moved into centralized marketing.

EXHIBIT 8   Marketing Reorganization Suggested Responsibilities

	Product Groups	*Either*	*Marketing Services*
Author/idea research	X		
Contract negotiations	X		
Product strategy	X		
Media choices	X		
Positioning	X		
Product development	X		
Packaging/covers	X		
Distribution channel selection	X		x
Pricing	X		x
Publicity		X	
Market research/analysis			X
Database management			X
Database analysis			X
Marketing plan	X		x
Service levels	x		X
Targeted usage	x		X
Marketing materials/catalogs	x		X
Electronic marketing	x		X
Advertising	X		x
Mail planning	x		X
Mailing			X
Telemarketing			X
Field sales			X
Distributor management		X	
Trade shows	X		X
Fulfillment data capture			X
Response analysis			X
Reporting			X

X = decision-making authority
x = the right to be consulted and provide input to a decision

Source: HBSP

In New Media, on the other hand, Little worked closely with Hughes on market planning; both found the process to be an easy one. The reasons were largely idiosyncratic, as Little noted: "New Media grew up in the organization at the same time as centralized marketing, so we've never had to work from a different model. I really don't have to change anything to collaborate with Joel and his staff."

Reprints

In the spring of 1995 HBSP was faced with the possibility of an unexpected shortfall in revenues and contribution. Hughes believed that he could make up the difference through a 30 percent increase in reprint sales—if he had marketing staff in place by July 1. He therefore took on responsibility for reprints outside the academic market. Unfortunately, it was not possible to get marketing staffed until the year was nearly over; in the meantime, a sudden collapse in the video market intensified the pressure to achieve his ambitious target.

One of the proposals generated by his new marketing organization was for a reprint-of-the-month service. The original proposal, made in December, was sketchy, but suggested that customers could specify an area of interest and would then receive two or three HBR reprints a month on their chosen topic. The service would be offered to HBR subscribers and advertised in HBR. It would cost slightly more than an HBR subscription and could be delivered electronically. Hughes thought he had covered the right ground organizationally with the idea, and was working within the guidelines of the decision matrix. He observed: "I was the product head for reprints, so I thought I had the authority to make the decision. Besides, we had sold reprint collections for 20 years."

Stone, however, was quite upset by the proposal. Given electronic technologies, Hughes's proposal had the potential, she thought, for being perceived as a customized subscription to HBR. If so, it was a new HBR product, directed at HBR subscribers, and not simply a way to sell more reprints. Even more critical, because it could be delivered electronically a reprint-of-the month service had enormous implications for the print version of HBR. Stone had herself begun exploring the idea of distributing HBR electronically, and her staff was investigating whether it made sense to offer customized subscriptions that could be delivered to the desktop over the Internet. But she was adamant about how the decision should be made:

I am not going to back inadvertently into offering an electronic version of HBR. While we might decide that is something we want to do, it is not my decision to make. Something with such important implications for print HBR should be discussed by the entire senior management group.

In Stone's view, the electronic content also made it irrelevant that HBSP had offered collections for years. In addition to edited books of HBR articles, HBSP had offered small collections of popular articles. But, she pointed out, "that was in the print age, and there was no way those collections could have cannibalized subscriptions to the Review. An electronic customized subscription is altogether different."

In the following months, there were several rounds of discussion involving Hughes, Stone, Doyle, and other members of the senior management group. They helped bring into focus several issues that had not been fully clear when the idea of centralized marketing was initially proposed. First was the narrow question of responsibility for reprints. Was it appropriate for someone in centralized marketing to have revenue responsibility for them? Second was the broader question of how product lines should be defined, especially for derivative products. Were HBR derivatives—of which reprints were a part—a separate product line? If not, should they be? Third, if derivatives were separate, what was their relationship to the originating group, HBR? Where did editorial oversight for derivatives reside? This issue was further complicated by the advent of the Web, which dematerialized product and blurred the distinction between electronic distribution of selected reprints and electronic delivery of an entire issue of HBR. Finally, there were issues of product group heads having responsibility without complete control. Were they, in fact, responsible for the P&L of their product group? Did the introduction of centralized marketing change these responsibilities in any way? One manager put the dilemma succinctly:

Publishing activities have always been separate from editorial at HBR. The primary difference now is that the business side reports to Joel. So is Nan still responsible for the P&L? Is Joel? To put it bluntly, if HBR suffers disappointing financial results, whom does Linda go see first?

Change Processes

OVERVIEW

Today, few business environments are stable and predictable. In industries as diverse as banking, consulting, computers, and telecommunications, disruptive forces routinely threaten the status quo. Some of these forces, such as competition, shifting consumer demands, and technological progress, have been with us for ages, but have recently accelerated in pace and intensity. Others are of more modern vintage. Powerful new forces include globalization, deregulation, collapsing industry boundaries, worldwide excess capacity, and the rapid spread of information technology.

In combination, these forces present formidable challenges for managers. Now, more than ever, adaptation and adjustment are essential to success. The required adjustments come in two forms: incremental and radical.[1] Incremental changes are small and evolutionary; for the most part, they involve fine-tuning. Typical examples include the addition of a new department or functional group, a product line extension, and the expansion of market coverage to a previously untapped geographical area. In each case, the basic organization remains the same, and implementation is largely a matter of refinement. Radical (also called frame-breaking, discontinuous, or transformational) changes are far more dramatic. They involve pronounced shifts in direction and simultaneous adjustments in strategy, structure, people, and processes. Here, the trigger is usually a fundamental change in the environment. Examples include repositioning the organization to take advantage of an innovative, breakthrough technology and responding rapidly to legislation that has rewritten the rules of the competitive game.

Both types of changes are necessary and desirable. In fact, the emerging scholarly consensus is that companies and industries typically progress through

---

[1]Michael L. Tushman, William H. Newman, and Elaine Romanelli, "Convergence and Upheaval: Managing the Unsteady Pace of Organizational Evolution," *California Management Review* 29 (1986), pp. 29–44.

alternating periods of evolution and revolution.[2] They enjoy long periods of relative calm, marked by fine-tuning and incremental change, only to find themselves confronted by brief periods of turmoil and upheaval. Then, driven by shifts in the underlying economics, technology, or dynamics of their industries, they initiate sweeping changes to ensure survival and continued prosperity.

Sometimes, dramatic changes are required simply because of growth.[3] As companies become larger, they face new and different challenges. Inspiration and creativity, so essential in the early years, are often associated with loose, informal management styles. As the number of employees increases and the company's scope expands, greater direction and control are required; they, in turn, produce demands for increased autonomy and delegation. Each stage of growth therefore produces its own distinct set of management challenges. Once solved, they result in a period of stability, which eventually leads to a new set of demands. This process continues indefinitely as "each evolutionary period creates its own revolution."[4]

In such settings, effectiveness at introducing and leading change becomes a critical skill—perhaps, *the* critical skill—for general managers. Applying that skill demands both knowledge and action, a deep understanding of the dynamics of change as well as the ability to move people and organizations quickly down the desired path. Managing change has four main components. General managers must have an awareness of the forces that prompt change (so that they can anticipate the time when adaptations are required); a sensitivity to the barriers impeding change (so that they can overcome likely employee resistance); an understanding of the broad stages of change (so that they can sequence activities appropriately); and skill at deploying the levers that shape behavior (so that they can improve the odds of successful implementation).

OUTLINE

"SAP America," the first case in the module, explores the change process associated with explosive growth. Between 1992 and 1996, the organization, a subsidiary of the German-based SAP AG, soared from relative obscurity to nearly a billion dollars in sales. For several years, revenues grew at over 100 percent annually, largely on the strength of a single, complex software product, the R/3 enterprise integration system. The case describes the management choices and strategic decisions that supported this remarkable growth, including a strong sales orientation, a flexible compensation system, dedication to a single product, and

---

[2]Connie J. Gersick, "Revolutionary Change Theories: A Multilevel Exploration of the Punctuated Equilibrium Paradigm," *Academy of Management Review* 16 (1991), pp. 10–36.

[3]Larry E. Greiner, "Evolution and Revolution as Organizations Grow," *Harvard Business Review* 50 (July–August 1972), pp. 37–46.

[4]Ibid., p. 38.

the outsourcing of critical implementation responsibilities to a network of partners. It also explores the legacy of this growth—a loosely managed organization with little discipline, limited consistency in policies across regions, and virtually no supporting infrastructure.

In April 1996, SAP America's senior managers recognized these weaknesses and launched a major change process. They reorganized, eliminating the company's regional structure in favor of a functional form with separate sales, consulting, and training organizations. They beefed up the human resources function and established formal job descriptions, clearly defined career paths, and a rigorous, market-based compensation system. They installed new leaders, who demanded increased discipline and accountability. Both employees and partners were affected by these changes. New skills and abilities were required because systems and controls now directed behavior, rather than informal guidelines. This shift is a common one for rapidly growing companies and marks the transition from entrepreneurial to professional management. It is a transition that is essential to becoming a successful large organization.

The second case in the module, "Millipore Corporation (A)," explores another, equally important transition. Millipore, a medium-sized manufacturer of membrane and filtering products, had, at the time of the case, already made the shift to professional management. Between 1960 and 1979, it grew from a small niche player, with a narrow product line and sales of $1 million, to a multinational corporation, with several thousand products and $195 million in sales. Shortly thereafter, it faced problems similar to those at SAP America: inefficiency, poor discipline, and lax controls. Profits fell sharply in 1980 and 1981; management responded by installing a new president at the largest division. He immediately tightened controls, reined in spending, and introduced formal processes, systems, and procedures. These changes led to sharp reductions in costs and improved profitability.

But there was fallout as well. Millipore's core skill—its ability to provide customers with tailored, innovative products—began to atrophy. There was also considerable grumbling in the ranks, especially among sales and applications experts, and sales growth slowed. Again, management responded by installing a new president at the largest division. His early actions provide a model of effective change leadership. In his initial few months, he reenergized the business with a series of symbolic and substantive moves: breaking down walls, approving new products, reallocating funds, shifting people around, and responding attentively to the concerns of key staff. Momentum built quickly, and, after several months, a new spirit and ethic are visible. Even bigger changes may still be needed, however, including a shift away from the current functional organization, and the division president remains undecided about the best way to move forward.

The third case in the module, "Harvey Golub: Recharging American Express," shifts the focus to large-scale, transformational change. The difference is one of scope and degree. Both SAP America and Millipore changed in fundamental ways, but neither was in the midst of a life-threatening crisis. American Express, on the other hand, faced just such problems in the early 1990s. Its strategy was weak and poorly defined; the organization was little more than a loose collection of inefficient, independent fiefdoms; political infighting was rife; and financial losses were mounting rapidly because of misguided acquisitions, customer defections, and a poorly managed entry into the credit-card business. Without changes on multiple fronts, the company's survival was in question.

In late 1991, Harvey Golub stepped into this environment as president of American Express and chairman and CEO of Travel-Related Services, the company's largest subsidiary. Over the next few years, he orchestrated a massive turnaround that proceeded through three distinct stages: fixing what's broken, creating a sense of direction, and consolidating the gains. He began by focusing on operating issues and financial improvements, including a reengineering program designed to remove $1 billion from the cost base, and only later shifted to strategic concerns, such as crafting a vision, pruning the portfolio of businesses, and stimulating growth.[5] Throughout, his primary goal was getting employees to think and act differently, to make decisions on the basis of principles rather than politics.[6] To that end, he employed a variety of powerful techniques. Golub intervened actively in managers' reasoning processes, asked provocative questions to deepen thinking and prompt vigorous debate, personally modeled the newly desired behaviors, and spent enormous amounts of time reviewing and evaluating senior managers' performance.

The next case in the module, "Pepsi's Regeneration, 1990–1993," provides an instructive contrast with American Express. It too describes a large-scale, transformational change process launched in the early 1990s, but in a completely different context. American Express was in the midst of financial crisis, while Pepsi-Cola was enjoying prosperity and healthy returns. Pepsi's profit growth, however, was beginning to slow, and Craig Weatherup, the president and CEO, recognized that dramatic changes in the environment were responsible. Over the previous decade, soft drink growth had softened, cola growth had become negative, private label competitors had seized market share, and growth in alternative beverages had mushroomed. Pepsi had also sharply increased its ownership of bottling companies, leading to a much greater need for operational excellence.

After studying these trends, Weatherup concluded that massive changes were necessary if Pepsi was to prosper in the years ahead. His primary challenge then became conveying his sense of urgency to others in the organization. Unlike Golub, Weatherup had to create dissatisfaction with the status quo, since at Pepsi there were few obvious signs of trouble. Urgency was lacking, and so was the motivation to change. Weatherup had to manufacture both, ensuring that all levels of the organization understood the rationale for change and the need for new

---

[5]Successful turnarounds often follow this pattern. See Richard C. Hoffmann, "Strategies for Corporate Turnarounds: What Do We Know About Them?" *Journal of General Management* 14 (1989), pp. 46–66, for further discussion.

[6]This goal—getting "a majority of individuals in an organization [to] change their behavior"—is, according to scholars, one of the defining features of large-scale, transformational change. See Barbara Blumenthal and Philippe Haspeslagh, "Toward a Definition of Corporate Transformation," *Sloan Management Review* 35 (Spring 1994), p. 101.

behaviors. He therefore designed a process with the primary goal of "selling" the need for change to employees.[7]

To begin, Weatherup focused on developing an integrated communication, education, and training package and insisted that it be rolled it out, level by level, to every member of the organization. The goal of these 90-day cycles, he observed, was to capture the "head, heart, and hands" of employees so that they would understand and embrace needed changes. Weatherup also devoted unusual attention to crafting his initial meetings with direct reports, devoting four full days to discussing the challenges the company faced, soliciting managers' views, incorporating their suggestions, and securing buy-in and commitment. He then asked the senior team to craft a new vision; once it was developed, he used it to drive change. But he moved much more slowly than Golub in redesigning the organization, modifying reporting relationships, and streamlining operations.

Despite these differences, there are strong similarities between the two CEOs' approaches. Both recognized that dramatic changes in culture and employee behavior were keys to successful transformation. Both were committed to process improvement and reengineering as tools for eliminating inefficiencies and changing the way the work was done. Both were impassioned teachers who engaged members of their organizations in extensive discussions of principles as a way of fostering aligned, coherent action. Both were thoughtful organizational architects who recognized the need to reshape incentives and rewrite reward systems in order to institutionalize new norms and embed them in the fabric of their organizations.

The final class in the module, "Leveraging Processes for Strategic Advantage," continues the comparative discussion. It consists of a roundtable on change management with four CEOs who pioneered the shift to process-based organizations: Paul Allaire of Xerox, Robert Herres of United Services Automobile Association (USAA), Jan Leschly of SmithKline Beecham, and Craig Weatherup of Pepsi-Cola. They represent diverse industries—document processing, insurance, pharmaceuticals, and soft drinks—yet each, at roughly the same time, launched a massive change process in response to fundamental shifts in the environment. These shifts ranged from technological upheavals to new customer requirements to sharp changes in the competitive backdrop. Yet, despite these differences, all four executives adopted surprisingly similar solutions, with a heavy emphasis on reengineering, process management, and organizational redesign.

The roundtable provides a rare, unfiltered view of the challenges of leading change as seen from high in the executive suite. Each CEO took an integrated approach. Each moved on multiple fronts simultaneously, altering strategy and then making corresponding changes in their organizations' structure, systems, and job assignments. Each focused special attention on the people side of the equation,

---

[7]For more on this critical activity, see Jay A. Conger, "The Necessary Art of Persuasion," *Harvard Business Review* 76 (May–June 1998), pp. 84–85, and Donald C. Hambrick and Albert A. Cannella, "Strategy Implementation as Substance and Selling," *Academy of Management Executive* 3 (1989), pp. 278–285.

investing heavily in the senior team. The result was considerable turnover, as well as pronounced changes in teams' composition and balance. Each also challenged the prevailing culture and norms, recognizing that a process approach required fundamentally different ways of thinking and acting. For this reason, the reading provides a fitting conclusion to the course as a whole, for it summarizes and highlights many of the differences between a process perspective and conventional management approaches.

THEMES

Predictable Transitions

As organizations grow, some changes are virtually inevitable. They arise in nearly all settings and reflect internal dynamics or industry forces that cannot be escaped. Probably the best known of these transitions is the shift from entrepreneurial to professional management.

Start-ups are normally informally and loosely run. They are led by passionate, committed entrepreneurs, who are more interested in getting their products out the door than in building formal organizations. Because they have few employees—all of whom can usually fit in the proverbial garage—start-ups have little need for structure, systems, policies, or procedures. The same core group makes most of the critical decisions, based on an instinctive feel for the business. Most communication is personal, and employees are intimately familiar with "the way we do things around here."

Increasing size, however, brings new requirements. As large numbers of employees are added, they can no longer be managed quite so informally. They are strangers, not yet steeped in the culture or attuned to unstated processes. To ensure that their behavior is consistent and productive, clear policies and guidelines must usually be articulated, detailed measurement and tracking systems must be added, and communications must be formalized and made more precise. Otherwise, control is likely to be quickly lost.

At some point in their growth, then, all companies have to switch from informal to formal management. The timing varies, depending on a host of idiosyncratic factors. But the transition must be made.[8] As both SAP America and Millipore illustrate, this is an exceedingly difficult process, requiring companies to develop unfamiliar practices and behaviors. Perhaps the most colorful

---

[8]For many years, People Express Airlines appeared to defy this rule. It was, in the words of a leading social scientist, "the transition that hasn't happened." Eventually, however, People Express's lack of formality and controls came back to haunt it, leading to severe financial problems and the company's eventual sale and loss of independence. See J. Richard Hackman, "The Transition That Hasn't Happened," in John R. Kimberly and Robert E. Quinn, *New Futures: The Challenge of Managing Corporate Transitions* (Homewood, IL: Dow Jones-Irwin, 1984), pp. 29–59, and Debra Whitestone and Leonard A. Schlesinger, "People Express (A)," Harvard Business School case 9-483-103, 1983.

description of the associated challenges comes from Daryl Wyckoff, who bundled them into "The Bermuda Triangle of Management."[9]

Wyckoff studied a representative industry—trucking—and found that operating ratios (expenses/revenues) varied systematically by company size. Small and large trucking companies were generally more profitable and efficient (i.e., had lower operating ratios) than midsized companies. Moreover, when the classification was further expanded to include approaches to management, companies that were informally managed generally did better at small sizes, while companies that were formally managed did better at large sizes. The broad crossover region, marking the transition from informal to formal approaches, corresponded to the midsized companies, which were inefficient precisely because they were in the midst of installing new policies, systems, and rules. Wyckoff named this region the "Bermuda Triangle of Management" after that infamous area in the Atlantic Ocean where, according to legend, ships and planes enter but never escape. Many firms, he argued, faced a similar scenario—never shifting successfully from informal, entrepreneurial approaches to formal, professional management and thus disappearing completely from the scene.

Nor is this the only transition that organizations face as they grow. Over time, most companies struggle to find the right balance between autonomy and control. Occasionally, they swing sharply from one pole to the other. These shifts may be internal to the firm or in relationships with partners. Within organizations, division general managers and department heads frequently clash with corporate leaders over constraints on their authority. Especially as local units grow ever more substantial, decentralization tends to become the preferred form. But increased local autonomy is a mixed blessing; it often results in duplication and inconsistency, leading to calls for greater centralization.[10] Both SAP America and Millipore show organizations shifting repeatedly between decentralized autonomy and centralized control.

Similar shifts occur within corporate networks and business ecosystems: broad collections of firms that collaborate to deliver complex products or services. Within these systems, each firm is responsible for an individual component, subsystem, or activity; together, they provide a complete, integrated package.[11]

---

[9]The phenomenon was first observed in the trucking industry, but has since been replicated in several other setting. See D. Daryl Wyckoff, *Organizational Formality and Performance in the Trucking Industry* (Lexington, MA: Lexington Books, D.C. Heath and Company, 1973); D. Daryl Wyckoff, "The Bermuda Triangle of Trucking," presentation to the IBM Executive Conference, November 3–5, 1976; and D. Daryl Wyckoff, "The Bermuda Triangle of Management," undated.

[10]Greiner, "Evolution and Revolution as Organizations Grow," pp. 42–43.

[11]The concept of a "business ecosystem" is discussed at length in James F. Moore, "Predators and Prey: A New Ecology of Competition," *Harvard Business Review* 71 (May–June 1993), pp. 75–86; James F. Moore, "The Four Stages of a Business," *Strategy & Business,* Third Quarter '96, pp. 44–50; and James F. Moore, *The Death of Competition* (New York: Harper Business, 1996). It is closely related to the idea of "network organizations" that has appeared in the academic literature. For an overview and summary, see Nitin Nohria and Robert G. Eccles, eds., *Networks and Organizations* (Boston: Harvard Business School Press, 1992).

Typically, systems evolve through four distinct stages: pioneering (in which relationships and interdependencies are established), expansion (in which the community expands its scope and market coverage), authority (in which the pioneer must often reestablish control over its partners), and renewal or death (in which the ecosystem struggles against obsolescence). SAP America is a classic example. From its inception, it worked closely with technology and consulting partners to design and deliver complete enterprise information systems. There was a clear division of labor: SAP America provided the software, while partners provided the hardware and systems expertise. For many years, these relationships were harmonious and productive. But at the time of the case, partners' interests have begun to diverge considerably from SAP's, and managers are trying to regain control of the installation and implementation process. They are wrestling with those challenges to authority that are so common in the third stage of systems evolution.

Other transitions are predictable, but only in hindsight. Profound, lasting changes in the environment nearly always require equally significant corporate adjustments; the difficulty is distinguishing them, when they first appear, from blips or temporary perturbations. Pepsi clearly faced this challenge, as did several of the companies featured in "Leveraging Processes." In the same spirit, flawed strategies usually lead to corporate reorientations; again, the difficulty is distinguishing a doomed strategy from one that merely requires more time to take hold. The problems at American Express clearly fall in this category.

Identifying and Overcoming Barriers to Change

Most people—and most organizations—are creatures of habit. They are settled in their ways and seldom embrace new ways of working without a fight. Change, after all, brings uncertainty, and uncertainty is stressful. Moreover, in the early stages of change potential losses are usually far easier to identify than potential gains. As Jack Welch, the CEO of General Electric, observed, the result is hardly surprising: "Change has no constituency"[12]

Except, perhaps, in the executive suite. The very best general managers try to stay on the leading edge of change, since they know that long-standing responses and routines can quickly become outdated. Like Golub at American Express and Weatherup at Pepsi, they stay attuned to emerging trends and sensitive to developing problems. Not surprisingly, they are often the first to recognize the need for adaptation and adjustment. But to be effective, they need another skill as well: the ability to identify and overcome barriers to change. Otherwise, their initiatives will lack supporters—whatever their merit.

---

[12]"Jack Welch's Lessons for Success," *Fortune,* January 25, 1993, p. 88.

There are five main barriers to change: anxiety, self-interest, lack of information, complacency, and cognitive bias.[13] Anxiety arises because most people fear the unknown. Faced with an uncertain future, they immediately ask, "What's going to happen to me?" If the answers are fuzzy or unclear, they seldom respond with great enthusiasm. Unfortunately, even the best-designed change programs produce enormous uncertainty. Especially when the associated changes are broad and sweeping, it is seldom possible to anticipate all consequences, especially for individual employees. In such settings, resistance is virtually inevitable.

Self-interest is a related barrier to change. Shifts in strategy and structure normally lead to changing roles and relationships; they, in turn, produce winners and losers. A supervisor's power may be reduced, as others are moved to more important, visible positions. A manager's competence may be undermined, as new skills become the calling card for success. An employee's identity may be threatened, as long-standing affiliations and associations are eliminated or disappear. Faced with these threats, both managers and employees are likely to cling to the status quo.

Sometimes, however, they simply don't know any better. Managers and employees who lack essential information—about customers, competitors, emerging technologies, or their company's financial performance—are likely to conclude that all is well. Based on the facts they have in hand, they will conclude that no changes are needed. With better, more complete information, however, often already available elsewhere in the organization, they might well come to very different conclusions. They are not necessarily knee-jerk resistors, fighting for parochial self-interest, just poorly informed.

Complacency is often a contributing factor. It has many roots: a tendency to look at the world through rose-colored glasses, an unwillingness to face hard truths, and ineffective warning systems. Often, these problems can be traced to the prevailing culture and norms. In far too many organizations, candor is discouraged. Managers "shoot the messenger" who brings bad news, providing little incentive to talk openly and honestly. Flawed measurement systems exacerbate the problem. By focusing on misleading or incomplete indicators, such systems present a rosy but distorted picture of the challenges ahead. Coupled with an all-too-human tendency—"unwillingness to indict one's past behavior and decisions"—those in command will seldom see the truth.[14] Without a sudden, undeniable crisis, they are almost certain to resist change.

---

[13]These barriers are drawn from the following sources: Michael Beer, "Leading Change," in John J. Gabarro, ed., *Managing People and Organizations* (Boston: Harvard Business School Publications, 1992), pp. 424–431; Gersick, "Revolutionary Change Theories," p. 18; John P. Kotter, *Leading Change* (Boston: Harvard Business School Press, 1996), chap. 1; John P. Kotter and Leonard A. Schlesinger, "Choosing Strategies for Change," in Gabarro, ed., *Managing People and Organizations,* pp. 396–400; David A. Nadler, "The Effective Management of Organizational Change," in Jay W. Lorsch, ed., *Handbook of Organizational Behavior* (Englewood Cliffs, NJ: Prentice-Hall, 1987), pp. 358–369; and Noel M. Tichy and David O. Ulrich, "The Leadership Challenge—A Call for the Transformational Leader," *Sloan Management Review,* Fall 1984, p. 61.

[14]Tichy and Ulrich, "The Leadership Challenge," p. 61.

Finally, cognitive biases often make it difficult to recognize the need for change, even when managers are trying to avoid complacency. Open-mindedness is a difficult-to-realize ideal, since information is nearly always processed selectively using time-tested filters and categories. In most cases, the associated categories are implicit or unstated; they have prevailed for so long that they exist only at a subconscious level. Examples include market boundaries—who is regarded as a competitor, and who is not—and the interpretation of competitors' behavior. These categories can quickly become outdated. Yet they often persist unnoticed, making it difficult to see the need for change, especially when fundamental or unforeseen shifts are underway.

These barriers are not insurmountable. Once recognized, they can be overcome by following a few simple guidelines. First, leaders must create a sense of urgency by generating deep and enduring dissatisfaction with the status quo.[15] They must convince employees that the present state of affairs is simply not good enough. Why is this step so important? Because dissatisfaction provides energy and the motivation to change. To get it, leaders can use a variety of techniques. They can highlight the gap between current reality and the desired future state, as Weatherup did at Pepsi when he contrasted the company's "mediocre" performance with the 15 percent annual profit growth expected in the future. They can set aggressive, stretch goals and targets that can only be reached through far-reaching changes, as Golub did at American Express when he proposed $1 billion in cost savings through reengineering. They can share painful, privileged data with employees and then lead "a frank discussion of potentially unpleasant facts," as Weatherup did with low customer and employee satisfaction ratings in his initial meetings with his senior team.[16]

Second, leaders must devote vast amounts of time to refining and communicating their messages. Resistance to change has an unfortunate side effect: It tends to make people hard of hearing. When uncertainty and anxiety are high, so are defenses. To break through, leaders need to "overcommunicate," repeating the same message again and again using diverse channels and media.[17] A single speech seldom does the trick. Instead, effective leaders incorporate their messages into everything they do: daily meetings, monthly plant visits, quarterly performance reviews, and annual question-and-answer sessions. They also keep their stories simple, drawing on powerful metaphors and a limited number of themes. Weatherup's "burning platform" speech at Pepsi is a classic example of this approach, as are several of the stories described in "Leveraging Processes."

Finally, leaders must ensure that an orderly process is in place. Change is seldom instantaneous; it usually involves a sequence of activities and events that unfold over

---

[15]Beer, "Leading Change," pp. 424–426, and Nadler, "The Effective Management of Organizational Change," p. 364.

[16]On comparing current and future states, see Richard Beckhard and Reuben T. Harris, *Organizational Transitions,* 2nd ed. (Reading, MA: Addison-Wesley, 1987), esp. chap. 4. On setting stretch goals, see Sumantra Ghoshal and Christopher A. Bartlett, *The Individualized Corporation* (New York: HarperBusiness, 1997), pp. 112–119. On discussing painful facts, see John P. Kotter, "Leading Change: Why Transformation Efforts Fail," *Harvard Business Review* 73 (March–April 1995), p. 60.

[17]Kotter, "Leading Change: Why Transformation Efforts Fail," p. 64.

time. Unfortunately, managers sometimes fail to describe this sequence or initiate the necessary steps. They "make the mistake of assuming that announcing the change is the same as making it happen," offering sweeping rhetoric rather than a detailed road map.[18] To be successful, they need to recognize, as the leaders of Millipore, American Express, and Pepsi did, that a well-defined process, especially one developed collaboratively, reduces anxiety and helps gain employees' commitment. But first, they must understand how the change process typically unfolds.

Stages of Change

Most scholars divide the change process into three broad stages.[19] The first stage is a period of questioning, challenging, goal setting, and designing. Here, the goal is to "unfreeze" the status quo, ensuring that employees are willing to move forward with new ways of thinking and acting.[20] Critical tasks include generating dissatisfaction, creating a sense of direction, and building a guiding coalition. It is at this stage that leaders need to craft a vision or plan that clarifies where the organization is headed. The vision can be abstract and uplifting, as it was at Pepsi, or concrete and operational, as it was at SAP America, Millipore, and American Express. But whatever the form, it must convey a picture of the future that is compelling and believable to employees.[21]

The second stage in the process is a period of changing, clarifying, and reinforcing. Here, the goal is to complete the tangible tasks of transformation, altering, as needed, the company's strategy, structure, systems, processes, and people. During this stage, leaders act on multiple fronts simultaneously, striving to make changes that are aligned and mutually supportive.[22] As the CEO of Xerox put it in "Leveraging Processes": "What you're after is congruence among strategic direction, organization design, staff capabilities, and the processes you use to ensure that people are working together to meet the company's goals."[23] Newly desired behaviors must also be signaled and then pursued aggressively. There are many routes: symbolic action, as at Millipore; repeated communication and reinforcement, as at Pepsi; and the identification and removal of resisters, as at American Express and the companies featured in "Leveraging Processes."

---

[18]Beer, "Leading Change," p. 427.

[19]For comparisons of several of the best-known three-stage models, see Rosabeth Kanter, Barry A. Stein, and Todd D. Jick, *The Challenge of Organizational Change* (New York: Free Press, 1992), pp. 375–377. There are a number of more refined models of change, which divide the process into seven or eight steps, but they are little different in substance from the three-stage models. Representative examples of the more refined models can be found in Kotter, *Leading Change,* and David A. Garvin, *Learning in Action* (Boston: Harvard Business School Press, 2000), pp. 125–137.

[20]Kurt Lewin, *Field Theory in Social Science* (New York: Harper and Brothers, 1951), pp. 228–229.

[21]David A. Nadler and Michael L. Tushman, "Beyond the Charismatic Leader: Leadership and Organizational Change," *California Management Review,* Winter 1990, pp. 82–83.

[22]Nadler, "The Effective Management of Organizational Change," pp. 359–360.

[23]David A. Garvin, "Leveraging Processes for Strategic Advantage," *Harvard Business Review,* vol. 73, September–October 1995, p. 78. Also see p. 609.

At this stage, two errors are common. Both involve overreaching. Executives sometimes focus so hard on the long run that they neglect present performance. Yet a series of "small wins" is often essential to building continued credibility and commitment. As a leading student of change has observed: "Most people won't go on the long march unless they see compelling evidence within 12 to 24 months that the journey is producing expected results."[24] Millipore and American Express clearly demonstrate the wisdom of this approach. A second error is forgetting that actions speak louder than words. Some executives get so caught up in rhetoric that they forget to attend to the messages they are sending through their mundane, daily behavior. Employees, however, pay enormous attention to the little things: how leaders allocate their time, ask questions, set agendas, and interact with others.[25] These actions are important because they are viewed as indicators of leaders' *real* priorities. At both Millipore and American Express, leaders clearly understood the power of these signals and worked hard to shape the ensuing messages so that they reinforced the change agenda.

Finally, the third stage of change is a period of consolidating, institutionalizing, and reviewing. Here, the goal is to make change stick, building it into the fabric of the organization so that it endures over time. Policies and structures must be formalized, reward systems must be reset, and programs must be reviewed and updated. Leaders must remember that change is fragile: It takes years to become firmly established. Instrumental leadership—"managing environments to create conditions that motivate desired behavior"—is therefore essential.[26] Leaders must ensure that all of the necessary structures, controls, and rewards are installed to prevent backsliding and the return of traditional ways of working. Every successful executive featured in this module was sensitive to this need and took action to institutionalize the changes they introduced.

This three-stage model has obvious implications for managers. It suggests that change processes unfold in a logical fashion, however chaotic they appear on the surface. It suggests that awareness—a sense of where companies are in the progression—is a powerful tool, since one can then "work with the flow of the tide rather than against it."[27] It suggests that completeness is a virtue, since successful transformations invariably progress through all three stages.

But the model has an important limitation. It is highly idealized. Change seldom proceeds in such a straightforward, linear fashion. There are invariably stops and starts. The stages frequently overlap; occasionally, they appear out of sequence. Tailoring is thus essential to success, since no two change challenges follow the same exact pattern. This, then, is why leading change is so difficult. It remains forever an art, in which skilled managers, at the right time and in the right measure, take step after necessary step.

---

[24]Kotter, "Leading Change: Why Transformation Efforts Fail," p. 65.

[25]Nadler and Tushman, "Beyond the Charismatic Leader: Leadership and Organizational Change," p. 87.

[26]Ibid., p. 85.

[27]Greiner, "Evolution and Revolution as Organizations Grow," p. 45.

Case 6–1

SAP AMERICA

In just three years, SAP America (the abbreviation stands for Systems, Applications, Programs in Data Processing, and is pronounced S-A-P) had gone from relative obscurity to being the phenomenon of the corporate computing world. By the mid-1990s, it was well on its way to becoming a billion-dollar company, and the derivative business powered by its engine was estimated at over $9 billion (see Exhibit 1). Such growth had placed great strain on the organization's regionally decentralized structure.

In April 1996, Jeremy Coote, the newly appointed president, called a meeting of senior executives to decide how to reorganize for the future. One of the resulting changes was that consulting activities became a separate line of business. Coote had subsequently charged Eileen Basho, consulting's new vice president, with two major tasks:

developing a professional services strategy that would allow the company to move from global to midtier markets, and significantly reducing the time and costs of implementation.

Company and Industry Background

SAP AG, the parent of SAP America, was the world's fifth largest software firm and the leading producer of real-time, integrated applications software for client-server computing. Its R/3 product had quickly come to dominate the enterprise

---

This case was prepared by Artemis March under the direction of David A. Garvin.

Copyright © 1996 by the President and Fellows of Harvard College. Harvard Business School case 397-057.

EXHIBIT 1   Annual Revenues (in millions)*

	91	92	93	94	95	As of 9/30/96 (9 months)
SAP-Global (DM)	707	831	1102	1831	2696	2372
Americas** (DM)	81	98	232	636	1010	921
Americas ($)	49	63	146	394	711	614
Exchange rate as of December 31	1.664	1.562	1.654	1.616	1.421	1.5
Americas % of Total Market	12%	12%	21%	35%	37%	39%

*In both Germany and America, the composition of revenues was roughly the same, and had been quite stable:

    70% licensing of software and maintenance
    20% implementation services by SAP's consultants
    10% training of partners and project teams

**Americas includes: Canada, U.S., Mexico, Latin America, and Australia. U.S. operations account for 80–90% of Americas operations.

Source: SAP America

information systems (EIS) segment of the client-server market. R/3 software functioned as the central nervous system of a company, allowing an entire global enterprise to communicate and exchange data instantaneously and seamlessly throughout (see Exhibit 2 for a more complete description of the product).

SAP AG was founded in Walldorf, Germany, in 1972 by four young software engineers whose vision of an integrated software package had been turned down by their employer, IBM. Seven years later, they launched their first major EIS product, R/2, which was designed for mainframe computers. In 1989, they took their company public. Five years later, SAP's market capitalization was $15 billion, and over 75 percent of the common stock was still owned by the founding families.

Three of the founders had remained active in the daily running of the company and continued to sit on the Executive Board. They were described as highly accessible, financially conservative, and as having kept the company "outrageously flat." They ran SAP AG on the basis of informal working relationships honed over long periods of time, consistently invested 20–25 percent of gross revenues in R&D, capitalized nothing, carried no debt, and did not book revenues until products were delivered. Almost 25 percent of the company's 7,000 employees were in R&D, and half were in professional services, which at SAP consisted of consulting and training.

The German (or AG) Executive Board was tightly linked to the product development organization and was involved in a variety of strategic decisions concerning the product, such as the functionality to be incorporated in new releases. Besides the founders, board members included the two top executives from the R&D organization, and Paul Wahl, who joined the company in 1991 as vice president for worldwide marketing but had spent most of his career in technology organizations.

Strategic Focus

In late 1991, prior to the R/3 launch, the AG board had spent at least two months discussing whether SAP should remain a product company, focused on selling software packages, or whether it should broaden to focus on solutions. Wahl, who had just joined the company, described the alternatives and some of the board's thinking:

> A product has a defined functionality, and you hope to sell a lot of copies. So as a product company, you earn your revenues from license fees. A solutions company, on the other hand, gets a lot more of its revenues from services, and provides a more complete package that includes implementation as well as a wide range of other services.
>
> But we knew that if R/3 were very successful and we were a solutions company, we would have to hire thousands of consultants. The board said, no; we are a product company. What we want is market penetration of our product. We want R/3 to become *the* business infrastructure, the de facto industry standard. So what we need to do is to sell as much software as we can, as fast as we can.
>
> To do that, we needed strong alliances with partners. There was some concern that this choice could put us in a fire-fighting mode, where we had to fix our partners' mistakes. Saying that we were a product company also hurt the feelings of our own consulting people. But the choice focused us, and put even more pressure on R&D to develop a superior product.

The board then had to decide how much of the services market generated by R/3 it would pursue itself, and how much of the business it would leave to partners. SAP, it decided, would seek only 20–30 percent of the R/3 implementation business. In the United States, it would initially pursue even less. R/3 was introduced in Europe on July 1, 1992, and three months later in America, where sales took off quickly and then skyrocketed in 1994.

Coming to America

SAP AG began to expand internationally in the late 1980s, and chose foreign subsidiaries as its vehicle. It established SAP America in 1988 as part of the Americas group, which also included Canada, Mexico, Latin America, and Australia. When the American subsidiary experienced management problems in mid-1992, top members of the German board

EXHIBIT 2   R/3

R/3 was a standard software package that helped companies reorganize around processes rather than functions. It employed a three-tier architecture whose robustness, scaleability, and flexibility allowed it to meet the diverse demands of global and smaller customers, as well as the needs of a broad range of industries. R/3's master file and client-server design made possible seamless and synchronous integration of data sharing across an enterprise, even through new releases of the product. This capability led SAP America's president Jeremy Coote to observe: "What you are buying from SAP is the breadth and scope of seamless integration, rather than a product."

By 1996, the cumulative investment in R/3 exceeded DM 3 billion, and had been fully expensed. The scope of R/3's reach was massive; it cut across the entire enterprise, linking over 80 percent of all activities. The global nature of the product was reflected in its ability to automatically calculate exchange rates and to operate in multiple languages. Revenues from R/3 came from licensing users at a particular site and from annual maintenance fees, which were a percentage of the original fee. Licensing fees depended on the number of users and their category of use; some users only read transactions, some carried out a limited set of transactions, while others used the full capacity of the system. Fees were higher for the more intensive categories of use.

R/3 was very open architecturally. This meant that a customer was not locked into an existing database, type of hardware, or any specific portion of their solution forever. R/3 could run on any of the major hardware platforms, operating systems, or relational databases. The product consisted of a large suite of applications modules in four broad areas—finance and control, materials management and production planning, sales and distribution, human resources—and the software took a process perspective on all of these activities. For example, on a quote-to-cash process, it delivered a quote on a product to a customer, priced it out, checked availability, procured materials, staged them, shipped the product, and collected the money.

The horizontal process orientation of R/3 was designed into the software through configuration tables. A table was an arrangement of default settings through which data ran automatically. A major process could involve a few hundred tables, and changing one table had ripple effects on scores of others. Although R/3 was designed as a standard package, the software could be customized by changing the settings in the tables. Based on its preferences and operating requirements, a company decided on the settings for each table. In this way, it tailored the software to its needs, but without changing any code.

Recently, the laborious process of changing every table by hand had been superseded by two major developments: SAP had encoded over 1,000 best practices into the software; and SAP had developed new modeling tools that automated the table-setting process. Best practices were scaleable business processes that had been drawn from 25 years of close collaboration between customers and developers. They were actually precise configurations of table settings that encoded the practices of industry leaders, serving as templates that other companies could use as a starting point for their own organizations.

New modeling tools such as Business Engineer also made it much easier to align standard templates with a customer's own processes. Business Engineer allowed customers to automatically reconfigure scores of tables to accommodate their changes to SAP processes. The tool allowed the application consultant to lift the template into the modeling tool, make it look like the customer's, and drive those parameters back into R/3. SAP had also developed a rapid implementation methodology called Accelerated SAP that drew from the best practices of field consultants, who collaborated to design the new methodology. It was specially tailored for midsized companies, who were unwilling to invest in extended implementation.

parachuted in. After the dust settled, Klaus Besier became president, Wahl joined the American board and Hasso Plattner, SAP's cofounder and de facto chief technologist, became chairman of the Americas organization, a position he continued to hold four years later. Besier soon added the title of chief operating officer; he became CEO early in 1994. Besier was described by a senior executive as a "dynamic leader, a marketeer par excellence, very directed and driven. He speaks well and has a strong physical presence. With Klaus, there is no pretense. What matters is getting the job done. His penchant is to build; the company has to be headed in a direction."

Charting a Course

To address the needs of the American market, Besier moved away from the German model in several respects, including the sales organization, target customer base, and organizational structure.

Commissioned Sales Force. SAP America had learned from R/2 that its product needed to be sold more heavily in America than in Europe, and that a strong sales force was required to compete effectively. Alex Ott, vice president of global partnering, recalled: "We had no customer base, no market share, a handful of people, and a new product which ran on a new technology. We concluded that we must be quick on our feet, and have more feet on the street than anyone else." SAP America's managers decided that they needed a commission plan for R/3. Besier moved aggressively, putting the entire sales force (rather than just a pilot group, as had been agreed by the board) on commission. He also recruited more and more of the sales force from the ranks of professional salespeople, rather than engineers.

Target Customers. Besier's aggressive, entrepreneurial sales force believed that it could close deals with very large companies. Their first multimillion-dollar sale, to Chevron, proved to be a watershed for SAP. The deal closed in December 1992; it punctured the belief that multinationals were married to their mainframes. R/3 more than met Chevron's tests for scaleability, volume, and speed; in fact, it outperformed SAP's major competitor by

300–800 percent. The product's architecture was validated, opening a floodgate to other large accounts. SAP America then set its sights on global companies with revenues of at least $2.5 billion. Eric Rubino, general counsel, recalled:

> The product was validated as being so superior to competitors' that we thought it really could become the de facto standard—if we could get it out there fast enough. We believed that we had a window of opportunity when no one could compete with us, but a window of only about two years.

Regional Organization. To move product as quickly as possible, SAP America established in January 1993 autonomous regional offices in San Francisco, Chicago, Atlanta, and Philadelphia. SAP headquarters remained in Philadelphia, but the coporate office, which continued to handle events, public relations, and advertising, was separated organizationally from the Northeast Region. Each region became a separate P&L with its own presales, sales, consulting, and training services, all reporting to a regional vice president (RVP). Wahl explained:

> Initially, we thought about common resources for the regions. Then we decided that for each region to win strategic deals, we needed to give them all of the autonomy and tools they needed to close the sale, as well as the services required to support the client.

The regions had significant flexibility in deal making. If they were negotiating licenses, for example, and the customer thought the fee was too high, they could offer free training, or even free consulting to close the sale.

In 1995, each of the four regions was further divided into three districts, led by a district director. Like regional vice presidents, district directors were general managers who ran relatively complete businesses. Key aspects of the role were described by Robert (Bob) Salvucci, district manager for Philadelphia, and later, Coote's successor as RVP for the Northeast: "It's a fun job if you don't like a lot of structure and you like to handle a lot of things happening at once. You need high energy, a thick skin, and the ability to make rapid-fire decisions on the fly." Districts did not have a separate

P&L, however; for accounting and compensation purposes, they were considered part of the region. The compensation system was highly leveraged; that is, for regional, district, and other managers, it had a low base salary relative to market, but there was no cap on the upside potential. The variable portion of the compensation system was tied primarily to making individual, district, or regional software sales numbers. Because SAP stock was traded only in Europe, there were no stock options.

Resourcing Explosive Growth

The first Americas strategy meeting was held in Bermuda in the summer of 1993, and it became something of a landmark event. Market acceptance of R/3 was now assured, and enthusiasm for the product was so great that explosive growth was anticipated. The group set a $1 billion revenue target for SAP America, to be reached by 1997. To achieve such massive growth, the executives concluded that they had to do three things: create an industry strategy to penetrate markets and build the installed base, rethink and vastly expand their partnership strategy, and dramatically ramp up their service and support capabilities.

An Industry Strategy: ICOEs

The executives developed a vertical industry strategy, to be delivered through industry centers of expertise, or ICOEs. ICOEs were to serve as a bridge between R/3 customers and the product development organization in Walldorf. Each would work closely with users in a particular industry, defining and prioritizing their requirements, and then communicating them to developers to influence their design decisions and deployment of resources. This approach fit well with SAP's product philosophy. The base R/3 product was not expected to provide a 100 percent solution; it would meet only 80 percent of customers' needs, and ICOEs would provide the final 20 percent through customized software solutions and industry-specific consulting services.

At their meeting in Bermuda, the executives chose to establish ICOEs in six manufacturing sectors, including oil and gas, process industries, and high technology. By 1995, these markets accounted for 80 percent of SAP America's licensing revenues. Organizationally, the ICOEs were small, highly autonomous units, consisting of two to six presales and consulting experts, that nominally reported to a regional vice president. But they were in fact highly independent, and were led by directors who were extremely entrepreneurial and had been recruited because of their industry-specific knowledge.

Each of the six ICOE directors interpreted his role uniquely, giving different weight to one of three areas of activity: presales support, charting market direction, and liaison with product development. The High Tech ICOE, for example, concentrated on supporting customers and the SAP field sales force during the presales process, while the Process Industry ICOE built a formal, broad-based process to help customers define their requirements more clearly. These requirements were then prioritized for different user groups. User groups were highly organized within the SAP community; they had considerable power, and served as a critical source of information and feedback.

Most ICOE directors spent considerable time in Germany building strong ties with influential developers and SAP AG board members. As one of them put it: "SAP works like the Senate. Lobbying and influence are essential for getting your industry's needs met in the next release of the product." Prior to the 1996 reorganization, the six ICOE directors had never met as a group; typically, they operated independently of one another and had little contact.

Partnering

To realize the company's ambitious growth goals, the range of partners and their level of investment in SAP would have to shift to unprecedented levels. Ott was given the task of leveraging external resources in the sales and implementation of SAP, while also managing the business side of partner relationships. He worked to develop partnering relationships in four categories: alliance, platform, technology, and complementary partners (see Exhibit 3). Allen

EXHIBIT 3 Types of Partners

Type	Characteristics	SAP Certifies That:	Value to SAP	Value to Partner	Examples
ALLIANCE	Professional service firms that provide services and resources in sales and implementation of SAP products	Individuals in the firm have sufficient R/3 knowledge	Leverage client relationships Leverage industry expertise Allow SAP to sell high volume of R/3 fast Allow R/3 to become de facto industry standard	Huge, lucrative SAP practice area	Price Waterhouse Andersen Consulting ICS/Deloitte CSC Index DDS, Inc.
PLATFORM	Provide hardware on which R/3 runs	R/3 runs on the platform	Ensure that SAP's technology is in sync with current and future platform technology Provide multiple platform choices to customer Leverage large marketing budgets of platform companies	Ensure that its current and future technology will support R/3 SAP is a market leader that drives their commodity product, part of channel strategy Exploit SAP in their advertising	IBM* HP* Digital Apple AT&T Sun Microsystems Pyramid Telemarketing
TECHNOLOGY	Provide operating systems and databases through which R/3 runs	R/3 runs on operating system or under database	Provide multiple choices to customer Ensure current and future compatibility	R/3 is core business application that must be able to support	Oracle Microsoft Intel
COMPLEMENTARY	Wide range of applications and software tools that run on top of or with R/3	Interoperability of R/3 and third-party software	SAP does not provide 100% of software solution Leverage specialized software expertise of third parties	Use interoperability as marketing tool Use SAP as channel to sell product	

*Some partners, such as IBM or HP, have multiple partnering relationships with SAP—as providers of professional services, platforms, operating systems or middleware, and software products.

Source: SAP America

Brault, director of the U.S. Partner Program, described the resulting network as an "ecosystem":

> Everyone is intertwined, with each firm tied into everyone else's success. If any component fails, it ripples throughout the entire system. Ultimately, the failure can be traced back to SAP, because it means we have not worked closely enough with that partner.

Gaining Cooperation. SAP America chose to leverage alliance partner resources and expertise by leaving 80–90 percent of the consulting implementation business on the table. It would focus on selling the product and assisting with the initial installation; all other aspects of implementation or application were the province of partners. To pursue this business, partners had to make substantial investments in thier own SAP practices (Exhibit 4). After three years, the results were obvious; as Ott put it: "R/3 has been a gold mine for leading consulting firms." Brault explained why SAP had been so successful in getting these firms to invest in their SAP practices:

> Our approach is a complementary one, in that we have opened up a vast new business for our partners. We say, "We have a great product, and if you are willing to make the investment, we are not going to compete with you for the same consulting business." Traditionally, these firms have been reluctant to fund a practice around an outside vendor's product, because the vendors have often moved into consulting, making it difficult for them to compete effectively.

These relationships were further strengthened by changing business needs. In the early 1990s, the concepts and language of reengineering and business process redesign (BPR) became increasingly popular. Ott noted: "Consultants were talking about reengineering and BPR, but they did not yet have a tool to make their concepts fly." R/3 was just such a tool, for it could immediately embed redesigned processes in an integrated information system. R/3 could even lead the redesign process, as Coote observed:

> R/3 is packaged software, but it is so broad that it forces different parts of an organization to work together. Just to install the software and set the tables, every part of the company has to agree on some basic points: What is a customer? When do we do credit checks? What are the capacity limits of each of our factories?

In addition, R/3 included at least 800 best practices, which made it possible to shorten the BPR process and lower the risks associated with installing custom software and integration. Instead of coming

EXHIBIT 4   Alliance Partner Investment in SAP Practice: Number of SAP-Certified Consultants, circa Early 1996

	Worldwide	*U.S.*
Price Waterhouse	1,800	1,100 (500 to be added in '96)
Andersen Consulting	2,700 (100/month to be added in '96)	N/A
ICS/Deloitte & Touche	1,400 (600 to be added in '96)	900
CSC	1,000	200
SAP America	750	180

NA: not available

Source: Aberdeen Group

up with new process designs only to find that they could not be programmed into computer systems, designers could use R/3's process templates, which were preconfigured, and then modify them using automated modeling tools. Ott explained:

> The market will no longer pay for paper designs that can't be programmed. Our system is both very flexible and standardized: You can configure it according to customer needs, without modifying the underlying software or interfaces. For this reason, the big consulting firms have adopted R/3 into their BPR methodologies, and the process reengineers now design their "to be" scenarios with R/3 in mind.

Competency Centers.   The openness of R/3 and its reliance on client-server architecture meant that customers had to make platform and technology decisions that they had not faced with R/2. SAP had to help them assess their options, while remaining neutral about their choices. This required an intimate familiarity with the ever-changing capabilities and constraints of platform and technology partners, and an understanding of their ability to support R/3, which was itself constantly evolving. To address these needs, SAP America established Competency Centers with each of its platform and technology partners.

The Centers provided a range of presales information to customers and were a focal point for the flow of knowledge between SAP and its partners. They were usually located at SAP headquarters in Philadelphia, and occasionally on partners' premises. In each Center, the partner provided a dedicated team of technical and applications consultants who were highly knowledgeable about their own product as well as R/3. The team worked with customers on such matters as the sizing and configuration of the computer system they would need, and the required connectivity to other corporate systems. The Competency Centers had the systems in place to perform tests and benchmarking for R/3; these tests served as the basis for SAP's certification of hardware and technology partners. Certification was conducted by a group of 50 technologists based in Walldorf, under the direction of Wahl.

Managing the Relationship.   Complementarity between R/3 and partners' business focus was but one part of SAP's approach to alliance relationships. Ott described its key characteristics: There could be no financial ties between SAP America and its partners; the relationship had to be mutually beneficial; and it could not be exclusive. The company had also established "rules of engagement" for partnering activities. Three of the most important were equal treatment at the same level, making the highest level partnering status (called "logo partner") an earned one, and the establishment of clear criteria for promoting alliance partners to that status.

Every year, SAP America assembled its global alliance partners and shared with them its business plan and anticipated consulting needs. Forecasts were extremely accurate because SAP dominated the market, knew its pipeline, and was relatively certain of the deals that would close. It was then up to each of the partners to decide how much more they wanted to invest in training and how much additional resources, including the number of additional R/3 consultants, they would hire that year. Ott explained his approach:

> The cornerstone of the relationship is open, trustworthy conversations. I put our numbers on the table, and I never overstate our expectations. We have always hit our numbers; in fact, we've always exceeded them. In addition, I will not sign up new alliance partners to meet rising demand if the old ones can do it; I always give them rights of first refusal.
>
> Of course, our logo partners cannot plan together because that would be collusion. But by the size and nature of the large consulting firms, you have a pretty good idea of what they are likely to be willing to invest. I don't want to legally nail down these resources, however, because the relationship should be based on trust.

Ott's organization included a single global partner manager for each of the global alliance partners, as well as partner managers who were responsible for two or more smaller alliance relationships. The rules of engagement minimized conflict of interest by having each partner manager responsible for a single partner in a category. To ensure the best solution for customers, Ott insisted that his managers not be measured on the SAP-related revenue generated by partners. They were, however, responsible for managing all bilateral relationship issues of strategy, communication, education, and advocacy.

Under their direction, a master legal agreement was signed with each partner. It outlined SAP's obligation to train its partners, give them a copy of R/3 software, and assign partner managers. Partners were obligated to make "reasonable commercial efforts" to acquire and maintain a comprehensive knowledge of SAP and its products; live up to certain standards, such as keeping customer satisfaction above a threshold level; and dedicate a partner manager of their own to SAP. Alliance partners had to have a software implementation methodology that was appropriate for R/3. They were also required to attach a business plan to the legal agreement, outlining their expected commitments of resources for SAP consulting, broken down by markets and geography.

Partnership agreements could be terminated on a number of accounts; the most important was customer dissatisfaction. Based on an annual customer survey undertaken by an independent source, partners were rated on a 1–10 scale. Those whose weighted average scores exceeded a certain level achieved an award of excellence for the year; those

that fell consistently below were warned of the need to improve. SAP ratcheted up the standard annually, and was willing to use it to remove poor performers. In past years, two partners had been removed for this reason.

Professional Services

Professional services were those activities provided to customers for a fee; support activities, by contrast, had no fee attached. Consulting was the core of professional services, while training spanned both categories. It provided a source of revenue, but had historically been run on a breakeven basis.

Consulting.   While a few SAP consultants worked directly for a particular ICOE, most reported to the region that hired them. Their solid reporting line was either to the district director or to the services director in the region. Because of the company's explosive growth, the hiring rate for consultants had been exceedingly steep (see Exhibit 5). Considerable learning took place on the job, since only 10 weeks of training was provided. Although exact numbers were hard to come by, SAP believed that for every one of its own consultants, there were 8–10 in the outside SAP community. Basho, who had been district director in the New York metropolitan area before Besier named her vice president

---

EXHIBIT 5   SAP America Headcount

Year End	Sales	Consulting	Other	Total
1988	–	9	2	11
1989	5	22	12	39
1990	16	50	23	89
1991	30	114	43	187
1992	50	155	79	284
1993	118	220	73	411
1994	211	523	138	872
1995	230	679	361	1270
10/31/96	296	846	479	1621

Source: SAP America

of consulting (with dotted line control), in January 1996 compared SAP's and partners' consultants:

> There is nothing that we do that our partners don't. But you could best describe our consultants as deep and theirs as broad. Our consultants bring in-depth product knowledge, and are always a little further ahead than partners on the product's capabilities and requirements.

SAP's consultants did two main kinds of work: basis consulting and applications consulting. Basis consultants put R/3 and its support system in place and ensured that the software was functioning correctly in a network. They knew what hardware configurations were needed to support the volume of transactions, how to convert the data from legacy systems to R/3's client-server approach, and how to load the software. Basis consultants were extremely valuable, and their skills had to be well leveraged. For every basis consultant, there were at least three applications consultants. Their primary responsibility was to work with customers to identify their requirements, and then customize the software configuration to match those requirements.

Because growth was so rapid, SAP America needed experienced managers immediately; it therefore hired its consulting managers from outside. As William (Bill) Schwartz observed when he was hired as director of human resources in February 1996: "The expectation was that you were being brought in because you already knew the right thing to do, and you were expected just to do it." There was no career path for managers or consultants, and each region evolved its own definitions of managerial roles. Because of the long learning curve, it took nearly two years for SAP to begin getting a payback from its consultants. Unfortunately, with demand so high for anyone who knew anything about R/3, consultants began leaving in significant numbers by 1995. Some left to join a customer or a partner organization; more frequently, they left to set up their own R/3 consulting practices.

Training.   During 1992–93, SAP developed scores of modules on product functionality. The Northeast region sequenced a number of these modules into a basic 10-week package that was used to train SAP's own consultants; the approach was quickly adopted by other regions. A five-week version of the course was then developed for partners, and customized versions were presented to customers' project implementation teams. SAP declined to pursue the end-user training business for profit, even though by 1996 it was estimated to be a $600 million market.

To create a large-scale operation that could provide the quantity of external resources of the desired quality level, SAP America founded a Partner Academy in June 1994. Multiple locations were soon established in various parts of the country. The Academy's business side was under Ott's purview, and he ran it on a breakeven basis. Ott explained: "If our partners are going to invest so heavily in staffing up for R/3, I do not want to charge them on top of that." The cost of attending the Academy was set at $1,000 per seat, but the fee was not always collected. By mid-1996, 5,000 outside consultants had gone through at least one cycle of training at one of the Academy locations. Those who passed were certified as skilled for that release of the software.

Support and Infrastructure

One manager likened the 1993–95 period to "riding a rocket." During this period, very little attention was given to building infrastructure, except in the area of licensing and contracts.

Licensing and Contracts.   When Eric Rubino was hired as general counsel in 1991, he found no systems or procedures in place to support the sales process. He recalled: "I would get a license in and wouldn't even know where it came from." To create order, Rubino generated standardized license agreements and a clear-cut proposal process; he also copyrighted the product. He observed: "Contract management is a tangible thing. For example, you must have a consistent message across regions. you must have consistent discounting policies, and be consistent in your concessions to customers." Rubino developed tools for training new contract administrators, noting that, "If you are going to decentralize, you must put tools in place to empower contract administrators—who are not lawyers—to make business and legal decisions for the corporation, and train them to understand corporate positions."

Tools included standard pricing manuals that spelled out discounts and concessions, and a contract manual that spelled out, paragraph by paragraph, what the license agreement meant in lay terms. The manual described very clearly what terms could be modified, the exact terms that could be used or added, and what language and wording could not be deleted. Before new administrators were sent out to the regions, they worked side by side with senior administrators for a month. Rubino also held a great many joint staff meetings on a regional basis, ensuring that regional contract administrators were aligned and consistent in their policies.

Administration.   Between 1993 and 1995, there was little formal planning or budgeting. One result was great latitude in the interpretations of the few administrative systems that did exist. Meetings were rare, and offices were frequently empty because staff were in the field meeting with customers. In response, the regions got rid of the computers sitting on unused desks and gave every employee a laptop. Salvucci described the field environment:

> You were closing every deal you could, hiring people, opening offices, and building support. There were never enough resources to go around, so you were constantly finding and juggling resources, and being careful about the promises you made. Until Bill Schwartz came on board, all HR was outsourced, so there was no infrastructure you could turn to for new employees—or for new customers or resolving a problem. You were personally responsible for things like finding office space for new hires, getting them laptops, plugging into systems, and ensuring new people were trained.

Human Resources.   Prior to Schwartz's arrival, SAP America's major HR concern was recruitment. The company knew what it had to offer people to bring them in, but had little idea how its compensation system compared to others, let alone the percentile in which its base salaries should be. Salary

grades and job titles existed on paper, but adherence to guidelines varied across regions. Schwartz found that even many senior managers did not take a traditional business perspective or give much thought to how their activities might impact people outside their regions. He observed:

> A director will want to promote some consultants, and will justify it in terms of employee retention. They don't think about a cost justification, or revenues versus costs. I will push back: "You are adding costs, but are you making money? Is there a strategy about whom you want to retain and whom you don't? Have you talked to other business directors about this? Have you considered the impact of your requests on my office? For instance, if I approve your requests, what precedent will it set for other regions?"

Building Infrastructure.   By the spring of 1996, SAP America began paying far more attention to issues of organization, systems, and infrastructure. Schwartz had a one-word explanation for the change: "Kevin." Kevin McKay had joined the company in mid-1995 as CFO for the Americas, with a charter to build the internal side of the company and the goal of playing a major role in shaping strategic direction. Software, McKay emphasized, was a reference business, in which the need to build infrastructure was linked to the phase of the business. "Early on," he observed, "we needed some good toeholds, some key customer references. Our first big push was to establish our name and to position ourselves. That's the hull of the ship parting the waves." But he pointed out:

> Once you take ownership of a product, you must have a huge infrastructure to support it effectively. Behind the hull there has to be fuel and propulsion that is headed in the right direction. So we needed a hotline that follows the sun on a 7/24 [7 days a week, 24 hours a day] basis, consulting resources to size and implement the product, a whole group of partners to help position R/3 within the customer organization, and relationships with hardware partners to establish performance criteria on their platforms. We had to develop a curriculum to train people and build our own consulting organization to make sure the implementation was done right.

That was stage one. Now we are entering a different stage of maturity, where we have a huge responsibility to our installed base. Worldwide, we have 5,000 customers who are investing millions yearly in our product for their mission-critical activities. At this point we have to build the additional infrastructure to support our customer base.

To that end, McKay's first-year agenda in human resources included several initiatives: the creation of accurate, properly titled job descriptions, a market survey of salaries and benefits to serve as the basis for a total compensation strategy, and the development of a communications plan covering benefits and pay. Schwartz described the communications plan as "our effort to tell employees what they risk losing if they leave. We have very good benefits and profit sharing, but we just gave them to people. They weren't communicated, so they just became taken-for-granted entitlements. We need to tell people much more effectively what they've got here." Schwartz had also begun working on a long-term incentive plan, which included three-year vesting and a performance-unit plan pegged to SAP America's performance as a whole, and was actively recruiting someone to help direct career pathing, succession planning, and management development.

Sales and Implementation Process

Presales and Sales.   The decision to purchase R/3 was often part of a strategic choice to run one's entire company differently. As a result, the sales cycle was a long one, especially for global clients. It often took a year or more to build relationships to the point where an opportunity arose that could be used to gain access for the 12–18-month presales and sales process. Account executives had to be able to identify and position these opportunities, while building consensus across divisions, countries, and multiple levels of the organization. In many cases, customers had never before made an enterprisewide decision. Paul Melchiore, a global account executive, described the process:

> You hang out at the company for long stretches of time. You live there, building relationships,

understanding the organization's complexity, its politics, its readiness for change, and putting a strategy together for your unique selling proposition. Sometimes you do a small project; if it goes well, you develop allies, gain some exposure, and can then begin selling the vision of what SAP can do across the board. You may meet 200–300 people during the selling process, all of whom are potential influencers. It may take a year or more to get the credibility to sell your vision at the top executive level. And when you get to that level, you may only get the opportunity to present for an hour, once.

Because the potential savings and strategic benefit from implementing R/3 were so large, a formal justification process was seldom required. Instead, global companies requested demonstrations, tests, and benchmarking to prove that SAP would work in their environment. This often required the involvement of SAP's partners. Salvucci described the role of the district director in the process:

> You need to be present at the beginning of the sales cycle to position the product and develop executive contacts that you will need later. You also have to find resources for a presales team, a sales team, and a consulting team to manage the sales cycle for the software. Because there is a sales cycle for the consulting partner, hardware, and database, you must spend a lot of time with them as well, putting together strategies.

Implementation.   Although no two installations were alike, outside partners like Andersen and Price Waterhouse usually took the lead role in R/3 project management and implementation. Because they integrated SAP product knowledge with their own implementation methodologies, each handled the process a little differently. The partner's consultants and customer's team members were dedicated full-time to the project, working together day in and day out.

SAP's basis and applications consultants, by contrast, usually served on multiple projects at the same time. They therefore attended meetings intermittently, assisting in the implementation process and providing expert advice and coaching about the product to both customers and partners. Each region's consultants used their own implementation methodology. Some customers did not want to rely on outside partners, or required special skills; these installations SAP handled itself.

Organizational Challenges in a Shifting Market

Despite its success, SAP America was facing a number of challenges and problems. By 1995, internal and external pressures had resulted from the company's explosive growth, stronger competition, and new strategic demands.

Internal Issues

The regions had different approaches to billing, overtime, and training, and were not operating as a single company. Utilization of consultants, for example, could be 80–90 percent in one region, and half of that in another. There were similar discrepancies in utilization rates in training centers. Nor was learning being transferred throughout the organization. Coote summarized the consequences:

> We have not been leveraging our size, and have not been able to match our talent with the problem at hand. People are working separately on the same problem, so instead of fixing something once, we fix it four times.

Moreover, market perception was that SAP implementation was costly and lengthy. This perception was fueled by a number of damaging articles in the press that cited six-month projects taking four times longer than predicted, with an attendant rise in costs. The reality was more complex. As a backbone for all business processes, R/3 made possible projects of a scale that had not previously existed. When implementation was linked to the massive redesign of business processes, project scope escalated dramatically. As a result, it was difficult to disentangle the costs and time for implementing R/3 from the costs of effecting the major cultural and organizational changes associated with reengineering.

Strategic Shifts and Opportunities

By 1995, competitors' products had developed sufficient functionality to be considered viable alternatives to R/3. SAP's largest competitor, Oracle, had an excellent database to which it had added an EIS application. As one manager observed: "What they want to sell is their database, so they use their application as a loss leader to gain control of the account. They are getting very aggressive and will do whatever it takes." Other firms had taken a modular approach, developing, for example, a strong HR module to gain entry, which could then be leveraged to sell other products over time. Baan had emulated SAP in some respects, but in order to land the Boeing account, was reputed to have revised its base product considerably—a path SAP had refused to take to win any order.

By 1996, SAP America had approximately 500 customers and 700 installations in North America; about half were Fortune 500 companies. As McKay pointed out, one challenge was to harvest these accounts more completely: "We've sold modules and software to the top tier, but we haven't fully mined these accounts. We have the hunters out bagging the big global accounts, but now we have to bring in the farmer who works them over time." Coote identified another challenge: "We must dramatically increase the customer base so that we become the de facto standard." This meant continuing to close global deals, increasing sales in services markets, and moving into the midtier market where customers thought about R/3 in a very different ways. Bryan Plug, president of SAP Canada, elaborated:

> Because of the complexity of their businesses, and their cultural belief that they are the best, big companies feel that they must invent their own business practices. So they want an implementation method that explores all the nuances and niches of R/3 and allows them to extract all the flexibility and functionality they can. They assemble the best software, the best process experts, and the best implementers, and are willing to make the necessary investments to stay on the leading edge.
>
> Midtier companies, on the other hand, are more pragmatic. They don't presume they can do it best.

They are willing to find out what others have done, and see how closely it fits their situation. They are willing to adapt, and are looking for a guided tour through the software. All they want is a solution that will work for them.

The increased importance of the middle market had implications for the sales and implementation process as well. Salvucci explained:

You have to be able to pick up a phone, get to the top people, and get in the door. You are trying to close the order from the moment you arrive. You have to minimize the sales cycle, get a decision, and, if it isn't happening, move on.

Reorganization

On February 1, 1996, Besier resigned from SAP America to head an Internet startup. In the wake of his departure, a three-person Office of the President was formed. Wahl was named CEO, but still spent about half of his time in Germany. Coote, who had joined SAP in 1988, became CFO of SAP America in 1990, and was at the time RVP of the largest region, the Northeast, was named president and took responsibility for the line organization. McKay continued as CFO and was named, in addition, chief operating officer for the Americas, adding training, internal systems, hotline, and other support to his responsibilities. Both McKay and Coote reported to Wahl.

A New Structure

On Saturday, April 13, 1996, Coote called a meeting of senior managers to discuss the best way to realign the company for the next wave of growth. His two primary objectives were for SAP America to act more as one company, and to better leverage its size and skills. Coote's original proposal for the new organization was vertical industry segments, an idea that had been strongly favored by Besier. Some expectancy had built around this outcome, with the ICOE directors anticipating that they would become vice presidents. In presenting the proposal, Coote separated out the existing manufacturing ICOEs and also, for the first time, financial services, health care,

and government. He explained: "I wanted to give everyone the same view of where we make money today and in the future. Today 75–80 percent of our revenues come from manufacturing companies. But our future growth is in services."

Lines of Business.   After a modest amount of discussion, the group concluded that although SAP America should continue to work toward a vertical organization, it was not yet ready to make the leap. It simply did not have the people to fill many of the vertical roles, and managers were not clear about the criteria to be used to form segments. For example, how many and which industry slices should they have? On what basis would such segments be formed? To which markets did they really want to dedicate resources? There was concern as well that SAP might again splinter into a dozen or so pieces, driving up overhead. The group therefore agreed rather quickly that for the next 18–20 months, they would organize around three major lines of business: sales, consulting, and training. In the weeks following the meeting, a more detailed organizational plan was developed, coupled with a new compensation plan. For directors and above, a portion of variable pay was now based on the performance of their line of business, and a portion was based on SAP America's performance overall.

Sales.   Sales was further subdivided into its own three lines of business by size of account; a fourth line, emerging markets, which involved the three new services markets, was added as well (see Exhibit 6). Peter Dunning, formerly RVP for the Southern region and newly named executive vice president, described the increased focus the reorganization gave him and his account executives in Global Sales:

As RVP, I had 250 people; 80 percent of them were in consulting and support. The job was very maintenance intensive. Now I can focus on getting licensing revenues from large accounts. We've gotten rid of the distractions—like geographic barriers and different sized accounts—for people who are good at global deals.

EXHIBIT 6 SAP Organization Chart—May 1996

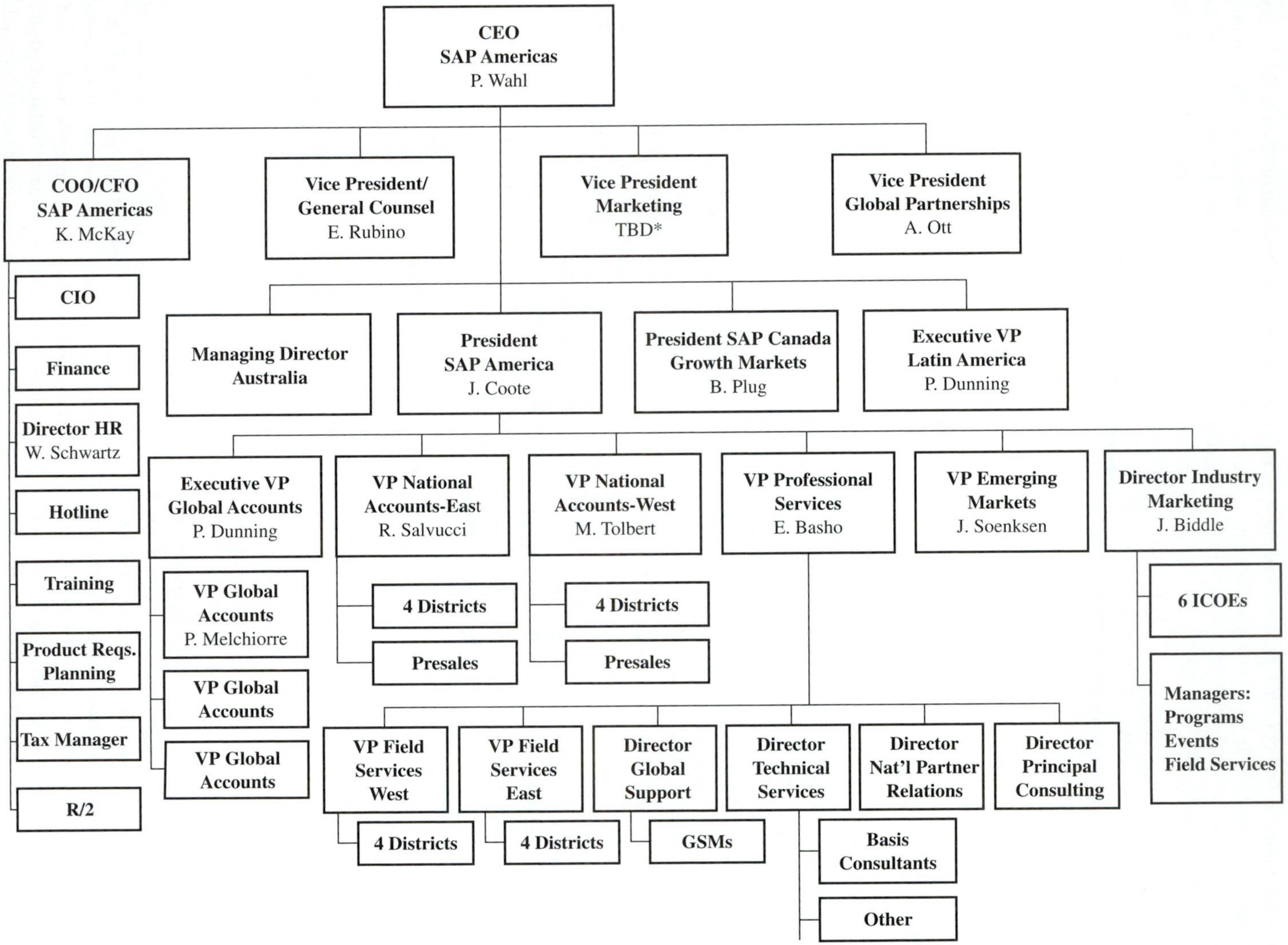

*TBD = To be determined

Source: SAP America

In anticipation of the next reorganization, Dunning set as one of his priorities the building of a virtual organization within Global Sales organized around industry expertise. More and more of his sales people would become specialists in particular industries.

ICOEs.   The throniest issue in the reorganization was what to do with the ICOEs. Coote outlined the situation:

> The ICOE directors were doing an excellent job, but they had each gone in separate directions. I wanted them to be more like program directors in a defense company or brand managers in a consumer products company who work across organizational boundaries. In reality, they were creating separate organizations within the company, and were beholden to no one. As a result, they were getting detached from the line. What we needed was to internalize their message into the mainstream of the organization.

After a great deal of discussion, the six manufacturing ICOEs became part of Jane Biddle's industry marketing group, reporting directly to Coote. Coote and Wahl had hired Biddle a few weeks earlier, anticipating that she would play a leadership role with the ICOEs. Biddle had 25 years experience in software development, systems implementation, and marketing, knew all the ICOE directors, and had been to Walldorf many times because SAP had for years been the largest client of her strategic marketing firm.

Biddle had two broad objectives: bringing consistency and standardization to ICOE practices, including a single face to customers and the field; and developing an integrated approach to marketing within the company by spreading ICOE knowledge throughout SAP. One of her vehicles was a formalized business planning process, which required the ICOE directors to develop plans and present slides in a common format. Her next step in planning was to help them turn their strategic plans into operational plans and budgets. To bring the ICOE's industry knowledge into the line organization, Biddle's first step was to develop "solutions guides." Each was a primer on an industry, and

crafted the information to accord with what a salesperson would want when talking with a potential customer. These guides were to be the basis for focused sales training, the first of its kind at SAP.

The Challenges in Professional Services

The reorganization gave Basho the 850-member consulting organization on a solid-line basis, rather than the dotted-line reporting she had had since January. She set as her top objective "to change both the myth and reality that SAP implementation is costly and complex." Coote had charged her as well with the goal of developing an implementation strategy for moving downmarket to midtier companies.

Professionalization
Even before the reorganization, Basho had taken steps to begin professionalizing the consulting organization. One of her first initiatives was to personally review each region. She first assembled a seven-page outline of the issues she intended to cover during her visit and sent it out several weeks in advance. She recalled: "The regions were shocked. First, because they got to see something in writing, and second, because I sent them the request ahead of time." Another first was the attention Basho devoted to productivity and consistency across regions. She requested information on consultants' billable hours and then established targets for the end of 1996. In addition, she assigned a cross-regional group to develop a single implementation methodology for midtier companies, and created another group to define an integrated set of consulting roles. Their work provided the input for Basho's recasting of the professional services organization and the development of multiple career paths.

Career Paths and Roles.   Basho subdivided her consulting force into four groups: technical services, field consultants, principal consultants, and global support managers. Her technical services people were grouped by functional expertise; they included SAP's 200 basis consultants and experts who worked with emerging technologies. The field consulting group mirrored the national accounts salesforce, and had a four-step career path: applications consultant, lead consultant, consultant manager, and services director. Basho aligned each of her field directors with an ICOE director, and made them accountable for bringing ICOE knowledge into the professional services organization. A new role, called principal consultant, was created for experienced consultants who aspired to excellence in consulting rather than positions in management. The role had considerable cachet; the first cadre of principal consultants immediately renamed themselves "platinum consultants" and created their own logo. Basho explained the importance of this option: "These were the people who were leaving SAP to establish independent practices. Within a couple of weeks of announcing the concept, a number of them had already contacted us and told us they want to come back."

Basho also split out the role of global support manager (GSM) and positioned GSMs at the front end of the sales process in a role equivalent to partner in a Big Six firm. There were 30 to 40 GSMs in total. Each was dedicated to a single account, mirroring the approach in sales. GSMs developed the overall implementation program for a new R/3 installation and coordinated SAP resources throughout the process.

Expectations and Behavior. Basho and Schwartz worked together to clarify roles, procedures, and lines of authority in the new organization. In May, Basho convened a two-day meeting with her directors and managers, where she and Schwartz shared the stage. He recalled:

> We were all in the room together, and Eileen said: "When you want to promote someone, I want to see it first, and I want a justification. Bill is the last stop in the process, so don't go around me. He will support me and simply send it back." And I stood there nodding my head, "Yes."

Schwartz then explained how the consulting organization would work with his field HR people; this time, Basho nodded in affirmation. Following the meeting, several people observed that they had learned more about what was expected of them in the preceding two days than they had in the previous two years.

Customer Alternatives and Involvement

The key objectives of moving into the middle market (called "national accounts" at SAP America) and controlling implementation time and costs were both addressed by a new approach. Basho explained:

> In national accounts, we are going to go in and help customers size the project during the presales period. Using an estimating tool, we can draw a baseline for time, costs, and resources. Then we are going to explore alternative project approaches, and increase the choices a customer has on implementation. If they choose to work with one of our global alliance partners, we will position the partner. If they choose Accelerated SAP [SAP's new rapid implementation methodology for national accounts], we can recommend a group of smaller partners who are certified implementers. Initially, I will have to subcontract these small partners in under me. Even though they have good people, they don't yet have a reputation for successful implementation.

Coote felt so strongly about getting a rapid implementation methodology in place that he had accelerated its timetable. Reorganizing by lines of business had made it easier, he thought, to adopt a strategy for the middle market that differed from past approaches. Salvucci, who now had national account sales responsibility, concurred:

> One of our strategies for selling in the middle market will be to engage our consulting organization early in the sales cycle, and put a stake in the ground for customers: If you want to use our methodology to install SAP, this is what you can expect in time and money. If our partners won't step up and meet these targets, we will do it ourselves. That does not mean we are going to go out and do all the consulting. We are not. What we are doing is putting a stake in the ground to increase our control over the process.

In the global market, Basho also intended to bring down implementation time and costs. She explained:

> I am also increasing our involvement with global accounts. From the beginning, global support managers are now strategically placed to deal directly with the customer's executive sponsor and to

educate the customer about how to use our partners more effectively. The GSM sets the implementation strategy, gets the right people onto the projects, and keeps the program from going off track.

Basho was keenly aware that this new approach would impact partner relationships, although she did not envision major changes in strategy. She observed: "Our partner strategy was and is sound. The problem is that we gave up too much control." Coote agreed, noting that SAP America's approach to global accounts was one of continuing evolution. He observed:

> We have to be more involved than in the past, and that means we have to refine the partnering model. In addition, our product has continued to evolve, and we have more tools available for automating some of the configuration work. Partners have to understand their changing role in the mix and that the relationship will continue to change.

Case 6–2

MILLIPORE CORPORATION (A)

Summer/Fall 1985

It was July 10, 1985, at the Bedford, Massachusetts, headquarters of the Millipore Corporation, a medium-sized firm (1984 worldwide sales of $332 million) engaged in the development, manufacture, and marketing of products used for the analysis and purification of fluids in critical applications. Fresh from a two-week vacation, chief financial officer John Gilmartin was called into a meeting with Millipore president John (Jack) Mulvany. He emerged with a new title: president of the Millipore Products Division (MPD). The new head of Millipore's largest operating division had these comments on his assignment:

> The whole change took me by surprise. I had just finished telling Jack about my vacation, when he announced that Fred Hildebrandt, the president of MPD, would be leaving and that I was the board's choice for the job. Jack said that things just didn't feel right in MPD. MPD was supposed to be growing at 15–20 percent worldwide but had stalled at 10–12

percent. Jack's feeling was that innovation had been made secondary, that job descriptions and cost controls and procedures all were inhibiting the development of new products and applications and markets. So the mandate was to get the top line moving, and one piece of that was putting together a more market focused, innovative, entrepreneurial setting. I didn't get any specifics from Jack and had no crisp four-point plan going into the job, although with six years in the company, I came with some strong suspicions. I felt a strong need to make an impact, to say someone's in charge and we'll be going in a different direction . . . though I didn't know what that direction would be.

Millipore and the Business of Separations Technology

Corporate History[1]

Millipore was founded in 1954 when chemist Jack Bush licensed a technology that had originated in Germany for microporous plastic membranes, based on a hunch that there was a market for it. By varying

---

This case was prepared by Shirley M. Spence under the direction of Paul R. Lawrence.

---

[1]*This section draws from Donald K. Clifford, Jr., and Richard F. Cavanaugh,* The Winning Performance: How America's High-Growth Midsize Companies Succeed *(New York: Bantam Books, 1985).*

the number of pores per square centimeter of the membrane, Millipore could filter just about any size of microscopic particle from just about any fluid. The challenge was to identify the most economic and high-potential applications. The key to success proved to be a customer-oriented strategy and a series of creative niche entries. Jack Bush, joined in the early 1960s by a Harvard MBA named Dee d'Arbeloff, traveled around the country talking to potential customers who provided a steady stream of ideas for high value-added applications. Over the years, the most important applications proved to be these: the purification of drugs by pharmaceutical manufacturers; the removal of defect-causing contaminants from integrated circuit-process fluids by microelectronics producers; the protection of patients from the complications of intravenous therapy by health care practitioners; the clarification of wine by the beverage industry; the bacteriological monitoring of drinking water supplies by public health agencies; gene harvesting by bioresearchers; and the purification of water for a wide range of industrial, research, and medical uses. For each application, Millipore custom-tailored a membrane-based solution to the customer's problem, creating niches for continued growth.

From 1960 to 1979, Millipore was one of the hottest high-tech stars. From a specialized filter manufacturer with scarcely more than $1 million in sales, it grew to a multinational corporation with sales of almost $195 million and operating profits of more than $35 million. The financial community came to rely on Millipore's predictable 20 percent–plus earnings growth, and the company's pride in this outstanding performance was evident in its high-energy, fast-paced work environment. Then came a modest decline in profits in 1980, followed by a steep drop in 1981. Millipore's difficulties could be traced to a number of external factors: deep recession in its key markets, international currency dislocations, and intensified competition. Some observers, however, pointed to four *internal* problem sources: (1) "indigestion" from acquisitions of technologically related businesses, which were acquired in pursuit of d'Arbeloff's vision of Millipore as a broad-based separations company; (2) confusion and bureaucracy

resulting from organizational experiments with dividing MPD into smaller divisions and adopting a formal matrix structure; (3) a shift at the operating level from emphasis on long-term, value-related goals, such as quality, innovation, and customer service, to emphasis on short-term financial goals; and (4) weak internal monitoring systems and financial controls.

In response to these problems, a dozen of Millipore's top managers met off-site in the fall of 1981 for a review of the company's values, objectives, and general direction. The result was a decision "to bite the bullet" and to take a series of action steps: reduction of expenses and staffing levels; sale of a division and use of proceeds to reduce long-term debt; reintegration of the Millipore Products Division; committee review and companywide reaffirmation of Millipore's core values; and control system improvements that involved the "cleaning up" of Millipore's balance sheet by chief financial officer John Gilmartin. Following these 1981 decisions, three years of steady improvements in operating profits culminated in a near-record performance in 1984, which also saw sales grow 14 percent. (See Exhibit 1 for financial details.)

Millipore's $332 million in sales made it a world leader in the field of high value-added separations technology. In 1984 the worldwide market was estimated at approximately $2 billion and was expected to grow 15 percent to 20 percent over the next five years. Millipore's product lineup (2,000 major products and systems backed up by 8,000 accessories, supplies, and consumables) encompassed three technologies that collectively addressed over 80 percent of the total separations market: membranes, ion exchange, and high-performance liquid chromatography.[2]

---

[2]*Although 30 companies sold products similar to Millipore's, no single competitor offered as broad a line. In 1984, Millipore's chief competitors were Pall and Gelman in membranes and Perkin Elmer, Varian, and Pharmacia in high-performance liquid chromatography. Also, Japanese manufacturers employing low-cost supplier strategies were a growing force in both of these technology segments.*

EXHIBIT 1 Millipore Ten-Year Summary of Operations (in thousands, except per share and employee data)

	1984	1983	1982	1981	1980	1979	1978	1977	1976	1975
Net sales	$332,102	$292,464	$271,835	$255,803	$234,363	$194,615	$158,013	$118,456	$88,636	$70,752
Cost of sales	153,463	133,433	126,635	125,914	100,036	79,770	62,110	46,280	34,806	28,848
Gross profit	178,639	159,031	145,200	129,889	134,327	114,845	95,903	72,176	53,830	41,904
Selling, general and administrative expenses	118,756	108,746	105,328	97,817	89,283	67,629	54,023	38,952	28,615	20,514
Research and development expenses	24,603	21,824	17,724	13,886	13,686	11,573	8,961	6,600	5,309	4,581
Operating income	35,280	28,461	22,148	18,186	31,358	35,643	32,919	26,624	19,906	16,809
Income before income taxes	36,289	28,235	22,880	13,740	27,834	33,372	31,864	26,226	19,852	16,462
Net income	30,493[a]	20,664	33,318	10,928	18,763	21,848	18,747	15,139	11,310	8,572
Net income per common share	2.21[a]	1.52	2.46	.81	1.40	1.67	1.45	1.18	.88	.70
Cash dividends declared per share	.43	.39	.35	.31	.27	.23	.19	.15	.11	.09
Average shares outstanding	13,776[b]	13,635	13,546	13,526	13,406	13,104	12,931	12,876	12,839	12,278
Financial Data										
Working capital	121,075	107,102	96,166	96,037	95,691	80,829	64,255	46,940	40,231	33,406
Total assets	300,714	275,199	256,802	252,319	239,204	183,828	148,270	108,262	85,284	68,203
Shareholders' equity	214,199	192,796	177,754	152,155	142,759	122,462	98,067	79,018	65,284	53,072
Number of employees at year-end	4,215	4,070	4,001	3,860	3,959	3,441	3,240	2,665	2,270	1,673

[a] Includes $4 million ($0.29 per share) nonrecurring DISC benefit.
[b] Distribution of ownership: 60 percent in hands of institutions (including Dow, the sole corporate owner, which owned over 9 percent) with balance owned by individuals and families. Only 2 percent was held by Millipore officers or directors.

Source: Millipore Corporation Annual Report

Millipore's broad technology base was believed to provide a competitive advantage in meeting a wide range of customer needs. Pharmaceutical, chemical, and food industry customers were Millipore's traditional stronghold and still accounted for more than half of total sales in 1984. Microelectronics and biotechnology were considered future growth markets. Millipore products were distributed in 60 countries, with foreign sales accounting for 47 percent total revenues in 1984.

In 1985, Millipore employees were working toward four long-term objectives: (1) 15 percent annual average revenue growth, (2) 10 percent return on sales, (3) creation of new and attractive niches in the field of high value-added separations, and (4) improvement of present applications. Jack Mulvany discussed Millipore's business strategy at a May 1985 meeting of the firm's shareholders. Mulvany described the application life cycle and the differing criteria for success in the early market development phase and in the subsequent competitive phase. (See Exhibit 2 for a follow-up interview published in the employee newsletter.) Mulvany closed on an upbeat note, predicting $1 billion in sales by the turn of the decade.

Just one month later, Millipore's mood was dampened by the death of Dee d'Arbeloff after a courageous seven-month battle with cancer. Although clearly a designated successor,[3] Mulvany stepped into the role of chairman of the board aware of the fact that some outsiders questioned whether Millipore could sustain its momentum without d'Arbeloff, a man described as a prototypical entrepreneur and the architect of Millipore's growth.

_____

[3]_Mulvany, who held degrees in chemistry and physics, was hired by d'Arbeloff in 1966 as a sales manager for Millipore's British subsidiary and subsequently became its managing director. In 1970, he joined the marketing department at corporate headquarters. He was elected president, chief operating officer, and a director in 1980, and succeeded d'Arbeloff to the chief executive post in February 1984._

Millipore Products Division

In 1983, the Millipore Products Division (MPD) was reassembled from smaller divisional units (i.e., business units with their own marketing, sales, and research and development responsibilities), which had been in place for approximately five years. In 1984 MPD, which had worldwide profit and loss responsibility for Millipore's membrane and ion exchange product lines, contributed approximately $30 million in operating profits on sales of $169 million. (See Exhibit 3 for MPD income statements.) The MPD mission statement read as follows:

> Millipore Products Division (MPD) is a worldwide leader in the applications of membrane-based products for the analysis and purification of fluids. MPD will enhance its market leadership position through exploiting new membrane-based opportunities. MPD will continue to focus on high value-added applications for membrane purification products in the pharmaceutical, electronics, and beverage markets, and on discovering new opportunities in other markets. MPD will pursue market needs for water purification by applying both membrane and ion exchange technology, and will continue to exploit existing and new opportunities in laboratory and health care applications.

MPD's core technology was the removal of particles from liquids and gases via filtration through membranes, which were thin plastic sheets with millions of pores per square centimeter. The company's first product was a simple filter disk used with a holder. Over the years, MPD had broadened its membrane technology to include three types of increasingly fine filtration materials—microporous, ultrafiltration, and reverse osmosis—which were packaged in convenient forms and tailored to specific applications. In 1985 MPD offered a variety of materials designed to suit the size of the particle to be filtered and the chemical properties of the fluid of interest. It also offered a number of configurations, including pleated cartridges, spiral-bound cartridges, and stacked disks. Membrane-filtration systems ranged from simple disposable plastic devices, for which the only hardware needed was a stainless steel housing, to sophisticated capital equipment.

EXHIBIT 2   Jack Mulvany: On Millipore's Strengths, Strategies, and Culture

Editor's note: At last month's annual shareholders meeting in Milford, Massachusetts, Millipore's President Jack Mulvany evaluated the company's success and talked about the directions he sees Millipore taking in the next few years. He touched on the growth of Millipore's markets, the company's ability to compete, and its business strategies. The interview below is a follow-up to that presentation; in his remarks here Mulvany elaborates on Millipore's strategies and directions, and discusses how the company will remain competitive and achieve its goal of an annual 15 percent growth rate. He also talks about Millipore's culture, and offers some personal insights about his role as CEO.

Milliscope: *In your remarks at the shareholders meeting you talked about there being a shift from defining Millipore in terms of technologies to defining the company in terms of "high value-added applications." Could you elaborate on this concept, and explain how it is different from what the company has done in the past?*

Jack Mulvany: It's important to understand that Millipore's strength is discovering new customer problems we can solve with our technological capabilities, and then providing the customer *solutions* to those problems. The term *applications* is a good word to describe what really drives us. There must be a continuous interaction between technology and the marketplace—you make those two things work for you to end up with a new product and application.

This concept is not different from what we've done in the past; it's different from how we've *talked* about ourselves in the past. What we've been doing for 30 years is discovering applications and using our technology to develop new products to serve those applications. But we've tended to talk about ourselves in technology terms as a chromatography company or a membrane company. We're really an applications-driven company.

Milliscope: *Isn't this focus on future needs and applications somewhat in conflict with what you described as the need for price and performance competition, and the need for efficiency?*

Mulvany: Yes, it would seem to be in conflict—unless you consider what I call the "applications life cycle." There are really two very different phases to an application; the market development phase, and the competitive phase. During the market development phase, a customer has a problem and doesn't know how to resolve it, so we come in with our solution and educate the customer. The education is an example of our "value added." At some point, as the customer begins to get educated, and the application is becoming widely used, a phase of rapid growth occurs. The customer says "I know what I want, because I have the application knowledge, and now I'm going to look for the best buy." That's when the competition frequently moves in.

If we develop the applications and aren't positioned to compete effectively, then we'll lose the major return. We must have a mind-set that recognizes there are times in every application when we have to be competitive. And during the development phase we need to prepare for the competitive phase, so that when it comes, we can win.

Milliscope: *So is Millipore's primary goal to be a low-cost producer, rather than a differentiated supplier?*

Mulvany: This applications life cycle pulls the concepts together and says we've got to be *both*. You can't say Millipore is always going to be differentiated and never be a low-cost producer, and you can't say we're going to be only a low-cost producer—because we'll never develop the new businesses that way. We've got to be a player for all seasons, if you will. There are times when we should educate and price accordingly, and there are times when we must be the most efficient producer and effectively compete. Both are legitimate; they're just different stages of the application life cycle.

Milliscope: *What does Millipore need to do to become a "low-cost producer" when that is appropriate?*

Mulvany: Actually, I prefer the term "most efficient producer" rather than "low-cost producer," which can be misinterpreted to mean low quality or minimal capability. The first thing we have to do, as I mentioned,

(continued)

EXHIBIT 2   (*continued*)

is *recognize* that there is a competitive phase and be innovative in thinking about designs that can be efficiently produced. Once into the competitive phase, we need to optimize manufacturing: What really ought to be the performance capability of this product? Have we designed it for efficient production? Are we making it in the right location? What can we do about uniformity between products so we maximize the use of common equipment and components, etc.?

Milliscope: *You issued two challenges in your talk: to give top priority to maintaining the ability to compete, and to remain committed to growth of at least 15 percent per year. How can Millipore meet these challenges?*

Mulvany: We're participating in markets with technologies that have inherent and sustainable growth. We have to continue to discover new applications for our technologies—and push our technologies to new levels of capability. We've also got to maintain our market share during that competitive cycle. We've got to be efficient, and be the best competitor in our industry. I think these challenges involve everyone in the company.

Milliscope: *What are the biggest obstacles to Millipore achieving that kind of growth?*

Mulvany: I don't think there are any big obstacles. The biggest *challenges* for us are maintaining an entrepreneurial, innovative environment, and not letting complacency or bureaucracy get in the way. We need to recognize that even though we're winners, we must work hard to keep our values and intensity alive.

Milliscope: *In describing Millipore's environment and the effort to keep this intensity alive, you talked about penalizing bureaucracy and rewarding risk. How would you define bureaucracy and risk?*

Mulvany: One example of bureaucracy is people putting in systems, procedures, and hurdles in business that are a function of minimizing risk and protecting themselves. It's the mentality that says cover yourself, and don't second-guess. We need to have an environment that climbs above that kind of thinking. I'd like everyone to ask themselves what they would do if it was their business, and they didn't have anyone looking over their shoulders. We all need to focus on the important things, and if something doesn't make sense, question it and escalate it.

Milliscope: *Isn't there a fine line, though, between fostering that kind of entrepreneurialism and maintaining a certain needed structure in a company that's growing as fast as Millipore?*

Mulvany: Yes, we've got to have certain systems and procedures; we don't want chaos. But we want to avoid *unproductive* behavior. It's hard to gain experience unless we attempt new hurdles, some of which we won't make first time around. But it's far better to make attempts that don't always work out, than to avoid making attempts because we are afraid to fail.

Milliscope: *You've been CEO for a little more than a year now; what has it been like for you? What have been your biggest challenges?*

Mulvany: I'd been with the company nearly 20 years, so it wasn't like walking into a brand new job. But I think the biggest challenge for me has been shifting from dealing with operational issues to thinking about the company long term, about how our goals and strategies are going to get us through the 1990s. I guess most people regard me as an operational type of person, but we've got a sound management team here, and I've been able to unhook myself from the operational level and really start thinking about how we leverage our capabilities, whether we're in the right markets, how to add to our technology base, and how we're going to meet our growth targets.

Milliscope: *What is the most fun part of your job?*

Mulvany: I think the most enjoyable part of my job is recognizing other people's successes. It really feels good to be in a position where you can say to an individual or a group, "That was a task well done. Thanks." I also really enjoy the challenges of the long-term market and technology issues. I like walking around the R&D labs and talking to people who deal with customers, finding out what's going on. That's exciting.

(*continued*)

EXHIBIT 2   *(concluded)*

Milliscope: *What are your personal goals for the company?*

Mulvany: I want to see us be an even more successful company than we have been. I want us to feel good about what we do. And as we grow I want us to keep the openness and the candidness you can have in a smaller environment. You know, Millipore is a super company, and I hope that we all will remain as proud of Millipore as we have been in the past.

EXHIBIT 3   MPD Income Statements (dollars in thousands)

			1985	
	1983 (Actual)	*1984 (Actual)*	*Budget*	*Projected*
Sales	$153,245	$169,240	$191,420	$176,730
Cost of sales	77,357	85,716	96,104	86,589
Gross margin	75,888	83,524	95,316	90,141
Selling, marketing & service expenses	35,059	30,062	32,762	32,347
General & administrative expenses	9,608	9,432	8,955	8,707
Research & development expenses	12,606	13,894	14,794	13,923
Corporate contribution	$18,615	$30,136	$38,805	$35,164

Source: Millipore Corporation

Millipore had acquired the Continental Water Conditioning Corporation and its ion exchange technology in 1979 to enable the company to better meet its customers' needs for high-purity water. The new product line consisted of ion exchange cartridges, which used a chemical process to remove salts from water. The customer could use the ion exchange cartridges for several days or weeks and then have them picked up and "regenerated" at local service centers. In addition to these local service centers, the acquisition included nationwide service centers from which Millipore's other traditional water products could be distributed and serviced.

In 1985 MPD offered more than 2,000 individual products (see Exhibit 4 for sampling) to research scientists, production and quality control engineers, and physicians. Most products were stock items ordered by mail or telephone from the MPD catalog. Traditionally, consumable products with unit prices of under $100 represented the bulk of MPD's business; the rest was accounted for by capital equipment ranging in price from $20 for a cartridge housing to $86,000 for an industrial-scale water system assembled from standard modules and accessories.[4] MPD management further grouped products into four broad application categories: (1) laboratory products, used in thousands of analytical and quality control

_____

[4]*Company observers noted that consumable sales had eroded from an optimal level of 80 percent of total revenues to under 65 percent in 1985.*

EXHIBIT 4   Sampling of MPD Products

Source: Millipore Corporation

applications by a highly fragmented customer base; (2) industrial products, used to clean or sterilize manufacturing process fluids by pharmaceutical, chemical, beverage, and electronics companies;[5] (3) water systems, used in a wide range of customer settings, and (4) OEM (original equipment manufacturer) medical devices, used as intravenous therapy filters by health care practitioners who purchased them from Millipore's customers, the hospital supply companies. (See Exhibit 5 for MPD sales by product category.)

---

[5]*Millipore was unique in offering both laboratory and manufacturing-scale filtration systems. At a process development scale-up facility in Bedford, MPD engineers helped customers move the processing of pharmaceutical and other products from the research laboratory into full-scale production.*

MPD Organization and Operations

Hildebrandt Era

Frederic (Fred) Hildebrandt began his three-year tenure as MPD president in 1982, following Millipore's worst year of performance. He held an engineering degree and had 20 years of work experience, including his most recent position as a divisional general manager at Foxboro Analytical Instruments. At Millipore, Hildebrandt had broad discretion in operating matters and full responsibility for MPD's worldwide business. Described as polite but distant, Hildebrandt brought to MPD a professional management style and an efficiency-oriented approach that clashed sharply with the division's freewheeling culture. Although his

EXHIBIT 5 MPD 1985 Product Line Sales by Quarter (Projected) (dollars in thousands)

Product Center[a]	Application	Worldwide					U.S. Only				
		Q1	Q2	Q3	Q4	Total	Q1	Q2	Q3	Q4	Total
(1) Chemical & Electronics	Industrial process (chemicals/semiconductors)	$ 5,175	$ 5,001	$ 4,243	$ 4,032	$ 18,450	$ 2,421	$ 2,228	$ 2,110	$ 1,725	$ 8,484
(2) Biological Filtration/Clarification	Industrial process (pharmaceutical/food & beverage)	7,842	7,893	7,479	8,208	31,422	3,976	3,613	3,616	3,669	14,874
(3) Tangential Filters		585	611	354	487	2,037	524	293	76	131	1,024
(4) Fabricated Filters	Laboratory research and analysis	5,673	5,923	5,221	5,898	22,715	2,302	2,379	2,216	2,288	9,185
(5) Analytical Filters	(industrial/medical/government)	11,920	11,932	10,955	11,479	46,286	5,951	6,031	5,699	5,576	23,257
(6) Water Systems	Water purification (all markets)	9,945	10,294	10,099	11,215	41,553	6,785	7,310	7,030	7,234	28,359
(7) Medical	Intravenous filters (OEM)	2,708	2,590	2,155	2,702	10,155	2,681	2,500	2,161	2,633	9,975
(8) Miscellaneous		1,125	951	752	1,284	4,112	31	−30	16	150	167
TOTAL		$44,972	$45,195	$41,258	$45,305	$176,730	$24,671	$24,324	$22,924	$23,406	$95,325

[a]Each product center included about a dozen major product lines tailored to a particular customer application.

Source: Millipore Corporation

success in instituting much-needed cost controls was widely acknowledged, Hildebrandt also drew criticism. In the words of a product manager:

> Fred was very strong on discipline: systems, structures, controls, organizational charts. He was a drastic change for a loose company where people were used to being independent and free to make decisions on new initiatives. It was apparent here in the trenches that people were losing their desire to do new things, that market creativity was being stifled. There was too much structure and control, and this affected morale.

According to a second marketing employee:

> Hildebrandt brought how Foxboro did things and tried to impose that on Millipore. His smokestack approach of leveraging the cost side and building systems makes sense in a predictable environment where you're being incremental. But it appeared inappropriate in a situation where new ideas are always coming up, where you need to be entrepreneurial and opportunistic. If we want to keep our customers on the leading edge of technology, we have to keep pace with the rate of change. Fred was lauded for bringing discipline, but at what cost? He did controls *instead* of innovation, but we need both. You don't need rules and procedures for that. You need a common understanding of goals, good communication, teamwork, and an atmosphere where opinions are valued. Hildebrandt's personal style was radically different from past senior managers. For example, he built a wall around his office area and put in executive parking places. The end result was that people got turned off and either left or kept their head[s] down.

When Hildebrandt arrived at MPD, he found it organized into four divisions described as "fiefdoms fighting over customers." The four profit centers were: (1) the industrial processing division, which marketed high-volume filtration systems to pharmaceutical, electronics, and beverage manufacturers; (2) the analytical products division, which served a wide variety of laboratory customers; (3) the medical products division, which sold devices used in the administration of intravenous solutions; (4) the water systems division,

which provided laboratory, medical, and industrial customers with water purification products capable of treating volumes of water ranging from 25 to 200,000 gallons per day. Noting that MPD's decentralized structure had resulted in considerable duplication of staff functions, Hildebrandt consolidated the four divisions and reorganized along functional lines. One MPD manager had these comments on the reorganization: "The rationale for the original move to smaller, market-focused divisions was that we weren't responsive enough to customer needs. Fred, though, saw a need to be more efficient and leaner. The new functional organization accomplished those objectives but also made communication among ourselves and with our customers more difficult."

In 1985 the MPD employee roster included about 2,000 persons, of whom 40 percent were professionals and 21 percent were located outside the United States. As division president, Hildebrandt reported to Jack Mulvany and supervised the heads of eight functional units: human resources, finance and administration, research and development, operations, North American sales, marketing, Europe, and Japan. (See Exhibit 6 for a partial organization chart.) Descriptions of these functional units follow.

Human Resources

Vice president of MPD human resources Wayne Kennedy described his role as follows: "I'm on the payroll to be proactive, to be a midwife to the organization, to make sure things are happening." His 15-person staff, which included a central services group and representatives assigned to specific functional areas, was responsible for U.S. personnel administration.

Finance and Administration

Financial support for MPD's worldwide business was provided by an 80-person group divided into three broad areas of responsibility—accounting, operations finance, and sales and marketing analysis—all of which reported to the division controller.

EXHIBIT 6 MPD Partial Organization Chart—June 1985

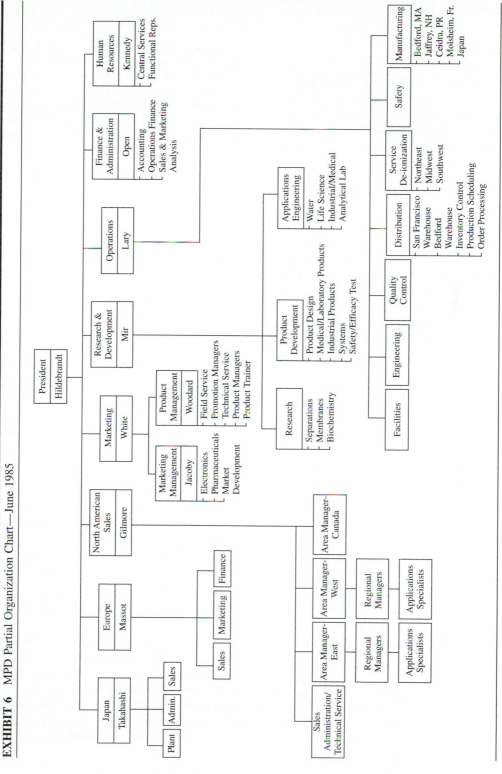

Source: Millipore Corporation

Research and Development

To maintain its traditional role as a leader in membrane separations technology, MPD supported a sizable internal research and development (R&D) organization and had also entered into some joint venture agreements. When Hildebrandt centralized the function, Leon Mir was assigned to the position of R&D vice president. Mir subsequently divided his organization into three activity-based sections: (1) research, which worked primarily to extend or enhance existing membrane technology and to develop new membrane materials; (2) applications engineering, which included four application-focused teams—water, life science, industrial/medical, and analytical laboratories—charged with finding new uses for existing and evolving technology; and (3) product development, which responded to new application needs by designing new configurations for MPD membranes and also developed hardware and accessories to incorporate membrane filters, modules, and devices into total separation systems. By 1985 Mir's Bedford-based organization had grown to 126 persons, was highly regarded, and attracted top research talent.

Although Millipore had broadened its membrane technology base over the years, microporous membranes remained, in 1985, the backbone of its business. The evolution of MPD's microporous technology and product line was described as follows by one R&D manager:

> For the first 20 years of our existence, we essentially lived off the original technology on which Jack Bush founded the company. By the 1970s, we were encountering strong competition worldwide. In that time frame, the Pall Corporation, always a worthy competitor, began offering a pleated membrane cartridge made out of a special nylon formulation, which had substantial competitive advantages. As we began to feel the impact in the market, we realized that we needed additional technological strengths. The edict from Dee d'Arbeloff was: "Develop a new membrane and products based on it." This sparked a major undertaking which, by the early 1980s, had resulted in the introduction of Millipore's Dura Pore

R product line. This product line is based on a polyvinyl fluoride membrane. When initially commercialized, product costs were high and profits low, but process improvements over the past few years have helped margins. Today, the Dura Pore R product line is a large success in the marketplace and an important contributor to MPD's sales and profits.

Traditionally, Millipore's product strategy was to offer a broad line of high-quality, differentiated products. MPD's ability to be the first to identify and respond to customer needs for membrane filtration remained an important competitive strength. Leon Mir offered these comments on new-product activity at MPD:

> If you develop a good membrane, which requires a fair amount of art as well as science, it can have a lifetime of 50 years. A new membrane material can take four to five years to develop but you'll get products out of it along the way. Currently, we put an R&D person in charge of each new-product project, which typically takes about two years to complete. It would be good to get marketing people involved, but their turnover is too high. Fred Hildebrandt wasn't deeply involved in the operations of research and development, and had limited impact on the choice of new products. In the fall of 1984, the senior marketing people and I decided we needed to plan to execute the new long-range plan, so we started a new-product committee that meets three or four times a year to discuss resource allocation issues.

In the early 1980s, senior management had begun to voice concern over a perceived slowdown in MPD's flood of new products, which historically generated about one-third of annual revenues. The problem was blamed on poor hand-offs in the product delivery process. Hildebrandt's solution was the addition of a pilot plant, which was credited with reducing product delays and improving efficiency. (See Exhibit 7 for a description of the six-step new-product delivery process.) In 1985, however, MPD's failure to field enough new products to meet growth targets remained an issue. Some managers

EXHIBIT 7   MPD New Product Delivery Process

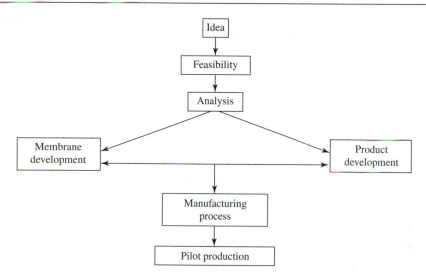

MPD's new-product development process was described as follows by one R&D manager:

The process starts with an *idea,* which may come from a laboratory person who sees an interesting and potentially useful new membrane property or from a marketing person who has identified a customer need and asks R&D to see if it can be satisfied. Next, R&D must confirm the *feasibility* of the product idea. If successful, we move to the *analysis* stage, where a decision must be made on whether or not to proceed with full-scale production and commercialization, based on our assessment of the product's market potential and the investment required to develop and launch it. If the project is a "go," we proceed along two paths that actually form an interactive loop: *membrane development,* where the basic membrane and a scale-up plan are developed; and *product development,* where engineers take the membrane and create a laboratory prototype of the final product. Next, a *manufacturing process* must be designed, followed by *pilot production* to debug the process and develop routines for full-scale production.

pointed to a lack of clear accountability for individual new-product projects. Other managers were more concerned by the fact that considerable effort was being expended on projects with questionable market potential. The then-head of MPD product development explained:

Millipore is the only place I've ever worked where there legitimately are too many opportunities. The issue is the dollar value of opportunities and whether we're doing the right thing strategically. We had delegated resource allocation for product development to marketing managers with a myopic view. The real decisions were made at lunchtime negotiations where the product manager who got along with the development people was the one whose stuff got done. I tried to break up this network by putting in forms that asked things like: "What will the product do? How many units will you sell?" But that smacked of bureaucracy and didn't work. The problem was that no one "owned" the new-product process. Department heads tried to work it out and make trade-offs, but it was hard to resolve conflicts.

Operations

Hildebrandt focused considerable attention on the operations area, where staff generally was supportive of his cost-control efforts. In the summer of 1985, vice president of operations Edward Lary oversaw a 1,200-person organization divided into seven broad responsibility areas:

1. *Manufacturing*—MPD conducted manufacturing operations in five locations: Bedford, Massachusetts, which served primarily as a pilot plant for new membranes and products; Jaffrey, New Hampshire, which specialized in industrial process products; Cidra, Puerto Rico, which produced high-volume products, including membranes, and was an automated plant; Molsheim, France, which fabricated membranes developed in the United States into filtration products tailored to Common Market customer needs; and Japan, which did custom work for the Pacific Basin and was a small facility.
2. *Engineering*—A staff of mechanical and industrial engineers based in Bedford addressed manufacturing issues for all MPD plants from a current product/technology standpoint and also worked with R&D on new-product development.
3. *Quality Control*—The MPD quality control group was responsible for production quality control and for regulatory affairs. It also managed the Acquisition of Customer Experience (ACE) program, which involved reviewing and reporting all customer complaints and suggestions.
4. *Safety*—Safety personnel monitored and worked to improve MPD safety standards and performance.
5. *Distribution*—The distribution group was responsible for the warehouses in San Francisco and Bedford. They performed production scheduling, inventory control, and order-processing functions. The order-processing staff quoted discounts, took telephone orders from customers for processing into MIS for shipment, and provided some minimal technical advice on customer applications.
6. *Service Deionization (SDI)*—SDI branches in 20 U.S. locations provided customers with on-site water purification. These service facilities included regeneration plants, where ion exchange cartridges were chemically treated for reuse; trucks for transportation of cartridges to and from customer sites; and service technicians for customer calls regarding problems such as equipment failure.
7. *Facilities*—Located in a wooded commercial park setting bought in 1960, Millipore's Bedford complex had grown to include five interconnected buildings housing both corporate and MPD divisional headquarters plus a membrane products pilot plant (see Exhibit 8 for floor plans). In 1985 space constraints were forcing the issue of another expansion.

North American Sales

MPD's 122-person North American sales organization consisted of the U.S. field sales force; Canadian subsidiary personnel; and a Bedford-based sales administration and technical service group, whose duties included responding by telephone to customers' application questions and technical problems. In 1984, Thomas Gilmore was hired as vice president of North American sales, bringing a background that included degrees in engineering and business administration, three years in the U.S. Navy, and nine years of marketing experience. One fellow MPD manager offered this assessment of Gilmore: "He was bright and very professional but had no sales experience. Also, he was from outside the industry and so lacked the relevant technology base."

In 1985 U.S. field sales responsibility was divided between Eastern and Western area managers. Each of these managers supervised four regional managers who in turn oversaw 8 to 12 application specialists who were responsible for selling all MPD products to all customer markets in their assigned geographic territories.[6] New field sales hires

---

[6]*In 1985, the average sales territory encompassed 50 customer accounts. Twenty percent of field representatives were dedicated to specific major accounts (e.g., Texas Instruments, Pfizer, IBM).*

EXHIBIT 8   Millipore's Bedford Facilities (Summer 1985)

First floor

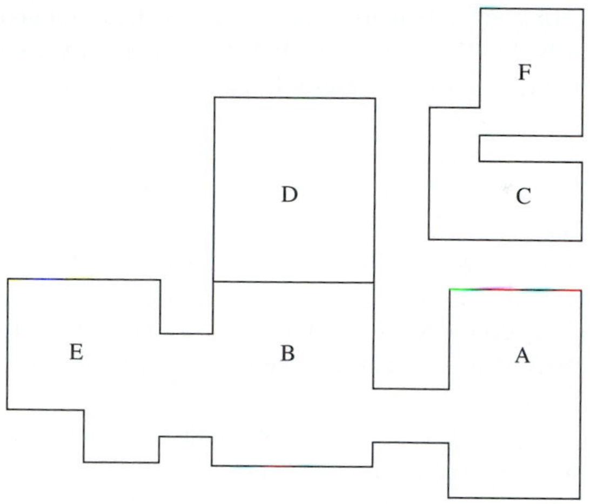

Second floor

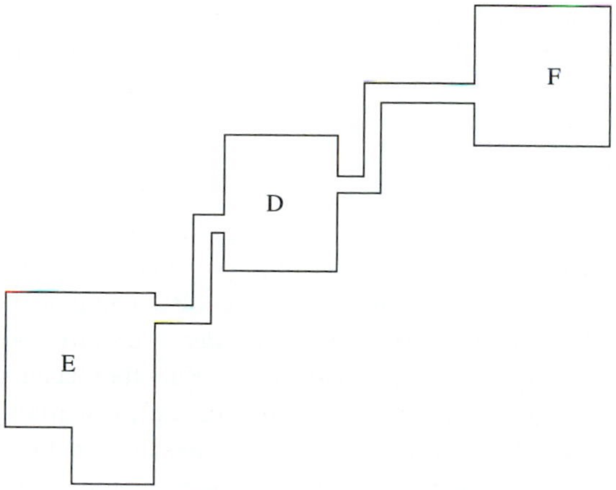

	First Floor	Second Floor
A	Research laboratories (separations/membranes/ biochemistry) Pilot production	
B	Drafting/central engineering Model shop Process and product development laboratories	
C	Membrane mixing/ drying	
D	Shipping Warehouse	MIS/computers
E	Product development and applications engineering laboratories Sales administration/ service Human resources Library/audiovisual Cafeteria Visitor's lobby	Finance and administration Marketing Executive offices
F	Controlled environment area Filter cutting/packaging/ quality control	Manufacturing offices

Source: Millipore Corporation

participated in a standardized training program at Bedford headquarters and then received in-field supervision from their regional managers. Field sales activities included servicing existing accounts, developing selected new market opportunities, and

following leads generated by promotion pieces, trade shows, referrals, or telephone inquiries. The 1985 compensation system, designed to attract and keep qualified specialists, offered such employees total earnings of $50,000 to $60,000, including a base salary of $30,000, plus commissions linked to achievement of sales quotas. Wayne Kennedy explained that compensation had become a major issue:

> Compensation was an issue because no one was making a nickel. The application specialists were very unhappy. Actually, it was the fault of the targeting system rather than the compensation system. The bottoms-up sales forecast for 1985 fell considerably short of the sales growth objectives targeted by senior management. Gilmore's solution was to divide the difference equally among his application specialists, so everyone's quota was raised by the same percentage regardless of geographic opportunities. This change in targets met with a lot of resentment and resistance. By midyear, the problems had been complicated by the fact that overall business was down due to slumps first in electronics and then in pharmaceutical and lab markets; targets then became a *cause célèbre.* Gilmore and I were unable to convince Hildebrandt that the problem was sufficiently acute to justify special adjustment in the incentive program.

Many MPD managers felt that the U.S. selling effort had been hurt by the 1982 switch from four divisional sales forces specialized by application area to a single (and smaller) sales organization that expected salespeople to cope with a broad range of customer needs. Sales force morale dropped, and many Ph.D.-trained application specialists left to be replaced by less technically expert "salespeople." By 1985, concern about sales-force competence had grown: "Our goal is to match Millipore technology with customer needs, yet our sales reps have a poor understanding of how our products work and what our customers' applications needs are." Struggling to cope with customers' very technical questions, field representatives frequently turned to MPD marketing managers for help.

Marketing

The demands of "firefighting" for the U.S. sales force left MPD marketers with little time for their assigned responsibilities: worldwide strategy formulation, new-product planning, and new-market development. Hildebrandt had tried to address the problem by dividing the marketing function into nuts-and-bolts product management and real marketing management. Marketing managers tended to be highly resistant to Hildebrandt's insistence that they focus on internal cost issues rather than on external growth opportunities. Morale sagged as the marketing department came under a barrage of criticism. International subsidiaries felt estranged; U.S. sales needed more support; new-product development wasn't being integrated with market needs; R&D efforts weren't being commercialized. Furthermore, as turnover increased, the age and experience of marketing staff dropped.

In partial response, Hildebrandt reinstituted the position of marketing vice president in 1985. Paul White, who was recruited from the Foxboro Company for the job of "pulling together marketing" and who held degrees in chemical engineering and business administration, had 20 years of work experience. In his new position, White directly supervised the heads of product management and marketing management. The 69-person product management group included promotion managers, who prepared sales literature; product managers, who were assigned to specific product lines; field service engineers, who were responsible for the installation and maintenance of capital equipment; and a product trainer, who educated sales hires on product positioning, applications, and other technical details. The small marketing management group included a market development manager charged with identifying new market opportunities, and managers for two specific customer markets—electronics and pharmaceuticals.

Europe

The general manager of MPD's European operations supervised a 167-person staff consisting of 65 sales representatives, a financial support group, and a marketing group that focused on the wine/beverage industry. Geoffrey Woodard, former director of marketing for MPD Europe, offered these observations six months into his new assignment at division headquarters in Bedford:

> There's much less customer responsiveness in Bedford relative to the subsidiaries, where the attitude that the priority is to serve the customer's needs permeates the organization. Maybe that's because of the size of the U.S. organization compared to the subsidiary, where everyone knows everyone. In the United States, there are more systems and less freedom. For example, Millipore has standard housings for membranes. In a subsidiary, if a customer wants different specs, a guy in a garage shop fixes it up in 15 minutes. A big part of Europe's success is because it will give the customer what he wants. In the U.S., there's a big long process, fussing with engineers, formal specs and so on. As a result, there's no risk taking here. For example, a product manager recently requested a test market for a new product that involved low quantities and no capital investment. A test market makes sense in a case where $400 million in tooling is required but not in this case. We need judgment. People ask: "Do you have any product failures?" I say: "We don't have enough." We should take risks. We have to in order to get the big wins. We must create an organization that tolerates failure. Everyone will make some mistakes.

Japan

Japanese subsidiary operations encompassed sales and administrative staff plus a small manufacturing facility geared to Pacific Basin market needs. The efforts of general manager Takahashi's 146-person organization were supplemented by extensive use of third-party distributors.

Summer of 1985

Business Trends

Midway through 1985, concern was mounting over MPD's lackluster business results. Worldwide sales had been reforecasted to amount to only $177 million in 1985, an increase of less than 5 percent from the preceding year and well below the original budget of $191 million. Regional business analyses showed healthy growth projections for Europe (+16 percent) and Japan (+10 percent) but

a disturbing 6 percent decline in U.S. sales. Mulvany's frustration with MPD management's failure to resolve U.S. business problems peaked at a late June meeting. Wayne Kennedy related the following account of the meeting:

> The background to the meeting was that Jack Mulvany was deeply concerned because he thought the average application specialist was spread too thin to understand or to cover all our markets. In addition, application specialists calling on large process customers weren't calling on the laboratory researcher at the front end. Jack believed that you needed to make the investment and get into the lab and felt MPD wasn't addressing the problem. As the result of discussions between Jack and Fred, a meeting was arranged with Jack, Fred, and Fred's staff. At this meeting, for which no agenda had been distributed, Jack's initial question was, "What are you doing about declining U.S. sales?" The response was silence. No one was prepared. Jack was asking good questions about sales, but getting few answers. Jack got frustrated and finally said, "It's clear to me you're unprepared for this problem," and walked out. Jack's loss of faith in Fred's ability to solve the sales growth problem, combined with Fred's lack of support from other senior managers and outside directors, eventually led to agreement that it would be in everybody's best interest for Fred to pursue other career opportunities.

Leadership Transition

At 4:30 P.M. on July 17, 1985, Fred Hildebrandt called together MPD department heads and informed them that he would be leaving Millipore due to irreconcilable differences in management philosophy between Jack Mulvany and himself. At department staff meetings early the next morning, MPD employees were informed that John Gilmartin would be assuming the position of president. Gilmartin, whose background included an MBA from Harvard plus 12 years of finance and general management experience at Pfizer, had joined Millipore as corporate controller in 1979 and had subsequently been promoted to senior vice president and chief financial officer. Shortly after these department staff meetings, the leadership change was publicly announced. The reaction was widespread surprise, as explained by corporate communications officer John Glass:

> Externally, no one realized anything was wrong with Fred. The financial community had just finished a few years of getting used to Fred and had come to like and respect him, so they were very surprised. The Gilmartin choice also raised some eyebrows. Shareholders were saying, "What? You're always telling us how important our customers and markets are, and now you put a finance guy in charge?" Security analysts knew John in his CFO role and liked the guy but also were skeptical, so I had them come in and talk to him. They asked, "How is it you have any business running a division?" He said, "Good question. Give me some time." Basically, he recognized their concerns as legitimate and went on to say he would take the time to learn and showed he had already done some learning by picking a few examples and digging in and describing technology and markets. He said that obviously the company had done many things right, so he wouldn't be tearing up plans but rather would reassess the current plan and put his mark on portions of it. Internally, too, there were questions about putting the CFO in charge of the family jewels. People on the board, especially Jack Bush, were sensitive to the fact that the MPD president's role involved more than managing the company's largest division and core business. It meant being custodian of the home office site, keeper of the faith, guardian of the corporate culture.

Gilmartin's First Steps

Getting Acquainted

John Gilmartin offered this account of his first days in the role of MPD president:

> The first thing I did was to knock down walls, literally. Senior management had walled itself in, and the walls had become symbols of the attitude "This used to be a fun place to work. Now, I do what I'm told." I also pulled up the executive parking place signs. These were symbolic moves intended to break down structure and show people we're all in this together. I wanted people to open up. My first staff meeting was indicative of just how tense things had become around here. The meeting started with a

capital spending request, which I approved. Then an old-time engineering guy put up a slide of an improved mold for a petrie dish. Everyone said: "Not yet. It's not worked out yet." It turns out that all the forms hadn't been filled out. Yet here it was July with no staff meeting scheduled for six weeks, so we would have lost time just because all the functional groups weren't signed off on it. I said, "Wait. What do you think? Do it. Place the order with the supplier and do the paperwork later." In the cafeteria at lunch, some manufacturing guys came up and said, "You really came through. We made a test, put up a proposal that was half-baked but clearly right. You really are going to change things. Word will go out." This was part of an interesting process of the organization—watching, testing, probing. At this point, I was still working on culture and attitudes and didn't see a clear direction yet.

Gilmartin eagerly launched into the task of learning about MPD, taking the high-visibility approach of informal visits to various departments, frequent attendance at meetings, and "just walking the halls." The normal budget cycle, which confirmed the urgency of the U.S. sales slump and provided evidence of a shrinking new-product flow, provided a natural forum for discussion of broad business issues with the marketing group. When Gilmartin turned to product and market managers, he discovered that they were spending most of their time on U.S. sales-support activities. The results of Gilmartin's observations were three budget themes for 1986—customer focus, investment in sales and marketing, and new-product planning—in addition to some important steps toward addressing organizational problems.

Focus on Sales

Gilmartin moved quickly to address U.S. business problems, turning to field personnel for answers:

> I went to a sales meeting in July and found most applications specialists getting up and saying they were going to come in well below target. I was probing and finally a regional manager said, "Look, this budget was given to me. I never thought it was right. Is it OK for me to tell you that?" I took them out to dinner and said, "I can't run this business without openness. Open up. Let's share our problems

and go forward." The story was that, by midyear, applications specialists knew they had no chance of making bonus. Actually, they knew that going into the year, because quotas were all out of whack, but a second quarter downturn in the electronics industry clinched it. Essentially, they had given up. The problem was clear from talking with applications specialists, who also were asking what I was going to do about it.

Sales Crisis Management.   Recognizing that the vice president of sales had lost all credibility with the field organization, Gilmartin replaced him with Henry (Hank) Clemente. Clemente, whose background included a degree in biochemistry and work experience as an analytical chemist, had joined Millipore in 1977 and had subsequently served in a number of sales and marketing positions domestically and abroad. Clemente described his first steps as head of MPD's North American sales group as follows: "I started by meeting with area and regional managers, 95 percent of whom I already knew. For three 12-hour days we focused on two questions: What are the problems? How do we solve them? Basically, the problems were people problems, motivational problems. The overriding complaint was that the organization was not sensitive to their needs in the field."

Over the second half of 1985, Gilmartin authorized approximately $1.5 million in incremental funding for three major initiatives: (1) a new bonus program that maintained established quotas but stepped up dollar incentives, (2) the addition of 12 sales representatives as part of Clemente's plan to reduce territory size and to specialize the field force by customer markets (which plan included creating a separate sales group for water systems products), and (3) a "Sales Action Millipore" system to replace a previously eliminated lead-qualifying program. Observers noted a dramatic improvement in morale under Clemente's leadership: "Clemente was a tough cookie and tolerated no sniveling. He commanded a lot of respect from the sales force and gave them someone to follow. Within three months, the sales force's attitude had turned 100 percent."

Clemente also identified some serious structural problems with the U.S. selling organization:

We had lots of people trying to help us, but the U.S. structure was getting in the way of our ability to respond to customer needs. For example, water systems are sold by my application specialists but serviced by engineers who report to operations, which causes huge delays when a customer with a service problem calls the rep who sold him the unit. As another example, one of our biggest semiconductor customers was asking for just-in-time inventory, a new thing for us. I called our California distribution center to say: "Let's experiment with $10,000 in inventory." Distribution, however, reports to purchasing, who began asking questions. Seven meetings and three months later, we got the go-ahead.

U.S. Sales Subsidiary.   Although there was broad consensus at MPD on the need to make the U.S. sales group more self-sufficient, the "U.S. Sales Subsidiary" concept was actually born of Gilmartin's efforts to address space problems at Bedford headquarters. Gilmartin explained his thinking this way:

We had outgrown our Bedford office space and so were considering leasing an adjacent building. The first idea was to split off the administrative group. But the more I thought of sales and the differences between our foreign and domestic selling operations, the more I thought that maybe we should physically separate the U.S. sales group from corporate headquarters in order to cut the amount of bureaucracy and make it easier to focus externally. The idea generated huge enthusiasm, and we put together a task force under Wayne Kennedy to design a sales organization that would bring together all our customer activity under Clemente's direction.

The 16-person U.S. Sales Subsidiary task force, which included functional representatives from every MPD department, had a clear objective: "To provide for a more customer-responsive integrated selling team in the U.S. market similar to the organization that exists in MPD's foreign subsidiaries." Subcommittees were formed to address the question of which pre- and postsales functions to add to the U.S. selling organization, to determine staffing requirements, and to delineate organizational interdependencies. Separate subcommittees simultaneously looked at space requirements, communications, MIS support needs, and financial requirements. The task force's final report recommended that the new organization include three major functions: field marketing, field sales, and sales support. The report also provided a financial schedule detailing incremental costs of $1.2 million over 1986 budget plans and presented an implementation timetable with a May 1986 target date for the move to new facilities. At an early December presentation to MPD and corporate management, the report met with overwhelming approval and the observation that the divisional marketing group would benefit significantly from the shifting of its current sales support duties to the new field marketing function. (See Exhibit 9 for U.S. Sales Subsidiary organization chart.)

Product Planning
Gilmartin believed that new products and innovation required involvement of the top officers of the organization. His early efforts to "come up to speed on technology" were noted with approval by R&D staff, who also commented on the difference in comparison with his predecessor's more distant role. Mir welcomed the greater top-management involvement as "helpful interference" that would help build companywide consensus and commitment to R&D efforts. By the end of 1985, company observers were seeing an improvement in MPD's new product flow: "Gilmartin went through all the R&D projects and dusted some off. So, it's not that he started a bunch of new initiatives. He just went back and said, 'That one in the corner looks good. Go for it.'"

Headquarters Reorganization
Over his first few months, Gilmartin struggled with the question of how to address problems in MPD's functional organization:

> When I got here, I found a strongly entrenched functional organization structure. People were doing a good job within their functional definitions, but there was a compartmental mentality. Coordination at lower levels probably was better than at middle or upper largely for survival reasons: They had to ship

something. The problem was that in the absence of upper-level involvement, lower levels were making almost all policy decisions. Another problem was that in all of the interface issues, customer needs got lost. We had got too caught up in managing ourselves versus managing the customer.

> I didn't want to be one of those funny stories about reorganizations, but I talked with Jack Mulvany, and he agreed we needed a fast switch from a functional to a divisional structure. The challenge was *how* to do it. I really wrestled with that because I knew we could lose a lot if it was done the wrong way. It was tremendously threatening to people, because they were married to their functions. Mulvany favored fully integrated divisions but I wasn't so sure, partly because there was still a sour taste from the small integrated divisions adopted in the late 1970s.

Current Situation

Early in the fall of 1985, Gilmartin announced that he intended to restructure MPD marketing with the objective of creating small units focused on the customer. The announcement, which prompted the marketing vice president's resignation, marked the beginning of a three-month organizational design effort led by Gilmartin:

> In September I signaled that we would be going to some sort of divisional structure. I said I would take several weeks, talk to all affected, listen to all opinions, and then make a decision. I saw a long line of people and probably made and unmade five or six organizations in the process. Part of the task was deciding how many divisions to create and which markets to focus on, but the fundamental dilemma was which functions to attach and which to keep separate. The research piece was the hardest because there were benefits to keeping R&D centralized under Mir, but our problems with new-product delivery seemed to argue for having R&D report directly to the divisions. I also had to think about who would head the new divisions. I wanted people who would think and act like general managers, but we didn't have any; one of the problems of a functional organization is that it breeds functional people. On the other hand, newcomers in high positions have such a high mortality rate here that I didn't want to bring in an outsider.

EXHIBIT 9 U.S. Sales Subsidiary Organization Chart

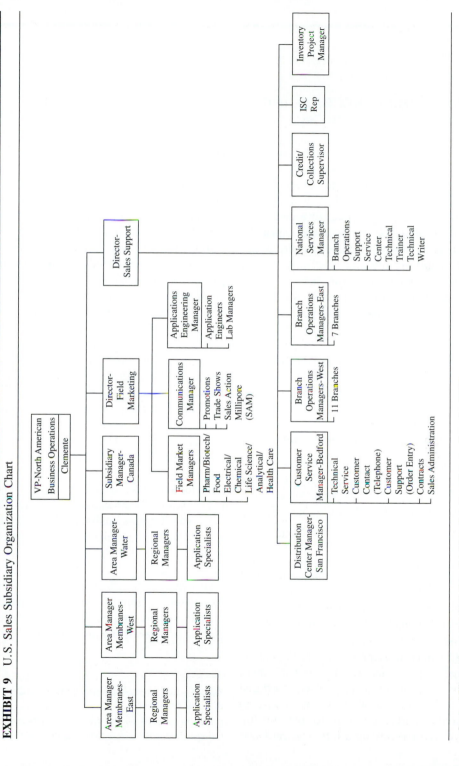

Source: Millipore Corporation (U.S. Sales Subsidiary Task Force Report—December 1985)

Case 6–3

HARVEY GOLUB: RECHARGING AMERICAN EXPRESS

In late October 1995, Harvey Golub, chairman and CEO of American Express, was preparing one of his quarterly memos to managers summarizing the state of the business. Golub had inherited a company with serious problems, but a new strategy, operating philosophy, personnel changes, and two successive waves of reengineering had succeeded in turning the tide. Recently, Warren Buffett, the legendary investor, had acknowledged the turnaround by purchasing 49 million shares of American Express, a 10.1 percent stake, for $2.2 billion. Still, the future remained uncertain, and there were a number of difficult challenges ahead. Golub believed that "the first task of a leader is to define reality." What, he wondered, should he say to his managers?

Company and Industry Background

American Express was founded in 1850 as an "express" company guaranteeing the safe and speedy delivery of packages in New York State. Forty years later, it created Travelers Cheques, signing up European banks, hotels, and tourist offices to accept them while assuming responsibility for losses due to theft, fraud, or fluctuating exchange rates. Over time, the company broadened its travel offerings to include trip planning, reservations, and ticketing, building on the themes of integrity, customer service, and peace of mind that had become hallmarks of the brand.

In 1958, American Express entered the charge card business, nine years after Diners Club inaugurated the concept. From the outset, it offered a charge card, not a credit card; there was no line of credit, and users had to pay in full within 30 days of receiving a bill. The card was positioned as a prestige product that offered travelers, especially business travelers, a convenient alternative to cash. It lost money for several years, but eventually became the most successful card in the industry, spawning a family of related products: Green, Gold, and Platinum Cards, each with its own level of services and annual fees. In 1970, American Express introduced a Corporate Card as part of a system that provided companies with expense information and consulting services to help manage their travel and entertainment expenses; in early 1994, it added a Corporate Purchasing Card to help companies manage their acquisition of supplies, equipment, and services. By 1995, the company also included American Express Bank, a network of 80 overseas banks in 37 countries that offered a range of international banking services, and American Express Financial Advisors, formerly Investors Diversified Services, that provided diversified portfolio planning and investment services.

Together, these businesses had a vast global reach, with 70,000 employees in 160 countries. American Express maintained relationships with over 4 million merchants and 25 million card-members, provided financial advice to 2 million people, and was the world's largest travel agent, with over 1,700 offices. In 1994, revenues were $14.3 billion, with 60 percent generated through fees associated with products and services and 30 percent by interest and investments (see Exhibit 1).

This case was prepared by Artemis March under the direction of David A. Garvin.

Copyright © 1996 by the President and Fellows of Harvard College. Harvard Business School case 396-212.

EXHIBIT 1   Selected Financial Data

Years Ended December 31 *(millions, except per share amounts)*	*1994*	*1993*	*1992*
NET REVENUES			
Commissions and fees	$ 8,591	$ 7,818	$ 8,817
Interest and dividends, net	4,120	3,395	3,975
Life insurance premiums	783	702	776
Other	788	739	687
Total	14,282	13,254	14,255*
EXPENSES			
Human resources	3,769	3,380	3,714
Provisions for losses and benefits:			
Annuities and investment certificates	1,173	1,259	1,315
Credit, banking and other	1,066	1,238	1,901
Life insurance	757	610	596
Marketing and promotion	1,063	1,091	1,113
Occupancy and equipment	1,058	965	1,167
Interest	1,011	864	939
Professional services	687	598	526
Communications	376	357	419
Other	1,431	1,345	2,375
Gain on sale of FDC	—	(779)	(706)
Total	12,391	10,928	13,359*
Pretax income from continuing operations before accounting changes	1,891	2,326	896
Income tax provision	511	721	318
Income from continuing operations before accounting changes	1,380	1,605	578
Discontinued operations, net of income taxes	33	(127)	(149)
Income before accounting changes	1,413	1,478	429
Cumulative effect of accounting changes, net of income taxes	—	—	32
Net income	$ 1,413	$ 1,478	$ 461
EARNINGS PER COMMON SHARE			
Income from continuing operations before accounting changes	2.68	$ 3.17	$ 1.12
Discontinued operations	.07	(.25)	(.31)
Income before accounting changes	2.75	2.92	.81
Cumulative effect of accounting changes	—	—	.07
Net income	$ 2.75	$ 2.92	$ .88

*Includes FDC revenues of $1,205 and expenses of $1,023 million.

Source: Annual Report

The Credit and Charge Card Industry

American Express's primary competitors in the card business were bank cards linked to two competing networks, MasterCard and Visa. Both were formed in the 1960s, but only became profitable years later. Issuers made most of thier money on the spread between interest rates charged cardholders on their revolving balances and the rates that they themselves paid to fund receivables, minus write-offs for losses. By the 1990s, the spread averaged 10 percent, allowing the roughly 5,000 bank card issuers to lower or drop their annual fees and offer low introductory rates in what was rapidly becoming a commodity market.

Several parties were involved in a transaction between merchants and cardholders. Card issuers, usually banks or large companies, issued cards to individuals; networks, primarily MasterCard and Visa, connected the participants; merchant banks owned the relationship with merchants; and merchant processors increasingly performed point-of-sale authorizations and transaction processing and billing. When customers used a bank card, merchants paid a discount fee that was divided among the participating network, card issuing bank, and merchant processor.

American Express, by contrast, did not share its fees and made money at every stage of the transaction process. Like other bank cards, it charged an annual fee to cardholders and a discount fee to merchants for every transaction. But because American Express owned the merchant relationship, acted as its own merchant processor, and did not participate in other networks, it kept the entire merchant fee rather than a small portion. This seamless, closed-loop system also provided access to a complete database of information on all customers, merchants, and transactions, which American Express increasingly used to design special promotions and targeted marketing initiatives.

The Robinson Years: 1977–1990

Building a Financial Supermarket

By the middle 1970s, American Express's principal businesses, travel and card operations, were highly profitable. But James Robinson III, who became CEO in 1977, had a larger company in mind. His first significant acquisition was Shearson Loeb Rhoades, an innovative and highly profitable brokerage house, purchased in 1981 for $1 billion. Over the next six years, Robinson strove to make American Express the largest "financial supermarket" in the world. In short order, he acquired The Boston Company, an institutional asset manager and trust company; Trade Development Bank Holdings S.A., a Swiss-based bank owned by Edmond Safra; Investors Diversified Services (IDS); First Data Resources, a merchant processor; and financially troubled Lehman Brothers Kuhn Loeb, the oldest investment banking partnership on Wall Street. In 1987, American Express paid $925 million for E. F. Hutton, a brokerage house on the verge of bankruptcy from prior deals; after the stock market crash in October, the purchase price was four times Hutton's book value.

Organization.   Robinson divided American Express into separate, largely autonomous businesses, each with its own chairman and CEO. The corporate parent became a holding company, and the pattern was repeated at several levels. For example, Travel Related Services (TRS), consisting of traveler's cheques, travelers services, and all cards, became a wholly owned subsidiary of American Express; TRS, in turn, was itself organized as a holding company with a number of independent subsidiaries. Each of these subsidiaries had its own staff groups, was further divided by product and function, and enjoyed considerable autonomy. Each card, for example, had its own management structure, credit process, financial organization, customer service organization or operations center, and data processing center, which installed and upgraded its own systems. Mike Monaco, CFO of the corporate parent since 1990, described the pattern: "Every time we came up with a different colored piece of plastic, we also came up with a completely separate, vertically integrated structure."

Culture and Management Style.   Both insiders and outsiders described the culture of the time as arrogant and complacent. Managers frequently treated bank cards as local shopping cards rather than serious competition; as Golub later observed: "Through our view of ourselves, we created Visa, the AT&T Universal Card, and the American AAdvantage program." For example, when American Airlines approached the company in 1984 about the possibility of collaborating on American AAdvantage, a co-branded card that would credit passengers with frequent flyer miles for every dollar they charged, managers spurned the offer. The airline launched the program with Citibank instead, triggering a steady exodus of customers.

Robinson was focused externally and was not a hands-on manager. One senior executive recalled:

Jim liked deals, and the strategy followed from the deals. You weren't really sure where things would go; debate and contention were the dominant mode of activity—"let's see where the chips fly." Jim looked at all the scenarios, letting people argue their positions and develop them all in detail. This Darwinian exercise was a killer to staff and very frustrating.

Politics were rife, and internal communication suffered because "you couldn't say certain things that carried implications about the leadership." Added another manager: "You could not challenge up." One executive who survived the period summarized it as

a triumph of form over substance. People were rewarded for thoughts and suggestions, not results. It was about how many options you could propose; there was no follow up on what you actually completed. There was no accountability, and lots of fiefdoms; we didn't work across the organization.

A Question of Survival

By the late 1980s, a host of problems converged, raising questions about American Express's long-term survival.

Strategic Failure. The financial supermarket approach produced a holding company with little clear direction. According to a manager who joined American Express at the time: "There was no strategy because people were so busy fighting fires. The

result was a bunker mentality in which everyone retreated to their own silo." Between 1987 and 1991 the company's stock lost half its value. Shearson had the most visible problems. Zealous overexpansion and poor deal making, coupled with stock and real estate market reversals, led to massive losses in 1989 and a billion-dollar write-down in 1990.

Competition in Cards. By the mid-1980s, bank cards' operations were profitable, and their marketing had become more aggressive. In addition, cobranding and the entry of large, nonbank players began to dramatically change the industry. In 1989, AT&T, in cooperation with Master Card, brought out its Universal Card with no annual fee; other companies quickly followed suit. A wide range of partnership programs emerged in which frequent flyer miles, discounts on hotels and car rentals, and other perquisites were linked to card usage. "The market shifted to the value-oriented customer," noted Monaco. "And prestige didn't cut it." Indeed, fully half of recent airline card billings were estimated to have come from defecting American Express customers.

Erosion of the Core Business. Although American Express's corporate card business continued to exhibit strong growth, the personal card business grew slowly during the 1980s and began to decline after 1990. In the next few years, the company's share of the $600 billion domestic charge and credit card market dropped from 25 percent to 16 percent; archrival Visa picked up 7 percent to command almost half of the total. Yet cards-in-force—the number of active American Express cards and a critical measure used by managers at the time—showed continued increases. The company soon discovered that this measure did not show the quality of cardholders: the average amount spent per transaction or the risk of nonpayment. Joe Keilty, executive vice president for human resources and quality, explained:

Cards-in-force doesn't really give you a true picture. As people were leaving, others were being rapidly added. But whom did we add? People who didn't use their cards or didn't pay their bills.

Meanwhile, merchants were increasingly unhappy about paying fees that averaged 100–150 basis points more than other cards'. Their displeasure came to a head in 1991 in the highly publicized "Boston Fee Party." Two Boston restaurant owners joined forces to boycott American Express, cutting up their cards before the media and fanning the perception that Boston merchants had en masse risen up against the company. American Express was forced to respond, arguing that many services its competitors handled separately were bundled into its fee, and that it delivered higher-spending customers. But the damage was done, and more and more merchants refused to accept American Express cards; others, who nominally accepted them, discouraged their use, a practice known as "suppression."

Problems in Consumer Lending.   Faced with increased competition, American Express entered the credit card business in 1987 with its Optima card. Optima was offered only to TRS customers in good standing, but four years later nearly 11 percent of its $7 billion receivables portfolio had to be written off—twice the industry average. In October 1991, to stabilize its portfolio and add to reserves, TRS took a $287 million write-down. One manager explained: "Our cash advances were too high, our data collection was poor, and we lowered our credit scoring to get our cards-in-force up." During the recession, some Optima cardholders withdrew their full lines of credit in cash to pay off loans or reduce balances on other cards. Small businesspeople and speculators also used the generous cash advances for purposes not originally intended.

Righting a Sinking Ship: 1991–1992

In July 1991, in the wake of these problems, Robinson asked Harvey Golub, who was running IDS, to become president of American Express. Three months later Golub added the posts of chairman and CEO of TRS. In February 1993, the board asked Robinson to step down and appointed Golub CEO of American Express; a few months later he was named chairman as well, relinquishing the presidency but retaining his TRS positions.

Harvey Golub

A graduate of NYU and for many years a senior partner at McKinsey, Golub's first contact with American Express was as a consultant on strategy and operations management. In 1984, he was recruited to become president and CEO of IDS; under his leadership, it enjoyed 40 straight quarters of 20 percent or more growth in earnings. Executives at American Express identified three hallmarks of his style: a commitment to principles; an intense focus on the reasoning process; and an insistence on open, issue-oriented, fact-based discussions.

Golub, one manager observed, was a man of "impeccable integrity" with a clear sense of the organization he desired:

> He wants a company with no rules or regulations, just principles, and you work within them. I can't remember Harvey ever telling anyone what to do. He pays more attention to *how* you think than anything else. He is always testing your thinking process. If he finds that you have thought about something really well, you get to go do it. If not, you get coached. He takes up his felt tip pen and goes to the board. Harvey loves to teach. But if you don't already have values, you are not teachable. Integrity is not a bargaining issue.

Golub was described as having very broad scope, brilliant at creating an overarching strategy and dissecting the minutiae of problems. He was conceptual and logical rather than emotional, but with the ability to tackle problems creatively and "come at things from a different angle." One manager observed:

> Harvey is the best counterintuitive thinker I have ever seen. If everyone agrees on something, he will ask, "Why?" For example, when everyone agreed that we should lower card fees, he spent two days with us discussing his counterproposal—that maybe we should raise them. I don't think he meant it seriously, but he certainly taught us how to think about fees.

Another manager added: "Harvey really has only two questions in business unit reviews: 'How did you think about that? And how would it be different if you thought about it this way instead?'"

Golub described the "teaching process" he employed:

> When you make a decision, you explain how you made it. For example, when you write a performance evaluation, you explain how you came to the assessment, and why you decided what you decided. You do not rely on unconscious competence. I do everything inductively, so I have to force myself to become deductive in order to explain things. The struggle is to tease out the reasoning process and make it clear.
>
> I am far less interested in people having the right answer than in their thinking about issues the right way. What criteria do they use? Why do they think the way they do? What alternatives have they considered? What premises do they have? What rocks are they standing on?

Golub would not tolerate information hoarding or hidden agendas, and insisted on issue-oriented discussions in which people told the truth. One manager noted:

> With Harvey, what you see is what you get. You can't go in with a hidden question. He's asking for reality in an organization that has historically had low tolerance for challenging up.

Another described the impact of this approach:

> Harvey wants to get to the bottom of issues, and in review meetings focuses on the deeper questions—he already knows the other stuff. When you meet to discuss a problem, he is always issue oriented, never personal. When he makes a suggestion, he wants you to think about it, not necessarily do something right away.

Another summed up Golub's philosophy: "Harvey sets the tone. Intellectually, he is very open, very logical, and demands rigor. You can have an opinion but you need to be clear about it. He wants you to distinguish opinion from fact and put a headline on it." Golub agreed, noting that he consciously tried to follow three rules: "Never beat up on anybody who brings bad news, never beat up on anybody who says 'I don't know,' but do beat up on those who bullshit." The contrast with

Robinson was stark, as a manager observed:

> Jim asked, "What's possible to do here? What are the risks and consequences?" Harvey asks, "What is the right thing to do here?" He wants people to understand the criteria for making decisions.

Changes in Performance Evaluation

To support his philosophy, Golub changed TRS's performance metrics and variable compensation system soon after assuming leadership. He observed: "If you get the metrics right, you'll get the behavior." In the past, over 90 percent of managers' evaluations was based on meeting individual and unit goals, with a focus on performance against budget. Drawing on the approach he had used at IDS, Golub shifted the mix to emphasize group and team incentives, judging performance not against budget but by

> what you should have done, given the circumstances. That reduces the manipulative component of the budget process and shifts people's focus from meeting negotiated planned targets to building a business. In making an evaluation, it's important to consider factors that arise after managers have put together a plan.

Golub's assessments were recorded in annual "report cards" that publicly graded managers from G1 (highest) to G5 based on their performance in five categories: shareholders, customers, employees, reengineering, and quality. Each category had a pre-assigned weight. Golub described this practice as

> a qualitative assessment of the numbers. By taking into account how the results were achieved, I made the criteria both more subjective and more objective at the same time. For example, if you meet your net income goals for the year but get them by cutting advertising expenses, you won't get a very high score.

Managers, he observed, had mixed reactions to the report cards: "People don't like the fact that the grades are clear, that I don't report them until the end of the year, and that they're public." Golub did, however, send long, quarterly memos describing the current state of the business to all bonus-eligible members of TRS, who were expected to share them with others. In these memos, he discussed what was going well in the business and what wasn't and explained his thinking about critical decisions and unresolved issues, but did not provide grades. The assumption underlying both memos and report cards, he noted, was that "you treat employees as adults. You tell them what's going on, and why, and how you came to the conclusions you did."

Triage at TRS

On becoming CEO of TRS, Golub immediately began to act. "Harvey does not sit and debate things," observed Monaco. "He comes up with a hypothesis, and then tries to prove it." On his very first day, Golub decided to centralize and consolidate TRS. He recalled: "We would have one CFO, one head of HR, and one general counsel; it was the first step in blowing up silos. I wanted coherence, and needed to know the facts and get things surfaced."

Yet data were not willingly shared. Golub found that he faced "destructive compliance"—his questions had to be framed precisely, because only the narrowly asked question was addressed. Even so, he began to develop a sense of the organization and its problems. He recalled:

> I was listening to reports, and although I had zero data, I did not believe what I was hearing. The way people talked did not match what I thought was reality, although I could not point to particulars.

Golub soon concluded that the basic card business was "in great danger of being marginalized. It felt like we were going to be another PanAm." At the same time, he began to assess TRS's readiness for change, based on

> how people were describing things to me. People use phrases that indicate their readiness levels. You get a sense for whether they know what to do but are simply unwilling to act, don't know what to do, or understand what needs to be done but don't know how to do it.

Golub's assessment was that readiness was low and strong leadership was required. "You can quickly

back off if your assessment turns out to be wrong. But most people find it punitive if you start by underleading and only later add structure."

He therefore articulated five broad priorities for halting the slide at TRS: fix the Optima credit problem, rebuild customer relationships, rebuild service establishment relationships, build the Cheque and Corporate Card businesses, and reduce the cost structure by $1 billion. At the same time, he observed:

> I was careful not to go too far. I could not give TRS a vision, at least not at the beginning, because it would have had zero credibility. But I did need to provide a sense of clarity so that we could fix what was broken.

Reengineering TRS: A $1 Billion Cost Cutting

The cost-reduction goal triggered an initial reengineering process that lasted from 1992 to 1994. Though lacking reliable data, Golub saw the target as roughly equal to the 100-basis-point spread between American Express and bank card merchant fees, and approximately 10 percent of TRS's costs. He formalized the target as "reducing the cost base by a billion dollars over a three-year time frame, based on 1991 volumes and mix," but did not assign goals to individual businesses. Most opportunities, he expected, would be across units; moreover, Golub believed that specific dollar goals would lead to traditional cost cutting that "rewarded" people for being sloppy in the past. He insisted instead that "we have to change how the work is done, not just tighten the screws." Initially, Golub recalled, there were few guidelines: "If I knew how to get there, it would have been a plan, not a goal." Vijay Parekh, senior vice president and chief credit officer for consumer lending, remembered how the message was received:

> There was wide variation throughout the organization. Those who had a "can do" attitude and could work without specific direction took up the challenge quickly, but the wait-and-watch group was on the fence.

Organization and Roles

Early in 1992, Golub appointed Randy Christofferson, a former consultant and strategic planner, as senior vice president of quality and reengineering (Q&R) for TRS and head of the reengineering initiative. A core team was established and a "virtual organization" formed to overlay the TRS reporting structure. Chaired by Christofferson, the core team included Golub, the business presidents, the EVPs of critical staff functions, plus Q&R professionals and outside consultants who participated on an as-needed basis. The core team identified a dozen or so areas of focus, selected project team leaders, and appointed steering committees, headed by executive owners, who were responsible for executing their project team's recommendations. Throughout the process, Q&R professionals functioned in an advisory and coaching role, introducing tools and training and reviewing reengineering proposals.

Golub's role was particularly critical, a Christofferson recalled: "I relied on the senior members of the core team to wield the big stick, but over time, I had to do it less often because Harvey gave the process legitimacy." Golub described his involvement:

I took ownership of the reengineering initiative; I did not delegate it. People had to feel it was theirs and my responsibility, and my behavior had to match the message. I went to reviews; I was present at project meetings; I attended training sessions. I contributed ideas and illustrated how to think about redesign. I did what was needed to get people on teams, get the right leadership, and get executives to understand that reengineering was part of their jobs. I ensured that monitoring and reporting systems were put in place, and expanded the compensation criteria to include reengineering. I encouraged people to join reengineering teams and made sure that they got good jobs when they came off of them. And I talked about reengineering all the time. That was hard for me. About the time I'm bored with a topic, others are beginning to understand it. I have to force myself to work the same ditch and not go on to something else.

Concepts and Frameworks

Two frameworks provided organization and guidance. First, all reengineering projects were assigned to categories, and each category was managed differently. *Cost* projects were expected to find cheaper ways of carrying out activities without major changes in processes or procedures. *Structural* projects would physically change how or where the work was done, and often focused on facility changes. *Strategic* projects would cut across organizational boundaries to redesign broad, crosscutting processes. Christofferson elaborated: "If one boss could make the decision, it wasn't a strategic project. My rule of thumb was that it wasn't a crosscutting process unless it touched at least three separate organizational units." Strategic projects, as well as large structural projects, were assigned to dedicated teams of line managers with their own steering committees; cost projects typically involved line personnel who continued in their regular jobs and were overseen on an ad hoc basis.

A second tool, the process blueprint, provided a more detailed map, although it was not mandatory (see Exhibits 2 and 3). It identified the five phases of reengineering—opportunity identification, opportunity assessment, project selection and design, implementation, and ongoing management—as well as the exit criteria for passing from one stage to the next. The primary goals of the first two phases were pinpointing gaps in performance and determining the likely payoffs. An 80/20 rule prevailed, with managers trying to identify the 20 percent of projects that would provide 80 percent of the cost savings. Several large strategic and structural opportunities emerged, including improved credit loss provisioning, greater reliance on outside sourcing, less duplication of data processing centers, less duplication of staff, and reduced interest expense to fund card receivables. Project leaders then spent several months assessing the extent of each opportunity and brainstorming possible solutions. They used process mapping to explore alternative structures and processes, and even tested a few complex scenarios. Q&R professionals played an important role during this phase, coaching

EXHIBIT 2 Overview of Process Management Blueprint

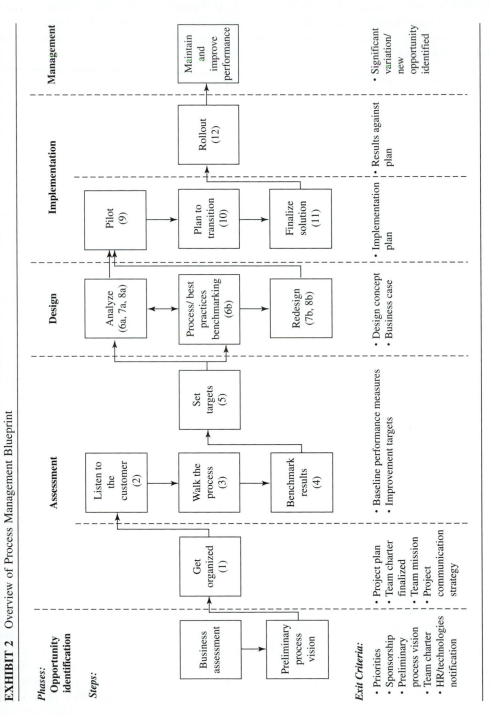

Phases:

Opportunity identification | Assessment | Design | Implementation | Management

Steps:

Business assessment → Preliminary process vision

Get organized (1)

Listen to the customer (2) → Walk the process (3) → Benchmark results (4)

Set targets (5)

Analyze (6a, 7a, 8a) ↔ Process/best practices benchmarking (6b) → Redesign (7b, 8b)

Pilot (9) → Plan to transition (10) → Finalize solution (11)

Rollout (12)

Maintain and improve performance

Exit Criteria:

- Priorities
- Sponsorship
- Preliminary process vision
- Team charter
- HR/technologies notification

- Project plan
- Team charter finalized
- Team mission
- Project communication strategy

- Baseline performance measures
- Improvement targets

- Design concept
- Business case

- Implementation plan

- Results against plan

- Significant variation/ new opportunity identified

Source: American Express

578

EXHIBIT 3 Detailed Description of Process Management Blueprint

Business Assessment
Preliminary Process Vision

Purpose:
- To assess and prioritize needs to build process capabilities

Key Activities:
- Document/map key business processes
- Synthesize and consolidate customer, process performance, and operational performance data from AEQL/Baldrige Assessment and other sources
- Catalog/evaluate existing improvement initiatives (existing portfolio)
- Identify new improvement initiatives
- Rationalize/prioritize list of existing and new improvement initiatives (planned portfolio)
- Complete organizational readiness assessment
- For selected initiatives:
  - secure executive sponsorship
  - develop preliminary process vision
  - create team charter
    - draft scope, objective, and deliverables
    - define required resources
    - determine communication/reporting requirements
  - notify HR/Technologies

Inputs:
- Strategic documents (strategic plan, vision, etc.)
- Customer, process performance, and operational results data from AEQL/Baldrige Assessment Categories 6 and 7 (Quality and Operational Results, Customer Focus and Satisfaction)

Exit Criteria:
- Priorities
- Sponsorship
- Preliminary process vision
- Team charter

1. Get Organized

Purpose:
- To launch Improvement team

Key Activities:
- Review/refine team charter and process overview (sponsor and team)
- Develop team mission statement
- Draft project plan
- Secure additional team resources (if necessary)
- Define roles, responsibilities, and teamworking principles
- Develop project communication strategy

Inputs:
- Team charter
- Sponsorship

Exit Criteria:
- Finalized team charter
- Team mission statement
- Project plan
- Project communication strategy

2. Listen to the Customers
3. Walk the Process

4. Benchmark Results
5. Set Targets

Purpose:
- To determine appropriate process performance improvement targets based upon customer requirements/expectations, current process performance/capability, and competitive/best of breed organizational performance

Key Activities:
- Determine customer data, process data, and benchmark results data requirements
- Prepare for and plan data collection efforts
- Collect/synthesize and analyze collected customer, process, and benchmark data
- Document baseline process performance measures
- Rate the health of the process
- Determine improvement priorities
- Set improvement targets
- Assemble and present the assessment findings

Inputs:
- Project plan
- Process overview

Exit Criteria:
- Baseline performance measures
- Improvement targets

(continued)

EXHIBIT 3 *(concluded)*

6a, 7a, 8a. Analyze 6b, 7b, 8b. Redesign	9. Pilot 10. Plan to Transition 11. Finalize the Solution	12. Roll out	Maintain and Improve Performance
Purpose:	**Purpose:**	**Purpose:**	**Purpose:**
• To develop the new improved process	• To finalize the design of the new process	• To implement the new process	• To ensure desired performance levels are maintained/improved
Key Activities:	**Key Activities:**	**Key Activities:**	**Key Activities:**
• Using the results from the assessment phase, determine what combination of analysis-driven methods or process redesign is necessary to attain the desired improvement targets	• Develop the pilot/simulation plan	• Organize and staff the implementation team (if necessary)	• Develop plan for ongoing measurement and tracking of process performance
	• Get buy-in from appropriate stakeholders	• Execute the implementation plan	• Determine appropriate next steps for team
	• Run pilot/simulation and examine results	• Develop/implement HR/organizational and technology framework	
• Prepare for, plan, and conduct a best practices/benchmarking study	• Finalize design of new process	• Monitor the roll out	
• For processes requiring more analysis-driven methods:	• Develop broader scale implementation plan		
- identify root causes of poor process performance	• Present pilot results and implementation plan		
• For processes requiring more of a redesign approach:	**Inputs:**	**Inputs:**	**Inputs:**
- develop/refine process vision statement	• Design concept	• Implementation plan	• Improvement targets
- determine key process characteristics/capabilities	**Exit Criteria:**	**Exit Criteria:**	**Exit Criteria:**
- conduct HR/organizational and technology enablement review	• Implementation plan	• Assessment of results against plan	• Ongoing process performance tracking system
• Prepare benchmarking study report			• Identification of significant variation or new opportunity
• Document/map the new process (at a macro level; the "design concept")			
• Document HR/organizational and technology implications of new process			
• Prepare business case for new process (financial/competitive/organizational impacts)			
• Present design concept and business case			
Inputs:			
• Baseline performance measures			
• Improvement targets (with supporting customer, process, and competitive information)			
Exit Criteria:			
• Design concept			
• Business case			

Source: American Express

managers on advanced quality methods and ensuring that new processes were not so streamlined that quality was threatened.

In phase three, senior management took a more active role, selecting projects, obtaining resources, and staffing project teams. They used a number of criteria to narrow the list of projects, including the 80/20 rule, potential profitability, and such customer-related goals as reducing attrition and increasing card usage. The chosen initiatives then had to be approved by both Christofferson and the appropriate executive owner before being transferred to line managers for the final two phases, implementation and ongoing management.

Tracking and Results

To assess progress, Christofferson worked with the CFO of TRS to establish a detailed tracking system. Savings were measured at three points in the process. An *identified* save was a project's estimated cost savings; it could not be claimed until the project exited the assessment phase. An *implemented* save indicated that physical changes in process or structure had taken place and TRS was now operating differently; it was not counted until the project exited the implementation phase. A *realized* save meant that net savings had actually been booked; it typically appeared in the ongoing management phase. All of the calculations were difficult, as Keilty pointed out: "The hardest part of reengineering was counting the saves, booking them, and making sure that we avoided double counting."

Between 1992 and 1994, TRS reduced its costs by $1.4 billion; in the following six months, it cut another $200 million from the cost base. About $500 million of the total came from improved credit loss provisioning, reflecting more sophisticated credit management instruments introduced as part of a fundamental process redesign. There were also significant savings in rent and personnel from consolidating six data processing centers into one. Some of these savings went directly to the bottom line; most, however, were used to fund decreases in merchant discount rates. Between 1992 and 1995, these rates declined 40 basis points to an average of 275 basis points; during the same period, bank card fees increased slightly to approximately 200 basis points.

Despite the magnitude of these savings, the first wave of reengineering was barely felt by many in the company. In part, the reason was geographic. Forty-eight hundred jobs were lost, but many were overseas. Derek Murphy, who assisted Christofferson, likened the effort to "stealth reengineering: nobody felt it; it wasn't bloody, and there weren't a lot of walking wounded." He elaborated:

> Someone had to come in with a sickle and a trailblazing mentality to clear the path. Then we could be more sophisticated about the way we manicured and groomed the business. Until the path was clear, it was difficult to determine what was value added, and what was not.

Turning the Ship: 1993–1994

With TRS's problems under control, Golub turned his attention to the parent company. As CEO of American Express, he focused on two themes: leveraging the brand, and developing a principles-driven organization.

Leveraging the Brand

Golub viewed the brand as "our biggest corporate asset," and saw himself as

> a brand manager, responsible for making sure that 10 years from now the American Express brand is worth more than it is today. To do that, I have to understand what actions are negative to the brand and stop them, what actions are neutral to the brand and make them positive, and what actions are positive to the brand and celebrate them. Being a brand-focused company also means that you start making choices on that basis. If you have a business that does not fit the brand strategy, you dispose of it even if it's doing well.

Since retail brokerage and investment banking did not fit these criteria, Shearson, Lehman, the Boston Company, and other noncore businesses were gradually sold or spun off. IDS was retained and renamed American Express Financial Advisors (AEFA).

At Golub's suggestion, the parent company also adopted the goal of becoming the "world's most respected service brand." This had important strategic and operating implications. Golub explained: "You start changing the criteria for running your businesses from, What are the economics? to, How does this support the brand and enhance its value?" AEFA was a prime example. After its renaming, AEFA introduced a new measurement system that, unlike its competitors, precisely tracked the quality of advice provided to clients; every one of its financial advisors was evaluated annually on the new criteria. In addition, AEFA advisors would soon be asked to stop cold calling. Golub noted:

> Nothing turns off prospects as much as getting a call at dinnertime from a stranger selling mutual funds. We will be the first company to eliminate the practice, and will develop other processes to attract new clients. We'll do it because it doesn't fit the brand.

To broaden their understanding of the brand, all American Express employees were being educated in its intellectual and emotional meanings. The intellectual training drew on extensive market research, which also shaped advertising, marketing, and product design. "The emotional training," Golub observed, "will go on forever. It's about internalizing the meaning of the brand so that employees can say, 'This feels like American Express,' or 'This does not.'"

The focus on the brand also provided a basis for classifying the company's diverse activities. A critical distinction was made between core and noncore businesses. These categories were developed by senior TRS managers at a lengthy off-site meeting in mid-1993. Golub explained:

> We had to be clear about roles and responsibilities even if people didn't like it. The sticking point was that everybody wanted to be considered a core business. Yet the reality is that not every business is core, so you can't treat them all alike. You don't put huge investments in noncore businesses; you don't look for significant growth.

Although the core/noncore distinction generated considerable discussion, the biggest surprise to managers was that relevance to the brand—and not simply profitability—was the primary basis for making the determination.

In a November 1993 speech entitled "Turning the Ship," Kenneth Chenault, recently named president of TRS/U.S. (and, in 1995, a vice chairman of American Express) introduced the resulting business framework (see Exhibit 4). Core consumer

---

EXHIBIT 4 TRS Business Framework

	Customers	
	Consumers	*Businesses*
Core Businesses:	Charge Card Lending Products	Corporate Card Purchasing Card Business Travel
Supporting Businesses:	Consumer Travel Financial Assets Traveler's Cheques	
Stand-alone Businesses:	Merchandise Services Publishing Epsilon Quattro	

Source: American Express

businesses were charge cards and lending products, while core corporate businesses were corporate card, business travel, and the soon-to-be released corporate purchasing card. Noncore businesses were divided into two categories, supporting and stand-alone. Supporting businesses were those like consumer travel and cheques that supported the brand, as well as core products and services. The objective of consumer travel was not to become the world's largest travel agency but to build a service network that supported cardmembers on a global basis. Stand-alone businesses, by contrast, were not critical to the brand; the company could easily survive without them. They had to be profitable and self-funding, requiring minimal resources and management attention. This classification scheme was reexamined periodically, and it was possible for businesses to migrate from one category to another. But none had done so by late 1995.

Building a Principles-Driven Organization

Golub hoped to turn American Express into a "principles-driven organization," where managers behaved according to principles and values rather than policies, rules, and procedures. Phillip Riese, president of TRS Consumer Card Group, explained:

> In very large, very complex organizations it is virtually impossible to give effective top-down direction on the multiplicity of decisions that have to be made daily. The notion of principles is a powerful alternative, particularly if you can find good techniques for cascading them down the organization.

An important step in this direction were the "guiding (operating) principles," originally articulated by TRS in 1994 but soon adopted by the entire company. They stated: "(1) We must provide a superior value proposition to all of our customer groups, (2) We must achieve best-in-class economics, and (3) Everything we do must enhance and support the brand." The first two principles were developed by Chenault, the third by Golub. Chenault explained the reasoning behind the first principle:

> In the past we were seen as customer service leaders, but still judged ourselves by internal

criteria. The real question now is, How do we stack up against the competition? How do we provide our customers with superior value?

The second principle represented a similar shift, from a focus on pure cost cutting to broader assessments that included costs and revenues. Best-in-class economics turned managers' attention to operating margins. Riese explained:

> What we want is corporate fitness, not corporate anorexia. It is important to consider revenues and costs together; otherwise, we might try to get costs down by reducing quality. New products present the opposite problem: They have traditionally focused on revenues alone, but now must be designed to produce best-in-class economics as well. This approach forces us to disaggregate costs and revenues to get at their subcomponents and drivers.

Both Golub and Chenault were conscious of the need to model how they wanted managers to employ the principles, as well as the necessity of making their actions transparent. Their skills were complementary, as Parekh explained:

> Both Harvey and Ken are driven by principles and values, are very able to articulate their veiws, and are focused on achieving goals. Both are visionary, but in a different sense. Harvey creates the vision through facts, while Ken does it through soft skills and relationships.

Even so, the transition to a principles-driven organization was expected to be difficult. If too much direction was provided, managers might lose their enthusiasm for the principles and their willingness to take initiative; if too little direction was provided, the organization might drift. Riese described the leadership challenge:

> In the past, we have not been effective in assessing where people needed direction and where we could pull back. Now, as we shift to being more principles driven, we have found that the questions people ask provide an important clue. You need to go in again and again, pulling out the questions people have and making sure that they are fed back to you. Then you need to be very clear in your answers to the questions, because you want to focus on

performance while giving people guidance for operating in a principles-driven manner.

Corporate Metrics

During this period, Health of the Franchise measures, consisting of shareholder, customer, and employee metrics, were introduced to the organization through a process that combined goal setting, ongoing tracking and reporting, and annual report card evaluations.

Customer Health of the Franchise (HOTF) Measures. To increase the company's focus on its customers, Golub led the effort to define customer success in terms of desired outcomes for such key groups as individual consumers, corporations, and service establishments. By focusing on specific behaviors and their determinants, rather than satisfaction alone, Golub ensured that improvements would be targeted in areas that would lead to measurable business results. This avoided the potential trap of only measuring satisfaction, since in the past American Express had received higher satisfaction scores than competitors even as its market share declined. Parekh explained:

> Harvey wanted to make sure that we understood how satisfaction translated into behaviors, like card usage, that were important to us. Now we have started to create measures so that each management level builds on those below it. We have begun to link the lowest level of transactional activity and the highest level HOTF measures.

Employee Values Survey. A similar approach was applied to employee measurement. The primary measure took the form of an annual survey in which employees assessed how well the company and its management were living the American Express values and addressing the drivers of employee satisfaction. (See Exhibit 5.) Golub established the goal of reaching world-class levels of employee satisfaction while closing gaps in satisfaction between males and females and between whites and other racial groups.

Keilty explained: "Employee success is as important as customer success; in fact, it contributes

to it." To reinforce this message, scores on the Employee Values Survey made up 25 percent of managers' performance ratings, making them equal in compensation weighting to customer performance. (The shareholder rating represented the other 50 percent.) A rigorous improvement process was also applied to employee survey results, including statistical analysis, focus group and qualitative feedback, root cause analysis, and clear action planning and follow-up from management.

To supplement and assist managers in improving their personal leadership behaviors, an additional, private, individually based upward feedback survey and report was prepared. It provided one-on-one information on demonstrated skills and work habits as seen by direct reports. (See Exhibit 6.) This process was repeated down through each succeeding level of direct reports to managers at all levels of the organization.

Report Cards. To ensure that the balanced set of measures was ingrained in management, Golub continued his practice of writing report cards after becoming CEO of the corporation in February 1993. At the end of the year, he spent nearly a month grading American Express's senior managers, checking his conclusions with a few key people. One reason for carefully rating people annually, he observed, was that:

> it takes time to make sure I'm right. I have to know a lot; how the results were achieved, how they compare to competitors', what exogenous factors impacted the results, and what trade-offs were made to get current performance. In many ways, this is the most important thing I do.

Setting a Course: 1994–1995

One Operating Company

In the fall of 1994, Golub articulated a new goal: American Express would become one operating company, rather than a collection of separate, loosely connected businesses. This was in keeping with his background and skills. Golub saw himself

EXHIBIT 5 Sample Employee Values Survey Report for an American Express Business Unit

AMERICAN EXPRESS 1995 ANNUAL SURVEY
Values and BPTW Dimensions Over Time
AMERICAN EXPRESS FINANCIAL ADVISORS
Consolidated (Y3)

Values and BPTW Dimensions	Percent Unfavorable				% Unfavorable Change		Percent Favorable				% Favorable Change[1]	
	1992	1993	1994	1995	1992 to 1995	1994 to 1995	1992	1993	1994	1995	1992 to 1995	1994 to 1995
Clients	11	8	8	9	−2	1	73	79	80	80	7	0
Quality	18	14	16	17	−1	1	61	65	64	65	4	1
People	14	11	11	11	−3	0	69	70	74	77	8	3
Integrity	22	20	17	14	−8	−3	52	52	60	62	10	2
Teamwork	18	18	17	16	−2	−1	59	57	62	65	6	3
Good citizenship	12	11	8	9	−3	1	54	57	68	69	15	1
Company commitment	11	9	11	15	4	4	66	67	67	64	−2	−3
People development	20	18	16	13	−7	−3	58	59	62	70	12	8
Job itself	12	9	8	9	−3	1	76	80	82	82	6	0
Meritocracy	22	19	20	21	−1	1	58	60	58	60	2	2
Management	25	25	20	19	−6	−1	51	50	56	62	11	6
Manager effectiveness	—	—	—	13	—	—	—	—	—	70	—	—
Diversity	—	13	9	8	—	−1	—	72	75	78	—	3
People satisfaction	—	6	6	7	—	1	—	76	78	78	—	0

NOTE: The first 11 dimensions contain three items common to all years except Management, which has four items. Manager effectiveness is a new dimension for 1995. The name of the Career Development dimension has been changed to people development. The diversity dimension contains three items common to all years. Longitudinal comparisons should be interpreted with caution when there are large differences between the sample sizes: 1992, N = 976; 1993, N = 7,497; 1994, N = 8,809; 1995, N = 9,116.
Unfavorable: Percent of people responding Disagree or Strongly Disagree
Favorable: Percent of people responding Agree or Strongly Agree
[1]Percent Favorable Change (1994 to 1995 only) values surrounded by a box indicate meaningful change. See *Survey Navigation Guide* for guidance on interpreting these results.

Source: American Express

EXHIBIT 6   Sample Page of Individual Upward Feedback Report

Character

	Direct Reports							Colleagues						
	Number Responding / Date	Highly Dissatisfied (1)	Dissatisfied (2)	Neither Satisfied nor Dissatisfied (3)	Satisfied (4)	Highly Satisfied (5)	Your Average / TRS Average / Your Percentile—TRS / Blue Box Average / Your Percentile—Blue Box	Number Responding / Date	Highly Dissatisfied (1)	Dissatisfied (2)	Neither Satisfied nor Dissatisfied (3)	Satisfied (4)	Highly Satisfied (5)	Your Average / TRS Average / Your Percentile—TRS / Blue Box Average / Your Percentile—Blue Box
27. Argues positions fairly and objectively	5 4/93	-	1	-	3	1	3.8 3.9 / 3.8 49 46	5 4/93	-	1	1	2	1	3.9 3.9 / 3.6 29 29
	6 12/91	-	-	2	1	3	4.2	3 12/91	-	-	-	3	-	4.0
	6 2/91	-	-	-	4	2	4.3	8 2/91	-	-	-	4	4	4.5
37. Encourages you to stand up for what you believe	5 4/93	-	-	1	2	2	3.9 3.9 / 4.2 75 73	4 4/93	-	-	-	3	1	4.0 4.0 / 4.3 82 80
	6 12/91	-	1	1	2	2	3.8	2 12/91						
	6 2/91	-	-	-	3	3	4.5	7 2/91	-	-	-	5	2	4.3
51. Avoids "playing favorites" or siding with friends	5 4/93	-	-	1	3	1	3.7 3.7 / 4.0 75 74	3 4/93	-	-	-	2	1	3.7 3.7 / 4.3 94 92
	6 12/91	-	1	1	3	1	3.7	2 12/91						
	6 2/91	-	-	3	2	1	3.7	4 2/91	-	-	1	2	1	4.0
54. Supports agreed-upon decisions	5 4/93	-	1	1	1	2	4.1 4.1 / 3.8 30 29	4 4/93	-	-	-	3	1	4.0 4.0 / 4.3 79 78
	6 12/91	-	-	1	4	1	4.0	3 12/91	-	-	1	2	-	3.7
	6 2/91	-	-	-	5	1	4.2	8 2/91	-	-	1	4	3	4.3
59. "Practices what he/she preaches"	5 4/93	-	-	-	5	-	3.9 3.9 / 4.0 67 67	4 4/93	-	-	-	1	3	3.9 3.9 / [4.8] 99 [99]
	6 12/91	-	-	1	3	2	4.2	3 12/91	-	-	-	3	-	4.0
	6 2/91	-	-	-	3	3	4.5	7 2/91	-	-	1	4	2	4.1
64. Admits mistakes readily	4 4/93	-	-	1	2	1	3.7 3.7 / 4.0 73 72	3 4/93	-	-	-	2	1	3.7 3.7 / 4.3 94 93
	6 12/91	-	-	3	2	1	3.7	2 12/91						
	6 2/91	-	-	2	2	2	4.0	7 2/91	-	-	3	2	2	3.9

Source: American Express

as an operating executive, best suited to leading a single, integrated business. He observed:

> I don't know what a corporate strategy is; I'm not sure I've even seen one. Besides, the brand drove the idea. One operating company comes right out of our focus on the brand.

Golub's intention was to leverage the brand while redesigning the organization around "shared utilities," common processes and platforms that would support diverse products and functions. These concepts aligned neatly with a second wave of reengineering already underway at TRS, and they also triggered a reassessment of corporate staff functions.

A Second Wave of Reengineering: "POA-II"

During the first half of 1994, TRS rigorously analyzed the performance of its U.S. operations. A leading consulting firm conducted benchmarking studies; it found large competitive gaps in costs, time to market, and flexibility in meeting customer needs. To close the gaps and develop critical capabilities, a group led by Chenault concluded that a second wave of reengineering was needed. TRS had to redesign its processes so that its businesses were better linked and its customers were served on a relationship, rather than a product, basis. This goal was defined as a "point of arrival" (POA); it indicated the kind of company American Express wished to become. Using this terminology, the second round of reengineering was designated POA-II, and the first round was renamed POA-I. Chenault compared the two:

> When we started POA-I, few people thought that we could take $1 billion out of our costs. Success built confidence, but the focus was strictly cost reduction. POA-I was a matter of survival; we were falling off a cliff. When we exceeded our original goal, many people said that the organization wasn't ready for another challenge; it was time to take a breather. Harvey and I said no, we need to define the reality of winning. Our present success can at best last two years. It is not fundamental, and it is not market-based. We want sustainable success based on the right cultural values, operating in

light of the principles, with improvements on both the cost and revenue sides. The objective of POA-II is to become a winner.

To direct and manage the process, Chenault chose James Cracchiolo, who returned to TRS after serving as Shearson's CFO, and appointed him Senior Vice President of Quality, Reengineering, and Business Strategy. After reviewing the benchmarking studies, the two set ambitious cost-reduction goals. All reengineering projects would be cross-functional, cross-business, and cross-card, and work would proceed in three concurrent phases. To begin, TRS's various businesses would quickly implement industry best practices, such as paperless transactions with merchants. Shared utilities, such as operating centers, would then be established, consolidating activities that were common to multiple products and businesses in order to realize economies of scale. Finally, critical business and support processes would be reconfigured and redesigned to take advantage of the new utilities.

Organization and Roles.   Because of its broad scope, POA-II required strong sponsor support, clear priorities, and the ability to work hand-in-hand with the line. Chenault established a centralized structure in which reengineering heads, each responsible for redesigning a single large process, were pulled from their line jobs and committed 50 percent of their time to reengineering. They reported directly to Cracchiolo; he, in turn, reported to Chenault. Each process also had an executive reengineering owner, who was responsible for implementation of the new process design. In addition, there was a program office with a dozen experts in human resources, finance, technology, and communications to ensure that the work proceeded smoothly and was integrated with larger company activities, as well as steering committees for each process composed of high-ranking executives who were knowledgeable about their processes' daily functioning. Cracchiolo met with each steering committee monthly; if problems arose, he took them to Chenault and his direct reports, who also, he observed, "called the big decisions like closing an operations center."

Chenault took personal responsibility for POA-II, was deeply involved in creating, championing, and selling the initiative, and expected to be evaluated by Golub and the board on its results. He personally selected the reengineering heads and worked with them to assemble the necessary resources. Parekh recalled:

> Ken asked each of us, "What resources do you need, what team structure do you need, and which individuals do you need from each functional area?" Then he went to the presidents of each TRS business and said, "How do we free up these resources?"

Concepts and Frameworks.   Drawing on the first round of reengineering, POA-II used the same five-phase process blueprint, but made it mandatory. The focus was almost exclusively on strategic projects. In spring 1994, a broad-based team of managers and consultants identified 13 crosscutting processes as candidates for redesign. They fell into three categories: customer-focused processes, like cardmember acquisition, that involved direct customer contact and deliverables, and support and enabling processes, like risk management and supplier management, that supported one or more customer-focused processes. (See Exhibit 7.) Once reengineering heads had been assigned to each of these processes and formed their teams, they began identifying opportunities and establishing targets for improvement. A key step was the mapping of cost centers against processes, a complex piece of financial analysis. Because costs had historically been reported on a functional basis, they had to be disaggregated and then restated in process terms. This effort showed precisely how competitive gaps could be closed and resulted in a series of targets for each process, expressed not only in dollars but also in time (e.g., time to market, time to process new cardmembers) and required resources (e.g. staffing levels, number of processing centers).

The other concept guiding POA-II was shared utilities. It was a direct outgrowth of Golub's goal of one operating company and was also, as Chenault pointed out, a way to overcome the apparent contradictions in the three guiding principles, ensuring that all three could be achieved simultaneously. Chenault had virtually mandated the adoption of shared utilities in the face of strong resistance; the primary counterargument was that each of TRS's businesses could reach best-in-class economics on their own. In the corporate area, Golub had issued a similar mandate, requesting that his executive vice presidents share activities in order to achieve best-in-class economics in their staff functions.

Functional heads responded by eliminating duplication, pulling experts from separate businesses and pooling them in "centers of excellence." These new centers provided services to all American Express units, regardless of product, business, geography, or subsidiary status. For example, in 1992 there were 29 geographically dispersed controllers' offices in TRS, a central TRS controller's office, and another controller's office at the corporate level. To eliminate redundancies, the finance group first reassessed its work in process terms. It distinguished two types of activities: factorylike transactions that required speed and accuracy, and analytical and consulting services that needed to be customer focused. The former were consolidated into shared utilities, three newly constructed financial resource centers in India, the United Kingdom, and the United States. Twenty-six of the 29 TRS controllers' offices were then closed.

Similar consolidations occurred at the corporate level. In the legal function, Louise Parent, executive vice president and general counsel, had earlier commissioned benchmarking studies and discovered that American Express was not the low-cost provider of legal services. She had then reduced the number of outside law firms from 300 to 60, but had maintained a full range of in-house services in both New York and Minnesota. Each business had also continued to operate with its own general counsel. Following Golub's directive, Parent and her colleagues consolidated offices, creating individual "Blue Box" centers of excellence in real estate, regulatory matters, compensation and benefits, employment law, and technology. The many general counsels were also eliminated. Parent recalled: "The hardest thing I've ever done was

EXHIBIT 7   POA II: The 13 Crosscutting Processes

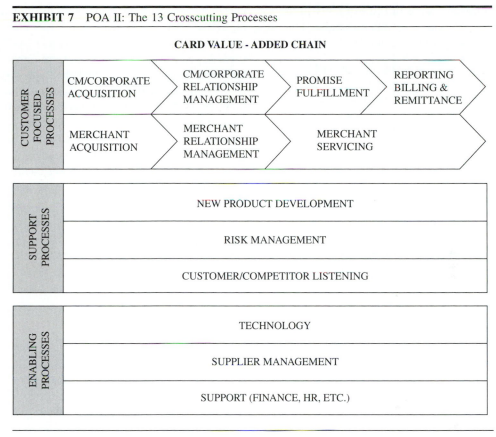

CARD VALUE - ADDED CHAIN

Source: American Express

reengineer this office. A billion-dollar acquisition is easy by comparison." The next challenge, she noted, was "convincing the survivors that this is a good place to work, even though it doesn't feel the same, and even though the brass ring [becoming a general counsel] is gone."

Tracking and Results.   To support POA-II and improve alignment across levels of the organization, a new set of metrics was developed. The development process was broad and participatory, and included Golub, Chenault, Cracchiolo, the reengineering heads, and assorted consultants, financial experts, and representatives of other functions. High level Health-of-the-Franchise measures were

disaggregated and translated into narrower activities that defined the role and performance expectations of each and every manager. Eventually, these metrics were expected to focus on individual transactions. The new measures were also designed to help managers think holistically, with a broader business perspective. For example, the goal of collection units had historically been to collect a certain number of dollars annually. The new metrics focused instead on "yield management," the absolute dollar yield for a given receivable quality, as well as the cost of collection for every dollar received. Such measures required managers to examine all aspects of their business, and suggested the possibility of doing work differently. Most of the new measures were linked explicitly to the 13 crosscutting processes. Parekh summarized the cumulative impact of these changes:

> With the new metrics in place, people making decisions in a functional capacity will focus on the overall impact of their decisions. Our new processes will become institutionalized and a basis for continuing improvement.

By late 1995, POA-II was beginning to have an impact. Five of the eight U.S. operating and customer service centers were being closed and their operations consolidated at the other three, eliminating about 4,000 jobs. Shared utilities for staff functions were expected to eliminate another 2,000 positions. Most redesigned processes were moving into the implementation phase, and dramatic improvements were expected. The new cardmember acquisition process, for example, was designed to cut cycle times from 14–16 weeks to four. Yet there was still considerable uncertainty about the future and questions about how the new processes would work. As one manager put it: "In this process you commit yourself to targets without knowing how you'll get there."

Case 6–4

PEPSI'S REGENERATION, 1990–1993

Pepsi-Cola and Coca-Cola were the Goliaths of the soft drink industry. Seemingly forever, the two companies had battled for prominence, often through vivid television advertisements promoting their flagship brands or new products. By the 1990s the competitors were squaring off through celebrities, with Pepsi extolled by singing superstar Michael Jackson, basketball superstar Shaquille O'Neal, and musical legend Ray Charles and the Rayettes, who introduced the phenomenally popular refrain, "You've Got the Right One, Baby, Uh-huh." The goal of these advertisements was to stimulate primary demand, as well as increase share. In 1990 Coke held roughly 40 percent of the domestic cola market, and Pepsi held 30 percent.

Traditionally, Pepsi had focused almost exclusively on selling products under the Pepsi brand name, including Pepsi-Cola, Diet Pepsi, and Caffeine-Free Pepsi. By 1990, however, the company began to face several competitive challenges (see Exhibit 1). Overall, soft drink growth was softening, with the cola market slipping even further.

Private-label colas were both gaining share and depressing industry prices. Alternative beverages, including bottled water, ready-to-drink tea, and fruit drinks, were growing in popularity. Finally, Pepsi confronted a growing volume gap versus Coke. Because of its more extensive distribution in restaurants like McDonald's, Coke realized an expanding volume advantage over Pepsi each year. Throughout the 1980s Pepsi had continued to meet its aggressive financial goal of 15 percent annual earnings increases. But now few opportunities remained for further cost reductions, and Pepsi's president and CEO, Craig Weatherup, feared that annual profit improvement could slip 5–10 percent (see Exhibit 2 for financials).

The shape of the company had also changed. In the late 1980s the majority of Pepsi bottlers were

---

This case was prepared by Donald N. Sull under the direction of David A. Garvin.

EXHIBIT 1   Pepsi's Competitive Situation: 1983–1993

Soft-drink category growth was softening…

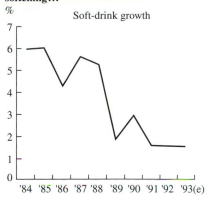

… with the cola segment slowing even more.

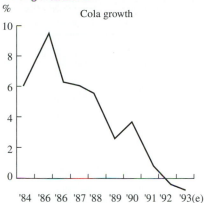

Private label soft drinks started taking off in supermarkets…

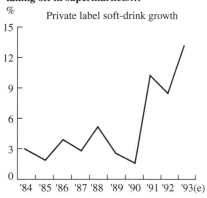

… and growth in alternative beverages accelerated.

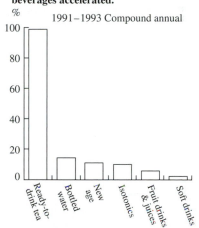

Pepsi-Cola's net prices continued to lag inflation…

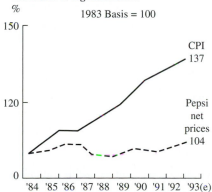

… while company-owned bottling operations expanded considerably.

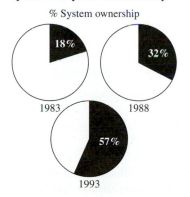

Source: P. Kay Coleman, "Pepsi's Road to the 'Right Side Up' Company," *Insights Quarterly* (CSC Index) 5, no. 3 (Winter 1993), p. 21. Reprinted with permission.

EXHIBIT 2   Financial Results ($ in millions)

	1989	1990	1991	1992	1993
Revenue					
Concentrate	$1,351.2	$1,181.8	$1,183.2	$1,199.9	$1,183.1
Bottling	3,272.1	3,852.7	3,991.3	4,285.3	4,735.0
Domestic Revenue	4,623.3	5,034.5	5,174.5	5,485.2	5,918.1
International Revenue	1,153.4	1,488.5	1,743.7	2,120.4	2,720.1
Total Revenue	5,776.7	6,523.0	6,918.2	7,605.6	8,638.2
Operating Profit					
Domestic*	577.6	673.8	746.2	801.7	936.9
International**	98.6	93.8	117.1	141.9	172.1
Total Op. Profit	676.2	767.6	863.3	943.6	1,109.0
Operating Margin					
Domestic*	12.5%	13.4%	14.4%	14.6%	15.8%
International**	8.5%	6.3%	6.7%	6.7%	6.3%
Total Op. Margin	11.7%	11.8%	12.5%	12.4%	12.8%
Beverage Sector					
Identifiable Assets	6,198.1	6,465.2	6,832.6	7,857.5	9,105.2
Capital Spending (1)	267.9	334.1	425.8	343.7	491.3
Acq. & Inv. in Affiliates (2)**	n/m	n/m	285.2	717.5	711.5
Amortization***	n/m	n/m	118.3	137.6	157.4
Depreciation***	n/m	n/m	251.7	290.6	358.5
Domestic Allocation					
Indentifiable Assets	4,960.6	4,989.9	5,110.5	5,666.9	6,238.0
Capital Spending (1)	214.4	257.9	318.5	247.9	336.6
Acq. & Inv. in Affiliates (2)***	n/m	n/m	213.3	517.5	487.5
Amortization***	n/m	n/m	88.5	99.2	107.8
Depreciation***	n/m	n/m	188.3	209.6	245.6

*Excludes restructuring charge of $115.4 in 1992.
**Excludes restructuring charge of $29.6 in 1992 to streamline an acquired business in Spain.
***Accounting changes in 1993 resulted in changes to these accounts that were not restated prior to 1991 due to lack of materiality.
(1) Includes capital leases.
(2) Includes noncash amounts related to treasury stock and debt issues, $367 in 1993, $110 in 1992, and $13 in 1991.

Source: Company records

independent. But in 1990, after an aggressive acquisition campaign, Pepsi was distributing 51 percent of its soft drink products through company-owned bottlers, with an additional 16 percent through joint ventures with franchisees. Weatherup observed:

> That was a $4 billion bet to control distribution. We went from a company with 600 customers—our

franchised bottlers—to 600,000 customers: those serviced through our newly acquired bottlers. Today we are a company that lives or dies . . . based on the 250,000 times a day it interacts with its customers.

The newly increased importance of the bottling operations challenged Pepsi's culture, which traditionally applauded individual heroics and "big picture" coups like the Jackson and O'Neal promotions. One senior vice president described the typical Pepsi manager as "an individual gunslinger," whose philosophy was "you make things happen, you take the ball and run with it. If you can take the ball from someone else and run with it, all the better." The bottling business, with its emphasis on the nuts and bolts of operations, presented a stark contrast. According to Weatherup: "It was incorrectly tagged as a second-class citizen—it had a 'loser' image, a grease-under-the-fingertips stereotype."

By June 1990 Weatherup felt that "things weren't right"—and had to change. He began to interview customers, employees, and outside experts on organizational change, while carefully analyzing the company's financials. The remainder of this case describes the three-year "Pepsi Regeneration" effort that he spearheaded. The most critical events are summarized in Exhibit 3. Weatherup later dubbed the major categories of change Pepsi's "Four Aces."

Launch

After months of data gathering and analysis, Weatherup presented his findings to his 10 direct reports in September 1990. He framed the meeting as a "soul-searching session," held off-site at the Point Resort in upstate New York. His primary goal was to convince his management team of the need for change. "I had taken months working through this," he explained, " and they were being asked to do it overnight. I worried that they wouldn't have enough time to internalize it." He added:

> People are generally all over the map in where they want to go. I knew that this was a situation where we couldn't afford the luxury of everyone flopping around. I wanted everybody to start the same book, on the same page, at the same time.

"Pains, Trains, and Radical Change"

During the first day of the Point meeting, Weatherup used vivid metaphors to create a sense of crisis. He described the financial, customer, and organizational pain facing the organization, concluding the session with his "freight train" speech: "There's a freight train out there, and it's called 15 percent earnings. We're standing on the track, and we'd better figure out something or it will run us right over."[1] The management team faced accepting mediocrity—accepting, and then explaining, to PepsiCo management that bottling was a 5–10 percent business—or embarking on a journey of radical change to achieve 15 percent earnings growth. Weatherup asked them to "sleep on" these two alternatives and come prepared to discuss their decision in the morning.

On the second day, the team began by unanimously voting to embark on a radical change program. Mark Wheless, senior vice president of operations, recalled: "The decision was, Did we want to be a mediocre company, or did we want to be one of the premier companies in the U. S.? To a person, we said we did not sign up for mediocrity." Weatherup then listed a series of questions for the group to debate: Did his data ring true? What were the important areas of doubt? What were the implications for Pepsi and the team? Finally, an outside consultant talked with the group about the factors differentiating winners from losers when introducing organizational change.

The group spent the third day brainstorming the systemic changes needed to achieve 15 percent annual earnings growth. To begin, they generated a list of 35 possible change levers, which they then distilled into 10 broad categories. After extensive discussion, each participant voted for the three most promising levers, with the five options receiving the most votes designated for further analysis (see Exhibit 4).

The last day of the meeting was devoted to task assignments and ground rules. Weatherup created

---

[1]*Brian Dumaine, "Times Are Good? Create a Crisis,"* Fortune, *June 28,1993, p. 123.*

EXHIBIT 3 The Four Aces Chronology

	1990	1991	1992	1993	1994
	JASOND	JFMAMJJASOND	JFMAMJJASOND	JFMAMJJASOND	JFMAM

The Right Side Up Vision

Point (11): CW and 10 direct reports agree on need for change and draft the screen	(9/90–12/90)
Hyatt (70): Point group enrolls their direct reports	(12/90–3/91)
Saddlebrook (400): Hyatt group enrolls their direct reports	(3/91–7/91)
Marriott (1,200): Saddlebrook group enrolls their direct reports	(7/91–1/92)
Dallas (5,500): Marriott group enrolls their direct reports	(1/92–3/92)
Team 20,000: one-day video presentation by top management of the screen to all employees	X (3/92)
HR develops new competencies and integrates them into performance evaluation	(4/91–10/92)

Process Improvement

Task	Timing
Process improvement one of 10 teams in Hyatt (70) enrollment	(12/90–3/91)
65 incremental process improvements (Three-Steps) conducted by Saddlebrook (400) teams	(3/91–7/91)
350 incremental process improvements (Three-Steps) conducted by Marriott (1,200) teams	(7/91–1/92)
16 Core Work processes defined	X (8/91)
16 core processes prioritized into 4 Enhanced Core Work processes	(first quarter 1992)
5 HQ macro-processes defined and improved through Three-Step conducted for Core Work processes by Dallas (5,500) teams	(6/91–12/92)
Reengineering effort of four major processes	(1/92–3/92)

The Total Beverage Company Strategy

Task	Timing
Pepsi Cola announces JV with Ocean Spray to distribute and develop juice products	X (9/91)
Pepsi Cola announces JV with Lipton to distribute Lipton products	X (12/91)
Pepsi enters into 75-year JV with Lipton to jointly produce ready-to-drink iced tea	X (4/92)
Total Beverage Company strategy unveiled as part of Pepsi's strategic planning cycle	X (Summer 1992)
Crystal Pepsi, a color-free cola, rolled out nationwide in the U.S.	X (1/93)
Roll out All Sport isotonic drink	X (2/94)

The Right Side Up Reorganization

Task	Timing
Craig Weatherup commissions his direct reports to design new organization	X (4/92)
Team analyzes current organization and recommends new design	(4/92–9/92)
Reorganization announced and rolled out nationally	(9/92–10/92)

Source: Company records

594

EXHIBIT 4 Summary of the Candidates for Change from the Point Meeting

	C. Weatherup	B. Barnes	M. Feiner	M. Pages	M. Lorelli	M. Wheless	R. Tidmore	J. Bronson	D. Novak	J. Montle	C. Hallenbeck	TOTAL VOTES			
Customer Focus												8			
Creating value for the customer															
Quality of transactions and exchange, both internally and externally															
Product/service quality															
Employee Empowerment												6			
Cultural vision															
Utilizing empowered workforce															
Improving internal and external communication															
Trusting															
Level of effectiveness															
Bottling Profit and Loss												6			
Get the bottling P&L in order (controllable costs)															
Buy franchisees															
CAPEX group = $100 million															
Organizational Effectiveness												6			
Improving internal and external communication															
Trusting															
Area ownership of businesses															
Lean and mean															
Team orientation															
Churn and burn of employees															
Cross-system consistency and alignment															
Fixing vicious circles in the planting process: manage consequences															
Targeted Volume Priority												5			
Growing share															
Marketing impact through a stronger marketing platform															
Win by focus/picking battlefields															
Become #1 in diet, category, and food store channel															
Achieve parity in fountain beverage channel															
Enter water segment															
15% NOPAT (we're doing all this to make 15%)												2			
Rallying Cry												0			
Rekindle "winning attitude/passion"															
Theme . . . rallying cry															
Most profitable company as candidate for rallying cry															
Premier company . . . special															
Quality												0			
Quality of transactions and exchange, both internally and externally															
Product/service quality															
Growing Distribution												0			
Buying Franchises												0			

Source: Company records

five "Point" teams and assigned two members of his staff to each one. "Their assignment," he recalled, "was to prove that their option was the Holy Grail. They had to prove it using facts, not just that this was their passion." Weatherup also charged the teams with dedicating half of their time during the following six weeks to the task, including interviewing customers and employees personally. Then, everyone agreed to plan and lead a meeting in December to enroll the next level of management in the vision that emerged. Brenda Barnes, senior vice president for special projects at the time and later chief operating officer for the South and West regions, summarized the Point session: "There was very little denial or challenge—just a brutal realization that things had to change and a big dose of reality. If we were going to change, it would be very, very difficult." To remind his team of the situation's urgency, Weatherup later gave each of them a model train with 15 percent painted on the side and 10 small figures standing on the tracks staring in terror as it approached.

Turning Pepsi "Right Side Up"

Six weeks after the Point meeting and a host of work sessions, Weatherup's direct reports reconvened for two days in Chicago to choose among the options explored by the five Point teams. Wheless recalled:

> The five alternatives were all false starts because they were created as individual solutions to the problem. Then we realized that you have to satisfy the customer, the employee, and the shareholder *simultaneously*. We had always traded off one against the other. The key "Aha" was the need to draft a strategy to do them all at once.

A vision of the future Pepsi then began to emerge. "We realized that we had a 'wrong-side-up' organization," Barnes observed, "where the front-line performers catered to managers at the top, instead of worrying about how to support customers." The team converged on the need to turn the company "right side up" by aligning the organization with customers' needs. Weatherup encouraged them to translate this broad consensus into a concrete vision statement.

While there was agreement on the basic thrust of "Right Side Up," the management team struggled over the specifics. Both concepts and language caused problems. Barnes recalled:

> We agreed that we would not move forward until we were all aligned, until everyone supported it 100 percent. We would stop frequently for 'alignment checks' to make sure that we had all contributed, we had all had the opportunity to be heard, and that we were all committed to support the decision. It consumed our lives. By the time we were done, we had written it, rewritten it, and argued over every word. By the time we were done, it was tattooed on our chests.

The result was the Right Side Up (RSU) vision statement (see Exhibit 5). The idea was to invert the traditional organizational pyramid so that customers were on top and managers were on the bottom, supporting front-line workers.

Enrolling the Organization

The team then began preparing to enroll other managers in the Right Side Up campaign. The first enrollment, which consisted of the 70 direct reports of the Point group executives, was kicked off with a three-day meeting in December 1990. Weatherup began the meeting by explaining that Pepsi's earnings growth was not sustainable, and by conveying the customer, employee, and financial pain that demanded radical changes. To put the needed changes in context, he used a story with another vivid metaphor, the "burning platform," borrowed from an organizational consultant advising the company:

> It seems that a few years ago a North Sea oil rig caught fire. One worker, trained not to jump from the 150-foot-high rig into the icy sea but to wait for help no matter how bad things got, leaped anyway. He survived. Asked afterward why he stepped off the edge, the worker said he looked behind him and saw an approaching wall of fire and looked down and saw the sea: "I chose probable death over certain death."[2]

---

[2] *Ibid., p. 124.*

EXHIBIT 5   The Right Side Up Vision

PEPSI-COLA...THE RIGHT SIDE UP COMPANY

We dedicate ourselves to creating a truly outstanding Pepsi-Cola Company, broadly recognized as a great Company to do business with, as a great place to work and as the driving force in making PepsiCo one of the best long-term investments.

**WE WILL BE AN OUTSTANDING COMPANY BY EXCEEDING CUSTOMER EXPECTATIONS
THROUGH EMPOWERED PEOPLE, GUIDED BY SHARED VALUES.**

_____THIS REQUIRES:_____

A consistent
CUSTOMER FOCUS
for our company which all of our people understand and feel passionate about

An

EMPOWERED ORGANIZATION
which is both motivated and supported to satisfy customers to the fullest extent of their capabilities.

A set of
SHARED VALUES
which guides all of our decisions and actions.

To make this a reality, we must turn the company "right side up". A "right side up" company, places the **CUSTOMER** (anyone who buys or sells our product) at the top, thereby acknowledging everything starts with the customer. The voice of the customer drives our actions. It's understood that everyone listens to our customer, understands what the customer needs, and delivers against those needs. Processes are developed which add value to our customer, and activities are eliminated that do not. Over time, this will enable us to build mutually beneficial partnerships with our customers. This will be our long-term sustainable, competitive advantage.

Those employees closest to the customers are at the top of the organization. They must be **EMPOWERED** to satisfy customer needs. The rest of the organization's role is to help those closest to the customers by providing resources and removing obstacles. Empowered employees exercise their freedom to act within their area of competence — take responsibility, accept accountability, exercise initiative, and deliver results. Empowering leaders create the environment by providing the vision, and latitude for action. Empowered people see themselves as owner-operators, recognizing what is good for the customer is good for the company and good for them as individuals.

A "right side up" company is guided by **SHARED VALUES**. The shared values we will live by are:

Diversity — We respect the individual and will seek, value and promote differences of race, nationality, gender, age, background, experience and style.

Integrity—We will do what we say.

Honesty — We will speak openly and directly, with care and compassion, and work hard to understand and resolve issues.

Teamwork — Working on real customer needs, we will combine functional excellence and cross-functional teamwork to produce exceptional results.

Accountability — We all understand what is expected of us, and are fully committed to meeting those expectations.

Balance — We will respect the decisions individuals make to achieve professional and personal balance in their life.

By living these shared values everyday, we will build mutual trust.
On this foundation we will build the outstanding Company that our customers, our shareholders, and our employees want and expect. Through customer focus, empowerment, and shared values we will be the "right side up" Company.

Members of the Point group then introduced the Right Side Up vision as the means to move the organization forward, and presented their findings from customer and employee interviews. The Point managers also led "table buzz" sessions, where the participants broke into smaller groups and discussed their immediate reactions to the Right Side Up vision in short sessions.

The final day of the meeting was devoted to assigning work for the managers to complete in the three months that followed. The Point managers divided the group into 10 teams of seven managers apiece, and assigned each team a particular problem, such as forecasting accuracy, productivity improvement, and employee satisfaction. They were also charged with planning and leading the enrollment for the next layer in the organization.

Subsequent enrollments followed the Hyatt meeting's three-part format: Weatherup's "burning platform" speech; a presentation of the RSU vision, often coupled with a brief training session; and dividing participants into teams that would do "real work." All groups were given 90 days to complete their work, which included interviewing customers, charting work processes, and preparing to lead the next enrollment. Weatherup concluded each enrollment meeting with a rousing send-off, his "head, heart, hands" speech. In it, he explained that for change to occur, people needed to do three things: develop a conceptual understanding of the rationale and proposed direction of change (head), internalize and commit emotionally to the new vision (heart), and begin to do the work necessary to develop new skills and ensure that the vision was realized (hands).

Although an effort was made to ensure consistency in enrollment meetings, there were subtle changes as each group tried to incorporate new learnings. Barnes recalled: "It was hell, because we couldn't map out everything in advance. We didn't know what we were going to do tomorrow until we'd lived it today. Finally, we realized, 'We'll know as we go.'" After several iterations, the enrollment process culminated in "Team 20,000," a one-day session in which every front-line employee saw a series of presentations from top management and then broke into small groups locally to discuss the RSU vision.

Weatherup's management team had called the RSU vision "the screen," because people were to screen their behavior for consistency with the vision statement. While Pepsi managers ultimately felt the approach had worked, they noted some cases of "screen abuse," where employees measured their actions selectively against certain parts of the screen while ignoring others. (See Exhibit 6 for the results of a 1993 survey measuring the company's overall progress on RSU goals.)

To translate the Right Side Up vision into changes in employees' daily behavior, Pepsi's human resource group gathered detailed examples that illustrated the tenets of customer focus, employee empowerment, and shared values in action. Outstanding performers were asked to describe critical incidents in performing their jobs and explain in great detail exactly what they did. These examples of specific behavior were synthesized into competencies, which became the building blocks of the Right Side Up implementation. "Building business partnerships," for example, represented one of the four competencies that supported customer focus. It consisted of such behaviors as "explaining to customers and suppliers the rationale behind proposals and recommendations using appropriate facts and data," and "building personal relationships with counterparts in customer organizations."

Once the broad maxims of the Right Side Up vision had been translated into these more specific terms, Pepsi used them to drive human resource decisions in a coordinated fashion. Employee selection, placement, training, performance evaluation, and compensation were all affected. In the performance review process, for example, managers were expected to cite specific illustrations of employees' behavior and calibrate them against the new standards. These evaluations also impacted employees' bonuses and merit raises. In 1993 a typical manager's bonus was 15–25 percent of his or her base salary; its components were the financial performance of the business unit (50 percent), success in achieving the department's or unit's Right Side Up goals as measured by the employee survey (25 percent), and progress against individual development goals (25 percent).

Process Improvement

Like many other companies undergoing radical change, Pepsi began to focus on processes as a means of improving operating efficiency. Such efforts typically require careful mapping of workflows and the introduction of new measures to

EXHIBIT 6   1993 Pepsi-Cola North American Survey Results USA

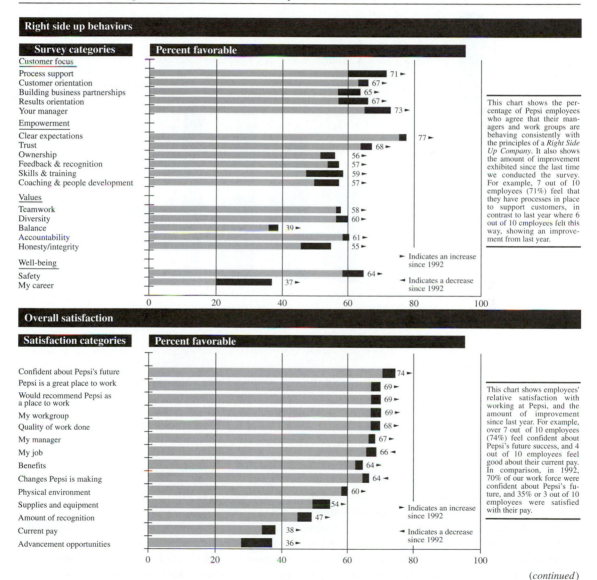

(continued)

EXHIBIT 6   *(concluded)*

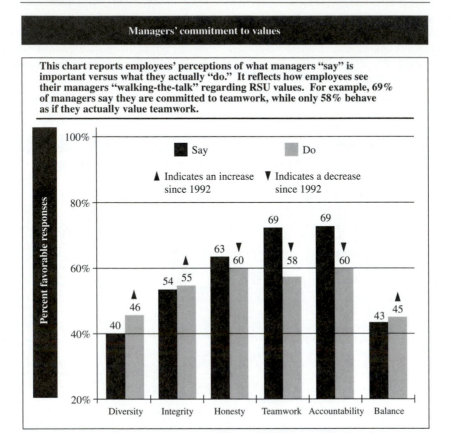

Managers' commitment to values

This chart reports employees' perceptions of what managers "say" is important versus what they actually "do." It reflects how employees see their managers "walking-the-talk" regarding RSU values. For example, 69% of managers say they are committed to teamwork, while only 58% behave as if they actually value teamwork.

Source: Company records

---

identify needed changes in the way that work is actually accomplished.

Rejecting Process

Although it later emerged as a critical part of Pepsi's regeneration, process thinking was initially resisted. Weatherup recalled the early response of his management team: "They felt that process was beneath them . . . it was a dirty word in this company." Added Barnes, "Process was rejected like an organ transplant. People said, 'We hate it, it's garbage, we're action-biased and it will slow us down.'" Indeed, as David Novak, senior vice president for marketing at

the time and later chief operating officer for the East and Central regions, noted:

> One of the things you loved about Pepsi was there wasn't a whole hell of a lot of process. We were more "this is what we want to get done, let's go get it done," and everybody had their own way of getting it done . . . Process was pretty informal, and not something that we really talked about a lot.

Over time, however, customer interviews and the process maps that were developed during later enrollment sessions hammered home the importance of process. Chuck Alpuche, director for continuous process improvement, observed that managers only realized the level of customer discontent "when they heard their customers, in their own words, say how unhappy they were with our overall service . . . now it was not a headquarters-driven initiative, but a local issue." Managers observed first-hand the amount of non-value-added work generated by current operating practices. One recalled: "This forced us to find out what the hell we were doing. I thought I knew, but I didn't have a clue." He remembered observing truck loading: "It was terrible. What really made the system work was individual heroics. Finding a trailer in the yard should be a simple thing, but it wasn't. It was amazing we made any money at all!" Ultimately, as Weatherup explained, "We realized that we needed to understand processes to improve them. Trying harder, and yelling and screaming, wasn't going to fix anything. It required fundamentally managing and planning the work."

The Process Journey

Early in the enrollment sessions, Wheless developed a method for mapping and improving processes, known as Three-Step, that was taught to all participants (see Exhibit 7). By the summer of 1991, Three-Step teams were analyzing more than 350 separate processes. Wheless and Barnes suspected overlap, and confirmed this hunch in focus groups with employees conducting Three-Step analyses. Wheless recalled: "When we talked to the teams, themes of needs emerged. If you take 350 projects, a few processes were surfacing over and over again. Take all the projects people were starting and you could categorize them real fast."

Thus, after sorting through the customer interviews and process improvement efforts, Wheless and Barnes boiled customers' goals down to a simple formula: customers wanted "the right product, in the right place, at the right time." They then analyzed

---

EXHIBIT 7   The Three-Step Method for Customer Valued Process Improvement

1. Start with the customer

    A. Understand their needs, and select the highest priority need, e.g., speed of delivery
    B. Establish measures and success criteria
    C. Select the process with the greatest impact on the chosen need

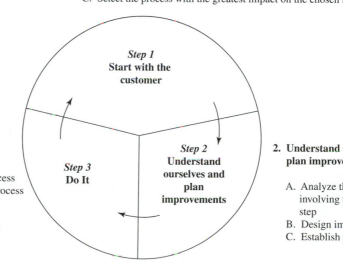

Step 1
Start with the customer

3. Do it

    A. Pilot test improved process
    B. Implement improved process
    C. Stabilize process
    D. Go to Step 1
       (continuously improve)

Step 3
Do It

Step 2
Understand ourselves and plan improvements

2. Understand ourselves and plan improvement

    A. Analyze the current process, involving the workers at each step
    B. Design improved process
    C. Establish process measures

Pepsi's operations and identified 16 processes that had to be executed flawlessly to avoid such failures. These 16, dubbed "Core Work," followed steps in delivering the product: forecasting demand, loading trucks, delivering product, invoicing customers, and so forth.

But collecting data, tracking, and improving even 16 processes proved burdensome. Wheless therefore aggregated the Core Work procedures into four "megaprocesses" that most directly affected customers. They were termed Enhanced Core Work and included defining customer needs, making the product, delivering the product, merchandising, and tracking customer satisfaction. New measures were then developed to track performance against these goals (see Exhibit 8).

A National Best Practices program was later established to identify and disseminate the most efficient practices throughout the company. Pepsi also embarked on a massive reengineering effort, designed around information technology, for invoicing, purchasing, equipment repair, and financial reporting processes. Because its goal was tenfold improvement, the effort was dubbed "10X."

"Real Men Talk Process"

Process initiatives introduced standardization to a company that had historically prided itself on individuality. Nevertheless, some differences existed in the definition of processes and process thinking and their organizational impact.

According to Weatherup,

We needed to develop a common language around process and how the work gets done. Before, the view at Pepsi was that "real men don't talk process."

Novak:

Process is the way we go about delivering against customer needs . . . the Three-Step [method] was a smart way to teach the company marketing. It allows people to focus on marketing without calling it that.

EXHIBIT 8   Core Work Processes and Measures

Process	*Measure*
1. Determine customer product needs	Deal lead time met
	Deal communicated effectively
	Forecast accuracy
	Right equipment expectations
2. Make product	Product specifications met
	Taste vs. gold standard
	Every route loaded as ordered
	Equipment reliability
3. Deliver product	Every delivery window met
	Correct in-store invoice
	Satisfied drivers
4. Service/merchandize product	Orderly backroom
	Proper merchandizing
	No surprises on equipment and installation
	Properly operating equipment
	No equipment downtime

Source: Company records

Barnes:

It's [process thinking] important because you're keeping an eye on what you put in place and making changes based on what the data tell you.

The Total Beverage Company Strategy

In the summer of 1992, as the Right Side Up enrollment and process initiatives progressed, Pepsi unveiled a "Total Beverage" strategy. Novak explained:

For a considerable time, Right Side Up was viewed as *the* strategy, but then people realized it was simply an operating philosophy. We had this Right Side Up company, and it needed to *do* something. Total Beverage tells the company what to do . . . A great strategy means you have new sources of growth built in, and Total Beverage has them.

With its Total Beverage strategy, Pepsi would offer a preferred beverage for any occasion throughout the day, targeting customers' "need states" at different times, such as early morning or before bedtime, and during different activities, such as exercise or eating. This meant moving aggressively beyond colas to develop alternative beverage segments, including bottled waters, ready-to-drink teas, isotonics (e.g., Gatorade-type drinks), and possibly milk and coffee products. Pepsi hoped to achieve one-half of its revenue growth from alternative beverages, which would total $2 billion by 1995. To begin, the company formed partnerships with Lipton and Ocean Spray to launch and distribute new products.

Pepsi's thrust into noncola beverages marked a divergence between its strategy and Coke's, which continued to emphasize its flagship cola. Weatherup recalled the in-house reaction to Total Beverage:

Fifty percent of the people in Pepsi said, "It's about time, let's go after those guys." The other 50 percent said, "That's the dumbest thing I've ever heard, let's stick to our knitting. We're going through all of this Right Side Up stuff, and now you want us to carry another 30 SKUs we don't even know how to sell or produce. You're crazy."

Early market results for the Total Beverage strategy were encouraging: Pepsi was soon number-one in the tea category, and juice sales were meeting ambitious projections. By 1993 new businesses, including Lipton, All Sport, and Ocean Spray products, accounted for nearly $1 billion in sales at retail.

Operationally, however, the Total Beverage strategy strained Pepsi's ability to produce and distribute products. The number of SKUs increased by nearly 100 percent, going from roughly 120 at the end of 1992 to over 220 by 1994. Equally important, the number of product categories jumped from one to four. Because the production of tea and juice differed significantly from cola, SKU proliferation challenged established warehousing and logistics systems. The introduction of new products also complicated demand forecasting, which resulted in costly shortages and excesses. Salespeople accustomed to selling cola required additional training to sell tea, isotonics, and juice. Brian Swette, senior vice president for new business development, observed:

Total Beverage was not constructed as part of Right Side Up, but it was evident that it was a good fit. Customer-driven means giving the customers what they want, and Total Beverage does that . . . Even so, all along the supply chain, we've had significant unexpected glitches. For one reason or another, we either don't have labels, line times, bottles, concentrate, raw materials—the formulations aren't right and we need to make adjustments. We make too much and we have to throw product away. We've had significant start-up issues with physically handling the production as well as anticipating what we need to have to sell.

Reorganization

Weatherup had originally believed that the "Pepsi Regeneration" effort might be accomplished without reorganization. He explained:

An organizational change is the kind of mistake I'd suggest that an MBA student might make. It's the ultimate "grass is always greener on the other side." It doesn't change anything fundamental. The issue here is the internalization of where we want to go as a company, and understanding process thinking and what Right Side Up means.

Eventually, however, Weatherup recognized that a reorganization would be necessary to support the Right Side Up vision; the question was when.

Pepsi's traditional organization had been totally functional. At the top of the pyramid sat the president, the only general manager responsible for more than one function. The company contained four divisions, which were further divided into 24 geographic areas. Few were aligned with major markets. "Functional silos" ran through the areas and divisions. According to one executive:

> The 24 areas were all microcosms of the functional organization. It was all function heads, there was not a leader, even as a tie breaker between sales and manufacturing. The most senior person was the retail sales person, but they only had authority over sales. There weren't any general managers in place, and there were very few people who had been general managers. It was a flawed design, to say the least.

Managers also considered the company top-heavy. Weatherup observed:

> We valued work being done to support the top of the organization. We thought as the CEO, you need a good CFO, a good sales type, a good marketing manager. The CFO needs a corporate planning type, a controller, etc., and you keep going this way until you finally get down to the poor person who's doing the work.

Designing the Right Side Up Organization

The reorganization effort began in April 1992 with broad discussions by Weatherup's management team. To begin, Weatherup presented 18 principles that established expectations for what the reorganization should accomplish and provided criteria for evaluating alternatives (see Exhibit 9). The senior management team first debated and refined the initial principles, then used them to guide the design. Weatherup explained:

> The design had to be consistent with the principles, or we had to redesign, or we had to change the

principles. We went back to the organizational principles time and time again and agonized, "Were we willing to change the principles or change the organization?"

The formal redesign began with an analysis of the work done by front-line employees, with the organization designed backwards from the front line to the headquarters group in Somers, New York. Weatherup first created a task force to examine the 16 Core Work processes performed by front-line performers, and urged the team to structure positions around these processes. Once this group's analysis was well advanced, he created two other teams to reorganize business unit management and corporate headquarters functions, and explicitly charged them with designing these jobs in support of front-line employees. Each team was headed by one of Weatherup's direct reports.

In the reorganization, the 24 areas were dismantled and 107 new local Market Units were created based on customer markets rather than geographic convenience (see Exhibit 10). Run by a general manager with profit and loss responsibility, the Market Units "owned" the customers in their community and were responsible for flawlessly executing the core work. The Market Units were then consolidated into 16 Business Units, charged with providing resources to the Market Units and supporting them. Business Units were also responsible for serving large customers, such as regional grocery chains, that cut across individual Market Units. Headquarters was renamed the National Business Unit and given a new role: to create the processes and tools necessary for field personnel to serve their customers. The redesigned organization was rolled out nationwide within a month of its completion, following the approach used for enrollment in the RSU vision.

Top management was pleased with the results. Deeper in the company, however, there was some concern about the pace and magnitude of change. Ken Kimmel, the Boston Market Unit manager, observed:

> Pepsi is the reorganization company from hell. I've been moved four times in five years. When the

---

EXHIBIT 9   Guiding Principles for the Reorganization

---

1. Establish organization around *the work* vs. departments and/or functions and/or geography and/or people.

2. Start with the work as defined *by our customers,* e.g., "I want one person I know is responsible for my store."

3. A learning orientation is valued behavior throughout the organization.

4. Our basic Front Line Work Unit (FLWU) "owns" the *customer* accounts that serve the units' *consumers,* e.g., Orlando, Jacksonville, Miami, Tampa, etc.

5. The number one people criteria is an organization populated by the right people as defined by the customer, e.g., local knowledge vs. international experience.

6. Extraordinary clarity of roles and how they are to be executed is of *paramount* need and one of our biggest issues today. We need a precise organizational logic flow from our customers to our line organization to our support resources.

7. Roles need to reflect the right decision being made at exactly the right level in the organization, i.e., what people do we want thinking about what; where do we want what decisions made.

8. Get/give knowledge (current facts/data, i.e., Gotta Have It Summer Program Information) to people with experience to apply that knowledge to getting their work done.

   (The hypothesis being that the gap between the strong traits and yet weak performance of our people as identified by our customers is primarily a lack of knowledge, secondarily a lack of skill—a CEW only opinion.)

9. Every one of our 600,000 customers (an outlet/a store/an address) is owned by *someone.*

10. Organization is process/results, not task driven. Jobs measured on contribution/results (P&R measures) not activity/busyness.

11. Key is applying skills to the customer (our business)—work is 40/60, e.g., functional skills (40%) must be applied cross functionally to the customer (60%).

12. Jobs—need to recognize that people need to feel they can grow/learn/prosper without constant movement.

13. Support to Front Line Work Units should only exist where it provides critical work expertise (what and how) better than FLWU's could provide for themselves.

14. Maximize flexibility and adaptability of front line work unit. . . . people are flexible *and* work is flexible, e.g., a fluid/resilient organization that changes work with season and/or day of the week.

15. Clear alignment around vision with consistent articulation and behavior as seen by performers and customers.

16. Simplicity must be rigorously applied and complexity must be managed. (Approached judiciously, the management of complexity can become a powerful competitive weapon.)

17. Need to recognize and maximize franchised bottlers customer relationship.

18. + Your input.

Source: Company records

company reorganized last year, people were wound up tighter than cheap clocks because they didn't know what would come next.

Barnes acknowledged the difficulties of Pepsi's radical change: "People can only assimilate so many things. We haven't cratered the place because we've got a lot of resilient people, but we're pushing them to the edge."

New and Improved Pepsi?

In the wake of the reorganization, executives in the National Business Unit (NBU) believed that they

EXHIBIT 10   Partial Organization Chart, The Right Side Up Organization

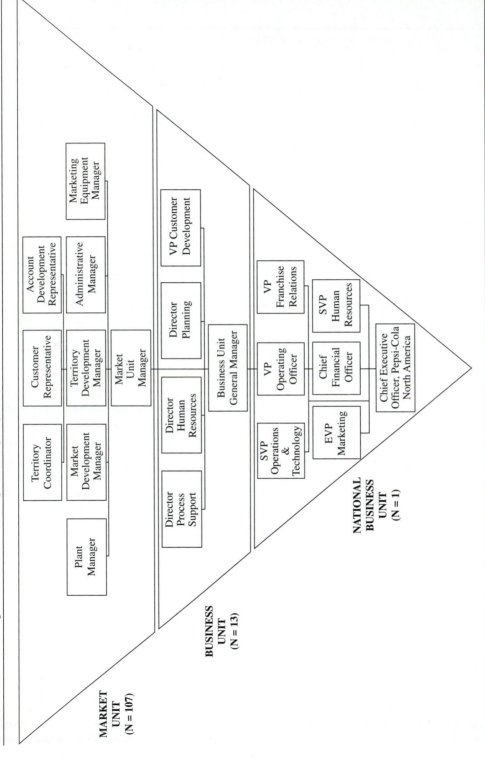

MARKET
UNIT
(N = 107)

BUSINESS
UNIT
(N = 13)

NATIONAL
BUSINESS
UNIT
(N = 1)

Plant
Manager

Territory
Coordinator

Customer
Representative

Account
Development
Representative

Marketing
Equipment
Manager

Market
Development
Manager

Territory
Development
Manager

Administrative
Manager

Market
Unit
Manager

Director
Process
Support

Director
Human
Resources

Director
Planning

VP Customer
Development

Business Unit
General Manager

SVP
Operations
&
Technology

VP
Operating
Officer

VP
Franchise
Relations

EVP
Marketing

Chief
Financial
Officer

SVP
Human
Resources

Chief Executive
Officer, Pepsi-Cola
North America

Source: Company records

spent more time listening to customers and employees so as to support the Business and Market Units in serving their customers. Novak elaborated:

> In the old Pepsi, you might not go out to the marketplace—the customers would come to you. During the visit people would present to you: It was ceremonial and all geared around serving managment's needs. Now our orientation is, How can we serve you?

But there was still concern that the NBU did not understand all of the complexities in the field, and some field personnel complained that they were receiving memos from the NBU addressed to them with incorrect names and titles.

Business Units (BU) also provided functional expertise and support to the Market Unit (MU) managers. Most BU managers preferred to delegate authority to these managers rather than dictate decisions from above. Barbara Bureck, vice president for customer development in the New England BU, compared the process of setting prices before and after the reorganization:

> In the old days, one or two people sitting around at six at night would scribble a price on an envelope, throw it out into the market, and see what would stick. In the new world, pricing is considered part of the Deal Creation and Communication process, and the whole process has changed—who's involved, what to consider, the level of effort and analysis, and how we communicate to customers and the ultimate consumer. Today we send out binders describing the process to Market Unit Managers, and then they execute.

Such activities raised questions for some managers about the role of the Business Units within Pepsi. One executive commented on his management style when he had served as a BU manager:

> I let the Market Unit managers define what their boundaries of decisions are. I very rarely stepped in and changed decisions. In the old days you had to get an act of Congress to spend $20,000; I just told them, "Spend it." . . . But if we're truly building capability at the Market Unit level, and I think we are, then why would we add these Business Units at all?

The greatest impact of the reorganization had, in fact, come from the Market Units. There were now 107 new general manager positions. Each ran a small business, with sales reaching hundreds of millions of dollars. According to Novak: "People love these jobs! They are very hard, but people know that they're really running a piece of the business; they like having the profit and loss responsibility." Barnes also emphasized the breadth of the position:

> They are dealing with everything—every function, every customer, every personnel-related issue, unions, freezes, hurricanes, earthquakes. You talk to the Market Unit manager in San Fernando, California, and his life was hell because his whole warehouse and Market Unit was destroyed by the earthquake in California. All of a sudden it's, "How do I get the building inspected? How do I treat my employees who are homeless?" You name it, and they have to deal with it . . . It's not a behind-the-desk job, it's out there, it's in the markets, it's on the routes, it's in the community.

Most of the newly minted MU managers came from sales or marketing positions. Some of them were still grappling with the demands of their new roles. Novak explained:

> Our business starts early and ends late. You need to be there when you open up in the morning. When you're going to bring everybody together for a meeting, you have to do it at 6:00 A.M. because people have to get to work. Plus you get to be part of the community—which means you've got to go to the Chamber of Commerce meeting at night.

Ken Kimmel described the challenges of his position a bit differently:

> The Market Unit manager job is a funnel: It's a hopper and everything is going in. I've really struggled with how information gets distributed. It all gets thrown into the funnel and lands on the Market Unit manager's desk. You get 43 binders from the National Business Unit, providing a template for marketing programs or giving a to-do list for a new product rollout. I'm not saying that the tools are bad—they're great—but I don't have the capability to process them all. It's death by a million pinpricks.

Case 6–5

LEVERAGING PROCESSES FOR STRATEGIC ADVANTAGE

David A. Garvin

Reengineering efforts are sweeping the country as companies shift from purely functional organizations to those that better accommodate horizontal work flows. Broad, crosscutting processes such as product development and order fulfillment have become the new organizational building blocks, replacing narrowly focused departments and functions. Managers, in turn, have begun to develop new ways of working. But much remains to be learned about how these new organizations are crafted and led. The critical questions involve strategy and management practice. Which strategic purposes are best served by processes? How do the roles and responsibilities of senior managers change in these new organizations? What skills are required to manage through processes?

To address those questions, I invited four senior executives who have pioneered the shift to process-based organizations to a roundtable discussion of their experiences. The group consisted of Paul Allaire, chairman and CEO of Xerox; Robert Herres, chairman and CEO of United Services Automobile Association (USAA); Jan Leschly, chief executive of SmithKline Beecham; and Craig Weatherup, president and CEO of Pepsi-Cola North America. They represent diverse industries—document processing, insurance, pharmaceuticals, and soft drinks—and a wide range of competitive challenges. But their observations about processes and process management are strikingly similar. The discussion was held at the Harvard Business School in Boston, Massachusetts.

David A. Garvin: In recent years, there has been an enormous surge of interest in processes. What caused you and your organizations to make the shift?

Jan Leschly: The customer completely changed on us. In the past, we were always a physician-driven business; now we're payer driven. In the United States today, employers and insurance companies pay our bills; in Europe, the government pays. So we figured we'd better find out how to satisfy these new customers, and that led us to a powerful realization: The way we do business had to change completely.

For a long time, we had four separate businesses—pharmaceuticals, consumer health care, animal health, and clinical laboratories—each working in silos, independent of the others, developing strategies of their own. But when we looked at the health care system as a whole and tried to understand how it was changing, we had trouble fitting these businesses into the new world. We simply had no idea which parts of the system to participate in and which to avoid. After a fair amount of work, we decided to focus on three key areas: care delivery, care management, and care coverage. Each is a collection of broad processes driving the health care system rather than a narrowly defined business. We then defined strategies for each area and looked into the capabilities that were necessary for success. We ended up with a list of six critical capabilities: pioneer discovery, product development, low-cost production, customer intimacy, alliance building and continuous improvement.

Eventually, that list led us to processes. Why? Because we realized that a capability comes only by combining a competence with a reliable process. To be a leader in biotechnology, you first need the best cellular and molecular biologists in the world. But that isn't enough. You must also have a reliable, repeatable discovery and development process; otherwise, products won't emerge regularly from the pipeline. These larger processes are themselves divided into many smaller ones—in the case of product development, more than 3,000 in all. Today each of these processes is charted and on the way to being repeatable and controllable. But I believe that we have at least five years to go before we become a fully process-oriented organization.

Paul Allaire: The incentive for us to shift to processes was similar: a fundamental change in customers' requirements and competitive forces. You can't survive if you don't respond to those new conditions. But first you have to understand them, so we began in 1989 with a broad review of trends in our environment. We called the review Xerox 2000 and used it to generate and examine assumptions about technology, markets, customers, and competitors over the coming decade. After studying position papers and meeting with experts in each of those areas, our senior team created a list of some 60 possible assumptions about the future. Then we voted on the ones that we deemed most likely to prove valid. Some of the assumptions were particularly thorny, such as whether paper would continue to be widely used in offices or whether digital technology would replace analog products altogether. The validated assumptions led us to a new set of imperatives—things we must do to succeed in the future—as well as to a new strategic direction, which we call the Document Company. Our goal shifted from being a manufacturer of copier, printer, and facsimile products to becoming a provider of document tools and services that enhance our customers' productivity. We soon realized that the organization had to be redesigned to reflect our strategy, and that's when we began focusing on processes.

So your motivation for shifting to processes was fundamentally strategic?

Allaire: Absolutely. You can't redesign processes unless you know what you're trying to do. What you're after is congruence among strategic direction, organizational design, staff capabilities, and the processes you use to ensure that people are working together to meet the company's goals. So you start by looking at the competition and reviewing your strategic direction; then you figure out how to organize to achieve the new goals. Today the toughest competition comes from smaller companies. Unless large companies like ours are able to change the way we operate, smaller companies will win because they are able to react to the marketplace so quickly.

We decided to respond to competitive forces by breaking our business into smaller pieces. But, at the same time, we didn't want to lose the effectiveness of a large organization. We wanted to be more customer focused but no less efficient. That, we found, is the magic of processes—you can have it both ways. A process orientation allows you to take huge amounts of cost out of the system while still improving customer satisfaction. It keeps your eye on both objectives simultaneously. Today we have nine separate divisions, each drawing on common research laboratories, a shared sales force, and a set of aligned processes. We realized pretty quickly that the only way to manage this kind of structure was to focus on core processes.

Craig Weatherup: Our motivation was a bit more internal, although I suppose it could also be traced to a changing environment. We've competed against Coke forever. But, in the late 1980s, we made a $4 billion bet, buying up many of our independent bottlers to gain more control over distribution. Almost overnight, we went from a company with 600 customers—the franchised bottlers—to a company with 600,000 customers. And we moved aggressively into a wide range of alternative beverages, such as juices and teas, and added lots of new packaging. All of a sudden, we had an explosion of complexity in various shapes, forms, and sizes. To give one example, between 1990 and 1992 we introduced eight new stock-keeping units; in the next two years we introduced 110.

At the same time, we were still a company with a "big event" marketing mentality. Our entire mind-set was geared to superstar entertainers such as Michael Jackson and Ray Charles. However, we now had several hundred thousand customers, and we weren't spending enough time thinking about them. The complexity was a huge challenge and drove us to this compelling commitment: to devote as much time, energy, and passion to operations and service as we had historically devoted to marketing. That quickly pointed us toward processes. As we got into it, we began to recognize the tremendous leverage that we would gain by improving our operating skills. We had processes, of course, since we were producing and selling every day. But they weren't working well enough. We have focused over the last four years on installing the context, tools, training, and incentives to make all our processes more effective.

Couldn't the changes you three have described been made years ago?

Allaire: Yes and no. The concept of processes really isn't that new. Effective managers have long known that you manage by processes—they're an essential tool for getting things done. What's different now is the enabling technology. Today's information systems allow you to do things that weren't possible in the past, such as accessing information simultaneously from multiple locations and diverse functional groups. With that ability, you can enjoy the efficiency of a process orientation without losing the responsiveness of a divisional orientation. The less developed information systems that supported command-and-control structures couldn't do that. In fact, those structures—which can probably be traced to the church and to the military as far back as Caesar—persisted precisely because for many years they were the *only* way to manage large, complex organizations.

Robert Herres: When I was taking management courses, we used to describe management as a process. I'm not sure that everybody got it. But the old rule that you plan, organize, direct, and control always seemed to me to be a pretty good description of what management is all about.

At USAA, we have always had processes linking together our basic activities. There's an underwriting process, a rate-setting process, a loss-management process, a catastrophe-management process, as well as the usual collection of functional processes. They've been there for years, although we haven't always been conscious of them. In fact, in some cases I think those processes were working in spite of our organizational structure.

Like Xerox, we were helped enormously by new developments in information technology. How? They forced us to think about the most effective ways of managing by process. We found that if you really want to exploit new technology—and for us, that includes both communications and information systems—you have to analyze how the work in your organization actually gets done and decide which steps can be tailored to a machine and which are best left to people. To do that, you have to develop detailed process maps and get the whole organization thinking in process terms.

Could you say a bit more about the links between information technology and processes?

Herres: Let me begin with a bit of history. USAA was started in 1922 as a direct writer of insurance. We never had agents; everything was done by mail and telephone. In fact, at one time we were the largest mail-order house in the country, maybe even in the world. Everything came to one centralized location in San Antonio, Texas, where the paperwork was processed. When we began to think about new technology, we discovered that lots of traditions had built up in this administrative organization, and many unnecessary steps. Paper was forever getting lost. My predecessor tells a wonderful story of trying to break into one of our processes. He was prowling the corridors one night when he looked into an office and noticed stacks of piled-up folders. None of them had been touched since his last visit a few evenings earlier, so he took a folder to see if anybody would notice. It was his way of testing whether our processes were under control. Unfortunately, many of them weren't, which meant that we had much cleaning up to do before we could meld those processes with modern information systems.

Technology also forced us to think about how and where our processes intersect. Alignment across businesses is critical for us because our goal is to exploit the efficiencies of centralized information management while we decentralize service delivery. Someone has to be master-at-arms to ensure that we don't have one of our companies—say, life insurance—creating systems and processes that don't interface well with the corporate system. Otherwise, we'd have a terrible time leveraging technology across the company.

Let me give you an example. About four years ago, I decided that the company needed to do something about address changes. Our customers are a mobile group; they move once every three years. And they didn't enjoy having to call each and every one of our lines of business to register the same change of address. They kept asking, "Don't you guys ever talk to one another?" Unfortunately, at the time the answer was no. It took us a year and a half to get the necessary systems and processes lined up so that a person could call any of our lines of business, report an address change, and have it posted immediately in our other businesses as well. It sounds like a simple process—changing addresses. But we found that the process cut across all parts of the organization.

Leschly: I think Bob raises an important point. Process improvement isn't limited to large-scale reengineering or fixing macro processes. Real power comes from working with small processes—that's where the inefficiencies are. For example, we examined the problem of changing business cards when our sales representatives move from one of our sales forces to another. It typically took a couple of weeks; today it takes 24 hours. That may seem insignificant until you realize that we

have 2,000 sales reps. Then the savings in time, money, energy, and communication with customers become quite substantial.

As you make these shifts, you are implicitly changing the company's culture and behavior patterns. Organizations, after all, are more than collections of processes; they are made up of people who have become accustomed to long-standing norms and ways of working together. How have the members of your organizations responded to the increased attention to processes?

Weatherup: We struggled at first. Pepsi has always been an action-oriented organization with a "take-the-hill, get-it-done, can-do" mentality. Results were what mattered, whether you got them in an ad hoc or an orderly fashion. At the start, people were afraid that processes would slow them down. They feared they would lead to standardization, bureaucracy, and less freedom to act. It took time to overcome those concerns.

Allaire: I think there's a danger of falling into a trap here, of thinking of processes as a constraint. At Xerox, we're very keen on empowering people and unleashing their creative juices—and we see processes as liberating. After all, if you have processes that are in control, you know how the organization is working. There's no guesswork because variances are small and operating limits are well defined. Couple that with objectives that are consistent with your strategy and communicated all the way down the line—to individuals on the production floor as well as to those who deal directly with customers—and you get quality output without a lot of checking. You don't need the old command-and-control approach, which was designed to keep people in line; instead, you can tell people to do their own thing provided they respect the process. You wind up with an environment that frees people to be creative. This connection to empowerment turned out to be critical for us: If people don't understand it, they tend to resist a process approach because they think it will restrict their creativity. But it does exactly the opposite.

Beyond Total Quality Management and Reengineering: Managing through Processes

Virtually all efforts to redesign business processes today have their roots in two movements: total quality management (TQM) and reengineering. Both have provided managers with a powerful means of reshaping individual processes so that they serve existing categories of customers more efficiently. Reengineering, in particular, has helped managers harness the formidable power of information technology to improve process performance. But a growing number of managers are discovering that TQM and reengineering have three severe limitations.

First, these techniques assume that process redesign can be divorced from rethinking business strategy. Most TQM and reengineering programs take a strong operational view of improvement. They target processes that have grown with little rationale or planning; measure progress by reductions in cycle times, defect rates, and costs; and define success as better or faster execution. Those are laudable goals. But, in an era of volatile and rapidly changing markets and technologies TQM and reengineering can generate a much improved process for competing in an environment that no longer exists.

Second, while TQM and reengineering are powerful tools for redesigning individual business processes, they often treat processes as unconnected islands. But the success of most businesses depends on how a bundle of their critical processes interact—something that TQM and reengineering programs often don't address.

Third, TQM and reengineering efforts typically focus on redesigning business processes and ignore management processes—the ways senior managers make, communicate, implement, monitor, and adjust decisions, and measure and compensate performance. But senior managers' role in a process-oriented organization is radically different than in a functional, command-and-control hierarchy. Unless management processes are redesigned, too, chances are the company will not come close to reaping the full benefits of its TQM or reengineering plan.

When I say that TQM and reengineering have limitations, I do not mean that they are inherently flawed. I am merely arguing that they are tools for achieving operational improvements, not total solutions. But the level of disappointment among companies that have embraced TQM or reengineering—reengineering experts report failure rates as high as 70 percent—suggests that many managers see them as panaceas rather than as tools for fixing particular problems.

Thus, before setting out to redesign a critical process, a manager first should ask whether the chief problem is the quality, cost, or speed of the process or, rather, the fundamental inability of the process to support the strategy. In other words, should the process be improved or should it be radically transformed to accommodate strategic requirements?

Consider a semiconductor manufacturer that has historically competed in slow-moving niche markets with limited competition. The company's managers describe its traditional resource-allocation process as "covering the roulette table"—avoiding difficult choices by spreading R&D dollars among a large number of small-scale, low-payoff projects. Product development has always been a leisurely and extended affair: Work on a product's next generation would begin only after work on its predecessor had been completely finished.

Today, however, changes in underlying technologies and customer preferences mean that instead of selling components, the company now must bundle components into complex systems. The required level of research per product is therefore rising rapidly, at the same time that product life cycles are shrinking from 10 to 15 years to 3 to 5 years. The company's mainstay customers have also changed. Formerly a virtually exclusive supplier to many companies in niche markets, the manufacturer now serves a handful of automakers and disk-drive producers and faces aggressive competition.

In short, the new strategy requires that the company excel at two tasks: making a few large R&D investments that can generate significant payoffs and developing new generations of products concurrently. Does the company need to adapt its resource-allocation and product-development processes to accommodate this strategy? If so, in what ways? Neither TQM nor reengineering experts deal with those questions, beyond

(*continued*)

suggesting that the two processes be made swifter, more productive, and less prone to error. Neither would necessarily lead the company to create a new resource-allocation process—one that is capable of identifying and funding a few high-impact investments. Such a process would require a more elaborate system for gathering customer information as well as revised procedures for choosing among investment proposals.

Nor would TQM and reengineering naturally bring about the radical changes in the product-development process that are critical for carrying out the new strategy. Because the company's product life cycles are much shorter, it needs a development process that enables it to work simultaneously on current and future generations of products. Such a process means engineers must develop new forms of collaboration and better ways to communicate across projects.

Managers should also try to answer a second question before redesigning a critical process: How much of the problem stems from the individual process and how much from the complex interaction among processes? Few processes unfold in isolation; most depend heavily on one another for information and resources. A greatly improved product-development process won't generate the desired results if the market-research process is not aligned to provide timely information about customers. Similarly, strategic planning is a mere exercise if the resource-allocation process uses different criteria to rank investment proposals. (In the case of the semiconductor company, the two processes remain distinct. The two top-level executives, both industry veterans, are continuing to rely mostly on their instincts, rather than on the company's formal strategic analysis, to place bets.) Before redesigning a process, therefore, managers need to make sure they understand the upstream and downstream linkages among processes; they must learn to think about processes as a collective organism rather than as isolated streams of activity.

Finally, managers should consider whether existing management processes will be compatible with the redesigned business processes. Most management processes are woven into the organizational fabric of a company. For this reason, they profoundly influence the likely success of reengineering initiatives. It makes little sense to reengineer a logistics process around information technology that allows rapid, autonomous

decision making in the field if the company's norms and incentives continue to require sign-offs from corporate staff. Nor is a redesigned service process likely to deliver superior advice to customers if the evaluation system continues to judge telephone representatives on their efficiency and productivity.

Will senior management groups need to relinquish authority to ensure that processes function as planned? Will they have to change the rules and the systems for accessing information to ensure that everyone needing to share it can do so? How do senior managers plan to interact with processes once inefficiencies have been eliminated? Will the reward system support the team behavior required of new processes? As Christopher Meyer noted in "How the Right Measures Help Teams Excel" (*Harvard Business Review,* May–June 1994), traditional measurement and reward systems for governing hierarchical, functional organizations often disempower teams charged with executing cross-functional processes.

TQM and reengineering experts—other than saying the goal should be to eliminate waste and minimize deviations from standard—are virtually silent on the subject of how to manage business processes once they have been improved. There is a wide range of possible approaches, depending on the nature of the process, the company's culture and management style, the organization's size, and competitive demands. Consider the strategic-planning process of Emerson Electric, an $8.6 billion company that competes in a wide range of stable, cost-competitive businesses. Charles F. Knight, the company's chairman and CEO, is the architect of the company's strategy and its strategic-planning process, including its accompanying performance-measurement system. By committing 50 percent of his time to planning and review meetings that focus on financial performance, he shapes the way that the process unfolds. In these meetings he rigorously questions the division presidents' goals and assumptions, but the division heads are ultimately responsible for devising and executing their own plans.

Standing in sharp contrast is the way the strategic-planning process needs to be managed at small, narrowly focused high-technology companies contending with rapid change. Their senior managers

(continued)

need to track real-time operating data, such as shipments. They also need to develop multiple strategic alternatives simultaneously; they cannot wait for review meetings to redirect misguided strategies and must play a much more hands-on role in crafting their businesses' strategies.

When a company has "fixed" its processes through TQM or reengineering, it hopes to end up with superior processes. But those processes still have to be managed. *How* they are managed will determine whether the company realizes their full potential.

Weatherup: I agree with you 1,000 percent. A process approach *is* liberating. It helps us build reliability and winning consistency, and our people love to win. So over time, they've bought in completely. But our starting point was totally different. People felt that processes meant standardization and less freedom. I'm curious to know how you dealt with that at USAA.

Herres: We decided to keep our experiments with processes focused in the early stages and designated the Great Lakes area as our test region for business-process improvement. That allowed us to work the bugs out of new ideas before we exposed them to the total membership; in addition, it helped us ensure consistency and seamless service. It was also a great opportunity to provide career-broadening experiences for promising managers, and it gave us a new way for us to think about change. Once the process approach was proven in the test region—and the goal there was revolutionary rather than evolutionary change—it could be rolled out to the rest of the organization with much less resistance.

Leschly: Sometimes you can get the same results by changing the players. I came to SmithKline Beecham in June 1990, just a year after the merger took place. I was a newcomer who had no association with the previous cultures and was put in charge of the worldwide pharmaceutical business. There were about 12 people on my management team. Today, I have to admit, only two of them are left. It was a gradual process. Some people retired; some didn't think the job was fun any longer; a few enjoyed it and stayed. We found that we needed people who were capable of adapting to a completely new way of running the business and who weren't wedded to either of the premerger cultures.

Weatherup: Bless you! It's good to know I have company. I also had 12 people reporting to me at the start of our change process. That was four years ago, and today only two of them remain.

Leschly: Unfortunately, people don't recognize these shifts at the top, because nobody in our position is going to stand up and say, "I'm proud to report that management has changed." But even with new people at the top, we found that we had to work hard on education and training. People have a tough time understanding what it means for processes to be reliable, repeatable, and in control. Every one of our employees was asked to embrace a set of problem-solving and process-improvement tools, which we've labeled a "Simply Better Way" of working. We now have 57 coach-trainers, who teach our trainers, plus 170 country/site trainers, who ensure a local presence in every country and major site. They, in turn, have trained 1,200 frontline facilitators, who support our process-improvement teams. And we still think it's going to take us years before we can honestly say that all 50,000 people at SmithKline Beecham understand what it means to standardize and improve a process. It's important to note that the trainers are not full-time; they all wear two hats. We have avoided having an organization within the organization to manage process improvements.

Weatherup: We actually developed a formal enrollment process to win acceptance of our changes. It took us 15 months—from December 1990 to March 1992—with separate meetings for each level of the organization. Every three months we worked with a different group, starting with the 70 people who are on the rung below my direct reports, moving to larger groups of 400 and 1,200, then to a huge meeting of 5,500 in Dallas, and finally to a one-day video presentation to all 20,000 of our front-line employees.

Every enrollment had the same format. The process was kicked off with a 3-day meeting, followed immediately by a 90-day work period. I always opened up the meeting with a "burning platform" speech that I borrowed from a consultant of ours to get people tuned in to the need for change. Apparently, a few years ago there was a fire on a North Sea oil rig. Because the rigs were 150 feet high, the workers had been instructed not to jump but to wait for help, no matter how bad things got. Despite the injunction, one worker jumped—and survived. Asked later to explain his actions, he said that he had looked behind, seen an approaching wall of fire, then looked down and seen the icy sea below. His rationale? "I chose probable death over certain death." Only 11 others survived the fire, out of several hundred workers.

That image set the stage. I then made the case for change with detailed data on the financial, market, and organizational pains we were facing. Members of the previous enrollment group followed, describing our new vision and reporting their findings from interviews with customers and employees. After discussion, training was presented; most of the time was devoted to basic process analysis. Participants then divided into teams to plan their "real" work. All groups were given 90 days to complete assigned activities, which included interviewing customers, charting work processes, and designing and leading the enrollment meeting for the next group of employees.

That last step was the secret for us. We ended up calling it "head, heart, hands" because we believed that for change to occur, people had to do three things: develop a conceptual understanding of the rationale and proposed direction of change, internalize and commit emotionally to the new vision, and acquire new skills to ensure that the vision would be realized. Each group had 90 days to get comfortable, to think about what was said and digest it, to conduct their own little process-improvement projects, and to work through the vision statement and company values. Not that you could get fully comfortable in 90 days. But our basic message was, Don't go underground. Either sign up or we'll be happy to give you a nice severance package—and you can go to work for somebody else.

It sounds as if a new type of manager with a different set of skills is required to work effectively in a process environment.

Leschly: Twenty years ago, it was simple to select people. You just looked at results. Anybody who could bring home the bacon was, by definition, a terrific person. Today we go through an elaborate selection process that goes well beyond bottom-line numbers. It focuses more on soft skills, on communication and the ability to work as a team player. All those skills are necessary if you are going to oversee or participate in cross-functional processes. And there are the intangibles that don't show up on a résumé—things like intelligence, judgment, a sense of humor, and energy level. Those are the qualities I use to pick my own team. Take a sense of humor. If there is no smile, no laugh, you can bet the candidate isn't any good with people and won't be able to create the right atmosphere. We also don't want any clones. We want some mavericks who are different—but still aligned. Because then you can create a team of wide-ranging differences that is more than the sum of its parts.

Herres: We've recognized the growing importance of technical skills. One of our biggest problems in the past was the gulf that separated our information technology people, who are centralized, from our lines of business. The business people had a simple approach to technology: They defined their business requirements, threw them over the transom to information services, and told them to call back when they were finished. That was okay when systems requirements were easy to define, but not today when complex processes are involved. I've seen it time and time again with the programs that have gotten into trouble. They all lacked a continuing, interactive dialogue between systems developers and the business people who wound up using the technology.

So we decided to foster an understanding of systems in the minds of our business people, especially those in key positions. I just announced a replacement for the head of our property and casualty group, and I picked someone who understands information technology. He hasn't been a technologist all his life, but he has a good grasp of systems design and systems analysis. For those employees who don't yet have the background, we've launched an ambitious program to subsidize their purchase of personal computers. Because it's open to any USAA employee, it's going to cost us a few million dollars. But it's worth it. Computer literacy is essential for succeeding in business today.

Weatherup: When I was considering someone for promotion a few years ago, I looked at only two criteria. One was idea leadership. The person had to have the ability to find, create, borrow, steal, or reshape ideas, especially big ideas, because that was the essence of our culture. The other thing I looked for was people leadership. Pepsi's managers had to be able to mobilize the troops and energize the organization, to get it moving fast and aggressively. Today we've added a third category, capability leadership, by which I mean a manager's ability to build and institutionalize the capabilities of people, the organization, and systems. To do that well requires a focus on core processes.

Have you assigned individuals or created special roles for overseeing processes?

Allaire: Right now, we're trying to reengineer four key processes: market to collection, or the order-fulfillment cycle; time to market, which is really the product-delivery process; integrated supply chain; and customer service. Each of these efforts has both a process champion and a process owner. The process owner is responsible for orchestrating the daily details of redesign and improvement; it's a full-time job for a vice president. Process champions, in contrast, are members of my senior team, with broad oversight responsibilities.

We have assigned process champions to each of the four major processes being reengineered. The symbolism is important; their mere existence makes senior management more process oriented. But champions are more than figureheads. Sometimes process owners, who sit one organizational level below our business-division presidents, run into interference. Their efforts stall, perhaps because of local loyalties or because a division manager is reluctant to provide funding for the additional investments required to upgrade a process. Traditionally, in situations like these, process owners had no recourse since they were outranked by the division presidents. But now there is a senior champion to turn to, a representative from the corporate office who understands the issues and has the clout to work across the entire business. With these people in place, our reengineering efforts no longer get sidetracked.

Leschly: We have a similar approach but use slightly different terms. We call them owners and sponsors. Ownership means that you jump into the soup: You roll up your sleeves and get intimately involved in improving the process. Sponsorship means that you manage the process: You have responsibility, but you don't necessarily get your hands dirty. That sounds like Paul's description, although sometimes—especially for a core process such as drug development—a member of the corporate management team serves as sponsor and owner simultaneously.

It sounds as though processes are becoming an accepted management responsibility even at senior levels. That poses a problem of evaluation. Companies have years of experience evaluating the performance of department and function heads but are still novices in evaluating process responsibility. How do you accurately judge the work of someone who is overseeing a cross-functional process? What measures do you use, and how do you conduct an assessment?

Allaire: For process owners, we use outcome-oriented measures such as quality and productivity. The only difference is that they apply to total processes rather than to individual functions or units. For example, the integrated supply chain has all the usual customer satisfaction, inventory, and efficiency metrics that a business division does. In this case, however, the process owner has companywide responsibility, and his numbers are the sum total of those reported by all divisions and departments. This part of the evaluation is pretty straightforward, although it took us a while to develop the right measurements. For individuals who are overseeing reengineering projects, we add other objectives that are geared to project management, like meeting budgets and progressing according to preset milestones.

Weatherup: My focus right now is on evaluating the members of my executive team, who have responsibility for broad, systemic processes. Take my senior vice president of marketing. To get a good evaluation, he first needs to "own" the Super Bowl, to have the most talked-about, memorable ads, the best copy, and great reviews in the popular press. That's still important, and if he doesn't deliver he gets a bad grade. But now he is also responsible for a process we call single-voice communication. It governs how we go to market with promotional campaigns and new products. A tremendous amount of material has to be sent to the field each trimester in a coordinated fashion, so that all market units are able to act in concert. Otherwise, we don't get the necessary alignment, and the phones start ringing with complaints.

In the past, this process didn't exist. Our advertising was terrific, but we broke down in execution. Now the senior vice president of marketing owns the process. It's one of his top four priorities and figures heavily in the calculation of his annual bonus. That makes a huge difference. We discuss the process regularly, and I evaluate him on the timeliness and completeness of his communications to the field. The subject also comes up at our weekly senior-staff meetings. Remember, this is a core process. If the materials don't show up in the field, it's not merely of passing interest; it's a disaster. Feedback from angry customers tends to pour in pretty quickly.

Does the shift to processes alter your concept of how senior managers should work together?

Allaire: I think the challenge now is that, for the first time, you must have a team at the top. We always *talked* teams, but today they really are necessary to make companywide processes work effectively. It's not just the people reporting to me but those several layers down, as well. I have six direct reports who form the top management team. But we also have nine division heads, who run their own businesses yet depend on the same laboratories and sales force. They therefore share processes and have to make joint decisions for the betterment of the company. In their minds, we're giving them contradictory advice: Be independent, but cooperate and work together.

At a minimum, they need to buy into what we're trying to do as a company. That's why the strategic intent has to be crystal clear. But, at the same time, they need to understand that even though they're running their own divisions, their success very much depends on the success of the larger organization and its core processes.

Leschly: I would love to get some input here, because we've hit a roadblock in moving toward a team-based organization. No matter how much we emphasize teams, individual managers still want to make their bonuses and tend to stay focused on their personal and departmental goals. How do you develop an incentive system that makes it worthwhile for people to work in teams?

Allaire: When we shifted to our new organization, we also put a new compensation plan in place. In a traditional plan, you get rated against your objectives in three areas—how the corporation does, how your division does, and how you as an individual perform—with the ratings then added together to determine your bonus. But ultimately what happened with this approach was that bonuses varied little year to year and became virtual entitlements at Xerox.

Not anymore. Now the ratings are multiplied together rather than added. We use a simple graph with two axes. The vertical axis represents performance against corporate objectives, which have been set for the whole company. They're not just financials—although they're a big part of it—but also include market share, customer satisfaction, and employee satisfaction. The horizontal axis reflects how your division has done and how you have performed against personal objectives. That's usually where we pick up the process dimension. For instance, process owners will be evaluated according to their progress against milestones that are part of their personal objectives. To compute the overall bonus factor, we multiply the horizontal and vertical ratings together.

With this system, if you perform well but the company doesn't, you're not going to do very well financially. Because if you achieve 100 percent of your goals and the company as a whole only performs at 80 percent, you're only going to get a score of 80. One result of this system is that the variability of bonuses has gone way up—they've been as low as 35 percent of target and as high as 250 percent—so that people have begun to pay more attention to the drivers of performance. Risk taking and entrepreneurship are more likely because the payoffs for success have increased so dramatically. The multiplicative factor also encourages managers to broaden their focus beyond their own needs to consider the needs of other departments and divisions. That has been especially important for our division presidents, who compete for resources yet must work together to oversee common processes like selecting R&D projects.

Let's turn now to your own jobs. How has a process orientation affected the work you do and the way you spend your time?

Weatherup: It has changed *everything* about my job, as well as the jobs of my senior team. Our focus is completely different. Let me give you an example. We spend every Monday morning in a senior-staff meeting, and much of the time is now devoted to discussions of our core, capability-building processes. Whether it's new-product development, single-voice communication, or coaching

and support for sales, we're constantly asking, How do we leverage these processes for maximum advantage? It's not as though we'd asked these questions before; they never came up. We were much too tactical and reactive.

At a personal level, there's even a difference in the questions I ask. As soon as I stepped off the plane on field visits, my first question used to be, "Are you going to deliver your volume and NOPAT [net operating profits after taxes] for the month?" You can imagine the message that sent. Now the questions are completely different: "Are we giving great customer service? How is our relationship with Wal-Mart? Where are you on coaching and support for sales? Were there any problems with the rollout of this trimester's promotion?" The focus is much more on the doing, much more attuned to our major processes. I never would have asked those questions before. Why? Because I grew up under the old Pepsi philosophy that said, Here's the big idea. Run with it and carry the flag up the hill. That's fine for getting things started. But if you don't create structured, repeatable processes, you don't develop a long-term capability, and the work doesn't get done.

Perhaps most important, processes have brought us discipline. They force you to be very precise about what you're looking for and how you make decisions. In the past, I could usually get away with vague advice or meddling because I was the boss. Take new-product development. Before we had a well-defined process, people would come to me with partially developed plans for review. I would usually propose changes, but they weren't always helpful. I might say, "I like the new flavor, but try to make it sweeter. Why don't you experiment with a few additional variables and get back to me as soon as you can?" In hindsight, those instructions weren't very clear. They often required guesswork by employees and resulted in repeated visits and requests for clarification.

Today we have a structured seven-step process that governs all product and package development. There are exit criteria for each stage, which lay out the hurdles that a new idea has to clear before it can move from one stage to the next. These hurdles are crystal clear, and all fuzziness and guesswork are gone. For instance, new products are not allowed to move beyond test marketing unless they are able to produce a 60/40 win in blind taste tests against the competition. Criteria like these force me to be more disciplined in my responses and more attentive to implementation. Either I override the exit criteria consciously—and live with the consequences—or allow the remainder of the process to unfold as planned.

Leschly: Like Craig, I'm also restructuring my work habits. I now spend about 90 percent of my time on strategic issues and 10 percent on operational issues. I am almost totally disengaged from day-to-day, tactical implementation. But that doesn't mean I'm removed from processes. I remain heavily involved in the development and measurement of the capabilities of our key management and business processes, and devote special attention to two of them—innovation, for which I am the process sponsor, and alliance formation. Both are tightly linked to our major strategic initiatives.

It seems that there has been a subtle shift at the top, from managing by results to managing through direction setting and processes. Direction setting is establishing the "where": It's making sure that everyone is working toward achieving the same goals. Processes are the "how": They ensure that the work gets done efficiently and effectively.

Leschly: That's right, but you still have to keep score. Maybe it goes back to my competitive tennis-playing days, but I have always felt that if you don't keep score, you're just practicing. And that requires very clear objectives. We have 1-year, 3-year, and 10-year plans, and we know exactly what has to be achieved for each one.

Herres: We also put great effort into setting objectives. But we've learned that you can't set them and then just walk off and assume they're good forever; there's a constant process of adjustment and change. That's especially true of new products because customers' needs are always evolving.

Managers need to be careful not to get completely captured by the customer-driven perspective. I spend a lot of time on customers' expectations and evaluations; I even try to sign the response to every complaint letter addressed to me. Two or three times a week, a small team and I meet to review the most recent letters, and at almost every session I hear something that inspires me to start a project that will fix a problem or hone a process. So we listen to our customers. But at the same time, when it comes to new and better products for the future, the customer doesn't know enough to tell us what to do. The minivan is a good example. The American public didn't know it wanted minivans until they were out on the market, and then it seemed that nearly every family had to have one. Our job is to anticipate what customers will want three or four years from now, before they can articulate it.

Let me play devil's advocate for a moment. Suppose we had been sitting around this table 25 years ago. I bet we would have heard the very same things from chief executives then. That they try to spend their time on strategic issues, not operational issues. That they focus on direction setting and keeping score. That they attend to innovation, product development, and customers' needs because of their links to strategic goals. What really is different today? Has process thinking had an impact? Or is the job the same as always?

Allaire: There's definitely a difference. But to understand it, you need to define processes more precisely. We've actually been talking about three very different kinds of processes. At the highest level, there are management processes—how the CEO runs the company, how management interacts with employees, how decisions get made, and how communication takes place. Those processes set the organizational context and style of working, like "the IBM way." Then there are business processes, which are the focus of reengineering efforts. Business processes are large, crosscutting collections of activities, like product design, order fulfillment, and customer service. Finally, there are work processes, which are the basic building blocks of business processes. Work processes are focused and operational; they are how the work actually gets done. Examples include such activities as prototype development, finished-goods warehousing, and purchasing.

With these definitions, we can distinguish the old from the new. Chief executives have always focused on management processes. They're the way you get things done. What's different now is that senior managers are also involved in business and work processes. Today those processes are explicit rather than implicit, and senior managers are examining them from a perspective that encompasses the entire company. For the first time, they are reshaping business and work processes to align them with strategy while making them more customer oriented and efficient.

There are good reasons for this shift. In the past, most processes were divided up on a functional basis. They were unintegrated, and the pieces were allowed to operate independently, without tight links. Because functional expertise was regarded as the key to success, there was little place for senior-management involvement. Now, however, we are trying to focus our processes on the customer. That requires much tighter integration and the involvement of a higher level of management. Unless each function has a different customer—and in our business, they don't—you have to link together activities that were always run separately. They're not going to integrate themselves; they haven't for a hundred years.

Herres: I think Paul's three-level map has real merit. It not only fits our own approach but also suggests another reason why senior managers are more involved with processes today. As technology improves and the pace of change accelerates, all three types of processes become faster moving and more interactive. Decision-making cycles tighten, feedback loops are shorter, and there's less room for error. The risks go up because you can get left behind a lot more quickly. For that reason alone, managers now have to pay more attention to

processes. In the past, the pace was less intense—you could plan, organize, direct, and control processes in a more leisurely fashion.

As you reflect on the changes you have described, what advice would you offer other chief executives about to embark on the same path?

Leschly: First and foremost, if you're not willing to go through the pain, do something else. I mean that seriously. Getting people to change is extremely difficult—exciting, yes, but terribly painful. Second, recognize that in the final analysis success rests on selecting the right people to work with. If you have the right people, the rest will follow.

Weatherup: I second Jan's comments. If you aren't willing to be relentless and persevere, don't even think about launching a change process. It takes years of hard work, and you have to be the one driving it forward. At the same time, make sure that you understand your company's culture. Leverage the strengths of the culture—it's your only advantage—while working around or eliminating the weaknesses. Finally, make sure that your message reaches the grass roots. We shut down all locations for a day to enroll our 20,000 front-line employees in our new vision. These are the people who do the work day in and day out. If they're not on board, you aren't going to make much progress.

Herres: I'd also suggest paying attention to the human side of the equation. Try to establish the notion that change is a way of life and that success in the new environment requires the sharing of obligations. At USAA, we now expect that in a 20- to 25-year career, a typical employee will hold six different jobs. We want to keep our employees when we shift to new processes. They come with assets like loyalty, commitment to customers, and understanding of our culture and our mission. We've therefore struck a bargain: We'll provide them with the training they need if they're willing to do their part and invest in self-development and education. CEOs need to accept the challenge of retraining their employees just as they retool their machinery and equipment.

Allaire: Changes in culture are what make the shift to processes so difficult. They can't be mandated; instead, they have to be formed over time through continual reinforcement. Communication becomes enormously important yet incredibly difficult. In fact, every time we make one of these changes, we find that we undercommunicate it. After four or five times repeating the same message, we assume that it has been heard. In reality, many people have not absorbed the information. It takes a lot of time to win understanding and acceptance of major changes.

Index